WILD FLORIDA

Hiker's Guide to the Sunshine State

Florida A&M University, Tallahassee
Florida Atlantic University, Boca Raton
Florida Gulf Coast University, Ft. Myers
Florida International University, Miami
Florida State University, Tallahassee
University of Central Florida, Orlando
University of Florida, Gainesville
University of North Florida, Jacksonville
University of South Florida, Tampa
University of West Florida, Pensacola

A blue-blazed trail leading hikers around the rapids at Camp Branch, along the Suwannee River west of White Springs.

WILD FLORIDA

edited by M. Timothy O'Keefe

Books in this series are written for the many people who visit and/or move to Florida to participate in our remarkable outdoors, an environment rich in birds, animals, and activities, many exclusive to this state. Books in the series will offer readers a variety of formats: natural history guides, historical outdoor guides, guides to some of Florida's most popular pastimes and activities, and memoirs of outdoors folk and their unique lifestyles.

30 Eco-Trips in Florida: The Best Nature Excursions (and How to Leave Only Your Footprints),
    by Holly Ambrose (2005)
Hiker's Guide to the Sunshine State, by Sandra Friend (2005)

Hiker's Guide to the Sunshine State

Sandra Friend

Foreword by M. Timothy O'Keefe

University Press of Florida
Gainesville
Tallahassee
Tampa
Boca Raton
Pensacola
Orlando
Miami
Jacksonville
Ft. Myers

10 09 08 07 06 05   6 5 4 3 2 1

A record of cataloging-in-publication information is available
from the Library of Congress.
ISBN 0-8130-2858-2

The University Press of Florida is the scholarly publishing agency
for the State University System of Florida, comprising Florida A&M
University, Florida Atlantic University, Florida Gulf Coast University,
Florida International University, Florida State University, University
of Central Florida, University of Florida, University of North Florida,
University of South Florida, and University of West Florida.

University Press of Florida
15 Northwest 15th Street
Gainesville, FL 32611-2079
http://www.upf.com

To my friends in the Loxahatchee Chapter of
the Florida Trail Association, who kept asking,
"So when will you tell us where *all* of the trails are?"

Contents

Regions

Series Foreword

With Florida already ranked as one of the most populous states and hundreds of thousands more moving here every year, it seems impossible that truly wild places can remain anywhere in such a densely inhabited region. Yet in spite of the tremendous influx of people wanting to enjoy the Sunshine State's warm climate and active outdoors lifestyle, significant sections of the original, natural Florida do still endure.

In fact, the amount of Florida set aside for preservation surprises many people, especially first-time visitors and newly arrived residents. As this is written, Florida terrain is protected by 3 national forests, 11 national parks, 157 state parks, and 28 national wildlife refuges. In addition, individual Florida counties have designated their own protected public lands, providing for pristine rivers and sheltered coastline.

Yes, there is quite a lot of Florida that hasn't been paved over or badly disturbed by development. And it never will be.

The University Press of Florida celebrates the essential natural qualities of Florida, its environment, its creatures, and its people through the broad-ranging series Wild Florida.

In *Hiker's Guide to the Sunshine State*, Sandra Friend takes readers into wild Florida by the most traditional and time-honored method, by foot.

Friend covers a tremendous amount of territory: 490 of the state's approximately 600 hiking trails, with 2,273 miles of footpaths. And these are true hiking trails, not multiuse trails where walkers might encounter cyclists or riders on horseback and their telltale left-behinds. In other words, this is a guide to enjoying natural Florida without unnecessary, unnatural distractions.

Ironically, with Florida offering so many hiking trails, it's sometimes difficult literally to know where to start. Which trails are the most interesting? What are the highlights of each one? How does one differ from another? Which are suited for long hikes or for short walks? Which have camping available? Where are pets allowed?

All these considerations and more are addressed in a clear and succinct manner throughout the guide. An introductory chart provides extensive information for all 490 trails. Individual walk descriptions are limited to a single page so that all the essentials are available quickly and conveniently in an at-a-glance format.

This user-friendly arrangement offers some eye-opening information. For instance, how many residents realize that two of the highest-population regions, Central Florida and the south Atlantic Coast, also lead in the number of walking trails? And that, statewide, more paths welcome dogs on a leash than ban them? Since Florida basically is a flat spit of sand without mountain vistas, some might consider hiking in the Sunshine State a boring prospect. After all, doesn't everything look almost the same?

Not at all.

As Friend points out, Florida has more than eighty different natural communities, although the transition from one to the next is rarely dramatically obvious. The interpretive signs along many trails, however, provide an effortless education that allows everyone to be aware of and appreciate the diversity of Wild Florida.

Although the likelihood of real danger is remote, hikers do need to keep in mind that there always is the chance for a truly wild encounter of some sort. Friend's suggestions for dealing with snakes, alligators, mosquitoes, and seasonal weather patterns are well worth noting, particularly if you're hiking with a child or a pet. Small dogs, after all, are among alligators' favorite foods.

As for getting lost, the latitude and longitude coordinates listed for most trailheads eliminate that embarrassment if you have a GPS. And, with some exceptions in the Everglades, a cellular telephone will bring help quickly anywhere in Florida, a comforting consideration for families, though this safety advantage does tend to diminish the sense of adventure.

Too many adventures occur when individuals encounter an unexpected condition or circumstance they don't know how to control. The firsthand knowledge shared by Friend in *Hiker's Guide to the Sunshine State* should prevent risky situations from ever cropping up.

When you set out on the trail, it's your responsibility to bring along the water, snacks, and insect spray. Sandra Friend has furnished everything else.

M. Timothy O'Keefe
Series Editor

Acknowledgments

I spent a full year sweeping across the Sunshine State looking for hiking trails and involved a lot of friends along the way. Thanks to Gary and Millie Buffington, Morena Cameron, Barb Dunn, Ruth Gardner, Willie Howard, Phyllis Malinski, Linda Patton, Warren Resen, and Rob Smith for sharing my hiking adventures; to Edwin McCook for logistical support; to Steve Bass, Cathy Briggs, Vernon Compton, Bob Coveney, Jim and Nancy Escoffier, Marsha Kearney, Tom Moody, Lee Parker, Kathi Rader-Gibson, Mike Richards, Susan and David Roquemore, Susan and Thomas Schmidt, and Terry Tenold for sharing their knowledge of their local trails; to Kurt Gephardt and John Street for taking me on personal tours at their parks; and to Linda and Jerry Benton, Gary and Millie Buffington, Morena Cameron, Bob and Bonnie Coveney, Carla Lewis, Phyllis Malinski, Daisy Palmer and Jim Auchterlonie, Linda Patton, Susan and Thomas Schmidt, Barbara Schmucker, Amy and Treacy Stone, Ted and Trudy Winsburg, and Kathy Wolf for providing a roof over my head as I wandered the length of Florida.

In addition, I could not have researched as much as I did and traveled so far without a helping hand from Visit Florida and its many partners. Thanks to Leon Corbett with Visit Florida, as well as Nicole Evans, Sarasota CVB; Alton Fish, Highlands County CVB; Anita Gregory, Apalachicola CVB; Nancy Hamilton, Lee County VCB; Zaneta Hubbard, Clearwater and the Beaches; Jayna Leach, Panama City CVB; Abby Montpelier, Kissimmee CVB; Kathy Newby, Santa Rosa County TDC; and Paula Ramsey Pickett, Visit Gulf. Thanks to the hospitality of Wakulla Lodge at Edward Ball Wakulla Springs State Park; Adventures Unlimited, Milton; Gibson Inn, Apalachicola; Palm Pavilion Inn, Clearwater Beach; Horse and Chaise B&B, Venice; Kenilworth Lodge, Sebring; Tarpon Lodge, Pine Island; and the Comfort Inn, Kissimmee.

Special thanks to Daisy Palmer, Bob Coveney, and Warren Resen for the idea of including latitude and longitude coordinates for each trailhead for Global Positioning System (GPS) and OnStar users—our gift to geocaching enthusiasts (www.geocaching.com) of a virtual cache of Florida's hiking trails. GPS coordinates are provided for *most* of the trails in this book. Shawn Riley, Virginia Lane, and Mark Nickerson scrambled to help me collect some of the trailhead coordinates at the last minute. And thanks to Amy Stone for suggesting the graphical at-a-glance chart!

Introduction

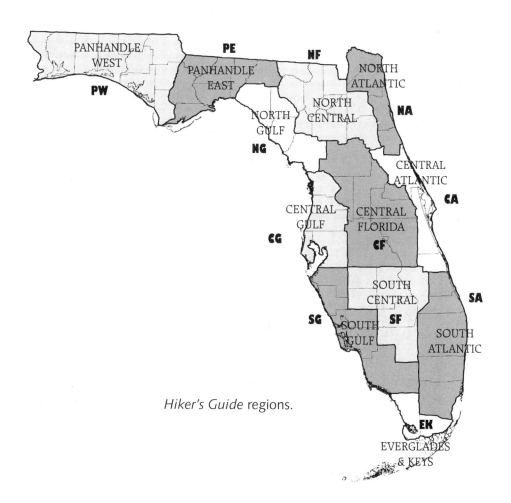

PANHANDLE WEST
PW

PE PANHANDLE EAST

NF

NORTH ATLANTIC **NA**

NORTH GULF **NG**

NORTH CENTRAL

CENTRAL ATLANTIC **CA**

CENTRAL GULF **CG**

CENTRAL FLORIDA **CF**

SOUTH CENTRAL

SOUTH GULF **SG**

SF

SOUTH ATLANTIC **SA**

EK
EVERGLADES & KEYS

Hiker's Guide regions.

Hike Florida?

After researching hiking trails for a couple of years, I was flabbergasted one morning when a reporter from a big-city Florida paper called me and in all earnestness asked, "Why would I want to hike in Florida?" He had learned to hike, as I had, in the Appalachian Mountains, and didn't see much merit in hiking the Sunshine State. Where are the mountains? Where are the views?

I explained to him why Florida's hiking trails are so special, and why I found more pleasure in hiking in Florida than I had on any of my recent trips to the Appalachians. Diversity of habitats is the key to Florida's natural beauty, with more than eighty different natural communities stretching across the state, ranging from the tangled tropical forests of gumbo limbo and mastic in the Keys and the haunting dwarf cypress plains of Big Cypress to the broad open prairies of Central Florida, the undulating ancient sand dunes of the Lake Wales Ridge, and the rhododendron-lined streams of the Western Panhandle. Your surroundings change with only a few inches of elevation change, allowing some trails to showcase as many as five or six different habitats within a single mile! Scrambling up the steephead ravines along the Apalachicola River rivals any climb found in the lower Appalachians, and clambering in and out of the floodplain levees of the Suwannee River will have you tired out after a full day of backpacking. Florida is a marvel of natural diversity, and our state's hiking trails showcase its beauty well.

White-topped pitcher plants in bloom at Garcon Point.

Using This Book

When I first started researching hiking trails in Florida, I discovered more than 250 trails and 2,500 miles of hiking across the Sunshine State. When I actually started traveling around to hike these trails, and several more years elapsed, I found nearly 600 hiking trails, from interpretive boardwalks to long-distance backpacking trips. Thanks to aggressive natural lands preservation programs in many Florida counties, our hiking opportunities continue to expand. This book encompasses 490 hikes covering 2,273 miles, including chunks of the 1,300-mile Florida Trail, the National Scenic Trail that is the granddaddy of all Florida hiking trails, first blazed in 1966. I have broken up the completed portions of the Florida Trail on public land into distinct segments, organized regionally throughout the book.

The focus of this book is on *hiking* trails, not multiuse trails. To keep the book to a manageable size, I include only clearly designated hiking trails that offer you a place to get out and enjoy Florida's natural habitats. If a route is shown on a map as a nature trail or blazed as a hiking trail, you'll find it here, no matter how long or short it is—short but informative interpretive trails rate as much attention as long backpacking loops. Some of the trails may have been established primarily for hiking but allow other uses; I note that in the text. I specifically *do not* include trails that I perceive have been established primarily for equestrian or bicycle use, which eliminates many trails in Florida State Forests as well as trails created by bicycle clubs. Nor do I include paved rail-trails or unmarked trails (such as suggested walks on forest roads in Wildlife Management Areas and state forests), unmarked beach walks, or exercise/fitness trails. To find the trails outlined in this book, I used public information sources such as brochures for Florida State Parks and state forests, trail guides issued by various water management districts, information from National Forests and National Wildlife Refuges, brochures and online information from county websites, county natural lands programs, city park information in urban areas, and recommendations from friends, as well as just spending a lot of time wandering around the state tracking down trails. To verify the existence of these trails, I've walked at least a portion of all of the trails described in this guidebook, with the exception of a few trails scouted by my friends.

Documenting all of Florida's hiking trails is an open-ended task. Although I have attempted to be comprehensive, I couldn't track down every trail I heard of—not if the book was ever to get into print. Look for additions in the next edition. Also, information can slip through the cracks, new trails open before the book is published, and old trails vanish through lack of use, hurricane damage, or forest restoration programs. I appreciate your feedback as to errors and trails that I might have missed; please e-mail me at **hike@sandrafriend. com** with your comments and suggestions for the next edition, or write to me at University Press of Florida, 15 NW 15th Street, Gainesville, FL 32611.

Sections

To make exploring Florida's hiking trails easier, this book divides the state into sections. Because of the sheer volume, the trails are numbered within each section rather than assigned an overall number for the state. Cross-references include a two-character code as a prefix for the hike number to indicate the section to which the hike belongs.

Section 1	Panhandle West	PW	33 hikes
Section 2	Panhandle East	PE	32 hikes
Section 3	North Gulf Coast	NG	19 hikes
Section 4	North Central	NF	45 hikes
Section 5	North Atlantic Coast	NA	31 hikes
Section 6	Central Gulf Coast	CG	42 hikes
Section 7	Central Florida	CF	87 hikes
Section 8	Central Atlantic Coast	CA	38 hikes
Section 9	South Gulf Coast	SG	43 hikes
Section 10	South Central	SF	17 hikes
Section 11	South Atlantic Coast	SA	72 hikes
Section 12	Everglades and Keys	EK	31 hikes

Each section includes an overview map showing the locations of all hikes listed in the section and a listing of hikes by overview map number within county.

Reading the Entries

If multiple trails link to each other to create a trail system, I group them together into a single hike, even if there are multiple trailheads that permit access to the trail system. If a piece of public land (like a state park) has trails starting from different trailheads that are far enough apart that you must drive between them, I keep each of those as a separate hike. If distinct trails start from the same trailhead but go off in separate directions, I group them together as one hike if you park in one place and can then hike off in various directions. I present hikes roughly in geographic order, from northwest to southeast, across each regional map. Check the regional locator map at the beginning of each section to determine the location of a particular trail.

Icons at the top of each entry depict trail features:

F   Trail built and maintained by the Florida Trail Association

$ Fee charged

    Interpretive information available

    Restroom near trailhead

    Trail at least partially wheelchair accessible

    Developed campground near trailhead

    Tent camping near or along trail

    Good trail for small children

    Pets on leash permitted on trail

    One of Florida's don't-miss hikes

Location: Nearest town [GPS coordinates for trailhead]. Coordinates are WGS-84 latitude-longitude provided in minute decimal (DD°MM.MMM'). To translate coordinates into other formats, **http://jeeep.com/details/coord** provides an excellent online resource. If using NAD-27, remember to enter West readings as minus.

Length: Distance of shortest and longest possible hikes on this trail, plus whether the hike is linear (one-way), round-trip, or loop. The distance of each hike may have been accurately measured with a measuring wheel or a GPS unit, or may rely on the official published measurement provided by the land manager or the Florida Trail Association. Unverified measurements are shown in italics in the overview chart.

Map: Where you can find a map for this trail.

Contact Information: Land manager or agency responsible for this trail.

Directions: Driving directions to the trailhead.

The Hike: An explanation of the hiking possibilities on this trail.

Highlights: Interesting stuff you should stop and see along the trail.

Logistics: Special concerns about parking, permits, and camping; tips for backpackers, including water sources.

Other Activities: Any of numerous outdoor activities that can be enjoyed on this same piece of public land. When fishing is mentioned as an activity, assume you'll need either a Florida freshwater or saltwater fishing license to cast a line; the only absolute exception in Florida is for those who use a bamboo pole. Visit an outfitter or a local department store, or check **www.florida conservation.org** to purchase a fishing license. Seniors (age sixty-five and over) are eligible for a free fishing license, but you must register and obtain your license before fishing.

Overview Chart—Hiker's Guide to the Sunshine State

	Trail	Public Land	County	Location
Panhandle West				
1	—	Tarklin Bayou Preserve State Park	Escambia	Perdido Heights
2	—	Big Lagoon State Park	Escambia	Chanticleer
3	Edward Ball Nature Trail	University of West Florida	Escambia	West Pensacola
4	Florida Trail	Fort Pickens Unit, Gulf Islands Natl Seashore	Escambia	Pensacola Beach
5	—	Fort Pickens Unit, Gulf Islands Natl Seashore	Escambia	Pensacola Beach
6	—	Naval Live Oaks Area, Gulf Islands Natl Seashore	Escambia	Gulf Breeze
7	Florida Trail	University of West Florida Dunes Preserve	Escambia	Pensacola Beach
8	Bear Lake Trail	Blackwater River State Forest	Santa Rosa	Munson
9	Juniper Creek Trail	Blackwater River State Forest	Santa Rosa	Holt
10	Chain of Lakes Nature Trail	Blackwater River State Park	Santa Rosa	Holt
11	Garcon Point Hiking Trail	Garcon Point Preserve	Santa Rosa	Milton
12	Florida Trail	Eglin Air Force Base (West)	Santa Rosa	Holley
13	Florida Trail	Santa Rosa Area, Gulf Islands Natl Seashore	Santa Rosa	Navarre Beach
14	Wiregrass Trail	Blackwater River State Forest	Okaloosa	Blackman
15	Jackson Red Ground Trail	Blackwater River State Forest	Okaloosa	Red Rocks
16	Florida Trail	Eglin Air Force Base (East)	Okaloosa	Crestview
17	Turkey Creek Nature Trail	—	Okaloosa	Niceville
18	—	Fred Gannon Rocky Bayou State Park	Okaloosa	Niceville
19	Henderson Nature Trail	Henderson Beach State Park	Okaloosa	Destin
20	Morris Lake Nature Trail	Topsail Hill Preserve State Park	Walton	Sandestin
21	—	Grayton Beach State Park	Walton	Grayton Beach
22	—	Ponce de Leon Springs State Park	Holmes	Ponce de Leon
23	Florida Trail	Pine Log State Forest	Bay	Ebro
24	—	Pine Log State Forest	Bay	Ebro
25	Pine Flatwoods Trail	St. Andrews State Park	Bay	Panama City Beach
26	Gator Lake Nature Trail	St. Andrews State Park	Bay	Panama City Beach
27	—	Falling Waters State Park	Washington	Chipley
28	Florida Trail	Econfina Creek Water Management Area	Washington	Fountain
29	St. Joseph Wilderness Preserve	St. Joseph Peninsula State Park	Gulf	Cape San Blas
30	St. Joseph Bay Trail	St. Joseph Peninsula State Park	Gulf	Cape San Blas
31	Maritime Forest Nature Trail	St. Joseph Peninsula State Park	Gulf	Cape San Blas
32	Caverns Trail System	Florida Caverns State Park	Jackson	Marianna
33	Lakeview Trail	Three Rivers State Park	Jackson	Sneads

Trail Miles	F	$	📖	🚻	⛺(camp)	tent	♿	👪	dog	❄
Panhandle West										
4.0	—	—	—	—	—	—	—	—	dog	❄
4.3	—	$	📖	🚻	⛺	—	—	👪	dog	—
1.0	—	—	📖	🚻	—	—	—	👪	—	—
4.2	F	$	📖	🚻	⛺	—	—	👪	—	—
1.1	—	$	📖	🚻	⛺	—	♿	👪	—	—
7.8	—	—	📖	🚻	—	—	—	—	dog	—
3.8	F	—	—	🚻	—	—	—	—	—	❄
4.0	—	$	—	🚻	⛺	—	—	—	—	—
8.8	F	$	—	🚻	⛺	tent	—	—	dog	❄
1.2	—	$	📖	🚻	⛺	—	—	—	dog	—
4.1	F	—	—	—	—	—	—	—	dog	❄
12.0	F	—	—	—	—	tent	—	—	—	—
7.1	F	—	—	🚻	—	—	—	—	—	—
12.8	F	—	—	🚻	⛺	tent	—	—	dog	—
21.5	F	—	—	🚻	⛺	tent	—	—	dog	—
49.0	F	—	—	—	—	tent	—	—	—	❄
1.8	—	—	📖	🚻	—	—	♿	👪	—	—
4.0	—	$	📖	🚻	⛺	—	—	👪	dog	—
0.8	—	$	📖	🚻	⛺	—	—	—	dog	—
2.5	—	$	📖	🚻	—	—	—	—	dog	❄
0.8	—	$	📖	🚻	⛺	—	—	👪	—	—
0.6	—	$	📖	🚻	—	—	—	👪	dog	—
6.1	F	$	—	—	⛺	tent	—	—	dog	—
7.0	—	$	—	—	⛺	—	—	—	dog	—
0.6	—	$	📖	🚻	⛺	—	—	👪	dog	—
0.4	—	$	📖	—	⛺	—	—	👪	—	—
2.0	—	$	📖	🚻	⛺	—	—	👪	—	—
17.9	F	—	—	—	—	tent	—	—	dog	❄
14.0	—	$	—	—	⛺	tent	—	—	—	❄
0.9	—	$	—	🚻	⛺	—	—	👪	—	—
0.7	—	—	📖	—	—	—	—	👪	—	—
1.5	—	$	📖	—	⛺	—	—	—	—	❄
2.0	—	$	—	—	⛺	—	—	—	—	—

	Trail	Public Land	County	Location

Panhandle East

	Trail	Public Land	County	Location
1	Terry L. Rhodes Trail System	Lake Talquin State Forest	Gadsden	Bloxham
2	Torreya State Park Trail	Torreya State Park	Liberty	Rock Bluff
3	Weeping Ridge Trail	Torreya State Park	Liberty	Rock Bluff
4	Garden of Eden Trail	Apalachicola Bluffs and Ravines Preserve	Liberty	Bristol
5	Camel Lake Trail	Apalachicola National Forest	Liberty	Estiffanugla
6	Trail of Lakes	Apalachicola National Forest	Liberty	Estiffanugla
7	Florida Trail	Apalachicola National Forest (west)	Liberty	Estiffanugla
8	Wright Lake Trail	Apalachicola National Forest	Franklin	Sumatra
9	Fort Gadsden Historical Site	Apalachicola National Forest	Franklin	Sumatra
10	Dwarf Cypress Boardwalk	Tate's Hell State Forest	Franklin	Carrabelle Beach
11	High Bluff Coastal Nature Trail	Tate's Hell State Forest	Franklin	Carrabelle Beach
12	—	Apalachicola Natl Estuarine Research Reserve	Gulf	Apalachicola
13	Gap Point Trail	St. George Island State Park	Franklin	St. George Island
14	—	Ochlockonee River State Park	Franklin	Sopchoppy
15	—	Bald Point State Park	Franklin	Bald Point
16	Fort Braden Trail	Lake Talquin State Forest	Leon	Tallahassee
17	Silver Lake Habitat Trail	Apalachicola National Forest	Leon	Tallahassee
18	Butler Mill Trail	Lake Jackson Mounds Archaeological State Park	Leon	Tallahassee
19	Eleanor Klapp-Phipps Park Trail	Eleanor Klapp-Phipps Park	Leon	Tallahassee
20	Stevenson Memorial Bird Trail	Tall Timbers Research Station	Leon	Bradfordville
21	Florida Trail	Apalachicola National Forest (East)	Wakulla	Sopchoppy
22	—	Leon Sinks Geological Area	Wakulla	Woodville
23	—	San Marcos de Apalache Historic State Park	Wakulla	St. Marks
24	Sally Ward Spring Trails	Wakulla Springs State Park	Wakulla	Wakulla
25	Plum Orchard Pond Trail	St. Marks National Wildlife Refuge	Wakulla	Newport
26	Primitive Walking Trails	St. Marks National Wildlife Refuge	Wakulla	Newport
27	Florida Trail	St. Marks National Wildlife Refuge	Wakulla	Newport
28	Mounds Pool Interpretive Trail	St. Marks National Wildlife Refuge	Wakulla	Newport
29	Lighthouse Levee Trail	St. Marks National Wildlife Refuge	Wakulla	Newport
30	Florida Trail	Aucilla River Sinks	Jefferson	Lamont
31	Ladell Brothers Center	North Florida Community College	Madison	Madison
32	Florida Trail	Suwannee River West	Madison	Lee

North Gulf

	Trail	Public Land	County	Location
1	Dallus Landing Nature Trail	Big Bend Wildlife Management Area	Taylor	Steinhatchee
2	Steinhatchee Trail	Steinhatchee Falls Water Management Area	Taylor	Tennille

Trail Miles	F	$	📖	🚻	☉	⛺	♿	👥	🐕	✳

Panhandle East

Trail Miles	F	$	📖	🚻	☉	⛺	♿	👥	🐕	✳
6.2	—	$	📖	🚻	—	—	♿	👥	🐕	—
14.5	F	$	—	🚻	☉	⛺	—	—	🐕	✳
1.0	—	$	📖	—	☉	—	—	—	🐕	✳
3.3	—	—	📖	—	—	—	—	—	—	✳
1.0	—	$	📖	🚻	☉	—	—	—	—	—
4.0	—	$	—	🚻	☉	—	—	—	—	—
34.9	F	—	—	—	☉	⛺	—	—	🐕	—
4.5	—	$	—	🚻	☉	—	—	—	—	—
1.1	—	$	📖	🚻	—	—	—	👥	🐕	—
0.2	—	—	—	—	—	—	♿	👥	—	—
1.6	—	—	—	—	—	—	—	—	🐕	—
0.6	—	—	📖	🚻	—	—	♿	👥	—	—
5.0	—	$	📖	🚻	☉	⛺	—	—	—	—
2.1	—	$	📖	🚻	☉	—	—	👥	🐕	—
0.5	—	—	📖	🚻	—	—	—	👥	🐕	—
11.0	F	$	—	🚻	—	⛺	—	—	🐕	—
1.3	—	$	📖	🚻	—	—	—	—	🐕	—
1.5	—	$	📖	🚻	—	—	—	👥	🐕	—
6.7	F	—	—	—	—	—	—	—	🐕	—
1.0	—	—	📖	—	—	—	—	—	—	—
32.2	F	—	—	—	—	⛺	—	—	—	✳
5.4	—	$	📖	🚻	—	—	—	—	🐕	✳
0.6	—	$	📖	🚻	—	—	—	👥	—	—
2.8	—	$	📖	🚻	—	—	—	👥	🐕	—
0.5	—	$	📖	🚻	—	—	♿	👥	—	—
12.0	—	$	—	—	—	—	—	—	—	—
41.0	F	$	—	—	—	⛺	—	—	—	—
1.4	—	$	📖	🚻	—	—	—	—	—	✳
0.3	—	$	📖	—	—	—	—	👥	—	—
17.2	F	—	—	—	—	⛺	—	—	—	✳
1.8	—	—	📖	—	—	—	—	👥	—	—
18.0	F	—	—	—	—	⛺	—	—	—	✳

North Gulf

Trail Miles	F	$	📖	🚻	☉	⛺	♿	👥	🐕	✳
1.2	—	—	📖	🚻	—	—	—	—	—	✳
3.3	—	—	—	🚻	—	—	—	—	🐕	—

	Trail	Public Land	County	Location
3	Fish Bone Nature Trail	Lower Suwannee National Wildlife Refuge	Dixie	Shired Island
4	Salt Creek Nature Trail	Lower Suwannee National Wildlife Refuge	Dixie	Suwannee
5	Basswood Trail	Andrews Wildlife Management Area	Levy	Fanning Springs
6	Buckeye and Turkey Track Trails	Andrews Wildlife Management Area	Levy	Fanning Springs
7	Florida Maple Trail	Andrews Wildlife Management Area	Levy	Fanning Springs
8	Persimmon Trail	Andrews Wildlife Management Area	Levy	Fanning Springs
9	Bluff Oak Trail	Andrews Wildlife Management Area	Levy	Fanning Springs
10	River Birch Trail	Andrews Wildlife Management Area	Levy	Fanning Springs
11	North End Trail System	Manatee Springs State Park	Levy	Chiefland
12	Sink Trail Loop	Manatee Springs State Park	Levy	Chiefland
13	Suwannee River Boardwalk	Manatee Springs State Park	Levy	Chiefland
14	River Trail	Lower Suwannee National Wildlife Refuge	Levy	Fowler Bluff
15	Shell Mound	Lower Suwannee National Wildlife Refuge	Levy	Cedar Key
16	East Trail System	Cedar Key Scrub Reserve	Levy	Cedar Key
17	West Trail System	Cedar Key Scrub Reserve	Levy	Cedar Key
18	Railroad Trestle Nature Walk	—	Levy	Cedar Key
19	Atsena Otie Key	Cedar Keys NWR	Levy	Cedar Key
North Central				
1	Big Oak Trail	Suwannee River State Park	Hamilton	Ellaville
2	Florida Trail	Holton Creek Wildlife Management Area	Hamilton	Holton Spring
3	Disappearing Creek Loop	—	Hamilton	White Springs
4	Florida Trail	Stephen Foster Folk Culture Center State Park	Hamilton	White Springs
5	Big Shoals Trail	Big Shoals Public Lands	Hamilton	White Springs
6	Long Branch Trail	Big Shoals Public Lands	Hamilton	White Springs
7	Milford A. Clark Nature Trail	—	Suwannee	Dowling Park
8	—	Suwannee River State Park	Suwannee	Ellaville
9	Anderson Springs Loop	Twin Rivers State Forest	Suwannee	Falmouth
10	Florida Trail	Little Shoals	Columbia	White Springs
11	—	Falling Creek Falls	Columbia	Falling Creek
12	—	Alligator Lake	Columbia	Lake City
13	Limestone Trail	O'Leno State Park	Columbia	High Springs
14	River Sink Trail System	O'Leno State Park	Columbia	High Springs
15	Old Bellamy Road	O'Leno State Park	Columbia	High Springs
16	—	Ichetucknee Springs State Park	Columbia	Fort White
17	Mount Carrie Wayside	Osceola National Forest	Columbia	Olustee
18	—	Big Gum Swamp Wilderness	Columbia	Deep Creek

Trail Miles	**F**	$	📖	🚻	⛺(camp)	⛺(tent)	♿	👫	🐎	❄
0.5	—	—	—	—	—	—	—	—	🐎	—
0.2	—	—	—	—	—	—	♿	👫	—	—
0.5	—	$	—	—	—	—	—	—	🐎	—
2.3	—	$	—	—	—	—	—	—	🐎	—
1.5	—	$	📖	—	—	—	—	—	🐎	—
1.1	—	$	📖	—	—	—	—	—	🐎	—
1.8	—	$	📖	—	—	—	—	—	🐎	—
1.8	—	$	—	—	—	—	—	—	🐎	—
6.0	—	$	📖	—	⛺	—	—	—	🐎	—
0.6	—	$	📖	—	⛺	—	—	—	🐎	—
0.4	—	$	—	🚻	⛺	—	♿	👫	—	—
0.6	—	—	📖	—	—	—	—	👫	—	—
1.6	—	—	📖	🚻	⛺	—	—	—	—	—
4.0	—	—	—	🚻	—	—	—	—	🐎	—
8.0	—	—	—	—	—	—	—	—	🐎	—
0.6	—	—	📖	—	—	—	—	👫	🐎	—
1.2	—	—	📖	🚻	—	—	—	—	—	—

North Central

Trail Miles	**F**	$	📖	🚻	⛺(camp)	⛺(tent)	♿	👫	🐎	❄
12.5	**F**	$	—	🚻	⛺	⛺	—	—	🐎	—
7.8	**F**	—	—	—	—	⛺	—	—	🐎	❄
1.5	**F**	—	—	—	—	⛺	—	—	🐎	❄
4.0	**F**	$	📖	🚻	⛺	—	—	—	🐎	—
2.2	—	$	📖	🚻	—	—	—	—	—	❄
2.5	—	$	📖	🚻	—	—	—	—	🐎	—
2.0	—	—	—	—	—	—	—	—	🐎	—
3.4	—	$	📖	🚻	⛺	—	—	👫	🐎	❄
5.2	—	—	📖	—	—	—	—	—	🐎	—
4.4	**F**	—	—	—	—	⛺	—	—	🐎	❄
0.4	—	—	—	—	—	—	—	👫	—	—
6.5	—	—	📖	🚻	—	—	—	—	—	—
0.6	—	$	📖	—	⛺	—	—	—	—	—
13.8	—	$	📖	🚻	⛺	⛺	—	—	🐎	—
2.2	—	—	📖	🚻	—	—	—	—	🐎	—
3.7	—	$	📖	🚻	—	—	♿	👫	🐎	—
1.0	—	—	📖	—	—	—	—	👫	🐎	—
4.9	—	—	—	—	—	⛺	—	—	🐎	—

	Trail	Public Land	County	Location
19	Florida Trail	Osceola National Forest	Baker	Olustee
20	Nice Wander Trail	Osceola National Forest	Baker	Olustee
21	—	Olustee Battlefield Historic State Park	Baker	Olustee
22	Florida Trail	Lake Butler Forest	Union	Lake Butler
23	New River Nature Trail	Chastain-Seay Park	Union	Worthington Springs
24	Fire and Water Nature Trail	Jennings State Forest	Clay	Middleburg
25	—	Gold Head Branch State Park	Clay	Keystone Heights
26	—	Black Creek Ravines Conservation Area	Clay	Middleburg
27	—	Bayard Conservation Area	Clay	Green Cove Springs
28	Florida Trail	Etoniah Creek State Forest	Putnam	Florahome
29	Florida Trail	Rice Creek Sanctuary	Putnam	Palatka
30	—	Ravine Gardens State Park	Putnam	Palatka
31	—	Welaka State Forest	Putnam	Satsuma
32	Beecher Run Nature Trail	Welaka National Fish Hatchery	Putnam	Welaka
33	St. Johns Loop	Cross Florida Greenway	Putnam	Rodman
34	—	San Felasco Hammock Preserve State Park	Alachua	Gainesville
35	—	Devil's Millhopper Geological State Park	Alachua	Gainesville
36	—	Gum Root Swamp Conservation Area	Alachua	Gainesville
37	—	Morningside Nature Center	Alachua	Gainesville
38	—	Bivens Arm Nature Park	Alachua	Gainesville
39	La Chua Trail	Paynes Prairie Preserve State Park	Alachua	Gainesville
40	Bolens Bluff Trail	Paynes Prairie Preserve State Park	Alachua	Micanopy
41	—	Paynes Prairie Preserve State Park	Alachua	Micanopy
42	—	Lake Lochloosa Conservation Area	Alachua	Cross Creek
43	—	Fort White Mitigation Park	Gilchrist	Bell
44	—	Hart Springs Park	Gilchrist	Hart Springs
45	Fanning Springs Hiking Trail	Fanning Springs State Park	Gilchrist	Fanning Springs

North Atlantic

	Trail	Public Land	County	Location
1	Cary Nature Trail	Cary State Forest	Nassau	Bryceville
2	Willow Pond Nature Trail	Fort Clinch State Park	Nassau	Fernandina Beach
3	Blackrock Trail	Big Talbot Island State Park	Duval	Big Talbot Island
4	Island Hiking Trail	Little Talbot Island State Park	Duval	Little Talbot Island
5	Campground Nature Trail	Little Talbot Island State Park	Duval	Little Talbot Island
6	—	Pope Duval Park	Duval	Whitehouse
7	Ortega Stream Valley Trail	Ringhaver Park	Duval	Orange Park
8	—	Westside Regional Park	Duval	Orange Park

Trail Miles	F	$	Book	Restrooms	Camp	Tent	Wheelchair	Family	Dogs	Winter
20.7	F	—	—	—	Camp	—	—	—	Dog	—
1.8	F	—	—	Restroom	—	—	Wheelchair	Family	Dog	—
1.1	—	—	Book	Restroom	—	—	Wheelchair	Family	—	—
17.6	F	—	—	—	—	Tent	—	—	Dog	—
0.6	—	$	—	Restroom	—	—	—	Family	Dog	—
1.8	—	$	Book	—	—	—	—	—	Dog	—
5.0	F	$	Book	Restroom	Camp	Tent	—	—	Dog	—
7.8	—	—	Book	—	—	Tent	—	—	Dog	—
5.0	—	—	—	Restroom	—	Tent	—	—	Dog	—
13.9	F	$	—	Restroom	—	Tent	—	—	Dog	—
5.6	F	—	—	—	—	—	—	—	—	—
2.1	—	$	Book	Restroom	—	—	—	—	—	—
9.0	—	$	Book	—	—	Tent	—	Family	—	—
0.8	—	—	Book	—	—	—	—	Family	—	—
3.6	—	—	Book	—	—	—	—	—	Dog	—
12.2	—	$	Book	Restroom	—	—	—	—	Dog	—
0.9	—	$	Book	Restroom	—	—	—	—	—	—
2.6	—	—	Book	—	—	—	—	Family	—	—
4.8	—	—	Book	Restroom	—	—	—	Family	—	—
1.1	—	—	Book	Restroom	—	—	Wheelchair	Family	—	—
4.2	—	—	Book	Restroom	—	—	—	—	—	—
2.8	—	—	Book	—	—	—	—	Family	Dog	—
16.8	—	$	Book	Restroom	Camp	—	Wheelchair	Family	—	—
1.5	—	—	—	—	—	—	—	—	Dog	—
3.9	—	—	Book	—	—	—	—	—	—	—
1.0	—	$	—	Restroom	Camp	—	Wheelchair	Family	—	—
0.9	—	$	Book	Restroom	—	—	—	Family	Dog	—

North Atlantic

Trail Miles	F	$	Book	Restrooms	Camp	Tent	Wheelchair	Family	Dogs	Winter
1.4	—	$	Book	Restroom	—	Tent	—	Family	Dog	—
0.6	—	$	Book	Restroom	Camp	—	—	Family	—	—
1.0	—	—	—	—	—	—	—	—	Dog	—
3.8	—	$	—	Restroom	Camp	—	—	—	—	—
0.8	—	$	Book	Restroom	Camp	—	—	Family	Dog	—
0.8	—	—	—	Restroom	—	—	Wheelchair	—	—	—
2.0	—	—	—	Restroom	—	—	Wheelchair	Family	Dog	—
2.4	—	—	Book	Restroom	—	—	Wheelchair	Family	Dog	—

Trail		Public Land	County	Location
9	—	Pumpkin Hill Creek Preserve State Park	Duval	New Berlin Park
10	—	Arlington Lions Club Park	Duval	Jacksonville
11	Hammock Nature Trail	Fort Caroline National Monument	Duval	Jacksonville
12	—	Theodore Roosevelt Area, Timucuan Preserve	Duval	Jacksonville
13	—	Kathryn Abbey Hanna Park	Duval	Mayport
14	Robert W. Loftin Nature Trails	University of North Florida Wildlife Sanctuary	Duval	South Jacksonville
15	—	Stokes Landing Conservation Area	St. Johns	St. Augustine
16	—	Guana River State Park	St. Johns	S. Ponte Vedra Beach
17	Ancient Dunes Trail	Anastasia State Park	St. Johns	St. Augustine Beach
18	—	Moses Creek Conservation Area	St. Johns	Dupont Center
19	Accessible Nature Trail	Fort Matanzas National Monument	St. Johns	Crescent Beach
20	Nature Trail	Faver-Dykes State Park	St. Johns	Colfax
21	Mala Compra Trail	Washington Oaks Gardens State Park	Flagler	Hammock
22	Bella Vista Trail	Washington Oaks Gardens State Park	Flagler	Hammock
23	—	Malacompra County Park	Flagler	Hammock
24	Red Trail	Princess Place Preserve	Flagler	Colfax
25	Blue Trail	Princess Place Preserve	Flagler	Colfax
26	Green Trail	Princess Place Preserve	Flagler	Colfax
27	—	Graham Swamp Conservation Area	Flagler	Palm Coast
28	—	Wadsworth Park	Flagler	Flagler Beach
29	Joe Kenner Nature Trail	Gamble Rogers Memorial State Recreation Area	Flagler	Flagler Beach
30	Bulow Creek Trail	Bulow Plantation Ruins SP / Bulow Creek SP	Flagler	Ormond Beach
31	—	Haw Creek Preserve	Flagler	Bunnell

Central Gulf

1	Ecowalk	Crystal River Preserve State Park	Citrus	Crystal River
2	Eagle Scout Trail	Crystal River Preserve State Park	Citrus	Crystal River
3	Churchhouse Hammock Trail	Crystal River Preserve State Park	Citrus	Crystal River
4	Redfish Hole	Crystal River Preserve State Park	Citrus	Crystal River
5	Oxbow Trails	Withlacoochee State Forest	Citrus	Citrus Springs
6	Johnson Pond Trail	Withlacoochee State Forest	Citrus	Citrus Springs
7	—	Potts Preserve	Citrus	Inverness
8	—	Fort Cooper State Park	Citrus	Inverness
9	Citrus Hiking Trail	Withlacoochee State Forest	Citrus	Inverness
10	Rooks Trail	Withlacoochee State Forest	Citrus	Chassahowitzka
11	—	Chassahowitzka Wildlife Management Area	Hernando	Chassahowitzka
12	—	Perry Oldenburg Mitigation Park	Hernando	Brooksville

Trail Miles	Ⓕ	$	📖	🚻	●	⛺	♿	👪	🐴	❄️
0.8	—	—	—	—	—	—	—	—	🐴	—
1.1	—	—	—	🚻	—	—	♿	👪	🐴	—
1.3	—	—	📖	🚻	—	—	—	👪	—	—
4.2	—	—	📖	🚻	—	—	—	👪	🐴	—
2.7	—	$	📖	🚻	●	⛺	—	👪	—	—
4.9	—	—	📖	—	—	—	♿	👪	—	—
3.0	—	—	📖	—	—	—	—	👪	🐴	—
9.0	—	—	📖	🚻	—	—	—	—	🐴	❄️
0.7	—	$	📖	🚻	●	—	—	👪	🐴	—
14.0	—	—	—	—	—	⛺	—	—	🐴	—
0.5	—	—	📖	🚻	—	—	♿	👪	—	—
0.5	—	$	📖	🚻	●	—	—	👪	🐴	—
0.7	—	$	📖	🚻	—	—	—	👪	🐴	—
1.8	Ⓕ	$	📖	🚻	—	—	—	👪	🐴	—
0.5	—	—	—	🚻	—	—	—	—	🐴	—
2.2	—	—	📖	—	—	⛺	—	—	—	—
1.0	—	—	📖	🚻	—	⛺	—	👪	—	—
0.8	—	—	📖	—	—	⛺	—	👪	—	—
1.0	—	—	—	—	—	⛺	—	—	—	—
0.2	—	—	—	🚻	—	—	♿	👪	🐴	—
0.7	—	$	📖	🚻	●	—	—	👪	🐴	—
13.4	Ⓕ	$	📖	🚻	—	⛺	—	—	🐴	❄️
1.6	—	—	📖	🚻	—	⛺	—	👪	—	—

Central Gulf

Trail Miles	Ⓕ	$	📖	🚻	●	⛺	♿	👪	🐴	❄️
2.3	—	—	📖	—	—	—	—	👪	🐴	—
0.5	—	—	—	—	—	—	—	—	🐴	—
1.0	—	—	—	🚻	—	—	♿	👪	—	—
1.6	—	—	—	—	—	—	—	—	—	❄️
1.0	—	—	—	—	—	⛺	—	—	🐴	—
2.7	—	—	📖	—	—	—	—	👪	🐴	—
12.3	Ⓕ	—	—	—	—	⛺	—	—	—	—
3.0	—	$	📖	🚻	—	—	—	👪	🐴	—
43.3	Ⓕ	—	—	—	●	⛺	—	—	🐴	❄️
2.7	—	—	—	—	—	—	—	—	🐴	—
1.5	—	$	—	—	—	—	—	—	🐴	—
1.6	—	—	📖	—	—	—	—	—	🐴	—

	Trail	Public Land	County	Location
13	McKethan Lake Nature Trail	Withlacoochee State Forest	Hernando	Brooksville
14	Croom Hiking Trail	Withlacoochee State Forest	Hernando	Ridge Manor
15	—	Weekiwachee Preserve	Hernando	Hernando Beach
16	—	Crews Lake Park	Pasco	Spring Hill
17	Florida Trail	Withlacoochee State Forest	Pasco	Ridge Manor
18	Florida Trail	Green Swamp West	Pasco	Dade City
19	—	Withlacoochee River Park	Pasco	Dade City
20	Upper Hillsborough River Hiking Trail	Upper Hillsborough River Water Mgmt Area	Pasco	Zephyrhills
21	Nature Trail	Werner-Boyce Salt Springs State Park	Pasco	New Port Richey
22	—	J. B. Starkey Wilderness Park	Pasco	New Port Richey
23	—	Key Vista Nature Park	Pasco	Holiday
24	—	Caladesi Island State Park	Pinellas	Dunedin
25	—	Honeymoon Island State Park	Pinellas	Dunedin
26	—	John Chesnut Sr. County Park	Pinellas	Oldsmar
27	The Friends Trail	Brooker Creek Preserve	Pinellas	Tarpon Springs
28	—	Moccasin Lake Nature Park	Pinellas	Clearwater
29	—	Sawgrass Lake Park	Pinellas	Pinellas Park
30	—	Boca Ciega Millennium Park	Pinellas	Seminole
31	—	Weedon Island Preserve	Pinellas	St. Petersburg
32	—	Boyd Hill Nature Park	Pinellas	St. Petersburg
33	Barrier Free Nature Trail	Fort De Soto Park	Pinellas	Tierra Verde
34	Soldiers Hole Trail	Fort De Soto Park	Pinellas	Tierra Verde
35	Arrowhead Nature Trail	Fort De Soto Park	Pinellas	Tierra Verde
36	—	Morris Bridge Park	Hillsborough	New Tampa
37	—	Trout Creek Park	Hillsborough	New Tampa
38	—	Hillsborough River State Park	Hillsborough	Thonotosassa
39	—	J. B. Sargeant Sr. Memorial Wilderness Park	Hillsborough	Thonotosassa
40	—	Lettuce Lake Park	Hillsborough	Temple Terrace
41	—	Alderman's Ford Park	Hillsborough	Lithia
42	—	Little Manatee River State Park	Hillsborough	Wimauma
Central Florida				
1	Sandhills Nature Trail	Rainbow Springs State Park	Marion	Dunnellon
2	Florida Trail	Cross Florida Greenway	Marion	Dunnellon
3	—	Hálpata Tastanaki Preserve	Marion	Dunnellon
4	Ross Prairie Loop	Cross Florida Greenway	Marion	Dunnellon
5	Land Bridge Loop	Cross Florida Greenway	Marion	Ocala

Trail Miles	F	$	📖	🚻	◉	⛺	♿	👫	⛺shelter	❄
1.9	—	$	—	🚻	—	—	—	—	🏠	—
23.7	F	—	—	—	◉	⛺	—	—	🏠	—
14.3	—	—	📖	🚻	—	—	—	—	—	—
1.1	—	—	📖	🚻	—	⛺	—	👫	🏠	—
31.5	F	—	—	—	—	⛺	—	—	🏠	—
17.9	F	—	—	—	—	⛺	—	—	🏠	—
7.9	F	—	📖	🚻	—	⛺	—	👫	—	—
4.0	F	—	—	—	—	⛺	—	—	—	—
0.5	—	—	📖	🚻	—	—	—	👫	🏠	—
14.0	—	—	📖	🚻	◉	⛺	—	👫	🏠	—
1.5	—	—	📖	🚻	—	—	—	👫	🏠	❄
3.5	—	$	📖	🚻	—	—	—	—	—	❄
2.5	—	$	📖	🚻	—	—	♿	👫	🏠	—
1.8	—	—	📖	🚻	—	—	♿	👫	🏠	—
1.8	—	—	📖	—	—	—	—	—	—	—
1.0	—	$	📖	🚻	—	—	♿	👫	—	—
1.9	—	—	📖	🚻	—	—	♿	👫	—	—
1.3	—	—	📖	🚻	—	—	♿	👫	🏠	—
4.7	—	—	—	🚻	—	—	♿	👫	—	—
4.0	—	$	📖	🚻	—	—	♿	👫	—	—
0.4	—	—	📖	🚻	◉	—	♿	👫	🏠	—
1.7	—	—	📖	—	◉	—	—	—	—	—
1.4	—	—	📖	🚻	◉	—	—	👫	🏠	—
1.9	—	$	📖	🚻	—	—	♿	👫	—	—
0.8	—	$	—	🚻	—	—	♿	👫	—	—
6.0	F	$	📖	🚻	◉	⛺	—	👫	🏠	—
0.6	—	$	📖	🚻	—	—	♿	👫	🏠	—
1.1	—	$	📖	🚻	—	—	♿	👫	🏠	—
7.0	—	$	—	🚻	—	⛺	♿	👫	🏠	—
6.5	F	$	—	—	—	⛺	—	—	—	❄
Central Florida										
2.1	—	$	—	🚻	◉	—	—	—	—	—
32.0	F	—	—	—	—	⛺	—	—	🏠	—
4.5	—	—	—	—	—	—	—	—	🏠	—
3.5	F	—	—	🚻	◉	⛺	—	—	🏠	—
2.2	F	—	—	🚻	—	⛺	—	—	🏠	—

	Trail	Public Land	County	Location
6	Historic Ship Canal Trail	Cross Florida Greenway	Marion	Santos
7	Brick City Quarry	Brick City Park	Marion	Ocala
8	Nature Trail	Coehadjoe Park	Marion	Ocala
9	Florida Trail	Ocala National Forest	Marion	Salt Springs
10	Bear Swamp Trail	Ocala National Forest	Marion	Salt Springs
11	Salt Springs Loop	Ocala National Forest	Marion	Salt Springs
12	Lake Eaton Trails	Ocala National Forest	Marion	Lake Eaton
13	Silver Glen Springs	Ocala National Forest	Marion	Silver Glen Springs
14	The Yearling Trail	Ocala National Forest	Marion	Silver Glen Springs
15	Juniper Creek Nature Trail	Ocala National Forest	Marion	Juniper Springs
16	Silver River Connector Trail	Cross Florida Greenway	Marion	Silver Springs
17	—	Silver River State Park	Marion	Silver Springs
18	Marshall Swamp Trail	Cross Florida Greenway	Marion	Silver Springs
19	—	Carney Island	Marion	Ocklawaha
20	Nature Trail	Lake Griffin State Park	Lake	Fruitland Park
21	—	Sabal Bluff Preserve	Lake	Leesburg
22	—	Flat Island Preserve	Lake	Leesburg
23	—	Lake Louisa State Park	Lake	Clermont
24	—	Sara Maude Mason Nature Preserve	Lake	Howey-in-the-Hills
25	—	Tavares Nature Park	Lake	Tavares
26	—	Sawgrass Island Preserve	Lake	Umatilla
27	—	Hidden Waters Preserve	Lake	Eustis
28	—	Palm Island Park	Lake	Mount Dora
29	Timucuan Indian Nature Trail	Ocala National Forest	Lake	Astor
30	Sandpine Scrub Forest Nature Trail	Ocala National Forest	Lake	Astor Park
31	St. Francis Hiking Trail	Ocala National Forest	Lake	Deland
32	Florida Trail	Seminole State Forest	Lake	Sorrento
33	Rock Springs Run Trail	Rock Springs Run State Reserve	Lake	Sorrento
34	Hog Island Nature Trail	Withlacoochee State Forest	Sumter	Nobleton
35	Croom Hiking Trail	Withlacoochee State Forest	Sumter	Nobleton
36	Pine Flatwoods Trail	Dade Battlefield Historic State Park	Sumter	Bushnell
37	—	Oakland Nature Preserve	Orange	Oakland
38	—	Tibet-Butler Preserve	Orange	Lake Buena Vista
39	Nature Trail	Bill Fredrick Park at Turkey Lake	Orange	Orlando
40	—	Mead Gardens	Orange	Winter Park
41	—	Orlando Wetlands Park	Orange	Christmas

Trail Miles	F	$	📖	Restroom	Camp	Tent	♿	People	Shelter	Playground
0.5	—	—	📖	—	—	—	—	People	Shelter	—
0.7	—	—	—	Restroom	—	—	♿	—	Shelter	—
0.7	—	—	—	Restroom	—	—	—	People	Shelter	—
71.3	F	—	—	—	Camp	Tent	—	—	Shelter	✳
1.2	—	$	—	Restroom	Camp	—	—	People	Shelter	—
1.9	—	—	📖	—	—	—	—	People	Shelter	—
4.1	—	—	📖	—	—	—	—	—	Shelter	—
2.8	—	$	📖	Restroom	—	—	—	People	—	—
6.0	F	—	—	—	—	Tent	—	—	Shelter	—
1.0	—	$	📖	Restroom	Camp	—	—	People	—	✳
1.8	—	—	📖	Restroom	—	—	—	—	Shelter	—
8.3	—	$	📖	Restroom	Camp	—	—	People	Shelter	—
4.3	F	—	📖	—	—	—	—	People	—	—
4.0	—	$	📖	Restroom	—	—	—	People	—	—
0.4	—	$	📖	Restroom	Camp	—	—	People	—	—
5.0	—	—	—	—	—	—	—	—	Shelter	—
3.5	F	—	📖	—	—	Tent	—	—	Shelter	—
7.4	—	$	📖	—	Camp	—	—	People	Shelter	—
0.6	—	—	📖	—	—	—	—	People	—	—
2.1	—	—	📖	—	—	—	—	—	Shelter	—
3.0	—	—	—	—	—	Tent	—	—	Shelter	—
1.0	—	—	📖	—	—	—	—	People	Shelter	—
1.0	—	—	📖	—	—	—	♿	People	—	—
1.1	—	$	📖	Restroom	Camp	—	♿	People	—	—
0.3	—	—	📖	—	—	—	—	People	—	—
7.7	F	—	📖	—	—	Tent	—	—	Shelter	—
16.4	F	$	—	—	—	Tent	—	—	Shelter	—
13.2	F	$	—	—	—	Tent	—	—	Shelter	—
1.6	—	—	📖	Restroom	Camp	—	—	—	—	—
6.8	F	—	—	Restroom	Camp	—	—	—	Shelter	—
0.7	—	$	📖	Restroom	—	—	—	People	Shelter	—
1.1	—	—	📖	Restroom	—	—	♿	People	—	✳
3.5	—	—	📖	Restroom	—	—	—	People	—	—
1.6	—	$	—	Restroom	Camp	—	—	People	Shelter	—
1.5	—	—	—	Restroom	—	—	—	People	Shelter	—
6.0	F	—	📖	—	—	—	♿	—	—	—

	Trail	Public Land	County	Location
42	Florida Trail	Seminole Ranch Conservation Area	Orange	Christmas
43	Florida Trail	Tosohatchee Reserve State Park	Orange	Christmas
44	—	Hal Scott Regional Preserve	Orange	Bithlo
45	—	Split Oak Forest Mitigation Park	Orange	Narcoossee
46	Sandhill Nature Trail	Lower Wekiva River Preserve State Park	Seminole	Sanford
47	—	Wekiwa Springs State Park	Seminole	Longwood
48	—	Sabal Point Sanctuary	Seminole	Longwood
49	—	Lake Lotus Park	Seminole	Altamonte Springs
50	—	Big Tree Park	Seminole	Winter Springs
51	Florida Trail	Spring Hammock Preserve	Seminole	Winter Springs
52	—	Spring Hammock Preserve	Seminole	Winter Springs
53	—	Lake Jesup Wilderness Area	Seminole	Sanford
54	East Lake Jesup Tract	Lake Jesup Conservation Area	Seminole	Oviedo
55	Bear Creek Nature Trail	—	Seminole	Winter Springs
56	Florida Trail	Little-Big Econ State Forest	Seminole	Oviedo
57	—	Geneva Wilderness Area	Seminole	Geneva
58	—	Lake Proctor Wilderness Area	Seminole	Geneva
59	Nature Trail	Lake Mills Park	Seminole	Chuluota
60	—	Econ River Wilderness Area	Seminole	Oviedo
61	Florida Trail	Bull Creek Wildlife Management Area	Osceola	Holopaw
62	Florida Trail	Prairie Lakes Wildlife Management Area	Osceola	Lake Marian
63	Sunset Ranch Interpretive Trail	Prairie Lakes Wildlife Management Area	Osceola	Lake Marian
64	—	Osceola County Environmental Education Center	Osceola	Poinciana
65	—	Disney Wilderness Preserve	Osceola	Poinciana
66	—	Lake Marion Creek Wildlife Management Area	Osceola	Poinciana
67	Florida Trail	Green Swamp East	Polk	Rock Ridge
68	—	Gator Creek Preserve	Polk	Gibsonia
69	Tenoroc Hiking Trail	Tenoroc Fish Management Area	Polk	Lakeland
70	Saddle Creek Park Nature Trail	Saddle Creek Park	Polk	Lakeland
71	—	Lakeland Highlands Scrub	Polk	Lakeland
72	—	IMC Agrico Peace River Park	Polk	Fort Meade
73	Nature Trail	Fort Meade Outdoor Recreation Area	Polk	Fort Meade
74	Norton Agey Nature Trail	Street Audubon Center	Polk	Winter Haven
75	—	Catfish Creek Preserve	Polk	Dundee
76	—	Lake Kissimmee State Park	Polk	Lake Wales
77	Caloosa Nature Trail	Ridge Audubon Center	Polk	Babson Park

Trail Miles	Ⓕ	$	📖	🚻	camp	tent	♿	👫	horse	❄
4.9	Ⓕ	—	—	—	—	tent	—	—	horse	—
11.3	Ⓕ	$	—	—	—	tent	—	—	horse	—
5.1	Ⓕ	—	—	—	—	tent	—	—	horse	—
8.5	Ⓕ	—	📖	—	—	—	—	—	—	—
2.5	Ⓕ	—	📖	—	—	—	—	👫	horse	—
13.5	Ⓕ	$	📖	🚻	camp	tent	—	—	horse	—
7.0	—	—	📖	—	—	—	—	—	horse	—
1.7	—	—	📖	🚻	—	—	♿	👫	—	—
0.3	—	—	📖	🚻	—	—	♿	👫	horse	—
1.1	Ⓕ	—	—	🚻	—	—	—	—	horse	—
4.0	—	—	—	🚻	—	—	—	👫	horse	❄
2.7	—	—	📖	—	—	—	—	—	—	—
1.3	—	—	—	—	—	tent	—	—	horse	—
0.3	—	—	—	—	—	—	—	—	horse	—
7.3	Ⓕ	$	—	—	—	tent	—	—	horse	❄
3.2	—	—	—	🚻	—	tent	—	👫	horse	—
6.0	—	—	📖	—	—	—	—	👫	horse	—
0.8	—	—	📖	🚻	camp	—	—	👫	—	—
4.0	—	—	📖	—	—	—	—	👫	horse	—
23.7	Ⓕ	—	—	—	—	tent	—	—	horse	—
31.3	Ⓕ	$	—	—	—	tent	—	—	horse	—
2.0	—	$	📖	—	—	—	—	—	horse	—
5.3	—	—	📖	🚻	—	—	♿	👫	—	—
6.0	—	$	📖	—	—	—	♿	👫	—	—
4.2	—	—	—	—	—	tent	—	—	horse	—
13.9	Ⓕ	—	—	—	—	tent	—	—	horse	—
2.5	—	—	📖	—	—	—	—	👫	horse	—
6.0	Ⓕ	$	—	🚻	—	—	—	—	—	—
2.4	—	—	📖	🚻	camp	—	—	—	horse	—
0.6	—	—	—	🚻	—	—	—	—	horse	—
0.5	—	—	📖	🚻	camp	—	♿	👫	—	—
0.3	—	—	—	🚻	—	—	—	—	—	—
1.0	—	—	📖	🚻	—	—	—	👫	horse	—
9.0	—	—	—	🚻	—	—	—	—	horse	❄
16.3	Ⓕ	$	📖	🚻	camp	tent	—	👫	horse	❄
0.3	—	—	📖	—	—	—	—	👫	—	—

Trail	Public Land	County	Location
78 Jenkins Trail	Tiger Creek Preserve	Polk	Frostproof
79 George Cooley Trail	Tiger Creek Preserve	Polk	Babson Park
80 Pfundstein Trail	Tiger Creek Preserve	Polk	Babson Park
81 Bay Loop Trail	Lake Wales Ridge State Forest	Polk	Frostproof
82 Scrub-Jay Loop Trail	Lake Wales Ridge State Forest	Polk	Frostproof
83 Reedy Creek Trail	Lake Wales Ridge State Forest	Polk	Frostproof
84 Old Cabin Nature Trail	Lake Wales Ridge State Forest	Polk	Frostproof
85 —	Crooked Lake Prairie	Polk	Frostproof
86 North Loop	Hickory Lake Scrub	Polk	Frostproof
87 South Loop	Hickory Lake Scrub	Polk	Frostproof
Central Atlantic			
1 Nature Trail	Tomoka State Park	Volusia	Ormond Beach
2 —	DeLeon Springs State Park	Volusia	De Leon Springs
3 —	Lake Woodruff National Wildlife Refuge	Volusia	De Leon Springs
4 Indian Mound Nature Trail	Hontoon Island State Park	Volusia	Deland
5 Pine Island Hiking Trail	Blue Spring State Park	Volusia	Orange City
6 Buncombe Hill Interpretive Trail	Tiger Bay State Forest	Volusia	Daytona
7 —	Lyonia Preserve	Volusia	Deltona
8 —	Lake Ashby Park	Volusia	Lake Ashby
9 Kratzert Tract	Lake Monroe Conservation Area	Volusia	Sanford
10 —	Spruce Creek Park	Volusia	Port Orange
11 —	Smyrna Dunes Park	Volusia	New Smyrna Beach
12 Turtle Mound Trail	Canaveral National Seashore	Volusia	Bethune Beach
13 Eldora Hammock Trail	Canaveral National Seashore	Volusia	Bethune Beach
14 Castle Windy Trail	Canaveral National Seashore	Volusia	Bethune Beach
15 Seminole Rest Trail	Canaveral National Seashore	Volusia	Oak Hill
16 Scrub Ridge Trail	Merritt Island National Wildlife Refuge	Brevard	Merritt Island
17 Oak and Palm Hammock Trails	Merritt Island National Wildlife Refuge	Brevard	Merritt Island
18 Visitor Center Boardwalk	Merritt Island National Wildlife Refuge	Brevard	Merritt Island
19 Cruickshank Trail	Merritt Island National Wildlife Refuge	Brevard	Merritt Island
20 —	Wuesthoff Park	Brevard	Titusville
21 Canaveral Marshes Trail	Canaveral Marshes Conservation Area	Brevard	Titusville
22 —	Enchanted Forest Sanctuary	Brevard	Titusville
23 —	Pine Island Conservation Area	Brevard	Courtenay
24 Hammock Nature Trail	Lori Wilson Park	Brevard	Cocoa Beach
25 Nature Trail	Rotary Park—Merritt Island	Brevard	Merritt Island

Trail Miles	🅕	$	📖	🚻	♲	⛺	♿	👫	🐴	❄
1.0	—	—	—	—	—	—	—	—	—	❄
0.8	—	—	📖	—	—	—	—	👫	—	❄
7.6	🅕	—	—	—	—	—	—	—	—	—
1.5	—	$	—	—	—	⛺	—	—	🐴	—
2.7	—	$	—	—	—	—	—	—	🐴	—
18.7	🅕	$	—	—	♲	⛺	—	—	🐴	—
1.0	—	$	📖	—	—	⛺	—	—	🐴	—
4.6	—	—	📖	🚻	—	⛺	—	—	🐴	—
0.4	—	—	📖	—	—	—	—	👫	🐴	—
0.3	—	—	📖	—	—	—	—	👫	🐴	–
Central Atlantic										
0.7	—	$	📖	🚻	♲	—	—	👫	🐴	—
5.5	🅕	$	📖	🚻	—	—	♿	👫	—	—
6.0	—	—	📖	🚻	—	—	—	—	—	—
3.3	—	$	📖	🚻	♲	—	—	—	🐴	—
7.3	—	$	📖	🚻	♲	⛺	—	—	—	—
2.1	—	—	📖	—	—	⛺	—	—	🐴	—
2.5	—	—	📖	🚻	—	—	—	👫	—	—
1.5	—	—	📖	🚻	—	⛺	♿	👫	—	—
3.0	—	—	—	—	—	⛺	—	—	🐴	❄
1.5	—	—	📖	🚻	♲	—	♿	👫	🐴	—
1.4	—	$	📖	🚻	—	—	♿	👫	🐴	—
0.3	—	$	📖	—	—	—	—	👫	—	—
0.5	—	$	📖	—	—	—	—	👫	🐴	—
0.7	—	$	📖	🚻	—	—	—	👫	🐴	—
0.3	—	—	📖	🚻	—	—	♿	👫	🐴	—
0.9	—	—	📖	🚻	—	—	♿	👫	—	—
2.7	—	—	📖	—	—	—	—	👫	—	—
0.4	—	—	📖	🚻	—	—	♿	👫	—	—
4.8	—	—	📖	🚻	—	—	—	—	—	—
1.0	—	—	📖	🚻	—	—	—	👫	🐴	—
3.9	🅕	—	—	—	—	—	—	—	—	—
2.5	—	—	📖	🚻	—	—	♿	👫	—	❄
2.5	—	—	—	🚻	—	—	—	—	—	—
0.3	—	—	📖	🚻	—	—	♿	👫	—	—
0.3	—	—	📖	🚻	—	—	♿	👫	—	—

Trail	Public Land	County	Location
26 —	Wickham Park	Brevard	Melbourne
27 Nature Trail	Erna Nixon Park	Brevard	Melbourne
28 —	Turkey Creek Sanctuary	Brevard	Palm Bay
29 —	Malabar Scrub Sanctuary	Brevard	Malabar
30 Flatwoods Loop	Micco Scrub Sanctuary	Brevard	Malabar
31 —	St. Sebastian River Preserve State Park	Brevard	Fellsmere
32 —	Coconut Point Sanctuary	Brevard	Melbourne Beach
33 —	Maritime Hammock Sanctuary	Brevard	Melbourne Beach
34 Nature Trail	Sebastian Inlet State Park	Brevard	Sebastian Inlet
35 Centennial Trail	Pelican Island National Wildlife Refuge	Indian River	Orchid Island
36 —	Wabasso Island Environmental Learning Center	Indian River	Wabasso Island
37 —	Oslo Riverfront Conservation Area	Indian River	Vero Beach
38 —	Fort Drum Marsh Conservation Area	Indian River	Yeehaw Junction

South Gulf

Trail	Public Land	County	Location
1 —	Emerson Point Park	Manatee	Snead Island
2 —	Rye Wilderness Park	Manatee	Parrish
3 —	De Soto National Memorial	Manatee	Bradenton
4 —	Coquina Baywalk	Manatee	Leffis Key
5 —	Quick Point Nature Preserve	Sarasota	Longboat Key
6 Nature Trail	Phillipi Estate Park	Sarasota	Sarasota
7 Canopy Walk	Myakka River State Park	Sarasota	Sarasota
8 Birdwalk	Myakka River State Park	Sarasota	Sarasota
9 Myakka Hiking Trail	Myakka River State Park	Sarasota	Sarasota
10 Caspersen Beach Nature Trail	Caspersen Beach Park	Sarasota	Venice
11 Nature Trail	Shamrock Park	Sarasota	South Venice
12 North Trail System	Oscar Scherer State Park	Sarasota	Osprey
13 South Trail System	Oscar Scherer State Park	Sarasota	Osprey
14 —	T. Mabry Carlton Jr. Memorial Reserve	Sarasota	Venice
15 —	Lemon Bay Park	Sarasota	Englewood
16 —	Jelks Preserve	Sarasota	North Port
17 —	Myakkahatchee Creek Environmental Park	Sarasota	North Port
18 —	Cedar Point Park	Charlotte	Englewood
19 —	Alligator Creek Preserve	Charlotte	Punta Gorda
20 Old Datsun Trail	Charlotte Harbor Environmental Center	Charlotte	Punta Gorda
21 —	Cayo Costa State Park	Lee	La Costa Island
22 Little Pine Island Hiking Trail	Charlotte Harbor Preserve State Park	Lee	Pine Island Center

Trail Miles	F	$	📖	🚻	🏕(C)	⛺	♿	👫	🐕	❄
4.0	—	—	—	🚻	🏕	—	—	—	🐕	—
0.5	—	—	📖	🚻	—	—	♿	👫	—	❄
1.6	—	—	📖	🚻	—	—	♿	👫	—	❄
5.0	—	—	—	🚻	—	—	♿	—	—	—
3.2	—	—	—	—	—	—	—	—	🐕	❄
2.4	—	—	📖	🚻	—	⛺	—	—	🐕	—
1.0	—	—	—	—	—	—	—	👫	—	❄
2.5	—	—	—	—	—	—	—	—	—	—
0.5	—	—	📖	—	🏕	—	—	—	—	—
0.8	—	—	📖	—	—	—	♿	👫	—	—
2.0	—	—	📖	🚻	—	—	♿	👫	—	—
3.0	—	—	📖	—	—	—	—	👫	—	❄
3.0	—	—	—	—	—	⛺	—	—	—	—

South Gulf

Trail Miles	F	$	📖	🚻	🏕(C)	⛺	♿	👫	🐕	❄
3.0	—	—	📖	🚻	—	—	—	—	🐕	—
4.0	—	—	📖	🚻	🏕	—	—	—	—	—
1.1	—	—	📖	🚻	—	—	♿	👫	🐕	—
0.8	—	—	📖	—	—	—	♿	👫	🐕	❄
0.8	—	—	📖	—	—	—	—	👫	🐕	—
0.3	—	—	📖	🚻	—	—	♿	👫	🐕	—
0.9	—	$	📖	🚻	🏕	—	—	👫	—	❄
0.4	—	$	📖	—	🏕	—	♿	👫	—	—
39.0	F	$	—	—	—	⛺	—	—	—	❄
0.4	—	—	📖	🚻	—	—	—	👫	🐕	—
0.5	—	—	—	🚻	—	—	—	—	🐕	—
7.5	—	$	📖	🚻	🏕	—	—	—	🐕	—
5.0	—	$	📖	🚻	🏕	—	♿	👫	🐕	—
1.8	—	—	📖	🚻	—	—	♿	👫	—	—
2.7	—	—	📖	🚻	—	—	♿	👫	🐕	—
3.3	—	—	📖	—	—	—	—	—	—	—
2.5	—	—	📖	🚻	—	—	—	👫	—	—
3.5	—	—	📖	🚻	—	—	—	👫	—	—
3.0	—	—	📖	🚻	—	—	—	👫	—	—
1.7	—	—	📖	—	—	—	—	—	—	—
6.5	—	$	📖	🚻	—	⛺	—	—	—	—
2.0	—	—	📖	—	—	—	—	—	—	—

Trail	Public Land	County	Location
23 —	Caloosahatchee Regional Park	Lee	Alva
24 —	Hickey's Creek Mitigation Park	Lee	Alva
25 —	Four Mile Cove Ecological Preserve	Lee	Cape Coral
26 —	Calusa Nature Center	Lee	Fort Myers
27 —	Six Mile Cypress Slough Preserve	Lee	Fort Myers
28 —	Winkler Point, Estero Bay Preserve State Park	Lee	Fort Myers
29 —	Bailey Tract, Ding Darling Natl Wildlife Refuge	Lee	Sanibel Island
30 Indigo Trail	Ding Darling National Wildlife Refuge	Lee	Sanibel Island
31 Wulfert Keys Trail	Ding Darling National Wildlife Refuge	Lee	Sanibel Island
32 Shell Mound Trail	Ding Darling National Wildlife Refuge	Lee	Sanibel Island
33 —	Sanibel-Captiva Conservation Foundation	Lee	Sanibel Island
34 —	Mantanzas Pass Preserve	Lee	Fort Myers Beach
35 Black Island Trail	Lovers Key State Park	Lee	Lovers Key
36 —	Estero Scrub Preserve	Lee	Estero
37 Nature Trail	Koreshan Historic State Park	Lee	Estero
38 CREW Marsh Trail System	CREW ManagementArea	Collier	Lake Trafford
39 —	Corkscrew Marsh Sanctuary	Collier	Immokalee
40 Sabal Palm Trail	Picayune Strand State Forest	Collier	Naples
41 Royal Palm Hammock Trail	Collier-Seminole State Park	Collier	Royal Palm Hammock
42 Collier-Seminole Hiking Trail	Collier-Seminole State Park	Collier	Royal Palm Hammock
43 Big Cypress Bend Boardwalk	Fakahatchee Strand Preserve State Park	Collier	Copeland

South Central

Trail	Public Land	County	Location
1 —	Paynes Creek Historic State Park	Hardee	Bowling Green
2 —	The Preserve at Sun n' Lakes	Highlands	Sebring
3 Hickory Trail	Highlands Hammock State Park	Highlands	Sebring
4 Young Hammock Trail	Highlands Hammock State Park	Highlands	Sebring
5 Cypress Swamp Trail	Highlands Hammock State Park	Highlands	Sebring
6 Ancient Hammock Trail	Highlands Hammock State Park	Highlands	Sebring
7 Allen Altvater Trail	Highlands Hammock State Park	Highlands	Sebring
8 Bobcat, Eagle, and Deer Trails	Lake June-in-Winter State Park	Highlands	Lake Placid
9 Tomoka Run Trail	Lake June-in-Winter State Park	Highlands	Lake Placid
10 Florida Scrub Nature Trail	Archbold Biological Station	Highlands	Lake Placid
11 Bee Island Boardwalk	Istokpoga Park	Highlands	Lorida
12 Florida Trail	Upper Kissimmee River	Highlands	Lorida
13 Florida Trail	Hickory Hammock	Highlands	Lorida
14 —	Platt Branch Mitigation Park	Glades	Venus

Trail Miles	🅕	$	📖	👫	⛺︎(fire)	⛺	♿	🧒	🐕	❄
3.4	—	$	📖	👫	—	⛺	♿	🧒	—	—
5.7	—	$	📖	👫	—	—	♿	🧒	—	—
1.2	—	—	📖	👫	—	—	♿	🧒	—	—
2.1	—	$	📖	👫	—	—	♿	🧒	—	—
1.4	—	$	📖	👫	—	—	♿	🧒	—	❄
5.0	—	—	—	—	—	—	—	—	—	—
1.1	—	—	📖	—	—	—	—	—	—	—
4.0	—	$	📖	👫	—	—	♿	—	—	—
0.5	—	$	—	—	—	—	—	—	—	—
0.4	—	$	—	—	—	—	♿	—	—	—
3.0	—	$	📖	👫	—	—	—	🧒	—	—
2.0	—	—	—	—	—	—	♿	🧒	—	—
5.0	—	$	📖	👫	—	—	—	—	—	—
5.5	—	—	—	—	—	—	—	—	—	—
0.5	—	$	📖	👫	🔥	—	—	🧒	🐕	—
5.0	—	—	—	👫	—	⛺	—	—	—	—
2.3	—	$	📖	👫	—	—	♿	🧒	—	❄
3.5	—	—	—	—	—	⛺	—	—	—	—
0.9	—	$	📖	👫	🔥	—	—	—	—	—
6.5	🅕	$	—	—	🔥	⛺	—	—	—	❄
1.2	—	—	📖	—	—	—	♿	🧒	—	❄

South Central

Trail Miles	🅕	$	📖	👫	🔥	⛺	♿	🧒	🐕	❄
2.9	—	$	📖	👫	—	—	—	🧒	🐕	—
4.0	—	—	—	—	—	—	—	—	🐕	—
2.9	—	$	📖	👫	🔥	—	—	🧒	🐕	—
0.6	—	$	📖	—	🔥	—	—	🧒	🐕	—
0.4	—	$	📖	—	🔥	—	♿	—	—	❄
0.6	—	$	📖	—	🔥	—	—	🧒	🐕	❄
0.6	—	$	📖	—	🔥	—	—	🧒	🐕	—
3.3	—	$	—	—	—	—	—	—	🐕	—
0.3	—	$	📖	👫	—	—	—	🧒	🐕	—
0.5	—	—	📖	👫	—	—	—	🧒	—	—
0.4	—	—	—	👫	—	—	—	—	—	—
29.2	🅕	—	—	—	—	⛺	—	—	🐕	—
9.1	🅕	—	—	—	—	⛺	—	—	🐕	❄
5.0	—	—	📖	—	—	—	—	—	🐕	—

Trail	Public Land	County	Location
15 Florida Trail	Lake Okeechobee	Glades	Moore Haven
16 Florida Trail	Lower Kissimmee River	Okeechobee	Fort Basinger
17 Florida Trail	Seminole Section	Hendry	Clewiston
South Atlantic			
1 —	Indrio Savannas Natural Area	St. Lucie	Indrio
2 —	Jack Island Preserve, Fort Pierce Inlet State Park	St. Lucie	Fort Pierce
3 Coastal Hammock Trail	Fort Pierce Inlet State Park	St. Lucie	Fort Pierce
4 —	Pinelands Natural Area	St. Lucie	Fort Pierce
5 —	Sweetwater Hammock Natural Area	St. Lucie	Fort Pierce
6 —	Oxbow Eco-Center	St. Lucie	Port St. Lucie
7 Halpatiokee Nature Trail	St. Lucie River Preserve State Park	St. Lucie	Port St. Lucie
8 Ocean Bay Nature Trail	—	St. Lucie	Hutchinson Island
9 Turtle Beach Nature Trail	—	St. Lucie	Hutchinson Island
10 —	Oak Hammock Park	St. Lucie	Port St. Lucie
11 —	Spruce Bluff Preserve	St. Lucie	Port St. Lucie
12 —	Savannas Preserve State Park	Martin	Jensen Beach
13 Hawks Bluff Nature Trail	Savannas Preserve State Park	Martin	Jensen Beach
14 Florida Trail	Dupuis Management Area	Martin	Indiantown
15 —	Halpatiokee Regional Park	Martin	Stuart
16 —	Phipps Park	Martin	Stuart
17 South Fork Hiking Trail	South Fork St. Lucie River Management Area	Martin	Stuart
18 —	Seabranch Preserve State Park	Martin	Hobe Sound
19 Sand Pine Scrub Oak Trail	Hobe Sound National Wildlife Refuge	Martin	Hobe Sound
20 Florida Trail	Jonathan Dickinson State Park	Martin	Hobe Sound
21 Hobe Mountain Trail	Jonathan Dickinson State Park	Martin	Hobe Sound
22 Kitching Creek Nature Trail	Jonathan Dickinson State Park	Martin	Hobe Sound
23 Rafael Sanchez Trail	Okeechobee Ridge Park	Martin	Port Mayaca
24 Florida Trail	J. W. Corbett Wildlife Management Area	Palm Beach	Royal Palm Beach
25 Hungryland Boardwalk and Trail	J. W. Corbett Wildlife Management Area	Palm Beach	Royal Palm Beach
26 —	Riverbend County Park	Palm Beach	Jupiter Farms
27 —	Blowing Rocks Preserve	Palm Beach	Jupiter Island
28 —	Jupiter Ridge Natural Area	Palm Beach	Jupiter
29 —	Juno Dunes Natural Area	Palm Beach	Juno Beach
30 —	Frenchman's Forest Natural Area	Palm Beach	Palm Beach Gardens
31 Satinleaf Trail	John D. MacArthur Beach State Park	Palm Beach	Singer Island
32 North Trail System	Grassy Waters Preserve	Palm Beach	West Palm Beach

Trail Miles	𝐅	$	📖	🚻	campfire	tent	♿	👫	dog	❄
109.0	𝐅	—	—	🚻	●	tent	—	—	dog	—
30.6	𝐅	—	—	—	—	tent	—	—	dog	—
36.1	𝐅	—	—	—	—	tent	—	—	—	-
South Atlantic										
5.0	—	—	—	—	—	—	—	—	—	—
5.0	—	—	—	—	—	—	—	—	—	—
0.4	—	$	📖	🚻	—	—	—	👫	—	—
6.0	—	—	—	—	—	—	—	—	dog	—
0.4	—	—	📖	—	—	—	—	👫	dog	—
4.0	—	—	📖	🚻	—	—	♿	👫	dog	❄
0.8	—	—	📖	—	—	—	—	—	—	—
0.3	—	—	📖	—	—	—	—	👫	dog	❄
1.0	—	—	📖	—	—	—	—	👫	—	—
1.5	—	—	—	🚻	—	—	—	👫	dog	—
2.0	—	—	📖	—	—	—	—	—	dog	—
1.5	—	—	📖	🚻	—	—	—	—	dog	—
1.1	—	—	—	—	—	—	—	—	—	❄
15.6	𝐅	$	—	—	—	tent	—	—	dog	—
1.3	—	—	📖	🚻	—	—	—	—	dog	—
1.0	—	—	—	—	●	—	—	—	—	—
2.1	𝐅	—	—	—	—	tent	—	—	—	—
5.1	𝐅	—	—	🚻	—	—	—	—	dog	—
0.4	—	—	📖	🚻	—	—	—	👫	—	—
17.0	𝐅	$	📖	🚻	●	tent	—	—	dog	❄
0.4	—	$	📖	—	●	—	—	👫	—	—
1.3	—	$	📖	🚻	●	—	—	👫	dog	—
5.0	𝐅	—	—	—	—	—	—	—	—	—
17.0	𝐅	$	—	—	—	tent	—	—	—	—
1.1	—	$	📖	—	—	—	—	👫	—	—
2.5	𝐅	—	—	🚻	—	—	♿	👫	—	—
2.0	—	$	📖	🚻	—	—	—	—	—	—
2.3	—	—	📖	🚻	—	—	♿	—	—	❄
0.7	—	—	📖	—	—	—	♿	👫	—	—
2.7	—	—	📖	—	—	—	♿	—	—	—
0.3	—	$	📖	🚻	—	—	—	👫	dog	—
1.6	—	—	—	—	—	—	—	—	—	—

Trail	Public Land	County	Location
33 Raincatcher Boardwalk	Grassy Waters Preserve	Palm Beach	West Palm Beach
34 —	Royal Palm Beach Pines Natural Area	Palm Beach	Royal Palm Beach
35 Okeeheelee Nature Trail	Okeeheelee Park	Palm Beach	West Palm Beach
36 Wetland Hammock Trail	Pine Jog Environmental Education Center	Palm Beach	West Palm Beach
37 Custard Apple Trail	John Prince Park	Palm Beach	Lake Worth
38 —	Rosemary Scrub Natural Area	Palm Beach	Boynton Beach
39 —	Seacrest Scrub Natural Area	Palm Beach	Boynton Beach
40 —	Loxahatchee National Wildlife Refuge	Palm Beach	Boynton Beach
41 —	Wakodahatchee Wetlands	Palm Beach	Delray Beach
42 Nature Trail	Morikami Park	Palm Beach	Delray Beach
43 —	Delray Oaks Natural Area	Palm Beach	Delray Beach
44 —	Gumbo Limbo Nature Center	Palm Beach	Boca Raton
45 Spanish River Boardwalk	James A. Rutherford Park	Palm Beach	Boca Raton
46 —	Serenoa Glade Preserve	Palm Beach	Boca Raton
47 —	Sugar Sand Park	Palm Beach	Boca Raton
48 Cathy Burdett Nature Trail	South County Regional Park	Palm Beach	Boca Raton
49 —	Doris Davis Foreman Wilderness Area	Broward	Parkside
50 —	Tall Cypress Natural Area	Broward	Coral Springs
51 —	Deerfield Island Park	Broward	Deerfield Beach
52 Pond Apple Trail	Tradewinds Park South	Broward	Coconut Creek
53 —	Fern Forest Nature Center	Broward	Coconut Creek
54 —	Colohatchee Natural Park	Broward	Wilton Manors
55 Habitat Restoration Nature Trail	Easterlin Park	Broward	Oakland Park
56 Beach Hammock Trail	Hugh Taylor Birch State Park	Broward	Ft Lauderdale Beach
57 Exotic Trail	Hugh Taylor Birch State Park	Broward	Ft Lauderdale Beach
58 —	Secret Woods Nature Center	Broward	Dania
59 —	Woodmont Natural Area	Broward	Tamarac
60 Barrier Island Nature Trail	John U. Lloyd Beach State Park	Broward	Dania Beach
61 Ann Kolb Memorial Trail	Plantation Heritage Park	Broward	Plantation
62 —	Tree Tops Park	Broward	Davie
63 Ann Kolb Nature Center	West Lake Park	Broward	Hollywood
64 —	Greynolds Park	Miami-Dade	North Miami Beach
65 —	Arch Creek Park	Miami-Dade	North Miami
66 —	Bear Cut Nature Preserve	Miami-Dade	Key Biscayne
67 Nature Trail	A. D. Barnes Park	Miami-Dade	Miami
68 Hammock Trail	Matheson Hammock Park	Miami-Dade	Coral Gables

Trail Miles	Ⓕ	$	📖	🚻	♲	⛺	♿	🧒	🐕	❄
0.8	—	—	📖	🚻	—	—	♿	🧒	—	❄
3.6	—	—	📖	🚻	—	—	♿	🧒	—	—
2.0	—	—	📖	🚻	—	—	♿	🧒	🐕	—
0.5	—	—	📖	🚻	—	—	—	🧒	—	—
1.0	—	—	—	—	♲	—	—	🧒	🐕	—
0.4	—	—	📖	—	—	—	♿	🧒	—	—
1.0	—	—	📖	—	—	—	♿	🧒	—	—
1.2	—	$	📖	🚻	—	—	—	🧒	—	❄
0.8	—	—	📖	—	—	—	♿	🧒	—	—
0.6	—	—	📖	🚻	—	—	—	—	🐕	—
1.0	—	—	📖	—	—	—	—	🧒	—	—
1.0	—	—	📖	🚻	—	—	♿	🧒	—	—
0.7	—	—	—	—	—	—	♿	🧒	—	❄
0.5	—	—	📖	🚻	—	—	♿	🧒	—	—
1.2	—	—	📖	—	—	—	—	🧒	🐕	—
0.6	—	—	📖	🚻	—	—	♿	🧒	—	—
0.5	—	—	📖	—	—	—	—	🧒	—	—
0.5	—	—	📖	🚻	—	—	♿	🧒	—	—
1.3	—	—	📖	🚻	—	—	—	—	—	—
0.5	—	—	📖	—	—	—	—	—	—	❄
2.2	—	—	📖	🚻	—	—	♿	🧒	—	❄
0.3	—	—	📖	🚻	—	—	♿	🧒	—	—
0.9	—	—	📖	🚻	—	⛺	—	—	🐕	—
0.3	—	$	📖	—	—	—	—	🧒	🐕	—
0.5	—	$	📖	🚻	—	—	—	🧒	🐕	—
1.0	—	—	📖	🚻	—	—	♿	🧒	—	—
0.4	—	—	📖	—	—	—	♿	🧒	🐕	—
0.5	—	$	📖	🚻	—	—	—	🧒	—	—
0.2	—	—	—	🚻	—	—	—	🧒	🐕	—
3.1	—	—	—	🚻	—	—	♿	🧒	🐕	—
1.0	—	—	📖	🚻	—	—	♿	🧒	—	—
1.7	—	—	—	🚻	—	—	—	—	—	—
0.3	—	—	📖	🚻	—	—	—	🧒	🐕	—
2.2	—	$	📖	🚻	—	—	♿	🧒	—	—
0.6	—	—	📖	🚻	—	—	♿	🧒	🐕	—
1.4	—	—	📖	—	—	—	—	—	🐕	—

Trail	Public Land	County	Location
69 Old Cutler Hammock Nature Trail	Bill Sadowski Park & Nature Center	Miami-Dade	Cutler Ridge
70 Nature Trail	Kendall Indian Hammocks Park	Miami-Dade	Kendall
71 —	Castellow Hammock Park	Miami-Dade	Redland
72 —	Bill Baggs Cape Florida State Park	Miami-Dade	Key Biscayne
Everglades and Keys			
1 Florida Trail	Alligator Alley to Big Cypress Seminole Reservn	Collier	Ochopee
2 Florida Trail	Oasis to Alligator Alley	Collier	Ochopee
3 Fire Prairie Trail	Big Cypress National Preserve	Collier	Ochopee
4 Florida Trail	Loop Road to Oasis	Monroe	Pinecrest
5 Tree Snail Hammock Trail	Big Cypress National Preserve	Monroe	Pinecrest
6 Bobcat Boardwalk	Shark Valley, Everglades National Park	Miami-Dade	Shark Valley
7 Otter Cave Hammock Trail	Shark Valley, Everglades National Park	Miami-Dade	Shark Valley
8 Anhinga and Gumbo Limbo Trails	Everglades National Park	Miami-Dade	Royal Palm Hammock
9 Old Ingraham Highway	Everglades National Park	Miami-Dade	Royal Palm Hammock
10 Pinelands	Everglades National Park	Miami-Dade	Long Pine Key
11 Pa-hay-okee Overlook	Everglades National Park	Miami-Dade	Long Pine Key
12 Mahogany Hammock Trail	Everglades National Park	Miami-Dade	Long Pine Key
13 Mangrove Trail	West Lake, Everglades National Park	Miami-Dade	Flamingo
14 Snake Bight Trail	Everglades National Park	Miami-Dade	Flamingo
15 Rowdy Bend Trail	Everglades National Park	Miami-Dade	Flamingo
16 Bear Lake Trail	Everglades National Park	Miami-Dade	Flamingo
17 Christian Point Trail	Everglades National Park	Miami-Dade	Flamingo
18 Eco Pond Loop	Everglades National Park	Miami-Dade	Flamingo
19 Coastal Prairie Trail	Everglades National Park	Miami-Dade	Flamingo
20 —	Biscayne National Park	Monroe	Homestead
21 —	Key Largo Hammock Botanical State Park	Monroe	Key Largo
22 Mangrove Trail	John Pennekamp Coral Reef State Park	Monroe	Key Largo
23 Wild Tamarind Trail	John Pennekamp Coral Reef State Park	Monroe	Key Largo
24 —	Windley Key Fossil Reef Geological State Park	Monroe	Windley Key
25 —	Lignumvitae Key Botanical State Park	Monroe	Lignumvitae Key
26 Golden Orb Trail	Long Key State Park	Monroe	Long Key
27 Layton Trail	Long Key State Park	Monroe	Long Key
28 Silver Palm Trail	Bahia Honda State Park	Monroe	Bahia Honda Key
29 Wilderness Trails	National Key Deer Refuge	Monroe	Big Pine Key
30 —	Torchwood Hammock Preserve	Monroe	Little Torch Key
31 —	Fort Zachary Taylor Historic State Park	Monroe	Key West

Trail Miles	● F	$	📖	👫▢	◉	⛺	♿	👫▢	🐕	✽
0.4	—	—	📖	👫▢	—	—	—	👫▢	—	—
0.7	—	—	📖	—	—	—	—	👫▢	🐕	✽
0.5	—	—	📖	👫▢	—	—	—	👫▢	🐕	—
2.0	—	$	—	👫▢	—	—	—	—	🐕	–
Everglades and Keys										
14.9	● F	—	—	👫▢	—	⛺	—	—	—	—
28.8	● F	—	—	👫▢	—	⛺	—	—	—	—
5.2	—	—	—	—	—	—	—	—	🐕	—
7.8	● F	—	—	👫▢	—	⛺	—	—	—	—
0.3	—	—	📖	—	—	—	—	👫▢	—	—
0.3	—	$	📖	👫▢	—	—	♿	👫▢	—	—
1.0	—	$	—	👫▢	—	—	—	—	—	—
1.2	—	$	📖	👫▢	—	—	♿	👫▢	—	✽
22.0	—	$	—	—	—	⛺	—	—	—	—
0.4	—	$	📖	—	◉	—	♿	👫▢	—	—
0.2	—	$	📖	—	—	—	♿	👫▢	—	—
0.4	—	$	📖	—	—	—	♿	👫▢	—	—
0.4	—	$	📖	👫▢	—	—	♿	👫▢	—	—
3.6	—	$	—	—	—	—	—	—	—	—
5.2	—	$	—	—	—	—	—	—	—	—
3.5	—	$	—	—	—	—	—	—	—	—
3.6	—	$	—	—	—	—	—	—	—	—
0.5	—	$	📖	👫▢	◉	—	♿	👫▢	—	—
14.0	—	$	📖	—	◉	⛺	—	—	—	—
9.0	—	—	📖	👫▢	—	⛺	—	—	—	—
1.1	—	$	📖	👫▢	—	—	♿	👫▢	—	—
0.8	—	$	📖	👫▢	◉	—	♿	👫▢	—	—
0.3	—	$	📖	👫▢	◉	—	—	👫▢	🐕	—
1.4	—	$	📖	👫▢	—	—	—	👫▢	—	✽
3.5	—	$	📖	👫▢	—	—	—	—	—	—
1.2	—	$	📖	👫▢	◉	—	—	—	—	✽
0.2	—	—	📖	—	◉	—	—	—	—	—
0.6	—	$	📖	👫▢	◉	—	—	👫▢	—	—
1.1	—	—	📖	—	—	—	♿	👫▢	—	✽
0.4	—	—	📖	—	—	—	—	—	—	—
1.2	—	$	📖	👫▢	—	—	—	👫▢	—	—

Public Lands in Florida

Florida State Parks

Avid hikers will certainly get their money's worth from a Florida State Parks annual pass; for $40 (individual) or $80 (family) you receive unlimited access to more than 140 state parks. In many parks, the nature trail is too short to warrant the cost of entering the park, so be sure to take advantage of the other activities offered, such as picnicking, swimming, canoeing, and the like.

Florida State Forests

Florida's state forest system encompasses hundreds of thousands of acres of recreational resources in Florida. The Florida Division of Forestry Trailwalker Program encourages you to hike designated trails in Florida's state forests. For a Trailwalker application, visit any of the designated Trailwalker trailheads for a brochure, call 850-414-0871, or visit the website at **www.fl-dof.com/Recreation/Trailwalker/**. As you complete each hike, you send in a postcard to the program, and after ten hikes you receive a patch and a certificate. The vast majority of the Trailwalker trails are multiuse. Some notable exceptions are included in this book. Most state forests charge a day-use recreation fee; an annual pass is available for families for $30.

Florida Trail

From its humble roots in the Ocala National Forest in 1966, the Florida Trail has grown to a state-spanning resource encompassing more than 1,400 miles of linear hiking from the Big Cypress National Preserve to Gulf Islands National Seashore. In 1986 the trail was designated one of only eight National Scenic Trails in the United States. Although incomplete in places, the trail utilizes blazed walks on roads to connect completed sections. Members of the Florida Trail Association (FTA) build and maintain sections of the Florida Trail throughout the state as well as many of the loop trails provided in Florida State Parks and State Forests. Look for the "FT" sign at the trailhead for trails built and maintained by the FTA. Local FTA chapters hold meetings with an outdoor recreation focus and lead guided hikes on many trails. The FTA maintains a statewide trail inventory and creates detailed maps for backpacking, which are updated annually and sold in regional and state sets ($24.95 for most regions, $135.45 for a complete set). For more information on the FTA and to purchase maps, visit the website at **www.floridatrail.org**, call 877-HIKE-FLA, or write to Florida Trail Association, 5415 SW 13th Street, Gainesville, FL 32608.

Wet prairie along the Florida Trail, Corbett Wildlife Management Area.

National Forests in Florida

There are three National Forests in Florida. The Ocala National Forest, the first national forest created east of the Mississippi, protects more than 500,000 acres of the Big Scrub. The Osceola National Forest is a mosaic of pine flatwoods, pine plantations, cypress swamps, and gum swamps along the Georgia border, and the Apalachicola National Forest around Tallahassee is known for its extensive pine flatwoods, swampy bays, and pitcher plant savannas. National forests are open for twenty-four-hour use. There are usually fees for the use of developed recreation areas. Hikers may camp off trail anywhere within a national forest except where the land use is otherwise posted—and except for hunting season, when camping is limited to designated campsites as marked on the Florida Trail maps.

National Parks in Florida

In Florida the national park system affords hikes in Everglades National Park, with its array of interpretive and hiking trails; Big Cypress National Preserve, hosting the Florida Trail; Biscayne National Park, a scattering of protected islands across Biscayne Bay; and Gulf Islands National Seashore, where the Florida Trail intersects with a few interpretive trails. National Parks are open twenty-four hours, but parking access may be limited to daylight hours.

National Wildlife Refuges

Florida is the birthplace of the National Wildlife Refuge (NWR) system, where President Theodore Roosevelt dedicated the Pelican Island NWR in 1903. There are now more than twenty national wildlife refuges in Florida alone. Most, but not all, provide access via interpretive trails. St. Marks NWR is the only refuge that permits overnight camping, for backpackers along the Florida Trail, but you must obtain a permit in advance before backpacking. NWR hours are from dawn to dusk unless otherwise posted.

Natural Lands Programs

Many Florida counties have natural lands programs, which enable counties to purchase undisturbed wilderness space and protect it from development. Since the concept of "natural lands" is habitat preservation, hiking tends to be the primary recreational use on natural lands. Both Palm Beach County and Polk County have extensive natural lands programs, more so than most other counties in the state, and provide access to most of their natural lands via hiking trails.

Office of Greenways and Trails

A division of the Department of Environmental Protection, the Office of Greenways and Trails oversees development of dedicated greenway corridors throughout the state. While many of these focus on paved biking trails, others, such as the Marjorie Harris Carr Cross Florida Greenway, are broad strips of preserved land that include natural-surface hiking trails as well.

Water Management District Lands

All five of Florida's water management districts encourage hikers to enjoy their public lands. In most cases, water management districts do not establish hiking-only footpaths; they create multiuse trails by blazing existing forest roads and jeep trails on their land. Only those WMD lands where hiking is the primary use are listed in the book. There are no usage fees for WMD lands but, in general, groups of seven or more who intend to camp together must arrange for a camping permit in advance. For more information on WMD recreation, contact the regional WMD for a recreation guide.

Wildlife Management Areas

The Florida Fish and Wildlife Conservation Commission (FWC) oversees wildlife management areas (WMAs) and mitigation parks throughout Florida. WMAs are generally managed for hunting, with nonconsumptive recreation a secondary consideration. Hikers are welcome to utilize the forest roads within any WMA for recreation, but a complex set of rules covers the use of these areas; for information on any specific WMA, dig through the regulations posted on **www.floridaconservation.org** for details. Many WMAs are closed to hiking during general gun-hunting season, which usually falls during optimal hiking season. Only WMAs with established hiking trails are listed in this book. Entrance fees to WMAs run $3–4 per person or $6 per carload.

Military Installations

Both Avon Park Air Force Range and Eglin Air Force Base offer hiking along the Florida Trail. At Avon Park, hikers must call in advance (863-452-4254 on weekdays 7:30–3:30, or 941-452-4119 for a recorded message) to confirm that the range is not closed because of military operations. At Eglin, you must obtain an Eglin Recreational Use Permit in advance of your visit. Permits are good for one fiscal year, starting September 1, and cost $7. You may obtain the permit in person at the Jackson Guard office on SR 85 (Mon–Thu 7:00–4:30, Fri 7:00–6:00, Sat 7:30–12:30); you will be required to watch a brief video on recognizing ordnance (unexploded bombs). If you plan to backpack, you must also purchase a camping permit for an additional $5 fee; this may be paid at a trailhead kiosk. To obtain either of the permits by mail, write

Eglin Natural Resources Branch
107 Highway 85 North
Niceville, FL 32578

Include a photocopy of your driver's license, or other ID with current address and date of birth, and a check or money order for $7, payable to DFAS-LI Eglin AFB. When hiking in Eglin AFB, you are also required to sign in at each trailhead kiosk by completing a user self-registration card. Carry the bottom half with you at all times.

When hiking on a military installation, carry a photo ID in case you are stopped by military personnel. If you come across unexploded ordnance—grenades, bombs, missiles—call the contact for that base immediately to report its position, and give it a wide berth.

Universities

The University of North Florida (Jacksonville) and the University of West Florida (Pensacola) maintain hiking trails on their campuses. The University of Central Florida (Orlando) has a pleasant unmarked trail system adjoining its arboretum, but I understand the natural area is imperiled by expansion of the campus. The University of Florida (Gainesville) has unmarked paths and boardwalks along the floodplain forests of Lake Alice off Museum Road.

Hiking in Florida

Thanks to the diversity of ecosystems across our state, hiking in Florida is not like hiking anywhere else in the United States. There are special considerations, including an awareness of our climate, seasonal weather patterns, flora, and fauna. The following precautions should be observed when planning a hike in Florida.

Precautions

Animal Encounters

With the exception of encounters with **snakes**, most animal encounters in Florida tend to be benign and exciting—who wouldn't want to claim they saw a Florida **panther** or a Florida **black bear** in the wild? In general, animals hear you coming and get out of your way. Notable exceptions are **cottonmouth moccasins**, which tend to be aggressive and stand their ground, and **rattlesnakes**, which also can be territorial. Although many hikers worry about Florida's **alligators**, alligators that have not been habituated to human presence will tend to get out of your way immediately. If an alligator or snake blocks the trail, do not approach it. Give it a wide berth. When backpacking, consider "bear bagging" your food, especially in the national forests and in St. Marks National Wildlife Refuge, and not just for the sake of the bears—**raccoons** cause much more grief to campers.

Climate

Florida's temperate winters are a draw for hikers from around the country but, yes, we still experience freezing temperatures, especially in the Panhandle! Backpackers and day hikers should plan accordingly, carrying layers when temperatures are cool. Our summer climate makes it tough to do more than a couple of miles at daybreak—humid air and temperatures in the nineties are not conducive to pleasant hiking. Plan your outings for optimal conditions by hiking from October through April; summer trips should be short and early in the day.

Dangerous Plants

Florida has a lot of plants not found anywhere else in the United States, thanks to the subtropical habitats of South Florida. Some may cause you problems if brushed against when hiking. **Poison ivy** is found throughout the state. But have you ever heard of **poisonwood**? It's ten times as toxic as poison ivy and belongs to the same family, but it's a tropical tree, found in the Everglades and the Keys. **Manchineel** is in the same family and even more toxic—it can cause temporary blindness if you rub your eyes after brushing against the tree. When hiking in these areas, get to know what these toxic trees look like. A major problem through South and Central Florida is the invasive exotic **Brazilian pepper**, which will cause reactions in anyone sensitive to poison ivy. South Florida's bane, the **melaleuca**, is an invasive exotic that takes over wetlands, crowding out cypresses. It can cause respiratory problems. A more common annoyance throughout the state is tread-softly, also known as **stinging nettle**. It has a beautiful white flower atop a tall stem, but its leaves are covered with tiny stinging hairs. Avoid brushing bare skin against it.

Heat and Dehydration

When hiking in Florida, it is very easy to become dehydrated before you ever realize it. Dehydration and long exposure to the sun can cause heat exhaustion, which starts with nausea, chills, and dizziness, and can lead to deadly heat-stroke. If you feel any of these symptoms, stop hiking and drink as much fluid as possible. You should always carry enough water for your hike, based on your knowledge of your personal needs, the air temperature, and the amount of sun exposure you expect. On a day hike, I carry a minimum of one liter per four miles, and twice that when temperatures are over 80°F.

About Pets

Many of Florida's habitats are not suitable for pets—open shadeless scrub will dehydrate you and your pet quickly, and floodplain forests and cypress swamps are risky places to take your dog, thanks to our large alligator population. If a land manager permits pets but I perceive that the particular hike would not be good for a pet, I do not include the 🐕 icon. Please note that although Florida state parks generally permit pets on leash on their trails, pets are usually not welcome overnight in state park campgrounds. To clarify any questions you have about bringing your pet along, please contact the land manager in advance of your visit.

Hunting

Florida's prime hiking season is also the state's prime hunting season. Hunting in Florida is managed by the Florida Fish and Wildlife Conservation Commission, which maintains a website with all hunting dates and restrictions on all state lands: **www.floridaconservation.org/**. Check this website before hiking on lands where hunting is permitted. Hunting is *not* permitted in county parks or state parks. During deer season, wear a lightweight blaze orange vest when hiking in any area where hunting is permitted.

Insects

There's no avoiding them—Florida probably has more insects per square inch than anywhere else on the North American continent. So, savvy hikers need to know their defenses. First, hike in the winter months. After the first freeze, most insects are dead. And what of those places where it never freezes? That's why insect repellent was invented! **Mosquitoes** are once again the nasty disease carriers they were a century ago, spreading malaria and West Nile virus through portions of the state. Use an insect repellent with DEET to fend off these bloodsuckers, and minimize exposed skin—wear long pants and a long-sleeved lightweight shirt. Carry a mosquito net if you know you're headed into a heavy concentration, such as what you'll encounter in Everglades National Park no matter the time of year. If you have problems with DEET, a natural antimosquito remedy is to rub wax myrtle leaves on exposed skin. Some guides claim it works; I haven't had such luck. To fend off **chiggers**, those microscopic insects that attach themselves to bare skin to feed and cause a terrible itch thereafter, dust your socks and shoes with sulfur powder, available from a compounding pharmacist or under the brand name Chigg Away. Got chiggers? Soak your feet and legs in hot water for at least fifteen minutes to kill them off and ease the itch. Spraying your clothes (not yourself) with permethrin before hiking will help keep off both chiggers and **ticks**. Always check yourself after a hike (especially a hike along the Suwannee River in spring) for ticks; remove carefully with tweezers and watch the removal site for several days for swelling and a "bulls-eye" mark. See a doctor if this mark appears. To minimize picking up unwanted travelers when you sit, carry a plastic garbage bag to sit on when you take your breaks. **Fire ants** can be a major problem if you step in their nest—they swarm and inflict ferocious bites. Keep a cortisone-based anti-itch medicine in your first aid kit as a basic remedy, and if you are sensitive to insect bites, ask your doctor what would be best for you to carry in the event of an emergency.

Leave No Trace

Practice proper wilderness ethics when hiking. Pack out all trash. Do not bury it; animals will dig it up. If nature calls, find a spot well away from the nearest water source. Dig a "cathole" at least six inches deep to deposit solid waste and bury afterwards. Leave the wilderness as you found it—take only pictures, leave only footprints.

Water

Florida experiences severe extremes with water: we usually have either too much or too little of it. During drought years, many habitats undergo extreme stress, making them more prone to forest fires and deadfall. In a year with heavy rains, trails along our rivers may be dangerously flooded. Be aware of the type of season the region is experiencing before you set out on a hike. If there has been a lot of rain, expect trails to be flooded, especially in the pine flatwoods. Always check on river conditions before planning a long riverside hike. Expect to get your feet wet on a lot of Florida hikes, so wear shoes that can stand up to the challenge. You don't need heavy hiking boots for most Florida hiking. Running shoes that dry out quickly and wick away sweat are a good choice.

When seeking drinking water in the woods, water sources should be considered suspect, with the exception of first-magnitude springs. Backpackers should boil, filter, or chemically treat water before drinking it or using it to prepare food. Be especially wary of water sources contaminated by agricultural runoff from citrus groves, sugarcane fields, and cattle ranches. In dry upland areas, you may want to cache water in advance for a multiday trip.

Weather

Be aware that Florida's dry season is in the winter and its wet season in the summer. In South Florida you'll encounter flooded trails during summer months. Afternoon thundershowers are the norm all over the state during the summer months, and their violent fronts can spawn strong winds and tornadoes. Darkening skies signal it's time to retreat to the relative safety of your car. If you are caught out in the open during a storm, attempt to reach cover as quickly as possible. Pay attention to weather forecasts during hurricane season (June to early November) so you do not plan a multiday backpacking trip in risky weather.

Understanding Florida's Habitats

One of the greatest joys of hiking in Florida is immersing yourself in the variety of habitats found across our vast state. From the bluffs and ravines of the Panhandle to the tropical hammocks and coastal berms of the Keys, you won't run out of interesting and unique places to explore. Here are general descriptions of some of the major habitats you'll encounter while hiking in Florida, each with a representative hike that showcases the habitat.

Coastal Habitats

Coastal berm: Salt-rich low dunes that develop between the mangroves surrounding the Florida Keys and the sea, where salt- tolerant vegetation thrives. [EK-26]

Coastal dunes: Wind-driven sand piled up along the sea in a complex, shifting environment around an anchor such as sea oats. [PW-20]

Coastal pine flatwoods: Forests of slash pine that thrive along the shoreline, growing right up to the water's edge along bays or to the edge of the coastal dunes. [PW-21]

Coastal prairie: Vast open prairie, unique to the Everglades and the Keys, where buttonwood (a member of the mangrove family) and pickleweed thrive on a base of sticky marl mud. [EK-19]

Coastal scrub: Rolling dunes where sand pine thrives and Florida rosemary is a common component of the understory. [SA-18]

Bearded grass-pink blooming in a prairie at Jonathan Dickinson State Park.

Coastal strand: Low dunes that develop between the sea and the coastal dunes, supporting salt-tolerant vegetation like railroad vine. [NA-4]

Estuary: Coastal marsh, also known as a **coastal savanna**, with tidal waterways threading through stands of needlerush and the occasional island hammock topped with cabbage palms. [NG-1]

Mangrove forest or **mangrove swamp:** Thickets of red, white, and black mangroves that cluster along the waterways of the barrier islands and keys of Florida. Mangroves grow as far north as Cedar Key on the West Coast and the Matanzas River on the East Coast. [SG-25]

Maritime hammock: A canopy of windswept live oaks and red bay over an understory dominated by saw palmetto. [CA-33]

Salt flats or **salt marshes:** Open coastal mud flats exposed by tides, a favorite place for wading birds like roseate spoonbills and ibises to feed. [CG-4]

Transition zone: A desertlike salt-rich habitat based on coral rock that sometimes forms between the coastal berm and the mangrove forests of the Florida Keys, supporting rare vegetation like the bay cedar. [EK-26]

Open habitats

Freshwater marsh: A marsh forming along a lake or river drainage, often dominated by willows and cattails. Many of Florida's marshes have been "impounded," or trapped behind dikes to prevent flooding. [SA-40]

Prairie: A swath of grassland that may be seasonally inundated with water but harbors a diverse collection of colorful wildflowers [SG-9]. Hidden in the prairie grasses may be a seepage slope, where a trickle of ground water feeds a bog of pitcher plants or other carnivorous plants like sundew and butterwort [CF-44]. Savannas of pitcher plants form in wet grasslands edged by pine flatwoods [PW-11]. Sawgrass prairies are vast open wetlands of impenetrable sawgrass [EK-6].

Scrub: Florida's oldest plant communities, analogous to a desert, forming on well-drained loose sand deposited along ancient shorelines [CF-80]. In sand pine scrub, short-lived but tall sand pines dominate [SA-19]. Oak scrub is the favorite habitat of the Florida scrub-jay, where wizened Chapman, myrtle, and sand live oak thrive [CA-7]. Rosemary scrub has an unusual look, with Florida rosemary bushes up to eight feet tall growing out of a white sand base [PE-12].

Wetland: A shallow grassy basin amid open prairie and scrub habitats, supporting aquatic plants and wildlife and sometimes rare grasses like cutthroat grass [CF-84]. Wetlands include ephemeral ponds, which fill with water during the rainy season, as well as flatwoods ponds created from trickling runoff after a rain in the pine flatwoods.

Swamp Forests

Bay or **basin:** A swampy interior forest of cypress, bay magnolia, and mixed hardwoods where water collects from feeder streams before draining off. The Apalachicola National Forest has many swampy bays. [PE-21]

Bayhead: A low, wet depression usually found in pine flatwoods, where sweet bay magnolia and loblolly bay thrive. [CF-38]

Cypress dome: A cluster of bald cypress forming a dome-shaped forest in a low depression in open prairie. [CF-62]

Cypress strand and **slough:** Depressions where near-surface bedrock collects water, and bald and pond cypress thrive. Strands are shallow, broad depressions; sloughs (pronounced "slews") tend to be long, linear, and deep. [SG-27]

Floodplain forest: A forest found along a river or other drainage. The floodplain forest can be a riot of color in winter, since red maples and sweet gum, two dominant trees, have showy "fall" leaves. Cypress and members of the bay magnolia family are also found in this usually wet habitat. [CF-31]

Hydric hammock: A dense thicket of palms with slight elevation over the surrounding marshes, generally flooded when water levels are high. [SF-13]

Upland Forests

Bluffs and **ravines:** Microclimates shaped by rivers. Along river bluffs, the forests are dominated by oaks, tupelo, southern magnolia, and American holly [NF-5]. Ravines are created by the flow of tributaries into rivers, forming deep natural bowls with dense vegetation [NF-26]. Steephead ravines, fed by the steady drip of spring water down a slope, have unique vegetation including a diversity of ferns. [PE-4]

Hardwood hammock: A mixed forest of hardwoods such as oak, elm, hickory, and dogwood; a catch-all term. An upland hardwood hammock has similarities to the river bluff forest, with southern magnolia, American holly, and sparkleberry dominant. [CF-4]

Oak hammock: Florida's climax forest, usually live oak shading an understory of saw palmetto, appearing as islands of vegetation in habitats where fire plays a key role in keeping the oaks from dominating. [CF-76]

Pine flatwoods: Florida's dominant forest, with pines covering nearly half of the natural land in the state [NF-20]. Pine flatwoods can be xeric (dry), mesic (sometimes wet), or hydric (very wet). Interesting variants are pond pine flatwoods [CA-5], the cabbage palm flatwoods found in low-lying areas of South Florida [SG-19], and pine rocklands, where pines grow on exposed limestone karst [EK-10].

Sandhills and **clayhills:** Gently rolling hills of white to orange sand (or, in

North Florida and the Panhandle, orange to red clay) topped with longleaf pines and wiregrass, with scattered stands of turkey oak and sand live oak. [NF-37]

Scrubby flatwoods: A transition zone between pine flatwoods and scrub, with a relatively open canopy of scattered pines over a dense understory of gallberry and other scrubby plants. [CF-45]

Tropical hardwood hammock: A hammock, found from Merritt Island south, that starts with a subtropical base of strangler figs and cabbage palms and transitions to the hardwoods of the West Indies, such as gumbo limbo, mastic, paradise tree, and mahogany. [SA-31]

Field Guides and Trip Planning Resources

Alden, Peter, Rich Cech, and Gil Nelson. *National Audubon Society Field Guide to Florida.* New York: Knopf, 1998.

Andersen, Lars. *Paynes Prairie: A History of the Great Savanna.* Sarasota, Fla.: Pineapple Press, 2001.

Bartlett, R. D., and Patricia Bartlett. *Florida's Snakes: A Guide to Their Identification and Habits.* Gainesville: University Press of Florida, 2003.

Bartram, William. *The Travels of William Bartram.* Edited by Mark Van Doren. 1928. Reprint, New York: Dover, 1955.

Belleville, Bill. *River of Lakes: A Journey on Florida's St. Johns River.* Athens: University of Georgia Press, 2000.

Brown, Paul Martin. *Wild Orchids of Florida.* Gainesville: University Press of Florida, 2002.

Friend, Sandra. *50 Hikes in Central Florida.* Woodstock, Vt.: Backcountry Guides, 2002.

———. *50 Hikes in North Florida.* Woodstock, Vt.: Backcountry Guides, 2003.

———. *50 Hikes in South Florida.* Woodstock, Vt.: Backcountry Guides, 2003.

———. *Along the Florida Trail.* Englewood, Colo.: Westcliffe, 2003.

———. *The Florida Trail: The Official Hiking Guide.* Englewood, Colo.: Westcliffe, 2004.

Green, Deborah. *Watching Wildlife in the Wekiva River Basin.* Longwood, Fla.: Sabal Press, 1999.

Grow, Gerald. *Florida Parks: A Guide to Camping in Nature.* Tallahassee, Fla.: Longleaf Publications, 2002.

Hammer, Roger L. *Everglades Wildflowers.* Guilford, Conn.: Globe Pequot Press, 2002.

Molloy, Johnny. *The Hiking Trails of Florida's National Forests, Parks, and Preserves.* Gainesville: University Press of Florida, 2001.

Nelson, Gil. *The Ferns of Florida.* Sarasota, Fla.: Pineapple Press, 2000.

———. *The Shrubs and Woody Vines of Florida.* Sarasota, Fla.: Pineapple Press, 1996.

———. *The Trees of Florida.* Sarasota, Fla.: Pineapple Press, 1994.

Ripple, Jeff. *The Florida Keys: The Natural Wonders of an Island Preserve.* Stillwater, Minn.: Voyageur Press, 1995.

———. *Southwest Florida's Wetland Wilderness: Big Cypress Swamp and the Ten Thousand Islands.* Gainesville: University Press of Florida, 1996.

Stamm, Doug. *The Springs of Florida.* Sarasota, Fla.: Pineapple Press, 1994.

Taylor, Walter Kingsley. *Florida Wildflowers in Their Natural Communities.* Gainesville: University Press of Florida, 1998.

Tebeau, Charlton W. *Man in the Everglades: 2,000 Years of Human History in the Everglades National Park.* Coral Gables: University of Miami Press, 1968.

Tekiela, Stan. *Birds of Florida Field Guide.* Cambridge, Minn.: Adventure Publications, 2001.

Yarlett, Lewis L. *Common Grasses of Florida and the Southeast.* Spring Hill, Fla.: Florida Native Plant Society, 1996.

Web Resources

Florida Department of Environmental Protection, Office of Greenways and Trails: **www.dep.state.fl.us/gwt/guide/index.htm**
 Online guide with maps and directions to hikes on public lands throughout the state.

Florida Division of Forestry: **www.fl-dof.com**
 Information about Florida state forests, maps, and descriptions of hikes in the Trailwalker program.

Florida Fish and Wildlife Conservation Commission:
www.floridaconservation.org
 Details on hunting regulations, plus information on wildlife-watching hikes throughout the state.

Florida State Parks: **www.floridastateparks.org**
 Everything you need to know about visiting any of the 140-plus award-winning state parks. Make camping reservations online.

Florida Trail Association: **www.floridatrail.org**
 Descriptions of hikes on the Florida Trail and a resource for purchasing maps and guidebooks.

National Forests in Florida: **www.fs.fed.us/r8/florida/**
Information on camping and all recreational resources in the Ocala, Osceola, and Apalachicola National Forests.

U.S. Fish and Wildlife Service **http://southeast.fws.gov/maps/fl.html**
Directions to and descriptions of the national wildlife refuges in Florida.

A Hiker's Checklist

Day Hiking

☐ Water

☐ Food

☐ Map, plus compass or GPS for longer trips

☐ Rain gear

☐ Hat

☐ First aid kit with bandages, antibiotic cream, and items you need for your personal health and safety

☐ Insect repellent

☐ Sunscreen

☐ Sunglasses

☐ Small flashlight

☐ Optional personal items such as a camera, sketch pad, or field guide

Backpacking

All of the elements needed for a day hike, plus:

☐ Water filtration method

☐ Adequate food for the length of the trip

☐ Camp stove and fuel

☐ Cooking pot and fork or spoon

- [ ] Tent, hammock, or bivy
- [ ] Sleeping bag and pad
- [ ] Headlamp or other light source with spare batteries
- [ ] Duct tape for emergency repairs
- [ ] Bandana
- [ ] Biodegradable soap or alcohol-based hand cleaner
- [ ] Spare set of dry clothes, especially socks

Panhandle West

Escambia, Santa Rosa, Okaloosa, Walton, Holmes, Bay, Washington, Gulf, Jackson, Calhoun

Along the Sinkhole Trail boardwalk at Falling Waters State Park.

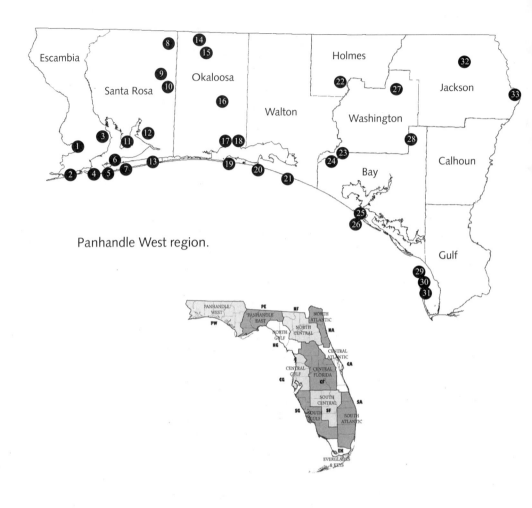

Panhandle West region.

Escambia
- PW-1 Tarkiln Bayou Preserve State Park
- PW-2 Big Lagoon State Park
- PW-3 Edward Ball Nature Trail, University of West Florida
- PW-4 Florida Trail, Fort Pickens Unit, Gulf Islands National Seashore
- PW-5 Fort Pickens Unit, Gulf Islands National Seashore
- PW-6 Naval Live Oaks Area, Gulf Islands National Seashore
- PW-7 Florida Trail, University of West Florida Dunes Preserve

Santa Rosa
- PW-8 Bear Lake Trail, Blackwater River State Forest
- PW-9 Juniper Creek Trail, Blackwater River State Forest
- PW-10 Chain of Lakes Nature Trail, Blackwater River State Park
- PW-11 Garcon Point Hiking Trail, Garcon Point Preserve
- PW-12 Florida Trail, Eglin Air Force Base (West)
- PW-13 Florida Trail, Santa Rosa Area, Gulf Islands National Seashore

Okaloosa
- PW-14 Wiregrass Trail, Blackwater River State Forest
- PW-15 Jackson Red Ground Trail, Blackwater River State Forest
- PW-16 Florida Trail, Eglin Air Force Base (East)
- PW-17 Turkey Creek Nature Trail
- PW-18 Fred Gannon Rocky Bayou State Park
- PW-19 Henderson Nature Trail, Henderson Beach State Park

Walton
- PW-20 Morris Lake Nature Trail, Topsail Hill Preserve State Park
- PW-21 Grayton Beach State Park

Holmes
- PW-22 Ponce de Leon Springs State Park

Bay
- PW-23 Florida Trail, Pine Log State Forest
- PW-24 Pine Log State Forest
- PW-25 Pine Flatwoods Trail, St. Andrews State Park
- PW-26 Gator Lake Nature Trail, St. Andrews State Park

Washington
- PW-27 Falling Waters State Park
- PW-28 Florida Trail, Econfina Creek Water Management Area

Gulf
- PW-29 Wilderness Preserve Hiking Trail, St. Joseph Peninsula State Park
- PW-30 St. Joseph Bay Trail, St. Joseph Peninsula State Park
- PW-31 Maritime Forest Nature Trail, St. Joseph Peninsula State Park

Jackson
- PW-32 Caverns Trail System, Florida Caverns State Park
- PW-33 Lakeview Trail, Three Rivers State Park

Tarkiln Bayou Preserve State Park

PW-1 🦅 ❄️

Location: Perdido Heights.

Length: Up to 4 miles round-trip in two trails.

Map: No map available yet, but kiosk at gate has information on this brand-new state park.

Contact Information: Big Lagoon State Park (850-492-1595), 12301 Gulf Beach Highway, Pensacola, FL 32205.

Directions: From US 90 west of Pensacola, drive south on SR 293 (Bauer Road) to the park entrance on the right.

The Hike: Two trails lead you through unique habitats on the edge of Florida—a coastal scrub along a bayou of Perdido Bay, and open pine savannas guarding marshlands with pitcher plants. Follow the scrub trail to a boardwalk through a titi swamp, emerging on the edge of the bayou, or continue along the pinelands trail out to its end on Pensacola Bay.

Highlights: This new state park preserves a critical habitat on the Florida-Alabama border: the Perdido Pitcher Plant Prairie, one of the highest concentrations of white-topped pitcher plants along the Gulf Coast. Don't miss the blooms in March and April!

Logistics: Expect bugs and heat along the bayou. Bring lots of water and wear your insect repellent!

Other Activities: Birdwatch along the trails.

Note: This hike sustained major damage during Hurricane Ivan and may no longer be open. Please contact the land manager for the current status of the trail.

Big Lagoon State Park

PW-2 $ 🔲 👫 🅒 👫 🐾

Location: Chanticleer [N30°19.707' W087°21.052'].

Length: 4.3 miles in three trails.

Map: Rough sketch of hiking trails in park brochure.

Contact Information: Big Lagoon State Park (850-492-1595), 12301 Gulf Beach Highway, Pensacola, FL 32205.

Directions: From Pensacola, follow US 90 west to SR 173 (Blue Angel Parkway). Continue south to SR 292 (Sorrento Road); turn right. Drive 2.7 miles to SR 293 (Bauer Road); turn left to reach the park entrance at the end of the road.

The Hike: The 0.8-mile Yaupon Trail loops through the maritime hammock along Big Lagoon. The linear Long Pond Trail starts at the campground and traverses the sand pine scrub out to Grand Lagoon, where the pine trees grow in dense thickets along the linear Grand Lagoon Trail.

Highlights: The trails offer great views of both lagoons, and a unique introduction to a windswept coastal scrub.

Logistics: Park at the Governor's Pavilion to access the Yaupon Trail and the Long Pond Trail, and park near the picnic area to access the Grand Lagoon Trail.

Other Activities: Enjoy camping, paddling, swimming, and fishing. The park is also a gateway for the Great Florida Birding Trail.

Note: This hike sustained major damage during Hurricane Ivan and may no longer be open. Please contact the land manager for the current status of the trail.

Edward Ball Nature Trail

University of West Florida

PW-3 📖 🚻 🧑‍🤝‍🧑

Location: West Pensacola [N30°33.051' W087°13.300'].

Length: 1-mile loop.

Map: Trail shown on campus map behind Crosby Hall (Building 13).

Contact Information: University of West Florida (850-474-2230), 11000 University Parkway, Pensacola, FL 32514.

Directions: From US 98, follow Nine Mile Road west to University Parkway. Turn right and drive 0.5 mile to the university entrance. Stop to obtain a parking pass, map, and directions to the trailhead, which is behind Lot 20.

The Hike: The trail starts and ends behind Building 13. Follow the paved path past the nature trail sign to the boardwalk, which leads you out along Thompson's Creek, a tributary that flows into the Escambia River within a mile.

Highlights: The boardwalk traverses numerous fern-lined ponds along the floodplain of the crystal-clear creek, which is lined with mountain laurel and hemlock.

Logistics: The boardwalk may be slippery when wet. Numerous benches make this an easy walk. Restrooms are available in Building 13.

Other Activities: Canoes are available for students and their guests.

Florida Trail

Fort Pickens Unit, Gulf Islands National Seashore

PW-4 **Ⓕ** **$** 🕮 🚻 Ⓒ 👫

Location: Pensacola Beach [N30°19.718' W087°17.374'].

Length: 4.2 miles linear.

Map: Rough sketch of trail on park map; detailed backpacking map available from Florida Trail Association.

Contact Information: Gulf Islands National Seashore (850-934-2600), 1801 Gulf Breeze Parkway, Gulf Breeze, FL 32561-5000.

Directions: From Pensacola Beach, follow Fort Pickens Road west into Gulf Islands National Seashore. Depending on what portion of the trail you are hiking, park at Parking Area 22 (0.2 mile east of the National Seashore), Langdon Beach, Battery Langdon, the campground store, or Fort Pickens.

The Hike: Entering Gulf Islands National Seashore (Fort Pickens Unit), the Florida Trail takes to the beach. You walk on the brilliant white sands along the Gulf of Mexico to reach Langdon Beach, where the trail crosses to the bay side and continues through coastal pine flatwoods and coastal scrub, skirting freshwater marshes and passing through the campground en route to the trail terminus at Fort Pickens.

Highlights: This is the northern terminus of the Florida Trail. The trail passes numerous points of historical interest and showcases the coastal flatwoods habitat.

Logistics: Walking along the beach can be a bit difficult when you encounter soft sand. The trail is shared with bicycles between Battery Langdon and Fort Pickens. Don't miss the trail crossover at Langdon Beach, where the trail crosses the park entrance road. There are benches at numerous stops between Battery Langdon and Fort Pickens.

Other Activities: Take a tour of historic Fort Pickens, or take a swim in the emerald green waters of the Gulf of Mexico. There are also two nature trails (PW-5) that start near the campground store.

Note: This hike sustained major damage during Hurricane Ivan and may no longer be open. Please contact the land manager for the current status of the trail.

Fort Pickens Unit

Gulf Islands National Seashore

PW-5 $ 📖 🚻 📷 ♿ 🧑‍🧒

Location: Pensacola Beach [N30°19.147' W087°16.235'].

Length: 1.1 miles in two loops.

Map: Rough sketch of trails in Gulf Islands National Seashore brochure.

Contact Information: Gulf Islands National Seashore (850-934-2600), 1801 Gulf Breeze Parkway, Gulf Breeze, FL 32561-5000.

Directions: From Pensacola Beach, follow Fort Pickens Road west into Gulf Islands National Seashore. Park your car at the "Dunes Nature Trail" sign across from Battery Langdon, or at the campground store.

The Hike: Two nature trails can be accessed from the campground store area: a 0.5-mile loop on the Blackbird Marsh Trail and a 0.6-mile round trip or loop on the Dunes Nature Trail. The Blackbird Marsh Trail rings a large freshwater marsh in the coastal flatwoods. The Dunes Nature Trail is a broad boardwalk through the coastal scrub habitat, where Florida rosemary grows in the shade of stands of sand live oaks gnarled by the salt breeze. Vegetation shrinks in size as you rise up into the coastal strand. After 0.3 mile, you emerge onto the beach at the Gulf of Mexico.

Highlights: The beach is an unbroken, undeveloped ribbon of sugar white sand stretching off as far as the eye can see, set against a backdrop of emerald green waves. At dawn and dusk, watch for the tiny Santa Rosa beach mouse; it makes its home in these sparkling white dunes.

Logistics: Only the boardwalk portion of the Dunes Nature Trail is wheelchair accessible. The trailhead for the Blackbird Marsh Trail may be a little difficult to find. Walk into the campground to the end of Loop A, and keep to the south fork (the north fork is the Florida Trail). On the Dunes Nature Trail, return along the same boardwalk or walk along the beach to the next crossover to make a loop.

Other Activities: Enjoy swimming, sunbathing, fishing, camping, and touring historic Fort Pickens and its outlying batteries. The Florida Trail (PW-4) also passes through the park.

Note: This hike sustained major damage during Hurricane Ivan and may no longer be open. Please contact the land manager for the current status of the trail.

Naval Live Oaks Area

Gulf Islands National Seashore

PW-6 📖 🚻 🏕

Location: Gulf Breeze [N30°21.832' W087°07.829'].

Length: 7.8-mile trail system.

Map: Trail guide available at Naval Live Oaks Preserve visitor center.

Contact Information: Gulf Islands National Seashore (850-934-2600), 1801 Gulf Breeze Parkway, Gulf Breeze, FL 32561-5000.

Directions: From Pensacola, follow US 98 east over the Pensacola Bay Bridge to Gulf Breeze. Continue east into the preserve and park at the visitor center. The Breckenridge Nature Trail starts behind the center near the lookout over Santa Rosa Sound; other trails can be accessed from this one.

The Hike: Utilizing the various footpaths and the historic Pensacola–St. Augustine Road, you can put together hikes of varying lengths and difficulty ranging from 0.3 mile to nearly 8 miles, stretching from Pensacola Bay to Santa Rosa Sound. On the south side of US 98, you walk through a mixed upland forest of hickory, cedar, and magnolia, with the namesake oaks on the bluffs. On the north side of US 98, the trails meander through pine flatwoods, coastal scrub, and oak hammocks.

Highlights: Enjoy great views of both Pensacola Bay and Santa Rosa Sound, and take the time to read the interpretive markers around the majestic live oaks, as the markers explain how the navy once used the oaks in their ship-building. There is also a beaver dam at the north end of the Beaver Pond Trail!

Logistics: Use caution crossing US 98, as drivers whizzing past don't expect to see hikers. Take a map along, since there are plenty of cross trails (most with clear signage) to explore.

Other Activities: Bank fishing is permitted on both bodies of water. Bicycles are permitted on some trails.

Florida Trail

University of West Florida Dunes Preserve

PW-7

Location: Pensacola Beach [N30°21.096' W087°01.941'].

Length: 3.8 miles linear.

Map: Detailed map available from Florida Trail Association.

Contact Information: University of West Florida (850-474-2230), 11000 University Parkway, Pensacola, FL 32514.

Directions: From Pensacola Beach, follow SR 399 east toward Navarre. This segment of the FT is on the bay side of the road between the beginning of the Pensacola Bicycle Trail and Parking Area 9. Look for the "Florida National Scenic Trail" sign at the trail crossing from the beach, best accessed from Parking Area 9.

The Hike: Bring your hiking poles! This is a rugged but beautiful stretch of the Florida Trail, one of the rare places in Florida where hiking on the dunes is permitted. Windblown sand obscures the footpath, so as you reach each blazed post, look for the next one. The trail winds over near a calm beach on Pensacola Bay before climbing a series of enormous dunes. It passes through a shady maritime hammock and crosses several needlerush marshes, giving a nice diversity of coastal habitats to explore.

Highlights: Enjoy the views from the tops of the dunes, and pause at the Oasis, a shady spot under the cedars.

Logistics: Day use only. Bring plenty of water. Walk softly in this fragile environment; attempt to follow the beaten path. Do not disturb the metal traps used for monitoring the endangered Santa Rosa beach mouse. There are restrooms available at the beach parking area.

Other Activities: Bring your bicycle and head west on the Pensacola Bicycle Path, or bring your swimsuit and hit the beach!

Note: This hike sustained major damage during Hurricane Ivan and may no longer be open. Please contact the land manager for the current status of the trail.

Bear Lake Trail

Blackwater River State Forest

PW-8 $ 🚻 🅒

Location: Munson [N30°51.727' W086°49.984'].

Length: 4-mile loop.

Map: Rough map in Blackwater River State Forest brochure; detailed map on trailhead kiosk.

Contact Information: Blackwater River State Forest (850-957-4201), 11650 Munson Highway, Milton, FL 32570.

Directions: From the junction of SR 191 and SR 4 in Munson, drive east 2 miles to the Bear Lake Recreation Area entrance on the left side of the highway. Continue 0.6 mile down the entrance road to the trailhead kiosk; park near the kiosk.

The Hike: Shaded by pine flatwoods and river bluff forests, the trail circles Bear Lake, a reservoir that flows down into Sweetwater Creek. Connector trails lead to Krul Recreation Area (1.5 miles west on the Sweetwater Trail, a Trailwalker trail) and, for backpackers, 2 miles east to the Jackson Red Ground Trail (PW-15).

Highlights: As you circle Bear Lake, there are great views and good opportunities for birdwatching. Swallow-tailed kites are frequently spotted in springtime.

Logistics: Day-use fee is $1 per person. Be alert for alligators along the trail. No hunting is permitted in this part of Blackwater River State Forest.

Other Activities: Fishing and boating are available on Bear Lake, and camping in the lakeside campground.

Juniper Creek Trail

Blackwater River State Forest

PW-9 **F** $ 👫 🅒 ⛺ 🏕 ❄️

Location: Northern terminus, Red Rock [N30°47.113' W086°53.205']; southern terminus, Holt at Deaton Bridge [N30°42.264' W086°52.997'].

Length: 8.8 miles linear.

Map: Rough map in Blackwater River State Forest brochure; detailed backpacking map available from Florida Trail Association.

Contact Information: Blackwater River State Forest (850-957-4201), 11650 Munson Highway, Milton, FL 32570.

Directions: For the northern trailhead, follow SR 191 north from US 90 through Milton toward Munson to the turnoff for Red Rock Picnic Area. You must hike 0.3 mile east from the picnic area along the road to reach the trail. For the southern trailhead at Deaton Bridge, drive north from US 90 (east of Milton) on Deaton Bridge Road at Harold for 3.5 miles to the trailhead on the left just before the bridge, within Blackwater River State Park.

The Hike: This is the most scenic hike in Blackwater River State Forest, starting out (from the northern terminus) in rolling clayhills of longleaf pine and wiregrass on high bluffs above Juniper Creek, gradually dropping down into the river bluff forests with the creek mere feet away, where rhododendron crowds its banks. The trail traverses numerous titi swamps on puncheons, and crosses bridges over several ravines.

Highlights: Be sure to take the blue blaze to the west to look over the sixty-foot clay bluffs above Juniper Creek. Backpackers will delight in the sandy beach and natural swimming area adjacent to the Bluffs Campsite shelter area.

Logistics: Blackwater River State Park has a parking fee. Overnight parking must be arranged at the campground. Parking overnight at Red Rock Picnic Area is not recommended. There is a restroom at the riverside picnic area in Blackwater River State Park, at the southern terminus of the trail. The trail may flood if the creek is high.

Other Activities: There is swimming in the creeks, and seasonal hunting. The Chain of Lakes Trail (PW-10) starts on the other side of the Blackwater River at Deaton Bridge.

Chain of Lakes Nature Trail

Blackwater River State Park

PW-10 $ 📖 🚻 Ⓐ 🐾

Location: Holt [N30°42.264' W086°52.870'].

Length: 1.2-mile loop.

Map: Rough map in park brochure.

Contact Information: Blackwater River State Park (850-983-5363), 7720 Deaton Bridge Road, Holt, FL 32564.

Directions: From I-10 exit 31, follow SR 85 for 1.3 miles north to US 90; turn right. Continue 5.5 miles east on US 90 to the turnoff at Holt for Deaton Bridge Road, across from the small store. Drive 3.2 miles north to the Deaton Bridge parking area, where a self-pay fee is required.

The Hike: While the trail starts out by paralleling the beautiful Blackwater River through the river bluff forest, providing access to a broad sandy beach, it turns away after 0.3 mile into the floodplain forest to follow a chain of oxbow lakes that once were another branch of the river. Walking along the oxbows, you circle floodplain ponds with tall cypresses. After the trail makes a sharp turn uphill to leave the chain of lakes, it climbs into a longleaf pine forest and turns back toward Deaton Bridge to complete the loop.

Highlights: Enjoy great views of Blackwater River, as well as catfaced longleaf pines carved into by turpentiners in the last century to tap for sap, as well as an amazing number of songbirds in the longleaf pine forest.

Logistics: The trail may be muddy in places, and will flood if the river is high. Mosquitoes can be fierce because of standing water in the oxbows; wear repellent. Numerous side trails can confuse you by leading you to the river's edge until the trail turns to follow the oxbow lakes.

Other Activities: The beach, accessed by the boardwalk at the beginning of the trail, is extremely popular. Canoes and kayaks can be rented at the outfitter near the park entrance. The Juniper Creek Trail (PW-9) starts on the other side of the river at the picnic area.

Garcon Point Hiking Trail

Garcon Point Preserve

PW-11 **F** 🐾 ⚜

Location: Milton [N30°27.544' W087°05.546'].

Length: Up to 4.1 miles of hiking, including a 1.7-mile loop.

Map: Displayed and available in interpretive brochure at trailhead kiosks.

Contact Information: Northwest Florida Water Management District (850-539-5999), 81 Water Management Drive, Havana, FL 32333-4712.

Directions: From I-10 exit 22, drive south on CR 281 (or from exit 26, drive south on CR 191 to CR 281) and continue 0.7 mile to the north entrance of the preserve on the left. Use this entrance if you plan to hike the 4.1-mile trip; otherwise, drive another 0.9 mile to the south entrance, just before the toll plaza, to directly access the 1.7-mile loop trail.

The Hike: Starting out in pine flatwoods from the southern trailhead, a short spur trail leads from the kiosk to the blue-blazed loop. Turn left to walk clockwise to emerge out into the pitcher plant savannas within the first 0.3 mile. Keep left at the fork to walk along the spur trail out into the wide open savanna to see hundreds of pitcher plants around and on the trail. If you stay to the right to continue around the loop, the trail passes through open prairies and wet flatwoods and along the edge of the tidal marsh of Blackwater Bay before returning to the beginning of the loop.

Highlights: This is one of the most spectacular spots in the Southeast to see pitcher plants, most notably the endangered white-topped pitcher plant. Visit in March or April to see the plants in bloom. Sundews, butterworts, and bladderworts grow here as well.

Logistics: Since you're hiking in and around wet savannas, expect to get your shoes wet and to wade in places. And where there are carnivorous plants, there are insects—use your repellent!

Other Activities: Birdwatchers will delight in looking for Henslow and Le Conte sparrows as well as harriers, bluebirds, and dozens of other species.

Florida Trail

Eglin Air Force Base (West)

PW-12 🅕 ⌂

Location: North trailhead: [N30°33.076' W086°54.126']; south trailhead: Holley [N30°26.497' W086°52.005'].

Length: 12 miles linear.

Map: Trail shown on Eglin Air Force Base recreational map; detailed backpacking map available from Florida Trail Association.

Contact Information: Eglin Natural Resources Branch (850-882-4164), 107 Highway 85 North, Niceville, FL 32578.

Directions: From I-10 exit 31, follow SR 87 south 6.1 miles to the northern trailhead, just south of the Yellow River on the right before the turnoff for Buck Pond. Parking is possible at Buck Pond. The southern trailhead is at Holley at the East Bay River.

The Hike: This segment of the Florida Trail rises up and over the high sandhills east of East Bay, losing elevation as the trail draws closer to the East Bay River. Paralleling SR 87, the trail starts north of Buck Pond and spends half its route in the longleaf pine and wiregrass forests before crossing SR 87 to head down into hardwood forests along tributaries feeding the East Bay River.

Highlights: Enjoy an immersion in the longleaf pine and wiregrass habitat, and a nice campsite at Dean Creek.

Logistics: Before hiking in Eglin, call 850-882-0007 to ensure the base is open: FPCON DELTA status means the base is closed to public access. You must sign in at the trailhead kiosk and fill out a camping permit if camping. All hikers (with the exception of Florida Trail thru-hikers, who need a letter from the Florida Trail Association asserting their status) must carry an Eglin Recreational Permit; good for one year, it is available by mail or at the Jackson Guard station. Important: contact Eglin AFB Security Forces (850-882-2502) immediately if you see anything resembling munitions.

Other Activities: If you have an Eglin Recreational Permit, you are welcome to fish, bicycle the jeep roads, and participate in seasonal hunting.

Florida Trail

Santa Rosa Area, Gulf Islands National Seashore

PW-13 **F** 👫

Location: Navarre Beach [N30°21.339' W087°00.634'].

Length: 7.1 miles linear.

Map: Detailed backpacking map available from Florida Trail Association.

Contact Information: Gulf Islands National Seashore (850-934-2600), 1801 Gulf Breeze Parkway, Gulf Breeze, FL 32561-5000.

Directions: From Navarre, follow SR 87 across the causeway to CR 399. Drive west on CR 399 to find parking areas on Santa Rosa Island. The trail continues to the east and west along the beach, starting on the east from the Navarre Bicycle Trail and connecting on the west to the UWF Dunes Preserve (PW-7).

The Hike: While minimally blazed because of its location, this segment of the Florida Trail is unique in that it follows the brilliant white sand beaches of Santa Rosa Island. Tall dunes screen the nearby roadway, and the rumble of the surf lets you tune out any passing traffic.

Highlights: The Florida Trail is the only National Scenic Trail that leads hikers out onto the beach!

Logistics: There are numerous small beach-access parking areas along CR 399, but Opal Beach (fee required) is the one with restrooms, showers, and picnic pavilions. Walk close to the water, as soft sand can make for tough hiking. Since this is a linear segment, you may want to have someone drop you off so you can walk back to your car. There is no shade, so use plenty of sun protection and carry a lot of drinking water.

Other Activities: Swim and sunbathe on one of the state's most beautiful beaches.

Wiregrass Trail

Blackwater River State Forest

PW-14 🅕 🚻 🅒 ⛺ 🐾

Location: Northern terminus, Alabama State Line [N30°59.805' W086°46.551']; southern terminus, Blackman [N30°54.298' W086°41.934'].

Length: 12.8 miles linear.

Map: Rough map in Blackwater River State Forest brochure; detailed map available from Florida Trail Association.

Contact Information: Blackwater River State Forest (850-957-4201), 11650 Munson Highway, Milton, FL 32570.

Directions: For the southern trailhead, follow SR 189 north from US 90 to Karick Lake Recreation Area. Use the Jackson Red Ground Trail to connect to the Wiregrass Trail (5 miles hiking). Alternatively, access the trail via Hurricane Lake Recreation Area: follow SR 189 north to CR 28; turn west and follow signs to Hurricane Lake.

The Hike: An excellent overnight backpacking trip, the Wiregrass Trail traverses rolling hills topped with stately longleaf pines and wiregrass, broken up occasionally by titi swamps in depressions along sand-bottomed creeks. After rounding Hurricane Lake, a large impoundment, the trail passes through an area with labeled native plants en route to paralleling the Blackwater River's white sand beaches. Climbing away from the river, the trail ascends through sandhills to meet the Jackson Red Ground Trail.

Highlights: There are great views of the Blackwater River along the southern section of the trail, as well as opportunities for swimming, and a waterfall off the trail near Kennedy Bridge.

Logistics: The trail connects to the Jackson Red Ground Trail as part of the Blackwater section of the Florida Trail. Expect to get your feet wet wading across a couple of titi swamps. For safety, leave cars inside campground either at Karick Lake North or Hurricane Lake; let the campground host know when you plan to return. Restrooms at campgrounds. Footing can be rugged along the Blackwater River, and the trail can flood.

Other Activities: Swimming in the creeks, camping at developed campgrounds, fishing in the lakes and creeks, seasonal hunting.

Jackson Red Ground Trail

Blackwater River State Forest

PW-15 **F** 🚻 🌀 ⛺ 🏕

Location: Northern terminus, Blackman [N30°53.788' W086°38.512']; southern terminus, Red Rock [N30°47.123' W086°53.179'].

Length: 21.5 miles linear.

Map: Rough map in Blackwater River State Forest brochure; detailed map available from Florida Trail Association.

Contact Information: Blackwater River State Forest (850-957-4201), 11650 Munson Highway, Milton, FL 32570.

Directions: For the northern trailhead, follow SR 189 north from US 90 to Karick Lake Recreation Area. For the southern trailhead, follow SR 191 north from US 90 toward Munson; turn off at signs for Red Rock Picnic Area. The southern trailhead has no protected parking area.

The Hike: Rugged, rolling clayhills make this a great backpacking trip from Karick Lake to Red Rock in the hills between the Blackwater River and Sweetwater Creek, following part of the historic trail used by General Andrew Jackson in 1818 when he marched 1,200 men from the Apalachicola River to Pensacola in eighteen days. Mountain laurel and rhododendron grow along the streams, and depressions with titi swamps are traversed.

Highlights: Enjoy miles of longleaf pine and wiregrass, rugged climbs up and over clay bluffs, swimming in Big Juniper Creek, vast fields of blueberries and blackberries ready to pick in late spring. Watch for seepage slopes with hooded pitcher plants.

Logistics: Use the two designated shelter areas along the trail, or pitch a tent anywhere within the state forest. Connections to Wiregrass Trail, Juniper Creek Trail, and Sweetwater Trail: the Jackson Red Ground Trail is part of the Blackwater section of the Florida Trail. Expect to get your feet wet wading through marshy sections. For safety, leave cars inside campground at Karick Lake North; let the campground host know when you plan to return. The campground has a restroom.

Other Activities: There is swimming in the creeks, camping at developed campgrounds, fishing in the lakes and creeks, and seasonal hunting.

Florida Trail

Eglin Air Force Base (East)

PW-16 🅵 ⛺ 🏕

Location: Western terminus, Crestview [N30°41.174' W086°34.279']; eastern terminus, De Funiak Springs [N30°37.097' W086°07.043'].

Length: 49 miles linear.

Map: Trail shown on Eglin Air Force Base recreational map; detailed backpacking map, available from Florida Trail Association, highly recommended for this section.

Contact Information: Eglin Natural Resources Branch (850-882-4164), 107 Highway 85 North, Niceville, FL 32578.

Directions: From I-10 exit 56, follow SR 85 south for 2.5 miles to reach the western terminus on the left, just south of the Shoal River. The eastern terminus is on US 331, 5 miles south of I-10 exit 85.

The Hike: This is one of the most beautiful backpacking trails in Florida, following the northern edge of the base through old-growth forest with developed campsites spaced 8–12 miles apart. Sandhills, river bluff forest, titi swamps, and pine flatwoods are all part of the mosaic of habitats found along this rugged but satisfying hike.

Highlights: Look for pitcher plant bogs on seepage slopes, ancient hickory, elm, and oak trees, and burbling tannic streams lined with rhododendron.

Logistics: Before hiking in Eglin, call 850-882-0007 to ensure the base is open: FPCON DELTA status means the base is closed to public access. You must sign in at the trailhead kiosk and fill out a camping permit if camping. All hikers (with the exception of Florida Trail thru-hikers, who need a letter from the Florida Trail Association asserting their status) must carry an Eglin Recreational Permit; good for one year, it is available by mail or at the Jackson Guard station. Important: contact Eglin AFB Security Forces (850-882-2502) immediately if you see anything resembling munitions.

Other Activities: If you have an Eglin Recreational Permit, you are welcome to fish, bicycle the jeep roads, and participate in seasonal hunting.

Turkey Creek Nature Trail

PW-17 📖 🚻 ♿ 🚻

Location: Niceville [N30°31.421' W086°29.873'].

Length: 1.8 miles round-trip.

Map: Interpretive brochure with map available at Niceville City Hall.

Contact Information: City of Niceville (850-729-4062), 212 N Partin Drive, Niceville, FL 32578.

Directions: The trail is located along SR 20 in Niceville just west of SR 85 on the north side of the highway, immediately before the bridge across Turkey Creek.

The Hike: This boardwalk trail parallels Turkey Creek, a clear tannic stream draining sixty-seven square miles of forest in the sandhills encompassed by Eglin Air Force Base. You're walking amid the floodplain forest of tall cypress, sweet gum, red bay, and Atlantic white cedar, passing a bayhead swamp at 0.6 mile as the boardwalk crosses the creek. At the fork, turn left to walk down the Path of Memories to a shaded pavilion along the creek, or follow the right fork to the boardwalk's end at a landing beneath the cypresses.

Highlights: The creek is clear and has healthy tapegrass and other aquatic plants, making it a joy to just stand and watch the fish and turtles drift by on the current of the creek.

Logistics: The boardwalk may be slippery when wet. Watch out for groups of kids racing down the boardwalk with inner tubes in hand! This isn't a quiet place, but if you love to spot planes, they're coming in overhead every few minutes.

Other Activities: Numerous landings make the trail an access point for swimming and for float trips down Turkey Creek.

Fred Gannon Rocky Bayou State Park

PW-18 $ 📖 🚻 Ⓐ 👫 🐾

Location: Niceville.

Length: 4 miles in three trails.

Map: Rough map of trails provided in park brochure.

Contact Information: Fred Gannon Rocky Bayou State Park (850-833-9144), 4281 SR 20, Niceville, FL 32578.

Directions: The park is located on SR 20 east of Niceville, west of SR 293. Follow the park entrance road into the camping area and park at the end to access the Sand Pine and Rocky Bayou Trails. The short Red Cedar Trail starts at the picnic area on Rocky Bayou.

The Hike: The longest of the trails, the Sand Pine Trail loops through sand pine scrub along the length of finger-shaped Puddin Head Lake, and the Rocky Bayou Trail clambers through river bluff forest of magnolia, oaks, and red buckeye above the shores of Rocky Bayou. The Red Cedar Trail is a very short loop through a grove of red cedar.

Highlights: This state park is a former World War II bombing practice range, and has one of the "test" concrete bombs dropped by Jimmy Doolittle's squadron in March 1942. Beavers have been sighted along Puddin Head Lake.

Logistics: Expect some soft sand along the Sand Pine Trail.

Other Activities: Picnic along the shores of Rocky Bayou, launch your boat or try some bank fishing, or let the kids run around and enjoy the playground. The forty-two-site campground includes two ADA-compliant campsites.

Henderson Nature Trail

Henderson Beach State Park

PW-19 $ 📖 🚻 Ⓐ 🐕

Location: Destin [N30°23.051' W086°26.928'].

Length: 0.8-mile loop.

Map: Rough map provided in state park brochure.

Contact Information: Henderson Beach State Park (850-837-7550), 17000 Emerald Coast Parkway, Destin, FL 32541.

Directions: The park is 1.2 miles west of SR 293 on the south side of US 98 in Destin.

The Hike: Starting just behind the playground, the nature trail leads you up and over a chain of ancient dunes through a coastal scrub and maritime forest, where windswept oaks create small shady hammocks interspersed between stretches of open sand. Benches provide overlooks across the Gulf beaches and scrub habitat.

Highlights: There are great sweeping views from the tops of the dunes. Look closely at the scrub vegetation, as several endangered plant species are protected here, including Gulf Coast lupine and Godfrey's golden aster.

Logistics: Ask for an interpretive guide to the nature trail at the ranger station when you enter the park. Expect soft sand and difficult climbs on the dunes in places. There is little shade along the trail; wear sun protection and bring plenty of water.

Other Activities: This is a very busy and popular beachfront getaway for sunning and swimming, and the campground is almost always packed in the winter.

Morris Lake Nature Trail

Topsail Hill Preserve State Park

PW-20 **$** 📖 🕴 🏠 ⚘

Location: Sandestin [N30°22.058' W086°17.949'].

Length: 2.5-mile loop.

Map: Rough maps in park brochure and in interpretive guide available at trailhead; map also displayed on trailhead kiosk.

Contact Information: Topsail Hill Preserve State Park (850-267-0299), 7525 W Scenic Highway 30A, Santa Rosa Beach, FL 32459.

Directions: The entrance to this section of the state park is 0.3 mile east of Mack Bayou Road on US 98. Drive south along Topsail Hill Road for 0.5 mile to reach the trailhead. Parking is limited and may be crowded with beachgoers on weekends.

The Hike: Shaded by a coastal pine forest behind the backside dunes next to Morris Lake, this trail winds its way along the lakeshore in the ecotone between sand pines and slash pines to a lily-dotted marsh bridged by a broad boardwalk. The boardwalk ends on the dunes, where the trail continues to the right well above the lakeshore, creating a loop through the Florida scrub topping the white quartz dunes above the lake.

Highlights: There are great views of Morris Lake, and good birding along the boardwalk; the coastal dune habitat is one of the most excellent examples you'll find on this developed coastline.

Logistics: Be alert for alligators along the lakeshore. After you cross the boardwalk, you enter open dunes with little to no shade; use sun protection and carry lots of water. The restrooms (a composting toilet) are located at the very end of Topsail Hill Road.

Other Activities: This is a popular beach for sunbathing and swimming.

Grayton Beach State Park

PW-21 $ ▭ ⛹ Ⓐ ⛹

Location: Grayton Beach [N30°19.488' W086°09.221'].

Length: 0.8-mile loop in two trails.

Map: Interpretive brochure with map available at ranger station.

Contact Information: Grayton Beach State Park (850-231-4210), 357 Main Park Road, Santa Rosa Beach, FL 32459.

Directions: The park is along SR 30A west of Seaside and east of Grayton Beach.

The Hike: Starting at the east end of the parking area, follow the Barrier Dune Nature Trail up and over the dunes into the brief shade of a maritime hammock before dropping down through the dunes to the edge of Western Lake, where you start the Pine Woods Loop on a boardwalk along the lake. At 0.5 mile the trail leaves the boardwalk to follow a path on the pine duff, which takes you around past adjacent houses to face the Gulf. At the trail fork, either keep to the right to complete the loop back into the pine flatwoods, or turn left to take a beach crossover to the Gulf and walk along the beach to return to the parking area.

Highlights: For a short trail, you'll encounter a nice variety of habitats, including coastal strand, maritime hammock, freshwater marsh, saltwater marsh, and coastal pine flatwoods.

Logistics: You'll encounter very soft sand in quite a few spots along the trail. Please try to minimize your impact on the dunes by staying within the well-worn footpath.

Other Activities: Enjoy swimming or sunning at one of the most beautiful beaches on the Emerald Coast!

Ponce de Leon Springs State Park

PW-22 $ 📖 🚻 🚻 🏠

Location: Ponce de Leon [N30°43.251' W085°55.850'].

Length: 0.6 mile in two loops.

Map: Rough map in park brochure.

Contact Information: Ponce de Leon Springs State Park(850-836-4281), Route 2 Box 1528, Ponce de Leon, FL 32455.

Directions: From I-10 exit 96 at Ponce de Leon, drive north on SR 81 to US 90; turn right. Continue to SR 181A and turn right; follow the signs to the park entrance.

The Hike: The hike consists of two short nature trail loops. Starting at the spring, the 0.3-mile Spring Creek Trail follows a tannic sand-bottomed stream with sandy beaches through a river bluff forest, circling a peninsula created by the creeks. Walk a little farther down through the picnic area to reach the Sandy Creek Trail, a 0.3-mile loop following the creek flowing from the spring out to Spring Creek through a cypress floodplain forest.

Highlights: It's a wonderful waterside walk along Spring Creek and Sandy Creek with lots of scenic views. Look for spruce pine growing along the creek banks.

Logistics: Walk down to the spring and cross the bridge to access the trail system. Bridges can be slippery when wet. The Sandy Creek Trail may be muddy in places.

Other Activities: Swim in the spring, and picnic under the trees.

Florida Trail

Pine Log State Forest

PW-23 Ⓕ $ Ⓒ ⛺ 🏕

Location: Ebro [N30°25.745' W085°52.911'].

Length: 6.1 miles one-way.

Map: Displayed on trailhead kiosk; rough map of trail also shown as Orange Trail in state forest brochure; detailed backpacking map available from Florida Trail Association.

Contact Information: Pine Log State Forest (850-872-4175), 715 W 15th Street, Panama City, FL 32401.

Directions: Starting from the intersection of SR 20 and SR 79 in Ebro, drive south on SR 79 past the main entrance to Pine Log State Forest. Turn right and follow Environmental Road to the recreation area entrance on the right. Pay the entrance fee and park at the Sand Pond trailhead. Walk down to the kiosk next to the pond to access the trail system.

The Hike: Stretching east and west from the trailhead kiosk, the Florida Trail traverses the width of Pine Log State Forest. To the west, the trail climbs through sandhills with an open understory, circling a series of ponds before exiting at Subdivision Road. To the east, the trail passes through pine plantations before crossing SR 79 and entering a mosaic of pine flatwoods, cypress domes, and titi swamps along Pine Log Creek.

Highlights: There are beautiful cypress-lined ponds along the western portion of the trail.

Logistics: Prescribed burns may make it hard to follow the blazes in places. Expect to get muddy shoes in the titi swamps.

Other Activities: Camping, picnicking, fishing, and paddling are offered, as well as several shorter loop trails (PW-24) that intersect with the Florida Trail.

Following the Florida Trail around cypress-lined Sand Pond at Pine Log State Forest.

Pine Log State Forest

PW-24 $ 🅐 🐎

Location: Ebro [N30°25.745' W085°52.911'].

Length: Two loops totaling 7 miles, with shortcuts available.

Map: Displayed on trailhead kiosk; rough map in state forest brochure.

Contact Information: Pine Log State Forest (850-872-4175), 715 W 15th Street, Panama City, FL 32401.

Directions: Starting from the intersection of SR 20 and SR 79 in Ebro, drive south on SR 79 past the main entrance to Pine Log State Forest. Turn right and follow Environmental Road to the recreation area entrance on the right. Pay the entrance fee and park at the Sand Pond trailhead. Walk down to the kiosk next to the pond to access the trail system.

The Hike: Start at the trailhead kiosk and take your pick: both the Campground Loop Trail (2 miles) and Dutch Tiemann Trail (5 miles) are loops that begin and end at this point, traversing pine plantations, pine flatwoods, and sandhills.

Highlights: Climbing through the sandhills above the cypress-lined ponds to enjoy scenic views.

Logistics: The Campground Trail is blazed red, the Dutch Tiemann Trail blue. Both trails cross the Florida Trail (PW-23) twice. Gravel carries the Dutch Tiemann Trail through the low-lying titi swamps. Bicycles share the Dutch Tiemann Trail. There are benches to make this an easier hike.

Other Activities: Options include camping, picnicking, fishing, and paddling, as well as hiking on the Florida Trail. There is also an extensive bicycle trail (Crooked Creek) to the south on SR 79.

Pine Flatwoods Trail

St. Andrews State Park

PW-25 $ 📖 🚻 🅰 🚻 🐴

Location: Panama City Beach [N30°07.875' W085°43.838'].

Length: 0.6-mile loop.

Map: Rough map in park brochure.

Contact Information: St. Andrews State Park (850-233-5140), 4607 State Park Lane, Panama City Beach, FL 32408-7323.

Directions: From US 98 in Pensacola Beach, follow SR 392 east to its end at the park entrance. Continue along the park entrance road and make a left at the store. The parking area for the Pine Flatwoods Trail is on the right near the fishing pier and restrooms.

The Hike: Starting behind the replica turpentine plant, the trail meanders through coastal pine flatwoods into dunes topped with rosemary scrub and around freshwater marshes formed in the swales between the dunes. As the trail loops around, you walk along a salt marsh on the shore of Grand Lagoon, with boardwalks leading you across the marshes.

Highlights: Enjoy great views of Grand Lagoon, beautiful marshes, and explore a replica of an old-time turpentine-processing plant.

Logistics: You may encounter soft sand in places.

Other Activities: Swim or surf along the white sand beaches, fish from the pier, camp at one of two campgrounds on Grand Lagoon, or hike along the Gator Lake Nature Trail (PW-26).

Gator Lake Nature Trail

St. Andrews State Park

PW-26 $ 📖 🅰 👫

Location: Panama City Beach [N30°07.707' W085°43.978'].

Length: 0.4-mile loop.

Map: Rough map in park brochure.

Contact Information: St. Andrews State Park (850-233-5140), 4607 State Park Lane, Panama City Beach, FL 32408-7323.

Directions: From US 98 in Pensacola Beach, follow SR 392 east to where it ends at the park entrance. Continue along the park entrance road and make a right at the store. The parking area for Gator Lake is on the left.

The Hike: Leading you up and over relict dunes topped with maritime hammock, this trail ducks beneath rows of windswept sand live oaks while showing off the hammock and its surrounding rosemary scrub.

Highlights: Enjoy great views of Gator Lake (which is indeed a freshwater lake on this barrier island, and you will see alligators in it!) and the surrounding dunes.

Logistics: The trail is rugged in places, and you'll encounter soft sand, especially near the beginning. It can be easy to lose the trail as it turns away from the lake; keep alert for trail markers.

Other Activities: Swim or surf along the white sand beaches, camp at one of two campgrounds on Grand Lagoon, or hike along the Pine Flatwoods Trail (PW-25).

Falling Waters State Park

PW-27 $ 📖 👫 🅰 👫

Location: Chipley [N30°43.517' W085°31.744'].

Length: From a 0.3-mile loop up to a 2-mile round trip.

Map: Rough map in park brochure.

Contact Information: Falling Waters State Park (850-638-6130), 1130 State Park Road, Chipley, FL 32428.

Directions: Take I-10 exit 120 and drive 0.7 mile south on SR 77. Turn left on CR 77A (State Park Road) and continue to the park entrance. After paying your entrance fee, follow the road to its end and park near the picnic pavilion and playground.

The Hike: Follow the paved path downhill to the Sinkholes Trail, and turn right to walk down to the park's namesake waterfall, the tallest in Florida by virtue of its 73-foot drop into a cylindrical sinkhole. Leaving the waterfall, turn left and follow the Sinkhole Trail loop for a quarter mile around five different sinkholes of varying depths. Climb up the stairs to the Wiregrass Trail for a walk along the lip of the sinkhole area through the longleaf pine ecosystem, continuing out to the lake that feeds Branch Creek (which flows into the sinkhole). The Terrace Trail continues steeply uphill through the longleaf pine forest to the campground.

Highlights: If you've ever wondered about sinkholes, this is a great place to check them out safely! When the water is flowing over the waterfall, it's a pretty spectacular sight.

Logistics: The trail system connects to the campground via the swimming area. Boardwalks may be slippery when wet. When conditions are dry, the waterfall does not flow.

Other Activities: There's swimming in the lake (be aware that alligators have been seen here) as well as fishing and canoeing.

Florida Trail

Econfina Creek Water Management Area

PW-28 **F** ⛺ 🏕️ ✳️

Location: Eastern terminus, north of Fountain [N30°32.936' W085°26.147'];
western terminus, at SR 20 west of Pitt Spring [N30°25.683' W085°36.570'].

Length: 17.9 miles linear.

Map: Rough map in Northwest Florida Water Management District booklet
Exploring District Lands; detailed backpacking map available from Florida
Trail Association.

Contact Information: Northwest Florida Water Management District (850-
539-5999), 81 Water Management Drive, Havana, FL 32333-4712.

Directions: From US 231 north of Fountain, take Scott Road west 2 miles to
the eastern terminus. The western terminus is 10 miles west of Fountain on
SR 20, north side of the highway.

The Hike: This rugged riverside section of the Florida Trail provides a good
overnight backpacking trip as it follows the flow of Econfina Creek south.
The creek carves out a deep gorge beneath the pines and river bluff forest,
and the trail provides great scenic views, crossing the creek three times along
the way.

Highlights: You'll feel like you've been dropped into the Great Smoky Mountains, with rugged bluffs to clamber over, waterfalls to marvel at, and the
sweet aroma of mountain laurel in the springtime.

Logistics: If the creek is high, do not attempt the log bridge crossings, which
are tricky to begin with. They will be replaced by standard bridges in the near
future.

Other Activities: Equestrian trails also run along the creek, and there are developed recreation areas at Devil's Hole and Rattlesnake Lake.

Wilderness Preserve Hiking Trail

St. Joseph Peninsula State Park

PW-29 $ 🅐 ⛺ ❄

Location: Cape San Blas [N29°47.337' W085°24.385'].

Length: Up to a 14-mile round trip to the west end of Cape San Blas.

Map: Rough map, showing distances between points and beach access cross-overs, available from park ranger.

Contact Information: St. Joseph Peninsula State Park (850-227-1327), 8899 Cape San Blas Road, Port St. Joe, FL 32456.

Directions: From Port St. Joe, follow SR 30A to SR 30E; continue on SR 30E until it ends in the state park. Follow the state park entrance road to the very end to reach the trailhead for the wilderness preserve.

The Hike: One of the few places in Florida where you can camp in a wilderness setting along a sandy strand by the sea, this spectacular hiking trail system showcases coastal pine flatwoods, coastal scrub, coastal strand, and beaches with powdery white sand.

Highlights: Tall dunes, spindly oaks, and broad, uncluttered vistas of the Gulf of Mexico greet you on a private beach all your own for the night.

Logistics: Only twenty-five hikers are permitted overnight in the wilderness area at any particular time. You must check in and check out at the ranger station and pay a nominal camping fee. There is no water available—you must pack in all you need. Pack out all garbage, including toilet paper. Small campfires are permitted, but not on the beach. Interior trails are marked with yellow carsonsite posts. Bicycles are permitted but not recommended on soft sand; soft sand may also make for difficult hiking in places.

Other Activities: Two additional nature trails (PW-30 and PW-31) invite you, plus spectacular beaches, camping, picnic areas, fishing, and paddling in St. Joseph's Bay.

St. Joseph Bay Trail

St. Joseph Peninsula State Park

PW-30 $

Location: Cape San Blas [N29°46.595' W085°24.128'].

Length: 0.9-mile loop.

Map: Rough map in park brochure.

Contact Information: St. Joseph Peninsula State Park (850-227-1327), 8899 Cape San Blas Road, Port St. Joe, FL 32456.

Directions: From Port St. Joe, follow SR 30A to SR 30E; continue on SR 30E until it ends in the state park. Follow the state park entrance road to the picnic area past the dunes to the Bayside Picnic Area. Park and walk down along the bay to the boardwalk that leads to the nature trail loop.

The Hike: Immediately after crossing the boardwalk over a tidal creek, the trail splits three ways. Turn right to keep to the outer loop, walking out to the shoreline. Follow the arrows around the coastal fringe, where the trail squeezes down a narrow strip between the bay and cabins. After 0.4 mile an arrow directs you to the left into a hilly stretch of relict dunes, creating a loop back to the main trail.

Highlights: On the climb up through the relict dunes, Florida rosemary and Chapman oak grow like bonsai in a diminutive scrub forest.

Logistics: You'll encounter soft sand in some places, but there are numerous benches to make this an easy walk, and several shortcuts to make it a shorter walk for small children. Be alert for alligators along the bayshore; walking your dog is *not* recommended.

Other Activities: There's another nature trail (PW-31) plus a backpacking trail (PW-29), as well as spectacular beaches, camping, picnic areas, fishing, and paddling in St. Joseph's Bay.

Maritime Forest Nature Trail

St. Joseph Peninsula State Park

PW-31 📖 👫

Location: Cape San Blas [N29°44.754' W085°23.681'].

Length: 0.7-mile loop.

Map: Rough map in park brochure.

Contact Information: St. Joseph Peninsula State Park (850-227-1327), 8899 Cape San Blas Road, Port St. Joe, FL 32456.

Directions: From Port St. Joe, follow SR 30A to SR 30E; continue on SR 30E until it ends in the state park. The trailhead is on the right just before the ranger station, outside the park gates.

The Hike: Creating a loop through a coastal hammock on the shores of St. Joseph's Bay, this beautiful short trail starts out beneath the pines as a boardwalk across a freshwater marsh before rising up onto relict dunes beneath the sand pines. Turn left and follow the trail through a stretch of open scrub before entering the deep shade of a maritime hammock. At 0.3 mile, walk out to the bluffs for a view of the bay. The trail makes a loop between the bluffs and a marsh, beneath bay and cedar trees, completing the loop at 0.4 mile. Continue on the linear portion of the trail, retracing your steps to the trailhead.

Highlights: There are fabulous vistas along St. Joseph's Bay, and middens beneath the pines.

Logistics: You'll encounter soft sand in places.

Other Activities: Inside the park gates (where you'll pay a fee to enter), there is an additional nature trail (PW-30) plus a backpacking trail (PW-29), as well as spectacular beaches, camping, picnic areas, fishing, and paddling in St. Joseph's Bay.

Caverns Trail System

Florida Caverns State Park

PW-32 $ 🕮 🅒 ❄

Location: Marianna [N30°48.628' W085°13.628'].

Length: 1.5-mile outer loop.

Map: Displayed and available at trailhead kiosk.

Contact Information: Florida Caverns State Park (850-482-9598), 3345 Caverns Road, Marianna, FL 32446.

Directions: From US 90 in Marianna, follow SR 166 north to the park entrance, just beyond the golf course on the left. Once within the park, keep to the left at the fork and park in the same parking area as you would for a visit to the caverns.

The Hike: The trail system encompasses seven short hiking trails on limestone bluffs above the floodplain of the Chipola River. Start off on the Floodplain Trail at the far end of the parking lot, which leads you to Tunnel Cave. After you duck through the tunnel (or bypass it using the Short Cut Trail), the rugged Bluffs Hiking Trail follows the edge of the bluff, passing numerous cave entrances. You meet up with the Magnolia-Beech Trail and turn left, walking above the main caverns through a lush river bluff forest on a loop through the forest to emerge behind the visitor center.

Highlights: The Floodplain Trail is the only hiking trail in Florida to go right through a cave—and, yes, there is light at the end of Tunnel Cave, but it is dark in there and the floor may be wet and slippery. Needle palms grow lushly along the exposed karst, and in early spring you'll see the blooms of columbine and trillium.

Logistics: Although it's a short nature trail, the Bluffs Hiking Trail should not be taken lightly. It involves scrambles up boulder-strewn slopes, which will be slippery when wet, and careful foot placement along some narrow stretches.

Other Activities: Don't miss Florida's only cavern tour ($5 adult, $2.50 child, in addition to park entrance fee). The park features swimming at Blue Hole, the Chipola River to kayak, large picnic shelters, a campground, and the extensive multiuse Upper Chipola Trail System at the north end of the park.

Lakeview Trail

Three Rivers State Park

PW-33 $ 🅲

Location: Sneads [N30°44.789' W084°55.906'].

Length: 2-mile loop.

Map: Displayed at trailhead kiosk; rough map in park brochure.

Contact Information: Three Rivers State Park (850-482-9006), 7908 Three Rivers Park Road, Sneads, FL 32460.

Directions: From US 98, follow SR 271 north to the park entrance. Continue on the park entrance road until it reaches an intersection; turn left and follow the signs into the campground.

The Hike: This loop trail provides a scenic walk through a shady hardwood forest on the shores of Lake Seminole, a reservoir formed at the confluence of the rivers that create the Apalachicola River. When you reach the fork, keep left to enjoy the lakeshore first, walking beneath massive spruce pine, elm, beech, southern magnolia, and hickory trees. The trail loops around and continues back through the shady forest (farther up the bluffs) to the trailhead.

Highlights: You'll enjoy great views of Lake Seminole along much of the hike, and the hickories, elms, and magnolias of this river bluff forest are simply immense.

Logistics: Hikers who are not registered campers should park in the open area near the playground and restrooms. Look for the trailhead to the west of the boat ramp. Be cautious of alligators where the trail draws close to the lakeshore.

Other Activities: Down at the picnic area on Lake Seminole there is also the 0.5-mile Half Dry Creek Trail [N30°44.334' W084°55.000'], which was closed to hiking at the time of my research but may reopen. Enjoy great fishing, boating, and camping, but don't take a kayak out there—Lake Seminole is known for its dense alligator population!

Panhandle East

Gadsden, Liberty, Franklin, Leon, Wakulla, Jefferson, Madison

Rugged slopes on the Garden of Eden Trail, Apalachicola Bluffs and Ravines Preserve.

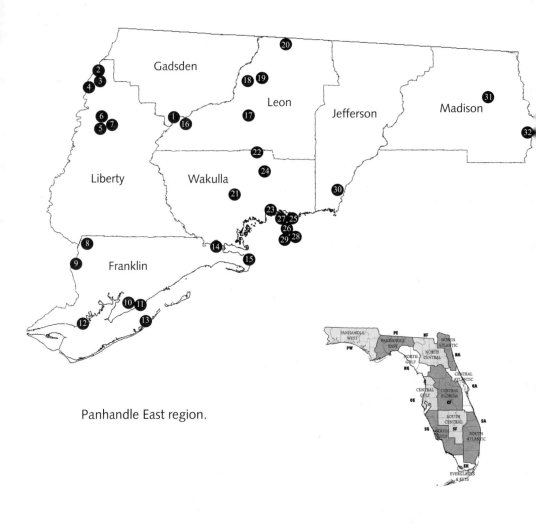

Panhandle East region.

Gadsden
  PE-1   Terry L. Rhodes Trail System, Lake Talquin State Forest
Liberty
  PE-2   Torreya State Park Trail, Torreya State Park
  PE-3   Weeping Ridge Trail, Torreya State Park
  PE-4   Garden of Eden Trail, Apalachicola Bluffs and Ravines Preserve
  PE-5   Camel Lake Trail, Apalachicola National Forest
  PE-6   Trail of Lakes, Apalachicola National Forest
  PE-7   Florida Trail, Apalachicola National Forest (West)
Franklin
  PE-8   Wright Lake Trail, Apalachicola National Forest
  PE-9   Fort Gadsden Historical Site, Apalachicola National Forest
  PE-10 Ralph G. Kendrick Dwarf Cypress Boardwalk, Tate's Hell State
         Forest
  PE-11 High Bluff Coastal Nature Trail, Tate's Hell State Forest
  PE-12 Apalachicola National Estuarine Research Reserve
  PE-13 Gap Point Trail, St. George Island State Park
  PE-14 Ochlockonee River State Park
  PE-15 Bald Point State Park
Leon
  PE-16 Fort Braden Trail, Lake Talquin State Forest
  PE-17 Silver Lake Habitat Trail, Apalachicola National Forest
  PE-18 Butler Mill Trail, Lake Jackson Mounds Archaeological State Park
  PE-19 Eleanor Klapp-Phipps Park Trail, Eleanor Klapp-Phipps Park
  PE-20 Harry M. Stevenson Memorial Bird Trail, Tall Timbers Research
         Station
Wakulla
  PE-21 Florida Trail, Apalachicola National Forest (East)
  PE-22 Leon Sinks Geological Area
  PE-23 San Marcos de Apalache Historic State Park
  PE-24 Sally Ward Spring Trails, Wakulla Springs State Park
  PE-25 Plum Orchard Pond Trail, St. Marks NWR
  PE-26 Primitive Walking Trails, St. Marks NWR
  PE-27 Florida Trail, St. Marks NWR
  PE-28 Mounds Pool Interpretive Trail, St. Marks NWR
  PE-29 Lighthouse Levee Trail, St. Marks NWR
Jefferson
  PE-30 Florida Trail, Aucilla River Sinks section
Madison
  PE-31 Ladell Brothers Outdoor Environmental Center, North Florida
         Community College
  PE-32 Florida Trail, Suwannee River West

Terry L. Rhodes Trail System

Lake Talquin State Forest

PE-1 $ 📖 🚻 ♿ 🚻 🐾

Location: Bloxham [N30°28.571' W084°37.523'].

Length: 6.2 miles in three trails radiating from trailhead: the Bear Creek Trail, 3 miles, blazed orange; the interpretive 2.5-mile Ravine Trail, blazed blue; and the Living Forest Trail, a 0.7-mile ADA-compliant trail.

Map: Trail system map posted on trailhead kiosk; maps and interpretive brochures for Ravine Trail available at kiosk or from park office.

Contact Information: Lake Talquin State Forest (850-488-1871), 865 Geddie Road, Tallahassee, FL 32304.

Directions: From I-10 exit 181, drive south 4.5 miles on SR 267 to the entrance of the Bear Creek Tract on the left.

The Hike: The paved Living Forest Trail provides the gateway into this extensive hardwood forest north of Lake Talquin, the reservoir created by the damming of the Ochlockonee River. Follow the Ravine Trail to enjoy a rugged walk along a ravine created by a creek draining into the lake, or hike the Bear Creek Trail into the drier upland pine flatwoods and sandhills.

Highlights: Walk along the creek on the Ravine Trail; it loops around a pond with a dam (once a beaver dam, now man-made) at one end.

Logistics: Hours are dawn to dusk, admission fee $1 per person. Both the Bear Creek and Ravine Trails are moderately strenuous. The Ravine Trail is part of the Florida State Forests Trailwalker program.

Other Activities: Picnic in pavilions at the trailhead. Just north of the state forest, there are numerous fish camps on the lake.

Torreya State Park Trail

Torreya State Park

PE-2 **F** $ 🚻 🅒 ⛺ 🐕 ❄

Location: Rock Bluff [N30°34.628' W084°56.945'].

Length: 14.5 miles in two loops: the River Bluff Loop Trail of 7.3 miles, and the Rock Creek Loop Trail (used to extend the hike into a backpacking trip) of 7.2 miles.

Map: Trails shown in park brochure; detailed backpacking map available from Florida Trail Association.

Contact Information: Torreya State Park (850-643-2674), Route 2, PO Box 70, Bristol, FL 32321.

Directions: From the I-10 exit for Bristol, follow SR 12 south to CR 270. Follow signs along CR 270 west to the park. There is one trailhead on the left immediately after the pay station for the park, and you can also access the trail system (per the above coordinates) in front of the Gregory House at the end of the park entrance road.

The Hike: One of the most rugged hikes in Florida, the Torreya State Park Trail treats you to an undulating landscape of bluffs and ravines, rising to 300 feet above the Apalachicola River at Logan's Bluff. The unusual landscape means unusual plant communities as well, including some of the rarest species in the state in the ravines. You'll climb through hardwood hammocks and pine flatwoods and down into floodplain forests.

Highlights: You'll find scenic views across the Apalachicola River to the flatlands on the far side, remains of Confederate earthwork gun batteries used to shell passing ships from the high bluffs, and rare plants such as the Ashe magnolia, the torreya ("stinking cedar"), and the Florida yew tree. Visit in late spring for optimal magnolia blooms—there are several rare varieties that grow only along these bluffs. Pause at the Red Rock scenic area to enjoy the cliffs.

Logistics: Stop in at the Gregory House to let rangers know if you plan to backpack the loop; there is a small fee for primitive camping. Potable water is available at the park entrance parking lot, campground, picnic area, and Gregory House; boil or treat all surface water sources.

Other Activities: Tour the historic Gregory House, a pre–Civil War plantation house. Camp in the developed campground, picnic, and hike the Weeping Ridge Trail (PE-3).

Weeping Ridge Trail

Torreya State Park

PE-3 $ 📖 🅐 🐕 🎿

Location: Rock Bluff [N30°34.108' W084°56.823'].

Length: 1 mile round-trip.

Map: Trail shown in park brochure.

Contact Information: Torreya State Park (850-643-2674), Route 2, PO Box 70, Bristol, FL 32321.

Directions: Follow SR 12 south from the I-10 exit for Bristol to CR 270. Follow signs along CR 270 west to the park. Make a left onto the campground road, and park on the left at the trailhead sign.

The Hike: The trail heads immediately downhill from the parking area, passing under a power line as it enters the lush hardwood forest. You reach a junction with a side trail from the campground; turn left and head down a steep slope that shows a good bit of erosion. The open understory lets you see what's coming as the trail continues to drop down the ridge. After 0.5 mile you make a sharp left to come to the end of the trail at a lookout over the ravine. Retrace your steps to return.

Highlights: It's an extraordinarily rugged nature trail, but the payoff is big—at the end, you find yourself mesmerized by the twenty-five-foot waterfall dropping off the ridge. Needle palms grow in the humid microclimate created by the waterfall, and a young torreya tree (looking like a broad-needled hemlock) grows on the hillside above the trail.

Logistics: The trail is blazed blue and may be muddy and slippery after a recent rain. Consider using hiking sticks—these are rugged slopes for Florida!

Other Activities: There are tours of the historic Gregory House, a pre–Civil War plantation house, camping in the developed campground, picnicking, and backpacking or day hiking portions of the Torreya State Park Trail (PE-2).

Garden of Eden Trail

Apalachicola Bluffs and Ravines Preserve

PE-4 📖 ❖

Location: Bristol [N30°27.282' W084°58.226'].

Length: Up to 3.3 miles round-trip and loop.

Map: Displayed and in brochure at trailhead kiosk.

Contact Information: The Nature Conservancy (850-643-2756), PO Box 393, Bristol, FL 32321.

Directions: Follow CR 12 north of Bristol to the entrance on the left.

The Hike: From the parking area, follow the trail down through the sandhills to the trailhead kiosk and pick up a trail map. After 0.4 mile the trail suddenly drops down out of the longleaf pines to make a steep descent through a shady river bluff forest into a steephead ravine. Climbing back up the ravine wall, you walk along the edge of another ravine and down stone stairs into a second ravine, crossing a stream. The trail climbs into the upland sandhills, where plants and trees are identified with markers. After 1.4 miles you reach Alum Bluff, looking out over the Apalachicola River. Return from this point or turn left to follow the loop through an extraordinarily rugged roller-coaster climb in and out of lush ravines along the Apalachicola bluffs, which returns you to the sandhills to exit on the path through the first two ravines.

Highlights: Only adjacent Torreya State Park can provide a similar Florida hiking experience—you'll hardly believe you're still in the Sunshine State with these rugged ravine climbs. The Alum Bluff overlook on the Apalachicola River provides an unparalleled panorama.

Logistics: The preserve is open dawn to dusk. Bring lots of water (you'll be exerting yourself much more than usual) and use hiking sticks! Take extreme caution on the narrow portions of the trail above the steephead ravines and on the steep climbs. Springs can make the trail wet and slippery in places.

Other Activities: Birdwatch in the ravines and along the bluffs of the Apalachicola River.

Camel Lake Nature Trail

Apalachicola National Forest

PE-5 **$** 📖 🚻 Ⓒ

Location: Estiffanugla [N30°16.629' W084°59.184'].

Length: 1-mile loop.

Map: Rough map in brochure for Camel Lake Recreation Area.

Contact Information: Apalachicola National Forest, Apalachicola Ranger District (850-643-2282), Revell Building, SR 20, Bristol, FL 32321.

Directions: From SR 20 in Bristol, follow CR 12 south for 11 miles to the turnoff on the left for Camel Lake Recreation Area. Drive another 2 miles east on FR 105 to the Camel Lake entrance road. Follow the signs back to the day-use area for parking. The nature trail starts at the far end of the picnic area.

The Hike: Follow the footpath around Camel Pond and take the second loop around Little Camel Pond, walking through longleaf pine flatwoods and oak hammocks along the water's edge.

Highlights: The ponds, with nice views, are especially good for birding.

Logistics: There is a $3 day-use fee per vehicle at the self-pay station. The trail may be muddy or under water in places.

Other Activities: Enjoy picnic facilities, fishing, canoeing, and the lakeside campground. The day-use area is also the place to park for access to the Florida Trail (PE-7) and the Trail of Lakes (PE-6).

Trail of Lakes

Apalachicola National Forest

PE-6 $ 👫 Ⓒ

Location: Estiffanugla from Camel Pond [N30°16.629' W084°59.184'] to the Florida Trail [N30°17.766' W084°58.530'].

Length: 4-mile linear trail that can be connected to the Florida Trail to create a 9.4-mile loop.

Map: Rough map in Camel Lake Recreation Area brochure; details on Florida Trail Association backpacking map for this area.

Contact Information: Apalachicola National Forest, Apalachicola Ranger District (850-643-2282), Revell Building, SR 20, Bristol, FL 32321.

Directions: From SR 20 in Bristol, follow CR 12 south for 11 miles to the turnoff on the left for Camel Lake Recreation Area. Drive another 2 miles east on FR 105 to the Camel Lake entrance road.

The Hike: Follow the blue blazes east from the picnic area to enter the longleaf pine forests and sandhills surrounding Camel Pond, crossing several forest roads before you drop down into a drainage area where streams, including cypress-lined Big Gully Creek, are flowing toward Shuler Bay. The trail skirts Sheep Island Lake and climbs over the sandhills of Sheep Island before rounding Bonnet Pond. Take the Florida Trail west to create a loop (leaving the Florida Trail at the signpost with the blue blazes pointing you back to Camel Lake from Memery Island), or retrace your route back to the trailhead.

Highlights: You'll find pitcher plant bogs near Sheep Island Lake and Bonnet Pond, and deep shade along the waterways.

Logistics: There is a $3 day-use fee per vehicle at the self-pay station. The trail passes around many lakes, ponds, and deep bogs and may require some serious wading. Carry a hiking stick and use it to steady yourself through the muck.

Other Activities: Enjoy picnic facilities, fishing, canoeing, and the lakeside campground. The day-use area is also the place to park for access to the Florida Trail (PE-7) and the Camel Lake Nature Trail (PE-5).

Florida Trail

Apalachicola National Forest (West)

PE-7 **F** Ⓐ ⛺ ⚒

Location: Western terminus, Estiffanugla at CR 12 [N30°17.899' W085°01.114']; eastern terminus, Porter Lake Campground [N30°10.606' W084°40.618'].

Length: 34.9 miles linear.

Map: Trail shown, as dashed line, on overall Apalachicola National Forest map; detailed backpacking map, available from Florida Trail Association, is recommended.

Contact Information: Apalachicola National Forest, Apalachicola Ranger District (850-643-2282), Revell Building, SR 20, Bristol, FL 32321.

Directions: For the western terminus, follow CR 12 south from Bristol for 10 miles to the trailhead area just north of the Apalachicola National Forest work center. For the eastern terminus, take CR 375 south from SR 20 at Bloxham for 15 miles to FR 13. Turn right and cross the Ochlockonee River; the camping area is on the left.

The Hike: This is a rugged backpacking trip that rewards you with miles of splendid longleaf pine forests, tangled titi swamps, and wet savannas full of carnivorous plants, especially west of SR 65 and around Memery Island.

Highlights: The wildflowers here are incredible, from red and yellow blooms on the pitcher plants in spring to the dainty pink blossoms of bearded grass-pink in the flatwoods. The trail passes through the ghost town of Vilas; look for building remnants and a railroad siding in this once-thriving turpentine town.

Logistics: The trail passes around many lakes, ponds, and deep bogs and may require some serious wading. Carry a hiking stick and use it to steady yourself through the muck. There are a few long bridges to help you cross some of the deeper sloughs. Camping is permitted anywhere, except during hunting season, when you must use designated campsites.

Other Activities: The trail passes through the Camel Lake Recreation Area, with campground and restrooms; for its various activities, see PE-5.

Wright Lake Trail

Apalachicola National Forest

PE-8 $ 🚻 🄰

Location: Sumatra.

Length: 4.5-mile loop.

Map: Posted at trailhead; available in brochure at kiosk.

Contact Information: Apalachicola National Forest, Apalachicola Ranger District (850-643-2282), Revell Building, SR 20, Bristol, FL 32321.

Directions: From SR 20 in Bristol, follow CR 12 south to SR 65. Continue south past Sumatra for 2.5 miles to FR 101. Follow the signs down the back roads to the recreation area entrance.

The Hike: Starting out from the campground, the blue-blazed trail makes a loop around Wright Lake, traversing floodplain forests, river bluff forests, and pine flatwoods, crossing cypress-lined Owl Creek and bringing you into open wet savannas with pitcher plants to the north of FR 101B. Passing through sandhills and pine flatwoods, you reach a boardwalk along Wright Lake that leads you back to the campground.

Highlights: You'll find a boardwalk through a swamp of sweet gum on the edge of the lake, a colony of red-cockaded woodpeckers in the longleaf pine flatwoods, and pitcher plant savannas to be savored.

Logistics: There is a $3 day-use fee per vehicle at the self-pay station. The white-blazed trail is a short interpretive nature trail that intersects this longer walk twice.

Other Activities: Swim and picnic at the lakeside campground; fish and canoe on Wright Lake.

Fort Gadsden Historic Site

Apalachicola National Forest

PE-9 $ ▢ 🚻 👥 🐾

Location: Sumatra [N29°56.423' W085°00.674'].

Length: 1.1-mile loop.

Map: Roughly accurate map in brochure at kiosk.

Contact Information: Apalachicola National Forest, Apalachicola Ranger District (850-643-2282), Revell Building, SR 20, Bristol, FL 32321.

Directions: From SR 20 in Bristol, follow CR 12 south to SR 65. Continue south past Sumatra to the forest road entrance on the left. Follow the signs down the back roads to the park entrance.

The Hike: From the parking area, follow the footpath past historic markers and an extensive interpretive kiosk, passing a screen of cypress swamp along the river's broad curve before emerging from the pine flatwoods into the open ground that was once Fort Gadsden. After a look from the bluff commanding a sweeping view of the Apalachicola River, turn and walk through the outline of the fort, past the Union Jack, to cross a small bridge. The trail continues as a mowed path through the longleaf pine forest, where wildflowers grow in profusion. After 0.9 mile the trail emerges at the park entrance road. Turn left and walk along the grassy berm to the parking area.

Highlights: Read the interpretive kiosks for information on the important history of this place, where on the morning of July 27, 1816, the well-aimed cannonade of Duncan Clinch killed 270 people by blowing up the powder magazine inside the old British fortress. In the woods, the trail passes a marker and burial vault at the Renegade Cemetery, where the people who died in the explosion are buried.

Logistics: There is a $3 day-use fee per vehicle at the self-pay station. The trail may be wet in places.

Other Activities: Enjoy the picnic facilities, and fishing along the bank of the Apalachicola River.

Ralph G. Kendrick Dwarf Cypress Boardwalk

Tate's Hell State Forest

PE-10 ♿ 👬

Location: Carrabelle Beach [N29°50.152' W084°47.579'].

Length: 0.2 mile round-trip.

Map: On kiosk.

Contact Information: Tate's Hell State Forest (850-697-3734), 1621 US 98 East, Carrabelle, FL 32322.

Directions: From SR 65, follow the signs into Tate's Hell State Forest High Bluff Tract along 4.5 miles of rough forest roads (passable by car, but barely) to the parking area just off Dry Bridge Road. A trickier approach is via John Allen Road off US 98 just 7 miles west of Carrabelle Beach, but you'd better have a map of the state forest roads to work your way back the 4.3 miles to Dry Bridge Road; take a left and continue 1.5 miles to the parking area on the left.

The Hike: It's a short walk but long on scenery. The dwarf cypress forest of Tate's Hell appears to sit in a broad rounded basin rimmed by pine forest. It is a strange and beautiful place. The boardwalk rises up to an observation tower overlooking the entire bay, with a side boardwalk to an observation platform at canopy level. Many of the "hat rack" cypresses are covered with fine wisps of old-man's beard.

Highlights: Look out across a canopy of trees that are several centuries old but less than six feet tall. Lily pads float on black, still water. Hydrology was restored to this area in the last decade; it will be interesting to see if the trees flourish.

Logistics: Be cautious on the drive back to the trail, as you'll cross several narrow bridges popular for fishing and encounter a lot of deep ruts in the often muddy back road.

Other Activities: Tate's Hell is a popular canoeing area, and fishing is permitted along the creeks.

High Bluff Coastal Nature Trail

Tate's Hell State Forest

PE-11 🐾

Location: Carrabelle Beach [N29°48.559' W084°43.744'].

Length: 1.6-mile loop.

Map: On kiosk.

Contact Information: Tate's Hell State Forest (850-697-3734), 1621 US 98 East, Carrabelle, FL 32322

Directions: Drive 2.7 miles west from Carrabelle Beach on US 98. The trailhead is on the north side of the highway.

The Hike: Part of the Florida State Forests Trailwalker program, this trail showcases the rare and unique coastal pine forests of the Gulf of Mexico, passing through relict dunes covered with scrub plants like Florida rosemary and scrub mint under a canopy of sand pines. Starting off from the parking area, follow the orange blazes to the blue-blazed loop. A side trail to the left leads to a catfaced pine with a metal cup still attached. The loop trail continues through sand pine scrub and saw palmetto stands, passing distant cypress domes and titi swamps.

Highlights: This hike provides an up-close look at coastal scrub vegetation, plus remnants of turpentine history. Look carefully at the footpath to identify tracks from deer and bobcats.

Logistics: Orange blazes mark the main trail, blue blazes mark the loop trail. As you emerge from the dense forest on the return trip, it isn't apparent which way the trail goes. Take the first soft right down the narrow path rather than following the broader path ahead of you, which is a firebreak. Despite this being a scrub habitat, the footpath lies lower than the surrounding land in places and can be mucky.

Other Activities: You're welcome to roam the unmarked roads and firebreaks through this forest, but take a map and compass if you do—they're easy to mistake for one another. There are several benches and a picnic table along the trail.

Apalachicola National Estuarine Research Reserve

PE-12 📖 🚻 ♿ 👫

Location: Apalachicola [N29°43.932' W084°59.748'].

Length: 0.6 mile round-trip.

Map: None available.

Contact Information: Apalachicola National Estuarine Research Reserve (850-670-4783), Florida Department of Environmental Protection, 350 Carroll Street, Eastpoint, FL 32328.

Directions: Follow Market Street through Apalachicola to its north end; the nature center is on the left past the marina.

The Hike: Starting off on a hard-packed shell and rock path, the trail meanders through a hardwood hammock to a boardwalk into a bayhead, where willows and wax myrtle crowd closely. At the fork in the boardwalk, keep right; you cross a freshwater wetland surrounded by cypresses, cabbage palms, and bay trees. Rising up through a cedar grove, the boardwalk climbs to its end at an observation deck, where a telescope is trained on the distant shore of the Apalachicola River.

Highlights: There is a sweeping view of the estuary from the observation deck at the end of the trail.

Logistics: The nature center (with restrooms) is open Mon–Fri 8:00–5:00; the trail is open at all times. Wheelchair-bound visitors will need assistance to traverse the short shell rock portion of the trail.

Other Activities: The nature center is a great place to bring the kids, with hands-on exhibits, open tanks with turtles and fish, and regularly scheduled activities. This is also an excellent site for birding—songbirds are everywhere!

Gap Point Trail

St. George Island State Park

PE-13 $ 📖 🚻 🅰 ⛺

Location: St. George Island [N29°43.134' W084°44.975'].

Length: 5 miles round-trip.

Map: Rough map in park brochure; more detailed map (showing benches every half mile) on trailhead kiosk.

Contact Information: St. George Island State Park (850-927-2111), 1900 East Gulf Beach Drive, St. George Island, FL 32328.

Directions: From Apalachicola, follow US 90 east into Eastpoint to take the causeway to St. George Island. Drive east on SR 300 to where it ends in the state park. Continue another 4.5 miles past the ranger station to the campground one-way loop; park at the trailhead parking area adjacent to the playground.

The Hike: This broad, linear trail parallels the East Slough, a finger of Apalachicola Bay, to scenic Gap Point, where you are permitted to camp overnight. En route, you walk through a coastal pine forest, the pines gnarled and shaped by persistent coastal winds. The trail also meanders around salt marshes and through delicate coastal scrub and coastal strand habitats.

Highlights: The trail meanders through an excellent example of the Florida rosemary scrub habitat, a desertlike landscape of large puffy rosemary bushes. Gap Point is a scenic and wild spot to set up camp. Pay attention to the interpretive information, and you'll learn a lot about the history of naval stores along Florida's shores.

Logistics: Backpackers must check in at the ranger station before and after their hike. You must pack all water in and garbage out; this is a very sensitive coastal environment. The sand is very soft in places and hiking can be a little difficult. The rumbles you hear are likely not thunder but the roar of Air Force jets from nearby Eglin and Tyndall Air Force Bases.

Other Activities: Enjoy the gulfside beaches, the shaded campground, fishing, sea kayaking (there are several outfitters on the island), and picnicking under the pines.

Ochlockonee River State Park

PE-14 $ 📖 🚻 Ⓐ 👫 🐾

Location: Sopchoppy [N30°00.244' W084°28.385'].

Length: 2.1 miles, in two one-way trails that connect to form a full loop: the 1.1-mile Pine Flatwoods Nature Trail and the 1-mile Ochlockonee River Nature Trail.

Map: On kiosk at trailhead for Pine Flatwoods Nature Trail.

Contact Information: Ochlockonee River State Park (850-962-2771), PO Box 5, Sopchoppy, FL 32358.

Directions: The park is on US 319 south of Sopchoppy. Follow the park entrance road past the ranger station (ask for a park map showing the trails if anyone is on duty) and past the campground to the parking area at the end. Drive around the loop; the trailhead is nearest the last parking space on the right.

The Hike: Winding through pine flatwoods with an understory of sand live oaks and scattered titi swamps, the Pine Flatwoods Nature Trail passes through a colony of red-cockaded woodpeckers in the longleaf pines. Look for the white-banded trees. Several benches along the way provide rest stops with scenic views. To create a loop, turn left on the Ochlockonee River Nature Trail at the junction (the Pine Flatwoods trail continues to a dead end from which you can return to this point). After crossing the park entrance road, the trail reaches the river and follows it downstream to the picnic area.

Highlights: Enjoy walking along the waterfront on the Ochlockonee River as it flows into Ochlockonee Bay; view red-cockaded woodpeckers emerging from their nests in the early morning light.

Logistics: Since the Pine Flatwoods Trail winds through mesic pine flatwoods, the footpath will be flooded in summer and after a strong rain. This is Florida black bear territory—be alert.

Other Activities: There is fishing from the pier and riverbanks, a picnic area with shelters and playground, and a canoe launch.

Bald Point State Park

PE-15   📖   🚻   👫   🐕

Location: Bald Point [N29°56.707' W084°20.419'].

Length: 0.5-mile designated nature trail plus two longer trail systems under development.

Map: On kiosk at Sunrise Beach parking area; rough map in park brochure at kiosk.

Contact Information: Bald Point State Park (850-349-9146), 146 Box Cut, Alligator Point, FL 32346.

Directions: From US 98 west of Ochlockonee Bay, follow SR 370 for 3.5 miles to Bald Point Road. Turn left and continue to the end, passing trailheads under development at Sunrise Beach (1.3 miles along Bald Point Road) and just outside the park entrance.

The Hike: The nature trail runs perpendicular to the parking area within the park gates at the end of Bald Point Road. Park near the middle of the area and look for the hiker signs. To the north, the trail leads out into the needlerush marsh and onto a boardwalk. To the south, the trail traverses the coastal scrub and dunes out to the Gulf of Mexico. At Sunrise Beach and just outside the park gates, it's also possible to walk abandoned roads (popular with local bicyclists) into the pine flatwoods; a more formal trail system from these trailheads is under development.

Highlights: Enjoy a sweeping view of Ochlockonee Bay and its surrounding estuary from the boardwalk, as well as great birding.

Logistics: The area is prone to flooding. Use caution when driving.

Other Activities: Bald Point State Park provides the only public beach access on Alligator Point. Bicycling is permitted on old roads abandoned by developers; look for trailhead symbols and small parking areas on the north side of Bald Point Road, including one directly across from Sunrise Beach. You can fish and picnic in a developed section of park at the end of the road.

Fort Braden Trail

Lake Talquin State Forest

PE-16 **F** **$** 🚻 ⛺ 🐕

Location: Tallahassee [N30°26.426' W084°29.712'].

Length: Three loops of 3.3, 4.2, and 11 miles.

Map: Basic map available at kiosk; detailed backpacking map available from Florida Trail Association.

Contact Information: Lake Talquin State Forest (850-488-1871), 865 Geddie Road, Tallahassee, FL 32304.

Directions: Drive 8.5 miles west of Capital Circle West on SR 20 to the entrance on the north side of the road.

The Hike: The Fort Braden Trail system includes the Central, East, and West Loops, all of which qualify for the Florida State Forests Trailwalker program. The three hiking loops provide a variety of options; the East Loop is the shortest walk. Trails wind through a shady hardwood forest of southern magnolia, white oak, American holly, and beech along sloping clay hills, where small but vigorous streams cascade down toward Lake Talquin. The open understory makes it easy to see wildlife, especially deer, and you will glimpse the lake long before the trail actually approaches it. The trail junctions are well marked with signs, and bright pink paint adorns footpath perils such as nasty roots.

Highlights: The two primitive campsites, each with fire rings and logs for sitting, have great views of Lake Talquin. Most of the hardwood forest is southern magnolia, so be sure to visit in late May or June, when the fragrance of magnolia blossoms fills the air. In late April, blueberry bushes drip with fruit.

Logistics: There is a day-use fee of $1 per person, payable at a self-pay station at the entrance. If you plan to backpack the trail, fill out the form at the self-pay station and include appropriate payment for your camping permit. At each campsite, you must camp within the area delineated by trees with white bands.

Other Activities: A covered picnic pavilion with barbecue grill adjoins the parking area. There are biking trails and equestrian trails. Fishing is allowed in Lake Talquin—launch boats from nearby public boat ramps.

Silver Lake Habitat Trail

Apalachicola National Forest

PE-17 $ 📖 🚻 🐴

Location: Tallahassee [N30°24.338' W084°24.324'].

Length: 0.8-mile loop and 0.5-mile (round trip) spur.

Map: Rough map in Silver Lake Recreation Area brochure.

Contact Information: Apalachicola National Forest, Wakulla Ranger District (850-926-3561), 1773 Crawfordville Highway, Crawfordville, FL 32327.

Directions: From Tallahassee, follow SR 20 west 3.5 miles from Capital Circle West to Silver Lake Road. Turn left and drive 3.2 miles south to the recreation area entrance. Park near the restrooms and walk down to the lakeshore picnic area, where the trail starts.

The Hike: The trail begins as a short boardwalk out along the shores of Silver Lake and then meets a fork that starts the loop. Stay right and follow the orange blazes along the river bluff forest and into oak hammocks and pine flatwoods. You meet the Pine Spur Trail, which leads off to the right to a large loblolly pine on the banks of a stream. Return to the loop and continue through a climax laurel oak forest and upland hammock to finish the loop at the boardwalk.

Highlights: There are nice views of Silver Lake from the boardwalk, and great interpretive signs explaining the habitat and plant life along the trail.

Logistics: There is a $3 day-use fee per vehicle at the self-pay station. The trail may be a little difficult to follow in places. Benches provide places to rest.

Other Activities: Enjoy picnic facilities, fishing (nonmotorized boats permitted), swimming, and canoeing.

Butler Mill Trail

Lake Jackson Mounds Archaeological State Park

PE-18 $ 📖 🚻 🧒 🐴

Location: Tallahassee [N30°30.041' W084°18.836'].

Length: 1.5-mile loop.

Map: On kiosk at park, near restrooms.

Contact Information: Lake Jackson Mounds Archaeological State Park (850-922-6007), 1022 DeSoto Park Drive, Tallahassee, FL 32301.

Directions: Take I-10 exit 199, Tallahassee, and drive north on US 27. Turn right on Crowder Road and continue 1 mile to Indian Mounds Road. Turn right and follow the road into the park. The trail starts at the far end of the parking lot.

The Hike: Amble through the deep shade of a hardwood bluff forest, following Butler Creek as it carves a ravine on its way down to Lake Jackson. As you explore the forest (which was part of a plantation in the mid-1800s), look for plants that require deep shade, such as columbine, trillium, and rattlesnake fern. The loop crosses the creek and returns along an earthen dike that was part of an irrigation system used by the plantation to keep the fields flooded.

Highlights: The "newest" historic site in the park is an early-1800s gristmill site located along the trail on the creek.

Logistics: The trail sometimes washes out after a heavy rain.

Other Activities: Explore the intriguing Lake Jackson Mounds, a complex of six ceremonial earthen temple mounds dating back to the Fort Walton culture of AD 1200–1500. There is a picnic grove near the restrooms.

Eleanor Klapp-Phipps Park Trail

Eleanor Klapp-Phipps Park

PE-19 Ⓕ 🏇

Location: Tallahassee [N30°32.200' W084°16.797'].

Length: 6.7-mile loop with many shorter options.

Map: Basic map offered in box at trailhead parking lot; detailed backpacking map available from Florida Trail Association.

Contact Information: City of Tallahassee (850-891-3975), 912 Myers Park Drive, Tallahassee, FL 32304.

Directions: Follow Meridian Road north from Tallahassee past the park's main entrance to Miller Landing Road. Turn left off Miller Landing Road at the sign for the Meadows Soccer Complex. Make an immediate right into the hiking and biking trails parking area.

The Hike: From the trailhead, walk down to the "FT" sign, follow the white blazes to the next sign, and turn left to follow the connector to the loop trail, which follows the gently rolling hills down to the shores of Lake Jackson. Four major loops make up the trail: Coonbottom, Swamp Forest, Oak Hammock, and Creek Forest, passing through hardwood forest, relict clayhill habitat, planted pines, and open meadows in this former game-hunting preserve along Lake Jackson.

Highlights: Enjoy a beautiful hardwood forest with a sand-bottomed stream along the Swamp Forest Loop, a cathedral of planted pines on the Oak Hammock Loop, and a stroll along the edge of massive Lake Jackson, an unusual lake that vanishes every twenty-five years or so by draining into a sinkhole.

Logistics: The park is open for day use only, sunrise to sunset. The hiking trail is blazed yellow, multiuse sections blazed white, horse trails blazed with pink horseshoes, and the mountain bike trail blazed blue.

Other Activities: Horseback riding and mountain biking are permitted on separate trail systems within the park.

Harry M. Stevenson Memorial Bird Trail

Tall Timbers Research Station

PE-20 📖

Location: Bradfordville [N30°39.324 W084°12.570'].

Length: 1 mile round-trip.

Map: May be available in interpretive guide.

Contact Information: Tall Timbers Research Station (850-893-4153; www.ttrs.org), 13093 Henry Beadel Drive, Tallahassee, FL 32304.

Directions: Tall Timbers is located 3.2 miles east of Meridian Road on CR 12, or 2.6 miles west of US 319. Turn south on Henry Beadle Drive and follow the signs to the visitor parking area.

The Hike: The trail starts at the base of the hill below the Beadel House, immediately entering the pine flatwoods on the clayhills that fringe Lake Iomonia, with tall loblolly pines overhead. Dropping down steeply to join a jeep road, the trail goes around scenic Gannet Pond to the Bird Watch Education Center, where you can relax in wicker chairs and look out across the marsh. A short loop takes you farther up the hill to rejoin the main trail; retrace your route back uphill to the parking area.

Highlights: The vast open understory makes it easy to spot birds—and wildlife.

Logistics: Tall Timbers is open Mon–Fri 8:00–4:30. Interpretive markers correspond to a brochure available at the Science Education Center behind the parking area. The Beadel House is open for tours once a month on the third Sunday.

Other Activities: As the name suggests, this is a fabulous spot for birding. The sound of birdsong is constant throughout the pine flatwoods, from the rattle of pileated woodpeckers to the sweet song of pine warblers.

Florida Trail

Apalachicola National Forest (East)

PE-21 ⒻⓁ 🏕️ ❄️

Location: Western terminus, Porter Lake Campground [N30°10.606' W084°40.618']; eastern terminus, Sopchoppy at US 319 [N30°04.565' W084°24.584'].

Length: 32.2 miles linear.

Map: Trail shown, as dashed line, on overall Apalachicola National Forest map; for more detail, get backpacking map from Florida Trail Association.

Contact Information: Apalachicola National Forest, Wakulla Ranger District (850-926-3561), 1773 Crawfordville Highway, Crawfordville, FL 32327.

Directions: For the western terminus, take CR 375 south from SR 20 at Bloxham for 15 miles to FR 13. Turn right and cross the Ochlockonee River; the camping area is on the left. For the eastern terminus, follow US 319 west from US 98 in Medart to the trail crossing.

The Hike: The Florida Trail through the eastern Apalachicola National Forest provides an interesting array of hiking experiences for backpackers and day hikers alike. Along the Sopchoppy River, delight in walking the high bluffs above the black water. Bradwell Bay is a 7-mile-wide section of mostly flood-plain forest, requiring strenuous wading through sometimes chest-deep water. Along the Ochlockonee River, the trail visits the historic Langston Homestead before crossing Smith Creek and following steephead bluffs.

Highlights: Visit in spring for optimal wildflowers; fragrant azaleas, buckeye, pitcher plants, and Florida anise all bloom then. Wade Bradwell Bay to see a hidden island of ancient virgin loblolly pines and cypresses.

Logistics: Bradwell Bay should not be entered alone; call the ranger district before you hike to ensure that water levels are at safe. Camping is permitted anywhere, except during hunting season, when you must use designated campsites. Use the forest roads to access particular portions of the trail if you do not want to backpack the entire route.

Other Activities: See the Apalachicola National Forest map and brochure for the many activities available throughout the forest, from hunting and fishing to equestrian, bike, and paddling trails.

Hiking the Florida Trail along the Sopchoppy River in the Apalachicola National Forest.

Leon Sinks Geological Area

Apalachicola National Forest

PE-22 $ 📖 👫 🐕 ⚘

Location: Woodville.

Length: 5.4 miles, the 3.1-mile Sinkhole Trail forming a loop with either the 0.5-mile Crossover Trail or the 2.3-mile Gumswamp Trail.

Map: In brochure at trailhead kiosk.

Contact Information: Apalachicola National Forest, Wakulla Ranger District (850-926-3561), 1773 Crawfordville Highway, Crawfordville, FL 32327.

Directions: From Tallahassee, follow US 319 south from Capital Circle for 5.5 miles to the preserve entrance on the right.

The Hike: This hike through the Woodville Karst Plain provides an excellent introduction to how sinkholes interconnect through the limestone bedrock beneath your feet to the water-filled Floridan Aquifer. Walk counterclockwise from the trailhead to meander through the sandhills past a series of sinks, some water-filled, some dry, and along the lush forests of Fisher Creek. The Gumswamp Trail below Fisher Creek Sink leads you through low-lying swamps to complete the loop; the Crossover Trail provides a shortcut.

Highlights: Pause at the observation deck to look down into Big Dismal Sink, and climb down along the boardwalk to look into Hammock Sink. Pay special attention to Fisher Creek, which disappears beneath the trail and rises again to the north.

Logistics: There is a $3 day-use fee per vehicle at the self-pay station. Benches provide places to rest.

Other Activities: Birdwatch along the trails; watch for wildlife around the sinks.

San Marcos de Apalache Historic State Park

PE-23 $ 📖 🚻 👫

Location: St. Marks [N30°09.158' W084°12.615'].

Length: 0.6-mile loop.

Map: Interpretive brochure and map at trailhead kiosk.

Contact Information: San Marcos de Apalache Historic State Park (850-922-6007), 1022 Desoto Park Drive, Tallahassee, FL 32301.

Directions: From US 98, follow Port Leon Road south through St. Marks to its end.

The Hike: An interpretive walk through a significant historical site, the trail (with markers keyed to the brochure) leads you through layers of ruins of various fortresses that once stood on this spot. Following the edge of the peninsula, it provides great views of the rivers.

Highlights: Completed by the Spanish in 1679, the original wooden stockade fort was destroyed by a hurricane which drowned the garrison. Walk the side trail down to the confluence of the Wakulla and St. Marks Rivers for an excellent view of the estuary, framed by gnarled cedars.

Logistics: The park is closed Tuesday, Wednesday, Christmas, and New Year's Day. Pay the entrance fee at the museum.

Other Activities: Before beginning your walk, tour the museum for a better understanding of the history of this site. There is an adjoining boat ramp. St. Marks State Trail, a 35-mile bicycle trail to Tallahassee, starts in adjacent Riverfront Park.

Sally Ward Spring Trails

Wakulla Springs State Park

PE-24 $ 🕮 🚻 👬 🐎

Location: Wakulla [N30°14.028' W084°18.134'].

Length: 0.9 mile for short loop (Hammock Trail), 2.8 miles for long loop (Hammock Trail and Sally Ward Trail).

Map: Rough map in park brochure.

Contact Information: Wakulla Springs State Park (850-224-5950), 550 Wakulla Park Drive, Wakulla Springs, FL 32305.

Directions: From US 98, follow CR 365 (from the west) or SR 267 (from the east) to SR 267 west of CR 363. The park entrance is on the left. Follow the entrance road in and park at the Wakulla Springs Lodge. Look for the hiker symbol to the left of the main entrance to the lodge; walk over to it and follow the open pathway to the sign marking the trailhead.

The Hike: The trail system encompasses two major trails plus a handful of minor connector trails. The Sally Ward Trail is a linear trail that leads through shady hardwood forests out to the Sally Ward Spring at the park entrance. Crossing the park road to head west, the Hammock Trail loops through upland hammocks of magnolia and beech, skirting floodplain forests of cypress, bay, and red maple. The Loop Trail boardwalk leads you out on the floodplain forest to meet the intersection of the two major trails.

Highlights: There are ancient cypresses and dark floodplain forests along the Hammock Trail.

Logistics: Watch for alligators rising out of Sally Ward Spring, which forms one of the Wakulla River's few tributaries. This is a floodplain forest and can be very buggy at dawn and dusk—wear plenty of mosquito repellent.

Other Activities: Wakulla Springs offers numerous recreational opportunities, from glass-bottom boat rides over the deepest spring in Florida to swimming, diving, equestrian trails, and the only lodge in the Florida State Park system—a 1930s gem. Don't miss the marble-topped soda fountain at the gift shop!

Plum Orchard Pond Trail

St. Marks National Wildlife Refuge

PE-25 $ 📖 🚻 ♿ 🧑‍🧒

Location: Newport [N30°09.052' W084°08.812'].

Length: 0.5-mile loop.

Map: Trail route noted on park map.

Contact Information: St. Marks National Wildlife Refuge (850-925-6121), 1255 Lighthouse Road, St. Marks, FL 32355.

Directions: Enter the refuge from US 98 east of Newport. Follow Lighthouse Road south to the visitor center; the trail starts behind the center along the pond.

The Hike: Follow the loop counterclockwise to walk along a boardwalk through the mesic flatwoods under tall longleaf pines, emerging at the shores of Plum Orchard Pond. The trail continues along the shore of the pond to complete the loop.

Highlights: There are pleasant views across the pond. Watch for alligators!

Logistics: Benches along the route make this an easy walk.

Other Activities: This is one of the top places in Florida for birding, and the hiking trails (PE-25 through PE-29) off Lighthouse Road provide great access to the vast open impoundments on the marshes.

Primitive Walking Trails

St. Marks National Wildlife Refuge

PE-26 $

Location: Newport [N30°08.461' W084°08.326'].

Length: Nested loops of 6 and 12 miles.

Map: Available at trailhead.

Contact Information: St. Marks National Wildlife Refuge (850-925-6121), 1255 Lighthouse Road, St. Marks, FL 32355.

Directions: Enter the refuge from US 98 east of Newport. Follow Lighthouse Road south to the visitor center, and continue another 4 miles to the trail entrance on the left.

The Hike: The 12-mile Deep Creek Trail and the 6-mile Stoney Bayou Trail consist of tram roads and levees designated as primitive walking trails, traversing pine flatwoods, oak hammocks, floodplain forests, and the open impoundments.

Highlights: Enjoy great views from the impoundments.

Logistics: Both trails are intended for day use only. Be certain when you start hiking the loop that you will have the time to complete it. Use sun protection, carry plenty of water, and wear insect repellent! Be alert for alligators sunning along the levees.

Other Activities: This is one of the top places in Florida for birding, and the hiking trails (PE-25 through PE-29) off Lighthouse Road provide great access to the vast open impoundments on the marshes.

Florida Trail

St. Marks National Wildlife Refuge

PE-27 **F** $ ⌂

Location: Eastern terminus, Newport on US 98; western terminus, Panacea [N30°04.453' W084°23.347'].

Length: 41 miles linear.

Map: Trail route noted on park map; for backpacking, purchase detailed map from Florida Trail Association—you'll need the logistical information!

Contact Information: St. Marks National Wildlife Refuge (850-925-6121), 1255 Lighthouse Road, St. Marks, FL 32355.

Directions: Enter the refuge from US 98 east of Newport. Follow Lighthouse Road south 4 miles from the visitor center to the trail crossing.

The Hike: Traversing a vast array of habitats from floodplain forest, palm hammocks, and freshwater marshes to salt marshes, pine flatwoods, and oak hammocks, the Florida Trail through St. Marks provides a unique coastal backpacking experience.

Highlights: Enjoy fabulous views from the open dikes, the grandeur of the Cathedral (a palm hammock), the ruins of Port Leon, and beautiful Shepard Spring.

Logistics: The visitor center, with interpretive information, is open Mon–Fri 8:00–4:00, Sat–Sun 10:00–5:00. If you plan to backpack across the refuge, a permit is required in advance; call the above phone number. You *must* use the designated campsites. Be very conscious of food handling, as bears roam the refuge.

Other Activities: This is one of the top places in Florida for birding, and the Florida Trail as well as other hiking trails (PE-25 through PE-29) throughout the refuge work well for tracking down birds.

Mounds Pool Interpretive Trail

St. Marks National Wildlife Refuge

PE-28 $ 📖 🚻 ❄️

Location: Newport [N30°05.279' W084°09.866'].

Length: 1.1-mile loop with 0.3-mile (round-trip) spur.

Map: Trail shown on park map and in interpretive guide at trailhead.

Contact Information: St. Marks National Wildlife Refuge (850-925-6121), 1255 Lighthouse Road, St. Marks, FL 32355.

Directions: Enter the refuge from US 98 east of Newport. Follow Lighthouse Road south to the visitor center, and continue another 6 miles to the Mounds Pool area on the left.

The Hike: This trail loops around several of the Mounds Pool impoundments, offering a shady walk along the rim of one pool and sunny, breezy walks out along the salt marshes. Climbing a hill past the fire tower, it drops down through coastal pine flatwoods to take you to an observation deck over a tidal marsh. The trail loops back around the salt marshes.

Highlights: This trail affords great views from many different vantage points, including across the broad sweep of salt marshes that make up the Big Bend.

Logistics: The trail may be wet and muddy in several places. Wear sun protection and prepare for mosquitoes!

Other Activities: This is one of the top places in Florida for birding, and the hiking trails (PE-25 through PE-29) off Lighthouse Road provide great access to the vast open impoundments on the marshes.

Lighthouse Levee Trail

St. Marks National Wildlife Refuge

PE-29 $ 📖 👫

Location: Newport [N30°04.461' W084°10.816'].

Length: 0.3 mile round-trip.

Map: Available at trailhead.

Contact Information: St. Marks National Wildlife Refuge (850-925-6121), 1255 Lighthouse Road, St. Marks, FL 32355.

Directions: Enter the refuge from US 98 east of Newport. Follow Lighthouse Road south to the visitor center, and continue another 7 miles to the end of the road. Park in front of the lighthouse and follow the trail to the right, along the waterfront.

The Hike: This short interpretive trail follows the levee between the Gulf of Mexico and the Lighthouse Pool impoundment, ending at a bench overlooking the salt marshes surrounding the outflow of the St. Marks River.

Highlights: Take a look at the lighthouse, a national landmark built in 1831. Visit in October, when the saltbushes are covered with monarch butterflies stopping to feed during their migration to Mexico.

Logistics: There is no shade on this short trail. Use sun protection. Pick up an interpretive brochure at the trailhead. It is possible to keep following the levee around past the point and walk back through the boat trailer parking area to the lighthouse.

Other Activities: This is one of the top places in Florida for birding, and the hiking trails (PE-25 through PE-29) off Lighthouse Road provide great access to the vast open impoundments on the marshes.

Florida Trail

Aucilla Wildlife Management Area

PE-30 **F** ⛺ ❄️

Location: Southern terminus, at US 98 [N30°08.696' W083°58.212']; northern terminus, Lamont at CR 14.

Length: 17.2 miles linear.

Map: Detailed backpacking map available from Florida Trail Association.

Contact Information: Aucilla Wildlife Management Area (850-421-1883), Florida Fish and Wildlife Conservation Commission, 620 South Meridian Street, Tallahassee, FL 32399.

Directions: Follow US 98 west from Perry or east from Newport to reach the trailhead just east of the Aucilla River.

The Hike: There's nothing else in Florida quite like this stretch of trail—it parallels the Aucilla River, which along nine miles of its length disappears underground and appears sporadically flowing through broad and deep sinkholes. The trail follows the high ground between the sinkholes.

Highlights: Visit the river sink, and enjoy the scenic views along the trail. Watch for a tunnel-like trailside cavern and a natural bridge set within a deep sinkhole.

Logistics: Do not attempt this trail if the river is in flood stage, since the river will rise to swamp the trail, making it impossible to distinguish the trail from the sinkholes. Camping is best north of Goose Pasture Road.

Other Activities: Kayakers enjoy playing in the Aucilla River rapids.

Ladell Brothers Outdoor Environmental Center

North Florida Community College

PE-31 📖 👫

Location: Madison [N30°28.518' W083°25.362'].

Length: 1.8 miles of hiking, divided into three interconnecting loops, the shortest 0.5 mile.

Map: Interpretive guides and maps available in box at trailhead; if missing, consult large map sign at first trail junction.

Contact Information: Ladell Brothers Outdoor Environmental Center (850-973-1645), 1000 Turner Davis Drive, Madison, FL 32340.

Directions: Follow US 90 west from Madison to the entrance to North Florida Community College, on the north side of the road; park on campus near the Hamilton Library.

The Hike: Starting off on a boardwalk across a cypress swamp, you enter the deep shade of a dense hardwood hammock. Signs identify massive trees, and numbered posts correspond to the interpretive guide. At the trail junction, choose your route. Two loops lead through the dark hammock along the edge of cypress swamps; the third works its way around one end of the Wood Duck Pond. Frequent benches make it an easy hike for all ages.

Highlights: Bring your barbecue gear to enjoy the picnic tables with grills tucked back in the forest. Despite the trail's proximity to campus buildings, you feel you're in a different world—and you *will* see wildlife.

Logistics: It's a little tough to find this hike. From the Hamilton Library, orient yourself with the gazebo near the staff parking area. From the gazebo, walk between the Student Success Center and Building 5 (Biology) and along the edge of the Wood Duck Pond. The trailhead is hidden in the trees in a direct line back from the water's edge. Open sunrise to sunset.

Other Activities: Birdwatch on the open landscaped areas of campus; stop in at the library to borrow a pair of binoculars and browse through their field guides.

Florida Trail

Suwannee River West

PE-32 🅕 ⛺ ❄️

Location: Northern terminus, Suwannee River State Park (north section) [N30°25.514' W083°07.930']; southern terminus, Twin Rivers State Forest, south of Mill Creek Tract at River Road.

Length: 18 miles linear.

Map: Detailed backpacking map available from Florida Trail Association.

Contact Information: Twin Rivers State Forest (386-208-1462), 7620 133rd Rd, Live Oak, FL 32060; Suwannee River State Park (386-362-2762), 20185 CR 132, Live Oak, FL 32060

Directions: Follow US 98 east from Lee. Drive south on River Road (on the west side of the Suwannee River) to access the trail from the Mill Creek Tract of Twin Rivers State Forest. The trail can also be accessed from several points in Suwannee River State Park.

The Hike: One of the state's most scenic places to enjoy a weekend backpacking, the Florida Trail along the Suwannee River follows the river's natural levees, deeply shaded by river bluff forests of magnolia, beech, and hickory. You'll walk through the ghost town of Ellaville, where only bricks, clay pots, and the town's water source remain, as you follow this majestic river south to where the trail leaves the river at the Mill Creek Tract.

Highlights: Views are great from hundreds of vantage points along the trail, as it overlooks the Suwannee River along most of this segment. In the northernmost section of Suwannee River State Park, there is a natural bridge created by several adjacent sinkholes along the river.

Logistics: There are trail access points at Mill Creek (south on River Road from US 98), US 98 (at the Trailwalker sign), Suwannee River State Park, and CR 141. Do not attempt this trail if the river is in flood stage, since the river will rise to swamp the trail.

Other Activities: Twin Rivers State Forest has equestrian and bicycle trails as well as fishing, canoeing, and picnic tables along the trail at river access points. Suwannee River State Park also provides several excellent hiking trails (NF-01, NF-02, and NF-08).

North Gulf

Taylor, Lafayette, Dixie, Levy

River boardwalk through the floodplain forest at Lower Suwannee National Wildlife Refuge.

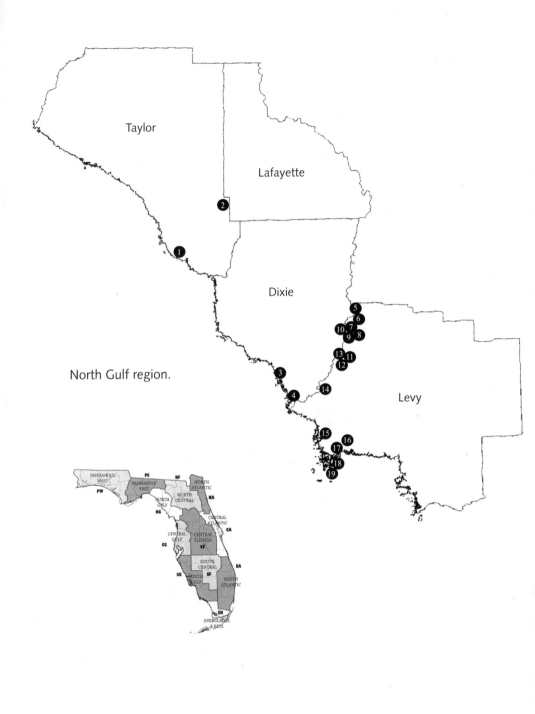

Taylor

Lafayette

Dixie

Levy

North Gulf region.

Taylor
  NG-1 Dallus Landing Nature Trail, Big Bend Wildlife Management Area
  NG-2 Steinhatchee Trail, Steinhatchee Falls Water Management Area
Dixie
  NG-3 Fish Bone Nature Trail, Lower Suwannee National Wildlife Refuge
  NG-4 Salt Creek Nature Trail, Lower Suwannee National Wildlife Refuge
Levy
  NG-5 Basswood Trail, Andrews Wildlife Management Area
  NG-6 Buckeye and Turkey Track Trails, Andrews Wildlife Management Area
  NG-7 Florida Maple Trail, Andrews Wildlife Management Area
  NG-8 Persimmon Trail, Andrews Wildlife Management Area
  NG-9 Bluff Oak Trail, Andrews Wildlife Management Area
  NG-10 River Birch Trail, Andrews Wildlife Management Area
  NG-11 North End Trail System, Manatee Springs State Park
  NG-12 Sink Trail Loop, Manatee Springs State Park
  NG-13 Suwannee River Boardwalk, Manatee Springs State Park
  NG-14 River Trail, Lower Suwannee National Wildlife Refuge
  NG-15 Shell Mound, Lower Suwannee National Wildlife Refuge
  NG-16 East Trail System, Cedar Key Scrub Reserve
  NG-17 West Trail System, Cedar Key Scrub Reserve
  NG-18 Railroad Trestle Nature Walk
  NG-19 Atsena Otie Key, Cedar Keys National Wildlife Refuge

Dallus Landing Nature Trail

Tide Swamp Unit, Big Bend Wildlife Management Area

NG-1 📖 🚻 ❄️

Location: Steinhatchee [N29°43.324' W083°29.182'].

Length: 1.2-mile loop.

Map: No map provided.

Contact Information: Big Bend Wildlife Management Area (850-838-1306), 663 Plantation Road, Perry, FL 32347.

Directions: From US 19/98 in Perry, drive 4.5 miles south to CR 361. Continue south along the Taylor County coast for 28 miles to the Dallus Creek entrance to Big Bend WMA on the right, 6 miles south of Hagen's Cove Road. (Alternatively, follow CR 361 north from Steinhatchee to Dallus Creek Road on the left.) Follow the rough dirt road 2.5 miles to the picnic area on the right. The trailhead is on the far side of the picnic area.

The Hike: Providing an excellent introduction to the Big Bend, this nature trail follows the edge of a salt marsh for 0.1 mile before turning away into the coastal pine flatwoods. Crossing a bridge, the trail continues into a coastal scrub habitat, with a side trail (worth the trip) leading to a scenic view of the estuary. Follow the trail markers through scrub and scrubby flatwoods to complete a 0.9-mile loop, and walk back along the salt marsh to end at the picnic area.

Highlights: The views of the Gulf coast salt marshes ringed with palm hammocks are spectacular.

Logistics: A portable toilet is provided at the end of the road near the boat ramp. The incoming road may be rough to negotiate in a car after a heavy rain. There are several benches at scenic points along the trail. Expect heavy mosquitoes at dawn and dusk and during the summer. The area is open for seasonal hunting; check on hunt status at www.floridaconservation.org before hiking.

Other Activities: Use the picnic grove or boat launch, go scalloping in the nearby bay, and fish from the bank of Dallus Creek. This is a stop along the 75-mile Big Bend Wilderness Paddling Trail.

Estuary views along the Dallus Landing Nature Trail.

Steinhatchee Trail

Steinhatchee Falls Water Management Area

NG-2 🚻 🐴

Location: Tennille [N29°46.461' W083°19.752'].

Length: 3.3 miles linear.

Map: None available.

Contact Information: Suwannee River Water Management District (386-362-1001), 9225 CR 49, Live Oak, FL 32060.

Directions: From US 19/98 in Tennille (north of Cross City, south of Perry), drive 0.5 mile south on SR 51 toward Steinhatchee. Turn left into the parking area. The trail starts at a trailhead sign at the edge of the pines.

The Hike: This linear hike meanders through public lands upstream from one of Florida's geologic wonders, Steinhatchee Falls, ending at the falls (which can also be accessed by road). Leaving the trailhead, you enter a pine plantation and continue into more natural habitats such as hardwood hammock, scrubby flatwoods, and upland forest with magnolias and hickories. The trail crosses and follows several forest roads along the way, and passes through an area once farmed, with plow lines still visible. After 3 miles you emerge onto the dirt road that leads to Steinhatchee Falls; turn left to walk down to the picnic area above the falls (open 8:00–7:00 daily).

Highlights: Enjoy spectacular wildflowers, including showy atamasco lilies, in spring and fall. A new loop trail takes you along the river above the falls.

Logistics: The trail is blazed with large white diamonds. Keep alert for blazes at road junctions and on the few short road walks. After 1.5 miles you'll encounter rocks and roots underfoot. Although primarily a hiking trail, the trail is open to equestrian use. Use two cars to set up a shuttle, or plan on a 6.6-mile round trip. Portable toilets are at both ends of the trail.

Other Activities: Steinhatchee Falls has a picnic area and canoe launch. Kayaking the river (in both directions) is a popular pastime, and float trips and rentals can be arranged through the Steinhatchee Outpost campground at SR 51 and US 19/98 in Tennille.

Fish Bone Nature Trail

Lower Suwannee National Wildlife Refuge

NG-3 🦴

Location: Shired Island [N29°25.523' W083°11.847'].

Length: 0.5 mile round-trip.

Map: None provided.

Contact Information: Dixie County Historical Society, PO Box 928, Cross City, FL 32628, or Lower Suwannee National Wildlife Refuge (352-493-0238), 16450 NW 31 Place, Chiefland, FL 32626.

Directions: From Cross City, drive south on CR 351 to CR 357, and continue south past the entrance to the Dixie Mainline Trail (a driving route through the California Swamp). The trail is on the left with a small parking area and sign.

The Hike: It's a short and pleasant walk in the shade along Fish Bone Creek (which flows into Shired Creek) through the maritime hammock to the site of the cemetery of the once thriving town of Fish Bone.

Highlights: The historic cemetery lies at the end of the trail; continue a little farther for a view out over the salt marshes surrounding Shired Island.

Logistics: Yellow flies and mosquitoes can be fierce in late spring and summer. The trail was built and is maintained by members of the historical society.

Other Activities: Drive two miles farther to Shired Island to enjoy a primitive campground on a secluded Gulf beach, with a restroom and nearby boat launch. Or drive north to take a slow nine-mile ride on the narrow Dixie Mainline Trail (which can be hiked or biked, but best driven except in the dead of winter) across the salt marshes and cypress swamps of the California Swamp to the town of Suwannee.

Salt Creek Trail

Lower Suwannee National Wildlife Refuge

NG-4 ♿ 👫

Location: Suwannee [N29°20.953' W083°08.615'].

Length: 0.2 mile round-trip.

Map: Trail shown in refuge brochure.

Contact Information: Lower Suwannee National Wildlife Refuge (352-493-0238), 16450 NW 31 Place, Chiefland, FL 32626.

Directions: From US 19/98 in Old Town, follow CR 349 south for 21.7 miles to the entrance to the Dixie Mainline Trail on the right. Drive 0.3 mile to the "Salt Creek Point" sign; turn left and follow the road to the parking area at the end.

The Hike: This is a short stroll out to a boardwalk and observation deck along Salt Creek, providing a sweeping view of the coastal savanna and islands of palm hammocks to the west of the town of Suwannee, where the Suwannee River meets the salt marshes.

Highlights: The panorama of the Gulf estuary along Salt Creek is fabulous.

Logistics: A crushed limestone causeway connects the parking area with the boardwalk, enabling wheelchair access (not guaranteed after a heavy rain) with assistance.

Other Activities: You can fish from the boardwalk, or drive the rugged nine-mile Dixie Mainline Trail through a mosaic of salt marshes and cypress swamps in the California Swamp, where there are several pulloffs for kayak launches.

Basswood Trail

Andrews Wildlife Management Area

NG-5 $ 🐎

Location: Fanning Springs [N29°34.176' W082°56.419'].

Length: 0.5 mile round-trip.

Map: Trail shown in WMA brochure available at entrance gate.

Contact Information: Florida Fish and Wildlife Conservation Commission (352-493-6020), 9550 NW 160th Street, Fanning Springs, FL 32693.

Directions: Follow US 19/98 north from Chiefland for 5.1 miles. Turn left on NW 160th Street at the "Great Florida Birding Trail" sign. When the road enters the park, turn right on Fort Fannin Road and follow it to its end at the gate. Park and do not block the gate. Walk down the road to access the trail on the left.

The Hike: This shady trail through the river bluff forest above the Suwannee River once led past an American basswood listed in the National Registry, but the grand tree has died. Instead, you walk through a grove of its offspring, young basswood (or linden) trees that sport fragrant white blooms in early summer. The trail connects to a forest road, inaccessible except on foot, at the far end.

Highlights: There are beautiful magnolia and basswood trees along the trail.

Logistics: There is a $3 per person entrance fee to this WMA. Seasonal hunting is permitted; check hunt dates before hiking. This area is known for being heavily infested with ticks—use strong repellent and wear light-colored clothing, or visit only in the dead of winter.

Other Activities: At the end of River Landing Road there is a picnic table overlooking the Suwannee River. Bank fishing is permitted along the river, and you can ride a bicycle on the forest roads. Or try any of the other short nature trails (NG-6 through NG-10) in this preserve.

Buckeye and Turkey Track Trails

Andrews Wildlife Management Area

NG-6 $ 🦌

Location: Fanning Springs [N29°33.392' W082°56.566'].

Length: 1.9-mile or 2.3-mile loop.

Map: Trails shown in WMA brochure available at entrance gate.

Contact Information: Florida Fish and Wildlife Conservation Commission (352-493-6020), 9550 NW 160th Street, Fanning Springs, FL 32693.

Directions: Follow US 19/98 north from Chiefland for 5.1 miles. Turn left on NW 160th Street at the "Great Florida Birding Trail" sign. Continue to where the road enters the park. Follow River Landing Road to Fort Fannin Road and turn left. Park on the left at the "Turkey Track Trail" sign; do not block the gate.

The Hike: Using the Buckeye Trail and the Turkey Track Trail, you can create a loop through the forest, with an optional walk down to the Suwannee River. Follow the Buckeye Trail east through the shady uplands, where American holly and magnolias dominate. As the trail curves to the right it becomes the Turkey Track Trail, passing through sandhills before entering the upland forest. Cross Fort Fannin Road (where you can use the road to complete the shorter loop) and continue down the straightaway to the Suwannee River. Turn right to explore the river bluffs and walk up River Landing Road to complete the loop.

Highlights: Enjoy a nice view of the Suwannee River from the end of the Turkey Track Trail.

Logistics: There is a $3 per person entrance fee to this WMA. Seasonal hunting is permitted; check hunt dates before hiking. This area is known for being heavily infested with ticks—use strong repellent and wear light-colored clothing, or visit only in the dead of winter.

Other Activities: At the end of River Landing Road there is a picnic table overlooking the Suwannee River. Bank fishing is permitted along the river, and you can ride a bicycle on the forest roads. Or try any of the other short nature trails (NG-5 through NG-10) in this preserve.

Florida Maple Trail

Andrews Wildlife Management Area

NG-7 **$** 🏇

Location: Fanning Springs [N29°32.770' W082°56.401'].

Length: 0.7 mile linear or 1.5-mile loop.

Map: Trail shown in WMA brochure available at entrance gate.

Contact Information: Florida Fish and Wildlife Conservation Commission (352-493-6020), 9550 NW 160th Street, Fanning Springs, FL 32693.

Directions: Follow US 19/98 north from Chiefland for 5.1 miles. Turn left on NW 160th Street at the "Great Florida Birding Trail" sign. Continue to where the road enters the park. Turn left on Fort Fannin Road and drive 1 mile. Look for the "Florida Maple Trail" sign on the right.

The Hike: This is the most beautiful of the short hikes in the preserve, leading you by yellow blazes through the river bluff forest along the rim of a series of sinkholes and past the base of a Florida Champion tree, a Florida maple last documented at 82" in circumference and 85' tall. When the trail emerges at Dick Slough Road, you can turn around and retrace your steps or walk up the shaded road to Fort Fannin Road to create a loop.

Highlights: Wildlife abounds in this part of the preserve. Keep alert, as you can see deer, owls, foxes, and wild hogs easily through the open understory.

Logistics: There is a $3 per person entrance fee to this WMA. Seasonal hunting is permitted; check hunt dates before hiking. This area is known for being heavily infested with ticks—use strong repellent and wear light-colored clothing, or visit only in the dead of winter.

Other Activities: At the end of River Landing Road there is a picnic table overlooking the Suwannee River. Bank fishing is permitted along the river, and you can ride a bicycle on the forest roads. Or try any of the other short nature trails (NG-5 through NG-10) in this preserve.

Persimmon Trail

Andrews Wildlife Management Area

NG-8 $ 🐴

Location: Fanning Springs [N29°32.591' W082°56.391'].

Length: 0.6 mile linear or 1.1-mile loop.

Map: Trail shown in WMA brochure available at entrance gate.

Contact Information: Florida Fish and Wildlife Conservation Commission (352-493-6020), 9550 NW 160th Street, Fanning Springs, FL 32693.

Directions: Follow US 19/98 north from Chiefland for 5.1 miles. Turn left on NW 160th Street at the "Great Florida Birding Trail" sign. Continue to where the road enters the park. Turn left on Fort Fannin Road and drive 1 mile. Turn right at the T and park on the left; do not block the gate. Walk up the open field to the trail entrance on the left.

The Hike: Follow the yellow blazes into the deep shade of an upland hammock past the Florida Champion persimmon, which was last documented as 90' tall and 60" around at its base. Wild coontie and ferns grow amid the open understory, where it's easy to spot wildlife. When the trail emerges at Randall Road, you can turn around and retrace your steps or turn left and walk up the shaded road to the trailhead parking area.

Highlights: I've never seen another persimmon tree come even close to the size of this one. It's awesome and definitely worth a look. The crown of this tree is up so high that you can hardly see it for the crowns of the understory trees.

Logistics: There is a $3 per person entrance fee to this WMA. Seasonal hunting is permitted; check hunt dates before hiking. This area is known for being heavily infested with ticks—use strong repellent and wear light-colored clothing, or visit only in the dead of winter.

Other Activities: At the end of River Landing Road, there is a picnic table overlooking the Suwannee River. Bank fishing is permitted along the river, and you can ride a bicycle on the forest roads. Or try any of the other short nature trails (NG-5 through NG-10) in this preserve.

Bluff Oak Trail

Andrews Wildlife Management Area

NG-9 $ 🦌

Location: Fanning Springs [N29°32.708' W082°57.424'].

Length: 1.8 miles round-trip.

Map: Trail shown in WMA brochure available at entrance gate.

Contact Information: Florida Fish and Wildlife Conservation Commission (352-493-6020), 9550 NW 160th Street, Fanning Springs, FL 32693.

Directions: Follow US 19/98 north from Chiefland for 5.1 miles. Turn left on NW 160th Street at the "Great Florida Birding Trail" sign. Continue to where the road enters the park. Turn left on Fort Fannin Road and drive 1 mile. Turn right and follow Dick Slough Road for 1.6 miles down to the trailhead parking on the left.

The Hike: The yellow-blazed trail starts out along a firebreak, rounding an open meadow before plunging into the upland forest. The trail becomes a narrow track through the hardwood forest as it circles around several broad sinkholes before entering a stand of southern magnolias. The shaggy-barked trees just beyond are the bluff oaks, which thrive on the limestone karst bluffs along the Suwannee River.

Highlights: A sign points out the Florida Champion bluff oak, and it's a biggie—it stands more than 105' tall and has a circumference of nearly 9' at its base.

Logistics: There is a $3 per person entrance fee to this WMA. Seasonal hunting is permitted; check hunt dates before hiking. This area is known for being heavily infested with ticks—use strong repellent and wear light-colored clothing, or visit only in the dead of winter.

Other Activities: At the end of River Landing Road there is a picnic table overlooking the Suwannee River. Bank fishing is permitted along the river, and you can ride a bicycle on the forest roads. Or try any of the other short nature trails (NG-5 through NG-10) in this preserve.

River Birch Trail

Andrews Wildlife Management Area

NG-10 $ 🦌

Location: Fanning Springs [N29°32.603' W082°57.862'].

Length: 1.8 miles round-trip.

Map: Trail shown in WMA brochure available at entrance gate.

Contact Information: Florida Fish and Wildlife Conservation Commission (352-493-6020), 9550 NW 160th Street, Fanning Springs, FL 32693.

Directions: Follow US 19/98 north from Chiefland for 5.1 miles. Turn left on NW 160th Street at the "Great Florida Birding Trail" sign. Continue to where the road enters the park. Turn left on Fort Fannin Road and drive 1 mile. Turn right and follow Dick Slough Road for 2 miles down to the gate for the River Birch Trail; park but do not block the gate.

The Hike: Follow the yellow blazes along a causeway through a tall stand of pond cypress. As the trail rises into the hardwood forest, you can see a ribbon of blue through the trees to your right—the Suwannee River. The trail veers away from the river, staying to the high ground on this island surrounded by floodplain forest. Beyond the old cattle pen, the trail becomes hard to follow. Use the "Designated Trail" signs.

Highlights: This hike is notable for how close it brings you to the Suwannee River. Although you don't walk along the river, you can see it in the distance through the tangled floodplain forest of sweet gum, maple, and cypress.

Logistics: There is a $3 per person entrance fee to this WMA. Seasonal hunting is permitted; check hunt dates before hiking. This area is known for being heavily infested with ticks—use strong repellent and wear light-colored clothing, or visit only in the dead of winter.

Other Activities: At the end of River Landing Road there is a picnic table overlooking the Suwannee River. Bank fishing is permitted along the river, and you can ride a bicycle on the forest roads. Or try any of the other short nature trails (NG-5 through NG-9) in this preserve.

North End Trail System

Manatee Springs State Park

NG-11 $ 📖 🅒 🐎

Location: Chiefland [N29°29.626' W082°58.397'].

Length: Up to 6 miles of hiking, with a minimum 0.9-mile loop and a 2-mile interpretive loop.

Map: Trail system map and interpretive brochure available at trailhead or from ranger station.

Contact Information: Manatee Springs State Park (352-493-6072), 11650 NW 115th Street, Chiefland, FL 32626.

Directions: From US 19/98 in Chiefland, follow SR 320 west for 6 miles to the park entrance. Continue down the park entrance road; the trailhead is on the right.

The Hike: At the trailhead kiosk use the map to determine the route you want to take through the shady upland forests above the Suwannee River. No matter where you walk, the understory is very open, great for wildlife watching. Habitats range from a river bluff forest of hickory, oak, and magnolia to cypress swamps in low-lying areas and longleaf pine flatwoods and oak hammocks along the uplands at the south end of the trail system.

Highlights: Shacklefoot Pond is a beautiful destination, a dark, primordial place ringed with tall cypresses. A historic graveyard lies at the southernmost point of the trail system.

Logistics: Numbers along the Scenic Trail (which makes a 2-mile loop using the Clay and Shacklefoot Trails) correspond to the interpretive brochure. Ticks are very prevalent in these woods—use a heavy dose of insect repellent on your socks, shoes, and lower legs. The trail is shared with bicyclists, who use the outer loop for the most part. The dead-end trails shown on the map do just that—dead-end without taking you to any particular points of interest.

Other Activities: There are two other trails (NG-12 and NG-13) to explore, plus swimming in the spring and paddling down the spring run to the Suwannee River.

Sink Trail Loop

Manatee Springs State Park

NG-12 $ 📖 🅒 🕸

Location: Chiefland [N29°29.197' W082°58.478'].

Length: 0.6-mile loop.

Map: Rough map in park brochure.

Contact Information: Manatee Springs State Park (352-493-6072), 11650 NW 115th Street, Chiefland, FL 32626.

Directions: From US 19/98 in Chiefland, follow SR 320 west for 6 miles to the park entrance. Continue down the park entrance road, passing the trailhead for the North End Trail System (NG-6) before reaching a small parking area on the left just before the campground road.

The Hike: Start at the "Sink Trail Loop" sign and follow this short but delightful walk through an upland forest of hickory, elm, and bluff oak along rugged limestone karst terrain full of sinkholes and caves. Keep to the right to follow the loop trail counterclockwise around the sinkholes; short side trails lead to vantage points where you can peer into these deep holes.

Highlights: This is a great short introduction to how sinkholes form in the limestone karst landscape, since many of the sinks along this trail are obviously aligned in a chain above an underground stream.

Logistics: Do not attempt to climb down into the holes. Restrooms are available up the road at the swimming area, and a short trail leads from the campground to this trail. Ticks are very prevalent in these woods—use a heavy dose of insect repellent on your socks, shoes, and lower legs.

Other Activities: In addition to the popular campground, there are two other trails (NG-11 and NG-13) to explore, plus swimming in the spring and paddling down the spring run to the Suwannee River.

Suwannee River Boardwalk

Manatee Springs State Park

NG-13 $ ⛹ 🅒 ♿ ⛹

Location: Chiefland [N29°29.336' W082°58.694'].

Length: 0.4 mile round-trip.

Map: Boardwalk shown on park map.

Contact Information: Manatee Springs State Park (352-493-6072), 11650 NW 115th Street, Chiefland, FL 32626.

Directions: From US 19/98 in Chiefland, follow SR 320 west for 6 miles to the park entrance. Continue down the park entrance road to where it ends at the large parking lot for the springs. Walk down to the springs and turn left; follow the pathway to the beginning of the boardwalk.

The Hike: The boardwalk winds its way through the floodplain forest along Manatee Springs Run, where tapegrass waves in the crystalline stream and deer browse through the wetlands beneath the maples and cypresses, before ending at a boat dock and covered observation deck along the lower Suwannee River.

Highlights: This is a shady, short, pleasant walk that shouldn't be missed on a visit to this park. Manatees can be spotted from the observation deck on the Suwannee River.

Logistics: It's possible to walk up and around the spring on a sidewalk and unmarked paths, but only the sidewalk and boardwalk are wheelchair accessible. Several benches provide spots to sit and savor the view. Mosquitoes may be a problem at dawn and dusk.

Other Activities: There are two other trails (NG-11 and NG-12) to explore, plus swimming in the spring and paddling down the spring run to the Suwannee River.

River Trail

Suwannee River National Wildlife Refuge

NG-14 📖 👫

Location: Fowler Bluff [N29°22.578' W083°02.625'].

Length: 0.6 mile round-trip.

Map: Trail shown in refuge brochure.

Contact Information: Lower Suwannee National Wildlife Refuge (352-493-0238), 16450 NW 31 Place, Chiefland, FL 32626.

Directions: From Cedar Key, follow SR 24 east to CR 347. Turn left and drive north 17 miles to the sign for the refuge headquarters. Turn left and park on the right at the trailhead.

The Hike: This is a short stroll through the floodplain forest of the lower Suwannee River, a watery swamp dominated by cypress, sweet gum, and red maple. Starting out as a footpath along a causeway through a hardwood forest, the trail meets a boardwalk and makes a sharp left to meander out to the river's edge.

Highlights: Watch for manatees and birds from the observation deck on the Suwannee River.

Logistics: Be cautious of the prolific poison ivy growing on the cypresses and hickories along the boardwalk—don't reach out and touch the trees!

Other Activities: Visitors are welcome to walk or bicycle more than ninety miles of forest roads throughout the refuge, most accessible from gates along CR 347.

Shell Mound Unit

Suwannee River National Wildlife Refuge

NG-15 📖 🚻 🅐

Location: Cedar Key [N29°12.427' W083°03.930'].

Length: Two loops totaling 1.6 miles.

Map: Trails shown in refuge brochure.

Contact Information: Lower Suwannee National Wildlife Refuge (352-493-0238), 16450 NW 31 Place, Chiefland, FL 32626.

Directions: From SR 24 east of Cedar Key, drive north on CR 347 for 2.3 miles to CR 326; turn left and follow the road until the pavement ends, just past the campground. The trailhead parking is on the left.

The Hike: Two trails radiate from this trailhead: the Dennis Creek Trail, which leads you across boardwalks to islands of palm hammocks in the midst of the estuary along Dennis Creek, and the Shell Mound Trail, which takes you up and over the largest and oldest Timucuan midden remaining on the Gulf Coast, a shell mound covering several acres and topped with a forest of oaks and cedars.

Highlights: Cool coastal breezes and fabulous views greet you on both trails, especially from the top of the twenty-eight-foot-tall Shell Mound. Birding is superb along the tidal flats circled by the Dennis Creek Trail.

Logistics: There is a portable toilet and a wheelchair-accessible fishing board-walk and observation pier at the very end of the road on the estuary, below Shell Mound.

Other Activities: You'll find a canoe and kayak launch at Shell Mound, fishing along the estuary, and camping along the salt marsh in Shell Mound County Park.

East Trail System

Cedar Key Scrub State Reserve

NG-16 👫 ⛺

Location: Cedar Key [N29°12.320' W082°59.296'].

Length: At least 4 miles of trails, with two spurs and a minimum 3-mile loop.

Map: Displayed and in brochure at trailhead kiosk.

Contact Information: Cedar Key Scrub State Reserve (352-543-5567), PO Box 187, Cedar Key, FL 32625.

Directions: Follow SR 24 east from Cedar Key to CR 347. Drive north 1 mile and park on the left at the "Cedar Key Scrub WMA" sign.

The Hike: The trail system is a series of blazed and signposted forest roads that loop through coastal scrub and coastal pine flatwoods, passing flatwoods ponds and oak hammocks.

Highlights: It's an immersion in the coastal scrub habitat, where you'll encounter numerous gopher tortoises and might spot birds of the scrub, such as rufous-sided towhees. Although there are Florida scrub-jays living to the west, they haven't migrated into this habitat yet.

Logistics: Although the trails are forest roads and considered multiuse, the soft sand makes them unappealing for equestrians and bicyclists. For hikers, walking can be downright difficult in several places along this loop. Open scrub also means little shade—wear sun protection and carry a lot of water. Seasonal hunting is permitted; check www.floridaconservation.org for dates and use appropriate precautions.

Other Activities: There is seasonal hunting, and a separate trail system (NG-17) within the same reserve.

West Trail System

Cedar Key Scrub State Reserve

NG-17 🐎

Location: Cedar Key [N29°11.656' W083°00.927'].

Length: At least 8 miles of trails, with two spurs and a minimum 0.5-mile loop.

Map: Displayed and in brochure at trailhead kiosk.

Contact Information: Cedar Key Scrub State Reserve (352-543-5567), PO Box 187, Cedar Key, FL 32625.

Directions: Follow SR 24 east from Cedar Key to CR 347. Drive north 1 mile and park on the left at the "Cedar Key Scrub WMA" sign.

The Hike: This system of blazed and signposted forest roads showcases a mosaic of habitats along the Gulf estuary, from freshwater marshes and open prairies to rosemary scrub, mesic flatwoods, and palm hammocks. For the most scenic route, about five miles long, follow Trail 10, Trail 6, and Trail 7 clockwise to make a loop around the scrub and prairies (using the white, red, blue, and orange blazes), with a side trip on Trail 8 through the palm hammocks to a view of the estuary.

Highlights: Expect to spot both gopher tortoises and Florida scrub-jays along the trail. Walk out to the edge of the salt marsh and enjoy sweeping views of the estuary. Wildflowers grow in profusion in the wet and dry prairies in the middle of the reserve.

Logistics: Although the trails are forest roads and considered multiuse, the soft sand in the scrub along the southwestern portion of the trail system makes these trails unappealing to equestrians and bicyclists. Open scrub also means little shade—wear sun protection and carry a lot of water. Seasonal hunting is permitted; check www.floridaconservation.org for dates and use appropriate precautions.

Other Activities: There is seasonal hunting, and a separate trail system (NG-16) within the same reserve along SR 24 to the east.

Railroad Trestle Nature Walk

NG-18 ![icon] ![icon] ![icon]

Location: Cedar Key [N29°08.681' W083°01.956'].

Length: 0.6 mile round-trip.

Map: None available.

Contact Information: Florida Nature Coast Conservancy (352-543-6352), PO Box 401, Cedar Key, FL 32625.

Directions: From US 19, follow SR 24 into Cedar Key. Within the mile after you pass the University of Florida Marine Science Center, watch for Grove Street on the left, just before the Blue Desert Cafe. Turn left. There is a small trailhead parking area immediately on the right.

The Hike: The interpretive kiosk at the trailhead explains the Florida Railroad, one of Florida's first railroads, connecting Fernandina and the Cedar Keys. The trailhead is at Kiss Me Quick, an old whistle-stop station along the route. The trail follows a short segment of the rail route, donated by Cedar Key Building & Development as mitigation for other projects. Vegetation has grown up since the railroad ceased operation in the 1930s, especially the mangroves. But cedars and silk bay have taken root too, and you'll find colorful blossoms of spiderwort and coral bean along the way. The trail ends at the original pilings for the railroad trestle that led to Depot Key, now downtown Cedar Key.

Highlights: Following the railroad grade, you get a very different perspective on the Cedar Keys, with sweeping views of the tidal flats. At trail's end, the trestle pilings date back to the 1850s.

Logistics: The trail is open dawn to dusk. There are only three trailhead parking spaces; if they are full, come back later.

Other Activities: Bring your binoculars—birdwatching is superb along this trail!

Atsena Otie Key

Cedar Keys National Wildlife Refuge

NG-19 📖 🚹

Location: Cedar Key [N29°07.496' W083°02.122'].

Length: 1.2 miles round-trip.

Map: Trail shown in refuge brochure.

Contact Information: Cedar Keys National Wildlife Refuge (352-493-0238), 16450 NW 31 Place, Chiefland, FL 32626.

Directions: From Cedar Key, you must either paddle or take a charter boat from the marina to reach Atsena Otie Key, which is less than a mile offshore from the historic dockside area.

The Hike: This linear trail (with several unmarked spurs to scenic overlooks) starts at the "Atsena Otie Key" sign at the dock and passes through landmarks of this former town, the original town of Cedar Key, abandoned in 1904 several years after a tidal surge destroyed the pencil mill that provided the residents' livelihood. Shaded by a maritime hammock of gnarled sand live oak and cedars, the trail ends along the estuary beyond the town's cemetery.

Highlights: Enjoy great views from many vantage points, a historic cemetery to explore, and great birding at the very end of the trail where it looks out over a vast estuary in the middle of the island, surrounded by coastal pine flatwoods.

Logistics: There is a composting toilet near the trailhead. Mosquitoes are fierce here most of the year; use plenty of insect repellent. Do not stray into the underbrush, as all of the islands off Cedar Key have an unusually high population of cottonmouth moccasins.

Other Activities: Walk on the beach, fish from the beach or the pier, or paddle around the island and marvel at its many secluded salt marshes.

North Central

Hamilton, Suwannee, Columbia, Baker, Union, Bradford, Clay, Putnam, Alachua, Gilchrist

Where the Suwannee River froths: Florida's only Class III whitewater, seen from the Big Shoals Trail.

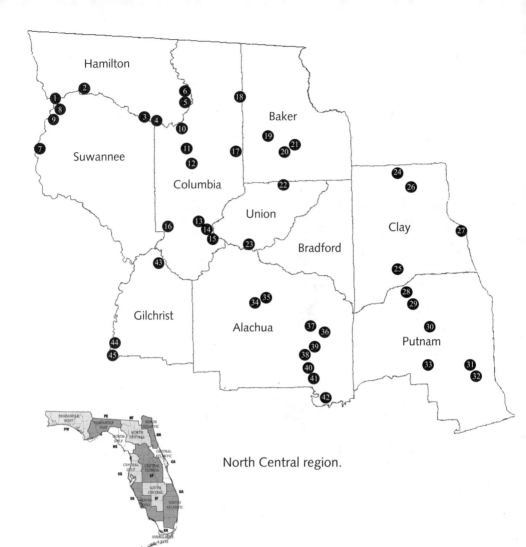

North Central region.

Hamilton
    NF-1   Big Oak Trail, Suwannee River State Park
    NF-2   Florida Trail, Holton Creek Wildlife Management Area
    NF-3   Camp Branch Disappearing Stream Loop
    NF-4   Florida Trail, Stephen Foster Folk Culture State Park
    NF-5   Big Shoals Trail, Big Shoals Public Lands
    NF-6   Long Branch Trail, Big Shoals Public Lands
Suwannee
    NF-7   Milford A. Clark Nature Trail
    NF-8   Suwannee River State Park
    NF-9   Anderson Springs Loop, Twin Rivers State Forest

Columbia
- NF-10 Florida Trail, Little Shoals
- NF-11 Falling Creek Falls
- NF-12 Alligator Lake
- NF-13 Limestone Trail, O'Leno State Park
- NF-14 River Sink / River Rise Trail System, O'Leno State Park
- NF-15 Old Bellamy Road, O'Leno State Park
- NF-16 Ichetucknee Springs State Park
- NF-17 Mount Carrie Wayside, Osceola National Forest
- NF-18 Big Gum Swamp Wilderness

Baker
- NF-19 Florida Trail, Osceola National Forest
- NF-20 Nice Wander Trail, Osceola National Forest
- NF-21 Olustee Battlefield Historic State Park

Union
- NF-22 Florida Trail, Lake Butler Forest
- NF-23 New River Nature Trail, Chastain-Seay Park

Clay
- NF-24 Fire and Water Nature Trail, Jennings State Forest
- NF-25 Gold Head Branch State Park
- NF-26 Black Creek Ravines Conservation Area
- NF-27 J. P. Hall Nature Preserve, Bayard Conservation Area

Putnam
- NF-28 Florida Trail, Etoniah Creek State Forest
- NF-29 Florida Trail, Rice Creek Sanctuary
- NF-30 Ravine Gardens State Park
- NF-31 Welaka State Forest
- NF-32 Beecher Run Nature Trail, Welaka National Fish Hatchery
- NF-33 St. Johns Loop, Cross Florida Greenway

Alachua
- NF-34 San Felasco Hammock Preserve State Park
- NF-35 Devil's Millhopper Geologic State Park
- NF-36 Gum Root Swamp Conservation Area
- NF-37 Morningside Nature Center
- NF-38 Bivens Arm Nature Park
- NF-39 La Chua Trail, Paynes Prairie State Park
- NF-40 Bolens Bluff Trail, Paynes Prairie State Park
- NF-41 Paynes Prairie State Park
- NF-42 Lake Lochloosa Conservation Area

Gilchrist
- NF-43 Fort White Mitigation Park
- NF-44 Hart Springs Park
- NF-45 Fanning Springs Hiking Trail, Fanning Springs State Park

Big Oak Trail

Suwannee River State Park

NF-1 **F** $ 👫 **C** ⛺ 🏕

Location: Ellaville [N30°23.138' W083°10.116'].

Length: 12.5 miles round-trip and loop.

Map: Rough map at trailhead; detailed backpacking map available from Florida Trail Association.

Contact Information: Suwannee River State Park (386-362-2746), 20185 CR 132, Live Oak, FL 32060.

Directions: From I-10 westbound, take exit 275, Live Oak / Lee. Follow US 90 for 5.1 miles west to the park entrance, on the right. From I-10 eastbound from Tallahassee, use exit 262, Lee. Head north on CR 255 for 2.9 miles to US 90. Turn right. Follow US 90 east for 8.9 miles, to the park entrance on the left just after the bridge over the Suwannee River.

The Hike: This is an excellent overnight introduction to the rugged bluffs of the Suwannee River, or a lengthy day hike. From the ranger station, the trail follows the park road out of Suwannee River State Park and crosses the old US 90 bridge over the Suwannee to the ruins of the Drew Plantation. Continue on the blue blazes to the Florida Trail; turn right and follow it along the Withlacoochee River, crossing the river on the CR 141 bridge. Follow the orange blazes back into the north side of Suwannee River State Park to meet the scenic loop; follow the blue blazes to the right to circle the peninsula between the two rivers.

Highlights: Attractions include campsites on the river bluffs, the Drew Plantation site and the ghost town of Ellaville, deep sinkholes, and, of course, the Big Oak. Look for where the footpath crosses a fallen log with diagonal lines cut into it; the tree over your head is the Big Oak.

Logistics: Sign in at the ranger station before starting off on this trail. Inform them if you plan to leave vehicles overnight; there is a small fee.

Other Activities: Suwannee River State Park features Confederate earthworks, beautiful interpretive trails (NF-8), a developed campground, and a put-in for boats and canoes.

Florida Trail

Holton Creek Wildlife Management Area

NF-2 **F** 🏕 🎣 🏕

Location: Holton Spring [N30°26.611' W083°04.586'].

Length: 7.8 miles linear.

Map: Detailed backpacking map available from Florida Trail Association.

Contact Information: Suwannee River Water Management District (386-362-1001), 9225 CR 49, Live Oak, FL 32060.

Directions: From I-10 exit 283, drive north on US 129 to CR 132; drive west on CR 132 to CR 249 and continue north across the Suwannee River bridge. Turn right onto Adams Grade Road and follow it to the turnoff for Holton Creek WMA on the right. Park near the hunt check station.

The Hike: Pick up the orange blazes behind the hunt check station and follow them through oak hammock and upland forest past large sinkholes to Holton Spring. The trail parallels the spring run past a camping area and continues around a series of cypress floodplain forests before reaching the Suwannee River. Follow the Suwannee upriver on the shady high bluffs to Mitchell Creek, which is spanned by a high bridge. The public section of the trail ends at the boundary of Holton Creek WMA.

Highlights: Enjoy the view of Holton Spring, the ancient cypresses on Holton Creek, and the rugged landscape along the Suwannee River.

Logistics: Since hunting is permitted throughout the preserve, check hunt dates before hiking and use all precautions. Do not attempt this hike if the Suwannee River is flooded. Only Florida Trail Association members may continue east along the river for a long day hike or backpacking trip; the trail crosses private lands to the east.

Other Activities: Birdwatching is excellent along the spring and spring run.

Camp Branch Disappearing Creek Loop

NF-3 **F** ⚠ 🏕 ❄

Location: White Springs [N30°22.685' W082°52.735'].

Length: 1.5 miles round-trip and loop.

Map: Detailed backpacking map available from Florida Trail Association. Map of access trail can be printed from Suwannee Bicycle Association website www.suwannneebike.org; look for information on Camp Branch.

Contact Information: Suwannee River Water Management District (386-362-1001), 9225 CR 49, Live Oak, FL 32060.

Directions: From I-75 exit 439, head east on SR 136 for 3 miles into White Springs and turn left at the light; drive three blocks, passing Stephen Foster Folk Culture Center State Park (NF-4). Turn left onto CR 25A and follow it for 8 miles. After it crosses I-75, the road makes a sharp bend to the right; the trailhead entrance is on the left before the next curve.

The Hike: From the Camp Branch trailhead for the bicycle trail system, follow the broad jeep road through upland forest until it intersects with the blue blazes of the Disappearing Creek Loop. Turn right and walk along the trail, which keeps to the high bluffs above the creek, providing a scenic view, before crossing the creek on a bridge and rope pull. Follow the trail back down the creek to watch the creek vanish. Use the jeep road to return to the parking area.

Highlights: When the water is flowing well, Camp Branch runs through rapids between the cypresses, cascading over small waterfalls before disappearing into a deep sinkhole. It flows underground to emerge as a spring along the Suwannee River.

Logistics: To cross the creek at the top of the loop, you need to be able to use the hanging rope to scramble up a steep hillside. If you cannot do this, retrace your steps back to the jeep trail. Since this trail is along the Suwannee River, do not hike here if the river is flooded. The trail connects with the main Florida Trail at the Suwannee River farther down the jeep road, past suitable sites for primitive camping.

Other Activities: There are mountain bike trails throughout Camp Branch.

Florida Trail

Stephen Foster Folk Culture Center State Park

NF-4 **F** **$** 📖 🚻 Ⓒ 🐕

Location: White Springs [N30°19.720' W082°46.148'].

Length: 4 miles linear.

Map: Detailed backpacking map available from Florida Trail Association; Carter Camp Trail map available from ranger station at park entrance.

Contact Information: Stephen Foster Folk Culture Center State Park (386-397-4331), P.O. Drawer G, White Springs, FL 32096.

Directions: From I-75 exit 439, head east on SR 136 for 3 miles into White Springs, and turn left at the light. The park entrance is down the hill on the left. The orange blazes start at the park entrance, but you can drive down to the gazebo parking lot and pick up the trail along the river's edge.

The Hike: This scenic portion of the Florida Trail follows the natural levees and floodplain channels of the northern shore of the Suwannee River, clambering up and down the bluffs in the deep shade of the upland forest as it parallels the river. You'll cross several cypress stands as well as tributaries of the Suwannee as they flow down from the bluffs.

Highlights: Hike in spring, when the fragrant azaleas are in full bloom; enjoy fabulous views all year.

Logistics: Hiking farther west along the Florida Trail is limited to Florida Trail members, as the trail crosses private land. Return along the same route from the state park boundary, or use the multiuse Carter Camp Trail to create an eight-mile loop back to the campground; the trail is marked with green-topped posts. If the Suwannee River is flooded, do not hike this section of trail. No overnight camping is permitted on this portion of the trail.

Other Activities: Visit the folk culture exhibits, picnic under the oaks, and enjoy the shady campground.

Big Shoals Trail

Big Shoals Public Lands

NF-5 $ 📖 🚻 🐕 🎋

Location: White Springs [N30°21.130' W082°41.257'].

Length: 2.2 miles round-trip.

Map: In park brochure and on trailhead kiosk.

Contact Information: Big Shoals Public Lands (386-397-2733), P.O. Drawer G, White Springs, FL 32096.

Directions: From I-75 exit 439, head east on SR 136 for 3 miles into White Springs. Turn right on US 41 and go south to CR 135 at the blinker. Turn left and follow CR 135 for 3.8 miles to SE 94th Street. Follow this dirt road 1.7 miles down to the trailhead.

The Hike: Start at the Trailwalker sign and follow the blazes into the hammock; the trail leads you to the river's edge near the piers of the old Godwin Bridge. Climbing atop a natural levee, the trail parallels the river down to the start of the Big Shoals rapids, providing scenic views of the river and the rapids along the way. The trail ends at a T intersection with a blue-blazed bicycle trail which continues further downstream.

Highlights: You won't see anything like this anywhere else in Florida—our only Class III whitewater, splashing through the limestone as the Suwannee River pours downstream. You can hear the rapids well before you see them.

Logistics: If the Suwannee River is low, the rapids will be a mere trickle. If the river is in flood stage, do not walk this trail. Seasonal hunting is permitted; check on hunt dates before hiking and use caution—wear blaze orange, and avoid the forest roads. Using forest roads and the single-track bicycle trail along the river, you can extend this hike into a 4.9-mile loop back to the Big Shoals overlook. This is a hike in the Florida State Forests Trailwalker program.

Other Activities: There are picnic tables and a canoe put-in for upriver journeys; canoes should portage the rapids via a trail on the south bank. Hike NF-6 starts along the river from the other end of the parking area.

Long Branch Trail

Big Shoals Public Lands

NF-6 $ 📖 🚻 🏕

Location: White Springs [N30°21.161' W082°41.259'].

Length: 2.5-mile loop.

Map: In park brochure and on trailhead kiosk.

Contact Information: Big Shoals Public Lands (386-397-2733), P.O. Drawer G, White Springs, FL 32096.

Directions: From I-75 exit 439, head east on SR 136 for 3 miles into White Springs. Turn right on US 41 and go south to CR 135 at the blinker. Turn left and follow CR 135 for 3.8 miles to SE 94th Street. Follow this dirt road 1.7 miles down to the trailhead.

The Hike: Starting at the canoe launch, the trail follows a mellow Suwannee River—broad and shaded by overhanging tupelo trees. Blazed blue, the trail leads through lush hardwood hammocks, into scrubby flatwoods and around cypress swamps, with side trails and overlooks heading out to the river. As it leaves the river, the trail heads into an upland hardwood forest of swamp chestnut, southern magnolia, and large live oaks, then through old farmers' fields and a pine plantation, before returning to the parking area.

Highlights: Stop and admire the river views. There is a live oak along the trail with a trunk so covered in bumps and bulges that it looks like a natural sculpture.

Logistics: Bicycles share this trail. The trail intersects with several jeep roads, so keep alert for the next blaze. Seasonal hunting is permitted; check on hunt dates before hiking and use caution—wear blaze orange, and avoid the forest roads.

Other Activities: There are picnic tables and a canoe put-in. Hike NF-5 starts along the river from the other end of the parking area.

Milford A. Clark Nature Trail

NF-7 🐎

Location: Dowling Park [N30°15.048' W083°14.603'].

Length: 2 miles linear, with trailheads at both ends.

Map: Map and interpretive guide available at Advent Village Lodge office at Village Square Shops on SR 136.

Contact Information: Advent Christian Village (800-371-8381) at Village Landing, CR 136 & CR 250, Dowling Park, FL 32064.

Directions: From I-10, head south from Lee on SR 255 to CR 250. Turn left and drive across the Suwannee River bridge; make a left on CR 136 and drive to Village Landing on the left. Start your walk behind the Village Lodge on the sidewalk along the river; turn right to walk upstream.

The Hike: Enjoy a scenic stretch of the Suwannee River along this peaceful community trail. Although the trail starts out as wheelchair-accessible pavement, the river dumps its high-water load of deep white sand across the footpath, making it a challenging walk in places. The deeply shaded trail sticks to the high river bluffs for most of the journey, providing numerous overlooks and access to unspoiled white sand beaches.

Highlights: Numerous benches and porch swings provide a perch from which to watch the river. Enjoy the huge white sand beach on the river's curve, 0.5 mile into the hike.

Logistics: Park your car at the Village Square Shops. Follow the paved walk northeast along the river toward the main Advent Village living facilities at Carter House to reach the south trailhead. The north trailhead is at Copeland Center. If you are hiking this as a round-trip, you can use a network of woods roads to shorten your return trip; consult the map. The trail is blazed with white diamonds and has mileage signs at decision points.

Other Activities: Enjoy canoeing and picnicking, or fishing from piers, landings, and beaches.

Suwannee River State Park

NF-8 $ 📖 🚻 🅒 🚻 🐕 ❄️

Location: Ellaville [N30°23.138' W083°10.116'].

Length: Several loops and a trail system providing 3.4 miles of interpretive trails.

Map: Rough map of trails in park brochure.

Contact Information: Suwannee River State Park (386-362-2746), 20185 CR 132, Live Oak, FL 32060.

Directions: From I-10 westbound, take exit 275 and follow US 90 for 5.1 miles west to the park entrance, on the right. From I-10 eastbound from Tallahassee, use exit 262 and head north on CR 255 for 2.9 miles to US 90. Turn right. Follow US 90 east for 8.9 miles to the park entrance on the left just after the bridge over the Suwannee River.

The Hike: Choose your interest and amble down any of these beautiful pathways through the forests above the Suwannee River. The Earthworks Trail leads through and past historic earthworks put in place by the Confederates during the Civil War; the Sandhills Trail winds through longleaf pine and wiregrass and past the old Columbus cemetery; and the Suwannee River Trail System provides scenic shaded walks along the river and its Lime Sink Run tributary.

Highlights: Explore beautiful cypress-lined Lime Sink Run along the Lime Sink Run Trail, walk to the confluence of the Withlacoochee and Suwannee Rivers on the Earthworks Trail, and look for Lime Spring and Balanced Rock along the river on the Suwannee River Trail. Spring wildflowers are spectacular along the Sandhills Trail.

Logistics: All trails can be accessed from the main parking area. The Earthworks Trail starts behind the ranger station; the Sandhills Trail has a trailhead on the parking lot; and the Suwannee River Trail System starts at the Nature Trail kiosk en route to the river. Wear insect repellent and long pants to fend off ticks.

Other Activities: Suwannee River State Park features Confederate earthworks, a developed campground, and a put-in for boats and canoes; the Big Oak Trail (NF-1) starts at the ranger station.

Anderson Springs Loop

Twin Rivers State Forest

NF-9 📖 🐎

Location: Falmouth [N30°21.201' W083°11.348'].

Length: 5.2-mile loop.

Map: Displayed and in brochure at trailhead kiosk.

Contact Information: Twin Rivers State Forest (386-208-1462), 7620 133rd Road, Live Oak, FL 32060.

Directions: From I-10 exit 275, drive west 5.6 miles, passing the entrance to Suwannee River State Park (NF-1 and NF-2) before reaching River Road. Turn left in front of the agricultural inspection station. Drive south on River Road for 2.1 miles to Twin Rivers State Forest, Anderson Springs Tract. Turn right and follow the narrow gravel track for 0.2 mile to the trail kiosk, and park on the left.

The Hike: Follow the blue blazes along this loop that takes you on a scenic tour of the Suwannee River's natural levees, the trail undulating up and down bluffs topped with hardwood forest and natural channels dense with saw palmetto. After 2.8 miles, you reach a junction with a sign "Loop Trail 1"; turn left and follow the yellow blazes away from the river and into the hardwood forest on the hiking-only footpath, which leads around several chains of sinkholes and through a couple of clear-cut areas before returning to the main trail only 0.1 mile from the trailhead.

Highlights: Enjoy fantastic river views, fascinating sinkholes, and a real workout for your leg muscles while climbing in and out of the natural levees and channels.

Logistics: Open 8:00 until dusk. If there is no parking at the trailhead, park at the spring access area and walk up the side trail. Wear insect repellent and long pants, as ticks are prevalent. This is a trail in the Florida State Forests Trailwalker Program.

Other Activities: Certified cave divers can explore Anderson Spring, and kayakers can launch at the put-in. You'll find a picnic table and grill at the parking area.

Florida Trail

Little Shoals

NF-10 🄵 ⛺ 🏕 🎆

Location: White Springs [N30°19.983' W082°43.390'].

Length: 4.4 miles linear.

Map: Detailed backpacking map available from Florida Trail Association.

Contact Information: Suwannee River Water Management District (386-362-1001), 9225 CR 49, Live Oak, FL 32060.

Directions: From I-10 exit 301, drive north on US 441 to the turnoff at the agricultural inspection station; follow the road back to the trailhead parking area at the end.

The Hike: Following the high bluffs above the Suwannee River, this deeply shaded section of the Florida Trail parallels the river's best section of whitewater, crossing the deep channels of several tributaries. There are several nice spots for camping above the river before you reach the end of the public portion of the trail, where it turns away from the river after 4.4 miles.

Highlights: The trail provides excellent views of the Little Shoals rapids as it follows the bluffs, and a true physical challenge as you climb up and down the bluffs.

Logistics: Since hunting is permitted in this area, check hunt dates before hiking and use all precautions. Do not attempt this hike if the Suwannee River is flooded. Only Florida Trail Association members may continue east along the river for a long day hike or backpacking trip; the trail crosses private lands to the east to reach Lassie Black Road. To the west, the trail enters White Springs.

Other Activities: This is a popular stretch of the Suwannee River for kayaking, thanks to the rapids between Big and Little Shoals; check with American Canoe Adventures in White Springs for rentals and shuttles. Bicycle trails parallel the Florida Trail on the lower bluffs.

Falling Creek Falls

NF-11 👫

Location: Falling Creek [N30°15.469' W082°40.118'].

Length: 0.4 mile round-trip.

Map: No map; kiosk at parking area explains significance of falls and history of area.

Contact Information: Suwannee River Water Management District (386-362-1001), 9225 CR 49, Live Oak, FL 32060.

Directions: From I-10 exit 301, drive north on US 441; immediately turn right on Falling Creek Road (CR 131) and drive 0.8 mile to the trailhead parking area on the right.

The Hike: It's a short stroll through an open meadow into the lush woods surrounding Falling Creek, where a boardwalk carries you into the shady floodplain forest of bald cypress, sweet gum, magnolia, and water oak. You hear the splashing water in the distance before you see it. The first observation platform overlooks the falls, while the second one provides a beautifully framed view of the limestone ledge and the falls through the forest.

Highlights: Stained dark with tannic acid, the falls look like root beer pouring from a mug as they bubble over the limestone ledge and drop more than ten feet, creating a frothy pool at the bottom of the cliff. Falling Creek then flows away over limestone boulders at the bottom of a deep gorge.

Logistics: The area, open dawn to dusk daily, has no facilities. Benches along the creek make this a pleasant stroll for hikers of all ages and abilities.

Other Activities: Use the picnic tables under the oaks; peer into historic structures on the property. Continue your drive up Falling Creek Road another 0.2 mile, just beyond the bridge over the creek, to see the old Methodist Church and graveyard, circa 1865, nestled in a curve of Falling Creek.

Alligator Lake

NF-12 📖 🚻

Location: Lake City [N30°10.008' W082°36.918'].

Length: 6.5-mile trail system.

Map: Displayed at trailhead kiosk.

Contact Information: Columbia County Parks and Recreation (386-755-4100), P.O. Drawer 1529, Lake City, FL 32055.

Directions: From I-75 exit 427, follow US 90 east for 2.4 miles to SW Baya Drive (SR 10A). Turn right and follow Baya Drive for 2.6 miles to SE Country Club Road. Turn right and continue 1.2 miles to the park entrance on the right.

The Hike: Check out the kiosk at the restroom parking area and pick a route through the trail system. For the longest loop, follow the Montgomery Trail from the end of the entrance road as it loops around the vast expanse of Alligator Lake and its impoundments. Shorter connectors and loops like the Possum Trot Trail, the Eagle Trail, and the Capybara Trail lead through pine flatwoods, along cypress swamps, and along Price Creek.

Highlights: Enjoy birdwatching along Alligator Lake, where egrets roost and nest on willow islands.

Logistics: The park is open Wed–Fri 11:00–7:00, Sat–Sun 8:00–7:00. Biking is permitted on preserve trails.

Other Activities: Kayak and canoe on the lake. Enjoy the picnic area and playground near the parking area by the restrooms.

Limestone Trail

O'Leno State Park

NF-13 $ 📖 �︎

Location: High Springs [N29°55.160' W082°35.388'].

Length: 0.6-mile loop.

Map: Rough map in park brochure.

Contact Information: O'Leno State Park (386-454-1853), Route 2, Box 1010, High Springs, FL 32643.

Directions: From I-75 northbound, use exit 399 and drive north on US 441 for 11.6 miles; from I-75 southbound, take exit 414 and drive south on US 441 for 5 miles. Follow SE Sprite Loop to the park entrance road.

The Hike: The trail makes an easy loop through the hardwood hammock around a large sinkhole, providing a shady walk through the forest. As the trail leaves the large sink, it loops around a smaller sinkhole and under a stand of dogwood trees before completing the loop.

Highlights: The sinkhole was once used as a quarry, where settlers carved out limestone blocks to build buildings and fireplaces.

Logistics: Park your car in the small parking spot on the right where the Dogwood Trail crosses the entrance road.

Other Activities: Continue down the entrance road to the main parking area, where you can enjoy swimming, picnicking, camping, and hiking along the trail system (NF-14) around River Sink and River Rise.

River Sink/River Rise Trail System

O'Leno State Park

NF-14 **$** 📖 🚻 ♿ ⛺ 🏕

Location: High Springs [N29°54.878' W082°34.775'].

Length: From 0.5 to 13.8 miles.

Map: Rough map in park brochure; more detailed map available at ranger station.

Contact Information: O'Leno State Park (386-454-1853), Route 2, Box 1010, High Springs, FL 32643.

Directions: From I-75 northbound, use exit 399 and drive north on US 441 for 11.6 miles; from I-75 southbound, take exit 414 and drive south on US 441 for 5 miles. Follow SE Sprite Loop to the park entrance road. Drive to the end of the road and park near the concession stand.

The Hike: Walk down to the Santa Fe River and start your hike by crossing the 1930s swinging bridge to the River Sink Trail, which parallels the river before heading through pine flatwoods to meet the 3-mile Pareners Loop Trail, which will take you past several sinks that display a portion of the Santa Fe River as it flows underground. Wire Road, a historic road, completes the loop, or you can continue to track the underground flow of the Santa Fe River through upland forests and cypress swamps via the Sweetwater Trail (passing a primitive campsite) to the River Rise and Black Lake Trails, where the river continues its aboveground course.

Highlights: As the Santa Fe River plays hide-and-seek through the limestone karst, look for it at River Sink, River Rise, and the many "karst windows" in sinkholes along the trail.

Logistics: If you are staying in the Dogwood Campground, the 1.4-mile (linear) Dogwood Trail connects the campground with the trail system. Inform the rangers if you plan to camp overnight at the Sweetwater campsite; there is a small fee.

Other Activities: Enjoy swimming, picnicking, camping, and hiking throughout the park.

Old Bellamy Road Interpretive Trail

O'Leno State Park

NF-15 □ 👫 🐎

Location: High Springs [N29°54.173' W082°35.089'].

Length: 2.2 miles round-trip.

Map: On kiosk at trailhead.

Contact Information: O'Leno State Park (386-454-1853), Route 2, Box 1010, High Springs, FL 32643.

Directions: North of High Springs on US 441, turn right on Bellamy Road; follow it 1.3 miles east to the park entrance and parking area on the left.

The Hike: This linear hike follows part of the route of the Bellamy Road, the first federally funded Florida highway to connect St. Augustine with Pensacola. Interpretive markers explain the associated historical events as you walk through the mixed hardwood forest.

Highlights: You're walking through a significant Florida historical site that's been forgotten by most residents and visitors. Built from 1824 to 1826, the Bellamy Road became the wagon route for settlers who migrated westward in the 1830s to found towns in this area, including the long-forgotten Keno (at the Santa Fe River's river sink) and High Springs.

Logistics: This trail is day use only. Bicycles and horses are permitted. Parts of the trail may flood seasonally.

Other Activities: Visit the main portion of O'Leno State Park for a variety of outdoor activities, including the hikes of NF-14, which connect to this trail, and NF-13.

Ichetucknee Springs State Park

NF-16 $ 📖 🚻 ♿ 🚼 🐾

Location: Fort White [N29°59.065' W082°45.748'].

Length: 3.7 miles in three trails.

Map: Available at ranger station and trailhead kiosk.

Contact Information: Ichetucknee Springs State Park (386-497-2511), Route 2, Box 5355, Fort White, FL 32038.

Directions: From I-75 exit 414, drive south on US 441 for 4.3 miles to CR 18; turn right and drive 6.4 miles to Fort White. Turn right and continue on US 27 to First Street (CR 47). Turn right and continue 2.2 miles, then make a left on CR 238. Drive 3.7 miles to the park entrance on the left. Follow the park entrance road down to the spring.

The Hike: In addition to a 1-mile round trip along a boardwalk and trail following the spring run down to Blue Hole Spring, there are two interpretive trails in the park: the 0.7-mile Trestle Point Trail, which leads down to an old river crossing for phosphate railroad carts, and the 2-mile Pine Ridge Trail, a loop through hardwood hammocks and up into the sandhills, skirting several phosphate pits now filled with forest.

Highlights: Walk down the Trestle Point Trail to see unusual limestone formations along the spring run; enjoy the many wildflowers in bloom in the sandhills in spring.

Logistics: You may encounter mosquitoes and muddy sections of trail en route to Blue Hole; use insect repellent.

Other Activities: Swim in Ichetucknee Spring and Blue Hole; go tubing and rafting down the crystalline spring run.

Mount Carrie Wayside

Osceola National Forest

NF-17 📖 🚻 🐴

Location: Olustee [N30°11.687' W081°30.425'].

Length: 1-mile loop.

Map: Trail shown on Osceola National Forest USFS map.

Contact Information: Osceola Ranger District Office (386-752-2577), PO Box 70, Olustee, FL 32072.

Directions: The trailhead is along US 90 east of Lake City, west of Olustee, across from a correctional facility.

The Hike: Established in 1952 and adopted by the Four Rivers Audubon Society, this trail winds through flatwoods with a scrubby understory topped by old-growth longleaf pines, home to a colony of red-cockaded woodpeckers, and around some bayheads.

Highlights: Trees marked with white bands contain red-cockaded woodpecker nests.

Logistics: A kiosk at the trailhead explains the role of fire in the pine flatwoods ecosystem. Others along the trail give further habitat information. Follow the hiker markers to stay on the trail.

Other Activities: Drive east on US 90 and stop at the National Forest visitor center for information about the other trails (NF- 18 through NF-22) in the area.

Big Gum Swamp Wilderness

NF-18 ⌂ 🏕

Location: Deep Creek [N30°21.444' W082°28.089'].

Length: 4.9-mile loop.

Map: Available from Osceola Ranger District office.

Contact Information: Osceola Ranger District Office (386-752-2577), PO Box 70, Olustee, FL 32072.

Directions: From I-10 exit 303, follow US 441 north 11.5 miles to Deep Creek. Turn right on NE Drew Road; the road turns to dirt and narrows to a single-lane jeep track, signposted as FR 262. After 9.2 miles, FR 262 ends at a T intersection with FR 232. Park your car at the trailhead across the road.

The Hike: Follow the silver dots into the longleaf pine flatwoods, along the trace of an old railroad grade into the pine forest on the edge of the Big Gum Swamp, an impassible tangle of sweet gum, bay, and cypress trees. The trail passes through a few areas that suffered from wildfires several years ago and follows the edge of the swamp before ending on FR 232; turn left and walk down the road to return to your car.

Highlights: At the creek crossing on the edge of Big Gum Swamp, a stand of yellow cannas competes for attention with large swamp hyacinths.

Logistics: The trail can be difficult to follow in places; keep watching for the next blaze. It is rarely maintained, so you may need to push through the vegetation in places. Be aware of seasonal hunt dates in the forest, and take appropriate precautions. Camping is permitted anywhere in the forest except during hunting season.

Other Activities: Hike on the Florida Trail (NF-19) through the forest.

Florida Trail

Osceola National Forest

NF-19 🄵 🄲 ⛺ 🏠

Location: Southern terminus, Olustee [N30°12.757' W082°23.345']; northern terminus, Deep Creek [N30°20.942' W082°36.476'].

Length: 20.7 miles linear.

Map: Trail shown on national forest map; detailed backpacking map available from Florida Trail Association.

Contact Information: Osceola Ranger District Office (386-752-2577), PO Box 70, Olustee, FL 32072.

Directions: The southern terminus is along US 90 at Olustee Battlefield; park on the left immediately after entering the park. The northern terminus is at the Deep Creek Trailhead, 0.7 mile east of US 441 on Drew Road, 10 miles north of Lake City.

The Hike: Beyond the first mile of trail (NF-20), the Florida Trail through the Osceola National Forest winds its way through established longleaf pine forests with colonies of red-cockaded woodpeckers, dense pine plantations, cypress swamps, and bayheads. You spend many miles amid the pines, where the open understory is ideal for wildlife watching.

Highlights: Take the blue blaze to Ocean Pond Campground for fresh water, restrooms, a picnic area, and a fabulous scenic view, especially at dusk. Hooded pitcher plants thrive in trailside bogs.

Logistics: Seasonal hunting is permitted; check hunt dates before hiking. Old forest roads are used to connect sections of the trail, so watch for blazes carefully. Camping is permitted anywhere in the forest, except during hunting season, when designated campsites must be used. There is a roofed shelter (with nearby privy) for camping at 9.2 miles.

Other Activities: The forest has an extensive network of equestrian trails, most of which start at West Tower. There is a hiking trail in Big Gum Swamp Wilderness (NF-18) and three additional hiking options at the southern trailhead (NF-20 through NF-22).

Nice Wander Trail

Osceola National Forest

NF-20 **F** ♿ 🚻 🐕 🚺

Location: Olustee [N30°12.757' W082°23.345'].

Length: Loop of 1, 1.3, or 1.8 miles.

Map: Trails shown on national forest map, at trailhead kiosk, and on detailed backpacking map for Osceola National Forest available from Florida Trail Association.

Contact Information: Osceola Ranger District Office (386-752-2577), PO Box 70, Olustee, FL 32072.

Directions: The trailhead is along US 90 at Olustee Battlefield; park on the left immediately after entering the park.

The Hike: This accessible loop in Osceola National Forest provides a gentle stroll through a mature longleaf pine forest with an open understory. Several cross trails permit shorter walks. At the north end of the longest loop, a boardwalk carries the trail over a bayhead swamp. The return trip is along a well-graded road.

Highlights: Bring your binoculars for this hike, as it passes through a heavy concentration of red-cockaded woodpecker nests, marked by white bands painted on the longleaf pines.

Logistics: The trail is a natural surface, wheelchair accessible with assistance. A restroom is available at the Olustee Battlefield visitor center, open Thu–Mon 9:00–5:00.

Other Activities: Visit adjacent Olustee Battlefield (NF-21) and its visitor center.

Olustee Battlefield Historic State Park

NF-21 📖 🚻 ♿ 👫

Location: Olustee [N30°12.860' W082°23.319'].

Length: 1.1-mile loop.

Map: Rough map in park brochure.

Contact Information: Olustee Battlefield Historic State Park (386-758-0400), PO Box 40, Olustee, FL 32072.

Directions: From I-75 exit 427, drive 18.6 miles east on US 90 to the state park entrance; from I-10 westbound, use exit 324 and follow US 90 west for 5.5 miles to the park entrance.

The Hike: From the visitor center, cross the road and continue past the kiosk to the first bench and interpretive marker, marking the start of the loop. Turn right and follow the path into the pine flatwoods, skirting scrubby flatwoods and bayheads as the trail winds through the forest.

Highlights: As you walk around the loop, the interpretive signs explain how this battle, the most significant Civil War battle in Florida, unfolded. White bands mark the trees with red-cockaded woodpecker nests.

Logistics: Red arrows on silver diamonds mark the trail route. Although the trail is a natural surface, it is wheelchair accessible with assistance, providing ramps and boardwalk bridges and a level grade.

Other Activities: The visitor center is open Thu–Mon 9:00–5:00 and features a twenty-minute film on the battle as well as exhibits about Florida's role in the Civil War. Three other trails start near US 90, all sections of the Florida Trail (NF-19, NF-20, and NF-22).

Florida Trail

Lake Butler Forest

NF-22 **F** 🏕 🏠

Location: Southern terminus, Lake Butler; northern terminus, Olustee [N30°12.757' W082°23.345'].

Length: 17.6 miles linear.

Map: Detailed backpacking map available from Florida Trail Association.

Contact Information: Office of Greenways and Trails (850-245-2052), Room 853 Douglas Building, 3900 Commonwealth Boulevard, Tallahassee, FL 32399-3000.

Directions: The northern terminus is along US 90 at Olustee Battlefield; park on the left immediately after entering the park. The southern terminus is at the south entrance to Lake Butler Forest along CR 231 north of SR 100, west of Lake Butler.

The Hike: Passing through private lands recently opened to the public under an agreement with the Office of Greenways and Trails, the trail roughly follows an old railroad route through pine plantations, with a mix of young plantings, older pines, and open clear-cuts marked with blazed posts. From Swift Creek north, the trail winds through both the pines and hardwood hammocks en route to its terminus at Olustee.

Highlights: Even if you're not camping along Swift Creek, pause to enjoy the pleasant setting. As you hike, watch for remnants of turpentine history—the clay cups used to collect tapped turpentine, and deep gashes on older pines where the turpentine was tapped.

Logistics: There are two designated campsites, one at Swift Creek and the other at FR 21A—look for the blue blazes leading east. Both have access to water, which must be filtered. Be aware that recent clear-cuts may obliterate the trail. Carry a compass or GPS and take a heading due north if you lose the trail markings.

Other Activities: Visit Olustee Battlefield (NF-21) at the northern terminus of the trail, which also connects with the Florida Trail (NF-19) through the Osecola National Forest.

New River Nature Trail

Chastain-Seay Park

NF-23 $ 🚻 🧑‍🧒 🐕

Location: Worthington Springs [N29°55.587' W082°25.539'].

Length: 0.6-mile loop.

Map: None provided.

Contact Information: Chastain-Seay Park (386-496-1006), SR 121 & Patton Avenue, Worthington Springs, FL 32697.

Directions: The trail begins just south of the intersection of SR 121 and CR 18, south of Worthington Springs along SR 121, on the west side of the north end of the New River Bridge.

The Hike: Leading into the river bluff forest from Worthington Spring (surrounded by a chain-link fence near the parking area), the boardwalk starting at the "Nature Trail" sign crosses waterways and ravines en route to the New River. Along the river, it becomes the Riverwalk, ending at the swimming area. Retrace your steps back to the side boardwalk, which ends in a picnic area. Walk through the island picnic area on a jeep road to meet up with the third and final boardwalk, which takes you back to the picnic area at the park entrance.

Highlights: Benches allow you to sit and enjoy the views of the New River and its tributaries, where cypresses reflect in the dark water. This is a good place for birding.

Logistics: The trail is open from 8:00 to sundown. An entry fee may be charged if an attendant is on duty at the front gate (likely on summer weekends)

Other Activities: There is swimming in the New River, a playground, and a picnic pavilion at the parking area.

Fire and Water Nature Trail

Jennings State Forest

NF-24 $ 📖 🐎

Location: Middleburg [N30°08.173' W081°52.922'].

Length: 1.8-mile loop.

Map: Displayed at trailhead kiosk; available in St. Johns River Water Management District's *Recreation Guide to District Lands* and in a Jennings State Forest brochure.

Contact Information: Jennings State Forest (904-291-5530), 1337 Long Horn Rd, Middleburg, FL 32068.

Directions: From Orange Park, take SR 21 south to CR 220A; turn right. Passing Long Bay Road, continue 1 mile to Live Oak Lane and turn right. Drive down the road for 1 mile, passing the Old Jennings Recreation Area before you reach the kiosk for the Fire and Water Nature Trail.

The Hike: This interpretive nature trail leads you through a variety of habitats amid the high sandhills south of Jacksonville, from marshy bayheads and floodplain forest to pine flatwoods of longleaf pine and wiregrass to seepage slopes and ravines. The lime green blazes follow old forest roads for the most part, veering off in several areas to traverse the habitats for a closer look.

Highlights: Visit the wildlife viewing blind to watch for wild turkey; poke around the hillside at marker 4 and you'll find patches of carnivorous pitcher plants. There is a nice view of a blackwater stream from the observation deck at marker 5—look straight down!

Logistics: Pick up an interpretive guide and map at the trailhead. Keep watching for the next blaze, as it's easy to lose the trail if you focus on walking down the roads. Be alert for pygmy rattlers; rangers note that they sometimes sun along the sand road leading into the loop. Seasonal hunting is permitted in this forest; check before you hike.

Other Activities: The 4.9-mile North Fork Black Creek Trail loop lies to the south with a trailhead at the Old Jennings Recreation Area; it is primarily used by equestrians and has a lot of difficult hiking in soft sand to get to the campsite near the creek.

Gold Head Branch State Park

NF-25 **F** $ 🏢 👫 🅖 ⛺ 🏕

Location: Keystone Heights [N29°50.811' W081°57.587'].

Length: More than 5 miles in four trails.

Map: Rough map in park brochure; detailed map available at park office; backpacking map available from Florida Trail Association.

Contact Information: Gold Head Branch State Park (904-473-4701), 6239 SR 21, Keystone Heights, FL 32356.

Directions: Follow SR 21 north from Keystone Heights for 6.6 miles to the park entrance on the left.

The Hike: There are three major trails in the park. The 3.3-mile linear Florida Trail works its way from the park entrance through the scrub down to follow Gold Head Branch, passing through a pine forest along Little Lake Johnson before it crosses a developed portion of the park en route through the sandhills to the South Gate. The 0.9-mile Loblolly Trail makes a loop through the ravines around Gold Head Branch, while Ravine Ridge leads you upstream to the deep steephead ravine and the Fern Loop boardwalk.

Highlights: Visit the Fern Loop at the base of the steephead ravine where Gold Head Branch begins; the boardwalk traverses a wonderland of ferns amid the outflow of numerous springs. Take the Florida Trail to Devil's Washbasin for a look at a huge sinkhole in the scrub habitat, and cross Gold Head Branch on a bridge near the old mill to enjoy the burbling stream cascading down into the forest.

Logistics: Follow the orange blazes to stay on the Florida Trail. If you plan to camp at the primitive campsite, you must contact the ranger station first and pay a small fee.

Other Activities: Swim in Little Lake Johnson, canoe on the lake, camp at either the developed campsites or in cabins, and picnic under the oaks.

Black Creek Ravines Conservation Area

NF-26 📖 ⛺ 🏕

Location: Middleburg [N30°03.501' W081°50.831'].

Length: 7.8 miles of trail, with loops of 2.1, 4, and 4.2 miles possible.

Map: Displayed at trailhead kiosk; available in St. Johns River Water Management District's *Recreation Guide to District Lands* and in a trail guide.

Contact Information: St. Johns River Water Management District (904-529-2380), PO Box 1429, Palatka, FL 32178-1429.

Directions: From SR 21 in Middleburg, drive east on CR 218 for 2 miles to Green Road. Turn left and follow the road for 0.9 mile to the parking area on the right.

The Hike: Follow the White Loop north through shady sandhills and scrub to access the Yellow Loop; both parallel the ravines above the creek and provide scenic overlooks, especially as the Yellow Loop draws close to the river's edge. A spur trail leads to a scenic view and campsite. On the south end of the preserve, the Red Loop circles a sandhill area where wildflowers thrive, with another spur trail out to the creek.

Highlights: There are several overlooks over the ravines along Black Creek. Beneath the power lines, look for vast seepage-slope bogs dense with hooded pitcher plants and terrestrial orchids. Especially in spring, the diversity of wildflowers along these trails is incredible. There is a high concentration of gopher tortoises in the sandhills.

Logistics: Although the trails are shared with equestrians, they display rough sections of sand only in the broad open area under the power lines. There is a primitive campsite on a hiking-only 0.7-mile spur trail out to a bluff above Black Creek.

Other Activities: Bank fishing is possible along several portions of the creek.

J. P. Hall Nature Preserve

Bayard Conservation Area

NF-27 🚻 ⛺ 🛖

Location: Green Cove Springs [N29°58.619' W081°38.358'].

Length: 5 miles of hiking trails, round-trip and loop; more than 8 miles of multiuse trails.

Map: Displayed at trailhead kiosk; available in St. Johns River Water Management District's *Recreation Guide to District Lands.*

Contact Information: St. Johns River Water Management District (904-529-2380), PO Box 1429, Palatka, FL 32178-1429.

Directions: From US 17 in Green Cove Springs, follow SR 16 east to the last turnoff on the right just before the St. Johns River bridge.

The Hike: From the trailhead, follow the blue-blazed hiking-only trail around bayheads and bogs in the pine flatwoods, meeting up with a multiuse trail briefly to access an observation tower. The hiking route continues on and off the multiuse trail through the flatwoods, passing a primitive campsite along a cypress-lined stream before emerging at a picnic area and restroom at an outdoor classroom from which two short loops radiate: the interpretive Legacy Trail and the Cougar Trail.

Highlights: Walk along the stream on the Cougar Trail. Watch for deer from the observation deck.

Logistics: The trails are low-lying and easily flood after a rain. Pay attention to blazing so you do not wander off on the equestrian trails (marked with colored diamonds) unless you want to; there's a beautiful campsite along the St. Johns River east on the red diamond trail.

Other Activities: Equestrians have an extensive trail system throughout the preserve. There is a canoe launch on the river near the bridge.

Florida Trail

Etoniah Creek State Forest

NF-28 **F** **$** 🚻 ⛺ 🚫

Location: Florahome [N29°45.802' W081°50.800'].

Length: 13.9 miles linear.

Map: Rough map in state forest brochure; detailed backpacking map available from Florida Trail Association.

Contact Information: Etoniah Creek State Forest (904-329-3772), PO Box 870, Hollister, FL 32147-0870.

Directions: From Palatka, drive west on SR 100 for 8 miles to Holloway Road. Turn right and follow the signs to the visitor center; the trail starts at a kiosk just outside the gate.

The Hike: From Holloway Road, follow the Florida Trail south through upland forests of magnolia, oaks, and holly along Falling Branch Creek, crossing the Iron Bridge and passing the campsite and shelter en route to the beautiful Etoniah Creek Ravine, where you can look down the steep slope and see the bottom of the clear stream. Farther north, the trail winds through diminutive scrub habitat and river bluff forest, crossing the creek on a long bridge near another campsite as it heads to the north end of the forest. To the north, the trail follows forest roads, winding through scrub and sandhills to the Tinsley Road trailhead.

Highlights: Walking along the bluffs above Etoniah Creek Ravine is especially fine when the dogwoods are in bloom in springtime. North of the ravine is a fairyland of delicate scrub plants.

Logistics: There are two campsites and a camping shelter along the trail. The trail exits the preserve at Old Starke Road to the east (no trailhead) and Tinsley Road to the northwest (where there is another trailhead). A pleasant day hike is to follow the trail from Holloway Road south along the creek and back.

Other Activities: There are extensive equestrian trails throughout the state forest, and a multiuse Trailwalker trail (the Longleaf Pine Trail) which forks from the Florida Trail off Scrub Road.

Florida Trail

Rice Creek Sanctuary

NF-29 **ⓕ**

Location: Palatka [N29°40.996' W081°43.887'].

Length: 4.4 miles linear plus a 1.2-mile loop.

Map: Posted at trailhead kiosk; detailed backpacking map available from Florida Trail Association.

Contact Information: St. Johns River Water Management District (904-529-2380), PO Box 1429, Palatka, FL 32178-1429.

Directions: The trailhead is along SR 100, 3 miles west of Palatka on the south side of the highway.

The Hike: From the pine plantations on either end of the preserve, the Florida Trail enters a wonderland of ancient cypresses along Rice Creek, where an indigo and rice plantation occupied a pre–Revolutionary War land grant. Man-made dikes break up the cypress swamp, and the trail features numerous bridges across them.

Highlights: The boardwalks through Hoffman Crossing lead you past grand cypress trees, and on the blue-blazed loop through the old indigo plantation, there are more massive cypresses along Rice Creek.

Logistics: Park at the trailhead and follow the forest roads into the preserve to find the blue-blazed loop trail, or access the orange-blazed main trail to the east along SR 100.

Other Activities: Birdwatch in the open understory beneath the pine plantations.

Ravine Gardens State Park

NF-30 $ 📖 🚻

Location: Palatka [N29°38.182' W081°38.777'].

Length: 2.1-mile loop.

Map: Rough map in park brochure; map of Bamboo Springs Trail available at trailhead.

Contact Information: Ravine Gardens State Park (386-329-3721), PO Box 1096, Palatka, FL 32712.

Directions: From the intersection of SR 19 and SR 100 in Palatka, drive 1.4 miles east on SR 100 to Mosley Avenue. Turn right, then left on Silver Lake Road. Follow the signs to the entrance.

The Hike: Starting from the formal gardens adjacent to the visitor center, the trails drop down into the ravine and circle around its edge and base. Start with the Bamboo Springs Trail, a short interpretive trail that showcases native plants as it circles the rim of the ravine, dropping down to an artesian spring in the bottom. Continue along the trail system to the Azalea Trail, which follows the far rim of the ravine through a thicket of planted azaleas. Numerous footpaths connect the two named trails.

Highlights: There are two 1930s suspension bridges across the ravine, and a tunnel of azaleas to walk through on the Azalea Trail. Fern-lined pools dot the bottom of the ravine.

Logistics: The trails are steep and slippery in places; be cautious along the far rim near the Azalea Trail.

Other Activities: Stroll the formal gardens, and enjoy a drive on the loop road around the ravine.

Welaka State Forest

NF-31 $ 📖 ⛺ 🚸

Location: Satsuma [N29°28.120' W081°39.614'].

Length: Up to 9 miles in various trails, with loops of 0.5, 1.7, 3, and 4.5 miles.

Map: Displayed at trailhead kiosks and available in state forest brochure.

Contact Information: Welaka State Forest (904-467-2388), PO Box 174, Welaka, FL 32193-0174.

Directions: From the intersection of US 17 and SR 40, drive north 19.1 miles to Crescent Lake. Turn left on CR 308 and follow it 8.4 miles to its end. Turn right and continue 2.1 miles on CR 309 to the Johns Landing trailhead at the fire tower, or 3.3 miles to the Mud Spring trailhead. Both are on the left.

The Hike: The trail system consists of the 1.7-mile Mud Spring Trail, which leads through pine flatwoods and hardwood hammocks to a picnic spot along Mud Spring; the 4.5-mile St. Johns Hiking Trail, which traverses wet flatwoods, dense hammocks, and river bluff forest; a connector trail past the fire tower that links the two; and many named trails that create loops and spurs from the St. Johns Trail. Children will enjoy the 0.5-mile Forest Education Trail that starts behind the fire tower, a boardwalk leading through the floodplain forest with "talking trees."

Highlights: Take the Mud Spring Trail to beautiful Mud Spring, a crystalline aquatic garden with an outflow into the St. Johns River. The Sulfur Spring side trail leads to a small sulfuric spring full of fish. The campsites at the ends of the spur trails along the Johns Landing loop provide scenic views of the St. Johns River.

Logistics: There is a $2 day-use fee, payable at the trailhead. Camping is by permit; contact the state forest in advance of your visit. Campsites are at Orange Point and Johns Landing. Anticipate spongy, soggy trails after a rain. The St. Johns Trail is not suitable for young children.

Other Activities: On the east side of CR 309 across from the fire tower, the Sandhill Horse Trail provides a place for equestrians to ride.

Beecher Run Nature Trail

Welaka National Fish Hatchery

NF-32 📖 👫

Location: Welaka.

Length: 0.8-mile loop.

Map: No map available; interpretive brochure, keyed to numbered stations, available at trailhead.

Contact Information: Welaka National Fish Hatchery (386-467-2374), PO Box 130, Welaka, FL 32193.

Directions: From US 17 south of Palatka, turn west on CR 308 in Crescent Lake. Drive 8.4 miles to the T intersection with CR 309. Turn right and drive 1 mile to the parking area on the right.

The Hike: This interpretive trail leads you through an upland pine forest surrounding a series of man-made wetlands that have, since 1926, served as a spawning ground for captured wild fish such as striped bass, redear sunfish, and bluegill, and as a nursery for their young.

Highlights: Enjoy panoramas across the wetlands from the observation tower, and stop at station 7 to see a catfaced pine from the turpentine era.

Logistics: The park is open for daylight use only. Keep making right turns at each junction to complete the loop. Be very cautious around station 8, where an active beehive is in a hollow tree along the trail.

Other Activities: This is a great spot for birding. The hatchery is open 7:00–4:00 daily.

St. Johns Loop

Cross Florida Greenway

NF-33 📖 🐎

Location: Rodman [N29°32.479' W081°43.643'].

Length: 3.6-mile loop.

Map: Available at visitor center on north side of Buckman Lock.

Contact Information: Florida Department of Environmental Protection, Office of Greenways and Trails (352-236-7143), 8282 SE Highway 314, Ocala, FL 34470.

Directions: From the intersection of SR 20 and SR 19 in Palatka, drive south 10 miles to Boys Ranch Road, just south of the bridge over the Cross Florida Barge Canal. Turn left and drive 1.9 miles to the St. Johns Loop trailhead sign. Turn left and follow the rough paved road for 0.4 mile to the parking area at Buckman Lock.

The Hike: Passing through oak hammocks, sandhills, and scrubby flatwoods, the trail reaches a loop along the cypress floodplain forests of the St. Johns River, where it narrows to a slight track through the ferns on the forest floor. Continue around the loop to emerge at an open area and return along the same loop.

Highlights: There are gopher tortoises in the oak hammocks and sandhills, and colorful bromeliads in the cypresses in the floodplain forest.

Logistics: Follow the paved road for 0.2 mile to the trailhead, then follow the hiker markers around the loop. Keep alert for trail markers when walking along the cypress floodplain. Expect mosquitoes along the river swamps; wear insect repellent.

Other Activities: The northern end of the Florida Trail through the Ocala National Forest (CF-09) also starts from this trailhead, as do equestrian trails along the Cross Florida Greenway. There is a picnic area adjacent to the parking area.

San Felasco Hammock Preserve State Park

NF-34 $ 📖 🚻 🏠

Location: Gainesville [N29°42.855' W082°27.653'].

Length: 12.2 miles in three loops.

Map: Rough map in park brochure; detailed map at trailhead kiosk.

Contact Information: San Felasco Hammock Preserve State Park (352-955-2008), 4732 Millhopper Rd, Gainesville, FL 32653.

Directions: From I-75 exit 390, follow CR 222 for 3.4 miles to NW 43rd Street. Turn left and drive 1 mile to NW 53rd Avenue (Millhopper Road). Turn left. Continue 4.5 miles, passing Devil's Millhopper (NF-35), to the parking area on the left.

The Hike: On the south side of Millhopper Road, the 1.5-mile Nature Trail leads through shady upland forests where streams and sinkholes have shaped the landscape. On the north side of Millhopper Road, there are two trails creating a figure-8 loop: the 5.7-mile Spring Grove Trail and the 5-mile Old Spanish Way. Both meander through upland forests, sandhills, and pine flatwoods; the Old Spanish Way circles a large pond and skirts numerous sinkholes, including deep Big Sink.

Highlights: Walking along the Nature Trail to Moonshine Creek, you'll encounter spring wildflowers rarely seen in this part of Florida, such as wakerobin, woodbine, and sundial lupine. There are sassafras trees and wild indigo along the Spring Grove Trail, which passes the site of the first county seat of Alachua County, Spring Grove—now a ghost town. In the woods off the Old Spanish Way is the site of the San Francisco de Potano mission, one of the first Spanish missions in the New World.

Logistics: Many areas of the preserve are off limits for off-trail exploration because of fragile vegetation, geology, and archaeological resources; please respect the signs. Rangers lead interpretive hikes and overnight backpacking trips to these special areas throughout the preserve.

Other Activities: There are extensive equestrian and bicycle trails at the north end of the preserve.

Devil's Millhopper Geological State Park

NF-35 $ 📖 🚻

Location: Gainesville [N29°42.324' W082°23.682'].

Length: 0.9-mile loop.

Map: Rough map in park brochure.

Contact Information: Devil's Millhopper Geological State Park (352-955-2008), 4732 Millhopper Rd, Gainesville, FL 32653.

Directions: From I-75 exit 390, follow CR 222 for 3.4 miles to NW 43rd Street. Turn left and drive 1 mile to NW 53rd Avenue (Millhopper Road). Turn left. The park entrance is on the right after 0.3 mile.

The Hike: A paved path leads to the visitor center, where the trail starts. When you reach the loop, turn right. From the hardwood hammock, the trail passes through sandhills and scrub as it follows the rim of the sinkhole, crossing a ravine with a creek that pours into the sink. A staircase leads down to the bottom of the sinkhole—232 steps—with pauses on several landings overlooking the splash of waterfalls down the sides of the sinkhole.

Highlights: Down in the bottom of the 120-foot sinkhole, it's another world—lush with ferns, with needle palms growing amid the rocks, water dripping off limestone ledges, and when the water table is high, tall cascades splashing down the sinkhole walls.

Logistics: There is a self-pay station in the parking lot. Guided tours are offered Saturday mornings at ten o'clock.

Other Activities: Visit the visitor center and watch the film before heading down into the sinkhole to understand the geology and history behind this site.

Gum Root Swamp Conservation Area

NF-36 📖 👫

Location: Gainesville [N29°41.104' W082°13.625'].

Length: 2.6-mile loop.

Map: Displayed at trailhead kiosk and available in St. Johns River Water Management District's *Recreation Guide to District Lands* (under Newnans Lake Conservation Area, North Tract).

Contact Information: St. Johns River Water Management District (904-529-2380), PO Box 1429, Palatka, FL 32178-1429.

Directions: From Gainesville, follow SR 26 (University Avenue) east through downtown. When the road splits, stay to the left to stay on SR 26. Passing Morningside Nature Center (NF-37), keep left at the next fork. Past the light at NE 27th Avenue, watch for the small Gum Root Swamp Conservation Area sign on the right.

The Hike: Three interconnected loop trails showcase the habitats surrounding this outdoor environmental education center. The Bobcat Trail meanders along the edge of a cypress swamp, creating a loop as it passes through sandhill habitat on the way back to the trailhead. The yellow-blazed Turtle Trail leads to and along cypress-lined Hatchet Creek. The Otter Trail crosses the creek twice on broad bridges and weaves between the cypress knees to ascend to a hardwood hammock island in the swamp.

Highlights: A spur trail off the Otter Trail leads to the edge of Newnan's Lake, known to the Seminoles as Pithlachocco, or "the place where boats are made." More than a hundred aboriginal canoes were found in 2000 as the waters receded from the muddy lake bottom; artifacts found around the lake date back to 3000 B.C.

Logistics: If water levels are high in the lake, the trails will be flooded. Expect mosquitoes—wear insect repellent!

Other Activities: Check out the model canoe in the environmental center; it's a replica of the canoes found in the bottom of Newnan's Lake.

Morningside Nature Center

NF-37 📖 🚻 👥

Location: Gainesville.

Length: Up to 4.8 miles in various loops.

Map: Detailed map available at educational center.

Contact Information: Gainesville Recreation and Parks Department (352-334-5067), Station 24, Box 490, Gainesville, FL 32602-0490.

Directions: From Gainesville, follow SR 26 (University Avenue) east through downtown. When the road splits, stay to the left to stay on SR 26. The entrance is on the left after 1.8 miles.

The Hike: The trail system provides a wide range of hikes through a variety of habitats. Start at the Education Center to select from trails such as the 3-mile Blue Loop, which works its way around the perimeter of the park; the 1.5-mile Yellow Loop through longleaf pine savannas, sandhills, and bayheads; the 0.2-mile Cypress Dome Boardwalk; and the 0.3-mile Gopher Loop Trail through a sandhill with gopher tortoises.

Highlights: Enjoy spectacular spring wildflowers throughout the park—and bring a field guide! You'll need it to identify the 270 varieties. There is a swamp overlook on a tupelo marsh off the Yellow Loop.

Logistics: There is an entrance fee on festival weekends. The Yellow and Blue Loops may have flooded or soggy footpaths after a rain. Some trails have two blazes where loops overlap.

Other Activities: Visit the living history farm, open Saturday and Sunday except in August, with original buildings from around the county and docents in period costume. There is a small fee. Two annual events, the Farm and Forest Festival and the Cane Boil, attract large crowds.

Bivens Arm Nature Park

NF-38 📖 🚻 ♿ 👫

Location: Gainesville [N29°37.200' W082°19.939'].

Length: 1.1-mile trail system.

Map: Displayed on kiosk at outdoor classroom.

Contact Information: City of Gainesville Recreation and Parks Department (352-334-5067), Station 24, Box 490, Gainesville, FL 32602-0490.

Directions: Driving 2.3 miles east from I-75 exit 382 on SR 331, you cross US 441. Get in the left lane and bear left at the fork onto Main Street (SR 329). You immediately pass the park on the left. Use the U-turn cutout to return to the park entrance.

The Hike: Starting at the outdoor classroom, follow the boardwalk around this finger of Bivens Arm, a landlocked marshy pond that is part of Paynes Prairie. At the trail junction, keep to the left to continue to walk around the pond. A side trail leads to the Marsh Observatory; the Hammock Trail continues straight. The trail crosses the outflow of this part of the marsh and leads to the Gator Gap Loop, a small loop through a forest of large loblolly pines and red maple. After you complete the loop and cross the bridge again, make a left to follow the rest of the Hammock Trail through the hammock and around to the picnic area near the entrance.

Highlights: There are tall loblolly pines and views across the marsh, plus great interpretive signage and inspirational quotes along the trails.

Logistics: The trail system is open 9:00–5:00 daily. The pavement and boardwalks are wheelchair accessible. Road noise is unavoidable throughout the preserve, given its location. Numerous benches along the trails make this an easy walk for all ages. The restroom is along the paved trail to the picnic area. There are cross trails providing shorter walks.

Other Activities: There are picnic tables next to the restrooms, and geocaches hidden in the forest.

La Chua Trail

Paynes Prairie Preserve State Park

NF-39 📖 🚻

Location: Gainesville [N29°36.453' W082°18.106'].

Length: 4.2 miles round-trip.

Map: Available at ranger station or visitor center.

Contact Information: Paynes Prairie Preserve State Park (352-466-3397), 100 Savannah Boulevard, Micanopy, FL 32667.

Directions: Driving 2.3 miles east from I-75 exit 382 on SR 331, you cross US 441. Get in the right lane and bear right at the fork. After 2 miles, turn right on SE 4th Street, and right again on SE 15th Street (CR 2043). Pass the entrance to Boulware Springs Park and turn right onto Camp Ranch Road. The trail starts at the far end of the parking lot.

The Hike: Rounding the deepest portion of Alachua Sink, the trail showcases the "drain" of Paynes Prairie, a series of sinkholes into which all of the prairie's waters flow. Follow the jeep trail to the left to see the broadest part of the sink. The trail continues along the jeep road on a dike just above the vast floodplains, and ends after 1.4 miles at an observation platform. Return along the same route.

Highlights: Looking for alligators? Alachua Sink has one of the highest concentrations of them you'll see outside of the Everglades. When the water in Paynes Prairie is low, you'll also see a waterfall dropping down into the deepest part of the sink, draining the prairie.

Logistics: The Camp Ranch Road entrance is open only on weekdays, and the gate is locked at 5:00 p.m. On weekends, use the paved trail from Boulware Springs to access the park. Sign in at the trailhead kiosk. Do not hike this trail if it is flooded. Do not take dogs or small children on this hike. Be alert for bison and wild horses. There is little shade once you walk around La Chua Sink. Use sun protection and carry adequate drinking water.

Other Activities: Visit the interpretive center before your hike. The Gainesville-Hawthorne Trail, a bike trail, passes through this end of the park, with the nearest trailhead just up the road at Boulware Springs Park.

Bolens Bluff Trail

Paynes Prairie Preserve State Park

NF-40 ▢ ▣ ⌂

Location: Micanopy [N29°33.395' W082°19.799'].

Length: 1.4-mile loop with a 1.4-mile spur.

Map: Trail shown in park brochure; more detailed map on trailhead kiosk.

Contact Information: Paynes Prairie Preserve State Park (352-466-3397), 100 Savannah Boulevard, Micanopy, FL 32667.

Directions: From I-75 exit 374, drive east on CR 234 for 1.3 miles to the T intersection at US 441, and turn left. The park entrance is on the right after 0.6 mile. Continue 3.4 miles past the park entrance to the trailhead parking on the right.

The Hike: Creating a loop through the shady upland forest on the bluffs above Paynes Prairie, the trail takes you past sinkholes and the remnants of an old farm. A 1.4-mile round-trip spur trail leads down the bluffs and into the prairie, where you'll encounter wildlife. The spur trail ends at an observation platform.

Highlights: This is a popular morning walk and a destination for birdwatching. Walk out to the observation platform for a nice view of the prairie.

Logistics: The trail is open from 8:00 to sunset. If the prairie is flooded, you will not be able to walk out to the observation tower. Be alert for wildlife as you walk. Give alligators and snakes a wide berth.

Other Activities: Continue your drive on US 441 and stop at the pulloff by the "William Bartram Trail" sign; walk out the boardwalk for some birdwatching and alligator observation. Or visit the trails in the main part of the park (NF-41), located south on US 441.

Paynes Prairie Preserve State Park

NF-41 $ 📖 🚹 🄲 ♿ 🚻

Location: Micanopy [N29°32.848' W082°17.640'].

Length: 16.8 miles in five trails, the shortest a 0.3-mile loop.

Map: Available at ranger station or visitor center.

Contact Information: Paynes Prairie Preserve State Park (352-466-3397), 100 Savannah Boulevard, Micanopy, FL 32667.

Directions: From I-75 exit 374, drive east on CR 234 for 1.3 miles to the T intersection at US 441, and turn left. The park entrance is on the right after 0.6 mile. Drive 2.6 miles on the entrance road (Savannah Boulevard) to the visitor center parking area.

The Hike: From this parking area, you can access most of the trails within the developed portion of the park. Follow the paved path for a walk on the Wacahoota Trail, which is wheelchair accessible to the observation tower. It continues to loop through upland forest for 0.3 mile. From the picnic area, 1.3-mile Jackson's Gap is a connector trail between the 6.2-mile Chacala Trail loop, which was created primarily for horses, and the 8.2-mile Cones Dike, which takes you out into the prairie. The 0.8-mile Lake Trail is a blazed forest-road connector between Savannah Boulevard and the picnic area at Lake Wauberg.

Highlights: Climb the tower on the Wacahoota Trail for a bird's-eye view of the prairie. Walk out on Cones Dike to see evidence of the wild horses and bison that live on the prairie. Walk to the overlook on Chacala Pond along the Chacala Trail.

Logistics: The visitor center is open Mon-Tue 10:00–4:00, Wed–Sun 9:00–5:00. Cones Dike has no shade—carry a lot of drinking water and wear sun protection. Although dogs are permitted on the trails, the presence of alligators (on all but the Wacahoota Trail) puts them at risk. The longer trails (Cones Dike, Jackson Gap, Chacala) are not recommended for small children.

Other Activities: Cones Dike, Jackson Gap, and the Chacala Trail are open to mountain biking; there is a special trailhead 1 mile from the entrance for the Chacala Trail, with a parking area large enough to accommodate horse trailers. To see alligators, head down to Lake Wauberg and walk the boardwalk over to the picnic area, where the Lake Trail ends.

Lake Lochloosa Conservation Area

NF-42 🐎

Location: Cross Creek [N29°28.653' W082°09.557'].

Length: 1.5 miles round-trip.

Map: Displayed at trailhead kiosk and available in St. Johns River Water Management District's *Recreation Guide to District Lands.*

Contact Information: St. Johns River Water Management District (904-529-2380), PO Box 1429, Palatka, FL 32178-1429.

Directions: From US 301 north of Citra, follow CR 325 west to Cross Creek. The trailhead is adjacent to the Cross Creek Fire Station, and you must enter the fire station grounds to get to the trailhead parking area.

The Hike: Starting out in a pine plantation, the trail twists and winds between the pines and drops down through a bayhead swamp before continuing down through a forest of pines and palms. You start to glimpse an open area beyond the trees on the left—Lake Lochloosa. After 0.7 mile you reach a boardwalk; turn left and walk out to the observation deck on the lake. Return along the same route.

Highlights: Take in the views of Lake Lochloosa, especially from the observation deck at the end of the trail.

Logistics: If Lake Lochloosa is high, the trail will flood in places. It's not always easy to follow the footpath, especially along the edge of the lake.

Other Activities: There is birdwatching along the lakeshore, and equestrian trails and a campsite are accessible from a trailhead off US 301 north of CR 325.

Fort White Mitigation Park

NF-43 📖

Location: Bell [N29°54.767' W082°46.492'].

Length: Separate loops of 0.9 mile and 3 miles.

Map: Displayed at both trailhead kiosks and available in an interpretive brochure.

Contact Information: Florida Fish and Wildlife Conservation Commission (850-488-5520), 620 South Meridian Street, Tallahassee, FL 32399-1600.

Directions: From US 27 east of Branford, drive south on US 129 for 4.2 miles and turn left on CR 138. Drive 3.2 miles east to NE 2nd Way; turn left on the broad dirt road. Continue 2.3 miles to the parking area on the right. The short South Loop starts beside the parking area; the North Loop starts across the road.

The Hike: Set aside to mitigate building along the Santa Fe River, this preserve protects waterfront along the river as well as crucial gopher tortoise habitat. The 0.9-mile South Loop follows the shoreline of the Santa Fe River for a half mile, passing through a shady river bluff forest before emerging up in the sandhills to make the return loop. The 3-mile North Loop meanders through sandhills, scrubby flatwoods, and scrub, with several cross trails providing shorter loop options.

Highlights: Enjoy walking along the banks of the Santa Fe River on the South Loop and looking for gopher tortoise burrows along the North Loop.

Logistics: Expect to walk through soft sand in places. The sandhills offer little shade; wear adequate sun protection and carry plenty of drinking water. The South Loop is blazed orange, the North Loop green. Blazes may be sporadic in places; use your good judgment or carry a GPS to keep track of the trailhead.

Other Activities: There are separate equestrian trails on both side of the road, and bank fishing on the Santa Fe River. A boat ramp is at the end of the road.

Hart Springs Park

NF-44 $ 👫 Ⓐ ♿ 👫

Location: Hart Springs [N29°40.565' W082°57.098'].

Length: 1-mile loop or round trip.

Map: None available.

Contact Information: Gilchrist County Parks Department (352-463-3444), 4240 SW 86th Avenue, Bell, FL 32619.

Directions: From US 19/98 in Fanning Springs, drive east 1.3 miles on SR 26. Turn left on CR 232. Continue north 4.2 miles to CR 334. Drive 1.5 miles to the park entrance on the right. Continue along the entrance road to the farthest parking area, near the picnic pavilions.

The Hike: Cross the bridge over the spring run and walk along the sidewalk to access the boardwalk, which starts 0.2 mile from the parking lot. Paralleling the crystalline waters of Hart Springs Run, the boardwalk follows the run through the cypresses to its confluence with the Suwannee River, then turns to the right to parallel the river for a stretch. The walk is open and breezy, with several overlooks. When the boardwalk turns away from the river, it crosses a willow marsh and winds through the cypress swamps before ending at the campground. Retrace your steps, or turn right and walk through the campground to create a loop.

Highlights: There are great views of both Hart Springs Run and the Suwannee River along the boardwalk. In the cypress swamp, look for two double-trunk cypresses growing so close together that they look like one massive tree with four trunks.

Logistics: There is an entrance fee of $2, seniors $1, children under five free. Plentiful benches along the boardwalk make this an easy walk for all ages. Wear insect repellent at dawn and dusk.

Other Activities: This is a popular swimming hole and picnic park, often busy with families. The campground provides a beautiful setting under the forest canopy near the Suwannee River.

Fanning Springs Hiking Trail

Fanning Springs State Park

NF-45 $ 📖 🚻 👫 🐕

Location: Fanning Springs [N29°35.258' W082°56.043'].

Length: 0.9-mile loop.

Map: Rough map in park brochure.

Contact Information: Fanning Springs State Park (352-463-3420), NW 115th Street, Chiefland, FL 32626.

Directions: The park entrance is along US 19/98 in Fanning Springs on the western side of the highway just south of the Suwannee River bridge.

The Hike: The trail starts at a kiosk above the swimming area and makes a loop through the shady upland forest, crossing a forest road twice. The mixed upland hammock has a high canopy of hickories, southern magnolias, and oaks. The trail passes a string of sinkholes in line with the underground stream that feeds Fanning Springs.

Highlights: Ferns grow lushly around the sinkholes, and the forest floor is open enough to make wildlife spotting easy—look for raccoons, deer, and wild turkeys.

Logistics: Wear insect repellent, as ticks are common in the bluff forests above the Suwannee River. The trail is shared with bicycles.

Other Activities: Swim in Fanning Springs, walk the boardwalk out to the Suwannee River, picnic under the oaks, and kayak along the river.

North Atlantic

Nassau, Duval, St. Johns, Flagler

Estuary of the Tolomato River, from the observation tower at Stokes
Landing.

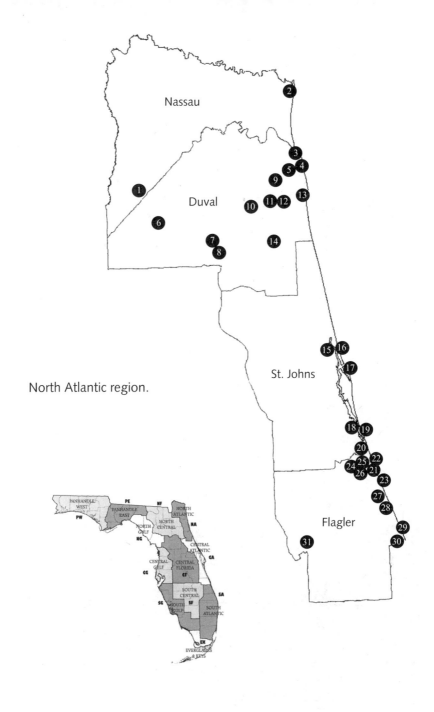

Nassau

Duval

North Atlantic region.

St. Johns

Flagler

Nassau
- NA-1   Cary Nature Trail, Cary State Forest
- NA-2   Willow Pond Nature Trail, Fort Clinch State Park

Duval
- NA-3   Blackrock Trail, Big Talbot Island State Park
- NA-4   Island Hiking Trail, Little Talbot Island State Park
- NA-5   Campground Nature Trail, Little Talbot Island State Park
- NA-6   Pope Duval Park
- NA-7   Ortega Stream Valley Trail, Ringhaver Park
- NA-8   Westside Regional Park
- NA-9   Pumpkin Hill Creek Preserve State Park
- NA-10 Arlington Lions Club Park
- NA-11 Hammock Nature Trail, Fort Caroline National Monument
- NA-12 Theodore Roosevelt Area, Timucuan Ecological and Historical Preserve
- NA-13 Kathryn Abbey Hanna Park
- NA-14 Robert W. Loftin Nature Trails, University of North Florida Wildlife Sanctuary

St. Johns
- NA-15 Stokes Landing Conservation Area
- NA-16 Guana River State Park
- NA-17 Ancient Dunes Trail, Anastasia State Park
- NA-18 Moses Creek Conservation Area
- NA-19 Accessible Nature Trail, Fort Matanzas National Monument
- NA-20 Nature Trail, Faver-Dykes State Park

Flagler
- NA-21 Mala Compra Trail, Washington Oaks Gardens State Park
- NA-22 Bella Vista Trail, Washington Oaks Gardens State Park
- NA-23 Malacompra County Park
- NA-24 Red Trail, Princess Place Preserve
- NA-25 Blue Trail, Princess Place Preserve
- NA-26 Green Trail, Princess Place Preserve
- NA-27 Graham Swamp Conservation Area
- NA-28 Wadsworth Park
- NA-29 Joe Kenner Nature Trail, Gamble Rogers Memorial State Recreation Area
- NA-30 Bulow Creek Trail, Bulow Plantation Ruins Historic State Park
- NA-31 Haw Creek Preserve

Cary Nature Trail

Cary State Forest

NA-1 $ ◻ 🚻 ⛺ 👫 🐕

Location: Bryceville [N30°23.991' W081°55.605'].

Length: 1.4-mile loop.

Map: In state forest brochure available at trailhead.

Contact Information: Cary State Forest (904-266-5021), Route 2 Box 60, Bryceville, FL 32209.

Directions: From I-10 exit 343 in Baldwin, drive north 9 miles on US 301 to Bryceville; the forest entrance is on the left. Follow Pavilion Road to its intersection with Fire Tower Road and park on the right next to the kiosk. The trail starts across Pavilion Road.

The Hike: This delightful short hike is a perfect place to learn about the mosaic of habitats that make up North Florida. From the kiosk, follow a short path past the education center and campground and, at the "Nature Trail" sign, follow the broad path into the longleaf pine forest, across a lengthy boardwalk through bayheads and cypress swamp, and onto a brief stretch of jeep roads to connect to the return portion of the loop, which circles pitcher plant bogs along cypress domes.

Highlights: Look for hooded pitcher plants along the ditches and off side trails on the return section of the loop. Savor the boardwalk through the cypress swamp. And don't miss the view from the top of the observation tower!

Logistics: Pay your $2 state forest usage fee at the self-serve kiosk. If you are camping, you must register with the forest in advance. The small campground is perfect for introducing children to tent camping, as there are restrooms within easy reach.

Other Activities: Visit the S. Bryan Jennings Environmental Education Center (when open) for more exploration of the habitats of this region. There is an eight-mile equestrian trail as well as miles of forest roads for riders to explore. Seasonal hunting is permitted.

Willow Pond Nature Trail

Fort Clinch State Park

NA-2 $ 📖 🚻 Ⓒ 👫

Location: Fernandina Beach [N30°41.900' W081°26.638'].

Length: Up to a 0.6-mile loop.

Map: In interpretive brochure available from ranger station or at trailhead kiosk.

Contact Information: Fort Clinch State Park (904-277-7274), 2601 Atlantic Avenue, Fernandina Beach, FL 32034.

Directions: Follow A1A south from Fernandina for 1.5 miles to the park entrance on the left. Continue 2.4 miles along the park entrance road to the Willow Pond parking area on the left.

The Hike: Start your hike by taking the trail to the left of the "Willow Pond" sign to walk the loop clockwise. As the trail drops downhill, you get a nice view of the pond; a side trail leads to an overlook, and the main trail follows a narrow slice of land between the ponds. The shortcut Willow Trail takes off to the right in an upland forest, while the perimeter Magnolia Trail continues through an undulating landscape of relict dunes and deep swales topped with maritime forest.

Highlights: Pause along the ponds, especially down the spur trail, for great birding. The northern end of the loop (Magnolia Trail) has some serious hill climbing on the relict dunes through the welcome shade of the maritime hammock.

Logistics: There is a guided nature walk every Saturday morning at 10:30; meet at the trailhead. Numerous benches make this an easy stroll for all ages. Be alert for alligators—there are several alligator slides between the ponds. Do *not* walk a dog on this trail (although it is permitted), and keep children away from the water.

Other Activities: There is an excellent mountain-biking loop trail as well as the historic fort, two full-service campgrounds, and miles of Atlantic oceanfront to enjoy.

Blackrock Trail

Big Talbot Island State Park

NA-3 🐎

Location: Big Talbot Island [N30°29.479' W081°26.524'].

Length: 1 mile round-trip.

Map: No map; trail shown in *Talbot Islands State Parks* brochure available at picnic area.

Contact Information: Talbot Island State Parks (904-251-2320), 12157 Heckscher Drive, Jacksonville, FL 32226.

Directions: From Amelia Island, drive south on A1A, crossing the bridge to Big Talbot Island. After you pass the "Big Talbot Island State Park" sign, drive 1 mile and look for the trail entrance on the left (there will undoubtedly be cars parked there).

The Hike: This broad beach-access trail leads you through coastal scrub and maritime hammock, beneath a stand of extremely tall and windswept live oaks, to emerge at the ever-changing shoreline of Blackrock Beach, a geological anomaly where the "rocks" are actually compacted humus and sand eroded into perfect replicas of rock—right down to the rounded shapes. Depending on the whim of wind and wave, you may see tidal pools, shoreline caves, or mounds of driftwood on the sand.

Highlights: This is one of the most visually intriguing beaches in Florida. Between the black "rock" and the black cliffs of humus crowded to the edge with saw palmetto, it looks like a beach scene from Hawaii.

Logistics: Since parking places are limited, it may be tough to find one on the weekend. Your alternative is to park at the Big Talbot Bluffs picnic area (fee) and walk down the beach 1 mile to the Blackrock Trail.

Other Activities: Visitors enjoy fishing from the beach, sunning on the beach, and sea kayaking along the shore. One of Florida's most colorful birds, the painted bunting, nests in the forest along this trail and can be spotted by keen eyes in late spring.

Island Hiking Trail

Little Talbot Island State Park

NA-4 $ 👫 Ⓐ

Location: Little Talbot Island [N30°27.619' W081°24.944'].

Length: 3.8-mile loop.

Map: Available at trailhead kiosk; trail shown in park brochure.

Contact Information: Talbot Island State Parks (904-251-2320), 12157 Heckscher Drive, Jacksonville, FL 32226.

Directions: From Jacksonville, follow SR 105 (Heckscher Drive) east along the St. Johns River to A1A, which merges in at the Mayport Ferry. Continue north 5 miles to the Little Talbot Island State Park entrance on the right. Park near the ranger station; the trailhead is just before the ranger station on the left.

The Hike: Follow the bark chip path down past the trailhead kiosk on a mowed corridor through the coastal scrub, descending into a shady maritime hammock. The trail becomes a causeway through a coastal pine flatwoods before rising into the open dunes, where the path is indistinct. At 2 miles, you reach a bench overlooking the sea. A sign at the shoreline says "Hiking Trail Return," with an arrow pointing to the right. Walk along the beach to return, using the dunes crossover after marker F and the park road to complete the loop.

Highlights: Although open and sunny, the dunes-traverse portion of the hike is the most scenic part of the walk, leading you through swales between tall dunes topped with cabbage palms out to the coastal strand.

Logistics: You must report in at the ranger station before and after the hike. Restrooms are located along the beach-access boardwalk on your return trip to the parking area. There are numerous benches along the trail. Since half the trail is in full sun, wear sun protection and carry a lot of water.

Other Activities: This is a very popular beach on weekends—sunning, swimming, sailing, fishing, it all happens here, just north of the mouth of the St. Johns River. The Campground Nature Trail (NA-5) is across A1A in the campground.

Campground Nature Trail

Little Talbot Island State Park

NA-5 $ 🚻 Ⓐ 🚸 🐕

Location: Little Talbot Island [N30°27.380' W081°25.253'].

Length: 0.8-mile loop.

Map: Detailed map in interpretive brochure in trailhead box.

Contact Information: Talbot Island State Parks (904-251-2320), 12157 Heckscher Drive, Jacksonville, FL 32226.

Directions: From Jacksonville, follow SR 105 (Heckscher Drive) east along the St. Johns River to A1A, which merges in at the Mayport Ferry. Continue north 5 miles to the Little Talbot Island State Park entrance on the right. At the ranger station, tell them you want to hike the Campground Nature Trail; they will give you directions. Park your car at the canoe launch and walk back to site 39 to find the trailhead.

The Hike: Follow the white blazes down a well-defined footpath, winding through cedars, yaupon, and large slash pines before you emerge on the edge of the estuary. Working its way along the edge of the vast needlerush marsh, the trail climbs up and over several relict dunes topped with a maritime forest of cedar and red bay before completing the loop.

Highlights: Panoramic views of the estuary are offered at several points along the trail.

Logistics: Unless you are a registered camper, you must obtain permission (and a gate combination) to visit the campground to hike this trail. Be sure to lock the gate behind you.

Other Activities: This is a very popular beach on weekends—sunning, swimming, sailing, fishing, it all happens here, just north of the mouth of the St. Johns River. The Island Hiking Trail (NA-4) is across A1A in the beach-access portion of the park.

Pope Duval Park

NA-6 🚻 ♿

Location: Whitehouse [N30°18.316' W081°54.206'].

Length: 0.8-mile round-trip boardwalk.

Map: None available.

Contact Information: City of Jacksonville Department of Parks and Recreation (904-630-CITY; www.coj.net), 851 North Market Street, Jacksonville 32202.

Directions: From I-10 exit 351, follow Chaffee Road north to US 90. Turn left and continue west 2.7 miles to the park entrance on the left. To get to the boardwalk, follow the rugged dirt road 0.9 mile, turning left at the underpass to parallel I-10. Turn right at the next road on the right, and park near the pond.

The Hike: Starting along the pond's edge at the picnic area, the boardwalk traverses pine flatwoods around the edge of the pond, then turns away from the water to meander through a forest of pines and cypress. After curving around a second pond, it passes through a dense pine forest and ends after 0.4 mile. An unmarked and ill-maintained trail continues into the woods, ending at an abandoned section of boardwalk.

Highlights: There are nice views of the flatwoods ponds.

Logistics: Restrooms are located in the building at the park entrance. At the boardwalk, if you continue past the end, be cautious of poison ivy. If you reach the abandoned boardwalk, do not attempt to use it; it is structurally unsound.

Other Activities: Picnic at the trailhead, or fish in any of the numerous fish management area ponds.

Ortega Stream Valley Trail

Ringhaver Park

NA-7 [♿] [♿] [♿] [🏇]

Location: Orange Park [N30°13.761' W081°42.943'].

Length: 2 miles in two interconnecting loops.

Map: None available.

Contact Information: Ringhaver Park (904-779-1519), 5198 118th Street, Jacksonville, FL 32244.

Directions: From I-295 exit 10 at Roosevelt Boulevard (US 17), follow US 17 north about 4 miles to Timuquana Road (SR 134). Turn left at the light and follow Timuquana for 1 mile across the Ortega River bridge. Turn left at the next light onto Ortega Farms Road. Follow this road south. Immediately after it makes a sharp right, look for the park entrance on the left. Drive all the way to the back of the park to find the trailhead, which adjoins a small picnic pavilion.

The Hike: From the trailhead, the Blue Loop (a narrow asphalt trail) leads you through pine flatwoods, crosses Ortega Stream on a boardwalk, and divides into a loop after 0.3 mile. Turn left to walk down to the long boardwalk over the Ortega River marshes; you reach the Ortega River at 0.7 mile. On the return trip, keep left at the fork to continue through sandhill habitat, where you meet the Orange Loop, a natural footpath that makes a separate 0.5-mile loop through the sandhills. Continue back on the Blue Loop to the trailhead.

Highlights: The nice long boardwalk over the tidal marshes of the Ortega River has a canoe launch platform at the end that gives you a view of the river down a snaking channel. Watch for gopher tortoises in the sandhills.

Logistics: At the trailhead there is a sign and a wooden trail marker. These chunky wooden posts have blue and orange stripes, indicating which trail you're on.

Other Activities: There are ballfields, large playgrounds, a picnic area, and a canoe and kayak put-in along the Blue Loop.

Westside Regional Park

NA-8 📖 👫 ♿ 👫 🏇

Location: Orange Park: Island Trail [N30°14.281' W081°41.932'], Sensory Trail [N30°14.307' W081°41.977'], Tower Trail [N30°14.305' W081°42.012'].

Length: Island Trail, 1.3 miles round-trip; Sensory Trail, 0.2-mile loop; Tower Trail, 0.9 mile round-trip.

Map: Available on City of Jacksonville website (www.coj.net) under Parks and Recreation, Westside Regional Park.

Contact Information: Westside Regional Park (904-573-2498), 7000 Roosevelt Boulevard, Jacksonville, FL 32244.

Directions: From I-295 exit 10 at Roosevelt Blvd, follow US 17 north for 3 miles to Yorktown Road. Turn left to enter the park. Follow the park entrance road to the very end and park near the nature center; all three trails start within sight of the center.

The Hike: The Island Trail offers the most rugged hiking experience in the park. It starts off with a short wheelchair-accessible section to a boardwalk over a slough, and then becomes a natural footpath through pine flatwoods and corridors of tall bamboo on the way to a loop around the island, a dry oak hammock surrounded by willow marshes off the Ortega River. The Sensory Trail is a learning experience: grab a blindfold at the nature center and follow the ropes through the forest, using your other senses to experience the outdoors. The Tower Trail heads out through oak hammocks to an observation tower overlooking a floodplain forest along the Ortega River.

Highlights: The Tower Trail follows a historic brick road. The Island Trail offers views of the marsh.

Logistics: The Island Trail is orange blazed; the Tower Trail is blue blazed. Many unmarked trails intersect both of these hikes, so use caution at trail intersections to watch for the next blaze—or go explore! Both trails start off with wheelchair-accessible segments.

Other Activities: Visit the nature center, or have a picnic with the family. There are separate biking and equestrian trails on-site, with trailheads closer to the park entrance.

Pumpkin Hill Creek Preserve State Park

NA-9 🐎

Location: New Berlin Park [N30°28.418' W081°29.241'].

Length: 0.8-mile hiking loop (Green Loop), plus four multiuse loops primarily used by equestrians: Purple (3.7 miles), Red (3.1 miles), Yellow (1.7 miles), and Blue (1.3 miles).

Map: Displayed at trailhead kiosk and available in St. Johns River Water Management District's *Recreation Guide to District Lands.*

Contact Information: St. Johns River Water Management District (904-529-2380), PO Box 1429, Palatka, FL 32178-1429.

Directions: From 9A north of the St. Johns River, exit on Heckscher Drive east. Turn left at the first traffic light onto New Berlin Road. Follow it 4 miles north to a Y intersection; bear right. Continue 5 miles along Cedar Point Road to make a left onto Pumpkin Hill Road. The trailhead is on the left just after the residential area ends.

The Hike: The trail system explores scrubby flatwoods, oak hammocks, and open scrub on a bluff above tidal marshes draining toward the St. Johns River. To access the Green Loop, cross Pumpkin Hill Road from the park entrance. This natural narrow footpath twists and winds through the pine flatwoods to the bluffs above the tidal marshes of the St. Johns River. The other four loops start at the trailhead kiosk. Because the soft sandy terrain is difficult, hikers should stick to the Blue and Green Loops, which provide a 2-mile circuit.

Highlights: Enjoy panoramas of the palmetto prairie in the scrubby flatwoods, and great sweeping views of the tidal marshes from both loops.

Logistics: Shade is severely lacking in the palmetto prairie—use sunscreen, a hat, and sunglasses! Expect to encounter equestrians anywhere but the Green Loop. Signs and color-tipped posts mark the trails. The Blue Loop is poorly blazed. After you turn at the gazebo onto the Blue Loop, make sure you take the first obvious right-hand turn within the next half mile.

Other Activities: The trails are open to equestrians and mountain biking, although the sandy entrance to the loops does not lend itself to biking. Birdwatching on the tidal marsh bluffs is great.

Nature Trail

Arlington Lions Club Park

NA-10 👪 ♿ 👫 🐕

Location: Jacksonville [N30°22.618' W081°37.108'].

Length: 1.1-mile loop.

Map: None available.

Contact Information: Arlington Lions Club Park (904-573-2498), 4322-1 Richard Denby Gatlin Road, Jacksonville, FL 32277.

Directions: From 9A south of the St. Johns River, exit on Merrill Road. Drive west 3 miles to University Boulevard. Turn right. Drive 2 miles north, past the entrance to Blue Cypress Park, to Denby Gatlin Road. Turn left. The park entrance is at the end of the road. Park your car in the first parking area on the left.

The Hike: Start at the "Nature Trail" sign and make a left to begin your walk on a natural footpath through a shady river bluff forest, where slash pine, southern magnolia, and sparkleberry dominate the forest. Ferns fill the damp spaces. After paralleling the park road, the trail begins its loop along the edge of a tidal marsh, passing through tall groves of pines. Frequent benches make this an easy walk for all ages. The natural surface ends after 0.5 mile. Turn left to follow a paved trail to the boardwalk along the St. Johns River and the tidal marsh. Turn left on the boardwalk to walk down to the observation platform at Blue Cypress Park. Return along the boardwalk to complete the loop.

Highlights: Extraordinarily tall, old trees—tupelo, magnolia, and slash pine—along the natural footpath make this a pleasant walk. The boardwalk provides great views of the St. Johns River.

Logistics: The park is open from sunrise to sunset. Wheelchairs cannot traverse the 0.5-mile natural segment of the trail, but if you make a right at the trailhead, you can follow the asphalt path around to enjoy the boardwalk section of the trail along the river.

Other Activities: You'll find a manatee exhibit at the boat ramp, plus picnic groves, a playground, and fishing from the pier at Blue Cypress Park.

Hammock Nature Trail

Fort Caroline National Memorial

NA-11 □ 🚻 👫

Location: Jacksonville [N30°23.141' W081°29.877'].

Length: 1.3-mile loop.

Map: Posted at trailhead kiosk.

Contact Information: National Park Service (904-251-3537), 12713 Fort Caroline Road, Jacksonville, FL 32225.

Directions: From SR 9A, take the Southside Connector exit and follow Fort Caroline Road 4.3 miles east to where it turns left at Mt. Pleasant Road. Continue 0.3 mile; the Fort Caroline entrance is on the left, and the Spanish Pond parking area (part of hike NA-12) is on the right.

The Hike: The trail starts at the kiosk to the right of the building. Stay right at the fork to walk down along the St. Johns River past a replica Timucuan village and the replica of Fort Caroline. Upon leaving the fort, turn right to continue along the nature trail into a maritime hammock where wax myrtle, yaupon holly, and witch hazel grow in profusion in the understory. The trail climbs up and over relict dunes, over a bridge through a needlerush marsh, and through coastal pine flatwoods before completing the loop.

Highlights: Enjoy panoramic views of the St. Johns River from several observation points, a visit to the reconstructed fort, and excellent interpretive signs depicting the interaction between the French, the Timucua, and the habitat.

Logistics: Fort Caroline is open 9:00–5:00 daily. Stop at the visitor center first for an overview of the important history of this region and of its varied coastal habitats. Restrooms are at the visitor center.

Other Activities: Drive to the end of Fort Caroline Road to visit the Ribault Monument, the site of the French landfall in Florida in 1562.

Theodore Roosevelt Area

Timucuan Ecological and Historical Preserve

NA-12 📖 👫 👫 🐕

Location: Jacksonville [N30°22.190' W081°28.992'].

Length: 1.5-mile to 4.2-mile loops in a network of trails.

Map: Posted at trailhead; available in brochure at kiosk.

Contact Information: National Park Service (904-251-3537), 12713 Fort Caroline Road, Jacksonville, FL 32225.

Directions: From SR 9A, take the Southside Connector exit and follow Fort Caroline Road 4.3 miles east to Mt. Pleasant Road. Continue straight on Mt. Pleasant Road for 1.2 miles to the "Theodore Roosevelt Area" sign on the left. Turn left through the second gate and drive down the entrance road to the parking area.

The Hike: Start out on the Willie Brown Trail, named for the generous man who deeded his family's settlement to the public as a preserve. Keep to the right at the next two forks to walk out to scenic Round Marsh. Return along the rugged Timucuan Trail through a cedar and oak forest atop a massive oyster shell midden, descending through coastal scrub into maritime hammock. The round-trip Spanish Pond Trail leads to an observation platform on the edge of the pond where, in 1565, Spanish soldiers camped on their way to attack Fort Caroline (along hike NA-11).

Highlights: Take in the panoramic views of the St. Johns River from the top of the midden (on the Timucuan Trail) and from the observation deck at the end of the Round Marsh Trail.

Logistics: The gate to the Theodore Roosevelt Area is an automatic gate, and its hours are posted—usually matching sunrise and sunset. Leave yourself ample time to exit before the gate closes. The Willie Brown Trail is shared with bicycles; the rest of the trails are not. It's possible to leave a car at the trailhead for the Spanish Pond Trail (off Fort Caroline Road) and walk one-way across the entire trail system.

Other Activities: There is a picnic area at the trailhead, and great birdwatching along both Spanish Pond and Round Marsh—bring your binoculars!

Kathryn Abbey Hanna Park

NA-13 $

Location: Mayport.

Length: 2.7-mile loop.

Map: Rough map in City of Jacksonville Department of Parks and Recreation's *Visitor's Guide to Oceanfront Parks*.

Contact Information: Kathryn Abbey Hanna Park (904-249-4700), 500 Wonderwood Drive, Jacksonville, FL 32333.

Directions: From downtown Jacksonville, take Atlantic Boulevard (SR 10) 12 miles east to A1A (Mayport Road). Drive 3.5 miles north on Mayport Road, continuing straight on SR 101 when A1A veers left. Turn right at Wonderwood Drive. After you pay your admission fee, drive all the way to the end of the entrance road to find the trailhead, and park by the sign that says "Trail G."

The Hike: Start your hike to the left of the parking area, following the orange blazes into the deep shade of the palm hammock. Paralleling (and sometimes crossing) an extensive system of biking trails, the hiking trail leads you through several lush palm hammocks, along sand-bottomed tannic streams, and through maritime hammocks and upland forest edging the shores of a large lake.

Highlights: Enjoy the view from the bluff above the lake, and savor the primordial feel of the palm hammocks, dense with ferns and yaupon holly. There is a pleasant picnic area just off the trail on an island in the Fish Management Area that the trail circles around.

Logistics: There is a $1 per person admission fee. To distinguish the hiking trail from the biking trail (since they often draw close together), the park has stenciled the letter H on many of the trees along the trail. Always look for the next H (and orange blazes) at trail intersections. Restrooms are not along the trail but are located at the beach crossovers.

Other Activities: An excellent mountain biking trail, both developed and primitive camping, fishing in the lakes, and miles of Atlantic Ocean beachfront are all here to enjoy.

Robert W. Loftin Nature Trails

University of North Florida Wildlife Sanctuary

NA-14 ⊔ ♿ 🚻

Location: South Jacksonville [N30°15.944' W081°30.694'].

Length: 4.9 miles in three loops: the Blueberry Trail (1.5 miles), the Goldenrod Trail (2.5 miles), and the wheelchair-accessible Red Maple Boardwalk (0.9 mile).

Map: Posted on trailhead kiosk and available in take-away brochure.

Contact Information: University of North Florida (904-620-2998), Department of Recreation, Division of Student Affairs, 4567 St. Johns Bluff Road, South Jacksonville 32224-2645.

Directions: From I-95 exit 344, drive east on J. Turner Butler Boulevard (SR 202). Exit on St. Johns Bluff Road north, and turn right into the first entrance to the University of North Florida. Park in the first parking lot on the right; parking fee is $2 weekdays, free on weekends.

The Hike: With three nested loops, the trail system around Lake Oneida offers plenty of options, from the short wheelchair-accessible portion of the scenic Red Maple Boardwalk to a 3-mile walk around the perimeter. The trails traverse a variety of habitats, from cypress swamps and hardwood hammocks along vernal streams to pine plantations and sandhills. Suggested midlength route: follow the Goldenrod Trail counterclockwise from the trailhead parking lot, and use the Blueberry Trail to loop around Lake Oneida.

Highlights: The humorous interpretive signs will have you laughing all the way around the loops. Stop and marvel at the 500-year-old cypress tree towering above the cypress swamp along the Goldenrod Trail; enjoy the views along Lake Oneida from the Red Maple Boardwalk and the Blueberry Trail.

Logistics: Colored arrows indicate which trail you're following at each junction: the Blueberry Trail in blue, the Goldenrod Trail in yellow, and the Red Maple Trail in red. No bicycles or dogs are permitted. Expect to run into some minor mucky spots along the southern portions of the Goldenrod Trail and the central Blueberry Trail.

Other Activities: Fish from the bridge to the island; picnic in the picnic grove along the lakeshore or on the island.

Hiking the trails at the University of North Florida Wildlife Sanctuary.

Stokes Landing Conservation Area

NA-15 📖 🚸 🐕

Location: St. Augustine [N29°59.993' W081°21.654'].

Length: 3-mile network of trails, with a minimum 0.5-mile loop.

Map: Displayed at trailhead kiosk and available in St. Johns River Water Management District's *Recreation Guide to District Lands.*

Contact Information: St. Johns River Water Management District (904-529-2380), PO Box 1429, Palatka, FL 32178-1429.

Directions: From St. Augustine, drive 6 miles north on US 1, past the airport, to Venetian Boulevard on the right. Follow Venetian Boulevard 0.3 mile to Old Dixie Drive. Turn right, then left on Lakeshore Drive, continuing 0.7 mile to the parking area on the right.

The Hike: Laid out by a Boy Scout troop, the trail system mainly utilizes forest roads to explore several habitats, from (wet) coastal pine flatwoods to oak hammocks, maritime hammock, saltwater estuary, and freshwater marshes. The Raccoon Run Loop is the main loop trail, with a spur trail, Marsh Point, leading off through the wet flatwoods to the edge of the estuary, and an unnamed spur trail to the north ending along a picnic area on a tidal creek.

Highlights: This hike offers panoramic views of the Tolomato River estuary, especially from the observation tower and the picnic area.

Logistics: The trails are blazed with white diamonds. Expect wet walking out to Marsh Point.

Other Activities: Birdwatchers have great opportunities on the observation tower and at the picnic area as well as the loop trail around the marsh near the parking area.

Guana River State Park

NA-16 📖 🚻 ⚐ ❄

Location: South Ponte Vedra Beach [N30°01.375' W081°19.741'].

Length: 9-mile perimeter loop enclosing a network of trails.

Map: Posted and in brochure at trailhead kiosk.

Contact Information: Guana River State Park (904-825-5071), 2690 South Ponte Vedra Boulevard, Ponte Vedra Beach, FL 32082.

Directions: From St. Augustine, follow A1A north from San Marco Boulevard through Vilano Beach into South Ponte Vedra Beach; the park entrance is on the right after 9.5 miles. Drive to the far end of the parking area and walk down the road across the dam to the treeline to find the trailhead.

The Hike: Circling a peninsula of land between the Guana River and the Tolomato River, the trail system (hiked clockwise) provides a breezy walk through maritime forests, a stroll on a bluff above the river and around salt marshes, and immersion in older pine flatwoods and oak hammocks before entering a mosaic of scrub, scrubby flatwoods, and open savannas at the north end of the peninsula.

Highlights: Explore the historic site of the first Spanish mission in the New World, flanked by Timucuan middens. Breathe the stiff salt breezes across the salt marshes. Enjoy the views along the Tolomato River, and the sheer variety of habitats traversed on this hike. Take a side trip, too: follow the middle Gray Trail from marker 3 briefly into Guana River WMA for a sweeping view of a freshwater savanna busy with wading birds foraging and roosting.

Logistics: All trails bear the names of colors. Although shared with bicyclists, the trails are in good shape. The three Gray trails lead into the adjacent Guana River WMA, which has its own system of blazed forest roads separate from the state park. Frequent benches, including several at key scenic points, add to the pleasure of walking the perimeter loop. The map is keyed to numbered trail marker posts that help you determine where you are.

Other Activities: Guana River State Park has several miles of beaches, farther north on A1A, plus launch points for canoes and kayaks, and bank fishing along the dam.

Ancient Dunes Trail

Anastasia State Park

NA-17 $ 📖 🚻 🅰 👫 🐕

Location: St. Augustine Beach [N29°52.006' W081°16.569'].

Length: 0.7-mile loop.

Map: Rough map in state park brochure.

Contact Information: Anastasia State Park (904-461-2033), 1340A A1A South, St. Augustine, FL 32080.

Directions: From old St. Augustine, follow A1A across the Bridge of Lions and continue 1.9 miles to the park entrance, on the left just past the St. Augustine Alligator Farm. Once inside the park, follow the park road to the campground; turn right and follow the campground road to its end at the parking area.

The Hike: Turn right at the trail sign to walk counterclockwise along the loop through a maritime hammock, climbing over dunes and through deep swales beneath the forest canopy. Massive southern magnolias and slash pines enter the botanical mix. Some of the dunes are so steep there are staircases to traverse them.

Highlights: The steep ups and downs make for fun hiking along this deeply shaded trail.

Logistics: Parking is limited at the trailhead; you may have to walk in from the parking area near the lagoon. Keep alert to where the trail leads, as side trails link to the campground.

Other Activities: This is a very popular park for near-the-beach camping, surfing, sailboarding, and fishing. The 8-mile round-trip walk along the beach out to a promontory overlooking St. Augustine is one of the most peaceful and pleasant beach walks in the state.

Moses Creek Conservation Area

NA-18 🛶 🏕

Location: Dupont Center [N29°45.440' W081°16.537'].

Length: 14 miles of linear trails.

Map: Displayed at trailhead kiosk and available in St. Johns River Water Management District's *Recreation Guide to District Lands.*

Contact Information: St. Johns River Water Management District (904-529-2380), PO Box 1429, Palatka, FL 32178-1429.

Directions: From I-95 exit 305, drive east 2.2 miles on SR 206 to Dupont Center, where you cross US 1. Continue 1.2 miles to the second trailhead on the left.

The Hike: Starting at the east trailhead (the west trailhead appears to be primarily for equestrian use), follow the blazes along a linear trail through scrubby flatwoods and scrub with side spurs to scenic views at Braddock's Point (the Youth Camping Area) and along the bluffs of Moses Creek. A connector trail ties into the equestrian trail system to lead out to the far end of the preserve, which is in scrubby flatwoods and maritime hammock along the salt flats of the Matanzas River.

Highlights: Enjoy scenic views from the bluffs. If you backpack out to the Murat Point campsite, you'll have a commanding view of the river and its estuaries.

Logistics: Expect soft sand where the two trail systems converge. If you walk out to the far end of the preserve, you'll have to wade across Moses Creek, normally ankle deep. Backpackers should carry plenty of water and pack out all trash.

Other Activities: Most of the trails are primarily used by equestrians. There is great birding from the bluffs along Moses Creek, as you overlook vast stretches of estuary. Bicycles are permitted but won't be able to traverse the soft sand in the scrub.

Accessible Nature Trail

Fort Matanzas National Monument

NA-19 📖 🚻 ♿ 🚼

Location: Crescent Beach [N29°42.916' W081°14.039'].

Length: 0.5-mile loop.

Map: Displayed and available in interpretive brochure at kiosk.

Contact Information: Fort Matanzas National Monument (904-471-0116), 8635 A1A South, St. Augustine, FL 32080.

Directions: From I-95 exit 305, Crescent Beach/Hastings, drive east on SR 206 to Crescent Beach. Turn south on A1A and continue several miles to the park entrance on the right, before the Matanzas Inlet bridge.

The Hike: A wheelchair-accessible boardwalk loop that lifts you over the sensitive coastal dune hammock, this shady trail provides a bird's-eye view of the forest floor and offers several observation areas along the tidal marsh for birding along Matanzas Inlet.

Highlights: Interpretive signs give you a good deal of information on the plants of the maritime hammock and on the history of Matanzas Inlet, where Pedro Menéndez de Aviles slaughtered captured French colonists from Fort Caroline.

Logistics: The boardwalk ends briefly to cross a service road; wheelchairs may need minor assistance across this section. Frequent benches make this a comfortable stroll, as do the persistent coastal breezes.

Other Activities: Board the ferry to Fort Matanzas (fee) to explore the fort and its important history lesson about the French and Spanish colonization of Florida in the 1500s.

Nature Trail

Faver-Dykes State Park

NA-20 $ 📖 🚻 Ⓐ 🧒 🐴

Location: Colfax [N29°40.198' W081°15.538'].

Length: 0.5-mile loop.

Map: Rough map in brochure available at kiosk at park entrance.

Contact Information: Faver-Dykes State Park (904-794-0997), 1000 Faver Dykes Road, St. Augustine, FL 32086.

Directions: From I-95 exit 298, drive north on US 1 to the first road on the right, Faver Dykes Road, located between two gas stations at the interchange. Follow the road for 1.5 miles to the park entrance. From the park entrance, continue along the one-way dirt road to a T intersection; turn right and make a right turn at the fork. The trailhead parking is on the right. Do not block the road leading back to the campsites.

The Hike: Starting behind the campsites, this short interpretive nature trail leads you along a footpath thick in pine duff through coastal pine flatwoods where yaupon, low-bush blueberry, wax myrtle, and saw palmetto dominate the understory. At 0.3 mile you reach the loop portion of the trail; follow the loop around a peninsula along the salt marsh.

Highlights: A bench provides a sweeping view of the Pellicer Creek salt marshes, a great spot for birdwatching. Pay close attention to the slash pines along the walk—some of them are enormous. The trail is broad and level and carpeted in pine needles.

Logistics: To find the trailhead, walk the road past the campsites to the second "Nature Trail" sign along the treeline near the salt marsh.

Other Activities: This is a paddlers' playground, popular for exploration of the salt marshes. A picnic pavilion and playground are across from the trailhead, with a fishing pier and launch point for kayaks and canoes nearby.

Mala Compra Trail

Washington Oaks Gardens State Park

NA-21 $ 📖 🚻 👫 🐕

Location: Hammock [N29°37.827' W081°12.541'].

Length: 0.7 mile round-trip.

Map: Park trails map available from ranger.

Contact Information: Washington Oaks Gardens State Park (386-446-6780), 6400 Oceanside Boulevard, Palm Coast, FL 32137.

Directions: The park is along the west side of A1A, south of Marineland and 4.1 miles north of the Hammock Dunes Bridge at Palm Coast. Drive in on the park entrance road and park at the Gardens parking area. The trailhead is just south of the visitor center.

The Hike: Paralleling the Matanzas River, the Mala Compra Trail leads you through a maritime hammock of cedar, red bay, live oaks, and cabbage palms. A spur trail with a fishing symbol sign leads out to a small mangrove-lined island in the river. The trail ends at the park's large picnic area beneath a canopy of oaks.

Highlights: Sit at the picnic table along the shoreline of the Matanzas River and watch the wading birds busily looking for their meals.

Logistics: Return along the same path for a 0.7-mile round trip.

Other Activities: Enjoy the picnic grove, stop at the visitor center, walk through the historic gardens, walk the Bella Vista Trail (NA-22), and don't miss the coquina beach across A1A, one of Florida's rare and scenic rocky shorelines.

Bella Vista Trail

Washington Oaks Gardens State Park

NA-22 **F** $ ▢ 🛉🛉 👫 🐾

Location: Hammock [N29°38.055' W081°12.515'].

Length: 1.8-mile loop.

Map: Park trails map available from ranger; detailed map available from Florida Trail Association.

Contact Information: Washington Oaks Gardens State Park (386-446-6780), 6400 Oceanside Boulevard, Palm Coast, FL 32137.

Directions: The park is along the west side of A1A, south of Marineland and 4.1 miles north of the Hammock Dunes Bridge at Palm Coast. Drive in on the park entrance road and park by the Bella Vista trailhead on the right.

The Hike: The trail leads you along the white-blazed Timucuan Loop through a shady maritime hammock of red bay, southern magnolia, and cabbage palms, crossing the pavement of old A1A before rising up into an oak hammock where the trees are shaped and gnarled by the constant coastal breezes. After entering an upland forest of holly and pines, you pass an enormous slash pine before emerging into an open, windswept coastal scrub. The trail continues along the loop to drop down into the maritime hammock again, crossing old A1A a second time before paralleling the Matanzas River to complete the loop.

Highlights: It's a pleasant walk all the way around. Note the massive slash pine in the upland forest, and pause at an overlook along the mangrove-lined shores of the Matanzas River.

Logistics: Old A1A, which cuts through the center of the trail loop, can be used as a shortcut and is open to bicycling. Restrooms are at the visitor center.

Other Activities: Stop at the visitor center, walk through the historic gardens, walk the Mala Compra Trail (NA-21) to a picnic grove along the Intracoastal Waterway, and don't miss the coquina beach across A1A, one of Florida's rare and scenic rocky shorelines.

Malacompra County Park

NA-23 🚻 🐕

Location: Hammock [N29°37.033' W081°11.469'].

Length: 0.5 mile loop.

Map: None available.

Contact Information: Flagler County Parks and Recreation (386-437-7490), 1200 East Moody Boulevard #3, Bunnell, FL 32110.

Directions: Drive 1.4 miles south of Washington Oaks Gardens State Park (hikes NA-21 and NA-22) to Malacompra Road; turn left at the Sea Breeze Sweet Shop. Follow the road for 0.7 mile to Malacompra County Park and turn left; park at the far end of the lot, past the restrooms.

The Hike: From the "No Motorized Vehicles" sign, follow the relatively straight and narrow sand-and-shell footpath along the coastal strand, just out of sight of the ocean amid the dense saw palmetto. After 0.2 mile the trail comes to a fork. To the left is a connector to the local community; keep right to climb up and over the dunes and out onto the beach. Return along the orange sand beach to create a loop.

Highlights: Savor the great sea breezes and the sound of the surf—and the opportunity to walk along one of Florida's few rocky shores. Here the Anastasia limestone formation outcrops in what is said to be the longest continuous stretch of rocky beach in Florida. (See hike SA-27 at Blowing Rocks Preserve for another major Anastasia limestone outcrop.)

Logistics: Only leashed pets are permitted. The footpath is in full sun, so use adequate sun protection.

Other Activities: Enjoy the beach for sunning and fishing, but swimming should be avoided because of the hidden rocks.

Red Trail / Orange Trail

Princess Place Preserve

NA-24 📖 ⛺

Location: Colfax [N29°39.142' W081°14.939'].

Length: 2.2-mile or 1.7-mile loop.

Map: Displayed at trailhead kiosk.

Contact Information: Flagler County Parks and Recreation (386-437-7490), 1200 East Moody Boulevard #3, Bunnell, FL 32110.

Directions: From I-95 exit 298, drive south on US 1 for 1.7 miles to Old Kings Road. Turn left and follow the road for 1.5 miles to the sign for Princess Place Preserve. Turn left and continue 1.6 miles to the parking area on the left. Start your hike at the trail kiosk and walk straight back to the first trail marker to follow the loop.

The Hike: This series of two nested loops leads you through habitats along the edge of Pellicer Creek, from sandhills to scrub and scrubby flatwoods. The decision point is at 0.7 mile: turn left for the shortcut Orange Trail, or right for the outer Red Trail loop, which leads you down to Pellicer Creek, providing nice views. The outer loop continues through oak scrub and past a freshwater marsh before rejoining the Orange Trail, then heads through an equestrian group campsite and open meadow to complete the loop.

Highlights: Observation decks overlook both the brackish estuary of Pellicer Creek and a freshwater marsh amid the pine flatwoods.

Logistics: The preserve is open Wed–Sun 9:00–5:00. Call ahead to reserve a site in the campground (tent camping only). Arrow-topped posts, with arrows painted the color of the trail name, serve as trail markers.

Other Activities: Tour the historic Cherokee Lodge and its grounds, which include Florida's first in-ground swimming pool (circa 1890), launch your kayak at the picnic area and explore the estuary between here and Faver-Dykes State Park (NA-20), or explore the other trails (NA-25 and NA-26) in the preserve. Equestrian trails, blazed with white diamonds, lead to adjacent Pellicer Creek Conservation Area and the new land bridge over I-95.

Blue Trail

Princess Place Preserve

NA-25

Location: Colfax [N29°39.472' W081°14.376'].

Length: 1-mile loop.

Map: Displayed at trailhead kiosk.

Contact Information: Flagler County Parks and Recreation (386-437-7490), 1200 East Moody Boulevard #3, Bunnell, FL 32110.

Directions: From I-95 exit 298, drive south on US 1 for 1.7 miles to Old Kings Road. Turn left and follow the road for 1.5 miles to the sign for Princess Place Preserve. Turn left and continue 2 miles to the parking area in front of the environmental education center.

The Hike: Leaving the environmental center, walk behind it and straight across through the oaks to the kiosk on the far side of the road. This short trail makes a loop through the upland forest and out to the edge of the estuary along Pellicer Creek.

Highlights: There is an observation deck at the confluence of Stiles Creek and Pellicer Creek, from which you can see kayakers slipping through watery corridors between the tall needlerush and observe birds wading through the marsh.

Logistics: The preserve is open Wed–Sun 9:00–5:00. Call ahead to reserve a site in the campground (tent camping only). Arrow-topped posts, with arrows painted the color of the trail name, serve as trail markers. Restrooms are near the carriage house by Cherokee Lodge.

Other Activities: Tour the historic Cherokee Lodge and its grounds, which include Florida's first in-ground swimming pool (circa 1890), launch your kayak at the picnic area and explore the estuary between here and Faver-Dykes State Park (NA-20), or explore the other trails (NA-24 and NA-26) in the preserve. Equestrian trails, blazed with white diamonds, lead to adjacent Pellicer Creek Conservation Area and the new land bridge over I-95.

Green Trail

Princess Place Preserve

NA-26 ⊔ △ ⛺

Location: Colfax [N29°39.420' W081°14.079'].

Length: 0.8-mile loop (or linear trip to campground).

Map: Displayed at trailhead kiosk.

Contact Information: Flagler County Parks and Recreation (386- 437-7490), 1200 East Moody Boulevard #3, Bunnell, FL 32110.

Directions: From I-95 exit 298, drive south on US 1 for 1.7 miles to Old Kings Road. Turn left and follow the road for 1.5 miles to the sign for Princess Place Preserve. Turn left and continue 2 miles, driving past the environmental education center to the turnoff on the right for the campground. Immediately turn left at the "Hiking Trailhead" sign and follow this one-lane road down past the canoe put-in to a parking area in front of the Green Trail kiosk.

The Hike: Follow the white posts (missing their green arrows) up the road and into the maritime hammock on the right, where a variety of trees flourish, providing a shady canopy. The trail reaches its loop at a pond after 0.3 mile; turn right to walk counterclockwise around this sulfur-spring-fed pond. A side trail leads to the campground. Continue around the pond and retrace your incoming path to exit.

Highlights: Numerous interpretive markers provide plant identifications of more unusual species (as well as the common ones), and the geyserlike artesian spring is interesting.

Logistics: The preserve is open Wed–Sun 9:00–5:00. Call ahead to reserve a site in the campground (tent camping only).

Other Activities: Tour the historic Cherokee Lodge and its grounds, which include Florida's first in-ground swimming pool (circa 1890), launch your kayak at the picnic area and explore the estuary between here and Faver-Dykes State Park (NA-20), or explore the other trails (NA-24 and NA-25) in the preserve. Equestrian trails, blazed with white diamonds, lead to adjacent Pellicer Creek Conservation Area and the new land bridge over I- 95.

Graham Swamp Conservation Area

NA-27 🏕

Location: Palm Coast [N29°32.257' W081°12.364'].

Length: 1 mile in two loops.

Map: Displayed at trailhead kiosk and available in St. Johns River Water Management District's *Recreation Guide to District Lands*.

Contact Information: St. Johns River Water Management District (904-529-2380), PO Box 1429, Palatka, FL 32178-1429.

Directions: From I-95 exit 289 in Palm Coast, drive east on the Palm Coast Parkway and turn right on Old Kings Road. Continue south 1.4 miles to the trailhead on the left.

The Hike: The red-blazed trail leads you along the south shore of a large pond in the sand pine scrub and into a cypress swamp, where the trail follows a waterway to another patch of sand pine scrub surrounding two more ponds. The trail briefly enters the shady lowlands along the cypress swamp as it passes a primitive campsite along the far loop.

Highlights: This is a rare freshwater basin only two miles from the Atlantic Ocean, with shady cypress floodplain forests and two beautiful lakes surrounded by sand pine scrub. Coontie grows in profusion in the understory.

Logistics: It's a good spot for a beginner's backpacking trip, to test out your gear. On the return loop around the first pond, be careful when crossing the outflow into the swamp. Alligators have been spotted sunning along both ponds. Expect mosquitoes all summer. Be cautious of the steep slopes down to the ponds.

Other Activities: Fishing is permitted along the ponds.

Wadsworth Park

NA-28 👫 ♿ 👫 🐕

Location: Flagler Beach [N29°28.803' W081°08.572'].

Length: 0.2 mile round-trip.

Map: None available.

Contact Information: Flagler County Parks and Recreation (386-437-7490), 1200 East Moody Boulevard #3, Bunnell, FL 32110.

Directions: From I-95 exit 284, Flagler Beach, drive 2.5 miles east on SR 100 to the park entrance on the left, just before the Intracoastal Waterway bridge. Keep right at both forks along the park road to follow the road around to the soccer field area, where the boardwalk starts.

The Hike: Look for the "Boardwalk and Canoe Launch" sign. This short wooden boardwalk drops down out of the pine flatwoods to follow a tidal creek, where the canoe launch juts out to allow put-in. The boardwalk continues winding its way through a palm hammock to the edge of the salt marshes, ending at an overlook.

Highlights: It's a great spot for birding. Don't miss the other (noncontiguous) section of the boardwalk, which goes over a freshwater pond filled with lilies; it starts directly across the parking area from the estuarine boardwalk.

Logistics: The park is open from 8:00 a.m. to 11 p.m. daily.

Other Activities: This is a large county park with a playground, batting cages, soccer and baseball fields, tennis courts, picnic pavilions, a skateboarding complex, and a special "Paw Park" for dogs. Unmarked trails lead through the dense forest behind the skateboarding complex.

Joe Kenner Nature Trail

Gamble Rogers Memorial State Recreation Area

NA-29 $ 📖 👫 🅐 👫 🐴

Location: Flagler Beach [N29°26.242' W081°06.559'].

Length: 0.7-mile loop.

Map: Rough map in park brochure available at ranger station.

Contact Information: Gamble Rogers Memorial State Park (386-517-2086), 3100 South A1A, Flagler Beach, FL 32136.

Directions: From I-95 exit 284, Flagler Beach / Bunnell, follow SR 100 west 3 miles to Flagler Beach. Turn south on A1A and continue 2 miles to park entrance on the right. Follow the park entrance road around to the right down a narrow dirt road along the waterway; park in the small parking area on the left.

The Hike: Named for a former interpretive guide with Florida State Parks, the beautiful Joe Kenner Trail treats you to an immersion in the maritime hammock habitat. Saw palmettos line the shady corridor, and yaupon and coontie rise from the forest floor. Watch for the spill of crushed shells in several places indicating where the trail clambers up and over middens. After 0.2 mile the loop begins, crossing a forest road several times and emerging briefly onto the open flats next to the Intracoastal Waterway before heading back into the densely vegetated forest.

Highlights: The trail is incredibly scenic for being almost entirely under a dense forest canopy. Walking through a shady tunnel of windswept live oaks, you will have to duck in places!

Logistics: The restrooms are right next to the trailhead. Frequent benches make this a pleasant stroll for all ages.

Other Activities: There's oceanfront camping and an orange sand beach across the street. A boat ramp and fishing pier adjoin the picnic area.

Bulow Creek Trail

Bulow Plantation Ruins Historic State Park/ Bulow Creek State Park

NA-30 **F** **$** 📖 🚻 Ⓒ 🐕 ❄️

Location: Ormond Beach [N29°26.094' W081°08.279'].

Length: 4-mile loop, 6.8 miles linear, or 13.4 miles round-trip, plus short nature trails at each end.

Map: Rough map in park brochure; detailed backpacking map available from Florida Trail Association.

Contact Information: Bulow Plantation Ruins State Park (386-517-2084), PO Box 655, Bunnell, FL 32110.

Directions: From I-95 exit 90, follow Old Dixie Highway east for 0.9 mile to Old Kings Road. Drive north 1.9 miles to Bulow Plantation Ruins State Park. Turn right. The trailhead sits just outside the park gate. To Bulow Creek State Park, follow Old Dixie Highway several miles, passing Walter Boardman Road before coming to the park entrance on the left.

The Hike: From the park gate, the trail winds through dense old-growth forest with a high canopy of large live oaks. Keep to the orange blazes when you reach the loop junction for a walk along a primeval creek and views of the marshes. Returning along Cisco Ditch, turn right to follow the blue-blazed loop (if hiking the loop) or left to continue past Boardman Pond, with its observation deck, following forest roads through pine plantations and hydric hammock and across a salt marsh to end up in front of the immense Fairchild Oak at Bulow Creek State Park.

Highlights: Plantation ruins, old-growth forest, giant-leather-fern-lined creek, dense undergrowth of wild coontie, birding on Boardman Pond, the 2,000-year-old Fairchild Oak.

Logistics: The trail can be hiked either as a scenic loop starting at the Bulow Plantation Ruins park gate, as a 6.8-mile one-way trip by parking a second car at Bulow Creek State Park, or as a 13.4-mile backpacking trip, utilizing the primitive campsite on Bulow Creek.

Other Activities: There's birding at Boardman Pond, and a canoe rental and put-in at Bulow Plantation Ruins. Interpretive trails include the Sugar Mill Trail (1-mile loop) at the historic site and Wahlin Trail (0.3-mile loop) at the Fairchild Oak.

Haw Creek Preserve

NA-31 📖 🚻 ⛺ 👥

Location: Bunnell [N29°23.703' W081°22.970'].

Length: 1.6 miles round-trip.

Map: None available.

Contact Information: Flagler County Parks and Recreation (386-437-7490), 1200 East Moody Boulevard #3, Bunnell, FL 32110.

Directions: From US 1 in Bunnell, follow SR 100 for 7.5 miles to SR 305. Turn left and drive south for 4.1 miles to CR 2006. Turn right and drive 1 mile, then left onto CR 2007, a dirt road that ends after 2.2 miles at Russell Landing, where the trail starts.

The Hike: This is a pleasant boardwalk through a floodplain forest of cypress, sweet gum, and red maple along the banks of Haw Creek, ending after 0.8 mile at a large grassy field with a group campsite tucked away on the far side behind an old gray building with a tin roof.

Highlights: There are numerous observation decks along the creek to help you spot alligators and watch the activities of wading birds. A patch of wild iris blooms in spring. Watch for migratory swallow-tailed kites that nest and roost in this area.

Logistics: It's possible to make a loop hike out of this walk by returning on a forest road from the clearing at the end of the boardwalk, but the road may be wet or under water in places as it passes through the floodplain forest. To reserve the tenting campsite, contact the county in advance of your visit.

Other Activities: There is a boat launch and picnic area at the trailhead. Paddling is not recommended, given the heavy alligator concentration.

Central Gulf

Citrus, Hernando, Pasco, Pinellas, Hillsborough

Virgin slash pine flatwoods, Caladesi Island.

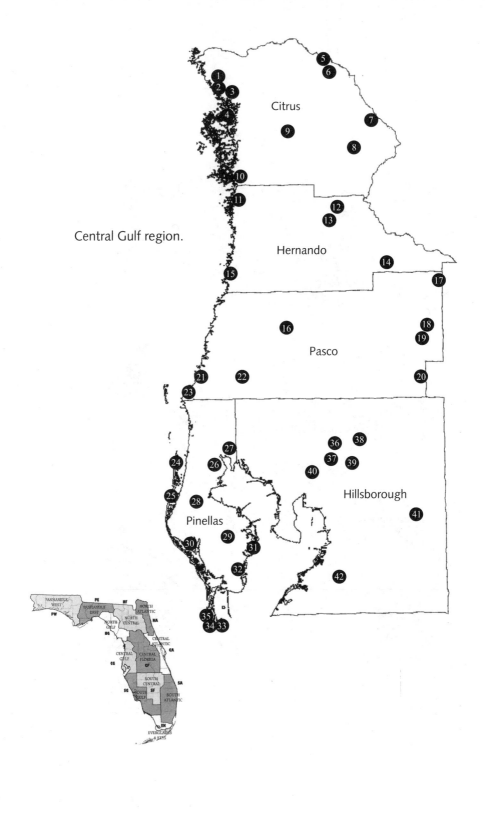

Central Gulf region.

Citrus
- CG-1 Ecowalk, Crystal River Preserve State Park
- CG-2 Eagle Scout Trail, Crystal River Preserve State Park
- CG-3 Churchhouse Hammock Trail, Crystal River Preserve State Park
- CG-4 Redfish Hole, Crystal River Preserve State Park
- CG-5 Oxbow Trails, Two Mile Prairie Tract, Withlacoochee State Forest
- CG-6 Johnson Pond Trail, Two Mile Prairie Tract, Withlacoochee State Forest
- CG-7 Potts Preserve
- CG-8 Fort Cooper State Park
- CG-9 Citrus Hiking Trail, Citrus Tract, Withlacoochee State Forest
- CG-10 Rooks Trail, Homosassa Tract, Withlacoochee State Forest

Hernando
- CG-11 Chassahowitzka Wildlife Management Area
- CG-12 Perry Oldenburg Mitigation Park
- CG-13 McKethan Lake Nature Trail, Withlacoochee State Forest
- CG-14 Croom Hiking Trail, Croom Tract, Withlacoochee State Forest
- CG-15 Weekiwachee Preserve

Pasco
- CG-16 Crews Lake Park
- CG-17 Florida Trail, Richloam Tract, Withlacoochee State Forest
- CG-18 Florida Trail, Green Swamp West
- CG-19 Withlacoochee River Park
- CG-20 Upper Hillsborough River Hiking Trail, Upper Hillsborough River Water Management Area
- CG-21 Nature Trail, Werner-Boyce Salt Springs State Park
- CG-22 J. B. Starkey Wilderness Park
- CG-23 Key Vista Nature Park

Pinellas
- CG-24 Caladesi Island State Park
- CG-25 Honeymoon Island State Park
- CG-26 John Chesnut Sr. County Park
- CG-27 Brooker Creek Preserve
- CG-28 Moccasin Lake Nature Park
- CG-29 Sawgrass Lake Park
- CG-30 Boca Ciega Millennium Park
- CG-31 Weedon Island Preserve
- CG-32 Boyd Hill Nature Park
- CG-33 Barrier Free Nature Trail, Fort De Soto Park
- CG-34 Soldiers Hole Trail, Fort De Soto Park
- CG-35 Arrowhead Nature Trail, Fort De Soto Park

Hillsborough

CG-36 Morris Bridge Park
CG-37 Trout Creek Park
CG-38 Hillsborough River State Park
CG-39 J. B. Sargeant Sr. Memorial Wilderness Park
CG-40 Lettuce Lake Park
CG-41 Alderman's Ford Park
CG-42 Little Manatee River State Park

Ecowalk

Crystal River Preserve State Park

CG-1 📖 👫 🐕

Location: Crystal River [N28°55.143' W082°38.069'].

Length: 2.3-mile loop.

Map: Displayed and in brochure at trailhead kiosk.

Contact Information: Crystal River Preserve State Park (352-563-0450), 3266 North Sailboat Avenue, Crystal River, FL 34428.

Directions: Northbound on US 19 from Crystal River, turn left on State Park Road and make an immediate right on North Tallahassee Road. Drive 2.4 miles to the park entrance on the left. From southbound US 19, turn right on Curtis Tool Road; the park entrance is immediately north on North Tallahassee Road.

The Hike: A pleasant broad mowed path leads you through oak hammocks past an incredible interpretive display. Not only are there plant identifications and habitat information, this very special trail has carved wooden interpretive stations that encourage you to pause and use your senses to connect with the environment around you.

Highlights: Pause and look for turtles and frogs at The Spring and Turtle Pond; enjoy the palm hammock at the Sabal Palm Oasis.

Logistics: Sign the trail register before you start, and follow the yellow arrows around the one-way loop.

Other Activities: Fish at the quarry (follow the limerock Quarry Trail) or bike the 9-mile Loop Trail.

Eagle Scout Trail

Crystal River Preserve State Park

CG-2 ⚐

Location: Crystal River [N28°54.925' W082°38.074'].

Length: 0.5 mile linear.

Map: None available.

Contact Information: Crystal River Preserve State Park (352-563-0450), 3266 North Sailboat Avenue, Crystal River, FL 34428.

Directions: From US 19 north of Crystal River, turn left on State Park Road and follow it into the preserve. When the road makes a sharp left turn, turn left and watch for the trailhead parking on the left, just beyond the trailhead.

The Hike: It's a rugged trail through a dense palm hammock along the Crystal River estuary, linking the 9-mile Loop Trail (primarily used by bikers) with additional riding along a limerock road.

Highlights: Carved into the deep shade of the palm hammock, this is a trail more suitable for a stroll than for the bikers who use it as a connector!

Logistics: The parking lot is beyond the trailhead. Follow the arrows back along the road to the trailhead.

Other Activities: The 9-mile Loop Trail (for mountain biking) heads north to connect with the Ecowalk (CG-1). Don't miss the excellent visitor's center at the end of State Park Road.

Churchhouse Hammock Trail

Crystal River Preserve State Park

CG-3 [👫] [♿] [🚻]

Location: Crystal River [N28 54.655' W82 36.450'].

Length: 0.3-mile boardwalk plus 0.7-mile loop trail.

Map: None available.

Contact Information: Crystal River Preserve State Park (352-563-0450), 3266 North Sailboat Avenue, Crystal River, FL 34428.

Directions: Directly across from the Crystal River Mall on US 19, north of downtown Crystal River.

The Hike: A wheelchair-accessible wooden boardwalk leads into junglelike cabbage palm flatwoods on the fringe of the Crystal River estuary north of Kings Bay, with a staircase to access the rugged portion of the trail that meanders through a bottomland hardwood forest with coontie and ferns in the understory and a lot of surface limestone. A side trail leads to an overlook.

Highlights: It's a pleasant walk through a shady palm hammock, with an overlook on the Crystal River estuary. Note the catfaced pines along the trail, indicators of this once being a turpentine plantation.

Logistics: Note the "Entrance" and "Exit" signs: although they imply a one-way trail, the trail is signposted in both directions. The trail system is still under construction and will eventually lead across boardwalks to an island in Crystal River. Follow the arrows to stay on the trail.

Other Activities: Picnic at the pavilion, birdwatch along the walkways.

Redfish Hole Trail

Crystal River Preserve State Park

CG-4 ✯✯

Location: Crystal River [N28°53.838' W082°37.159'].

Length: 1.6 miles round-trip.

Map: None available.

Contact Information: Crystal River Preserve State Park (352-563-0450), 3266 North Sailboat Avenue, Crystal River, FL 34428.

Directions: From US 19 south of downtown Crystal River, take Fort Island Trail west 3.8 miles to the trailhead parking area on the left.

The Hike: One of the most scenic hikes in this area, the Redfish Hole Trail follows a series of embankments around tidal flats, with sweeping views of the vast needlerush marshes and palm hammocks of the Crystal River estuary. Adding a bridge would make this a great loop hike; meanwhile, the trail stops abruptly where the berm ends along a tidal creek, and you must retrace your steps back to the trailhead.

Highlights: Look for a lone young mangrove rooting itself in the fine silt along the embankment. The estuary views are spectacular, and there are always shorebirds wading in the flats.

Logistics: This trail, open sunrise to sunset, has little shade; wear a hat and sunscreen. Blue arrow markers delineate the route. Although leashed pets are permitted, be aware that alligators do frequent these waterways, and a 'gator slide crosses the trail at one point.

Other Activities: This is a great site for birdwatching, and fishing is permitted.

Oxbow Trails

Two Mile Prairie Tract, Withlacoochee State Forest

CG-5 ⚐ ⛺

Location: Citrus Springs [N29°00.349' W082°23.268'].

Length: 1 mile in two loops.

Map: Map displayed and rough map available in brochure at trailhead kiosk.

Contact Information: Withlacoochee State Forest (352-754-6896), 15003 Broad Street, Brooksville, FL 34601.

Directions: Follow CR 39 south from US 41 in Citrus Springs or north from SR 200 at the Withlacoochee River; the trailhead is 2.5 miles north of SR 200, on the east side of the road.

The Hike: Meandering around a cypress swamp in a floodplain levee above the Withlacoochee River, the Oxbow Loop Trail leads out to campsites and picnic tables along the river bluffs. The Oxbow Nature Trail starts at the western campsite and creates a rugged loop in deep shade along a peninsula formed by an oxbow in the river.

Highlights: This trail provides great views of the Withlacoochee River near its confluence with the Rainbow River. Both sides of the river are protected land, and the cypresses are massive along the river banks.

Logistics: Be aware of river conditions, as the entire oxbow floods when the river is high. This is a floodplain area with a large number of mosquitoes.

Other Activities: There is tent camping and a canoe launch along the river beach.

Johnson Pond Trail

Two Mile Prairie Tract, Withlacoochee State Forest

CG-6 📖 👬 🐴

Location: Citrus Springs [N29°00.308' W082°23.044'].

Length: 2.7-mile loop.

Map: Displayed and in brochure at trailhead kiosk.

Contact Information: Withlacoochee State Forest (352-754-6896), 15003 Broad Street, Brooksville, FL 34601.

Directions: From SR 200 immediately west of the Withlacoochee River, drive north for 2.6 miles on CR 39 to the trailhead on the left.

The Hike: Starting at the kiosk, pass through the split-rail fence and follow the trail as it swings left onto a jeep road to rise into the sandhill habitat. Stay to the broad road at the fork, and it leads you after 0.7 mile to Johnson Pond, a cypress-lined pond dotted with lilies. The trail follows the edge of the pond, behind a screen of cypresses, as it continues through a pine plantation and a live oak hammock, briefly sharing the footpath with a blue-blazed horse trail. It winds through several stretches of rosemary scrub and ascends into a forest of longleaf pine and wiregrass before completing the loop.

Highlights: There are pretty patches of rosemary scrub amid the sandhills, and the expanse of Johnson Pond to enjoy, as well as showy wildflowers in the wiregrass.

Logistics: Be alert at trail crossings for the next orange blaze. Several benches along the way provide rest stops.

Other Activities: There is a picnic bench at the trailhead and near Johnson Pond. The observation deck at Johnson Pond is a popular place for birding. Equestrian and bicycle trails start from a trailhead off CR 491 on the south end of the tract.

Potts Preserve

CG-7 🅕 ⛺

Location: Inverness [N28°54.548' W082°16.764'].

Length: Several loops from 3.5 to 12.3 miles.

Map: See Southwest Florida Water Management District Recreational Guide; detailed backpacking map available from Florida Trail Association.

Contact Information: Southwest Florida Water Management District (800-423-1476), 2379 Broad Street, Brooksville, FL 34604.

Directions: From US 41 north of Inverness, take CR 581 east for 6.8 miles to Hooty Point Road. Turn right; the trailhead is 0.3 mile on the left.

The Hike: There are several loops within the preserve, providing easy day hikes and an overnight backpacking trip. Follow the white blazes through the riverside camping area into the shade of live oak hammocks, where you encounter the first decision point at the junction of the River Trail and the Lake Trail. The Lake Trail is the long backpacker's loop, passing through pine flatwoods, floodplain forests, scrub, and a vast meadow before reaching the river. Following the floodplain of the Withlacoochee River, the River Trail has two short loops and connects back to the Lake Trail to make the large loop.

Highlights: Along the Withlacoochee River, you'll see ancient cypresses with knees as tall as hikers, middens buried by the river bluff forest, and wildlife roaming the floodplain forests. There are Florida scrub-jay families living in the scrub along the George Washington Pasture.

Logistics: Permission is required in advance for tent camping along the Withlacoochee River; call the water management district.

Other Activities: There is camping along the Withlacoochee River, birdwatching along the river, and a network of equestrian trails throughout the preserve.

Fort Cooper State Park

CG-8 $ 📖 🚻 🚼 🛖

Location: Inverness [N28°48.691' W082°18.164'].

Length: 3 miles in two loops.

Map: Rough map in park brochure; more detailed map displayed at both trailheads.

Contact Information: Fort Cooper State Park (352-726-0315), 3100 South Old Floral City Road, Inverness, FL 34450.

Directions: From downtown Inverness, drive south on US 41 several miles to Old Floral City Road. Turn left, crossing the Withlacoochee State Trail, then turn right and drive 1.6 miles to the park entrance.

The Hike: Starting to the left of the picnic area, the Dogwood Trail loops through an upland forest along the edge of Lake Holathlikaha, passing phosphate pits dug in the early 1900s. A spur trail, the Coot Trail, leads to the marshy lakeshore. On the other side of the picnic area, the 2-mile Fort Cooper Trail starts at a kiosk at the upper parking area and follows the historic military trail to a replica of Fort Cooper, with a lengthy loop through the upland forest.

Highlights: You'll be treated to spectacular wildflowers in the sandhills, great views of the lake, and a real "walk through history" along the Fort King Military Trail.

Logistics: Follow the yellow arrows on the Fort Cooper Trail to keep to the route.

Other Activities: There is swimming in Lake Holathlikaha, a picnic grove, a playground—and, each April during Fort Cooper Days, a reenactment of a battle from the Seminole Wars.

Citrus Hiking Trail

Citrus Tract, Withlacoochee State Forest

CG-9

Location: Inverness [N28°48.167' W082°22.867'].

Length: 43.3-mile outer loop made up 4 loops, the shortest (Loop A) 7.5 miles.

Map: Basic map available from Withlacoochee State Forest; detailed backpacking map available from Florida Trail Association.

Contact Information: Withlacoochee State Forest (352-754-6896), 15003 Broad Street, Brooksville, FL 34601.

Directions: From the junction of SR 44 and CR 581 west of Inverness, turn south on CR 581 and drive 2.5 miles, passing the fire tower, to the sign for Holder Mine Recreation Area. Turn right and continue another mile into Holder Mine Recreation Area. Pass the hunt check station and campground. The trailhead is on the left, with an "FT" sign and kiosk.

The Hike: It's a don't-miss for serious backpackers—the longest loop trail in Florida within a single tract of land. It's also the state's most rugged backpacking loop, climbing up and over huge sandhills, in and out of karst valleys. Start your hike at the Holder Mine Campground, following a blue-blazed connector 0.9 mile to the main orange-blazed loop. Turn right, and begin your counterclockwise hike around the outer loop. Stay with the outer loop by following the orange blazes away from each clearly signposted loop trail junction. The frequently open understory of the sandhills impresses upon you the size of this forest. The official primitive backpacker-only campsites are spread thinly, making for long days to start. Since the terrain is unusually rugged for Central Florida, plan on at least three and probably four days to complete the outer loop.

Highlights: You'll encounter unusual karst formations, including trailside caves, steep ravines, and sinkholes—Lizzie Hart Sink being one of the most prominent geologic features in the forest.

Logistics: Be aware of hunting dates (posted on www.floridaconservation.org) and wear blaze orange; this is a popular deer hunting destination. You may want to cache water at trail crossings before starting your journey, since water is scarce.

Other Activities: There are extensive equestrian trails, hunting, fishing, camping, and caving.

Rooks Trail

Homosassa Tract, Withlacoochee State Forest

CG-10 🐎

Location: Chassahowitzka [N28°45.592' W082°34.553'].

Length: 2.7-mile loop.

Map: Displayed and in brochure at trailhead kiosk.

Contact Information: Withlacoochee State Forest (352-754-6896), 15003 Broad Street, Brooksville, FL 34601.

Directions: Follow US 19 south of Homosassa Springs to Burnt Bridge Road, on the right immediately after the fire tower. Turn right and drive down this rough dirt road, which narrows to one lane, for 1.7 miles until it ends at the trailhead parking area.

The Hike: Circling a hardwood swamp along the Gulf estuary, the trail meanders through oak hammocks, hardwood hammocks, and longleaf pine flatwoods, following old forest roads.

Highlights: Listen for songbirds throughout the open meadows along the forest roads.

Logistics: Operating hours are dawn to dusk. Follow the orange blazes for the main trail.

Other Activities: This is a popular birding trail.

Chassahowitzka Wildlife Management Area

CG-11 $ 𐃵

Location: Chassahowitzka [N28°38.939' W082°34.504'].

Length: Two loops, 0.8-mile Cypress Circle and 0.7-mile Wild Turkey Trace.

Map: Rough map in WMA brochure.

Contact Information: Chassahowitzka Wildlife Management Area (863-664-3203), US 19, Chassahowitzka FL.

Directions: Follow US 19 north 10 miles from SR 50 in Weeki Wachee to the park entrance on the left. Continue along the graded limerock forest road for another 1.5 miles to the trailhead.

The Hike: On the Cypress Circle, the footpath circles a large cypress dome, following brown hiker markers on green fence posts. Duck under the low canopy of scrub oaks and follow the trail through sandhills and scrub, down a corridor of saw palmetto, until it emerges on the edge of pine flatwoods. As you continue, the trail crosses a bog bridge over a marsh before reaching the end of the loop. The Wild Turkey Trace starts on the opposite side of the parking area and follows green markers, looping through hammocks of sand live oaks and turkey oaks in the sandhills.

Highlights: There is a boggy, fern-filled marsh along the Wild Turkey Trace.

Logistics: Entrance fee is $3 per person, $6 per carload.

Other Activities: There is a picnic table at the trailhead. Seasonal hunting is permitted. Check www.floridaconservation.org for dates and details. Wear blaze orange when hiking during hunt dates.

Perry Oldenburg Mitigation Park

CG-12 📖 ⚞

Location: Brooksville [N28°36.893' W082°19.920'].

Length: 1.6-mile loop.

Map: Displayed and in brochure at trailhead kiosk.

Contact Information: Florida Fish and Wildlife Conservation Commission (863-648-3203), 3900 Drane Field Road, Lakeland, FL 33811-1299.

Directions: From Brooksville, follow US 41 north 5 miles to Deer Run Road. Turn right and follow the road 1.3 miles to Government Road. Straight ahead there are two grassy tracks—take the one on the right, which leads to the parking area.

The Hike: Creating a loop around this 368-acre mitigation park, the trail leads you through sandhill and scrub habitats ideal for the inhabitant this land was preserved for—the gopher tortoise, a key species of the sandhill community.

Highlights: There is an incredible variety of oak tree species along the trail, from sand post oak to Chapman oak, and you will see many gopher tortoise burrows along the hike.

Logistics: In the open meadows, be cautious of small gopher tortoise burrows in the footpath.

Other Activities: Birdwatch along the open meadows.

McKethan Lake Nature Trail

Withlacoochee State Forest

CG-13 $ 🚻 ⛺

Location: Brooksville [N28°38.674' W082°20.136'].

Length: 1.9-mile loop.

Map: Displayed at trailhead kiosk and in brochure available at kiosk.

Contact Information: Withlacoochee State Forest (352-754-6896), 15003 Broad Street, Brooksville, FL 34601.

Directions: North of Brooksville on US 41, just north of the Withlacoochee State Forest visitor center on the west side of the highway.

The Hike: This is an interpretive nature trail circling McKethan Lake. Start at the trailhead kiosk on the south side of the entrance road and parking area, walking through a dense bottomland hardwood forest of magnolia, sweet gum, and hornbeam before rising onto a ridge in the sandhills. As the trail circles the lake, it drops down across a bridge and rises into a forest of hickory and cherry before entering a pine plantation on the edge of a natural longleaf pine forest. Walking through a short stretch of sand pine scrub, you complete the loop.

Highlights: The park has nice views of the lake, and a delightful number of dogwoods in bloom in the spring.

Logistics: To enter the park, open from 8:00 to sunset, there is a small fee. Restrooms are on the far side of the lake, near the picnic area.

Other Activities: There are picnic tables and grills, a canoe launch, and fishing from the lakeshore.

Croom Hiking Trail

Croom Tract at Silver Lake, Withlacoochee State Forest

CG-14 **F** **C** ⛺ 🎣

Location: Ridge Manor [N28°34.683' W082°13.091'].

Length: 3.7-mile access loop leading to 20-mile backpacking loop system with three stacked loops of 7, 9.9, and 8 miles.

Map: Rough map in brochure at kiosk; backpackers should obtain Florida Trail Association map 28, which notes campsites and water sources.

Contact Information: Withlacoochee State Forest (352-754-6896), 15003 Broad Street, Brooksville, FL 34601.

Directions: From I-75 exit 301, follow SR 50 east to the turnoff on the left for Croom Rital Road, just before the railroad trestle overpass. After 3.4 miles, turn right on a dirt road next to I-75. Keep to the left at the fork to reach the trailhead parking area.

The Hike: One of Central Florida's more rugged backpacking experiences, the Croom Hiking Trail scrambles up and down sandhills and bluffs along the Withlacoochee River and its tributaries, and through deeply wooded uplands. Folks come here to train for the Appalachian Trail! The access loop provides a scenic day hike along the river.

Highlights: If the water is low, don't miss the low-water route, which leads you along the river's edge through forests of massive cypresses. If you walk counterclockwise, at 0.6 mile you'll encounter a cypress with a base so large it swallowed the bases of two adjoining oaks.

Logistics: From the trailhead kiosk, follow the fence line down to the lake, and turn left to walk along the lakeshore under I-75. If the river is flooded, the trail may not be accessible from this trailhead; drive farther up Croom Rital Road to find the trail crossing at the Withlacoochee State Trail. The access loop is blazed blue; the backpacking loop is blazed orange, with cross trails blazed blue. Loop A is part of the Trailwalker program.

Other Activities: The Withlacoochee State Trail, a paved biking trail, intersects the hiking trail. Silver Lake is a popular fishing and boating destination. Withlacoochee State Forest permits seasonal hunting; see www.floridaconservation.org for details. Hikers should always wear blaze orange vests during hunting season.

Weekiwachee Preserve

CG-15 📖 🚻

Location: Hernando Beach [N28°29.428' W082°38.718'].

Length: 5-to-6-mile interpretive loop with 8.3-mile round-trip spur trail.

Map: Displayed on trailhead kiosk and available in Southwest Florida Water Management District Recreational Guide.

Contact Information: Southwest Florida Water Management District (800-423-1476), 2379 Broad Street, Brooksville, FL 34604.

Directions: From SR 50 and US 19 in Weeki Wachee, follow US 19 south to CR 595. Turn right and drive to CR 597 (Shoal Road). Turn right and continue 3 miles to the preserve entrance on the right. Start your hike at the gate.

The Hike: The loop trail circles around old limestone quarry pits, now filled with water and fish, sparkling aquamarine in the bright sunshine, with a soft haze of muhly grass around the edges. You have several options for hiking; follow the bear symbols and make your choices at the various trail intersections.

Highlights: The mounds of limestone boulders create habitats all their own, with plants like ladder brake fern flourishing between the rocks. The interpretive stations have nice explanations of habitat and creatures. Watch for bear paw prints in the sand!

Logistics: There is very little shade along the trail. Bring lots of water and wear sun protection. If you decide to follow the spur trail down into the sand pine scrub, there is a lot of soft sand to traverse and you are entering bear territory; be alert for bear activity.

Other Activities: Go birding around the edges of the ponds. This is one of the few places on the Gulf Coast where you might encounter least terns nesting. Do not disturb them.

Crews Lake Park

CG-16 📖 🚻 ⛺ 🏠 🧒

Location: Spring Hill [N28°22.604' W082°31.949'].

Length: 1.1-mile interpretive loop and perimeter multiuse loop trail.

Map: Available at park entrance kiosk.

Contact Information: Crews Lake Park (727-861-3038), 16739 Crews Lake Drive, Spring Hill, FL 34606.

Directions: From US 19, drive 9.2 miles east on SR 52, passing under the Suncoast Parkway, and continue another 0.6 mile east to Shady Hills Road. Turn left and drive 2.8 miles north to Crews Lake Road; turn right, and right again to enter the park. Follow the road to a turnoff on the right that leads to a parking area on the lake where the trails converge, near the boat ramp.

The Hike: Walk down to the boat ramp and begin a clockwise walk around the loop by turning right to enter the woods along the Gallery of Trees, a showcase of native trees that yields to a native hardwood hammock. After 0.3 mile you reach a junction with the perimeter loop, so make your decision whether to stick with the interpretive (inner loop) trail or walk the perimeter loop. Both trails traverse a variety of habitats, including sandhills, scrubby flatwoods, cypress domes, oak hammocks, and the shore of Crews Lake.

Highlights: It's a nice immersion in the sandhill habitat, where you'll see lots of spring and fall wildflowers. Although the trail loses its natural feel as it passes through the picnic areas along the lakeshore, the views are great.

Logistics: Pick up an interpretive guide at the kiosk near the restrooms at the boat ramp parking area. Raccoon footprints mark the interpretive stations.

Other Activities: This park has plenty to do in addition to hiking, with its fishing pier and shoreline fishing, paved bike trail, boat ramp and canoe launch, tent campground, numerous picnic areas and shelters, playground, and native plant garden.

Florida Trail

Richloam Tract, Withlacoochee State Forest

CG-17 🅕 ⚠ 🏕

Location: Ridge Manor [N28°30.017' W082°06.751'].

Length: 31.5-mile loop.

Map: Rough map available at kiosk; backpackers should obtain Florida Trail Association map, with details on water sources, campsites, and points of interest.

Contact Information: Withlacoochee State Forest (352-754-6896), 15003 Broad Street, Brooksville, FL 34601.

Directions: From I-75 exit 301, follow SR 50 east to Ridge Manor. After you cross US 301, continue 3 miles to Porter Gap Road, on the right. Turn right and drive 0.7 mile to the Richloam Fire Tower, where you'll find the trailhead kiosk and official parking area for the loop.

The Hike: This challenging backpacking loop, through floodplain forests and uplands along the Withlacoochee and Little Withlacoochee Rivers, traverses rugged terrain that is frequently flooded when the rivers are high.

Highlights: The range of attractions includes a eucalyptus grove along the southeastern part of the loop, a scenic stroll through a cypress swamp on the low-water trail along the Withlacoochee River south of Lacoochee Road, oak hammocks with centuries-old live oaks, and deep sinkholes along the northern portion of the trail.

Logistics: A map and GPS are recommended because of the many trail intersections (which do have signage). Pay attention to the different blaze colors. Blue blazes are connector trails leading to trailheads and campsites. Orange is the through trail—the Florida Trail's Western Corridor, which connects to Green Swamp West (CG-18) and Croom (CF-35). White is the loop trail. The through trail and loop trail are one and the same from the Green Swamp West connector near Devil's Creek to SR 50 along the southwestern part of the loop. You will cross both SR 50 and Lacoochee Road twice in different places.

Other Activities: Withlacoochee State Forest permits seasonal hunting; see www.floridaconservation.org for details. Hikers should always wear blaze orange vests during hunting season.

Florida Trail

Green Swamp West

CG-18 **F** ⌂ ⚞

Location: Dade City [N28°21.166' W082°07.510'].

Length: 17.9 miles linear.

Map: See Southwest Florida Water Management District Recreational Guide; detailed backpacking map available from Florida Trail Association.

Contact Information: Southwest Florida Water Management District (800-423-1476), 2379 Broad Street, Brooksville, FL 34604.

Directions: The southern trailhead is along SR 471, northeast of Zephyrhills. An intermediate trailhead is at the end of River Road, east of Dade City, and the northern end of the trail links into the Richloam Trail (CG-17).

The Hike: This backpacker's delight through the Green Swamp will introduce you to all of the varied habitats along the Withlacoochee River, from pine flatwoods and cypress forests to open prairies, sandhills, oak scrub, and hardwood hammocks. It's a varied, interesting trip that takes at least two full days to hike. A day hike from SR 471 to River Road is possible with two cars, but the more scenic portion of the trail is north of River Road.

Highlights: You'll find great views of the Withlacoochee River from high bluffs north of the Foster Bridge campsite, and fun traverses of waterways on boardwalks.

Logistics: This is a backpacking trail with few options for cutting your trip short. Plan accordingly. Parts of the trail through the cypress floodplain forest may be under water at times. You must have a permit (free) to utilize the four backpacking campsites; contact SFWMD at least two weeks in advance.

Other Activities: A network of horse trails crosses the Florida Trail throughout this area. Seasonal hunting is permitted; check www.floridaconservation.org for details and wear a blaze orange vest during hunting season.

Withlacoochee River Park

CG-19 **F** 📖 🚻 ⛺ 🚻

Location: Dade City [N27°55.660' W081°07.494'].

Length: Network including 5.4-mile trail into Green Swamp and 2.5-mile nature trail with cross trails and loops.

Map: Available at information center at park entrance and in Southwest Florida Water Management District Recreational Guide; detailed backpacking map available from Florida Trail Association for their section of the trail.

Contact Information: Withlacoochee River Park (352-567-0264), 12449 Withlacoochee Boulevard, Dade City, FL 33523.

Directions: From US 301 in Dade City, drive north on Truck Route 301 to River Road; turn right and follow River Road 4.5 miles to Auton Road. Turn right; the park entrance is the first road to the left. Stop at the kiosk at the entrance for a trail map and an interpretive guide.

The Hike: There are two separate but intersecting trails within the park. Both the Nature Trail and the Withlacoochee River Trail start at the canoe launch and follow the river upstream, diverging just beyond the main parking area. The rugged Withlacoochee River Trail heads east into Green Swamp, with a loop at the end that traverses wet prairies, floodplain forest, and oak hammocks, and passes two designated backpacking campsites. The gentle Nature Trail circles the edge of the developed park, through sandhills and oak hammocks, leading you to an observation tower and past two replica historic villages.

Highlights: The walk along the Withlacoochee River is the most beautiful and accessible part of the hike. Once you enter Green Swamp, you walk under bowers of ancient live oaks along the river's cypress floodplain forests. On the Nature Trail, you pass several points of interest, including some of the tallest gopher apple plants you'll see anywhere.

Logistics: Restrooms are at the main parking area. If you want to camp, contact the park in advance.

Other Activities: You'll find a canoe launch, an observation tower, and replicas of a Florida Cracker farm and a Creek Indian Village.

Upper Hillsborough River Hiking Trail

Upper Hillsborough River Water Management Area

CG-20 **F** ⚊

Location: Zephyrhills: North trailhead [N28°15.540' W082°06.848'], South trailhead [N28°13.381' W082°08.768'].

Length: 4 miles linear.

Map: See Southwest Florida Water Management District Recreational Guide; more detailed map available in trail register at either trailhead.

Contact Information: Southwest Florida Water Management District (800-423-1476), 2379 Broad Street, Brooksville, FL 34604.

Directions: From US 301 in Zephyrhills, take CR 54 east. After 2.4 miles, you reach CR 535 (Chauncey Road). The northern trailhead is another 2.1 miles east on the right, across from CR 35. For the southern trailhead, turn right on CR 535 and drive 2 miles to the trailhead on the left.

The Hike: This linear trail meanders through pine flatwoods, scrubby flatwoods, open fields, oak hammocks, and floodplain forests along the edge of the Hillsborough River basin.

Highlights: In fall, swallow-tailed kites gather in large numbers to migrate south from the Green Swamp to South America.

Logistics: A blue-blazed trail starts from the northern trailhead to meet the main trail. A permit (free) is required for use of the backpackers' campsite; contact the District in advance.

Other Activities: Be aware of seasonal hunting in the area; check www.floridaconservation.org for details and wear blaze orange during hunt dates.

Nature Trail

Werner-Boyce Salt Springs State Park

CG-21 📖 🚻 👪 🐕

Location: New Port Richey [N28°18.434' W082°42.346'].

Length: 0.5-mile loop.

Map: None provided.

Contact Information: Werner-Boyce Salt Springs State Park (727-469-5942), c/o Honeymoon Island State Park, #1 Causeway Boulevard, Dunedin, FL 34698.

Directions: From US 19 in New Port Richey, take Scenic Drive east to the park entrance; follow the signs.

The Hike: This short loop trail introduces you to a coastal bayhead and related habitats just a couple of miles from the Gulf of Mexico. Meandering past a red maple and cattail swamp into the scrubby flatwoods, the trail enters an oak hammock with older saw palmettos and tall live oaks; the understory is lush with ferns. An exceptionally large slash pine has a bench facing it. After 0.3 mile you emerge into the scrubby flatwoods and traverse the open habitat back to the trailhead.

Highlights: Relax at the bench along the red maple swamp, enjoying the crimson hues in December.

Logistics: Benches enable visitors of all ages to enjoy an easy stroll. The trail may be soggy or flooded in places after a rain. A composting toilet is provided at the trailhead.

Other Activities: There is a picnic table at the trailhead.

J. B. Starkey Wilderness Park

CG-22

Location: New Port Richey.

Length: 1.3-mile nature trail and 12.7-mile backpacking loop with shorter loops possible.

Map: Available at information center at park entrance, and in Southwest Florida Water Management District Recreational Guide.

Contact Information: J. B. Starkey Wilderness Park (727-834-3247), 10500 Wilderness Park Road, New Port Richey, FL 34652.

Directions: From US 19, take SR 54 east. Veer left onto Old SR 54 and drive 5 miles to Little Road (CR 1). Turn left and continue 1 mile to River Crossing Boulevard. Turn right and follow this road 1.8 miles to Starkey Road. Turn left and make an immediate right on Wilderness Drive. Check the park map for the two trailhead locations.

The Hike: The nature trail is a pleasant loop through several different types of habitat along the Pithlachascotee River floodplain, from cypress swamp to rosemary scrub. It connects via a bird-blazed trail to the backpacking trail system, but the main trailhead for the backpacking trail is near the horse corral. There are three stacked loops; pay close attention to trail intersections. The trail leaves the high sand pine scrub to follow the Anclote River east, meandering through vast open palmetto scrub. There are three backpacking campsites along the loop.

Highlights: Don't miss the nature trail for its interpretive information and diversity of habitats.

Logistics: The backpacking loop is blazed orange, and intersects with the equestrian trails in several places. It is in sand pine scrub and open palmetto scrub with little shade, and is not recommended for children—stick to the nature trail for the kids. All water must be packed in, as water sources are questionable at best and found only along the Anclote River floodplain. Be sure to check in with the park attendant before spending the night at one of the backpacking campsites.

Other Activities: This is a full-facility park with a paved biking trail, equestrian trails, developed campground, and picnic areas.

Key Vista Nature Park

CG-23 [icons]

Location: Holiday [N28°11.971' W082°46.782'].

Length: 1.5-mile perimeter trail with multiple shorter loops possible.

Map: None provided.

Contact Information: Key Vista Nature Park (727-938-2598), 2700 Ballies Bluff Road, Holiday, FL 34690.

Directions: From US 19 in New Port Richey, follow Moog Road west to Straber Memorial Highway. Continue south to the T intersection, and turn left on Pine View Road. The park entrance is on the right. The trail starts near the restrooms; walk past the picnic tables and into the woods.

The Hike: Traversing several habitats, from coastal pine flatwoods to sandhills, coastal scrub, coastal strand, and mangrove marsh, the trail system leads you out through the shady pine forest to the open scrub with a view of the Gulf of Mexico. A 0.2-mile spur boardwalk parallels the mud flats, crossing a tidal creek. From the top of the observation tower, you get a grand view of the shore and forest. The loop continues along a broad tidal creek lined with tall black mangroves and oyster flats, returning to the pine flatwoods near the parking lot, with options to follow the Rocky Creek Loop Trail and the Sleepy Lagoon Trail.

Highlights: The views of the Gulf are great, but you just won't encounter a bigger sand pine than the once–National Champion on the edge of the parking area: it has a circumference exceeding 99", a height of 75', and a crown of 52'. Although sand pines rarely survive more than seventy years, it's thought to be more than a century old.

Logistics: The park is open dawn to dusk.

Other Activities: There is excellent birding along the marshes, and numerous picnic tables scattered throughout the woods near the parking lot. An adjacent park just down the road has a canoe launch, boat ramp, and fishing pier.

Along a tidal creek, Key Vista Nature Park.

Caladesi Island State Park

CG-24 $ 📖 🚻 ❋

Location: Dunedin [N28°01.860' W082°49.222'].

Length: 3.5-mile trail system.

Map: Rough sketch in park brochure.

Contact Information: Honeymoon Island State Park (727-469-5942), #1 Causeway Boulevard, Dunedin, FL 34698.

Directions: Starting from Dunedin, drive north on US 19A to SR 589 (Causeway Boulevard); turn left and follow the causeway 2.8 miles to the park entrance. After you pay your entrance fee, continue along the park road to the first left and park. Take the ferryboat from here. Alternately, you can walk to the park, 4 miles north along Clearwater Beach, entering the trail system from the Beach Trail.

The Hike: From the ferryboat dock, walk up to and around the concession stand to the boardwalk leading to the beach. Turn left at the "Island Trail" sign to enter the trail system, which leads you into the coastal scrub. Grab an interpretive guide at the kiosk and continue through the scrub to the junction with the Hammock Loop and the Beach Trail. The Hammock Loop wanders out through a virgin pine forest to Dunedin Pass, passing a freshwater spring and the remains of the 1890s homestead. The Beach Trail is your route across the mangrove-lined lagoons to the beach. Return along the beach.

Highlights: Views are fabulous from the Hammock Loop as you walk through the pine forest out to Dunedin Pass. On the Beach Trail, you'll see many wading birds, including roseate spoonbills.

Logistics: Most visitors use the ferryboat ($7 round-trip) or paddle over in a kayak from the causeway. Do not miss the last ferryboat back to Honeymoon Island! There are restrooms near the beach and at the concession area.

Other Activities: This is a popular off-the-beaten-track beach for sunning and swimming along the Gulf.

Honeymoon Island State Park

CG-25 $ 📖 🚻 ♿ 🚸 🐎

Location: Dunedin [N28°04.300' W082°49.936'].

Length: 2.5-mile perimeter trail with several cross trails for shorter hikes.

Map: Rough sketch in park brochure.

Contact Information: Honeymoon Island State Park (727-469-5942), #1 Causeway Boulevard, Dunedin, FL 34698.

Directions: Starting from Dunedin, drive north on US 19A to SR 589 (Causeway Boulevard); turn left and follow the causeway 2.8 miles to the park entrance. After you pay your entrance fee, continue along the park road to its end and turn right into the parking area. Park at the end, near the "Nature Trail" sign.

The Hike: The Osprey Trail leads you through a virgin pine forest with an understory of coastal plants like the colorful necklace pod with its dangling yellow flowers. When you reach the Pelican Trail, follow it around the edge of the peninsula, walking along the Gulf of Mexico to the sound across from Pelican Point, following the thin ribbon of a mangrove marsh before you turn back up toward the pines to complete the loop.

Highlights: You can see a nesting colony of ospreys along the Osprey Trail, a nesting colony of pelicans from the Pelican Trail, and great views across the sound and the Gulf of Mexico.

Logistics: Only the Osprey Trail is wheelchair accessible (with assistance; it's a well-graded natural surface). There are numerous benches along both trails. The Pelican Trail may be muddy or flooded in places along the mangrove marsh.

Other Activities: This park has a long stretch of beaches for swimming and sunning, and sea kayaking along the bay. It is also the gateway to Caladesi Island (CG-24).

John Chesnut Sr. County Park

CG-26 📖 🚻 ♿ 👫 🐕‍🦺

Location: Oldsmar [N28°05.089' W082°42.148'].

Length: 1.8 miles in two loops.

Map: Peggy Park Nature Trail map available in guide at trailhead.

Contact Information: Pinellas County Parks Department (727-464-3347), 631 Chestnut Street, Clearwater, FL 33756-5336.

Directions: From Clearwater, follow McMullen Booth Road (CR 611) north to Oldsmar. North of SR 584, look for the park entrance on the left just after you cross Brooker Creek. Turn left when you enter the park and follow the road to the farthest parking area.

The Hike: The Peggy Park Nature Trail is a pleasant loop on a boardwalk and improved trail along the edge of Lake Tarpon, passing through a cypress floodplain forest and following the banks of Brooker Creek into an oak hammock. Starting at the boat ramp, there is also the Lookout Tower Trail, a boardwalk along Lake Tarpon through the cypresses, with side trails that lead to secluded picnic benches and to shaded observation decks along the lake.

Highlights: Both boardwalks provide a nice panorama of Lake Tarpon, but your best view is from the observation tower down the boardwalk from the boat ramp. Some of the trees along Brooker Creek are enormous!

Logistics: The park is open from sunrise to sunset. To connect the two trails, walk along the lakeshore (passing through several picnic areas) between the Peggy Park Nature Trail and the boat ramp.

Other Activities: Enjoy the extensive picnic groves, boat ramp, playground, and fishing from the boardwalk.

The Friends Trail

Brooker Creek Preserve

CG-27 📖

Location: Tarpon Springs [N28°07.767' W082°40.244'].

Length: 1.8-mile loop.

Map: Displayed and in brochure at trailhead; also see Southwest Florida Water Management District Recreational Guide.

Contact Information: Pinellas County Department of Environmental Management, Environmental Land Division (727-943-4000), 1001 Lora Lane, Tarpon Springs, FL 34689.

Directions: From McMullen Booth Road (CR 611), drive east on Keystone Road for 1.5 miles to Lora Lane. Turn right and drive 1 mile to the end of the road.

The Hike: Following a tannic stream in the pine flatwoods, the trail reaches a side trail after 0.2 mile. Turn left to walk out the short spur trail to an observation deck over a restored wetland and cypress dome. Continuing on the main trail, you make a left after 0.4 mile to start the loop. Crossing a horse trail, the trail narrows and enters a hammock dense with ferns, following the flow of Brooker Creek. After a mile, you cross the horse trail again and complete the loop through the flatwoods at 1.4 miles. Turn right to exit the loop.

Highlights: Enjoy the observation deck over the wetlands area, and the dark hammock along the creek.

Logistics: The trail is open dawn to dusk. No dogs are permitted. Numbers on red-tipped posts correspond to the interpretive brochure.

Other Activities: A separate equestrian trail departs from the same trailhead. The Brooker Creek Preserve Nature Center, farther east on Keystone Road, offers guided hikes of the trail system within the fenced portion of the preserve.

Moccasin Lake Nature Park

CG-28 **$** 📖 🚻 ♿ 🚻

Location: Clearwater [N27°58.574' W082°43.429'].

Length: 1-mile loop.

Map: None available.

Contact Information: City of Clearwater (727-462-6024), 2750 Park Trail Lane, Clearwater, FL 33759.

Directions: From McMullen Booth Road, take Drew Road west; from US 19, take Drew Road east. At Fairwood Avenue, turn north. Make a left on Park Trail Lane just after crossing the railroad tracks, and follow it to its end at the park.

The Hike: Winding through an oak hammock that appears to be about fifty years old, the trail system works its way beneath the forest canopy to the edge of a dammed stream that spills into a more natural fern-edged flow through the forest. A side trail, the Cypress Trail, leads to a bluff overlooking a large lake. The Brigham Dock is an observation deck on the lake from which the trail turns away from US 19 to parallel the railroad tracks, staying in the shady forest crossing long boardwalks to complete the loop.

Highlights: Enjoy the beautiful fern-lined streams that meander throughout the property.

Logistics: The park is open Sat–Sun 10:00–6:00, Tue–Fri 9:00–5:00; entrance $2 adult, $1 child; guided tours available. The trail system is a combination of boardwalk, pavement, and shellrock, suitable for strollers and wheelchairs. There are numerous benches along the route.

Other Activities: The nature center is full of activities and creatures for the kids to see. There is a butterfly garden, an aviary, and a water tower with solar panels.

Sawgrass Lake Park

CG-29   📖   🚻   ♿   🚼

Location: Pinellas Park [N27°50.359' W082°40.047'].

Length: 1.9-mile loop.

Map: See Southwest Florida Water Management District Recreational Guide, or ask for map and interpretive guide at environmental center.

Contact Information: Sawgrass Lake Park (727-217-7256), 7400 25th Street North, St. Petersburg, FL 33702.

Directions: From I-295 north of St. Petersburg, take exit 14B, heading west on 54th Avenue North. Turn right onto North 31st Street, then right onto 62nd Avenue North, which leads you back toward the interstate. Turn left at the traffic light just before the interstate overpass, onto North 25th Street. The road leads through a residential area and ends inside the park.

The Hike: Walk behind the education center and follow the sidewalk down to the canal. Cross the bridge to the boardwalk. At the fork, turn left to walk down the Sawgrass Trail, a loop through a floodplain forest dense with ferns; it leads to an observation tower overlooking Sawgrass Lake. Return to the fork to walk the Maple Trail and the Hammock Trail, which leaves the board-walk to meander through a dense hardwood hammock.

Highlights: Sit and watch the alligators and softshell turtles from the observation deck along the Sawgrass Trail; walk the maze of trails through the Oak Hammock when you step off the Hammock Trail.

Logistics: The park is open from 7:00 a.m. to sunset.

Other Activities: Explore the John Anderson Environmental Education Center for a close-up look at turtles, fish, and other creatures common to the habitats found in this park.

Boca Ciega Millennium Park

CG-30 📖 🚻 ♿ 👫 🐕

Location: Seminole [N27°49.922' W082°48.636'].

Length: 0.8-mile boardwalk loop plus 0.5-mile footpath loop.

Map: Available at www.pinellascounty.org/park/03_Boca_Ciega.htm.

Contact Information: Boca Ciega Millennium Park (727-588-4882), 12410 74th Avenue North, Seminole, FL 33772.

Directions: From US 19 in Pinellas Park, follow Park Boulevard (CR 694) west into Seminole, crossing US 19A. Continue west to 74th Avenue North (Old Oakhurst Road) and turn left. Turn left on 125th Street; the park entrance is on the right. Continue along the park road to the parking area for shelters 3 and 4. The boardwalk starts behind the restrooms.

The Hike: Follow the boardwalk to the T intersection, and turn left to walk down to an overlook over a small pond surrounded by large pines. Return along the boardwalk as it rises into the mangrove marshes, reaching the observation tower after 0.3 mile. Climb up and look over Boca Ciega Bay to the barrier islands. The boardwalk continues along the mangroves before looping into the maritime hammock on its return trip. Keep to the right at the fork to return to the correct parking area. The nature trail, the Fox Run Trail, starts in front of picnic pavilion 2 and loops through the pine flatwoods. It appears to have been abandoned, since the bridges are broken and you must hop across the creek twice to follow the posts with white arrows that mark the loop.

Highlights: The boardwalk provides a great view of the succession of coastal habitats, from pine flatwoods to maritime forest, coastal strand, and mangrove marsh.

Logistics: The park is open from 8:00 to dusk.

Other Activities: There is fabulous birding along the boardwalk, numerous picnic pavilions, a playground, a canoe launch, fishing along the shoreline, and a paved bicycle trail paralleling the entrance road past wetland areas.

Weedon Island Preserve

CG-31 🚻 ♿ 🚻

Location: St. Petersburg [N27°51.135' W082°36.561'].

Length: 4.7 miles of trails and boardwalks, including a 1-mile natural loop and two shorter boardwalk loops.

Map: In interpretive brochure at preserve entrance kiosk, and displayed on kiosk near trailhead.

Contact Information: Weedon Island Preserve (727-453-6500), 1800 Weedon Drive NE, St. Petersburg, FL 33702.

Directions: From I-275, follow Gandy Boulevard (SR 694) east for 3.1 miles to San Martin Boulevard, just past the greyhound racetrack. Turn right and drive 1 mile to Weedon Drive on the left. Turn left and follow the park entrance road for 1.1 miles to the first parking area on the left, which accesses the Boy Scout Loop and the northern section of the trail system.

The Hike: From the north end of the trail system, keep to the left at the first two decision points to walk the Boy Scout Loop, which traverses dikes around a saltwater lagoon, climbing up into oak hammocks and coastal scrub. After 0.4 mile you reach a well-marked decision point for following the footpaths down to the boardwalks along the mangrove marshes or completing the loop around the lagoon. The boardwalks can also be accessed via a wheelchair-accessible paved trail from the parking lot in front of the Cultural and Natural History Center.

Highlights: Enjoy great views across the mangrove-lined lagoons and from the tall observation tower, from which you can see the skylines of both Tampa and St. Petersburg on a clear day.

Logistics: The park is open dawn to dusk. Restrooms are at the Cultural and Natural History Center; the outside restroom is open when the building itself is not.

Other Activities: Visit the Cultural and Natural History Center, open Wed–Sun 10:00–4:00, for insights into the archaeological significance of this area. Free 3-mile, two-hour-long guided hikes are offered every Saturday morning at 8:50, starting at the center; call 727-453-6506 several days in advance to register. There is a 4-mile canoe trail circling the mangrove islands, and fishing off the pier at the end of the entrance road.

Boyd Hill Nature Park

CG-32 $ 📖 🚻 ♿ 👪

Location: St. Petersburg [N27°43.525' W082°38.992'].

Length: Trail system of nearly 4 miles with a 3-mile perimeter loop.

Map: Available at entrance station; self-guided trail book with interpretive information also available for a small fee.

Contact Information: Boyd Hill Nature Park (813-893-7326), 1101 Country Club Way South, St. Petersburg, FL 33705.

Directions: Follow I-275 north from St. Petersburg to exit 17. Drive 1.8 miles east on 54th Street to 9th Street South (Dr. Martin Luther King Street). Turn left and drive north for four blocks; make a left at the traffic light onto Country Club Way. The park is on the right.

The Hike: Originally built as a zoo and botanical garden for the city of St. Petersburg, this park evolved into a mosaic of natural habitats and wild tropical landscapes along the shores of Lake Maggiore. From the outer Main Trail, there are five side trails (mostly loops) showcasing specific habitats: the Swamp Woodlands Trail, Willow Marsh Trail, Lake Maggiore Trail, Scrub Island Trail, and Pine Flatwoods Trail.

Highlights: Enjoy the immersion in each habitat on the side trails, and the amusing giant armadillos along Wax Myrtle Pond.

Logistics: Opening hours are 9:00–5:00, with longer hours Tuesday and Thursday in summer. The main trails are paved or boardwalk. There is an admission fee of $1 adults, $0.50 children. The strategically placed cold-water stations around the park are a welcome relief on a hot day!

Other Activities: A paved bike path makes a loop through the park, and there is a wild bird aviary just inside the park entrance. Outside the park gates, enjoy the picnic area.

Barrier Free Nature Trail

Fort De Soto Park

CG-33 📖 🚻 🅰 ♿ 🚸 🚫🐕

Location: Tierra Verde [N27°37.330' W082°42.873'].

Length: 0.4-mile loop

Map: Interpretive guide available at trailhead.

Contact Information: Fort De Soto Park (727-866-2484), 3500 Pinellas Bayway South, Tierra Verde, FL 33715.

Directions: From I-275 in St. Petersburg, drive south to exit 17, Pass-a-Grille Beach. Head west on 54th Avenue South (Pinellas Boulevard), paying a 50-cent toll. Drive 2.5 miles to CR 679 south. Turn left, following CR 679 for 5.5 miles to the park entrance, just past the toll drawbridge. Continue into the park to the park headquarters; the trail starts at the edge of the parking lot.

The Hike: This trail through a palm hammock and coastal dunes features a graded path wide enough for two wheelchairs to pass, and six touch-activated speaker boxes at each of the interpretive stations. A concrete strip just before each station alerts the visually impaired to the location of the speaker box.

Highlights: There is a beautiful view of Tampa Bay from the dunes; you can see the Sunshine Skyway Bridge in the distance.

Logistics: Restrooms are inside park headquarters. Pick up an interpretive guide at the trailhead, and please return it to the box when you are done.

Other Activities: The campground (727-582-2267 for reservations) is one of the most beautiful on the coast, with shaded sites overlooking the bay. There are two other short trails (SG-34 and SG-35) within the park. Enjoy the beach on the Gulf, bayfront and pier fishing, and a tour of historic Fort De Soto.

Soldier's Hole Nature Trail

Fort De Soto Park

CG-34 📖 🏕

Location: Tierra Verde [N27°37.096' W082°43.597'].

Length: Loops of 1 mile and 1.7 miles.

Map: Check box on gate for interpretive booklet containing map.

Contact Information: Fort De Soto Park (727-866-2484), 3500 Pinellas Bayway South, Tierra Verde, FL 33715.

Directions: From I-275 in St. Petersburg, drive south to exit 17, Pass-a-Grille Beach. Head west on 54th Avenue South (Pinellas Boulevard), paying a 50-cent toll. Drive 2.5 miles to CR 679 south. Turn left, following CR 679 for 5.5 miles to the park entrance, just past the toll drawbridge. Continue into the park to the T intersection. Turn right; the trailhead is on the right down a dirt track.

The Hike: Follow the marked path along the mangrove forests sheltering Soldier's Hole, a secluded cove off Mullet Key Bayou. The numbered stations interpret the plants and creatures of the mangrove forest and coastal hammock. At station 11 you have the option of walking an extra 0.4 mile on a second loop out along the peninsula.

Highlights: It's a great spot to learn the differences between the three types of mangrove and the buttonwood tree. Overlooks give glimpses out to Mullet Bayou.

Logistics: Expect mosquitoes—wear plenty of insect repellent! Do not block the gate when you park by it.

Other Activities: The campground (727-582-2267 for reservations) is one of the most beautiful on the coast, with shaded sites overlooking the bay. There are two other short trails (SG-33 and SG-35) within the park. Enjoy the beach on the Gulf, bayfront and pier fishing, and a tour of historic Fort De Soto.

Arrowhead Nature Trail

Fort De Soto Park

CG-35 📖 🚶 Ⓒ 👫 🐕

Location: Tierra Verde [N27°38.582' W082°44.312'].

Length: 1.4-mile or 0.5-mile loop.

Map: Check trailhead kiosk for interpretive booklet containing map.

Contact Information: Fort De Soto Park (727-866-2484), 3500 Pinellas Bayway South, Tierra Verde, FL 33715.

Directions: From I-275 in St. Petersburg, drive south to exit 17, Pass-a-Grille Beach. Head west on 54th Avenue South (Pinellas Boulevard), paying a 50-cent toll. Drive 2.5 miles to CR 679 south. Turn left, following CR 679 for 5.5 miles to the park entrance, just past the toll drawbridge. Continue into the park to the T intersection. Turn right and follow the road down to the Arrowhead Picnic Area on the right.

The Hike: Winding through coastal flatwoods, maritime hammock, and mangrove swamp, this trail leads you through a sequence of interpretive stations; use the interpretive guide to "hike by numbers" on a route that takes you past a coastal savanna and along the edge of Bunce's Pass.

Highlights: Walk down to the water beneath the canopy of old mangrove trees along Bunce's Pass and savor the view.

Logistics: Expect mosquitoes—wear plenty of insect repellent!

Other Activities: The campground (727-582-2267 for reservations) is one of the most beautiful on the coast, with shaded sites overlooking the bay. There are two other short trails (SG-33 and SG-34) within the park. Enjoy the beach on the Gulf, bayfront and pier fishing, and a tour of historic Fort De Soto.

Morris Bridge Park

CG-36 $ 📖 👫 ♿ 🚻

Location: New Tampa [N28°05.938' W082°18.742'].

Length: 0.4-mile boardwalk loop on west side; 1.5-mile round-trip trail on east side.

Map: See Southwest Florida Water Management District Recreational Guide.

Contact Information: Hillsborough County Parks and Recreation Department (813-987-6209), 1101 East River Cove Street, Tampa, FL 33604-3257.

Directions: From I-75 exit 266, follow Morris Bridge Road (CR 579) north 3.5 miles to the park entrances on the left (west side) and right (east side), just before the bridge.

The Hike: The boardwalk loop traverses floodplain forest amid many meandering channels that make up the Hillsborough River. The hiking-only shell path on the east side follows a tram road that parallels the river through the floodplain forest, ending at a deck with benches, the "gazebo," along the river.

Highlights: This is a quiet place for contemplation amid the cypresses, both on the boardwalk and at the "gazebo" deck along the Hillsborough River.

Logistics: A donation of $1 per car is requested. No dogs or bikes are permitted.

Other Activities: Fishing is popular along the boardwalk and the banks of the river. There is a canoe put-in and a connector to the Wilderness Park bicycle trail on the east side of CR 579.

Trout Creek Park

CG-37 $ 🚻 ♿ 👫

Location: New Tampa [N28°05.535' W082°20.885'].

Length: 0.8-mile loop plus connectors to many miles of shared-use trails.

Map: See Southwest Florida Water Management District Recreational Guide.

Contact Information: Hillsborough County Parks and Recreation Department (813-987-6209), 1101 East River Cove Street, Tampa, FL 33604-3257.

Directions: From I-75 exit 266, follow Morris Bridge Road (CR 579) north 1 mile to the park entrance on the left.

The Hike: Start your walk near the restrooms and follow the wheelchair-accessible boardwalk on a loop along the cypress-lined shores of the Hillsborough River. Continue on the footpath along the parking lot to the "Nature Trail" sign behind the first picnic pavilion on the left. This 0.7-mile loop meanders through a shady hammock with an open understory of saw palmetto, into pine flatwoods, scrubby flatwoods, and along the edge of the floodplain forest. There are numerous connectors to the mountain bike trail; to stay on the loop, watch for the "Nature Trail" signs.

Highlights: Enjoy quiet time on a bench on the boardwalk, contemplating the wildlife along the Hillsborough River.

Logistics: Opening hours are 7:00 to sunset daily. A donation of $1 per car is requested.

Other Activities: There are picnic pavilions along the shady trail and overlooking the Hillsborough River, and a canoe launch. Fishing is permitted from the riverbanks and boardwalk. The mountain bike trail traverses the length of the park and connects to the lengthy Wilderness Park trail on the east side of CR 579.

Hillsborough River State Park

CG-38 $ ▯ ⛹ Ⓐ ⛺ ⛹ ⛺

Location: Thonotosassa [N28°08.916' W082°14.055'].

Length: 6-mile network of trails, with many shorter hikes possible.

Map: Rough map, with mileages for trails segments, in park brochure; detailed backpacking map available from Florida Trail Association.

Contact Information: Hillsborough River State Park (813-986-1020), 15402 US 301 North, Thonotosassa, FL 33592.

Directions: From I-75 exit 265, Temple Terrace, follow SR 582 east to US 301. Follow US 301 north 10.5 miles to the park entrance on the left. Inside, park at parking lot 2 near the rapids to start your hike.

The Hike: The River Rapids Nature Trail leads you through bottomland hardwood forest to the edge of the burbling rapids of the Hillsborough River. Follow the trail downstream, paralleling the river to reach a swinging bridge across to the north side, where the Baynard Trail makes a 1-mile loop through dense hardwood forests, connecting to the 3.2-mile Florida Trail loop. A single backpacking campsite sits off the trail down a blue blaze deep in the palm hammocks. The loop traverses dark hammocks before emerging along the river's edge to head upstream to rejoin the Baynard Trail.

Highlights: There aren't too many spots in Florida where you can see rapids, and this is one of them! Walk the Florida Trail loop to commune with ancient live oak trees, some of such size and girth they are easily many centuries old.

Logistics: Both the Baynard Trail and the Florida Trail traverse palm hammocks, where the footpath may be soft and damp (or even flooded) in places. Expect a lot of mosquitoes and prepare accordingly. If you plan to camp overnight, you must inform the rangers beforehand. There is a small fee for camping.

Other Activities: This is a large state park with two popular developed campgrounds, a swimming pool, a canoe outfitter, and Fort Foster State Historic Site, open for tours on weekends and holidays.

John B. Sargeant Sr. Memorial Wilderness Park

CG-39 $ ⊞ ⛌ ⛨ ⛌ ⛺

Location: Thonotosassa [N28°04.843' W082°17.117'].

Length: 0.6 mile in two round trips.

Map: See Southwest Florida Water Management District Recreational Guide.

Contact Information: Hillsborough County Parks and Recreation (813-987-6208), 1101 East River Cove Street, Tampa, FL 33604.

Directions: The park is 7.8 miles south of CR 535, Thonotosassa, on US 301.

The Hike: Starting from the parking area on the north side of the canal, the Nature Boardwalk creates a 0.3-mile loop beneath the shade of giant cypresses, following the access canal out to the confluence. On the opposite side of the canal, the Trail leads you along a rough path with many roots underfoot to another vantage point on the river, this in the midst of cypress knees in the river's floodplain.

Highlights: Both trails reach the scenic confluence of Flint Creek with the Hillsborough River.

Logistics: Opening hours are Mon–Fri 8:00–7:00, Sat–Sun 8:00–8:00. A donation of $1 for park use is requested. Although dogs are permitted in the park, keep in mind that alligators are present.

Other Activities: This is a launch point for canoe trips down the Hillsborough River into Tampa. Fishing off the boardwalk is a popular activity. Picnic tables provide a spot to have a snack, and a boat ramp is available for larger craft.

Lettuce Lake Park

CG-40 $ 📖 🚻 ♿ 👫 🐾

Location: Temple Terrace [N28°04.336' W082°22.551'].

Length: 0.9-mile boardwalk plus 0.2-mile nature trail.

Map: Available in interpretive brochure (fee) at Audubon Center.

Contact Information: Lettuce Lake Park (813-987-6204), 6920 East Fletcher Avenue, Tampa, FL 33637-0921.

Directions: From I-75 exit 266, drive west 0.8 mile to the park entrance on the right. Follow Lettuce Lake Park Road to the Audubon Center to reach the start of the boardwalk.

The Hike: The boardwalk meanders out into Lettuce Lake, a cypress swamp that is a broad lake in the Hillsborough River, with observation decks and benches over the tannic water. It also heads downstream along the river's edge to a tall observation tower, which gives a nice view of the park and river, and connects to the paved bike trail that circles around the park. Turn right and walk a short distance down the bike trail to reach the nature trail, a natural footpath through sandhill habitat.

Highlights: Climb to the top of the observation tower—the view is worth it!

Logistics: A donation of $1 is requested.

Other Activities: This is a popular picnic park, with bank fishing, a canoe launch, a playground, and the Audubon Resource Center, open Fri–Sun 12:00–5:00.

Alderman's Ford Park

CG-41 $ 🚻 ⛺ ♿ 🚼 🥾

Location: Lithia: Nature Trail [N27°52.022' W082°08.224'], Alafia River Corridor [N27°52.271' W082°08.141'].

Length: Trails range from easy 0.3-mile nature trail and paved trail to 7-mile loop in Alafia River Corridor Nature Preserve.

Map: Park trails map displayed on nature center kiosk; see also Southwest Florida Water Management District Recreational Guide.

Contact Information: Alderman's Ford Park (813-757-3801), 9625 Canoe Launch Loop, Lithia, FL 33547.

Directions: From the corner of Lithia-Pinecrest Road and CR 39 (12 miles south of Plant City), drive north 1.5 miles on CR 39 to park entrance on right.

The Hike: Starting off behind the nature center, cross the broad bridge over the willow-edged slough (watch for alligators!) and follow the footpath to the right to walk a gentle, kid-friendly loop on a broad shellrock path through the palmettos and oaks, which returns to the picnic pavilion. All around the picnic area and along the paved path, you'll find gray "Trail" signs that point out trailheads for unmarked paths that meander throughout the upland and floodplain forest habitats.

Highlights: Along the river's floodplain corridor, you are in deeply shaded hammocks, where massive cypresses and oaks rise above clear sand-bottomed streams in eroded gullies.

Logistics: The park is open 8:00–8:00; a $1 donation is suggested. You can get lost in here! GPS is recommended. The trailhead for the backpacking loop is at the north end of the Pinecrest Sports Complex just north of the park, but it is safer to leave your car inside the park if out on an overnight trip. An advance permit is required for backpacking; call the park for details. Numbered markers correspond to a map which may be available at the kiosk.

Other Activities: A paved bicycle path provides a connection to other parks along the Alafia River and leads to a boardwalk trail and numerous unmarked footpaths throughout the forest. The nature center, with children's activities, is open Sat–Sun 10:00–3:00. There are numerous picnic benches.

Little Manatee River State Park

CG-42 🄵 $ ⛺ 🔆

Location: Wimauma [N27°40.506' W082°20.921'].

Length: 6.5-mile outer loop, with 3-mile loop possible.

Map: Rough map in park brochure; detailed backpacking map available from Florida Trail Association.

Contact Information: Little Manatee River State Park (813-634-4781), 215 Lightfoot Road, Wimauma, FL 33598.

Directions: From I-75 exit 240A, Sun City, drive east on SR 674 for 3 miles to US 301. Head south on US 301 for 4.5 miles, crossing the Little Manatee River and turning on Lightfoot Road to the park's entrance.

The Hike: From the trailhead, follow the narrow footpath through a forest of ferns before reaching the orange-blazed main loop. Turn right to walk counterclockwise through this variety of ecosystems, which include old ranch land, oak hammocks, pine flatwoods, scrubby flatwoods, sand pine scrub, hardwood bottomlands, and floodplain forest as well as many minor variations in plant communities. You cross Cypress Creek at the halfway point, where a blue-blazed shortcut can trim the length of your hike. The backpackers' campsite is past Cypress Creek on the north end of the loop. The return trip along the loop parallels the scenic river floodplain with its many swampy side channels.

Highlights: This is one of the most beautiful loop trails in Florida. Enjoy the scenic views along Cypress Creek and along the river bluffs of the Little Manatee River.

Logistics: Before hiking this trail, register at the ranger station at the park's main entrance in order to obtain the combination to the lock on the parking area and directions on how to find it. Inform the rangers if you plan to use the backpackers' campsite, and pay the small fee. Parts of the trail are in full sun; use sun protection and carry adequate water for the length of this hike.

Other Activities: There are extensive equestrian trails on the south side of the river, as well as a developed campground, picnic areas, and a canoe outfitter with canoe launch. Paddling trips take about three hours.

Central Florida

Marion, Lake, Sumter, Orange, Seminole, Osceola, Polk

Corridor of cabbage palms through the Lake Jesup Wilderness.

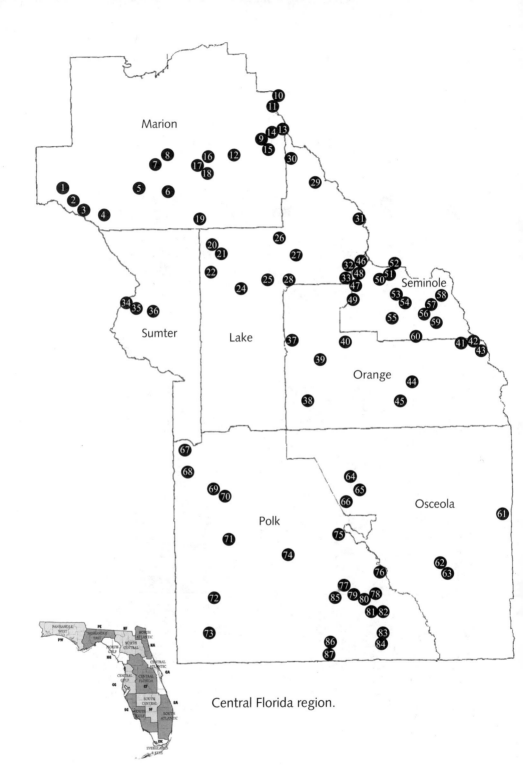

Central Florida region.

Marion

CF-1   Sandhills Nature Trail, Rainbow Springs State Park
CF-2   Florida Trail, Cross Florida Greenway
CF-3   Hálpata Tastanaki Preserve
CF-4   Ross Prairie Loop, Cross Florida Greenway
CF-5   Land Bridge Loop, Cross Florida Greenway
CF-6   Historic Ship Canal Trail, Cross Florida Greenway
CF-7   Brick City Quarry, Brick City Park
CF-8   Nature Trail, Coehadjoe Park
CF-9   Florida Trail, Ocala National Forest
CF-10   Bear Swamp Trail, Salt Springs Recreation Area, Ocala National Forest
CF-11   Salt Springs Loop, Ocala National Forest
CF-12   Lake Eaton Trails, Ocala National Forest
CF-13   Silver Glen Springs Recreation Area, Ocala National Forest
CF-14   The Yearling Trail, Ocala National Forest
CF-15   Juniper Creek Nature Trail, Ocala National Forest
CF-16   Silver River Connector Trail, Cross Florida Greenway
CF-17   Silver River State Park
CF-18   Marshall Swamp Trail, Cross Florida Greenway
CF-19   Carney Island

Lake

CF-20   Nature Trail, Lake Griffin State Park
CF-21   Sabal Bluff Preserve
CF-22   Flat Island Preserve
CF-23   Lake Louisa State Park
CF-24   Sara Maude Mason Nature Preserve
CF-25   Tavares Nature Park
CF-26   Sawgrass Island Preserve
CF-27   Hidden Waters Preserve
CF-28   Palm Island Park
CF-29   Timucuan Indian Nature Trail, Alexander Springs Recreation Area, Ocala National Forest
CF-30   Sandpine Scrub Forest Nature Trail, Ocala National Forest
CF-31   St. Francis Hiking Trail, Ocala National Forest
CF-32   Florida Trail, Seminole State Forest
CF-33   Rock Springs Run Trail, Rock Springs Run State Park

Sumter

CF-34   Hog Island Nature Trail, Hog Island Recreation Area, Withlacoochee State Forest
CF-35   Croom Hiking Trail, Croom Tract at Hog Island, Withlacoochee State Forest

CF-36   Pine Flatwoods Trail, Dade Battlefield Historic State Park

Orange
CF-37   Oakland Nature Preserve
CF-38   Tibet-Butler Preserve
CF-39   Nature Trail, Bill Fredrick Park at Turkey Lake
CF-40   Mead Gardens
CF-41   Orlando Wetlands Park
CF-42   Florida Trail, Seminole Ranch Conservation Area
CF-43   Florida Trail, Tosohatchee Reserve State Park
CF-44   Hal Scott Regional Preserve
CF-45   Split Oak Forest Mitigation Park

Seminole
CF-46   Sandhill Nature Trail, Lower Wekiva River Preserve State Park
CF-47   Wekiwa Springs State Park
CF-48   Sabal Point Sanctuary
CF-49   Lake Lotus Park
CF-50   Big Tree Park
CF-51   Florida Trail, Spring Hammock Preserve
CF-52   Spring Hammock Preserve
CF-53   Lake Jesup Wilderness Area
CF-54   East Lake Jesup Tract, Lake Jesup Conservation Area
CF-55   Bear Creek Nature Trail
CF-56   Florida Trail, Little-Big Econ State Forest
CF-57   Geneva Wilderness Area
CF-58   Lake Proctor Wilderness Area
CF-59   Nature Trail, Lake Mills Park
CF-60   Econ River Wilderness Area

Osceola
CF-61   Florida Trail, Bull Creek Wildlife Management Area
CF-62   Florida Trail, Prairie Lakes Wildlife Management Area
CF-63   Sunset Ranch Interpretive Trail, Prairie Lakes Wildlife Management Area
CF-64   Osceola County Environmental Education Center
CF-65   Disney Wilderness Preserve
CF-66   Lake Marion Creek Wildlife Management Area

Polk
CF-67   Florida Trail, Green Swamp East
CF-68   Gator Creek Preserve
CF-69   Tenoroc Hiking Trail, Tenoroc Fish Management Area
CF-70   Saddle Creek Park Nature Trail, Saddle Creek Park
CF-71   Lakeland Highlands Scrub
CF-72   IMC Agrico Peace River Park

CF-73   Nature Trail, Fort Meade Outdoor Recreation Area
CF-74   Norton Agey Nature Trail, Street Audubon Center
CF-75   Catfish Creek Preserve
CF-76   Lake Kissimmee State Park
CF-77   Caloosa Nature Trail, Ridge Audubon Center
CF-78   Jenkins Trail, Tiger Creek Preserve
CF-79   George Cooley Trail, Tiger Creek Preserve
CF-80   Pfundstein Trail, Tiger Creek Preserve
CF-81   Bay Loop Trail, Lake Wales Ridge State Forest
CF-82   Scrub-Jay Loop Trail, Lake Wales Ridge State Forest
CF-83   Reedy Creek Trail, Lake Wales Ridge State Forest
CF-84   Old Cabin Nature Trail, Lake Wales Ridge State Forest
CF-85   Crooked Lake Prairie
CF-86   North Loop, Hickory Lake Scrub
CF-87   South Loop, Hickory Lake Scrub

Sandhills Nature Trail

Rainbow Springs State Park

CF-1 **$** 🚻 Ⓐ

Location: Dunnellon [N29°06.065' W082°26.013'].

Length: 2.1-mile loop.

Map: Ask at park entrance for trail map and interpretive brochure.

Contact Information: Rainbow Springs State Park (352-465-8555), 19158 SW 81st Place Road, Dunnellon, FL 34432.

Directions: Follow US 41 north from Dunnellon, to the park entrance on the right.

The Hike: Starting off in an oak hammock beside the long-abandoned remains of spoil piles and pits from phosphate mining, the trail emerges into an open meadow to follow the treeline to a T intersection. Turn right and walk down a short spur trail to the Rainbow River. The trail follows a forest road/firebreak around the edge of the park property, circling a large natural sandhill area with tall longleaf pines and wiregrass before crossing the open meadow back into the woods to complete the loop.

Highlights: Walk along the edge of abandoned phosphate pits and tailings that create deep gullies down to the river; follow the short spur trail to the Rainbow River's edge. Don't miss the stunning fall wildflowers in the sandhills.

Logistics: The trailhead is a little difficult to find, as it's hidden away at the farthest corner of the developed portion of the park. Follow the old pathways through the botanical gardens past the waterfalls and uphill to the native plant garden on the old rodeo grounds. Continue through the native plant garden to a paved road; the "Nature Trail" sign faces the native plant garden across this road.

Other Activities: Stroll the botanical gardens (best in February with the azaleas in bloom). Go kayaking in a clear kayak across one of Florida's most beautiful first-magnitude springs. There's also swimming and picnicking.

Florida Trail

Marjorie Harris Carr Cross Florida Greenway

CF-2 **F** ⏴ 𝍐

Location: Pruitt Trailhead, Dunnellon [N29°02.823' W082°22.623']; Marshall Swamp Trailhead, Silver Springs [N29°11.015' W082°00.958'].

Length: 32 miles linear, with several intersecting trails (see CF-4, CF-5, CF-6, CF-18).

Map: Trail system map displayed at kiosks; detailed backpacking map available from Florida Trail Association.

Contact Information: Marjorie Harris Carr Cross Florida Greenway (352-236-7143), 8282 SE CR 314, Ocala, FL 34470.

Directions: Pruitt Trailhead: From I-75 exit 341 drive west on CR 484 for 15 miles to the trailhead on the left. Marshall Swamp Trailhead: see hike CF-18.

The Hike: This mile-wide corridor across Central Florida was once meant to be a barge canal expediting shipping across the peninsula. Instead it's been preserved for recreational enjoyment and wildlife habitat. This section of the Florida Trail traverses pine flatwoods, sandhills, scrub, oak hammocks, and former ranchland en route to the shady hydric hammocks of Marshall Swamp.

Highlights: Cross the nation's first land bridge over I-75; enjoy the views of the canal diggings in numerous spots along the trek. Pause for reflection at Stonehenge.

Logistics: Connector trails are blazed blue, and the main trail is blazed orange. In addition to the termini, trailhead parking with restrooms and potable water can be found at Ross Prairie (SR 200), SW 49th Avenue, Land Bridge Trailhead (CR 475A), Santos (SW 80th Avenue), and Baseline Road (CR 33). If you want to backpack this section, call in advance to advise the Office of Greenways and Trails where you plan to camp. You'll experience some rugged terrain, with switchbacks in the trail, thanks to the now-forested dirt piles left behind seventy years ago by the WPA during the construction of the Cross Florida Barge Canal.

Other Activities: There are separate equestrian and mountain biking trails. Access the equestrian trails from Pruitt, Ross Prairie, and Land Bridge, and the biking trails from Santos and Land Bridge.

Hálpata Tastanaki Preserve

CF-3 🐎

Location: Dunnellon [N29°01.679' W082°18.641'].

Length: 4.5 miles round-trip, connecting to 12 miles of multiuse trails.

Map: In Southwest Florida Water Management District Recreation Guide.

Contact Information: Southwest Florida Water Management District (800-423-1476), 2379 Broad Street, Brooksville, FL 34604.

Directions: Follow SR 200 south from Ocala, crossing CR 484. The trailhead is on the right after 2.4 miles, just before the entrance to the Spruce Creek golfing community.

The Hike: Follow the hiker markers from the hiking-only trailhead on SR 200 down a series of forest roads through former ranch land, oak scrub, sandhills, and oak hammocks into a loop trail that links to larger multiuse loops.

Highlights: An active Florida scrub-jay population inhabits the preserve, which also includes an archaeological site, the ghost town of Stockton, which was established after the end of the Second Seminole War.

Logistics: Be sure to sign the register before you start hiking. Large portions of the trail have no shade; bring plenty of water and use adequate sun protection. The out-and-back trail and loop connect to a system of multiuse (primarily equestrian) loops connecting to the Pruitt Trailhead on the Cross Florida Greenway (CF-2). Future plans are for picnic areas and a primitive campsite near the Withlacoochee River.

Other Activities: There are trails for mountain biking and equestrian use, and fishing along the banks of the Withlacoochee River. Enjoy great birding in the early morning.

Ross Prairie Loop

Marjorie Harris Carr Cross Florida Greenway

CF-4 🄵 🏻 🄯 △ 🏠

Location: Dunnellon [N29°02.323' W082°17.722'].

Length: 3.5-mile loop, which uses part of CF-2.

Map: Displayed at kiosk; detailed map of Florida Trail on Cross Florida Greenway available from Florida Trail Association.

Contact Information: Marjorie Harris Carr Cross Florida Greenway (352-236-7143), 8282 SE CR 314, Ocala, FL 34470.

Directions: Follow SR 200 south from Ocala, crossing CR 484. Look for the trailhead at the green sign 1.5 miles beyond CR 484 on the left. Follow the road around to park near the restrooms.

The Hike: As you leave the campground and hike northeast, the trail meanders through the shade of upland hardwood hammocks along the rim of Ross Prairie, a vast open grassland with small ponds. Rising through a pine forest, the blue-blazed trail meets the Florida Trail; turn left. Crossing SR 200, the trail continues along the far edge of Ross Prairie and climbs up onto the 1930s diggings above a segment of the Cross Florida Barge Canal. Watch for the blue blazes to the left to lead you back through the sandhills across SR 200 again to the trailhead.

Highlights: Enjoy the views of Ross Prairie; marvel at the ancient oaks; explore the canal diggings.

Logistics: The connectors to the campground (creating the loop) are blazed blue, and the main trail is blazed orange. To find the trail, climb the hill past the restrooms; the trail starts along the fence line dividing the day-use area from the campground.

Other Activities: There is an RV campground on-site, and separate trails for bicycling and horseback riding.

Land Bridge Loop

Marjorie Harris Carr Cross Florida Greenway

CF-5 **F** 🚻 ⛺ 🏕

Location: Ocala [N29°03.569' W082°09.307'].

Length: 2.2-mile loop, which uses part of CF-2.

Map: Displayed at trailhead kiosk; loop shown on Florida Trail Association map.

Contact Information: Marjorie Harris Carr Cross Florida Greenway (352-236-7143), 8282 SE CR 314, Ocala, FL 34470.

Directions: Pruitt Trailhead: From I-75 exit 341 drive east on CR 484 to the first traffic light. Turn left and drive 2 miles on CR 475A to the Land Bridge Trailhead on the left.

The Hike: Showcasing the nation's first land bridge, this loop trail provides a pleasant trip through oak hammocks and sandhills in the middle of the Cross Florida Greenway. From the Land Bridge Trailhead, start your hike at the "FT" sign at the fence and follow the orange blazes out through the oak hammocks. From the base of the land bridge, follow the blue-blazed trail which starts at the "FT" sign behind the kiosk; this narrow trail leads you back through shady hammocks and across an open field to return to the trailhead.

Highlights: Ancient oaks shade the beginning of the trail, and you'll have to duck and squeeze to get past some of them. Look for resurrection fern and orchids carpeting the oak limbs. When you reach the land bridge, climb up top and wave to the cars below!

Logistics: There are several benches along the trail. Because of the open section of trail, you'll want to use sun protection and carry adequate water. Insect repellent is recommended.

Other Activities: Separate equestrian and mountain biking trails leave this same trailhead. Camping is permitted at the trailhead; call in advance for permission.

Historic Ship Canal Trail

Cross Florida Greenway

CF-6 📖 🚻 🐕

Location: Santos [N29°06.299' W082°05.472'].

Length: 0.5 mile round-trip in a spur off CF-2.

Map: Displayed at kiosk near trailhead.

Contact Information: Marjorie Harris Carr Cross Florida Greenway (352-236-7143), 8282 SE CR 314, Ocala, FL 34470.

Directions: The trail is off US 441 north of Belleview, south of Ocala, on the island of forest between the divided sections of highway.

The Hike: Set in a shady upland forest, this short hike showcases a slice of history: it follows what would have been the route of US 441 across a bridge atop a set of four concrete piers poured in the 1930s in anticipation of construction of the Cross Florida Ship Canal.

Highlights: It's an interesting historic site. Be sure to check out the photos and information on the kiosk before you start your walk.

Logistics: The trailhead starts behind the Santos Sheriff Station. Use SW 80th Avenue to access the sheriff station parking lot. Do not block the helipad. Walk behind the building to find the trailhead sign.

Other Activities: There are several geocaches hidden in the forest along this trail.

Brick City Quarry

Brick City Park

CF-7 👫 ♿ 🐎

Location: Ocala [N29°09.922' W082°07.259'].

Length: 0.7-mile loop.

Map: No map, but easy to follow. Ask at adjoining Discovery Science Center for fact sheet.

Contact Information: Marion County Parks & Recreation (352-236-7111), 8282 SE CR 314, Ocala, FL 34470.

Directions: From US 27/301/441, turn east on SR 464. Make a right at the next major intersection, SE Magnolia Avenue. Drive south briefly to the "Brick City Park" sign on the left at SE 22nd Road; turn left and follow the residential street back to the park entrance on the left.

The Hike: From the parking area by the running track, walk along the fence to the distant kiosk that marks the start of the trail. Climb up on the boardwalk and turn left to walk clockwise around this deep pit, used between 1900 and 1952 as a limestone quarry for plaster making. Boardwalks with decks give you spectacular views of the vegetation-filled bowl and the willow marsh in its bottom. A bamboo forest surrounds one portion of the trail, which branches to allow you to climb down into the quarry and walk out on the deck at the base.

Highlights: There are great views into the quarry from the decks. The tunnel of dense bamboo is fun, and from the bottom of the quarry you can look up to see caves in the limestone walls.

Logistics: The area is open 8:00–6:00 daily, gated at other times. The adjoining Discovery Science Center has historical information, and restrooms. The upper boardwalk and old road are wheelchair accessible with assistance. Boardwalks will be slippery when wet.

Other Activities: You'll find a running track, a playground, and the Discovery Science Center, a small but fun children's museum focused on scientific discovery with both indoor and outdoor activities; museum admission is $2.

Nature Trail

Coehadjoe County Park

CF-8 👪 👫 🐕

Location: Ocala [N29°13.743' W082°04.539'].

Length: 0.7-mile loop.

Map: None available, but park caretaker will point out trail.

Contact Information: Marion County Parks & Recreation (352-236-7111), 8282 SE CR 314, Ocala, FL 34470.

Directions: Located in northeast Ocala, the park entrance is west of CR 35 on NE 35th Street, just before the railroad tracks, on the north side of the road. Follow the park road back past the caretaker's house to the far picnic area loop. The trailhead sign is across from the restrooms.

The Hike: Following a broad, level path through longleaf pine and wiregrass, the keystone species of the sandhill habitat, the trail comes to the edge of the property and reaches a T intersection. A spur to the left leads through the woods out to the park entrance; to stay on the loop, turn right to climb into open sandhill habitat, circling around the picnic area.

Highlights: The trail provides a glimpse into sandhill habitat, with large clumps of healthy deer moss and spring-blooming sandhill wildflowers like lupine and sandhill wireweed.

Logistics: The latter half of the trail is in full sun. The trail ends abruptly along the park entrance road; to return to the trailhead, turn right and follow the road back around past the restrooms.

Other Activities: There are tennis and racquetball courts, a small playground, and picnic pavilions.

Florida Trail

Ocala National Forest

CF-9 🅵 🅲 ⛺ 🏕 ❄

Location: Northern terminus, Buckman Lock near Palatka [N29°32.632' W081°43.725']; southern terminus, Clearwater Lake Recreation Area in Paisley [N28°58.620' W081°33.011'].

Length: 71.3 miles linear.

Map: Trail shown on USFS maps; for backpacking, purchase detailed maps from Florida Trail Association.

Contact Information: Ocala National Forest, Salt Springs Visitor Center (352-685-3070), 14100 North Highway 19, Suite A, Salt Springs, FL 32134.

Directions: Buckman Lock is located off SR 19, south of Palatka; follow Boys Ranch Road to the southern picnic area for the lock. Clearwater Lake Recreation Area is on SR 42 east of Altoona, west of Paisley.

The Hike: This is the longest unbroken section of the Florida National Scenic Trail, perfect for a week-long backpacking trip. As the trail follows the Ocklawaha River floodplain, you'll encounter floodplain forests up to Rodman Dam; southward, the trail skirts ponds in open prairie and scrub, sandhill and pine flatwoods. Most of the hike is through the Big Scrub, a mosaic of sand pine scrub and prairies. South of Alexander Springs, the trail traverses numerous hydric hammocks and rolling hills topped with longleaf pine.

Highlights: Stop for a refreshing dip in Hidden Pond. Set up camp along the breezy edge of Hopkins Prairie. The 8-mile section through the Juniper Prairie Wilderness is one of the most beautiful and secluded pieces of trail in Florida.

Logistics: Camp anywhere you like, except during hunting season, when backpackers must stay in designated campsites. Major trailheads are at the termini and at Alexander Springs, SR 19, Juniper Springs, Pat's Island, Hopkins Prairie, SR 316, Lake Delancy, and Rodman.

Other Activities: The trail passes through or near numerous recreation and camping areas such as Juniper Springs, Salt Springs, Rodman Dam, Alexander Springs, Buck Lake, and Hopkins Prairie, where you can camp, swim, paddle, or just kick back and relax.

Florida Trail in the Big Scrub, Ocala National Forest.

Bear Swamp Trail

Salt Springs Recreation Area, Ocala National Forest

CF-10 $ 𝍐 Ⓒ 𝍐 𝍐

Location: Salt Springs [N29°21.382' W081°43.925'].

Length: 1.2-mile loop.

Map: Campground layout map available at gatehouse.

Contact Information: Ocala National Forest, Lake George Ranger District (352-625-2520), 17147 East SR 40, Silver Springs, FL 34488.

Directions: From SR 19 in Salt Springs, enter the Salt Springs Recreation Area. Pay fee at gatehouse and turn left at the first stop sign. Make a right into the primitive camping area. Go left at the T intersection and park next to the closed restrooms, where you'll see the trailhead sign.

The Hike: From the "Bear Swamp Trail" sign, the trail leads you back to a kiosk. Keep right and head around the loop, walking on a broad footpath through a hardwood forest of oaks, magnolia, and hickory. After 0.5 mile the trail becomes a boardwalk out into Bear Swamp, a floodplain forest of Salt Springs Run, taking you past enormous cypresses. After 0.7 mile the trail becomes a footpath again and takes you around the rest of the loop through mixed pine and hardwood forest.

Highlights: Ancient cypress trees, easily five hundred years old, rise from the waters of Bear Swamp. Look up and notice the size of the galls on the trees: some are as big as a dining room table! Walk softly along the footpath, and you will see wildlife.

Logistics: There is a day-use fee of $4 if you're not camping in the campground.

Other Activities: Swim in Salt Springs, bicycle the forest roads, paddle Salt Springs Run. There are both tent and full hookup campsites; call 352-685-2048 for details.

Salt Springs Loop

Ocala National Forest

CF-11 📖 👫 🐕

Location: Salt Springs [N29°20.411' W081°43.738'].

Length: 1.9-mile loop.

Map: Displayed at trailhead kiosk.

Contact Information: Ocala National Forest, Lake George Ranger District (352-625-2520), 17147 East SR 40, Silver Springs, FL 34488.

Directions: From the junction of SR 314 and SR 19 in Salt Springs, drive south 0.5 mile on SR 19 to the trailhead entrance on the left.

The Hike: This short loop trail provides a good introduction to habitats found within the Big Scrub of the Ocala National Forest, from the oak and sand pine scrub with its gleaming white sand and trees laden in bromeliads to a bayhead and cypress floodplain forest along the edge of Salt Springs Run.

Highlights: Visit in spring to see dogwoods in bloom. The trail terminates at an observation platform on Salt Springs Run after crossing a boardwalk through the cypress floodplain; enjoy the view up and down the run.

Logistics: Parts of the trail nearest to Salt Springs Run may flood in times of high water.

Other Activities: Fish and birdwatch from the observation deck; go kayaking or canoeing on Salt Springs Run (access via CF-10).

Lake Eaton Trails

Ocala National Forest

CF-12 📖 🛖

Location: Lake Eaton [N29°15.795' W081°51.310'].

Length: 4.1 miles in two separate loops.

Map: Displayed at trailhead kiosk; trails shown on general forest map.

Contact Information: Ocala National Forest, Lake George Ranger District (352-625-2520), 17147 East SR 40, Silver Springs, FL 34488.

Directions: Drive north on SR 314 for 7.7 miles from its intersection with SR 40. Just after CR 314A and the "Hunter's Education Center" sign, turn right on right on FR 86, a dirt road, and follow it 1.1 miles to FR 79. Turn right; the trailhead parking is on the left after 0.3 mile. Both trails start from this parking area.

The Hike: The 2.3-mile Lake Eaton Trail, which starts across FR 79, leads downhill through the pine scrub to follow the edge of the floodplain forest surrounding Lake Eaton, with several spur trails and boardwalks out to the lake. The 1.8-mile Lake Eaton Sinkhole Trail also loops through the Big Scrub, but the attraction here is a geological one—a massive sinkhole, 462' in circumference and 122' deep. A spur trail takes you down a staircase into the depths of the sinkhole, which is filled with a hardwood forest.

Highlights: Walk the shady boardwalks along Lake Eaton, and be sure to walk down the staircase into the Lake Eaton Sinkhole and look back up!

Logistics: Both trails spend a good deal of time in open scrub, so wear sun protection and carry plenty of water. Use insect repellent to prevent bites from mosquitoes and chiggers.

Other Activities: Birders can look and listen for the songbirds of the scrub. Along both trails, listen for the chatter of Florida scrub-jays and the calls of rufous-sided towhees.

Silver Glen Springs Recreation Area

Ocala National Forest

CF-13 $ 📖 🚻 👫

Location: Silver Glen Springs [N29°14.766' W081°38.619'].

Length: 2.8 miles in two round-trips.

Map: Displayed on trailhead kiosks.

Contact Information: Ocala National Forest, Lake George Ranger District (352-625-2520), 17147 East SR 40, Silver Springs, FL 34488.

Directions: From the intersection of SR 40 and SR 19 in the Ocala National Forest, take SR 19 north 9 miles. Watch for the Silver Glen Springs Recreation Area on the right. Pay your fee and park near the concession stand.

The Hike: Two trails let you explore the flow of water. The 0.5-mile Spring Boils Trail, which starts in the picnic area adjacent to the Natural Well portion of Silver Glen Spring, leads to a boardwalk and observation decks over Jody's Spring, where numerous tiny bubbling springs kick up underwater sandstorms. The 2.3-mile Lake George Trail starts out along a line of Timucuan middens and works its way to the edge of Lake George, threading through floodplain forests out to sandy bluffs along the shore of the widest lake in the St. Johns River chain of lakes, three miles across.

Highlights: Enjoy panoramic vistas along the Lake George Trail and the fascinating tiny bubbling springs along the Spring Boils Trail.

Logistics: Pay your admission fee at the concession stand before hiking. Be alert for alligators along the Lake George Trail.

Other Activities: Swim in the spring, picnic under the live oaks, or rent a canoe or kayak to explore Silver Glen Run.

The Yearling Trail

Ocala National Forest

CF-14 **F** 📖 ⛺ 🏇

Location: Silver Glen Springs [N29°14.682' W081°38.897'].

Length: 3-mile and 6-mile loops.

Map: Displayed and in brochure at trailhead kiosk.

Contact Information: Ocala National Forest, Lake George Ranger District (352-625-2520), 17147 East SR 40, Silver Springs, FL 34488.

Directions: From the intersection of SR 40 and SR 19 in the Ocala National Forest, take SR 19 north 9 miles. Watch for the "Yearling Trail" sign on the left.

The Hike: It's a ramble around historic Pat's Island, a longleaf pine island in the Big Scrub where homesteads were established in the 1850s. Marjorie Kinnan Rawlings visited the Long family here and based *The Yearling* on her observations and their tales. The short loop passes by the sinkhole; the longer loop utilizes part of the Florida Trail in Juniper Prairie Wilderness, passing a beautiful old dogwood tree and one dry campsite.

Highlights: Visit numerous historic sites, including the Long Cemetery, a cattle dip vat, several homestead sites (one of which was used for the filming of the movie *The Yearling*), and a gigantic sinkhole.

Logistics: This is a dry trail; bring plenty of water. In the open scrub of the access trail you may see scrub-jays. Overnight campers can park at Silver Glen Springs ($3 fee) and walk across US 19 to access the trailhead.

Other Activities: Birdwatch, or swim and paddle at nearby Silver Glen Springs.

Juniper Creek Nature Trail

Juniper Springs Recreation Area, Ocala National Forest

CF-15 **$** 📖 🚻 Ⓐ 👫 🎋

Location: Juniper Springs [N29°11.014' W081°42.768'].

Length: 1 mile round-trip.

Map: Displayed on trailhead sign.

Contact Information: Ocala National Forest, Lake George Ranger District (352-625-2520), 17147 East SR 40, Silver Springs, FL 34488.

Directions: Juniper Springs Recreation Area is along SR 40 between Mill Dam and Astor.

The Hike: This gentle stroll along Juniper Run and Fern Hammock Run leads you through a junglelike forest where needle palms and ferns grow lushly in the understory and tall southern magnolias, cabbage palms, and oaks provide a shady canopy. When you arrive at Fern Hammock Springs, turn left to walk over and around the springs.

Highlights: Stand on the bridge over Fern Hammock Springs and be mesmerized by the play of colors and swirls of sand across the springs. Look up in the trees near the mill on Juniper Run to spot blonde squirrels, an aberration in the gray squirrel gene pool, perpetuated here for generations along Juniper Run.

Logistics: Pay your admission fee at the concession stand before hiking. There are numerous benches along the trail.

Other Activities: Swim in the spring, picnic under the live oaks, stay in the campground, or rent a canoe or kayak for an unforgettable journey down Juniper Run. The Florida Trail (CF-9) crosses the park entrance road on its way into the Juniper Prairie Wilderness, the most spectacular part of the trail.

Silver River Connector Trail

Marjorie Harris Carr Cross Florida Greenway

CF-16 📖 🚻 🐴

Location: Silver Springs [N29°13.131' W082°00.899'].

Length: 1.8 miles linear.

Map: Displayed and in brochure at trailhead kiosk.

Contact Information: Marjorie Harris Carr Cross Florida Greenway (352-236-7143), 8282 SE CR 314, Ocala, FL 34470.

Directions: From SR 40 in Silver Springs, drive east several miles to CR 315; turn left. Park your car at the Ocklawaha Visitor Center on the right. The trail starts from the northern end of the parking area.

The Hike: Leading you down to the Silver River, this linear trail passes through the northernmost cabbage palm flatwoods in Florida, where cabbage palms and slash pines dominate a habitat prone to flooding. After rounding a man-made pond, the trail passes under the massive piers of the SR 40 bridge over the Ocklawaha River and ends at the entrance road to the Ray Wayside Park.

Highlights: Pause at the pond to watch wading birds searching for food in the shallows. Enjoy the variety of ferns and bromeliads along the trail.

Logistics: Follow the orange footprint signposts. The trail may flood when the Silver River is high. Use plenty of insect repellent to ward off the mosquitoes!

Other Activities: Biking is permitted but difficult when there are puddles along the trail. Ray Wayside Park (fee) provides restrooms, a picnic area, fishing, and a launch point for boats, canoes, and kayaks into the Silver River.

Silver River State Park

CF-17 $ 🔲 🚻 Ⓐ 🚼 🐕

Location: Silver Springs: Sandhill Trail [N29°12.086' W082°02.974'], Sinkhole Trail [N29°12.056' W082°02.084'], River Trails [N29°12.061' W082°02.062'].

Length: 8.3 miles in two round-trip trails and two loops.

Map: Available at ranger station at park entrance.

Contact Information: Silver River State Park (352-236-1827), 1425 NE 58th Avenue, Ocala Florida 34470.

Directions: Drive south on SR 33 for 1.1 miles from the intersection of SR 40 and SR 33 in Silver Springs to the park entrance on the left. Continue along the park entrance road, where you'll see the Sandhill Nature Trail parking on the left, to the parking area near the Cracker village.

The Hike: The Sandhill Nature Trail (which can also be reached from the Sinkhole Trail) is a 1.7-mile loop through a longleaf and wiregrass sandhill habitat. The Sinkhole Trail starts next to the Cracker village and follows a 2.5-mile loop through scrub and sandhill, crossing the park entrance road to round a large sinkhole. An extension on the loop, the Old Field Loop, has an abundance of informative interpretive information about the sandhill habitat. Next to the environmental center are the trailheads for the two round-trip trails. The 2-mile Swamp Trail works its way through oak hammocks and floodplain forest to head out on a boardwalk along the Silver River; the 2.1-mile River Trail leads you down to the Silver River, with a loop through cabbage palm flatwoods along the river's floodplain forest of cypress, with several scenic views.

Highlights: Enjoy the river views from the Swamp and River Trails, and great interpretive information throughout the entire trail system.

Logistics: All trails can be accessed from the parking area near the Cracker village. The Swamp Trail is your best choice for taking small children on a walk.

Other Activities: The Silver River Museum has limited hours but is worth a visit to understand the natural history of the river. Wander through the Cracker village to see what life used to be like along the river. The Ross Allen Loop is a 5-mile biking trail starting near the campground.

Marshall Swamp Trail

Marjorie Harris Carr Cross Florida Greenway

CF-18 **F** 📖 👫

Location: Silver Springs [N29°11.015' W082°00.958'].

Length: 4.3 miles round-trip.

Map: On trailhead kiosk; available from Florida Trail Association.

Contact Information: Marjorie Harris Carr Cross Florida Greenway (352-236-7143), 8282 SE CR 314, Ocala, FL 34470.

Directions: From SR 40 in Silver Springs, drive south on SR 35 (Baseline Road), passing the entrance to Silver River State Park (CF-17). Turn left at the traffic light onto Sharpes Ferry Road (CR 314, or SW 7th Street). Trailhead parking entrance is on the right immediately after the Office of Greenways and Trails.

The Hike: Extending through the deeply shaded depths of Marshall Swamp, this linear trail features a rough gravel footpath and a series of bridges that keep you high and dry in even the wettest season. It's an excellent introduction to the hydric hammock ecosystem, dominated by cabbage palms and dotted with cypress swamps.

Highlights: Bridges span primeval cypress swamps; be sure to take the side trail to see a flag pond busy with frogs.

Logistics: Follow the orange footprint signposts and the orange blazes: this is also an official part of the Florida National Scenic Trail through the Cross Florida Greenway (CF-2). Backpackers may camp at the parking area with permission; contact the Office of Greenways and Trails in advance. The trail may flood when the Silver River is high. Use plenty of insect repellent—mosquitoes can be ferocious!

Other Activities: Biking is permitted but difficult on the gravel trail surface.

Carney Island

CF-19 $ 📖 🚻 👫

Location: Ocklawaha [29°00.884' W081°57.870'].

Length: 4 miles in three stacked loops and two connector trails.

Map: Displayed on kiosks at main and connector trailheads.

Contact Information: Marion County Parks & Recreation (352-236-7111), 8282 SE CR 314, Ocala, FL 34470.

Directions: Follow SR 25 south from Belleview toward Ocklawaha; watch for the park signs on the right. Follow signs to the park. Follow the entrance road all the way to the back of the park to reach the main trailhead.

The Hike: From the main trailhead, a 0.3-mile connector follows an earthen causeway into a floodplain forest to reach the first of the three loops, Fern Gully (1 mile), which circles a wetland area dense with ferns. The Quail Loop (2.2 miles) goes around a pine plantation surrounded by oak hammocks; a short spur trail, Whispering Pines, leads into the pines. The final loop is the Fox Trot Loop, which follows the edge of the peninsula into Lake Weir and gives the best view of the lake.

Highlights: There are old-growth live oaks and pines, great views of the lake, and the aroma of wild citrus blossoms wafting through the hardwood hammocks.

Logistics: There is a fee of $3 for up to 8 people in a car. The park is open Oct–Apr 8:00–5:00, May–Sep 8:00–8:00. The trail follows broad forest roads with good signage at every intersection and benches along the route. A 0.5-mile connector, Trail Between the Lakes, ties together the main trailhead and the swimming area.

Other Activities: A large sand beach on Lake Weir has picnic tables, volleyball, and a playground. Bank fishing is permitted.

Nature Trail

Lake Griffin State Park

CF-20 **$** 📖 🚻 ⛺ 🧒

Location: Fruitland Park [N28°51.507' W081°54.009'].

Length: 0.4-mile loop.

Map: Rough map in park brochure; map on trailhead kiosk.

Contact Information: Lake Griffin State Park (904-787-7402), 103 US 27/441, Fruitland Park, FL 34731.

Directions: On US 441 just north of Leesburg, the park entrance is on the east side of the highway. Follow the entrance road back to the parking lot near the boat ramp.

The Hike: Follow the boardwalk along the water's edge and climb up the hill past the restrooms to find the trailhead for this short walk through upland forest above the Dead River Marsh. A fence on the right discourages hikers from wandering into the marsh. A side trail leads to a bench under live oaks. Crossing the campground road, the trail continues down a wild corridor following a streambed; a side trail leads off to the right to the Live Oak Trail.

Highlights: On the extremely short Live Oak Trail, there is a massive live oak near the park entrance (outside the gates) with a crown 130' across and a trunk 10' in diameter.

Logistics: Follow the yellow hiker symbol. The trail passes through part of the campground.

Other Activities: This is a popular park for launching your canoe into the Dead River Marsh for a paddle to Lake Griffin. There are picnic facilities, a playground, and a campground.

Sabal Bluff Preserve

CF-21 🏠

Location: Leesburg [N28°49.853' W081°50.048'].

Length: 5 miles in four trails.

Map: Displayed on trailhead kiosk.

Contact Information: Lake County Water Authority (352-343-3777), 107 North Lake Avenue, Tavares, FL 32778.

Directions: From US 441 in Leesburg, follow SR 44 east to Mobile City Road. Turn left and drive 0.1 mile. Immediately before the mobile home park, turn right and follow the single-lane road down to the parking area.

The Hike: Follow the blue-blazed Bourlay Trail from the parking area through a pine plantation to the Wetlands Trail, which runs along the edge of the wetlands to connect to the Hammock Trail, where you can wander along a hydric hammock. The red-blazed Lake Griffin Trail follows a bluff above Lake Griffin where exotic fruit trees grow.

Highlights: The views from the twenty-foot-tall bluff overlooking Lake Griffin are great.

Logistics: The gates are open 7:00–7:00 daily.

Other Activities: Lake Griffin has picnic tables and a canoe launch.

Flat Island Preserve

CF-22 **F** 📖 ⛺ 🦌

Location: Leesburg [N28°46.721' W081°54.168'].

Length: 3.5-mile loop with several shorter options.

Map: Basic map in Lake County Water Authority brochure; detailed backpacking map available from Florida Trail Association.

Contact Information: Lake County Water Authority (352-343-3777), 107 North Lake Avenue, Tavares, FL 32778.

Directions: Drive south on US 27 from Leesburg to CR 25A; turn right and continue 0.5 mile, then turn left onto narrow Owens Road. After 0.6 mile you'll reach the preserve entrance.

The Hike: This shady and well-maintained trail creates a loop around an island of botanical diversity amid the vast Okahumpa Marsh; more than 110 species of plants have been identified here, from greenfly orchids to collybia mushrooms. The short linear Daubenmire Trail, named after the botanists who studied the island, leads to the Island Hiking Trail loop. Either 1.4 miles (counterclockwise) or 2.1 miles (clockwise) around the loop, there is a spur trail to a primitive campsite, often used by beginning backpackers.

Highlights: Take the side trip down to the canoe launch for a lookout over Okahumpa Marsh.

Logistics: The preserve is open from 8:00 to sunset. The cross trails are well marked. This area has a high concentration of mosquitoes, so apply the insect repellent liberally! The trail may be wet and muddy in places. The backpacker's campsite has benches and a pitcher pump.

Other Activities: Rent a canoe from the Lake County Water Authority (call in advance) and take off on an exploration of the Okahumpa Marsh.

Lake Louisa State Park

CF-23 $ ☐ Ⓒ 🚻 🐴

Location: Clermont [N28°27.632' W081°44.357'].

Length: 7.4 miles of interconnecting trails, with more under development.

Map: Displayed on kiosks; in brochure available at ranger station and at trailhead kiosks.

Contact Information: Lake Louisa State Park (352-394-3969), 12549 State Park Drive, Clermont, FL 34711.

Directions: Follow US 27 south of Clermont 10 miles to park entrance on west side of highway.

The Hike: Lake Louisa State Park provides a trail system with two trailheads, each kicking off with an interpretive nature trail. Nearest the ranger station, the Killdeer Trail connects to the trail system ranging across the broad open scrub restoration area; a more pleasant start is the Cypress Loop from the parking area by Lake Louisa. Most of the named trails follow old jeep roads, but are clearly marked with signs and intersection numbers that correspond to the map.

Highlights: View Lake Louisa and water-filled sinkholes from the high hills. Walk along cypress stands on the edge of Lake Louisa.

Logistics: Pets are permitted if on leash. The park is open from 8:00 to sunset. Most of the trail system is in full sun, so pick a cool day to hike it, and bring plenty of water. The trails nearest the lake may be soggy or flooded in places.

Other Activities: Biking is permitted on the hiking trail system; horseback riding is on a separate trail system on the south side of the park, near the campground. There is picnicking and fishing along Lake Louisa.

Sara Maude Mason Nature Preserve

CF-24 📖 👫

Location: Howey-in-the-Hills [N28°42.069' W081°45.844'].

Length: 0.6-mile loop, plus spur trail to side entrance.

Map: Posted on trailhead kiosk.

Contact Information: Sara Maude Mason Nature Preserve (352-324-2290), Howey-in-the-Hills, FL 34737.

Directions: From SR 19 in Howey-in-the-Hills, drive 0.9 mile on Rebel's Road. Turn right at Buckhill Road at the "Nature Preserve" sign; follow the red clay road 0.2 mile to the trailhead parking area on the left.

The Hike: This shady trail spends most of its time on a boardwalk over a floodplain forest along Little Lake Harris, where ferns grow in profusion beneath the sweet gum, maples, and cypresses. Looping back into a dense hardwood hammock, the boardwalk ends and the trail forks, with the right fork headed to a walking trail along Lakeshore Boulevard and the left fork following a forest road through the woods back to the main trailhead.

Highlights: It's a pleasant walk through the swamp without getting your feet wet. Bring binoculars for the view from the observation tower on the lake.

Logistics: The preserve is open dawn to dusk. Interpretive information is available at the kiosk. There's an additional entrance from Griffin Stormwater Park with a connecting paved trail to downtown.

Other Activities: The preserve has picnic tables and swings.

Tavares Nature Park

CF-25 📖 🐎

Location: Tavares [N28°47.145' W081°44.647'].

Length: 2.1 miles in two loops and a boardwalk trail.

Map: On trailhead kiosk.

Contact Information: City of Tavares (352-742-6319), 123 North St. Clair Abrams Avenue, Tavares, FL 32778.

Directions: From SR 19, turn south on Lake Dora Circle (one block west of Woodlea); after crossing the railroad tracks, turn right on Milwaukee Avenue, following "Tavares Nature Park" signs. The park is on the right just past Sunshine Lane.

The Hike: Starting at the kiosk, the short loop leads you into the pine flatwoods and emerges at a clearing with picnic tables along a pond covered in water lilies. To the right, the secondary loop heads out into agricultural land that is returning to natural habitat, including a pretty section of sand pine and rosemary scrub, as well as bayheads. To the left, the trail leads to a spur trail to a boardwalk on Lake Dora.

Highlights: There is a lengthy boardwalk along the northern shore of Lake Dora that follows the edge of the cypress floodplain forest and extends out into the lake, where you'll see cormorants roosting in the willows and cypresses, and alligators cruising the lake.

Logistics: Opening hours are 7:00 to dusk. The large grassy parking area may be muddy at times.

Other Activities: Equestrians and bicyclists are permitted on the trails but not on the boardwalk. Fishing from the boardwalk is permitted. Bring a picnic lunch!

Sawgrass Island Preserve

CF-26 ⛺ 🏠

Location: Umatilla [N28°57.184' W081°45.390'].

Length: Some 3 miles suitable for hiking in an 8-mile trail network.

Map: In brochure from Lake County Water Authority, with mileage listed for each trail segment.

Contact Information: Lake County Water Authority (352-343-3777), 107 North Lake Avenue, Tavares, FL 32778.

Directions: Follow CR 452 north from Eustis to Lake Yale; turn right on Em-En-El Grove Road. Follow it to the end and make a right onto Thomas Boat Landing Road. Turn left on Sawgrass Island Road and follow the one-lane track, which makes two sharp turns before ending at the parking area.

The Hike: From the parking area, follow the Sawgrass Causeway, which leads across the marshes to the east. In the hammock, follow the Bog Button Trail, the Hammock Trail, and the Cactus Trail for an introduction to the habitats. The North Loop Trail provides a short loop from the parking area into an oak hammock.

Highlights: There are great views of the sawgrass marsh along the causeway, with Lake Yale in the distance to the south.

Logistics: The preserve is open daily from 8:00 to sunset. Most of the trails are primarily used by equestrians, so you will encounter a lot of soft sand underfoot if you attempt the Bent Pine Trail or the Bear Prairie Trail. Primitive camping requires a permit (free) from the Lake County Water Authority.

Other Activities: The network of equestrian trails is extensive.

Hidden Waters Preserve

CF-27

Location: Eustis [N28°50.068' W081°39.279'].

Length: 1-mile loop.

Map: Displayed on trailhead kiosk.

Contact Information: Lake County Water Authority (352-343-3777), 107 North Lake Avenue, Tavares, FL 32778.

Directions: From US 441, take CR 44-B (Donnelly Road) north to Waycross Ave; turn left. After 0.7 mile you see Abrams Road on the left: the new eastern entrance is just up Abrams on the left. Continue down Waycross to Country Club Road for the main entrance. Turn left on Country Club, and watch for the entrance on the right.

The Hike: The Eichelberger Sink, the geological feature that dominates this property, is ringed by two trails. The Ravine Trail, blazed red, takes you down into the depths of the sinkhole through a lush forest. The Lake Alfred Trail, blazed blue, follows the edge of the freshwater marsh along the sinkhole lake. The damp north slope of the sinkhole shelters an Appalachian-like forest, while the south slope hosts a drier sandhill environment.

Highlights: Follow the Ravine Trail down as it drops into the sinkhole, paralleled by a burbling stream that ends up in the lake at the bottom.

Logistics: The preserve is open daily from 8:00 to sunset. There is an elevation change of more than a hundred feet in each direction as you climb down into the sinkhole and back out again, so be prepared to work those muscles!

Other Activities: Birdwatch around Lake Alfred, where local birders have spotted Cooper's hawks, a threatened species in Florida.

Palm Island Park

CF-28 📖 ♿ 🚻

Location: Mount Dora [N28°47.621' W081°38.509'].

Length: 1 mile of trails and boardwalks, with a 0.5-mile minimum walk.

Map: On trailhead kiosk.

Contact Information: City of Mount Dora Leisure Services, Recreation Division (352-735-7155), PO Box 176, Mount Dora, FL 32756-0176.

Directions: From US 441, follow Donnelly Street through downtown Mount Dora. Turn left on East 3rd Avenue, and right on South Tremain Street. Follow South Tremain Street to the parking area at the intersection with Liberty Avenue; the trail starts at the far end of the parking lot on the lakeshore.

The Hike: A boardwalk leads along a wild and wonderful undeveloped shoreline of massive pond cypresses to Palm Island, a dark hammock dominated by cabbage palms and live oaks. Once on the island, choose between using the boardwalks and meandering the wilder shaded paths through the forest, but don't miss the second stretch of lakefront boardwalk out on the island.

Highlights: Enjoy sweeping views of Lake Dora and excellent birding. As evidenced by white spots on the leaves, birds roost en masse in the shoreline cypresses at dusk. Watch for alligators cruising the shallows beneath the cattails. Do some exploring on the natural trails, and you'll discover a cypress with a hollow big enough to step into.

Logistics: The gate is open at 9:00, locked at sunset. Frequent benches make this an easy walk for visitors of all ages and abilities.

Other Activities: Fishing is permitted from the boardwalk except on weekends and holidays. There are picnic shelters with grills at the trailhead. Two parks adjoin: Grantham Point has fishing piers, the "Port of Mount Dora," and the Mount Dora lighthouse; Gilbert Park has a large playground, a camellia garden, and a short paved path along the landscaped cascades of Alexander Creek.

Timucuan Indian Nature Trail

Alexander Springs Recreation Area
Ocala National Forest

CF-29 $ 📖 🚻 🅐 ♿ 🚼 ⛺

Location: Astor [N29°04.851' W081°34.579'].

Length: 1.1-mile loop.

Map: In park brochure.

Contact Information: Recreation Resource Management, Inc. (352-625-0546), 26701 East SR 40, Silver Springs, FL 34488.

Directions: From SR 40 eastbound, turn south on the Astor Park Cutoff (or turn south on CR 445A from SR 40 westbound) and follow the signs. After 0.4 mile, turn left on CR 445 and continue south 5.7 miles. The park entrance is on the right immediately after the bridge over Alexander Run.

The Hike: Boardwalks and footpaths lead you on an exploration of habitats surrounding the headspring of Alexander Run, starting off with a hydric hammock with a junglelike feel. Keep to the right to walk counterclockwise around the loop by clambering up the sand path to walk through a river bluff habitat. A long boardwalk carries you across a hammock before the trail rises into the Big Scrub, introducing you to plants like rusty lyonia and silk bay. As you lose elevation, you enter a forest of ancient cypress trees, rejoining the boardwalk along Alexander Run. There are several observation decks along the run. Return along the boardwalk amid the palms to complete the loop.

Highlights: This is one of the most beautiful short trails in the National Forests in Florida, introducing you to the Ocala National Forest's major habitats in a very short stroll.

Logistics: There is a $4 *per person* entrance fee. Wheelchairs can access only the boardwalk section of the loop, approximately one-third of the trail.

Other Activities: This is a full-service facility, with concession stands and rentals. You can swim in the spring, canoe down Alexander Run, camp in the shady campground, picnic within sight of the sparkling water, or follow the blue-blazed trail from the campground to connect up with the Florida Trail (hike CF-9).

Sandpine Scrub Forest Nature Trail

Ocala National Forest

CF-30 📖 🚸

Location: Astor Park [N29°06.394' W081°37.889'].

Length: 0.3-mile loop.

Map: Available at trailhead kiosk.

Contact Information: University of Florida Extension, 4H Camp Ocala (352-759-2288), Institution of Food and Agricultural Services, Gainesville, FL 32611.

Directions: From the junction of SR 40 and SR 19 in the Ocala National Forest, drive south to 4H Camp Ocala on the right. Follow the entrance road into the camp and park on the left, across from the main buildings, to access the nature trail.

The Hike: This short interpretive trail leads you through a mature sand pine scrub with an understory of scrub oaks, with nineteen interpretive stations along the way.

Highlights: The weather station along the trail is one of only two in Florida, out of twenty-one in the United States, and collects data on the effects of climate change. Note the large number of gopher tortoise burrows in the forest.

Logistics: Access to the site may be limited when youth camps are in session.

Other Activities: Registered campers can enjoy fishing, canoeing, and camping.

St. Francis Hiking Trail

Ocala National Forest

CF-31 **F** 📖 ⛺ 🏕

Location: Deland [N29°00.763' W081°23.553'].

Length: 2.8-mile and 7.7-mile loops.

Map: Displayed at kiosk; detailed backpacking map available from Florida Trail Association.

Contact Information: Ocala National Forest, Lake George Ranger District (352-625-2520), 17147 East SR 40, Silver Springs, FL 34488.

Directions: From US 17 in Deland, drive west on SR 44 west over the Whitehead Bridge; turn right onto CR 42. Make the first right at the "River Forest Group Camp" sign on FR 542. The trailhead parking is on the left after 0.3 mile.

The Hike: The 2.8-mile yellow-blazed interpretive loop traverses bridges and boardwalks through the floodplain forest to the Rattlesnake Well Trail, which loops past a sulfuric spring. Use this trail to access the 7.7-mile main loop, which parallels the St. Francis Dead River through the floodplain forest to a road marking the boundary with the Alexander Springs Wilderness Area. This is the former site of the river town of St. Francis. The trail turns left to head through the now defunct town, and loops back to the parking area in a winding route through pine flatwoods and bayheads.

Highlights: It's always damp and humid along the riverside section of this trail, so many interesting varieties of fungi flourish on and in rotting logs and stumps. When you reach the ghost town of St. Francis (along the old road), take a couple of minutes to walk down to the right to the former landing along the river.

Logistics: Be cautious crossing on bridges and boardwalks, since most have a thin layer of algae. Backpackers should look for dry ground in the ghost town area. If the St. Johns River is high, the trail will be flooded; after a heavy rain, the pine flatwoods will be flooded.

Other Activities: Hunting is permitted; check hunt dates and wear blaze orange if you hike at those times, since this is a very popular hunting area, especially during deer season.

Florida Trail

Seminole State Forest

CF-32 Ⓕ $ ◿ 🛖

Location: Sorrento [N28°49.160' W081°25.686'].

Length: 7.4 miles linear plus 9-mile loop.

Map: Rough map in state forest brochure; detailed backpacking map available from Florida Trail Association

Contact Information: Seminole State Forest (352-360-6675), Leesburg Forestry Station, 9610 CR 44, Leesburg, FL 34788.

Directions: From I-4 exit 51, Sanford, drive 5.4 miles west on SR 46 to the forest entrance, just beyond the Wekiva River bridge on the right, to reach the southern trailhead. The northern trailhead is off SR 44 in Cassia, east of SR 44A.

The Hike: This segment of the Florida Trail provides an excellent day hike if you hike between two cars (place one at each trailhead) or a nice weekend backpacking trip if you utilize the loop trail. There are two designated campsites along the main route, and you walk through a variety of habitats, from pine flatwoods to open scrub to palm hammocks along waterways draining into the Wekiva River.

Highlights: Don't miss Shark Tooth Spring, where crystalline water pours out of a cave in the side of a hill and tiny fossilized shark's teeth glimmer in the sand bottom of the run.

Logistics: Be aware of hunting seasons and dress accordingly. The single shelter along the trail is not in good shape and should be used only in an emergency. The picnic table along Blackwater Run makes a great rest stop. Bring plenty of water, as the open scrub is a hot, dry place. This is bear country— use proper food handling techniques when camping. The main trail is blazed orange, the side loop white.

Other Activities: Canoe down Blackwater Run, fish in the streams, or camp at the primitive camps along the forest roads.

Rock Springs Run Trail

Rock Springs Run State Reserve

CF-33 **Ⓕ** **$** 🛶 ⛺

Location: Sorrento [N28°48.287' W081°27.224'].

Length: 7-mile and 13.2-mile loops.

Map: Map available from Florida Trail Association.

Contact Information: Wekiva Basin Geo Park (407-884-2009), 1800 Wekiwa Circle, Apopka, FL 32712-2599.

Directions: From I-4 exit 51, Sanford, drive 7.4 miles west on SR 46 to the park entrance on the left. After paying at the self-pay station, continue 0.6 mile to the hiker parking area on the right.

The Hike: Heading counterclockwise from the parking area, follow the white blazes along the North Loop through oak hammocks and vast pine flatwoods and out into the open scrub. This is the stomping ground of the Florida black bear, and chances are high you'll see bear tracks or bear scat along the trail. Signposts indicate the junction with the South Loop, which heads down to Rock Springs Run by following forest roads. The North Loop is more of a footpath, and as it swings around the loop, it follows shaded streams, skirts open meadows, and enters stretches of young oak hammock where Florida scrub-jay families live.

Highlights: There is a beautiful campsite right along the edge of Rock Springs Run, and the opportunity to see Florida scrub-jays in the scrub.

Logistics: The gates are closed from 6:00 p.m. to 8:00 a.m. to keep the bears *in*. If you plan to camp here, you must inform the rangers at Wekiwa Springs by phone. This is bear country—use proper food handling techniques when camping. The trails are closed to hiking during hunting season. Bring plenty of water, as you'll cross a lot of open scrub. Numerous cross trails can make this a confusing hike—a map and compass (or GPS) are recommended.

Other Activities: There are separate equestrian and bicycle trails; riding stables inside the park offer trail rides (407-735-6266).

Hog Island Nature Trail

Hog Island Recreation Area
Withlacoochee State Forest

CF-34 📖 👫 🅰

Location: Nobleton [N28°37.185' W082°14.465'].

Length: 1.6-mile loop.

Map: In interpretive guide at trailhead kiosk.

Contact Information: Withlacoochee State Forest (352-754-6896), 15003 Broad Street, Brooksville, FL 34601.

Directions: From US 301 in Bushnell, follow CR 476 west to CR 635. Turn left and drive 0.7 mile to the stop sign. Continue straight for 1 mile on the unpaved road to the entrance, and turn right into the recreation area. Continue past the Croom Hiking Trail trailhead 0.4 mile to the picnic area on the river on the right.

The Hike: This pretty little gem is nearly overshadowed by its nearby big brother, the Croom Hiking Trail (CF-35). Starting out from the trailhead kiosk, you come to a fork in the trail at the start of the loop. Keep to the left to walk amid the cypresses along a side channel of the Withlacoochee River along the edge of the river bluff forest. The trail loops past large sinks into the upland pine forests, crosses the entrance road, and joins the Croom Hiking Trail briefly to round some sinkholes before returning across the road to complete the loop.

Highlights: A riverside sink contains primeval giants, cypresses of incredible size. Several bluffs provide good views of the waterway.

Logistics: The trail is blazed mustard yellow; keep alert for when it briefly joins the Croom Hiking Trail (orange blazes) and then leaves it again. Benches make for a comfortable stroll, and numbered posts correspond to the interpretive brochure. The restrooms are at the nearby campground, not at the trailhead. The trail may be flooded in times of high water on the Withlacoochee River.

Other Activities: Cast a line or launch your boat at the picnic area after chowing down with the family. The quiet and deeply shaded Hog Island Campground is one of my favorites in the region.

Croom Hiking Trail

Croom Tract at Hog Island
Withlacoochee State Forest

CF-35

Location: Hog Island Recreation Area, Nobleton [N28°37.315' W082°14.549']; River Junction Recreation Area, Croom-a-Coochee.

Length: 6.8 miles linear.

Map: Rough map may be available in brochure at kiosk; for more detail, obtain a map from Florida Trail Association.

Contact Information: Withlacoochee State Forest (352-754-6896), 15003 Broad Street, Brooksville, FL 34601.

Directions: From US 301 in Bushnell, follow CR 476 west to CR 635. Turn left and drive 0.7 mile to the stop sign. Continue straight for 1 mile on the unpaved road to the entrance, and turn right into the recreation area. Trailhead parking is well marked on the right.

The Hike: Walk through shady hardwood forests, pine flatwoods, and up-lands along the Withlacoochee River floodplain, an ideal place to see wildlife. After leaving Hog Island, the trail meanders around open prairies, cuts through dense forests of southern magnolia, and skirts the edges of cypress swamps along the Withlacoochee River, emerging at the river's edge at Iron Bridge. More dense forest shades the trail en route to its end.

Highlights: The trail circles around old sinkholes under old-growth oaks near the Hog Island end of the trail. Take in the great river views around Iron Bridge, and a "natural arch" created by a bent magnolia down near River Junction.

Logistics: Both recreation areas open at 8 a.m. and lock their gates at 10:00 p.m. Restrooms are available in camping areas, not at the trailhead. This is a good one-way day hike if you have two cars available for shuttling. The trail briefly merges with a horse trail to cut under I-75. No overnight camping is permitted along the trail. Follow the orange blazes to stay on the main trail, which is intersected by the yellow-blazed Hog Island Nature Trail (CF-34).

Other Activities: There are canoe launches and camping at both recreation areas, as well as a few picnic tables along the water. Withlacoochee State Forest permits seasonal hunting; see www.floridaconservation.org for details. Hikers should always wear blaze orange vests during hunting season.

Pine Flatwoods Trail

Dade Battlefield Historic State Park

CF-36 $ 📖 🚻 👫 🐎 ♿

Location: Bushnell [N28°39.155' W082°07.689'].

Length: 0.7-mile loop.

Map: Rough sketch of trail in park brochure.

Contact Information: Dade Battlefield Historic State Park (352- 793-4781), 7200 CR 603 (South Battlefield Drive), Bushnell, FL 33513.

Directions: From US 301, take CR 476 west for 0.5 mile. Turn left on Battlefield Drive, which leads into the park. After paying your entrance fee, turn right into the first parking area. Follow the "Nature Trail" signs to the trailhead adjacent to the reenactment field.

The Hike: It's a gentle loop through the longleaf pine forest that saw one of the bloodiest moments in Florida history. On December 28, 1835, Seminole warriors who opposed the federal government's attempt to remove them from Florida waited in ambush for U.S. Army soldiers marching down the Fort King Military Road. The Seminoles' initial attack killed or wounded more than half of the 108 soldiers. After several hours, only three of the soldiers, thought dead, escaped to tell the tale. The incident sparked the Second Seminole War.

Highlights: The interpretive signs are unlike any seen in other state parks—they're artfully mounted on slices from trees. Blueberries abound in late spring. Note the many catfaced pines from the turpentine era, some with flashing still embedded in their trunks.

Logistics: There are numerous unmarked trail junctions within the trail system, so sticking to the loop is a little tough—pick a direction and go! All trails stay within the park and the understory of the forest is relatively open.

Other Activities: Visit the visitor center (open 9:00–5:00) for the full story on the Dade Massacre and the Seminole Wars. A separate trail on the opposite side of the park road leads past monuments commemorating the fallen. There are picnic pavilions (including a screened room), a playground, and a large grassy field that hosts the battle reenactment each December.

Oakland Nature Preserve

CF-37 　⊞　♦♦　♿　☆♦　❋

Location: Oakland [N28°33.302' W081°38.390'].

Length: 1.1 miles round-trip.

Map: Displayed on trailhead kiosk and available in park brochure.

Contact Information: Town of Oakland (407-737-2400; www.oaklandnaturepreserve.org), PO Box 98, Oakland, FL 34760.

Directions: From Florida's Turnpike exit for SR 50, Winter Garden, drive east 0.2 mile to Tubb Street. Turn left and drive to the stop sign at CR 438 (Oakland Avenue). Turn left and continue 0.5 mile to the preserve entrance on the right.

The Hike: This is a pleasant, meandering stroll along a broad boardwalk through floodplain forests on the edge of Lake Apopka. Dense oak hammocks yield to trees that prefer a little water—red maples and sweet gum—as the forest floor becomes more thickly carpeted with ferns. Shady shelters and benches make this an easy walk for anyone.

Highlights: Enjoy a fabulous view of the lake from the shaded observation platform at trail's end, and great wildflowers and ferns along the way. Interpretive plant identifications add to your experience.

Logistics: The reserve is for day use only. There is a portable toilet 0.1 mile along the trail, with formal restrooms planned. The boardwalk suffers occasional damage from fallen trees; take care to skirt problem areas.

Other Activities: The birding along the trail is superb! The preserve is also adjacent to the West Orange Trail, an extremely popular paved bicycle trail. A nature center and additional upland trails are planned for the future.

Tibet-Butler Preserve

CF-38 📖 🚻 👥

Location: Lake Buena Vista [N28°26.563' W081°32.476'].

Length: 3.5 miles in several loops, with shorter hikes possible.

Map: Displayed at trailhead kiosk and available in interpretive brochure.

Contact Information: Tibet-Butler Preserve (407-876-6696), 8777 SR 535, Orlando, FL 32836.

Directions: From I-4 exit 68, drive north on SR 535, passing the entrance to Walt Disney World at the first light before you turn left at the second light. Drive 5.3 miles to the park entrance on the right. The entrance road leads to parking in front of the environmental center.

The Hike: Preserving 440 acres of pine flatwoods along the Tibet-Butler chain of lakes, this preserve is all about hiking—even though you can hear the mournful whistle of the railroad in the Magic Kingdom just a mile or two away. Follow the adventuresome and sometimes soggy Palmetto Passage around the bayhead, or take the easy Pine Circle Trail through the flatwoods. The Fallen Log Crossing provides a boardwalk across the bayhead, leading to scrub habitat in the Tarflower Loop and a boardwalk over the cypresses on the Osprey Overlook.

Highlights: Enjoy scrambling over and under trees and roots on the Palmetto Passage, and breathing in the sweet scent of tarflowers on the Tarflower Loop.

Logistics: Opening hours are Wed–Sun 8:00–6:00, closed Mon–Tue. Sign in and out of the hiker register at the trailhead.

Other Activities: Before starting your trip, visit the educational center, where gopher tortoises roam the native plant garden. Bring your binoculars and settle in for some birdwatching from the observation deck on the Osprey Overlook along Lake Tibet. Have a picnic lunch and let the kids play at the trailhead.

Nature Trail

Bill Fredrick Park at Turkey Lake

CF-39 $ 👫 🅰 👫 🐕

Location: Orlando [N28°29.943' W081°28.565'].

Length: 1.6 miles round-trip.

Map: Handed out at entrance station.

Contact Information: Bill Fredrick Park at Turkey Lake (407-299-5581), City of Orlando, 1206 West Columbia Street, Orlando, FL 32805.

Directions: From I-4, take Conroy Road and drive north, crossing Kirkman and Turkey Lake Boulevard before turning right on Hiawassee. Continue 0.8 mile to the park entrance on the right. Follow the entrance road all the way through the park to where it reaches a T intersection; turn right and continue to the parking area for cabin and tent camping.

The Hike: The nature trail parallels Florida's Turnpike along a ribbon of sand pine scrub on the park's western border. There are benches and some shaded pavilions along the way, as well as a trailside restroom by the children's farm. "Nature Trail" signs point the way. The linear trail ends near a large picnic pavilion. You can use the paved bike trail to make a return loop, or walk back the way you came.

Highlights: It's a glimpse into the only significant sand pine scrub remaining within the City of Orlando. Look for plants that you won't see anywhere else in the city, like scrub hickory, scrub plum, and aromatic silk bay.

Logistics: The park is open 8:00–7:00. There is a $4 vehicle or $2 individual admission fee. The trailhead is a little tough to find. From the "Nature Trail" sign at the cabins, walk along the line of vegetation behind the cabins and cross the disc golf course to #17 to find the trailhead sign.

Other Activities: Come for the day and enjoy the swimming pool, volleyball courts, paved bike trail, children's farm, and lots of picnicking, as well as rental fishing gear and fishing boats. There are RV spaces, tent camping, and camping cabins on-site.

Mead Gardens

CF-40 🚻 🚸 🐕

Location: Winter Park [N28°35.050' W081°21.491'].

Length: Trail network with 1.5-mile loop.

Map: None available.

Contact Information: City of Winter Park (407-599-3334), 401 Park Avenue South, Winter Park, FL 32789.

Directions: From I-4 in Winter Park, take SR 426 (Fairbanks Avenue) east. After crossing US 17/92, turn right on South Denning Drive. Continue 0.5 mile and turn left on Garden Drive to enter the park. Drive down to the end of the circle and park near the "Braille Trail" sign.

The Hike: Opened in 1940 as a formal botanical garden, Mead Gardens is partially manicured, partially wild, offering a boardwalk loop over a floodplain forest and gentle paths along a cypress-lined crystalline creek that links lakes in Orlando and Winter Park. A forested sinkhole dominates the northeast corner of the park, with several unmarked rugged trails (created by bikers) down and up the rugged slopes.

Highlights: Blue flag irises bloom each spring along the boardwalk, ancient cypress trees tower over the creek, and there is a natural waterfall along the creek, a tiny cascade that burbles as it splashes over tree roots.

Logistics: Start your walk at the "Braille Trail" sign. Boardwalks may be slippery when wet.

Other Activities: Walk the sensory garden, or visit in early spring for a sensory overload when the azaleas and citrus are both in bloom. A paved biking trail crosses the north end of the park, and there are numerous picnic areas beneath the pines and oaks.

Orlando Wetlands Park

CF-41 🅕 📖

Location: Christmas [N28°34.220' W080°59.732'].

Length: 6-plus miles of hiking, in loops formed from shorter trails.

Map: Displayed and in brochure at trailhead kiosk; available in St. Johns River Water Management District's *Recreation Guide to District Lands.*

Contact Information: Orlando Wetlands Park, City of Orlando (407- 246-2288), 25115 Wheeler Road, Christmas, FL 32709.

Directions: From SR 50 in Christmas, take Fort Christmas Road north. At the sharp left curve, turn right onto Wheeler Road into the park entrance. Continue down the road to the parking area on the left.

The Hike: The extensive trail system through this maze of natural hammocks and man-made marshes includes the Florida Trail, which follows the northern edge of the park; the 1-mile linear South Woods Branch Trail, which tunnels through a shady palm hammock before emerging along the berm of a levee enclosing Lake Searcy, one of the water retention areas in the park; and the 0.9-mile North Woods Branch Trail, which links Lake Searcy with a 3-mile section of the Florida Trail. The Berm Trail creates several loops and leads to an observation deck along the deeper wetlands near Wheeler Road.

Highlights: There are great views across Lake Searcy and the other impoundments from many vantage points on the hiking trails and berms. Wildlife is abundant here—watch for deer, alligators, and thousands of birds.

Logistics: The park is open January 21 through September 30, from sunrise to a half hour before sunset; authorization is required to enter the park at other times. The Florida Trail, South Woods Branch Trail, and North Woods Branch Trail are open to hiking only. When dry, the Berm Trail is wheelchair accessible with assistance. Be alert to the activity of alligators along the berms.

Other Activities: Bike or jog on the dike trails, use the picnic pavilions at the front entrance, and spend plenty of time birdwatching!

Florida Trail

Seminole Ranch Conservation Area

CF-42 ⓕ 🏕 🦌

Location: Christmas [N28°34.152' W081°00.791'].

Length: 4.9 miles linear.

Map: In St. Johns River Water Management District's *Recreation Guide to District Lands*; detailed backpacking map available from Florida Trail Association.

Contact Information: St. Johns River Water Management District (904-529-2380), PO Box 1429, Palatka, FL 32178-1429.

Directions: The trail crosses SR 50 in Christmas in front of the Christmas RV Park. To park your car for a day hike, take Fort Christmas Road north from SR 50. At the sharp left curve, turn right onto Wheeler Road into the park entrance. Continue down the road to the parking area on the right. Follow the blue blazes to the hunt check station to meet the main trail.

The Hike: The trail follows a string of hydric hammocks in the St. Johns River floodplain, crossing bridges over slow-moving tannic streams with steep sand bluffs. Ferns sprout from the tops and trunks of the cabbage palms.

Highlights: This is a lush, humid environment presenting the full spectrum of green—from palm fronds to sphagnum moss, shoelace ferns to oak leaves. A secluded primitive campsite provides a getaway for hikers.

Logistics: As the trail is in a floodplain, it is prone to flooding. Check on water levels in the St. Johns River before walking this trail; expect muddy feet and wading in portions of the trail. Use insect repellent—this is a swamp forest! The trail connects to Orlando Wetlands Park (CF-41) at the north end.

Other Activities: Seasonal hunting is permitted; check www.floridaconservation.org for details and wear blaze orange when hiking during hunting season.

Florida Trail

Tosohatchee Reserve State Park

CF-43 🅕 $ 🏕 🦌

Location: Christmas [GPS] [N28°29.910' W080°59.805'].

Length: 11.3 miles linear, plus loop trails to designated campsites.

Map: Rough map in park brochure; detailed backpacking map available from Florida Trail Association.

Contact Information: Tosohatchee Reserve State Park (407-568-5893), 3365 Taylor Creek Road, Christmas, FL 32709.

Directions: From SR 50 in Christmas, follow Taylor Creek Road south to the park entrance on the left. Stop and pick up a park map, and drive in to the trailhead parking on Powerline Road. The trail can also be accessed from the end of Yates Road off SR 520; do not block the gate.

The Hike: Traversing vast pine flatwoods, the Florida Trail crosses Tosohatchee Reserve, a 28,000-acre tract of lands protecting the western edge of the St. Johns River floodplain. Walk through one of the state's oldest slash pine forests and the virgin cypress swamp at Jim Creek; stand beneath a canopy of ancient live oaks along a tannic creek. Side trails create loop possibilities for weekend backpacking.

Highlights: Jim Creek, a virgin cypress swamp, lies south of where the trail crosses Fish Hole Road. Wildlife encounters are common here—watch for deer, armadillos, foxes, and wild turkeys in the pine flatwoods.

Logistics: Hikers following the through trail must keep alert at intersections for signage, since the blazes are orange in all directions. The designated Tiger Creek Campsite is 0.3 mile west of the main trail along the Tiger Creek Trail. Most of the roads in the reserve have deep soft sand and may not be passable by passenger cars. Weekend backpackers must make reservations in advance for use of the campsites.

Other Activities: Seasonal hunting is permitted; check www.floridaconservation.org for hunt dates. Always wear a blaze orange vest when hiking during hunting season.

Hal Scott Regional Preserve

CF-44 🅕 ⟁ 🛖

Location: Bithlo [N28°29.180' W081°05.750'].

Length: 5.1-mile loop.

Map: Displayed at trailhead kiosk and available in St. Johns River Water Management District's *Recreation Guide to District Lands*; detailed backpacking map available from Florida Trail Association.

Contact Information: St. Johns River Water Management District (904-529-2380), PO Box 1429, Palatka, FL 32178-1429.

Directions: Leaving the Orlando International Airport area, drive east on SR 528 (Beeline Expressway). Take exit 24, Dallas Boulevard. Turn left at the end of the ramp, and drive 2.4 miles to the park entrance, on the left.

The Hike: Follow the trail that begins at the hiker symbol, which parallels the immense parking area before heading out into the pine flatwoods. Keep alert for the trail junction to the right. Turn right and follow the blue blazes through the pine flatwoods. At the T intersection, an optional 5-mile loop starts just beyond the creek on your right, but you'll have to wade to get to it. To stay on the main loop, turn left. A spur leads down to Curry Ford on the Econlockhatchee River, and a white-blazed loop leads to a campsite in an oak hammock.

Highlights: Savor the hooded pitcher plants in ditches, sundews in damp areas, red-cockaded woodpeckers in a grove of longleaf pines near the river, the visit to the river through a dark cypress swamp thick with bromeliads, the appealing campsite under the live oaks.

Logistics: Enjoy this trail as a very short backpacking trip, taking advantage of the campsite. Add five miles to the hike if you want to explore the northern loop, which primarily passes through more pine flatwoods. Some of the trail crosses drainage areas and may require wading after a heavy rain.

Other Activities: An extensive network of equestrian trails runs throughout the property, crossing the Econ River at Curry Ford. Bicycles are permitted on the trails, and you may fish in the reclaimed phosphate mine.

Split Oak Forest Mitigation Park

CF-45 🅵 📖

Location: Narcoossee [N28°21.200' W081°12.655'].

Length: Loops of 3.1, 4.2, and 1.2 miles, allowing an 8.5-mile perimeter hike, plus a 0.8-mile linear connector trail to Moss Park.

Map: Displayed and in brochure at trailhead kiosk; detailed map available from Florida Trail Association.

Contact Information: Florida Fish and Wildlife Conservation Commission (352-732-1225), 1239 SW 10th Street, Ocala, FL 34474-2797.

Directions: From Orlando International Airport, go east on SR 528 (Beeline) for 2.5 miles to CR 15 (Narcoossee Road) and turn south. Follow CR 15 south for 7 miles. Turn east onto Clapp-Simms-Duda Road. Go east 1.5 miles to the trailhead parking lot on the right.

The Hike: From the trailhead parking lot, hike east to the trail junction, where you can choose to hike the North Loop or the South Loop. The North Loop meanders through scrubby flatwoods, scrub, and pine flatwoods and out along Lake Hart and Bonnet Pond, circling the oak hammock in which you'll find the Split Oak. The South Loop traverses open prairies, oak hammocks, and scrub, rounding a large flatwoods pond with an observation deck. A cross trail connects the two.

Highlights: The namesake oak, several centuries old, was split down the middle by lightning and still survives. This is a great park for spotting wildlife along the prairies, especially the sandhill cranes for which this land was set aside.

Logistics: The park allows day use only, but camping is available at nearby Moss Park. The South Loop tends to flood after a heavy rain.

Other Activities: Equestrians may enter the preserve if they obtain a permit in advance. Adjoining Moss Park offers a wide range of outdoor recreational activities, including a campground, a playground, beaches, and picnic groves.

Sandhill Nature Trail

Lower Wekiva River Preserve State Park

CF-46 **F** 📖 👪 🐕

Location: Sanford [N28°48.920' W081°24.354'].

Length: 2.5-mile loop.

Map: Displayed on trailhead kiosk and in interpretive brochure.

Contact Information: Wekiva Basin Geo Park (407-884-2009), 1800 Wekiwa Circle, Apopka, FL 32712-2599.

Directions: From I-4 exit 51, Sanford, drive west 4.1 miles on SR 46 to the park entrance on the right.

The Hike: Providing a loop through a sandhill habitat, this gentle trail is a great introduction to the longleaf and wiregrass ecosystem that once covered the uplands of Central Florida.

Highlights: This preserve has great wildflowers in spring and fall, and plenty of opportunities to see wildlife.

Logistics: Do not block the entrance gate when parking. There are benches along the trail. The orange blazes are a section of the Florida Trail passing through this preserve en route to Seminole State Forest (hike CF-32), utilizing the southern side of the loop.

Other Activities: Picnic tables are provided.

Wekiwa Springs State Park

CF-47 **F** **$** 📖 🚻 🅰 ⛺ ⛺

Location: Longwood [N28°42.756' W081°27.603'] at springs; [N28°43.423' W081°28.398'] at Sand Lake

Length: 0.4-mile nature trail with connector trail to loop system of 8.4 miles, providing 13.5 miles of hiking, including a 10.2-mile loop out of Sand Lake.

Map: Available at ranger station; detailed map EC-1 available from Florida Trail Association.

Contact Information: Wekiva Basin Geo Park (407-884-2009), 1800 Wekiwa Circle, Apopka, FL 32712-2599.

Directions: From I-4 exit 49, Longwood, follow SR 434 west for 0.9 mile to Wekiwa Springs Road. Turn right and continue 5 miles to the park entrance on the right.

The Hike: At the springs, the Wet to Dry Nature Trail is a pleasant boardwalk off the main trail that leads through a hydric hammock down along the edge of the springs and river. The main trail (which for a loop hike should be accessed from the north parking area at Sand Lake) forms an 8.4-mile loop through sandhills, scrubby flatwoods, oak hammocks, cypress swamp, and hardwood hammocks along Rock Springs Run.

Highlights: Note the Florida champion sand pine (near the springs end of the trail). The loop provides a pleasant primitive campsite along Rock Springs Run.

Logistics: A permit is required for primitive camping; check at the ranger station. A large section of the habitat along the main loop near Sand Lake was devastated in an attempt to halt an infestation of southern pine bark beetles, so there is limited shade in the sandhills. Carry plenty of water. The cypress swamp portion of the loop may be flooded at times; check with rangers before hiking.

Other Activities: Enjoy swimming in the spring, canoeing down one of the finest rivers in Florida, or relaxing at the picnic groves.

Sabal Point Sanctuary

CF-48 📖 🐎

Location: Longwood [N28°42.686' W081°24.608'].

Length: 7 miles round-trip.

Map: Posted on trailhead kiosk and in St. Johns River Water Management District's *Recreation Guide to District Lands.*

Contact Information: Audubon of Florida (407-539-5700), 1331 Palmetto Avenue, Suite 110, Winter Park, FL 32789.

Directions: From I-4 exit 94, drive west on SR 434 for 0.9 mile to Wekiwa Springs Road. Turn right, then right again after 0.8 mile onto Sabal Palm Drive. Follow the curving road through the subdivision for 1.5 miles to Wilderness Drive, on the right. Drive to the end of the road.

The Hike: The hike follows an old logging tramway into the depths of the Wekiva River floodplain, immersing you in a floodplain forest of red maple and sweet gum without getting your feet wet. Needle palms grow lushly along the trail. The trail crosses Hog Island, a hammock with ponds in the middle of the swamp, before dropping down again to lead you to its end at the Little Wekiva River.

Highlights: Take the side trail on the right at 0.5 mile to see the enormous live oak, and spend a little time wandering the trails around the pond to watch for wildlife.

Logistics: The trail is for day use only, and parking is very limited. Do not block the gate.

Other Activities: Biking along the main trail is permitted.

Lake Lotus Park

CF-49 📖 🚹 ♿ 👫

Location: Altamonte Springs [N28°38.632' W081°25.522'].

Length: 1.7-mile trail system of boardwalks and natural footpaths.

Map: In brochure at kiosk near trailhead.

Contact Information: City of Altamonte Springs (407-293-8885), 225 Newburyport Avenue, Altamonte Springs, FL 32701.

Directions: From I-4, follow SR 414 (Maitland Boulevard) west for 3 miles to the park entrance on the right, across from Magnolia Homes Boulevard.

The Hike: The trail system provides a respite from surrounding suburbia, immersing you in the sights and sounds of Lake Lotus and its surrounding marshes and cypress swamps. Walk on the boardwalks amid the massive cypresses, or follow the footpaths between the ferns.

Highlights: Enjoy great views of Lake Lotus and opportunities to see ospreys nesting in the tall cypresses along the Little Wekiva River.

Logistics: Open Wed–Sun 8:30–dusk. There is limited parking, so visitors on weekends must leave their vehicles in the large parking area across SR 414 on Magnolia Homes Boulevard, taking a shuttle tram into the park.

Other Activities: Fishing is permitted from certain portions of the boardwalk. There are plenty of picnic tables and pavilions, a playground, and a butterfly garden.

Big Tree Park

CF-50 □ ⛑ ♿ ⛉ ⚲

Location: Winter Springs [N28°43.225' W081°19.892'].

Length: 0.3 mile round-trip on boardwalk.

Map: No map, but interpretive brochure at kiosk.

Contact Information: Seminole County Natural Lands Program (407-665-7352), Spring Hammock Preserve, 2985 Osprey Trail, Longwood, FL 32750.

Directions: From US 17/92 in Winter Springs, take General Hutchinson Parkway west for 1 mile to the park entrance on the left; the park is between US 17/92 and SR 427 in Longwood.

The Hike: As old Florida postcards can attest, this park has been a major tourist attraction for decades. The reason? The Senator, said to be the oldest living cypress in the United States. A boardwalk leads through the floodplain forest to circle around this massive cypress—note how large *all* of the trees are in the preserve—and continues on to a second giant cypress. Both are missing their tops, but their girth is incredible.

Highlights: These trees are truly awesome in size. Note the gall on the smaller cypress—it's as big as a car hood!

Logistics: The park is open 8:00–6:00.

Other Activities: Picnic at the pavilions.

Florida Trail

Spring Hammock Preserve

CF-51 **F** 🏃 🐴

Location: Winter Springs [N28°43.294' W081°18.414'].

Length: 1.1 miles linear.

Map: Detailed backpacking map available from Florida Trail Association.

Contact Information: Seminole County Natural Lands Program (407-665-7352), 1101 East 1st Street 3rd Floor, Sanford, FL 32771.

Directions: From US 17/92 in Winter Springs, turn right on SR 419 and drive east 0.7 mile to Soldiers Creek Park on the right. Park at the far end of the ball fields near the forest and look for the orange blazes leading into the woods.

The Hike: A shady walk takes you through a forest of ancient cabbage palms along Soldiers Creek.

Highlights: It's a beautiful example of a cabbage palm bottomland, with Soldiers Creek a clear but tannic stream cutting through the deep sand.

Logistics: Beware of bicyclists who switch over from their own trail system to ride down the hiking trail, although they are not supposed to. The restrooms are at the ball field complex.

Other Activities: Besides the ball fields, there are mountain biking trails.

Spring Hammock Preserve

CF-52 [icons]

Location: Winter Springs [N28°43.294' W081°18.414'].

Length: 4-plus miles of trails.

Map: Available at Environmental Education Center; overview map of trail system posted on sign near Center.

Contact Information: Seminole County Natural Lands Program (407-665-7352), Spring Hammock Preserve, 2985 Osprey Trail, Longwood, FL 32750.

Directions: From US 17/92 in Winter Garden, drive east 0.6 mile on SR 419 to the park entrance on the left. Enter the gates and park on the right.

The Hike: Start at the "Pine Woods Trail" sign to access the trail system, which provides numerous named trail options to work your way down to Soldiers Creek and Lake Jesup. You'll pass through dark palm hammocks with high bluffs above the creek, oak hammocks, pine flatwoods, and a broad meadow under the power lines. A boardwalk creates a loop out into the lush floodplain forest, adjacent to the Mud Walk, a popular destination for school groups. A linear boardwalk follows Soldiers Creek as it empties into Lake Jesup.

Highlights: Marvel at the giant cypresses along the boardwalk out to Lake Jesup—their girth and crowns rival those of the big trees at nearby Big Tree Park (CF-50).

Logistics: The gates close at dusk. Some trails are shared with bicyclists. Trails along Soldiers Creek and along the floodplain forest on the lakeshore may be seasonally flooded. There are numerous benches along the trails. Restrooms are open only when the center is open.

Other Activities: Visit the Environmental Education Center to see some of the inhabitants of these habitats, or bring a picnic and settle back in the picnic pavilion.

Lake Jesup Wilderness Area

CF-53 📖

Location: Sanford [N28°43.632' W081°15.812'].

Length: 2.7 miles in two loops and a T-shaped linear trail.

Map: Displayed and in brochure at trailhead kiosk.

Contact Information: Seminole County Natural Lands Program (407-665-7352), Lake Jesup Wilderness Area, 5951 South Sanford Avenue, Sanford, FL 32773.

Directions: From I-4 in Lake Mary, follow Lake Mary Boulevard east past SR 417 to Sanford Avenue. Turn right on South Sanford Avenue and drive to the end of the road, which enters the park.

The Hike: Passing through a wetland area along the edge of Lake Jesup, the loop trail leads you out to a canal where a bridge crosses over to an old dike which is now completed covered in a palm hammock. Walk either north or south on the dike, ducking beneath the dark bower of palm fronds. At both ends, the trail reaches a short loop off the dike.

Highlights: The "tunnel of palms" is especially scenic.

Logistics: The low-lying areas leading to the dike often flood when the lake is high. Expect to get muddy feet or wade in places. Watch for alligators in the canal.

Other Activities: There is a very busy boat ramp near the trailhead, and picnic tables under the oaks.

East Lake Jesup Tract

Lake Jesup Conservation Area

CF-54 ⚊ 🏕

Location: Oviedo [N28 43.238' W81 11.255'].

Length: 1.3-mile loop.

Map: Displayed at trailhead kiosk and available in St. Johns River Water Management District's *Recreation Guide to District Lands*.

Contact Information: St. Johns River Water Management District (904-529-2380), PO Box 1429, Palatka, FL 32178-1429.

Directions: From Florida Avenue in Oviedo, turn north on Elm Street and follow it across Howard Avenue. After 1 mile the pavement ends. Continue another 0.9 mile along the road, which narrows to a one-lane track, dead-ending in the parking area.

The Hike: Pass through the gate and follow the forest road along a pine plantation down to the kiosk to get your bearings. Continue along the forest road, passing the group campsite on the right and another turnoff on the right. At the second turnoff after the campsite, at 0.4 mile, turn right and walk into the cool shade of a dense oak and palm hammock. The trail emerges on the edge of the ring of freshwater marshes around Lake Jesup after 0.5 mile, and reaches the two-story observation tower after 0.6 mile. For the return trip, follow the white-diamond-blazed rugged path through the palm hammock. It comes to a T at 1 mile. Turn right. At the next T, turn left to complete the loop.

Highlights: Enjoy a great view from the observation tower, and a wonderland of ferns—including beds of sword ferns and ditches thick with giant leather ferns—along the return loop.

Logistics: The first portion of the trail, to the observation deck, is multiuse, open to horseback riding and biking. The park is day use only unless you have a permit for the group campsite. If the large parking area is flooded, do not attempt this hike—the trail will be under water. The last 0.3-mile stretch of the access road is rather rugged and single lane.

Other Activities: Bring your binoculars to scan the marshes. Camping is allowed with a group permit.

Bear Creek Nature Trail

CF-55 🏃

Location: Winter Springs [N28°40.669' W081°14.754'].

Length: 0.3-mile loop.

Map: None provided.

Contact Information: City of Winter Springs (407-327-6593).

Directions: From SR 426 in Oviedo, drive 1.5 miles south on Winter Springs Boulevard. The park is on the right, with a small parking corral with a brown sign.

The Hike: In a tiny slice of wilderness in the middle of suburbia, this rugged trail follows the bluffs above tannic Bear Creek, which flows through cypresses on its way to Lake Jesup. The forest is dense and shady, with oaks swaddled in wild pine, tall longleaf pines, and tall cabbage palms along the bottomlands. Boardwalks and bridges carry you across the wetlands.

Highlights: Burbling "rapids" are caused by cypress knees and downed logs in Bear Creek. Some visitors have seen otters playing in the creek.

Logistics: The trail is day use only. The parking lot is very small. Low areas may flood or may be muddy. The loop is not well marked, but the small size of the wilderness area will keep you from getting lost. Follow the creek as far as you can, then turn right to find a pathway to return along the uplands to the parking area.

Other Activities: None.

Florida Trail

Little-Big Econ State Forest

CF-56 **F** $ 🛶 🎣 ❄️

Location: Oviedo [N28°41.245' W081°09.558'].

Length: 7.3 miles linear.

Map: Displayed at trailhead kiosk and available in St. Johns River Water Management District's *Recreation Guide to District Lands*; detailed backpacking map available from Florida Trail Association.

Contact Information: Little-Big Econ State Forest (407-971-3500), 1350 Snow Hill Road, Geneva, FL 32732.

Directions: From downtown Oviedo, follow SR 426 east past Lockwood Road to Barr Street. Turn right and park in the grassy parking area on the left for the designated trailhead. There is also a trailhead off Snow Hill Road in Chuluota on the west side of the river, and the northern terminus of the trail segment is along Lockwood Road 0.5 mile east of SR 419.

The Hike: From the Barr Street trailhead, follow the trail to the north for 2.7 miles for a walk along the Econ River's floodplain forests and hydric hammocks out to Lockwood Road, or walk south along this segment for 4.6 miles along scenic river bluffs through shady hammocks of cabbage palms and oaks, passing campsites on sandy beaches.

Highlights: The scenery along the river bluffs is incredible, especially amid the palm hammocks. This section of trail was named one of the nation's top trails for families in 2004 by the American Hiking Society.

Logistics: The parking fee is payable to the iron ranger at the trailhead. Until the bridge over the Econlockhatchee River (leading down the old railroad bed to Snow Hill Road) is replaced, consider this a round-trip hike to the river crossing, or connect to the Geneva Wilderness Area via the 1.4-mile Flagler Trail to make a 3.8-mile trip between two cars.

Other Activities: Separate bicycle and equestrian trails also run through Little-Big Econ State Forest. The Econlockhatchee River is a hidden gem for paddlers.

Geneva Wilderness Area

CF-57 👫 ⛺ 👬 🐕

Location: Geneva [N28°42.528' W081°07.438'].

Length: 1.8-mile loop plus 1.4-mile linear spur.

Map: Posted and in brochure at trailhead kiosk.

Contact Information: Seminole County Natural Lands Program (407-665-7352), Geneva Wilderness Area, 3501 North CR 426, Geneva, FL 32732.

Directions: From downtown Oviedo, drive east on SR 426 for 6.1 miles (passing the Little-Big Econ State Forest trailhead for the Florida Trail); the park entrance is on the right.

The Hike: Two trails wind their way through the park. Starting at the trailhead and leading you through an oak scrub to the decision point, the Loop Trail circles the edges of the park's many ponds. Walk counterclockwise around the loop to cross scrub habitats, pine flatwoods, and oak hammocks along the ponds, passing a primitive campsite. Side trails lead back into the woods to catfaced pines and out to a chapel beside the pond. The linear Flagler Trail connects the Loop Trail with the Florida Trail (CF-56) along the Econlockhatchee River.

Highlights: There are nice views across the flatwoods ponds. Walk to the shore of the big pond to see hundreds of tiny carnivorous sundew plants in the soft mud.

Logistics: The Loop Trail is blazed with red diamonds, the Flagler Trail with yellow diamonds and blue blazes. Call in advance if you want to camp at either the North or South Camp.

Other Activities: The Ed Yarborough Nature Center, open the first Saturday of each month 9:00–noon, offers public workshops and hands-on exhibits.

Lake Proctor Wilderness Area

CF-58 ⬚ 👫 🐕

Location: Geneva [N28°43.599' W081°05.950'].

Length: 6-plus miles in a 2.6-mile main loop and three side trails.

Map: Posted and in brochure at trailhead kiosk.

Contact Information: Seminole County Natural Lands Program (407- 665-7352), Lake Proctor Wilderness Area, 920 West SR 46, Geneva, FL 32732.

Directions: From Sanford, follow SR 46 east through Geneva. Just beyond the intersection of SR 426 and SR 46, keep alert for the trailhead parking area on the left.

The Hike: Follow the red diamonds into the pine flatwoods to the white trail, which branches off to the left to meet the edge of the wetlands south of Lake Proctor. After you rejoin the red loop in the oak hammock, continue left on the blue trail to walk along the lake, rising back into oak hammocks. As the trail continues east, it climbs into sandhills and sand pine scrub, where the yellow trail loops the scrub.

Highlights: The trail along Lake Proctor offers broad views and great birding.

Logistics: The trails are shared in places with bicycles and local equestrians. Expect soft sand on some of the Red Loop trail.

Other Activities: Picnic tables are provided at the trailhead.

Nature Trail

Lake Mills Park

CF-59 📖 🚻 Ⓒ 👫

Location: Chuluota [N28°37.910' W081°07.461'].

Length: 0.8 mile round-trip.

Map: Information kiosk at trailhead.

Contact Information: Lake Mills Park (407-788-0609), 1301 Tropical Avenue, Chuluota, FL 32766.

Directions: From SR 419 in Chuluota, follow Lake Mills Road north to Tropicana Road. Turn left; the park is less than a mile along the road on the right. After you enter the park, turn left and park at the first parking area on the right.

The Hike: The trail follows a boardwalk through a mixed hardwood and bay swamp along Mill Branch Creek as it flows into Lake Mills. The trail leads out to the lakeshore, where alligator gars swim past the observation deck.

Highlights: Enjoy the pleasant walk along Mill Branch Creek, the scenic overlook on Lake Mills, and dozens of types of ferns.

Logistics: The park is open 8:00–sunset, closed Thanksgiving and Christmas. The nature trail starts near the entrance to the campground.

Other Activities: This is a fifty-acre park with plenty to do. The campground, tucked away in a forest, has inexpensive tent and RV sites, and there are picnic pavilions, a playground, fishing from the shore of Lake Mills, and canoeing and kayaking on the lake.

Econ River Wilderness Area

CF-60 📖 🚸 🐕

Location: Oviedo [N28°36.828' W081°10.448'].

Length: 3.2 miles in a loop and two spurs, with a 0.8-mile access loop.

Map: Displayed and in interpretive brochure at trailhead.

Contact Information: Seminole County Natural Lands Program (407-665-7352), Econ River Wilderness Area, 3795 Old Lockwood Road, Oviedo, FL 32765.

Directions: From the intersection of SR 434 (Alafaya Trail) and SR 50 near the University of Central Florida, drive east on SR 434 and turn right on East McCulloch Road. Drive 2 miles and turn left on Old Lockwood Road. The trailhead is on the right.

The Hike: Sign the trail register at the trailhead kiosk and follow the red arrow markers on a pleasant narrow natural footpath into open scrubby flatwoods with tall cordgrass broken up by hammocks of sand live oaks, rising into sandhills with turkey oaks, longleaf pines, and wiregrass. Where the access loop meets the Red Loop, turn left to follow a forest road down to the main part of the trail system, which leads you to the Flatwoods Loop and the River Swamp Loop.

Highlights: The footpaths are well maintained and pleasant to hike, with great views across the prairies and pine flatwoods.

Logistics: The River Swamp Loop may be flooded during the wet season.

Other Activities: Enjoy birdwatching along the prairies.

Florida Trail

Bull Creek Wildlife Management Area

CF-61 **F** 🛶 🏕

Location: Holopaw (US 192 trailhead) [N28°06.993' W080°55.951'].

Length: 20.5-mile loop or 23.7 miles linear.

Map: Displayed at trailhead kiosk and available in St. Johns River Water Management District's *Recreation Guide to District Lands*; detailed backpacking map available from Florida Trail Association.

Contact Information: St. Johns River Water Management District (904-529-2380), PO Box 1429, Palatka, FL 32178-1429

Directions: The trailhead for Bull Creek WMA is along US 192, 10 miles east of the junction with US 441 in Holopaw, on the south side of the highway. Do not block the gate.

The Hike: Weekend backpackers will enjoy a trip around the loop through Bull Creek WMA, as the trail follows Bull Creek on the east side of the preserve and meanders through miles of open pine flatwoods with an understory of saw palmetto stretching off to the horizon.

Highlights: Have fun walking the narrow bridges through the cypress swamps around Crabgrass Creek. Just south of the northern loop junction along the west loop, watch for patches of carnivorous pitcher plants growing in seepage bogs.

Logistics: Sign in at the register. If the creek is high, the trail will be flooded in places. During dry seasons, water can be difficult to come by, especially on the west loop. Long-distance hikers on the Florida Trail must connect this segment with Prairie Lakes WMA (CF-62) via a walk across private land in Forever Florida; you must be a Florida Trail member to traverse private land. There are two designated campsites, Jane Green and Little Scrub.

Other Activities: Seasonal hunting is permitted; check www.floridaconservation.org for hunt dates.

Florida Trail

Prairie Lakes Wildlife Management Area

CF-62 🅕 $ 🏕 🐾

Location: Lake Marian [N27°55.660' W081°07.494'].

Length: Intersecting loops of 5.5 and 5.6 miles, plus 31.3 miles linear between US 441 and SR 60.

Map: Detailed backpacking map available from Florida Trail Association.

Contact Information: Florida Fish and Wildlife Conservation Commission (863-648-3203), 3900 Drane Field Road, Lakeland, FL 33811-1299.

Directions: From the intersection of US 441 and CR 520 (Canoe Creek Road) in Kenansville, follow CR 520 north 8 miles to the WMA entrance on the left. Turn left and continue a short distance to the parking area.

The Hike: North of Canoe Creek Road, the trail crosses broad open prairies, circling cypress domes before it enters pine flatwoods and scrub to the north of Florida's Turnpike. To the south of Canoe Creek Road, enjoy a day hike or weekend backpacking trip on the figure-eight loop on the vast palmetto prairies, with forays into oak and palm hammocks.

Highlights: Wildlife watching and birding is superb on the prairies—watch for bald eagles, sandhill cranes, crested caracara, burrowing owls, and dozens of other species. Visit the observation tower on the North Loop for an eagle's-eye view.

Logistics: Except for Florida Trail thru-hikers, there is a charge of $3 per person or $6 per carload. Expect to wade along the trail south of Canoe Creek Road during the rainy season. A permit (free) is required for camping; contact FWC in advance.

Other Activities: Prairie Lakes permits seasonal hunting; see www.floridaconservation.org for details. Hikers should always wear blaze orange vests during hunting season.

Sunset Ranch Interpretive Trail

Prairie Lakes Wildlife Management Area

CF-63 $ 📖 🏇

Location: Lake Marian [N27°54.234' W081°05.892'].

Length: 2-mile outer loop and shorter inner loops.

Map: In brochure at trailhead kiosk.

Contact Information: Florida Fish and Wildlife Conservation Commission (863-648-3203), 3900 Drane Field Road, Lakeland, FL 33811-1299.

Directions: From the intersection of US 441 and CR 520 (Canoe Creek Road) in Kenansville, follow CR 520 north 7.5 miles to the trailhead parking area on the left.

The Hike: The broad, mowed, hiking-only path traverses scrubby flatwoods, sandhills, pine flatwoods, and open prairie en route to the edge of Lake Marian.

Highlights: Look out from the observation deck on Lake Marian, or hide in the wildlife blind to watch wild turkey and deer walk by.

Logistics: This short interpretive trail (watch for the brown fiberglass markers) has a whopping $3 per person or $6 per carload day-use fee.

Other Activities: Prairie Lakes WMA permits seasonal hunting; see www.floridaconservation.org for details. Hikers should always wear blaze orange vests during hunting season.

Osceola County Environmental Education Center

CF-64 📖 🚻 ♿ 👫

Location: Poinciana [N28°09.933' W081°26.793'].

Length: 5.3 miles in two round trips and a loop.

Map: Displayed near environmental center.

Contact Information: School District of Osceola County Environmental Center (407-870-4856), 817 Osceola Boulevard, Kissimmee, FL 34744-4495.

Directions: From SR 535 in Poinciana, follow Poinciana Boulevard south 14.1 miles to the park entrance on the right.

The Hike: There are three trails starting from the Environmental Center parking area: a 0.5-mile loop on the wheelchair-accessible Reedy Creek Boardwalk, which circles a cypress swamp and follows the edge of Reedy Creek; the 1.2-mile Indian Mounds Trail, leading through squishy floodplain forest alive with ferns to a midden along the creek; and the 1.8-mile linear Pine Flatwoods-Ecotone Trail, working its way along the edge of the floodplain forest along the creek to a trailhead across from Horse World on Poinciana Boulevard.

Highlights: Walk beneath the ancient cypress trees on the boardwalk and amid the dense floodplain forest along the Indian Mounds Trail.

Logistics: The park is open only on weekends: Sat 10:00–5:00, Sun 12:00–5:00.

Other Activities: Visit the center for an overview of the habitats and the effect of cypress logging on Reedy Creek. Enjoy birdwatching along the Reedy Creek Boardwalk—look for the pair of eagles that nests in one of the ancient cypress trees.

Disney Wilderness Preserve

CF-65 $ 📖 ♿ 🚻

Location: Poinciana [N28°07.726' W081°25.810'].

Length: 6-plus miles of trails in three loops and two spurs.

Map: Posted at trailhead and available at Learning Center.

Contact Information: The Nature Conservancy (407-935-0002), 222 South Westmonte Drive, Suite 300, Altamonte Springs, FL 32714.

Directions: From SR 535 in Poinciana, follow Poinciana Boulevard south 15 miles to Pleasant Hill Boulevard. Make the first left onto Old Pleasant Hill Road. Follow this road for 0.6 mile, turning left onto Scrub-jay Trail. Drive 1.6 miles to the Learning Center.

The Hike: Follow the sidewalk and gravel path around the pond to the main kiosk for the hiking trail system, where you can pick up a map and interpretive booklet. The 0.5-mile Pine Flatwoods Trail starts to the left, looping through a small stretch of pine flatwoods. Blazed with diamonds, the Red Trail and Blue Trail lead south from the kiosk. The Red Trail creates a 5.5-mile loop through pine flatwoods, bayheads, oak hammocks, and cypress domes; the Blue Loop samples these habitats on a 3.2-mile trek. Spur trails lead to Lake Russell and to a picnic area next to a cypress dome.

Highlights: Don't miss the overlook on Lake Russell, a pristine cypress-lined lake where ibises swoop low over the water.

Logistics: The preserve is open 9:00–5:00 daily, with early opening at 7:00 on Saturdays from January to March; closed on major holidays. There is an entrance fee of $2 adults, $1 children. Guided walks are offered at 10:00 a.m. on the first Saturday of each month, and swamp buggy rides on Sundays from September to June for an additional fee. Wheelchair access is limited to the paved trail around the pond.

Other Activities: The Learning Center includes interpretive exhibits, a bookstore, and rocking chairs to sit and relax in, as well as restrooms.

Lake Marion Creek Wildlife Management Area

CF-66 🏕 🐎

Location: Poinciana [N28°08.410' W081°31.381'].

Length: 4.2 miles round-trip.

Map: Displayed at trailhead, available in brochure and in South Florida Water Management District Recreational Guide.

Contact Information: South Florida Water Management District (800-250-4200), 205 North Parrott Avenue Suite 201, Okeechobee, FL 34973.

Directions: From the intersection of CR 531 (Pleasant Hill Road) and CR 580, drive 6 miles west of Poinciana toward Haines City to the trailhead entrance on the right.

The Hike: Following blazed forest roads, this trail passes through pine flatwoods, scrubby flatwoods, and a cypress swamp before climbing into open prairies and palmetto scrub to end in a loop around an oak-shaded campsite at 2.1 miles. Return along the same route.

Highlights: In the cypress swamp, wild irises bloom along a beautiful tannic stream.

Logistics: Do not block the gate when you park. Much of the trail is out in the open, so bring lots of water and wear adequate sun protection. A permit (free) is required to use the campsite.

Other Activities: There are picnic tables near trailhead and at the campsite. Seasonal hunting is permitted; check www.floridaconservation.org for details, and wear blaze orange during hunt seasons.

Florida Trail

Green Swamp East

CF-67 🅕 ⚠ 🏕

Location: Rock Ridge [N28°18.184' W081°55.120'].

Length: 11.3 miles linear, plus loops of 7.7 and 13.9 miles.

Map: Rough map in Southwest Florida Water Management District Recreational Guide; detailed backpacking maps available from Florida Tail Association.

Contact Information: Southwest Florida Water Management District (800-423-1476), 2379 Broad Street, Brooksville, FL 34604.

Directions: The northern trailhead is along SR 471, northeast of Zephyrhills, and links to Green Swamp West (CG-18). The southern trailhead is along Rock Ridge Road north of Providence.

The Hike: This is a wilderness trek through the wilds of the Green Swamp, which is not so much a swamp as a mosaic of habitats, from pine flatwoods to cypress domes and floodplain forests along the Withlacoochee River. The linear orange-blazed Florida Trail follows the Withlacoochee River's flow north, while the blue-blazed day loop and white-blazed weekend loop explore the pine uplands.

Highlights: Green Swamp East offers enjoyable walks along the Withlacoochee River's cypress forests, ancient oaks and pines shading the trail, and miles of wilderness to explore.

Logistics: This is a backpacking trail with few options for cutting your trip short. Plan accordingly. Parts of the trail through the cypress floodplain forest may be under water at times. You must have a permit (free) from SFWMD to utilize the backpacking campsites; contact them at least two weeks in advance of your trip.

Other Activities: A network of biking trails crosses the Florida Trail throughout this area. Seasonal hunting is permitted; check www.floridaconservation.org for details and wear a blaze orange vest during hunting season.

Gator Creek Preserve

CF-68 📖 🚸 🐕

Location: Gibsonia [N28°10.733' W081°59.403'].

Length: 2.5-mile loop.

Map: Displayed and in interpretive brochure at trailhead kiosk.

Contact Information: Polk County Natural Resources Environmental Lands Program (863-534-7377), 4177 Ben Durrance Road, Bartow, FL 33830.

Directions: From I-4 exit 32 in Lakeland, drive 6.8 miles north on US 98 to the park entrance on the right.

The Hike: Primarily following forest roads, this hiking loop introduces you to a tiny slice of the Green Swamp, a patchwork of flatwoods, sandhills, and cypress domes, uplands and lowlands covering more than 860 square miles, and the birthplace of four of Florida's rivers. Although this patch of land has been altered by drainage canals, the trail presents each of the habitats in turn.

Highlights: As you round the cypress domes, cypress knees jut out well into the grasslands around the swamps.

Logistics: Pay attention to the signs and trail markers as you work your way around the loop, since the forest roads head off in all directions. Expect to get your shoes wet in the low spots after a heavy rain.

Other Activities: Bring your binoculars—this forest is a breeding ground for the blue-gray gnatcatcher, the yellow-throated warbler, and the summer tanager. You'll see several species of woodpecker as well.

Tenoroc Hiking Trail

Tenoroc Fish Management Area

CF-69 **F** **$** 👥

Location: Lakeland [N28°06.422' W081°51.833'].

Length: 6-mile loop.

Map: Posted at main trail junction and available at park office; available in regional map packet from Florida Trail Association.

Contact Information: Florida Fish and Wildlife Conservation Commission (863-648-3203), 3900 Drane Field Road, Lakeland, FL 33811-1299.

Directions: From I-4 exit 38, follow SR 33 south to the first left, SR 659 (Combee Road). Drive 1.3 miles south, then turn left on Tenoroc Mine Road. Follow the road into the preserve. Stop at the ranger station to sign in, pick up a map, and pay your fee. Continue to the "Parking Lot / Picnic Area" sign on the left; turn in and park. The trailhead is in the corner of the lot.

The Hike: The trail consists of two stacked loops. A wide mowed path leads from the trailhead to the blue-blazed loop. When you reach the trail junction with the loop, turn right for a touch of adventure on Rattlesnake Ridge, a narrow ridge made up of spoil piles from the former phosphate mines that are the lakes throughout this preserve. Watch your footing on the ridge, as gullies cut through it. After 1.3 miles, you reach the eastern end of the loop at a kiosk. A short connector trail leads to the orange loop. Turn right to walk this loop along more high ridges, through oak hammocks and scrub. Returning to the kiosk, turn right to follow the more sedate north side of the blue loop back to the parking area.

Highlights: Walk narrow Rattlesnake Ridge for the scenic views, note the hilly slash pine forest, and look for fossils and phosphate nuggets on exposed slopes of the spoil piles.

Logistics: The preserve is open Fri–Mon 6:00–5:00. There is a $3 per person day-use fee.

Other Activities: This is a popular destination for anglers, and there are picnic tables in several places on the preserve.

Saddle Creek Park Nature Trail

Saddle Creek Park

CF-70 📖 🚻 🅰 🐕

Location: Lakeland [N28°03.848' W081°52.832'].

Length: 2.4 miles round-trip.

Map: Displayed at trailhead kiosk; may be available in interpretive brochure.

Contact Information: Polk County Parks & Recreation (863-534-4340), 515 Boulevard Street, Bartow, FL 33830.

Directions: From US 92 east of Lakeland, follow Saddle Creek Park Road for 1 mile past the campground; bear right and follow it as it turns to dirt past the maintenance yard and dead-ends at the trail kiosk.

The Hike: Following markers placed by Boy Scout Troop 123 of Winter Haven, the trail sticks to the high ground between the natural floodplain forest of Saddle Creek and the fish management impoundments of the park. Look for natural forests of red maple, sweet gum, and willow off to your left as you hike south along the trail, and the cattail- and reed-fringed edges of the ponds on the right. South of the observation tower, the trail has a small loop in its middle.

Highlights: An observation tower gives you an eagle's-eye view of the park impoundments; look for the egret rookeries along their eastern shores. Much of the trail follows burbling Saddle Creek. Enjoy great birding and alligator spotting along the impoundments.

Logistics: The trail can be a little tough to follow. Look for the beaten path. The marker posts correspond to an interpretive brochure.

Other Activities: There's plenty of fishing throughout the park—it's a fish management area. There are also playgrounds and picnic tables, and a shady campground.

Lakeland Highlands Scrub

CF-71 ⛹ 🐴

Location: Lakeland [N27°56.174' W081°55.428'].

Length: 0.6-mile hiking loop; also a 2.2-mile multiuse loop.

Map: Available at trailhead kiosk.

Contact Information: Polk County Natural Resources Environmental Lands Program (863-534-7377), 4177 Ben Durrance Road, Bartow, FL 33830.

Directions: From Polk Parkway (SR 570) exit 9, take Lakeland Highlands Boulevard (CR 37B) south. Reach CR 540 at 1.8 miles, and continue south another mile, crossing CR 540A. After crossing Crews Lake Road, Lakeland Highlands Boulevard becomes a dead-end dirt road at 3.6 miles; keep going to where the road ends at the trailhead at 4 miles.

The Hike: For the hiking-only loop, walk past the picnic bench in the oak hammock and keep left at the fork in the trail, walking beneath sand pines and sand live oaks heavily laden with Spanish moss. You pass a crowded forest of young longleaf pines in their spiky "candle" stage. There is a bench at 0.3 mile, just before you enter a sandhill habitat with beargrass and muscadine grapes in the understory. The loop ends just before the picnic bench. The multiuse trail starts off to the left and follows forest roads to create a loop through scrubby flatwoods, along bayhead swamps, and into the open palmetto prairie.

Highlights: It's a pleasant walk through the sandhill and scrub habitats, where you'll see numerous gopher tortoise burrows.

Logistics: The 2.2-mile trail is blazed blue, and the 0.6-mile loop is blazed orange. The blue trail becomes easily flooded after a heavy rain and may require wading across a creek crossing. On the orange loop, watch the blazing carefully, as unmarked paths intersect the main trail in several places.

Other Activities: Equestrians and bicyclists are welcome on the Blue Trail, but equestrians require a permit in advance. There is a picnic bench at the trailhead.

IMC Agrico Peace River Park

CF-72 📖 🚻 🅰 ♿ 🚼

Location: Fort Meade [N27°49.309' W081°48.266'].

Length: 0.5 mile round-trip on boardwalk; 0.3 mile round-trip between parking lot and boardwalk.

Map: None available.

Contact Information: Polk County Parks & Recreation (863-534-4340), 515 Boulevard Street, Bartow, FL 33830.

Directions: From US 17 south of Lakeland, take CR 640 east, following "Great Florida Birding Trail" signs for a mile to the park entrance on the left before the bridge over the Peace River.

The Hike: The site of an open-pit phosphate mine until the early 1980s, this reclamation project borders the Peace River floodplain, where the boardwalk winds through the floodplain forest out to the river. Interpretive signs give background information on the 1,800-square-mile Peace River basin. The forest becomes denser as you draw closer to the river, and water marks on the trees show how deeply this floodplain can flood. After a quarter mile, the boardwalk ends at a peaceful spot under the cypresses on the Peace River.

Highlights: The dense cypress floodplain forest and the overlook on the Peace River offer a striking contrast.

Logistics: The park is open 7:00–dusk. Either park in a pulloff along the road (if available) at the beginning of the boardwalk, or drive up the hill to the large parking lot.

Other Activities: There is picnicking, birding, and, at the upper entrance to the park, an equestrian trail and a campground.

Nature Trail

Fort Meade Outdoor Recreation Area

CF-73 🚻

Location: Fort Meade [N27°44.795' W081°46.671'].

Length: 0.3 mile round-trip.

Map: None available.

Contact Information: Polk County Parks & Recreation (863-534-4340), 515 Boulevard Street, Bartow, FL 33830.

Directions: Follow US 98 east from Fort Meade.

The Hike: Meandering along the edge of the Peace River, this short nature trail connects the picnic area with the canoe launch. As you walk along the bluffs, you'll skirt floodplain forests, walk under giant cypresses, and watch gators lazing on the far bank along this beautiful stretch of river.

Highlights: Although short, this trail offers a rare view of an unsullied portion of the Peace River.

Logistics: The trail may be under water at times of high water.

Other Activities: You'll find a playground, ball fields, shaded picnic pavilions, fishing along the river bank, and a 1-mile fitness circuit track. The canoe launch is the starting point for the 67-mile Peace River Canoe Trail; the state Office of Greenways and Trails (850-245-2052 or 877-822-5208; www.dep.state.fl.us/gwt) can provide specific details and a map of the route.

Norton Agey Nature Trail

Street Audubon Center

CF-74 📖 🚻 👫 🐾

Location: Winter Haven [N27°59.735' W081°40.023'].

Length: 1-mile loop, comprising a network of five trails, with several extensions.

Map: Map and interpretive guide available at Howe House and posted on kiosk behind the house.

Contact Information: Street Audubon Center (863-324-7304), 115 Lameraux Road, Winter Haven, FL 33884.

Directions: From Winter Haven, follow SR 540 (Cypress Gardens Boulevard) east. Turn left on Cypress Gardens Road, following the "Great Florida Birding Trail" signs. Turn right on Lameraux Road and drive 0.3 mile through a residential community to the entrance on the left.

The Hike: There are many different ways to approach the trail system, which makes a loop around the Howe House to showcase Lake Ned. From the parking area, the North Trail circles a pond and leads down to the lakeshore to meet the Lake Trail in a shady hammock with some non-native landscaping such as queen palms and bamboo; the splash of blue beyond the vegetation is Lake Ned. Lizard tail crowds the extremely narrow footpath. Passing the bird blind, you come to the junction of the Lake Trail with the South Trail, Main Trail, and Primitive Trail. The Main Trail makes a broad beeline for the Howe House, while the Primitive Trail provides another narrow footpath through dense vegetation back around to the parking area to complete the loop.

Highlights: Spend a little time in the Window on Lake Ned bird blind, a nice screened room that overlooks the lake and lets you watch for birds without being harassed by mosquitoes.

Logistics: Opening hours are Mon–Sat 9:00–3:00. Numbered posts correspond to the interpretive guide. There are benches in several places for you to sit and watch the birds.

Other Activities: Stop in the Howe House to see the exhibits and to browse through their library of field guides, and visit the butterfly garden in the yard.

Allen David Broussard Catfish Creek Preserve

CF-75 👫 🐕 🏕

Location: Dundee [N27°59.029' W081°29.810'].

Length: 9 miles in two nested loops.

Map: Posted on trailhead kiosk.

Contact Information: Lake Kissimmee State Park (863-696-1112) 14248 Camp Mack Road, Lake Wales, FL 33898.

Directions: From SR 17 north of Dundee, turn right on Lake Hatchinhea Road and drive 7.8 miles to the "FFA Training Center" sign at Fire Tower Road. Turn right and continue down the road to the trailhead on the left.

The Hike: The trail starts to the right of the kiosk, looping through what is considered a perfect example of Lake Wales Ridge scrub, with diminutive rare plants such as scrub plum, pygmy fringe tree, and scrub hickory, as well as scrub morning glory and cutthroat grass in the seepage slopes.

Highlights: Catfish Creek Preserve is so far off the beaten path that it is an amazingly peaceful and quiet place to hike, and the views from the ridge are superb.

Logistics: The preserve is open 8:00–sunset. There is a composting toilet at the trailhead. The longer loop is blazed white, with the cross trails (creating shorter loops) blazed blue. Hikers and equestrians share trails across a couple of short stretches. Leashed pets are permitted.

Other Activities: There is a shaded picnic table at the trailhead. Separate equestrian trails loop around the park. Visit the FFA (Future Farmers of America) Training Center at the end of Fire Tower Road for pontoon boat rides on Lake Hatchinhea and canoe and kayak rentals to explore Catfish Creek.

Lake Kissimmee State Park

CF-76 **F** **$** 📖 🚹🚻 🔆 ⛺ 👫 🐾 ❋

Location: Lake Wales [N27°56.534' W081°21.230'].

Length: 16.3 miles in three loops and a round-trip trail.

Map: Rough sketch in park brochure; detailed backpacking map available from Florida Trail Association.

Contact Information: Lake Kissimmee State Park (863-696-1112), 14248 Camp Mack Road, Lake Wales, FL 33853.

Directions: From US 27 in Lake Wales, drive east on SR 60 for 9.7 miles to Boy Scout Camp Road. Turn left and continue 3.5 miles to Camp Mack Road. Turn right and drive 5.4 miles to the park entrance, on the right. All trails can be accessed from the parking area adjacent to the marina.

The Hike: Small children will enjoy the 0.4-mile interpretive Flatwoods Pond Nature Trail, which meanders around a marshy pond in the pine flatwoods, explaining a succession of habitats. Backpackers flock to the Buster Island Trail, a 6.9-mile loop which stays mostly under the canopy of ancient oak trees before crossing scrub and prairie, and to the North Loop Trail, a 6.7-mile loop through similar habitats with an optional 2.2-mile round trip on the Gobbler Ridge Trail through open scrub and prairie to the edge of Lake Kissimmee.

Highlights: This is one of Florida's best parks for wildlife watching. Deer and wild turkey are abundant, and you'll see alligators lazing along the canal, sandhill cranes wandering the prairie, and Florida scrub-jays along the North Loop. Visit the observation tower near the playground for a bird's-eye view of the prairies around Lake Kissimmee.

Logistics: Inform the rangers if you plan to camp overnight on either the North Loop or Buster Island campsites; there is a small fee. Bring adequate water and pack out all trash.

Other Activities: Visit the 1876 Cow Camp for an immersion in the life of the Cracker cowmen who once roamed these prairies. Fish behind the marina, or picnic under the live oaks. The campground makes it possible to spend a weekend exploring the trails as day hikes.

Caloosa Nature Trail

Ridge Audubon Center

CF-77 📖 🚸

Location: Babson Park [N27°50.483' W081°32.023'].

Length: 0.3-mile loop.

Map: Trail guide with map available at trailhead kiosk.

Contact Information: Ridge Audubon Center (863-638-1355), South Scenic Highway at North Crooked Lake Drive, Babson Park, FL 33827.

Directions: The center is along SR 17 between US 27 and Babson Park, at the intersection of SR 17 and Crooked Lake Road.

The Hike: Starting in front of the nature center, this short loop trail has twenty-six interpretive stations that identify key plants of the Lake Wales Ridge, a narrow string of ancient islands topped with rare and unusual species like the scrub hickory and scrub plum. Look for these and others as you climb from scrub habitat into the sandhills and back down again.

Highlights: The identification markers and interpretive brochure let you put a face on rare native plants that you might have only heard of before, like garberia and Britton's beargrass.

Logistics: The center is open dawn to dusk.

Other Activities: Visit the nature center, and bring your field guides to identify birds—this is a stop along the Great Florida Birding Trail.

Jenkins Trail

Tiger Creek Preserve

CF-78 🏕️

Location: Frostproof [N27°49.894' W081°27.397'].

Length: 1-mile loop.

Map: Displayed and in brochure at trailhead kiosk; map covers George Cooley (CF-79) and Pfundstein (CF-80) trails as well.

Contact Information: The Nature Conservancy (863-635-7506), 222 South Westmonte Drive, Suite 300, Altamonte Springs, FL 32714.

Directions: From SR 60, drive 9 miles south on Walk-in-the-Water Road to Wakeford Road; or, from CR 630, drive 5.1 miles north to the same intersection. Turn west and follow the clay road 0.7 mile to the end of the road; the entrance to the preserve is on the left.

The Hike: A bark chip path connects the parking area with the hiking loop. Turn right when you reach the loop, just beyond the fence line. The trail follows a jeep road through scrubby flatwoods and palmetto prairie; the line of forest in the distance outlines the floodplain of Tiger Creek. Reaching the creek, the trail enters the deep shade of the hammocks and follows the creek's course for a third of the hike before rising back up into the scrub to complete the loop.

Highlights: Halfway along the trail, you can step to the edge of Tiger Creek and look down at the clear tannic sand-bottomed creek and its floodplain marshes; the walk along the creek is worth the hike on the jeep trails.

Logistics: The trail is blazed orange. Keep alert for several turns at the intersection of jeep roads in the scrub. Along the creek, the trail is rough and uneven with tree roots in the footpath. Half of this trail has no shade, so wear sun protection and carry water with you.

Other Activities: Bring your binoculars to watch for Florida scrub-jays and other scrub habitat birds.

George Cooley Trail

Tiger Creek Preserve

CF-79 📖 🚸 🏕️

Location: Babson Park [N27°48.404' W081°29.917'].

Length: 0.8 mile, comprising an 0.5-mile loop and several spur trails.

Map: Available at kiosk at Pfundstein Trail (CF-80) up the road.

Contact Information: The Nature Conservancy (863-635-7506), 222 South Westmonte Drive, Suite 300, Altamonte Springs, FL 32714.

Directions: From US 27 in Lake Wales, drive south to CR 640 east to reach SR 17. Drive south on SR 17 through Babson Park for 2 miles to North Lake Moody Road. Turn left, and then left again on Murray Road. At the "Dead End" sign, turn left on Pfundstein Road. The trail starts at the first power pole on the left.

The Hike: Follow the footpath away from the road and through a line of posts to enter the preserve. The trailhead has several benches around it. Turn right to follow the Circle Trail counterclockwise; it links to the various spur trails as you walk through oak scrub, down to a bayhead, through a rare cut-throat seep, to tannic Patrick Creek, and through pine flatwoods.

Highlights: An extraordinary diversity of habitat along a very short hike makes this a fun place to take the family to show them the "real Florida." Be sure to walk the spur trail down to a scenic spot along Patrick Creek.

Logistics: Two or three cars can fit along the road. Do not block the road. If necessary, drive up to the Pfundstein Trail trailhead and walk 0.2 mile back to this trail. Metal "Nature Conservancy" diamond-shaped markers serve as blazes. "End of Trail" signs mark the end of some of the spur trails.

Other Activities: Visit the other excellent trails in Tiger Creek Preserve—the Pfundstein Trail (CF-80) just up the road, and the Jenkins Trail (CF-78) at the north end of the preserve.

Pfundstein Trail

Tiger Creek Preserve

CF-80 **F**

Location: Babson Park [N27°48.479' W081°29.523'].

Length: Up to 7.6 miles in two loops.

Map: Displayed and in brochure at trailhead kiosk; map covers George Cooley (CF-79) and Jenkins (CF-78) trails as well.

Contact Information: The Nature Conservancy (863-635-7506), 222 South Westmonte Drive, Suite 300, Altamonte Springs, FL 32714.

Directions: From US 27 in Lake Wales, drive south to CR 640 east to reach SR 17. Drive south on SR 17 through Babson Park for 2 miles to North Lake Moody Road. Turn left, and then left again on Murray Road. At the "Dead End" sign, turn left on Pfundstein Road. Continue 0.3 mile to the preserve entrance on the left; park across from the kiosk.

The Hike: Providing a path into the heart of the Lake Wales Ridge, this trail system consists of a 1-mile linear connector from the trailhead and two loops. The blue-blazed 0.3-mile Patrick Creek Loop circles a hydric hammock along the creek. The orange-blazed 5.3-mile Highland Loop is a rugged footpath that traverses the ancient dunes, dropping down into bayhead swamps and circling prairies surrounded by scrub.

Highlights: This hike stands out because of its lack of human intrusion, especially along the Highland Loop; breezes wipe away the last footprints in the sand. There are no outside noises, just the birds and the wind and the ancient wonder of the Lake Wales Ridge.

Logistics: It is easy to lose the trail along the loop portion in the scrub, since the trail hops on and off jeep trails. Always check for the next blaze. Much of the trail has no shade. Wear sun protection and bring plenty of water. Expect to wade through several of the bayheads, and you will get your shoes wet and muddy along the Patrick Creek Loop.

Other Activities: Visit the other excellent trails in Tiger Creek Preserve—the George Cooley Trail (CF-79) just up the road, and the Jenkins Trail (CF-78) at the north end of the preserve.

Bay Loop Trail

Lake Wales Ridge State Forest

CF-81 **$** ⚠ 🏕

Location: Frostproof [N27°45.602' W081°27.918'].

Length: 1.5-mile loop, connecting to 4.7 miles of linear trails.

Map: Displayed and in brochure at trailhead kiosk.

Contact Information: Lake Wales Ridge State Forest (863-635-8589), 851 CR 630 East, Frostproof, FL 33843.

Directions: From the intersection of SR 17 and CR 630 in Frostproof, drive east for 4.8 miles on CR 630 to the trailhead kiosk on the left. En route, you will pass an entrance to the Hidden Pond Recreation Area and a kiosk for the Black Bear Trail before reaching the trailhead, which is also 0.8 mile west of Walk-in-the-Water Road.

The Hike: Follow orange-tipped posts along the 1.5-mile loop along jeep roads and footpath through sandhills and scrub on the Lake Wales Ridge. A quarter of the way along the loop counterclockwise you reach a junction with the 0.9-mile yellow-blazed Black Bear Trail. Follow it west, where a 0.5-mile spur trail leads to the Black Bear primitive campsite. At the north end of the loop, the Big Bay Trail leads 3.8 miles (one-way) to Hidden Pond Recreation Area, with the Wood Duck primitive campsite at its northernmost point.

Highlights: You'll see patches of ancient scrub with gleaming white sand, and cutthroat seeps in swales. You may see Florida scrub-jays amid the scrub oaks, and gopher tortoises in the sandhills.

Logistics: A fee of $2 per vehicle is required at the iron ranger. If camping overnight, it's better to access the trail system from the Hidden Pond Recreation Area. Seasonal hunting is permitted; be aware of hunt dates and wear blaze orange during hunting season. Carry in water to the campsites. This trail is part of the Florida State Forests Trailwalker Program.

Other Activities: Equestrian trails start at the state forest campground off Walk-in-the-Water Road, where tent camping is permitted. Visit the Scrub-jay Loop Trail (CF-82) up the road, or drive south to the Arbuckle Tract for more extensive hiking (CF-83, CF-84).

Scrub-Jay Loop Trail

Lake Wales Ridge State Forest

CF-82 $ 🏕

Location: Frostproof [N27°45.759' W081°27.189'].

Length: 2.7-mile loop.

Map: Displayed and in brochure at trailhead kiosk.

Contact Information: Lake Wales Ridge State Forest (863-635- 7801), 851 CR 630 East, Frostproof, FL 33843.

Directions: From the intersection of SR 17 and CR 630 in Frostproof, drive east for 5.5 miles on CR 630 to the trailhead kiosk on the left. The trailhead is on the left within sight of the intersection of SR 630, Walk-in-the-Water Road, and Blue Jordan Road.

The Hike: Follow the orange-tipped posts on a hike through broad, open scrubby flatwoods, cutthroat seeps, and the ancient scrub of the Lake Wales Ridge.

Highlights: The scrub uplands are prime Florida scrub-jay habitat: watch for scrub-jay families working their way through the young oaks and pines.

Logistics: This trail is also posted as the Long Pond Trail at the trailhead. A fee of $2 per vehicle is required at the iron ranger. Seasonal hunting is permitted; be aware of hunt dates and wear blaze orange during hunting season. This trail is part of the Florida State Forests Trailwalker Program.

Other Activities: Equestrian trails start at the state forest campground off Walk-in-the-Water Road, where tent camping is permitted. Visit the Bay Loop Trail (CF-81) up the road, or drive south to the Arbuckle Tract for more extensive hiking (CF-83, CF-84).

Reedy Creek Trail

Lake Wales Ridge State Forest

CF-83 **F** $ **©** △ ⌂

Location: Frostproof [N27°42.478' W081°26.752].

Length: Trail network providing loop hikes up to 18.7 miles.

Map: Posted and in brochure at several trailhead kiosks; backpackers should purchase detailed map from Florida Trail Association.

Contact Information: Lake Wales Ridge State Forest (863-635-7801), 851 CR 630 East, Frostproof, FL 33843.

Directions: From Frostproof, take SR 630 east to Lake Arbuckle Road. Turn right and follow the road 7 miles to Rucks Dairy Road. Turn right and follow this clay road to Reedy Creek. Keep left at the fork; the most accessible trailhead is on the left immediately after the bridge.

The Hike: Walk up School Bus Road to where the trail starts at an "FT" sign with a dedication plaque on a rock. The 3.9-mile Paula Dockerty Trail provides access to the loop, leading to Lake Arbuckle. The trail follows the lakeshore en route to a campsite in a hammock, which connects with the 2.7-mile Kellerman Trail to CR 64. Along the outer loop, the trail traverses broad palmetto prairies, pine flatwoods, pine plantations, and the high scrub of the Lake Wales Ridge along Reedy Creek and its tributaries; the 3-mile Lake Godwin Trail provides a cross trail across the middle of the trail system.

Highlights: Walk through ancient scrub habitats and around perpetually green patches of cutthroat grass, unique to the Lake Wales Ridge.

Logistics: There is a $2 per vehicle fee. Seasonal hunting is permitted; be aware of hunt dates and wear blaze orange during hunting season. There are three designated primitive campsites on the outer loop: Lakeside, Hidden Hammock, and Grave Island. Carry a water filter. This trail is part of the Florida State Forests Trailwalker Program.

Other Activities: Reedy Creek Campground adjoins the Dockerty trailhead. Visit the Old Cabin Nature Trail (CF-84) or the trails (CF-81, CF-82) in the Walk-in-the-Water Tract. Separate equestrian trails run throughout the state forest.

Old Cabin Nature Trail

Lake Wales Ridge State Forest

CF-84 **$** 📖 ⛺ 🏕

Location: Frostproof [N27°40.779' W081°24.997'].

Length: 1-mile loop.

Map: Posted at trailhead kiosk; map in brochure at kiosk is inaccurate.

Contact Information: Lake Wales Ridge State Forest (863-635-7801), 851 CR 630 East, Frostproof, FL 33843.

Directions: From Frostproof, take SR 630 east to Lake Arbuckle Road. Turn right and follow the road 7 miles to Rucks Dairy Road. Turn right and follow this clay road to Reedy Creek. Keep left at the fork and head down School Bus Road. After 2.5 miles, you reach the entrance for the Hunt Check Station; turn right and park near the kiosk in front of the old cabin.

The Hike: Start by walking from the trailhead kiosk behind the cabin to a second interpretive kiosk, and follow the nature trail sign to your right. The trail makes a loop around a vast wetland, crossing bridges on the inflow and outflow for the wetland; interpretive signs mark plants along the way, and several kiosks provide more extensive information about the habitats you're traversing: scrubby flatwoods, cutthroat seeps, and scrub.

Highlights: Walk right through the middle of a cutthroat seep, one of the rarest habitats in Florida, where the cutthroat grass stays green all year.

Logistics: There is a $2 per vehicle fee. The trail may be wet in places. Blazes are red in some places, blue in others: connector trails from the Reedy Creek Trail merge here, so follow the "Nature Trail" signs rather than the blazes. Seasonal hunting is permitted; be aware of hunt dates and wear blaze orange during hunting season. This trail is part of the Florida State Forests Trailwalker Program—don't forget to send in your postcard!

Other Activities: There are picnic benches in front of the old cabin, and a campground adjacent to the Dockerty trailhead of the Reedy Creek Loop (CF-83) on Rucks Dairy Road.

Crooked Lake Prairie

CF-85 📖 🚻 ⛺ 🐕

Location: Frostproof [N27°48.389' W081°33.569'].

Length: Trail network enabling loop hikes of 1.3 to 4.6 miles.

Map: Posted on trailhead kiosk and available in interpretive brochure.

Contact Information: Polk County Natural Resources Environmental Lands Program (863-534-7377), 4177 Ben Durrance Road, Bartow, FL 33830.

Directions: From the junction of SR 17 and CR 630 in Frostproof, drive north 3.8 miles to Cody Villa Road; turn left at the sign for Crooked Prairie Preserve. Follow the road to where it makes a sharp right; turn right and make an immediate left into the preserve. The entrance road leads through a citrus grove to the trailhead parking area.

The Hike: Follow the orange-blazed 1.3-mile Scrub Trail to explore the scrub habitats of the Lake Wales Ridge. The trail connects to the blue-blazed Piney Woods Trail, a 1.5-mile loop through pine flatwoods and pastureland with scenic views. The purple-blazed Lookout Trail is a 0.3-mile spur to a marsh. The yellow-blazed 1.2-mile Prairie Path offers vistas across a prairie, leading to a scenic oak hammock along the lake.

Highlights: Enjoy walking along the Piney Woods Trail, which provides excellent views of Crooked Lake, and meandering through the beautiful scrub of the Lake Wales Ridge.

Logistics: The reserve is open 5:00–7:00 standard time, 5:00–8:30 daylight savings time. Leashed pets are permitted. The restroom is a wheelchair-accessible portable toilet. Follow signs to the right of the gate for the shortest route to the picnic area. Primitive camping is allowed with a special-use permit; call in advance of your visit.

Other Activities: There is a picnic area on Crooked Lake, and fabulous birding along the lake.

North Loop

Hickory Lake Scrub

CF-86 📖 🚹🚺 🐕

Location: Frostproof [N27°41.837' W081°32.207'].

Length: 0.4-mile loop.

Map: Posted and in brochure at kiosk.

Contact Information: Polk County Natural Resources Environmental Lands Program (863-534-7377), 4177 Ben Durrance Road, Bartow, FL 33830.

Directions: Drive north on SR 17 from Avon Park toward Frostproof; the trailhead is on the left 0.5 mile after Hopson Road.

The Hike: After passing through open scrub with a carpet of spike moss and deer moss, the trail turns to follow the marshy edge of Hickory Lake. Continuing through scrubby flatwoods, it makes a sharp left onto a jeep trail to climb through the scrub to complete the loop.

Highlights: Beautiful natural gardens of rare scrub plants line the footpath: bring your field guide to identify scrub morning glory, Curtis's milkweed, scrub plum, Ashe's savory, and many others. Watch for gopher tortoises emerging from their burrows.

Logistics: Sign in at the trail register. The trail is marked with fat orange blazes and orange arrows. The footpath may be indistinct in places, and wet nearest the lakeshore.

Other Activities: Birdwatchers will find numerous wading birds in the shallow marshes along the lakeshore.

South Loop

Hickory Lake Scrub

CF-87 📖 🐎 🚻

Location: Frostproof [N27°41.653' W081°32.693'].

Length: 0.3-mile loop.

Map: Posted and in brochure at kiosk.

Contact Information: Polk County Natural Resources Environmental Lands Program (863-534-7377), 4177 Ben Durrance Road, Bartow, FL 33830.

Directions: From US 27 north of Avon Park, follow SR 17 north toward Frostproof. Turn left on Hopson Road; the trailhead parking and kiosk are immediately on the right.

The Hike: Starting out under the dense canopy of an oak hammock, the trail continues through deep shade up to the edge of the scrub habitat, where it begins the loop. Gaining elevation, it comes to the crest of a hill with a side trail to a view of a cutthroat seep, and then drops back down the hill to complete the loop.

Highlights: A natural green meadow of rare cutthroat grass grows beneath the sand pines at the far end of the loop. In the oak hammock, look for orchids on the oak limbs, and unusual mushrooms emerging from the forest floor.

Logistics: Sign in at the trail register. The trail is blazed reddish orange.

Other Activities: Equestrian trails start on the opposite side of Hopson Road.

Central Atlantic

Volusia, Brevard, Indian River

Oak hammock on the Kratzert Tract.

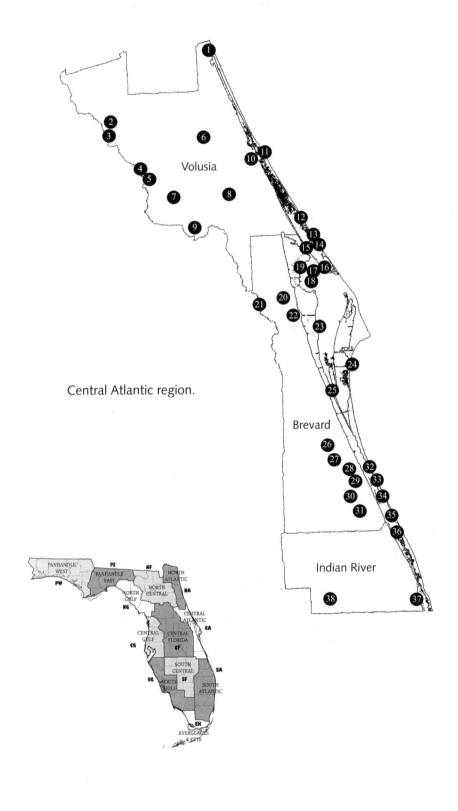

Central Atlantic region.

Volusia
- CA-1 Nature Trail, Tomoka State Park
- CA-2 DeLeon Springs State Park
- CA-3 Lake Woodruff National Wildlife Refuge
- CA-4 Indian Mound Nature Trail, Hontoon Island State Park
- CA-5 Pine Island Hiking Trail, Blue Spring State Park
- CA-6 Buncombe Hill Interpretive Trail, Tiger Bay State Forest
- CA-7 Lyonia Preserve
- CA-8 Lake Ashby Park
- CA-9 Kratzert Tract, Lake Monroe Conservation Area
- CA-10 Spruce Creek Park
- CA-11 Smyrna Dunes Park
- CA-12 Turtle Mound Trail, Canaveral National Seashore
- CA-13 Eldora Hammock Trail, Canaveral National Seashore
- CA-14 Castle Windy Trail, Canaveral National Seashore
- CA-15 Seminole Rest Trail, Canaveral National Seashore

Brevard
- CA-16 Scrub Ridge Trail, Merritt Island National Wildlife Refuge
- CA-17 Oak and Palm Hammock Trails, Merritt Island National Wildlife Refuge
- CA-18 Visitor Center Boardwalk, Merritt Island National Wildlife Refuge
- CA-19 Allan Cruickshank Memorial Trail, Merritt Island National Wildlife Refuge
- CA-20 Wuesthoff Park
- CA-21 Canaveral Marshes Trail, Canaveral Marshes Conservation Area
- CA-22 Enchanted Forest Sanctuary
- CA-23 Pine Island Conservation Area
- CA-24 Hammock Nature Trail, Lori Wilson Park
- CA-25 Nature Trail, Rotary Park–Merritt Island
- CA-26 Wickham Park
- CA-27 Nature Trail, Erna Nixon Park
- CA-28 Turkey Creek Sanctuary
- CA-29 Malabar Scrub Sanctuary
- CA-30 Flatwoods Loop, Micco Scrub Sanctuary
- CA-31 St. Sebastian River Preserve State Park
- CA-32 Coconut Point Sanctuary
- CA-33 Maritime Hammock Sanctuary
- CA-34 Nature Trail, Sebastian Inlet State Park

Indian River
- CA-35 Centennial Trail, Pelican Island National Wildlife Refuge
- CA-36 Wabasso Island Environmental Learning Center
- CA-37 Oslo Riverfront Conservation Area
- CA-38 Fort Drum Marsh Conservation Area

Nature Trail

Tomoka State Park

CA-1 $ 📖 🚻 🅰 👥 🐾

Location: Ormond Beach [N29°20.981' W081°05.274'].

Length: 0.7-mile loop.

Map: Rough map in park brochure.

Contact Information: Tomoka State Park (386-676-4050), 2099 North Beach Street, Ormond Beach, FL 32174.

Directions: From I-95, follow SR 40 east into Ormond Beach. Turn left on North Beach Street right before the Intracoastal Waterway bridge. Follow North Beach Street through a historic residential district to the park entrance on the right. Follow the park road back to the Visitors Center.

The Hike: This interpretive trail immerses you in a maritime hammock that was once the site of a Timucuan village, with wild coffee growing at one of its northernmost points in Florida. After 0.3 mile the trail reaches a parking lot and picnic area. Turn right to follow the Partnership Loop down to the edge of the salt marsh. At the fork, keep left, walking through the sand live oaks and cedars on a carpet of pine duff. Continue straight as you rejoin the shortcut trail, and bear right to go around the outdoor classroom.

Highlights: There are great views across the salt marsh canals, ideal for birding, and a steady breeze no matter what time of year. At one overlook, a tall pine tree stands suspended over the water, its exposed roots reaching out and down like a plumbing system.

Logistics: The trail starts to the left of the Visitors Center front door. Numerous benches make this an easy trail for all ages.

Other Activities: A trip to the Visitors Center (open 9:30–4:30 daily) will enlighten you about the culture of the Timucua people who once had a village in this hammock. Take a side trip to the Chief Tomokie sculpture, across the picnic area you reach at the halfway point of the trail. There is a full-service campground, a boat launch, canoe trails, picnic pavilions, and fishing.

DeLeon Springs State Park

CA-2 **F** $ 📖 🚻 ♿ 🚻

Location: De Leon Springs [N29°08.022' W081°21.682'].

Length: 5.5 miles, in 0.5-mile and 4-mile loops plus spur trail.

Map: Rough map in park brochure; more detailed map of Wild Persimmon Trail posted and in brochure at trailhead kiosk; highly detailed map in regional map set available from Florida Trail Association.

Contact Information: DeLeon Springs State Park (386-985-4212), PO Box 1338, De Leon Springs, FL 32130.

Directions: Follow US 17 north of Deland into De Leon Springs. Turn left on De Leon Springs Boulevard and follow it into the park. On the park entrance road, turn right at the fork and park near the bathhouses. The nature trail starts up the hill to the left.

The Hike: Start on the wheelchair-accessible paved nature trail, a 0.5-mile loop that leads you between tall azalea bushes beneath loblolly pines, and along the edge of the swampy floodplain forest. Leading west from the nature trail, the 1-mile round-trip Monkey Island Trail follows an old tramway through the blackwater floodplain forest, ending at an island along Spring Garden Run. Branching off the nature trail, the Wild Persimmon Trail is a rugged 4-mile loop through the junglelike hydric hammocks of the St. Johns River floodplain and adjacent upland forests and fields.

Highlights: Old Methuselah, a giant bald cypress, is thought to be at least a thousand years old. Pale pink and deep magenta azaleas bloom in February along the nature trail.

Logistics: Expect mosquitoes—this is a floodplain forest. Neither the Monkey Island Trail nor the Wild Persimmon Trail is recommended for small children. You must register at the ranger station if you are hiking the Wild Persimmon Trail. It floods frequently and may require some wading through the swamp to complete the loop. Follow the orange blazes.

Other Activities: Come and swim in DeLeon Springs, rent a canoe or kayak to explore Spring Garden Run, or take a guided ecotour on the river. But don't miss the popular Old Spanish Mill Restaurant, where you can make your own pancakes at your table!

Lake Woodruff National Wildlife Refuge

CA-3 📖 🚻

Location: De Leon Springs [N29°06.402' W081°22.268'].

Length: 6-plus miles of interconnecting trails.

Map: In park brochure and displayed on kiosk at primary trailhead.

Contact Information: Lake Woodruff National Wildlife Refuge (386- 985-4673), PO Box 488, De Leon Springs, FL 32130.

Directions: From US 17 in De Leon Springs, drive south on Grand Avenue and watch for the park signs; turn right on Mud Lake Road, which becomes a dirt road, and follow it to the end to reach the parking area nearest the impoundments.

The Hike: Most folks who visit the refuge walk the dike trails around the impoundments, but there's a lot more to explore. The Hammock Trail leads you through a dense upland hammock, and the Pine Island Trail heads out past the observation tower to the pine flatwoods of Jones Island, leading you down an old road to Pontoon Landing on Spring Garden Run.

Highlights: Walk the dikes slowly to observe alligators, gallinules, and deer; this is a great place for wildlife watching. The views are excellent across the impoundments.

Logistics: The refuge is open sunrise to sunset, the visitor center and bookstore Mon–Fri 8:00–4:30. Be alert for alligators along the impoundments. Where the trails leave the dikes, they are subject to flooding if the St. Johns River is high. Mosquitoes are fierce—wear insect repellent!

Other Activities: This is one of Central Florida's top birding sites, so bring your binoculars and roam the impoundments, where you might see limpkins, Louisiana herons, and sandhill cranes with their young.

Indian Mound Nature Trail

Hontoon Island State Park

CA-4 $ 📖 🚻 🄯 🐾

Location: Deland [N28°58.474' W081°21.434'].

Length: 3.3 miles round-trip.

Map: Rough map in park brochure, more detailed map displayed at trailhead.

Contact Information: Hontoon Island State Park (386-736-5309), 2309 River Ridge Road, Deland, FL 32720.

Directions: From US 17 in downtown Deland, take SR 44 west to Old New York Avenue. Signs direct you along the remainder of the 7.2-mile back-road route to the park. The parking lot is on River Ridge Road.

The Hike: Starting at the "Indian Mound Nature Trail" sign by the marina, follow the road down to the "Nature Trail" sign to enter the forest, where you walk on bog bridges and boardwalks under the shade of cabbage palms and massive live oaks, emerging briefly along the Hontoon Dead River before climbing up through pine flatwoods to the endpoint of the trail, high atop an ancient Timucuan midden.

Highlights: Surrender to the enchantment of the hydric hammock habitat, with live oaks and cabbage palms creating a cathedral-like feel. One particularly grand tree marks the end of the trail on the midden.

Logistics: You must take a ferryboat (free) from the parking area to and from the island unless you arrive by boat. If the river is high, the trail will be flooded—expect to wade.

Other Activities: Tent camping and cabins are available in the campground. There is a picnic grove on the St. Johns River, and a small museum to explore.

Pine Island Hiking Trail

Blue Spring State Park

CA-5 **$** 📖 🚻 Ⓒ ⛺

Location: Orange City [N28°56.569' W081°20.469'].

Length: 7.3 miles round-trip.

Map: Rough map in park brochure.

Contact Information: Blue Spring State Park (386-775-3663), 2100 West French Avenue, Orange City, FL 32763.

Directions: From US 17/92 in Orange City, you'll see a large overhead sign for the park. Turn and drive west on West French Street to the end of the paved road. The entrance is on the left. Continue down to the lower parking area (left at the fork) to find the trailhead near the end of the loop.

The Hike: Mostly following old forest roads, this hike introduces you to a variety of habitats as it circles a lagoon along the St. Johns River. You walk through oak hammocks, floodplain forests of cypress and sweet gum, hydric hammocks, pond pine flatwoods, open scrub, and scrubby flatwoods. The trail ends in a palm hammock with a river view and several campsites for backpackers.

Highlights: You'll find deep, dark cypress swamps, gopher tortoises and Florida scrub-jays in the open scrub, and the unusual-looking pond pines with tufts of needles emerging from their trunks!

Logistics: Register at the ranger station before you hike or backpack. The trail can be challenging—if the river is high, you'll be wading at least a quarter of the trail, especially close to the lagoon. The flatwoods retain a lot of water after a rain. Restrooms are found near the dock at the parking lot for the trailhead. There is a privy at the primitive camping area.

Other Activities: There is developed camping, picnicking, canoeing and kayaking, swimming, and tours of the historic Thursby House. Don't miss the 0.8-mile round-trip boardwalk up along Blue Spring Run to see Blue Spring. In winter, more than 150 manatees call this short waterway home.

Buncombe Hill Interpretive Trail

Tiger Bay State Forest

CA-6 📖 ⛺ 🎣

Location: Daytona [N29°09.975' W081°09.709'].

Length: 2.1-mile loop.

Map: Displayed at trailhead kiosk; available in brochure and in St. Johns River Water Management District's *Recreation Guide to District Lands.*

Contact Information: St. Johns River Water Management District (904-529-2380), PO Box 1429, Palatka, FL 32178-1429.

Directions: Drive west from Daytona Beach on US 92 to Indian Lake Road. Turn right and continue 1.8 miles to the state forest kiosk. Stop and sign in, then continue along the road, which makes a left turn. Make the first right turn to enter the parking lot at Indian Lake Recreation Area.

The Hike: Pick up an interpretive guide at the trailhead kiosk, and follow the wide trail through a corridor of sand pines into an oak hammock, where the trail narrows before emerging into a slash pine plantation with furrowed ground and the shards of turpentine cups. Weaving through the trees, the trail rises into a sand pine scrub. After 0.9 mile you enter the Buncombe Hill Turpentine Camp, an open area scattered with the remains of turpentine cups and mattress springs. Crossing Rima Ridge Road twice, the trail makes its way back through scrub and sandhill to complete the loop.

Highlights: The trail has interesting historic stops, like the turpentine camp and the old homestead—notice the chips of dishes and glass embedded in the sand. Come in the fall and you'll see hundreds of butterflies flitting around the profusion of wildflowers.

Logistics: Follow the mint green blazes. Seasonal hunting is permitted; check hunt dates before you hike. This is a trail listed in the Florida State Forests Trailwalker Program. The trail makes several tricky turns, so always confirm that you've found the next blaze before continuing on your assumed route.

Other Activities: Go kayaking on Indian Lake and birding around the lake.

Lyonia Preserve

CA-7 📖 🚻 👥

Location: Deltona [N28°55.812' W081°13.505'].

Length: 2.5 miles in three stacked loops.

Map: Displayed at trailhead kiosk; available from Volusia County Parks website and in brochure from public library.

Contact Information: Lyonia Preserve (407-736-5927), 2150 Eustace Avenue, Deltona, FL 32725.

Directions: From I-4 exit 114, Orange City, drive 2.5 miles south on SR 472 to Providence Boulevard; turn right. Continue 0.7 mile to Eustace Avenue; turn right. The entrance and parking for the preserve are shared with the Deltona Public Library on the left. Park on the right side of the building, near the trailhead kiosk.

The Hike: Preserving four hundred acres of relict sand dunes, this park is ground zero for the one of the state's densest populations of Florida scrub-jays. Walk along the Rusty Lyonia Trail, the Red Root Trail, and the Blueberry Trail to enjoy the young sand pine scrub where these colorful birds gather in family groups, squawking and quibbling in the trees and under the bushes.

Highlights: I know of no other place in Florida where you are virtually guaranteed to see a Florida scrub-jay up close. The preserve is also home to Volusia County's high point, at 75 feet. Walk the Blueberry Trail to climb 50 feet above sea level for a scenic view across the marshes.

Logistics: The trails are open and shadeless for the most part, so wear sun protection and bring plenty of water. Please do not feed the scrub-jays, as it interferes with their natural diet. The scrub-jays tend to be overly friendly and may land on your head. Resist the urge to touch them, as they will bite. Restrooms are in the library.

Other Activities: There is a picnic grove at the trailhead. Bring your binoculars, as Florida scrub-jays are only one of many species living at the preserve.

Lake Ashby Park

CA-8 📖 🚻 ⛺ ♿ 🚻

Location: Lake Ashby [N28°56.196' W081°05.024'].

Length: 1.5 miles in two trails.

Map: Displayed and in brochure at trailhead kiosk.

Contact Information: Lake Ashby Park (386-428-4589), 4150 Boy Scout Camp Road, New Smyrna Beach, FL 32168.

Directions: Follow SR 44 west 4.5 miles from I-95 (or east 10 miles from I-4) to its junction with CR 415 in Satsuma. Turn south and drive 4.2 miles on CR 415 to Lake Ashby Road. Turn left onto the narrow road. After 0.7 mile turn left on Boy Scout Camp Road. The road turns to dirt after 0.2 mile; continue another 0.3 mile through the oak hammock to the park entrance on the right.

The Hike: The trail starts immediately across the park road (next to the campground) from the kiosk and restrooms. Cross the road, turn right, and follow the meandering footpaths (with signs at various intersections) out to the impressive boardwalk, which traverses floodplain forest and goes out over Lake Ashby, and around past the picnic area to a rugged spur trail that follows the lakeshore to the property line, where you must turn around and return on the same path.

Highlights: Enjoy walking along the lake, with the cool breeze beneath the cypress trees.

Logistics: The park is open 7:00–6:00 daily. Be alert for alligators, especially along the Lakeshore Trail; although dogs are permitted in the park, I wouldn't recommend taking them on these trails.

Other Activities: There is a nice tent campground in an oak hammock within sight of the lake (great breezes!) as well as a picnic area on the lake and a small playground. Great birding from the lake boardwalk.

Boardwalk on Lake Ashby.

Kratzert Tract

Lake Monroe Conservation Area

CA-9

Location: Sanford [N28 49.913' W081 11.501'].

Length: 1.5-mile loop plus-1.5 mile linear trail to campsite.

Map: Displayed at trailhead kiosk; available in St. Johns River Water Management District's *Recreation Guide to District Lands.*

Contact Information: St. Johns River Water Management District (904-529-2380), PO Box 1429, Palatka, FL 32178-1429.

Directions: From SR 46, follow SR 415 north for 2.5 miles, crossing the St. Johns River bridge. Turn left onto Reed Ellis Road. Continue 0.6 mile to trailhead parking on left.

The Hike: Enter through the gate. The linear Oak Hammock Trail, which leads to the campsite, heads south from the kiosk; the White Loop trail starts and ends at the kiosk. Turn right to walk the loop counterclockwise, passing through planted longleaf pines in an old farmer's field before descending after 0.5 mile into oak and palm hammocks. The narrow footpath follows streams through the junglelike palm hammocks, climbing back up to the pine plantation at 1.3 miles. Continue straight to complete the loop.

Highlights: You'll find dense hammocks of tall cabbage palms decked in ferns, with meandering tannic sand-bottomed streams flowing toward Lake Monroe. Narrow bridges evoke "walking the plank." Citrus grows wild in the forest, adding splashes of color. An oak hammock provides a beautiful setting for the campsite. Expect to see deer!

Logistics: The White Loop Trail is narrow, blazed with white blazes, and has bridges suitable for hiking only. A camping permit is required for groups of seven or more. The trails and campsite may be flooded during times of high water in the St. Johns River.

Other Activities: Birdwatching, camping, and fishing are all possible.

Spruce Creek Park

CA-10 📖 🏃 🅲 ♿ 🚻 🐕

Location: Port Orange [N29°05.591' W080°58.394'].

Length: 1.5 miles round-trip.

Map: Map and brochure available at park office.

Contact Information: Spruce Creek Park (386-322-5133), 6250 South Ridgewood Avenue, Port Orange, FL 32123.

Directions: From I-95 exit 249A, drive east on SR 44 toward New Smyrna Beach; make the turnoff on the left to access US 1 via Business SR 44. Drive north 5.8 miles on US 1, passing the park entrance on the left (on the divided highway) before you get to a turnaround where you can head south and enter the park on the right. Drive up to the park office and turn right to park next to the picnic pavilion and playground.

The Hike: There are two trails in this park—a broad shell path circling the entire park, and the hiking trail out to Rose Creek. Start by crossing the boardwalk next to the playground, turn right on the shell path, then left to cross the bridge over Rose Creek for an enjoyable stroll through cedars and pines. The trail leads to an observation tower, with a rugged loop into the woods and a spur trail that takes you out on forest roads to Rose Bay.

Highlights: The views from the bridge and the observation tower are great. There are lots of picnic tables for you to take along a picnic lunch and enjoy it beside the estuary.

Logistics: The park is open 7:00–6:30. Wheelchairs can utilize only the shell path (with assistance) and the boardwalk and bridge leading across the estuary.

Other Activities: The park has camping, a playground, a picnic area, a canoe launch, and a large fishing pier.

Smyrna Dunes Park

CA-11 $ 📖 🚻 ♿ 🧎 🐕

Location: New Smyrna Beach [N29°04.002' W080°54.809'].

Length: 1.4-mile boardwalk loop, plus 1 mile of side trails, and walking on the beach to your heart's content.

Map: Posted on trailhead kiosk.

Contact Information: Smyrna Dunes Park (386-424-2935), Peninsula Boulevard, New Smyrna Beach, FL 32169.

Directions: To find the park, take I-95 exit 84, New Smyrna. Follow FL 44 east over the causeway into New Smyrna Beach, turning left on Peninsula Boulevard after 5.4 miles. Follow the road for 2.7 miles until it ends at the Coast Guard Station. Turn right to enter the park.

The Hike: For the most scenic walk, follow the boardwalk south through a shady maritime forest. The boardwalk emerges into a scenic panorama of rolling dunes, keeping you well above the fragile coastal terrain. As it follows the perimeter of the peninsula, you cross flatlands where the winds and waves have flattened the dunes, and other places where the dunes are rebuilding. A nice side trail leads through a mangrove swamp. The loop ends back at the parking area behind the restrooms.

Highlights: Follow the side trails (also boardwalks) to vantage points looking out over the ocean and inlet, and through the mangrove marshes on the west side of the peninsula. Climb the observation tower for a broader view.

Logistics: There is an admission fee of $3.50 per vehicle, and limited parking available. Since most of the boardwalk is in the sun, wear sun protection and carry plenty of water. The entire loop is wheelchair accessible, although the side trails to the beach are not—they involve scrambles along sand paths, or staircases up and over the dunes. If you walk your dog here, you must clean up after it.

Other Activities: Try fishing off the pier and the beach, sea kayaking in the inlet, and sunning on the sandy Atlantic beach. There are also numerous shaded picnic benches with grills along the boardwalk. Swimming is permitted, but this area has a high concentration of sharks.

Turtle Mound Trail

Canaveral National Seashore

CA-12 $ 📖 🚻

Location: Bethune Beach [N28°55.832' W080°49.542'].

Length: 0.3-mile round-trip boardwalk.

Map: Rough trail map in park brochure.

Contact Information: Canaveral National Seashore (386-428-3384; www.nps.gov/cana), 7611 South Atlantic Avenue, New Smyrna Beach, FL 32169.

Directions: From I-95 exit 249A, drive east on SR 44 until it turns into A1A; continue 7 miles south to where the highway leads into the park entrance. Continue 0.5 mile to the parking spaces on the right.

The Hike: After leading you out to the edge of the Indian River Lagoon, the trail climbs steeply up the side of an ancient Timucuan shell mound topped with a fragrant coastal hammock. At the top, the trail comes to a T intersection, and in both directions, the boardwalk ends at an observation platform overlooking the lagoon and ocean.

Highlights: There are fabulous views from the top of the shell mound, and a climb that'll get your heart pumping!

Logistics: The entrance fee is $5 per car, with receipt good for one week. Although this is a boardwalk trail, it is extremely steep and not recommended for wheelchairs.

Other Activities: Stop by the visitor center to learn about the park and its full range of activities, including swimming, surfing, fishing, sea kayaking, camping on the beach, and two other short trails (CA-13 and CA-14) inside the park, as well as a pathway to a historic site.

Eldora Hammock Trail

Canaveral National Seashore

CA-13 $ 📖 🚸 🏠

Location: Bethune Beach [N28°54.561' W080°49.113'].

Length: 0.5-mile loop.

Map: Rough trail map in park brochure.

Contact Information: Canaveral National Seashore (386-428-3384; www.nps.gov/cana), 7611 South Atlantic Avenue, New Smyrna Beach, FL 32169.

Directions: From I-95 exit 249A, drive east on SR 44 until it turns into A1A; continue 7 miles south to where the highway leads into the park entrance. At 1.4 miles along the park road, turn right on Eldora Road. Follow it past the Eldora Village Historic Site to the next parking area on the right.

The Hike: Entering an extraordinarily shady tropical hammock, the nature trail is crowded by understory plants like wild coffee, yaupon, and marlberry. Live oaks and large red bay trees create the canopy and are covered in resurrection fern. After 0.3 mile you drop down into a corridor of silvery saw palmetto, many of which are very old and tall.

Highlights: These are not your average interpretive markers—a good deal of research and thought went into them. Take the time to read them as you walk down this beautiful wild trail.

Logistics: The entrance fee is $5 per car, with receipt good for one week. The trail may be rugged and rough to follow in places. There are restrooms available at the Eldora Village parking area, a short walk back up the road.

Other Activities: Stop by the visitor's center to learn about the park and its full range of activities, including swimming, surfing, fishing, sea kayaking, camping on the beach, and two other short trails (CA-12 and CA-14) inside the park, as well as a pathway to a historic site.

Castle Windy Trail

Canaveral National Seashore

CA-14 **$** 📖 🚻 👫 🐕

Location: Bethune Beach [N28°53.895' W080°48.218'].

Length: 0.7 mile round-trip.

Map: Rough trail map in park brochure.

Contact Information: Canaveral National Seashore (386-428-3384; www.nps.gov/cana), 7611 South Atlantic Avenue, New Smyrna Beach, FL 32169.

Directions: From I-95 exit 249A, drive east on SR 44 until it turns into A1A; continue 7 miles south to where the highway leads into the park entrance. Continue down the park road to Castle Windy Beach, and park in the beach parking area on the left.

The Hike: Starting across the road from the beach parking, the trail is essentially a straight line through the undulating terrain of the barrier island's maritime hammock, with numbered posts keyed to an interpretive brochure available at the trailhead. After 0.3 mile you emerge into the sunlight at a picnic table along the Indian River Lagoon. Retrace your steps to the trailhead.

Highlights: There is a great view of the lagoon coastline from the end of the trail. Listen for armadillos nosing around beneath the underbrush.

Logistics: The entrance fee is $5 entrance fee per car, with receipt good for one week.

Other Activities: Stop by the visitor's center to learn about the park and its full range of activities, including swimming, surfing, fishing, sea kayaking, camping on the beach, and two other short trails (CA-12 and CA-13) inside the park, as well as a pathway to a historic site.

Seminole Rest Trail

Canaveral National Seashore

CA-15 📖 🚻 ♿ 🧑‍🧒 🐕

Location: Oak Hill [N28°52.197' W080°50.244'].

Length: 0.3 mile round-trip on boardwalk and pavement.

Map: Rough trail map in park brochure.

Contact Information: Canaveral National Seashore (386-428-3384; www.nps.gov/cana), 7611 South Atlantic Avenue, New Smyrna Beach, FL 32169.

Directions: From US 1 in Oak Hill (south of New Smyrna), turn left on Canal Avenue. Drive 1.3 miles east to the park entrance on the left.

The Hike: This easy stroll around Seminole Rest, a former plantation on the Indian River, overlooks the Eldora Hammock area of Canaveral National Seashore. It is built on a large Timucuan midden topped with cedars and an oak hammock. The trail follows the shoreline and then loops around the houses to parallel a mangrove-lined slough on the return trip.

Highlights: Enjoy great views of the Indian River Lagoon. Large interpretive markers tell the story behind this historical and archaeological site.

Logistics: The pavement is good for strollers and wheelchairs. Active restoration of the 1911 Wesley H. Snyder home is under way, so the trail may be rerouted at times.

Other Activities: Tours of the historic homes are offered; contact the park for details. There's a canoe launch nearby.

Scrub Ridge Trail

Merritt Island National Wildlife Refuge

CA-16 ▢ ▦ ♿ ▦

Location: Merritt Island [N28°41.699' W080°42.953'].

Length: 0.9-mile loop.

Map: In park brochure.

Contact Information: Merritt Island National Wildlife Refuge (321-861-0667), PO Box 6504, Titusville, FL 32782.

Directions: Take I-95 exit 220, Titusville, and follow SR 406 east for 8 miles over the causeway to Merritt Island. Take CR 402 east for 5.1 miles to SR 3. Turn left and drive north 3.8 miles to the entrance road on the right. Drive 0.4 mile down the dirt road to the trailhead.

The Hike: Starting behind the kiosk, the trail is a broad path through the young coastal scrub, headed toward a distant line of tall slash pines. Curving to the left, the trail comes to a T intersection with another unmarked path. Turn left to walk along the path to return. A wall of vegetation screens your view of the marsh. The road broadens after 0.7 mile as you return to the trailhead.

Highlights: Watch for Florida scrub-jays, as the young scrub is an ideal habitat for these rare birds.

Logistics: The refuge is open sunrise to sunset. The trail may be mushy in places.

Other Activities: Birdwatching is the top activity in the refuge, which is renowned for its diversity of species, especially during the winter migratory season. There are several other trails on which to explore the varied habitats of the refuge: see hikes CA-17, CA-18, and CA-19.

Oak and Palm Hammock Trails

Merritt Island National Wildlife Refuge

CA-17 📖 👫

Location: Merritt Island [N28°38.645' W080°42.996'].

Length: 2.7 miles in two loops.

Map: In park brochure.

Contact Information: Merritt Island National Wildlife Refuge (321-861-0667), PO Box 6504, Titusville, FL 32782.

Directions: Take I-95 exit 220, Titusville, and follow SR 406 east for 8 miles over the causeway to Merritt Island. Take CR 402 east for 4 miles, passing the visitor center, before reaching the trailhead on the left.

The Hike: From the trailhead, two paths radiate in opposite directions. To the right, the 0.7-mile Oak Hammock Trail is a family-friendly interpretive trail that loops through a tropical hammock on boardwalks and footpaths, emerging through a wonderland of sword ferns back to the parking area. To the left, the 2-mile Palm Hammock Trail is a loop for the more adventuresome hiker, as it winds it way through swamp forests, open marshes, and hydric hammocks, often under a dense canopy of cabbage palms.

Highlights: When you see the unusual forest of Simpson's stopper trees along the Oak Hammock Trail, you'll understand why their nickname is nakedwood. You're likely to see more birds and wildlife along the Palm Hammock Trail.

Logistics: The refuge is open sunrise to sunset. Expect the Palm Hammock Trail to be muddy, mucky, and even under water in places—not recommended for small children.

Other Activities: Birdwatching is the top activity in the refuge, which is renowned for its diversity of species, especially during the winter migratory season. There are several other trails on which to explore the varied habitats of the refuge: see hikes CA-16, CA-18, and CA-19.

Visitor Center Boardwalk

Merritt Island National Wildlife Refuge

CA-18 📖 🚻 ♿ 👫

Location: Merritt Island [N28°38.494' W080°44.143'].

Length: 0.4-mile loop.

Map: In park brochure.

Contact Information: Merritt Island National Wildlife Refuge (321-861-0667), PO Box 6504, Titusville, FL 32782.

Directions: Take I-95 exit 220, Titusville, and follow SR 406 east for 8 miles over the causeway to Merritt Island. Take CR 402 east for 2.8 miles to the visitor center; the trail starts behind the center.

The Hike: Meandering around clear freshwater ponds, the broad boardwalk follows the edge of an oak hammock to a roofed observation deck overlooking a pond before looping back through the forest.

Highlights: Look out across the panoramas on the open edge of the marsh.

Logistics: The trail can be accessed only when the visitor center is open, Mon–Fri 8:00–4:30, Sat–Sun 9:00–5:00. It is closed on Sundays from April through October, and on major holidays.

Other Activities: Check out the interpretive displays in the visitor center, and visit the gift shop for field guides! Birdwatching is the top activity in the refuge, which is renowned for its diversity of species, especially during the winter migratory season. There are several other trails on which to explore the varied habitats of the refuge: see hikes CA-16, CA-17, and CA-19.

Allan Cruickshank Memorial Trail

Merritt Island National Wildlife Refuge

CA-19 📖 🚻

Location: Merritt Island [N28°40.691' W080°46.310'].

Length: 4.8-mile loop.

Map: In park brochure.

Contact Information: Merritt Island National Wildlife Refuge (321-861-0667), PO Box 6504, Titusville, FL 32782.

Directions: Take I-95 exit 220, Titusville, and follow SR 406 east for 8 miles over the causeway to Merritt Island. Take CR 402 east for 3 miles and turn left on CR 406. Continue 1.4 miles to Black Point Wildlife Drive. Follow this scenic one-lane, one-way road around the impoundments for 3.4 miles to the parking area on the left.

The Hike: An on-foot adjunct to the Black Point Wildlife Drive, this trail takes you around a large impoundment on the shores of the Indian River Lagoon, past both brackish and freshwater marshes, mangrove-lined shores, and tall needlerush.

Highlights: Climb the observation tower for a bird's-eye view of the marshes, and expect to see birds along the entire length of the hike. Bring your binoculars!

Logistics: The refuge is open sunrise to sunset. The trail is open and breezy, with no shade. Wear sun protection and carry plenty of water. A portable toilet is provided at the trailhead. Several shaded benches offer places to rest along the walk.

Other Activities: Birdwatching is the top activity in the refuge, which is renowned for its diversity of species, especially during the winter migratory season. There are several other trails on which to explore the varied habitats of the refuge: see hikes CA-16, CA-17, and CA-18.

Wuesthoff Park

CA-20 📖 🚻 👫 🐕

Location: Titusville [N28°33.352' W080°49.563'].

Length: 1 mile of interconnecting trails.

Map: None available.

Contact Information: Wuesthoff Park (321-264-5105), 2000 Wuesthoff Street, Titusville, FL 32782.

Directions: From I-95 exit 215, Titusville, drive east on SR 50 to Barna Road. Turn right and make the immediate next right onto Wuesthoff Street. Follow the street to its end at the park.

The Hike: Walk past the Homer Powell Nature Center and start your hike by crossing a boardwalk over a cattail and willow marsh into a shady palm hammock, entering a system of nature trails that traverses this 25-acre park. The main trail rises into an oak hammock and a sand pine scrub, with numerous unmarked side and cross trails leading off into neighboring habitats.

Highlights: Although you're in the middle of suburbia, it only takes a few minutes to feel like you're immersed in a primeval forest.

Logistics: There is limited parking. Boardwalks are slippery when wet. Plant identification labels are mounted on PVC posts. Several benches provide places for a break.

Other Activities: The Homer Powell Nature Center has interpretive activities for kids and offers nature walks. There is a picnic table near the nature center.

Canaveral Marshes Trail

Canaveral Marshes Conservation Area

CA-21 🄵

Location: Titusville [N28°32.622' W080°53.790'].

Length: 3.9 miles round-trip, including 0.6-mile loop at end.

Map: Displayed at trailhead kiosk and available in St. Johns River Water Management District's *Recreation Guide to District Lands*; detailed backpacking map available from Florida Trail Association.

Contact Information: St. Johns River Water Management District (904-529-2380), PO Box 1429, Palatka, FL 32178-1429.

Directions: From I-95 exit 215, Titusville, drive 2.8 miles west on SR 50 to the conservation area entrance on the left, just before the bridge over the St. Johns River. The low sign is easy to miss. There is a second trailhead available, off Plantation Avenue inside the private Great Outdoors RV Park, that directly accesses the loop portion of the trail.

The Hike: Following a series of dikes across the broad open freshwater marshes of the St. Johns River floodplain, the trail leads you past former cattle ranches and a puzzle of marshlands along the Brevard County line. Crossing the historic Addison Canal (also seen at hike CA-22), the trail continues on to the second trailhead at Great Outdoors, where the loop trail through an oak hammock begins.

Highlights: You'll enjoy vast panoramas along most of this trail. The loop trail circles a large Timucuan midden.

Logistics: The main trail is blazed white, and side trails are blazed blue. There is a backpackers' campsite at the site of an old corral. Most of the trail is in full sun, so carry plenty of water and take appropriate precautions.

Other Activities: This is a fabulous spot for birding on the open marshes.

Enchanted Forest Sanctuary

CA-22 📖 🚻 ♿ 🚻 ❄

Location: Titusville [N28°32.001' W080°48.137'].

Length: 2.5 miles of interconnected trails.

Map: Displayed at trailhead kiosk.

Contact Information: Enchanted Forest Sanctuary (321-264-5185), 444 Columbia Boulevard, Titusville, FL 32782.

Directions: From I-95 exit 215, Titusville, drive east on SR 50 to the first traffic light, FL 405. Turn right and drive 2.5 miles to the park entrance on the left.

The Hike: With names like Lime, Orange, and Magnolia, the trails lead you through a variety of habitats on both sides of the Atlantic Coastal Ridge, atop which you'll find a coastal scrub habitat. Along the Orange Trail, high sand bluffs stand well above the Addison Canal, and the Magnolia Loop winds through a forest of giant southern magnolias and massive live oaks.

Highlights: Don't miss the spur trail to the old coquina quarry, which was dug out of an outcropping of Anastasia limestone several miles from the sea. The main road into the sanctuary follows the Hernandez-Capron Trail, a military trail built in 1837. The Addison Canal also provides a slice of history: started in 1912, it was meant to drain the wetlands between the St. Johns River and the Indian River Lagoon for development.

Logistics: The park is open Mon–Sat 9:00–5:00, Sun 1:00–5:00. A portion of the trail is wheelchair accessible.

Other Activities: Visit the educational center for information on the habitats in the sanctuary, or bring a picnic lunch and enjoy a picnic under the trees.

Pine Island Conservation Area

CA-23 🚻

Location: Courtenay [N28°29.558' W080°43.310'].

Length: 2.5 miles in two trails, accessed by a 1-mile round-trip walk.

Map: Displayed at trailhead kiosk and available in St. Johns River Water Management District's *Recreation Guide to District Lands* and in Pine Island Conservation Area brochure.

Contact Information: Brevard County EEL Program (321-255-4466), 5560 North US 1, Melbourne, FL 32940.

Directions: From I-95, follow SR 528 east 7 miles to SR 3; drive north on Merritt Island for 5.5 miles to Pine Island Road. Turn left and follow the road 2.5 miles to where it ends at the conservation area. Park your car in the small parking area near the entrance and walk down the berm along the Pine Island Canal for 0.5 mile to access the trailheads.

The Hike: The North Loop follows a straight line along a forest road through wet flatwoods to a loop through palm hammocks along Marsh Pond, where an observation deck enables you to watch manatees. The South Loop parallels the edge of the Indian River Lagoon to an observation point along a small cove.

Highlights: You'll see lots of birds along the South Loop. The North Loop enters a primeval forest full of giant leather ferns and marsh ferns under a screen of palm fronds.

Logistics: A portable toilet is provided at the trailhead. Both loop trails are prone to flooding, especially the North Loop—if there are deep puddles in the trail before you reach the loop, the loop itself may be knee deep or more. Be very careful of snakes and alligators if the trail is flooded.

Other Activities: There is a canoe launch, and fishing in canals and in the lagoon.

Hammock Nature Trail

Lori Wilson Park

CA-24 📖 🚻 ♿ 👫

Location: Cocoa Beach [N28°20.164' W080°36.469'].

Length: 0.3-mile loop.

Map: On sign at entrance to boardwalk loop.

Contact Information: Lori Wilson Park (321-868-1123), 1320 North Atlantic Avenue, Cocoa Beach, FL 32931.

Directions: From the intersection of SR 528 and SR 3 on Merritt Island, follow SR 528 into Cape Canaveral and Cocoa Beach. After 10 miles, look for the park on the ocean side.

The Hike: The maritime hammock feels close and intimate along this series of boardwalks beneath a tight-knit canopy of live oak and red bay, where interpretive markers clue you in to the plants, and benches invite you to sit and rest a spell in the shade.

Highlights: It's a dense, shady hammock smack-dab in the middle of the busy beachfront, an ideal getaway to sit and relax or read a book.

Logistics: The park is open 6:30–dusk. Many of the tree limbs are low—watch your head!

Other Activities: This is a seaside park with a beautiful beach for swimming and sunning. Be sure to stop in the nature center with the kids and take a look around—there are plenty of activities for them to explore.

Nature Trail

Rotary Park

CA-25 ▭ ⛹ ♿ 👫

Location: Merritt Island [N28°19.552' W080°41.128'].

Length: 0.3-mile loop.

Map: None available.

Contact Information: Rotary Park (321-455-1385), 1899 Courtenay Parkway, Merritt Island, FL 32952.

Directions: From the intersection of SR 520 and SR 3 on Merritt Island, drive 2.5 miles south to the park entrance on the right. Look for the Great Florida Birding Trail sign. Follow the entrance road to the back of the park, and turn left to park in front of the Nature Center.

The Hike: The family-friendly boardwalk creates a horseshoe around the nature center as it winds through pine flatwoods. Interpretive markers identify the plants along the shady path.

Highlights: There is a stand of older saw palmettos, their trunks arching well above the boardwalk, and a crossing of a willow marsh filled with cattails, spatterdock, and ferns.

Logistics: The boardwalk may be slippery when wet. There are lots of benches along the route.

Other Activities: You'll find picnic pavilions, a playground, ballfields, and a very nice nature center full of children's activities.

Wickham Park

CA-26   👫   Ⓐ   🐴

Location: Melbourne [N28°09.810' W080°39.587'].

Length: 4 miles of interconnected trails, some open to horseback riding and biking, others hiking only.

Map: Rough sketch of trail system in overall park map.

Contact Information: Wickham Park (321-255-4307), 2500 Parkway Drive, Melbourne, FL 32935.

Directions: From I-95 exit 183, Melbourne, follow Wickham Road (SR 518) south 7.3 miles to Parkway Drive. Turn left. Continue another 0.5 mile to the park entrance on the left. When entering the park, make a right and stop at the office for a map. Continue around the entrance road past the fitness trail, and make a left into the parking area; the "Multi-Use Trail" sign on the opposite side of the road marks the beginning of the trail system.

The Hike: Start at the "Multi-Use Trail" sign and make the first right to get away from the shared trail to a narrow hiking-only footpath that parallels a marshy slough. The trail rises and comes to a T intersection at a large pine tree; turn right. At the bridge, choose your route! Trails head out in numerous directions; all are narrow and provide excellent immersion in the habitats. There are no trail markers, so pay attention to landmarks as you pick your way through this mazelike network of shady trails.

Highlights: You'll encounter beautiful oak scrub heavily decorated with colorful lichens, and burbling waterways lined with ferns.

Logistics: Some of the trails are multiuse. It is very easy to get lost in this trail system, since there are few blazes and fewer signs. Consider carrying a compass or GPS and make sure to note the location of your car before hiking!

Other Activities: This is a full-service county park with a campground, picnic pavilions, swimming, and a disc golf course.

Nature Trail

Erna Nixon Park

CA-27 📖 🚻 ♿ 🚸 ❄️

Location: Melbourne [N28°05.480' W080°39.337'].

Length: 0.5-mile loop.

Map: Displayed at kiosk.

Contact Information: Erna Nixon Park & Nature Center (321-952-4525), 1200 Evans Road, West Melbourne, FL 32904.

Directions: From I-95, follow US 192 east to Evans Road. Drive north 2 miles on Evans Road to the park entrance on the left, two blocks past the Melbourne Mall.

The Hike: Pick up an interpretive guide at the kiosk before starting out on this short self-guided loop through several natural communities. Primarily a boardwalk, the trail ascends through pine flatwoods past a small stretch of scrub, rounds a marsh edged with red maples, and snakes through a hammock deeply shaded by a canopy of live oaks. Cabbage palms show off growths of shoelace fern and golden polypody, and wild coffee, marlberry, and Simpson's stopper flourish in the understory.

Highlights: Watch for gopher tortoises in the open scrub area, and alligators in the marsh. Look for butterfly orchids overhead where the oaks hang heavy with resurrection fern.

Logistics: The boardwalk may be slippery when wet. Benches make this an easy walk for hikers of all ages. The park is open 9:00–5:00 daily.

Other Activities: The hike begins at the Nature Center, which has exhibits on the region's natural communities.

Turkey Creek Sanctuary

CA-28 📖 🚻 ♿ 🚸 ❄️

Location: Palm Bay [N28°01.018' W080°36.281'].

Length: 1.6-mile loop with shorter hikes possible.

Map: Displayed at trailhead kiosk.

Contact Information: Turkey Creek Sanctuary (321-952-3433), 1502 Port Malabar Boulevard, Palm Bay, FL 32905.

Directions: From I-95 exit 176, take CR 516 (Palm Bay Road) east 2.3 miles to CR 507 (Babcock Street). Turn right and drive 1 mile to Port Malabar Boulevard. Turn left and continue 1.1 miles to Santiago Drive, just before the park sign. Turn right. Parking is on the right, across from the park entrance.

The Hike: Inside the park gates, the boardwalk zigzags through the sand pine scrub until it reaches a fork with the Hammock Trail. Turn right to follow the boardwalk on a loop down through the shady hammocks along Turkey Creek and up again through upland forests with marshes. When you complete the loop, continue along the main boardwalk to parallel the creek. It ends, but the path continues through sand pine and oak scrub to complete a loop back to the park gate.

Highlights: Enjoy great views from the high bluffs above Turkey Creek and from several observation decks. In spring and summer, look for manatees in the clear tannic waters of Turkey Creek as you walk along the boardwalk. Look overhead for blooming orchids nestled in the live oaks, and down to see if you know any of the names carved into the boardwalk.

Logistics: The park is open daily 7:00–sunset; the exact hour the gate will be locked is posted next to the gate. Sign the trail register when you enter. Most of the trail is a wheelchair-accessible boardwalk, but the return loop on the Sand Pine Scrub Trail is not.

Other Activities: Visit the Margaret Hames Nature Center for information about the habitats in the preserve. There is a jogging trail through one section of the park, a picnic area along the boardwalk, and a butterfly garden at the entrance. Folks arriving by canoe or kayak can take out at a dock along the boardwalk.

Malabar Scrub Sanctuary

CA-29 ♿

Location: Malabar [N28°00.104' W080°34.922'].

Length: 5-plus miles of trail in numerous loops and spurs, affording a 4-mile perimeter loop and many shorter hikes.

Map: Displayed and in brochure at kiosk.

Contact Information: Brevard County EEL Program (321-255-4466), 5560 North US 1, Melbourne, FL 32940.

Directions: From I-95 exit 173, drive east on CR 514 (Malabar Road) for 2.4 miles; watch for a fire station on the left. Turn left immediately after the fire station and follow the unmarked road to the preserve entrance. Turn left and park by the restrooms at the county park.

The Hike: A network of trails, each with signposts with graphical icons depicting the trail name, such as Acorn or Butterfly, provides access to this 400-acre tract adjacent to the sprawling subdivisions of Palm Bay. It's a peaceful place, resounding with birdsong. The trails lead through oak and sand pine scrub and scrubby flatwoods with several marshes.

Highlights: There are scenic flatwoods ponds with their own white sand beaches and numerous gopher tortoise burrows, and you'll hear the constant sound of birds amid the scrub oaks.

Logistics: As this land was going to be developed as a subdivision, a paved road runs down the middle and is suitable for wheelchair access or bicycling. Most of the trails run through scrub habitat and have no shade, so wear sun protection and sunglasses and carry plenty of water. Hiking may be difficult in several spots because of the soft sand.

Other Activities: Equestrians and bicyclists are permitted on the trails, excepting the boardwalks, but bicycling is not recommended because of the soft sand of the scrub habitat.

Flatwoods Loop

Micco Scrub Sanctuary

CA-30 🐎 🦋

Location: Malabar [N27°52.476' W080°36.847'].

Length: 3.2-mile hiking-only Flatwoods Loop; numerous multiuse trails crisscrossing the preserve enable shorter or longer hikes.

Map: Displayed and in brochure at trailhead kiosk.

Contact Information: Brevard County EEL Program (321-255-4466), 5560 North US 1, Melbourne, FL 32940.

Directions: Take I-95 exit 173, and drive east on Malabar Road to the first traffic light. Turn right on Babcock Street and drive south for 8.5 miles to Micco Road. Turn left on Micco Road and drive 0.5 mile to the trailhead, on the left side of the road.

The Hike: From the trailhead, follow the white arrows on brown signs as they lead you past a flatwoods pond and down a narrow corridor lined with saw palmetto into the sandhill and scrubby flatwoods ecosystems. On the far side of the power lines, the trail enters a vast open flatwoods where the saw palmetto stretches to the horizon. On the return loop, you walk through open scrub and cross numerous trails before paralleling the Sottile Canal back to the pine plantations, where the trail weaves its way through the forest back to the trailhead.

Highlights: Expect to see lots of wildlife along this trail, from deer and gopher tortoises to indigo snakes and armadillos.

Logistics: The preserve is open sunrise to sunset. With the exception of the Flatwoods Loop, the trails are marked with signposts with graphical icons depicting the trail name, such as Butterfly and Deer.

Other Activities: Equestrians and bicyclists are permitted on other trails within the sanctuary.

St. Sebastian River Preserve State Park

CA-31

Location: Fellsmere [N27°49.491' W080°35.780'].

Length: 0.3-mile and 2.1-mile interpretive loop trails, plus a vast network of multiuse trails.

Map: Posted on trailhead kiosks and available at park office and in St. Johns River Water Management District's *Recreation Guide to District Lands.*

Contact Information: St. Sebastian River Preserve State Park (321-953-5004), 1000 Buffer Preserve Drive, Fellsmere, FL 32948.

Directions: Take I-95 exit 156, Fellsmere/Sebastian. For the north entrance, follow CR 512 west several miles to Fellsmere and continue north on CR 507 for 4.2 miles to the park entrance on the right; follow the park road for 0.7 mile to the visitor center, where the interpretive trail begins.

The Hike: Start your hike at the interpretive trail kiosk, following the white blazes into the longleaf pine and wiregrass savanna. After 200 feet the trail splits; keep left. The footpath is rugged and narrow through the saw palmetto. At the T intersection, turn left to follow red blazes through the open savanna. At 0.5 mile the red loop begins; continue straight. The trail curves right into a scrub before coming to the return loop on the right, before the power line. The return loop is not well defined; watch for red blazes on the trees. At the junction with white blazes, turn left to finish off the short interpretive loop.

Highlights: The red loop circles a colony of red-cockaded woodpeckers; trees with nests are ringed with white paint. Visit early in the morning for optimal birdwatching.

Logistics: The preserve is open 8:00–5:00 daily. In addition to the interpretive trails, it has nearly forty miles of multiuse trails blazed with color-tipped posts. Backpacking is permitted, but you must check in at the park office. The longer trails have segments of difficult hiking over sugar sand. The main gate is locked at 5:00 p.m. daily; extended-hours parking is available just outside the north gate on CR 507.

Other Activities: Visitors enjoy an extensive equestrian trail system, numerous canal and riverside sites for birdwatching, and a manatee viewing platform on the south side of the preserve.

Coconut Point Sanctuary

CA-32 👫 ⚜

Location: Melbourne Beach [N28°00.710' W080°31.875'].

Length: 1-mile loop.

Map: Displayed and available in brochure at kiosk.

Contact Information: Brevard County EEL Program (321-255-4466), 5560 North US 1, Melbourne, FL 32940.

Directions: The trailhead is 6.1 miles south of US 192 on A1A in Melbourne Beach, on the west side of the road just beyond the Publix shopping center. Park your car on the east side of the road in the cleared area, which may be muddy.

The Hike: From the north entrance, the trail winds through an open coastal scrub before diving into shady hammocks of wind-sculpted sand live oaks en route to the Indian River Lagoon. The footpath enters a wetland area, crossing boardwalks through marsh grasses and fern-lined bayheads to the edge of a mangrove marsh, entering a tropical hammock with a spur trail to the Indian River Lagoon. Return through a shady hammock to emerge at the south entrance. To complete the loop, follow the bike path 0.2 mile north to the parking lot.

Highlights: There is a great variety of habitats for such a short hike. Take the kids out to the observation deck on the Indian River Lagoon where you can watch manatees.

Logistics: Beware of soft sand in parking areas and use caution crossing A1A.

Other Activities: Fish along the lagoon, or birdwatch from the observation deck and trails.

Maritime Hammock Sanctuary

CA-33

Location: Melbourne Beach [N27°57.382' W080°30.174'].

Length: 2-mile horseshoe with 0.5-mile connector via bike trail.

Map: Displayed and may be available in brochure at kiosk.

Contact Information: Brevard County EEL Program (321-255-4466), 5560 North US 1, Melbourne, FL 32940.

Directions: Follow A1A south 10.3 miles from US 192 in Melbourne Beach; watch for the trailhead on the right.

The Hike: Follow the bike trail down to the south entrance. From there the trail follows a fence line into a tropical hammock, where the low canopy of live oaks is festooned with bromeliads and orchids. The trail reaches an observation deck on a mangrove-lined cove of the Indian River, and then traces the edge of the mangrove forest to arrive at a dike on the north side of the reserve. After leaving the dike, the trail snakes through non-native tropical palms and plants, crossing a creek before emerging at the north entrance.

Highlights: The hammock is a hanging garden of bromeliads and orchids. Enjoy the views from the observation deck.

Logistics: The trail around the mangrove forest may be mucky and wet.

Other Activities: Fish and birdwatch from the observation deck.

Nature Trail

Sebastian Inlet State Park

CA-34 📖 🅐

Location: Sebastian Inlet [N27°52.527' W080°27.417'].

Length: 0.5-mile loop.

Map: Simple map in park brochure at kiosk near trailhead.

Contact Information: Sebastian Inlet State Park (321-984-4852), 9700 South A1A, Melbourne Beach, FL 32951.

Directions: Sebastian Inlet State Park encompasses both sides of A1A, 7 miles north of CR 510 (Wabasso Bridge from Sebastian). After you cross the inlet and pass the park's main entrance on the left, look for the next turnoff on the left. Park near the large kiosk and look for the start of the nature trail, hidden under the tree canopy.

The Hike: Starting out in a shady tropical hammock, the trail crosses an old forest road to reach a series of boardwalks and trails through mangrove forests and across mud flats, with interpretive signs identifying the plants and habitats along the edge of the coastal hammock.

Highlights: There are nice views of the Indian River Lagoon from the mangrove forest.

Logistics: The trail is marked with a raccoon paw print on brown signs.

Other Activities: Within the main portions of the state park (fee required) north of the nature trail, you'll find a full-service campground, a fishing pier, an outfitter, ecotours, and the McLarty Treasure Museum.

Centennial Trail

Pelican Island National Wildlife Refuge

CA-35 📖 ♿ 👫

Location: Orchid Island [N27°48.680' W080°25.540'].

Length: 0.8 mile round-trip.

Map: On kiosk along trail.

Contact Information: Pelican Island National Wildlife Refuge (561-562-3909), 1339 20th Street, Vero Beach, FL 32960.

Directions: From the junction of CR 510 (east of Sebastian) and A1A, follow A1A north 3.5 miles to the park sign on the left; turn left onto Jungle Trail and follow it 0.6 mile past the Jungle Trail parking area to the main entrance on the right. The paved Centennial Trail starts at the handicapped parking area.

The Hike: Rounding a large wetland area, the paved path leads up to a boardwalk climbing to an observation tower. Each plank along the boardwalk has the name and opening date of a National Wildlife Refuge engraved in it, in descending order from newest to oldest. The observation tower affords a great view of the Indian River Lagoon and Pelican Island.

Highlights: This is the nation's first National Wildlife Refuge, documented in 1858 as a breeding ground for brown pelicans, and the reason why can be seen from the observation deck at the end of the trail: 2.2-acre Pelican Island. Free binoculars let you watch the pelicans.

Logistics: Covered shelters and benches make this a very easy walk for all ages.

Other Activities: Two other trails within the refuge, Bird's Impoundment Trail and Pete's Impoundment Trail, are available for walking around the mangrove-lined impoundments but are primarily used for biking. Each is a 2.5-mile loop with no shade but plenty of birdwatching opportunities.

Wabasso Island Environmental Learning Center

CA-36 📖 🚻 ♿ 👪

Location: Wabasso Island [N25°45.469' W080°25.069'].

Length: 2-plus miles of trails in concentric loops.

Map: Available in *Trek & Tracks* interpretive field guide ($2) at visitor center.

Contact Information: Environmental Learning Center (772-589-5050; www.elcweb.org), 255 Live Oak Drive, Vero Beach, FL 32963.

Directions: From US 1 north of Vero Beach, follow CR 510 east across the Wabasso Causeway to Wabasso Island Road. Turn right on Live Oak Drive and follow it to the nature center on the right.

The Hike: Starting at the "Nature Walk" sign, follow the Mangrove Boardwalk, one of many interconnected trails throughout the property. You can create a loop by stringing the boardwalks and trails together, or just wander around where your interest takes you. Spur boardwalks lead through mangrove forests to wild walks in the mangrove community; a side trail crosses Live Oak Drive to reach another boardwalk on the Indian River Lagoon.

Highlights: Boardwalks and observation decks provide numerous overlooks on the Indian River Lagoon.

Logistics: The grounds are open daily 9:00–5:00; the nature center and gift shop is open Tue–Fri 10:00–4:00, Sat 9:00–12:00, Sun 1:00–4:00. There is an automatic gate that closes at 5:00 p.m.

Other Activities: Let the kids play at the hands-on interpretive education stations along the trails, and bring your birding guide for bird identification from the overlooks.

Oslo Riverfront Conservation Area

CA-37 □ ⚌ ⚌

Location: Vero Beach [N27°35.241' W080°22.477'].

Length: 3 miles of trail in several loops, the shortest 0.3 mile.

Map: Displayed at trailhead; available in brochure at kiosk and in St. Johns River Water Management District's *Recreation Guide to District Lands.*

Contact Information: St. Johns River Water Management District (904-529-2380), PO Box 1429, Palatka, FL 32178-1429.

Directions: From I-95 exit 147, follow SR 60 east to US 1 in downtown Vero Beach. Turn right and drive south 3.8 miles to CR 606 (Oslo Road). Turn left onto the dead-end road; the parking area is immediately on the left.

The Hike: Starting with the Herb Kale Nature Trail, sign the trail register and follow this network of trails into a lush tropical hammock dense with tall wild coffee, marlberry, and ferns. The first fork provides the shortest loop back to the trailhead. Turn left to venture farther into the preserve along a trail that winds through the forest. The next left connects to the Pine Flatwoods Loop; continue straight to head through the shady forest and across a bridge to the trail that circles the mangrove-lined impoundments on the edge of the Indian River Lagoon.

Highlights: There are more than twenty rare species of plants in this hammock. One of the world's largest slash pine trees, the Awesome Pine, has a trail leading to it from the Pine Flatwoods Loop. Bromeliads grow thickly on every tree in the forest.

Logistics: If the small parking area is full, use the adjacent shopping center as an alternative. The trail may be muddy or flooded in places through the hydric hammocks leading out to the impoundments. The Hammock Loop has green signs, the Coastal Wetlands Trail has blue signs, and the Pine Flatwoods Loop has yellow signs. Red signs lead to the Awesome Pine, and white ones to the Historic Quarry.

Other Activities: Bring your binoculars to watch birds from the observation deck on the impoundment.

Fort Drum Marsh Conservation Area

CA-38 🏕

Location: Yeehaw Junction [N27°36.822' W080°45.425'].

Length: 3 miles in two loops.

Map: Displayed at trailhead kiosk and available in St. Johns River Water Management District's *Recreation Guide to District Lands.*

Contact Information: St. Johns River Water Management District (904-529-2380), PO Box 1429, Palatka, FL 32178-1429.

Directions: From Florida's Turnpike exit 193, Yeehaw Junction, follow SR 60 for 9.2 miles to the entrance on the south side of the road. Continue south on a narrow dirt road for 2 miles to the parking area. The trail starts at the gate with a blue blaze.

The Hike: To walk around Horseshoe Lake, turn left. This loop trail leads you along man-made levees around the lake, with a bridge leading to an island in the middle of the lake, the site of a primitive campsite. To hike to Hog Island, turn right. Follow the jeep trail south to a boardwalk that leads across a cypress swamp to the island, where a loop trail circles the island, bordering the swamps and passing another primitive campsite.

Highlights: The boardwalk is a quiet place for contemplation and birdwatching, and a good short walk with children.

Logistics: Access during certain hunting seasons is limited to hunters. Check www.floridaconservation.org for details. The campsite on Hog Island has benches and a fire ring.

Other Activities: There is excellent birding around the lake and impoundments; watch for crested caracara in open areas. Horseback riding, fishing, biking, and hunting are permitted on-site.

South Gulf

Manatee, Sarasota, Charlotte, Lee, Collier

Royal Palm Hammock Trail, Collier-Seminole State Park.

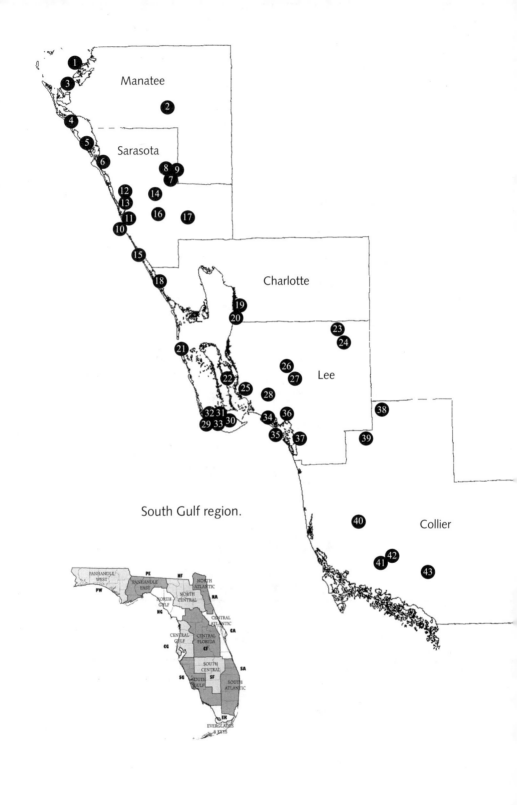

Manatee

Sarasota

Charlotte

Lee

South Gulf region.

Collier

PANHANDLE
WEST
PE
PANHANDLE
EAST
NF
NORTH
ATLANTIC
PW
NORTH
GULF
NORTH
CENTRAL
NA
HG
CENTRAL
ATLANTIC
CENTRAL
GULF
CENTRAL
FLORIDA
CA
CG
CF
SOUTH
CENTRAL
SA
SG
SF
SOUTH
ATLANTIC
SOUTH
GULF
EK
EVERGLADES
& KEYS

Manatee
- SG-1   Emerson Point Park
- SG-2   Rye Wilderness Park
- SG-3   De Soto National Memorial
- SG-4   Coquina Baywalk

Sarasota
- SG-5   Quick Point Nature Preserve
- SG-6   Nature Trail, Phillipi Estate Park
- SG-7   Canopy Walk, Myakka River State Park
- SG-8   Birdwalk, Myakka River State Park
- SG-9   Myakka Hiking Trail, Myakka River State Park
- SG-10 Caspersen Beach Nature Trail, Caspersen Beach Park
- SG-11 Nature Trail, Shamrock Park
- SG-12 North Trail System, Oscar Scherer State Park
- SG-13 South Trail System, Oscar Scherer State Park
- SG-14 T. Mabry Carlton Jr. Memorial Reserve
- SG-15 Lemon Bay Park
- SG-16 Jelks Preserve
- SG-17 Myakkahatchee Creek Environmental Park

Charlotte
- SG-18 Cedar Point Park, Charlotte Harbor Environmental Center
- SG-19 Alligator Creek Preserve, Charlotte Harbor Environmental Center
- SG-20 Old Datsun Trail, Charlotte Harbor Environmental Center

Lee
- SG-21 Cayo Costa State Park
- SG-22 Little Pine Island Hiking Trail, Charlotte Harbor Preserve State Park
- SG-23 Caloosahatchee Regional Park
- SG-24 Hickey's Creek Mitigation Park
- SG-25 Four Mile Cove Ecological Preserve
- SG-26 Calusa Nature Center
- SG-27 Six Mile Cypress Slough Preserve
- SG-28 Winkler Point, Estero Bay Preserve State Park
- SG-29 Bailey Tract, Ding Darling National Wildlife Refuge
- SG-30 Indigo Trail, Ding Darling National Wildlife Refuge
- SG-31 Wulfert Keys Trail, Ding Darling National Wildlife Refuge
- SG-32 Shell Mound Trail, Ding Darling National Wildlife Refuge
- SG-33 Sanibel-Captiva Conservation Foundation
- SG-34 Matanzas Pass Preserve
- SG-35 Black Island Trail, Lovers Key State Park
- SG-36 Estero Scrub Preserve
- SG-37 Nature Trail, Koreshan State Historic Site

Collier

Emerson Point Park

SG-1 📖 🚻 ⌂

Location: Snead Island [N27°31.918' W082°37.557'].

Length: Up to 3 miles in several trails.

Map: None available.

Contact Information: Manatee County Parks and Recreation Department (941-742-5923), 5502 33rd Avenue Drive, Bradenton, FL 34209.

Directions: From I-75 exit 224, Ellenton / Palmetto, follow US 301 south for 3.5 miles to its junction with US 41. Where US 301 turns to join US 41, continue straight on SW 10th Street, crossing business US 41. After 2.5 miles you cross a bridge onto Snead Island. Turn right on Tarpon Road, then left at the first stop sign, and follow the road into the park. Once you're inside the park gates, park on the left near the Portavant Temple Mound.

The Hike: The short interpretive Pioneer Trail leads up, over, and around the Portavant Temple Mound, and connects to the major loop around the park, the Restoration Trail, which is a shell path around restored wetlands where there has been active eradication of exotic plants. The Terra Ceia Trail is a don't-miss hikers-only footpath tunneling through the mangrove forests along the Terra Ceia Bay, with several observation points.

Highlights: The massive Portavant Temple Mound is part of a Timucuan village more than a thousand years old, overlooking the Manatee River. Enjoy the view from the observation tower on the other side of the park, overlooking Tampa Bay.

Logistics: The park is open 8:00–sunset daily. The Restoration Trail is shared with bicycles. It may flood in low places.

Other Activities: You'll find sea kayaking, fishing, picnic areas, and playgrounds.

Rye Wilderness Park

SG-2 📖 🚻 ⓐ

Location: Parrish [N27°30.806' W082°21.851'].

Length: 4-plus miles of hiking on fifteen named trails.

Map: Displayed on kiosk in middle of park near campground entrance.

Contact Information: Rye Wilderness Park (941-776-0900), 905 Rye Wilderness Trail, Parrish, FL 34219.

Directions: From I-75 exit 220A, follow SR 64 east for 2 miles. Drive north 3 miles on Rye Road. One section of the park is on the right just before the Manatee River bridge; the other is down the road to your right after you cross the bridge.

The Hike: It's a smorgasbord of short hikes, starting with the River's Edge Trail, which makes a loop down to the Manatee River and climbs back up through sand pine scrub, where you can connect it across the park road with the Sand Pine Scrub Trail to make a loop. Other trails create loops to the east through river bluff forest and scrubby flatwoods. From the picnic area along Rye Road, several linear trails lead to the river.

Highlights: There are great views of the flood-prone Manatee River (note the sandbars and scouring!) from many of the trails, and a pretty brook along the Sand Pine Scrub Trail.

Logistics: The park is day use only, 8:00–sunset, except for the campground, open Fridays and Saturdays at $10 per tent.

Other Activities: There is fishing along the river, horseback riding on a horse trail system, kayaking down the Manatee River, picnic tables, and a playground.

De Soto National Memorial

SG-3 ▢ ⚏ ♿ ⚏ ⚐

Location: Bradenton [N27°31.221' W082°38.669'].

Length: 1.1 miles round-trip.

Map: Displayed at trailhead kiosk and available in park brochure.

Contact Information: De Soto National Memorial (941-792-0458), PO Box 15390, Bradenton, FL 34280.

Directions: From I-75 exit 220B, follow SR 64 (Manatee Ave) west 12 miles to 75th Street West. Turn right and follow the road 2 miles to the parking area on the right, just before the park entrance. If the trailhead is full, proceed into De Soto National Memorial and start at the other trailhead, behind the visitor center.

The Hike: Starting from the Riverview Point Trail trailhead outside the park boundary, a broad shell path leads you through sand pines and a shady hammock before coming to the edge of the Manatee River, where there are two major memorials along the trail as it turns and enters the National Memorial grounds. At the loop, turn right and follow the trail around Shaw's Point, where boardwalks carry you through mangrove forests. After visiting the Memorial, continue around the loop and return along the same path.

Highlights: Walk through a bower of buttonwood in a coastal berm habitat, and enjoy many different perspectives on the Manatee River and Tampa Bay.

Logistics: The visitor center is open 9:00–5:00 daily except major holidays; trails are open dawn to dusk. Parking lot gates close at 5:00 p.m.

Other Activities: This is a significant archaeological site, worth the time to fully explore and learn about Timucuan culture on the Gulf and Hernando de Soto's march through Florida. The interpretive markers along the trail are elaborate and deserve pausing for—you'll learn a good deal of Florida's early history.

Coquina Baywalk

SG-4 ⬛ ♿ 👫 🐕 ✳️

Location: Leffis Key [N27°27.049' W082°41.439'].

Length: 0.8-mile loop.

Map: None available.

Contact Information: Manatee County Parks and Recreation Department (941-742-5923), 5502 33rd Avenue Drive, Bradenton, FL 34209.

Directions: The park is 3.2 miles south of the Anna Maria Causeway on East Bay Drive, just south of Bradenton Beach. The park entrance is on the left, across from the beach at the south end of the key.

The Hike: This is a fun little trail system that guides you through coastal habitats in a restoration area on Leffis Key, overlooking Sarasota Bay. Interpretive markers give specific details about the surrounding habitats, including those under water—you can see rock reefs with sponges and sea squirts, and seagrass beds in the clear water. Keep to the left as you walk through the trail system to enjoy the full perimeter loop.

Highlights: There are great views of the bay from observation decks hidden away in the mangroves—you feel like you're peeking out of tunnels! Climb to the top of the spoil piles for a sweeping view of the bay and the Gulf of Mexico.

Logistics: The park is open dawn to dusk. The shell paths and boardwalks are suitable for strollers or for wheelchairs with assistance. There isn't a lot of shade, except inside the mangrove forests along the water's edge. Restrooms are across the road at the beach.

Other Activities: Fish from the decks along Sarasota Bay, or head across the road to enjoy the beach.

Quick Point Nature Preserve

SG-5 📖 👫 🐕

Location: Longboat Key [N27°20.048' W082°34.978'].

Length: 0.8 mile round-trip.

Map: Displayed on kiosk at park entrance and found on town website; interpretive brochure available at kiosk.

Contact Information: Town of Longboat Key (941-316-1999), 501 Bay Isles Road, Longboat Key, FL 34228.

Directions: From the intersection of US 41 and the Ringling Causeway in Sarasota, follow the causeway out to St. Armands Key and drive north on CR 789. Make a left into the parking area immediately after crossing the drawbridge. There is a walkway beneath the drawbridge that leads to the park entrance.

The Hike: On this 34-acre peninsula between Sarasota Bay and New Pass, the trail meanders beneath a stand of Australian pines to enter natural habitats of mangrove marshes and tidal lagoons, passing through a forest of tall mangroves before emerging at the end of the trail at the Sarasota Bay Lookout, an observation deck over the bay.

Highlights: Watch fish and birds in the lagoons, or enjoy the view of the bay and the Sarasota city skyline from the end of the trail.

Logistics: Although most of the trail is boardwalk, the entrance to the trail system is across a soft sand beach. From trail's end, unmarked trails lead along the shoreline and into the mangroves but are dead ends.

Other Activities: Relax on the beach, or fish in New Pass. Birders can get up close to wading birds in the lagoons.

Nature Trail

Phillipi Estate Park

SG-6 📖 🚻 ♿ 🚼 🐕

Location: Sarasota [N27°16.203' W082°32.058'].

Length: 0.3-mile loop.

Map: None available.

Contact Information: Sarasota County Parks & Recreation (941-316-1172), 6700 Clark Road, Sarasota, FL 34241.

Directions: The park is on US 41 south of downtown Sarasota, north of Clark Road, on the west side of the highway. Take the left inside the park and drive down near the playground, where the trail starts.

The Hike: It's a gentle shellrock path, suitable for wheelchairs with assistance, looping through a palm hammock and along the edge of a mangrove marsh on an estuarine waterway.

Highlights: You'll hear lots of birdsong over the marshes, and see beautiful ferns beneath the palms and pines.

Logistics: Open dawn to dusk, the trail may be utilized by bicyclists. Numerous benches make this an easy walk for all ages.

Other Activities: There's a canoe launch, a playground, a bandstand, a fishing pier, picnicking, and the historic Edson Keith House to visit.

Canopy Walk

Myakka River State Park

SG-7 $ 📖 🚻 🅰 👫 ❄

Location: Sarasota [N27°14.785' W082°18.162'].

Length: 0.9-mile loop.

Map: Rough sketch in park map.

Contact Information: Myakka River State Park (941-361-6511), 3207 SR 72, Sarasota, FL 34241.

Directions: From I-75 exit 205, drive 9 miles east on SR 72 to the park entrance on the left. Follow the park entrance road. The trailhead is on the right just after you cross the Myakka River.

The Hike: This nature trail along the Myakka River provides a 0.9-mile loop through a mosaic of prairies, wetlands, and oak hammocks, as well as a spur trail leading to a canopy walk—a swinging bridge suspended forty feet in the air, enabling visitors to view the live oak hammock canopy at eye level.

Highlights: The canopy walk provides an up-close view of the inhabitants of the live oak canopy of this hammock, and a 72-foot-tall tower lets you look over the Myakka River and the prairies. Along the loop portion of the trail, you'll enjoy birdwatching from the boardwalks between the oak hammocks.

Logistics: The trail will flood when the river is high. If you have a problem with heights, don't try the canopy walk—stick to the loop trail instead. Restrooms are at the visitor center near the park entrance.

Other Activities: Enjoy more hiking (SG-8 and SG-9) in the park, take an ecotour on the Myakka River, or put in a kayak and head upriver. There is a developed campground near the park entrance, and plenty of picnic areas throughout the park, as well as a mountain bike trail system at the north end of the park.

Bird Walk

Myakka River State Park

SG-8 $ 📖 🅰 ♿ 🚻

Location: Sarasota [N27°16.510' W082°16.209'].

Length: 0.4 mile round-trip.

Map: Rough sketch in park map.

Contact Information: Myakka River State Park (941-361-6511), 3207 SR 72, Sarasota, FL 34241

Directions: From I-75 exit 205, drive 9 miles east on SR 72 to the park entrance on the left. Follow the park entrance road for 4.6 miles, keeping to the right at the fork. The trailhead is on the left.

The Hike: The boardwalk leads out into the lake under the shade of cypress trees, ending at an observation platform overlooking marshes in Little Myakka Lake along the Myakka River.

Highlights: This is a very scenic walk, and perfect for birdwatching.

Logistics: The boardwalk is wheelchair accessible. There are no restrooms at this stop; the nearest ones are at the Myakka Outpost.

Other Activities: Enjoy more hiking (SG-7 and SG-9) in the park, take an ecotour on the Myakka River, or put in a kayak and head upriver. There is a developed campground near the park entrance, and plenty of picnic areas throughout the park, as well as a mountain bike trail system at the north end of the park.

Myakka Hiking Trail

Myakka River State Park

SG-9 **Ⓕ** **$** 🏕 ⛺

Location: Sarasota [N27°16.453' W082°15.777'].

Length: 39-mile backpacking loop made up of four stacked loops, one of which (Bee Island Loop) can be walked as a long day hike.

Map: Available from park rangers; detailed backpacking map available in regional map set from Florida Trail Association.

Contact Information: Myakka River State Park (941-361-6511), 3207 SR 72, Sarasota, FL 34241.

Directions: From I-75 exit 205, drive 9 miles east on SR 72 to the park entrance on the left. Follow the park entrance road for 5.1 miles, keeping to the right at the fork. The trailhead is on the right. Unlock the gate and drive up the entrance road to the parking area.

The Hike: If you're looking for wilderness, you'll find it here along the Myakka Hiking Trail, with a mosaic of habitats to explore in the midst of the grand Myakka Prairies, grasslands more than two miles wide in places. Although the trails attempt to stay in shady oak hammocks, they do traverse the open prairies as well. There are five designated campsites along the way; Bee Island, the easiest overnight trip, is the most popular.

Highlights: You get a two-mile view across the grasslands on the Bee Island Loop!

Logistics: You must stop at the ranger station and register before using this trail (either day hiking or backpacking), and they will give you a gate combination. Before planning your trip, call and ask how wet it is out there, because when the Myakka River floods, so do the prairies and tributaries, and you may find yourself wading through waist-deep water along the sloughs. Campsites must be reserved in advance.

Other Activities: Enjoy more hiking (SG-7 and SG-8) in the park, take an ecotour on the Myakka River, or put in a kayak and head upriver. There is a developed campground near the park entrance, and plenty of picnic areas throughout the park, as well as a mountain bike trail system at the north end of the park.

Caspersen Beach Nature Trail

Caspersen Beach Park

SG-10 📖 🚻 🚼 🐕

Location: Venice [N27°03.434' W082°26.562'].

Length: 0.4-mile loop.

Map: Displayed on trailhead kiosk and available in interpretive brochure.

Contact Information: Sarasota County Parks & Recreation (941-316-1172), 6700 Clark Road, Sarasota, FL 34241.

Directions: From I-75 exit 193, follow Jacaranda Boulevard west 0.7 mile to Venice Avenue; turn right. Cross the bridge into downtown Venice and continue through the shopping district. Turn left on Harbor Drive North and follow it to the end, past the airport and several parks; it ends in the parking lot for Caspersen Beach Park.

The Hike: This short interpretive trail leads you through a palm hammock along the Intracoastal Waterway, passing a picnic area. Keep right to cross a bridge over a mangrove-lined canal, where the trail turns to parallel an inlet before rising back up to meet the entrance road and crossover to the dunes on the beach. Follow the boardwalk along the coastal strand back to the parking area.

Highlights: From the observation deck, you get a good view of the mangrove islands. Watch for birds picking through the dense tangle of roots.

Logistics: Mosquitoes may be a problem along the inlet—use insect repellent.

Other Activities: This is the best beach in Florida for finding sharks' teeth, and you can enjoy a pleasant walk on an unspoiled beach by walking south from the parking area.

Nature Trail

Shamrock Park

SG-11 ♦♦ ⚥

Location: South Venice [N27°03.200' W082°26.226'].

Length: 0.5-plus mile of natural footpaths connecting to 1-mile paved pathway.

Map: None available.

Contact Information: Shamrock Park (941-486-2706), 3900 Shamrock Drive, Venice, FL 34293.

Directions: From US 41 in South Venice, turn west on Shamrock Drive and drive 1.7 miles to the park entrance on the right. Follow the entrance road back to the nature center; the trailhead is a gap in the fence behind the playground.

The Hike: Starting behind the playground, the trail leads up onto the berm overlooking the Intracoastal Waterway. Turn left and walk through the coastal pine forest, following the berm until it ends on the edge of a scrub habitat. Head downhill and turn right to walk along the waterway to complete the loop, hooking up with any of several footpaths back up the berm or with the paved trail coming through the north end of the park.

Highlights: From the top of the berm, you can hear waves crashing against the shore at Caspersen Park on the other side of the waterway. Florida scrub-jays are resident in the scrub at the south end of the park.

Logistics: The trails in this park hook into the new Venice Waterway Park along the Intracoastal Waterway.

Other Activities: Shamrock Park has a paved bike trail, tennis courts, a large playground, and a nature center with activities for children.

North Trail System

Oscar Scherer State Park

SG-12 $ 📖 🚻 Ⓒ 🐴

Location: Osprey [N27°10.213' W082°28.441'].

Length: 7.5 miles in several loops.

Map: Displayed at trailhead and available at ranger station.

Contact Information: Oscar Scherer State Park (941-483-5956), 1843 South Tamiami Trail, Osprey, FL 34429.

Directions: The park entrance is on the east side of US 41, 1.7 miles north of SR 681 between Nokomis and Osprey.

The Hike: Of the many color-coded loops in the North Trail System, the 5-mile White Loop is the most scenic and the most likely to bring you close to Florida scrub-jays. It visits a nice range of habitats, from scrubby flatwoods and scrub to pine flatwoods, cypress domes, oak hammocks, and palm hammocks along the banks of a tannic creek. The Blue and Red Loops traverse scrub habitats and offer little shade.

Highlights: Protecting more than 1,300 acres of mostly coastal scrub and scrubby flatwoods, this park has one of the highest concentrations of Florida scrub-jays in South Florida. Hike in early morning to encounter scrub-jays foraging in the oak scrub.

Logistics: The trails are shared with bicycles, although soft sand in many places throughout the scrub makes the going impossible for bikes and tough for hikers. Benches throughout the park are numerically coded to the trail map and have a phone number for you to call in case you get lost.

Other Activities: In addition to the South Trail System (SG-13), the park has a nice campground, canoe rentals for a trip down South Creek, and a nature center at Osprey Lake.

South Trail System

Oscar Scherer State Park

SG-13 $ 📖 🚻 Ⓐ ♿ 👫 🐕

Location: Osprey [N27°10.503' W082°27.718'].

Length: 5 miles in several loops.

Map: Displayed at trailhead and available at ranger station.

Contact Information: Oscar Scherer State Park (941-483-5956), 1843 South Tamiami Trail, Osprey, FL 34429.

Directions: The park entrance is on the east side of US 41, 1.7 miles north of SR 681 between Nokomis and Osprey.

The Hike: The South Trail System consists of several trails, including the short, family-friendly and wheelchair-accessible Lester Finley Trail along South Creek, which offers observation decks and benches for resting and "ranger in a box" narrated interpretive stops; the Green Loop, which runs 3 miles through prime scrub-jay habitat; and the South Creek Trail, a shady walk along South Creek that connects the Green Loop and the Lester Finley Trail.

Highlights: Look for scrub-jays along the Green Loop, and savor the views from the many observation decks along South Creek.

Logistics: The Green Loop is shared with bicycles, although soft sand in many places throughout the scrub makes it impassible for bikes and tough for hikers. Benches throughout the park are numerically coded to the trail map and have a phone number for you to call in case you get lost.

Other Activities: In addition to the North Trail System (SG-12), the park has a nice campground, canoe rentals for a trip down South Creek, and a nature center at Osprey Lake.

T. Mabry Carlton Jr. Memorial Reserve

SG-14 📖 🚻 ♿ 👫

Location: Venice [N27°07.683' W082°20.014'].

Length: 1.8 miles in three loops, the shortest 0.3 mile.

Map: Displayed and in interpretive brochure at trailhead kiosk.

Contact Information: Sarasota County Parks & Recreation (941-316-1172), 6700 Clark Road, Sarasota, FL 34241.

Directions: From I-75 exit 193, Jacaranda Boulevard, drive north 0.6 mile to where the road ends at a T intersection. Brown signs direct you to the park; turn right onto Border Road. After you cross the Myakka River, the road comes to a T intersection at 2.5 miles. Turn left at the park sign; a broad drive leads into the reserve. At the next sign on the right, turn right to enter the public parking area, which is down a lengthy gravel driveway.

The Hike: Meandering through a mix of pine flatwoods, scrubby flatwoods, oak hammocks, and open prairies, the trails circle wet prairies and flatwoods ponds.

Highlights: Walk around the wet prairie and watch the wading birds busy at work.

Logistics: Gates close at 8:00 p.m. No dogs are permitted. A short segment of trail, paved with paving stones, is wheelchair accessible. Numerous benches make this an easy walk.

Other Activities: There is a picnic area with pavilions.

Lemon Bay Park

SG-15 📖 🚻 ♿ 🚻 🐾

Location: Englewood [N26°58.407' W082°22.448'].

Length: 2.7 miles in an extensive trail system.

Map: Available at park office and displayed on trailhead kiosks.

Contact Information: Lemon Bay Park (941-474-3065), 570 Bay Park Road, Englewood, FL 34224.

Directions: From CR 776 in Englewood, follow Dearborn Street west through old Englewood Village to Buchman's Landing, and turn right at the stop sign. After 0.5 mile, make a left on Stuart Street. After another 0.3 mile, turn right on Curtis Boulevard and make the first left on Brengel Avenue, which leads into the park entrance. Walk through the arbor at the end of the parking lot to access the trail system.

The Hike: Follow the Eagle Trail to enter a vast pine flatwoods for a walk under the pines, the open understory providing a sweeping view as you work your way up to the northern end of the preserve, with numerous options— the Fern Loop, the Bobcat Trail, the Gopher Tortoise Trail, and the Lupine Loop Trail—to provide peeks into a freshwater swamp, a forest of ferns, and the Intracoastal Waterway. The trails on the southern end are along the Lemon Bay Aquatic Preserve and include a boardwalk around a mangrove forest.

Highlights: A pair of eagles nest on the property and can be seen from a "scope" along the Eagle Trail. Enjoy the views along the Intracoastal Waterway.

Logistics: Much of the trail system has little to no shade, so wear a hat and sunscreen and bring lots of water. Both the paved block and asphalt trails on the south trail system are wheelchair accessible. Trail junctions are well signed.

Other Activities: A canoe launch and formal gardens add to the fun at this park. Visit the nature center for interpretive information about the habitats. The park office has brochures on other natural areas in the county.

Jelks Preserve

SG-16 📖

Location: North Port [N27°05.493' W082°20.269'].

Length: 3.3-mile perimeter loop with many shorter alternatives.

Map: Displayed and in interpretive brochure at trailhead kiosk.

Contact Information: Sarasota County Parks & Recreation (941-316-1172), 6700 Clark Road, Sarasota, FL 34241.

Directions: From I-75 exit 191, North Port, follow River Road south to the park entrance on the left. The trailhead is 0.9 mile north of Center Road.

The Hike: Meandering through pine flatwoods, scrubby flatwoods, and oak hammocks, this trail invites you to explore the uplands above the Myakka River. Numerous shortcut trails cut across the loop, allowing you to make a hike of as little as 0.8 mile. On the river side of the loop, expect pleasant shade under the oaks and pines; away from the river, the trail traverses open flatwoods and oak scrub, where you may spy Florida scrub-jays. Several seasonal marshes have showy wildflowers.

Highlights: You can reach the bluffs of the Myakka River via several side trails; don't miss the view from #2. Survey the flatwoods and river from the observation tower.

Logistics: The preserve is open 8:00–sunset. Brown signposts with red numbers correspond to points in the interpretive brochure. No dogs permitted.

Other Activities: There are picnic tables at the trailhead and on bluffs above the Myakka River.

Myakkahatchee Creek Environmental Park

SG-17 📖 🚻 👥

Location: North Port [N27°07.122' W082°11.763'].

Length: 2.5 miles, in a 1.3-mile main loop and two spur loops.

Map: Displayed and available as brochure at trailhead.

Contact Information: Sarasota County Parks & Recreation (941-316-1172), 6700 Clark Road, Sarasota, FL 34241.

Directions: From I-75 exit 182, North Port, head north on Sumter Boulevard. When you reach the T intersection after 1 mile, turn left on Tropicaire Boulevard. Brown signs lead the way to the park. After 0.3 mile turn right on Reistertown Road, and after 0.9 mile turn right into the park entrance. Park your car near the picnic area.

The Hike: Starting at the trailhead sign just beyond the picnic area, follow the yellow blazes of the Big Slough Trail for a scenic 1.3-mile loop walk along this picturesque natural waterway, on sand bluffs above the creek. The trail passes through oak hammocks and old fields, while two side loops—the white-blazed West Loop Trail and the red-blazed East Loop Trail, of 0.7 mile and 0.5 mile respectively and worth the extra walk—enter dense hammocks along restored wetlands.

Highlights: There are great views of the waterway as you walk along the bluffs along Big Slough. An observation deck and interpretive display overlook restored wetlands on the East Loop Trail.

Logistics: The park gate is locked at 8:00 p.m. No dogs are permitted. The composting toilet at the trailhead is not in the best of shape. Trails are marked with yellow, white, and red-tipped posts. They may be shared with horses and bikes, but hiking appears to be the primary use.

Other Activities: The park provides a picnic area, primitive group camping (by reservation), and a canoe launch. Enjoy great birding along the creek and wetlands.

Cedar Point Park

Charlotte Harbor Environmental Center

SG-18 📖 🚻 🚸

Location: Englewood [N26°55.512' W082°20.105'].

Length: 3.5 miles in six trails.

Map: Displayed on trailhead kiosk and available in brochure.

Contact Information: Cedar Point Park (941-475-0769), 5800 Placida Road, Englewood, FL 34224.

Directions: From US 41 in North Port, follow River Road south to Englewood. Continue south on Pine Street to SR 775, and soon after you cross SR 776, watch for the park entrance on the right.

The Hike: Along Lemon Bay Aquatic Preserve, this network of six hiking trails winds through the varied habitats of this 88-acre preserve, including a vast stretch of pine flatwoods with high points with oak scrub and scrubby flatwoods. Trails meander along the edge of salt marshes and through mangrove swamps out to the coast.

Highlights: The Mangrove Trail leads out to a scenic viewpoint on Lemon Bay, and the Crystal Trail loops through a mangrove forest along the water's edge.

Logistics: The park is open sunrise to sunset, the environmental center Mon–Fri 8:30–4:30. Guided tours are offered on Saturday and Sunday in winter. You'll find picnic tables and benches along the trails. Some trails are closed during eagle nesting season, as several eagle pairs raise their young in the pine flatwoods.

Other Activities: Besides the nature center, there's a picnic area and a nonmotorized boat launch.

Alligator Creek Preserve

Charlotte Harbor Environmental Center

SG-19 📖 🚻 👥

Location: Punta Gorda [N26°52.463' W082°01.747'].

Length: 3-mile network of trails with short loops possible.

Map: Map and interpretive guide available at trailhead kiosk.

Contact Information: Charlotte Harbor Environmental Center (941-575-5435), 10941 Burnt Store Road, Punta Gorda, FL 33955.

Directions: From I-75 exit 161, head west for 1.3 miles on CR 768, which becomes CR 765 (Burnt Store Road) just before crossing US 41. Continue another 1.2 miles to the park entrance on the right.

The Hike: The trail system is made up of the Eagle Point Trail, which loops through pine flatwoods and scrubby flatwoods before rounding a needlerush marsh and freshwater lake; the Flatwoods Trail, which immerses you in cabbage palm flatwoods dotted with cypress domes; and the Three Lakes Trail, which leads out to the edge of several mangrove-lined lagoons.

Highlights: Stop at the bird blind to observe warblers, sparrows, and other small songbirds visiting the various feeders; peer from the observation deck over the lake to look for alligators. Expect to see wading birds, especially ibises, along the Three Lakes.

Logistics: The center is open Mon–Sat 8:00–3:00, Sun 11:00–3:00, closed holidays. After hours, you can park outside the gate and walk in, adding 0.4 mile to your hike. There are many benches along the trails.

Other Activities: The kids will love the interactive exhibits in the Caniff Environmental Center, and if you pack a picnic lunch, there are several picnic benches in scenic spots along the Eagle Point Trail.

Old Datsun Trail

Charlotte Harbor Environmental Center

SG-20 📖

Location: Punta Gorda [N26°51.077' W082°01.326'].

Length: 1.7-mile loop.

Map: Map and interpretive guide available at trailhead kiosk.

Contact Information: Charlotte Harbor Environmental Center (941-575-5435), 10941 Burnt Store Road, Punta Gorda, FL 33955.

Directions: From I-75 exit 161, head west on CR 768 for 1.3 miles, which becomes CR 765 (Burnt Store Rd) just before crossing US 41. Continue another 2.7 miles, passing Alligator Point Preserve (SG-19) before reaching the trailhead parking on the right.

The Hike: Follow the mowed path to the fork, and keep right. The trail makes a broad loop around a large wetland area as it passes through cabbage palm flatwoods, palm hammocks, and oak hammocks.

Highlights: Pause and watch the bird activity in the wetlands. Yellow cannas grow in profusion in a clump along one part of the shoreline. In fall, there are beautiful wildflowers throughout the preserve.

Logistics: Arrows guide you along the trail. Take care as to where the trail goes, as some of the markers are missing. After a rain, expect the footpath to be wet or flooded in places.

Other Activities: Visit nearby Alligator Point Preserve (SG-19) and the Caniff Environmental Center.

Cayo Costa State Park

SG-21 $

Location: La Costa Island [N26°41.154' W082°14.743'].

Length: 6.5-mile network of trails.

Map: In park brochure and displayed at trailhead; detailed map available at visitor center.

Contact Information: Cayo Costa State Park (941-964-0375), PO Box 1150, Boca Grande, FL 33921.

Directions: From I-75 exit 143, follow SR 78 west to Pine Island. Turn right onto CR 767 (Stringfellow Road) and follow the signs that say "Cayo Costa Ferry."

The Hike: With names like Quarantine Trail and Pinewoods Trail, the various elements of this trail system lead you to unspoiled beaches and remote historic points on Pelican Bay and Boca Grande Pass. Walk through tropical hammocks, mangrove swamps, pine flatwoods, and coastal scrub, where you'll see gopher tortoises burrowing and bald eagles nesting.

Highlights: Take the Cemetery Trail north to a secluded cabbage-palm-lined beach on Boca Grande Pass, a perfect place to sit and relax. The scenic Gulf Trail takes you to the confluence of waters at the pass and the Gulf of Mexico.

Logistics: You must take a boat to this state park. The ferryboat round-trip fare runs a minimum of $21.20 per person including tax (cash only). Call in advance (941-283-0015) to reserve a spot on the ferry, which leaves at 9:30 each morning. If you're camping, let them know so you can be assured of a space on the appropriate return ferry. Day trippers must be back at the park dock by 3:00 p.m. for the return trip. The visitor center is open 8:00–5:00 daily.

Other Activities: If you've wanted to spend a day (or a week) on a deserted island, this is a great place to play beachcomber. Bring a tent or rent a cabin so you can kick back and relax on your own private beach.

Note: These trails were damaged by Hurricane Charley. Check with the land manager for status.

Little Pine Island Trail

Charlotte Harbor Preserve State Park

SG-22 📖

Location: Pine Island Center [N26°37.123' W082°05.409'].

Length: 2-mile loop.

Map: Displayed and in interpretive brochure at trailhead kiosk.

Contact Information: Charlotte Harbor Preserve State Park (941-575-5861), 12301 Burnt Store Road, Punta Gorda, FL 33955.

Directions: From I-75 exit 143, follow SR 78 west to Pine Island. After you pass through Matlacha, keep alert for a turnoff on the right for the trailhead parking, which is 3.5 miles past CR 765.

The Hike: It's a mucky walk through the estuarine tidal marsh, following markers that correspond to the interpretive brochure available at the trailhead, through high marsh, salt flats, and mangrove forests.

Highlights: You'll have a close-up look at tidal marsh plants, especially mangroves, and fiddler crabs scuttling into their holes.

Logistics: The trail is often wet and sticky because of the tides, and may be flooded at times of high tide or after a rain. There is deep mud in places—bring a change of shoes along.

Other Activities: Birdwatch from the mangrove overlook.

Caloosahatchee Regional Park

SG-23 $ 📖 🚻 ⛺ ♿ 👫

Location: Alva [N26°43.318' W081°39.081'].

Length: 3.4 miles in four interconnecting trails.

Map: Displayed and in brochure at trailhead kiosk.

Contact Information: Caloosahatchee Regional Park (941-693-2690), 18500 North River Road, Alva, FL 33920.

Directions: From I-75 exit 143, drive 3.3 miles east on SR 78 (Bayshore Rd). The road ends at a T. Turn left onto SR 31, and continue 1.2 miles to CR 78. Turn right on CR 78. After 6.6 miles, you pass the Northside Trails entrance (for equestrians and bicyclists). Keep alert for the main entrance on the right at 7.2 miles. The trails start near the restrooms.

The Hike: The Overlook Trail provides a short and easy path to an observation deck on the Caloosahatchee River. The River Trail winds through a dark hammock of cabbage palms and ferns, looping back to the Overlook Trail. For more rugged hiking, tackle the Shoreline Trail, which follows the edge of the river and splashes through several wetlands, and the Palmetto Path, which loops from pine flatwoods into a wet portion of the hydric hammock. In the wet season, you'll wade down these trails.

Highlights: Enjoy the dark and shady palm hammock along the River Hammock Trail.

Logistics: The park is open 8:00–sunset. Obtain a ticket from the automated machine for the parking fee ($0.75 per hour or $3 per day) and place it on your dashboard before starting your hike. Only the Overlook Trail is wheelchair accessible. If you're hiking with small children, stick to the River Hammock and Overlook Trails. Trail markers with wooden icons act as confirmation blazes on each route.

Other Activities: There is a rustic campground for tenting, and separate trail systems for equestrians and mountain bikers.

Hickey's Creek Mitigation Park

SG-24 $ 📖 🚻 ♿ 👫

Location: Alva [N26°42.762' W081°39.909'].

Length: 5.7 miles in three loops.

Map: Displayed and in brochure at trailhead.

Contact Information: Hickey's Creek Mitigation Park (941-728-6240), 17980 Palm Beach Boulevard, Fort Myers, FL 33920.

Directions: From I-75 exit 141, take SR 80 (Palm Beach Boulevard) east. After 8.5 miles, the road narrows. Keep alert for a small sign on the right indicating the location of the park entrance.

The Hike: Three loops comprise the trail system: the main Hickey's Creek Trail, the often wet North Marsh Trail, and the long Palmetto Pines Trail. The Hickey's Creek Trail is a 2.2-mile combination of footpath and boardwalk following the creek through a mixed forest of water oaks, laurel oaks, and cabbage palms. The North Marsh Trail is a 1-mile loop through a large open wetland area. The Palmetto Pines Trail follows a rugged and sometimes wet 2.5-mile loop through mostly open scrub.

Highlights: There is a garden of bromeliads in the trees above Hickey's Creek, and Florida scrub-jay families living along the Palmetto Pines Trail.

Logistics: Park hours run from 7 a.m. to 6 p.m., and are enforced by an automatic gate. Plan carefully if you arrive late in the day so you aren't locked in! Obtain a ticket from the automated machine for the parking fee ($0.75 per hour or $3 per day) and place it on your dashboard before starting your hike. A wheelchair-accessible trail of hard-packed shell and clay leads through the pine flatwoods to the edge of Hickey's Creek. While the Hickey's Creek Trail is suitable for families with young children, the other trails are best left to more adventuresome hikers with experience at route-finding.

Other Activities: There is a canoe launch on Hickey's Creek.

Four Mile Cove Ecological Preserve

SG-25 ▢ ⛹ ♿ 🚺

Location: Cape Coral [N26°36.521' W081°55.049'].

Length: 1.2-mile loop.

Map: Available at visitor center.

Contact Information: Lee County Parks and Recreation (941-461-7400), 3410 Palm Beach Boulevard, Fort Myers, FL 33916.

Directions: From US 41 in Fort Myers, drive west on Colonial Boulevard across the Midpoint Memorial Bridge to Cape Coral; stay in the right lane at the tollbooth and take the Del Prado exit. Make the right and follow the "Four Mile Eco Park" signs.

The Hike: Start your walk at the beginning of the boardwalk past the visitor center, following it through the coastal habitats of marshes and mangrove forest. You pass numerous benches and several overlooks out into the mangroves, including one on the narrow upper end of Four Mile Cove and an observation pier on the Caloosahatchee River. The boardwalk ends shortly after and you continue on a shell path lined by sand live oak and gumbo limbo back to the east end of the parking area.

Highlights: Tunnel into a mangrove forest, where many of the trees tower well overhead. Keep alert for birds roosting amid the tangled roots and limbs.

Logistics: No bicycles, food, or beverages are permitted on the trail. The boardwalk is wheelchair accessible down to the pier on the Caloosahatchee River. Use insect repellent, as you will encounter mosquitoes.

Other Activities: There is a fine kayaking route through the mangroves, and kayaks can be rented here on the weekends from September through May, 8:00–4:00. Fishing is permitted from the observation pier.

Mangrove forest at Four Mile Cove Ecological Preserve.

Calusa Nature Center

SG-26 $ 📖 🚻 ♿ 👥

Location: Fort Myers [N26°36.952' W081°48.759'].

Length: 2.1 miles in two loops.

Map: Trail map and interpretive guide available at admission desk.

Contact Information: Calusa Nature Center (941-275-3435), 3450 Ortiz Avenue, Fort Myers, FL 33905.

Directions: The Calusa Nature Center sits very close to I-75 on the eastern edge of Fort Myers. Coming from I-75 exit 136, drive west on Colonial Boulevard for 0.5 mile. Turn right on Ortiz Boulevard. Continue 0.2 mile north; the entrance is on the left.

The Hike: The wheelchair-accessible 0.6-mile Cypress Loop Trail winds through a cypress slough, joining up with the Pine Loop Trail to circle through the wet flatwoods. The swamp-tromping Wildlands Trail starts at a replica Calusa village and circles the property on a 1.5-mile walk along dikes and through the seasonal wetlands.

Highlights: This is a great place to bring the kids—let them enjoy the nature center before heading out into the woods to spot creatures in the wild. There are scenic views across the flag ponds.

Logistics: The nature center is open Mon–Sat 9:00–5:00, Sun 11:00–5:00, with an admission of $5 adults, $3 children, which includes the planetarium show. Expect to get your shoes wet (and perhaps even wade) on the Wildlands and Pine Loop Trails.

Other Activities: The nature center has an extensive herpetological exhibit with little-seen creatures like Florida's largest salamander, the greater siren, and Florida's only brackish-water turtle, the ornate diamondback terrapin. Don't forget to catch the planetarium show during the day. The small aviary showcases injured Florida birds of prey, such as the barred owl, the bald eagle, and the crested caracara, and there are ponds under the nature center with alligators and turtles.

Six Mile Cypress Slough Preserve

SG-27 $ 🔲 🚻 ♿ 🔭 🎋

Location: Fort Myers [N26°34.270' W081°49.567'].

Length: 1.4 mile loop.

Map: Posted and in brochure at kiosk at beginning of loop.

Contact Information: Six Mile Cypress Slough Preserve (941-432-2042), 7751 Penzance Crossing, Fort Myers, FL 33905.

Directions: From I-75 exit 136, drive west on Colonial Boulevard. Turn left on Six Mile Cypress Parkway. Continue 3.2 miles south to the park entrance on the left.

The Hike: A boardwalk loop through a small corner of the nine-mile-long Six Mile Cypress Slough, this accessible walk heads through a young cypress stand and circles a man-made lake before plunging into the depths of the swamp. Side trails lead to observation decks on flag ponds and to a bird blind along one of the ponds. A cross trail makes a shorter walk possible.

Highlights: This stroll through the cypress slough introduces you to the vibrant textures and colors of the swamp beneath a canopy of grand old cypresses. Take your time to savor the experience and explore the side trails down to the ponds.

Logistics: The park is open 8:00–8:00 daily. The front gate closes automatically at 8:00 p.m. Obtain a ticket from the automated machine for the parking fee ($0.75 per hour or $3 per day) and place it on your dashboard before starting your hike. On Wednesdays from July through October, arrive at 9:30 a.m. to enjoy a free guided walk of the preserve. Be cautious walking along the boardwalk in the shady sections or after a rain, as the boards can be slippery.

Other Activities: Stroll along the boardwalk and watch the wading birds, or cast for bass from the fishing platform.

Winkler Point

Estero Bay Preserve State Park

SG-28

Location: Fort Myers [N26°28.820' W081°53.899'].

Length: 5 miles in three loops.

Map: Displayed and in brochure at trailhead kiosk.

Contact Information: Estero Bay Preserve State Park (941-463-3240), 700-1 Fisherman's Wharf, Fort Myers Beach, FL 33931.

Directions: From US 41 south of downtown Fort Myers, turn west on Gladiolus Drive. Turn left on Summerlin Road. Take the first left, Winkler Drive, and follow it to the end of the pavement. The trailhead is on the right.

The Hike: The trail system consists of three stacked loops that provide up to 5 miles of hiking. The 1.1-mile Orange Trail loops through wet flatwoods that have been invaded by melaleuca; volunteers are actively working to remove the dense growth of trees. The loop passes two ponds, one of which has an observation deck. The 2.3-mile Blue Trail heads out along the edge of Hell Peckney Bay, following the tidal flats and providing another overlook over a large pond. The 1.6-mile Yellow Trail traverses the eastern edge of the tidal marsh.

Highlights: Look out across a cordgrass and needlerush marsh from the first observation deck; walk along the tidal flats on the Blue Trail.

Logistics: The park is open sunrise to sunset. As this area is an estuarine preserve, it is prone to tidal flooding. It is a trail for the adventuresome: expect to wade along portions of the trail and to slog through sticky mud.

Other Activities: Bring your binoculars and spend some time on the observation decks, where you'll see various wading birds and shorebirds.

Bailey Tract

J. N. "Ding" Darling National Wildlife Refuge

SG-29 📖

Location: Sanibel Island [N26°25.738' W082°04.826'].

Length: 0.3-mile to 1.1-mile loops.

Map: Displayed at trailhead kiosk.

Contact Information: J. N. "Ding" Darling National Wildlife Refuge (941-472-1100), 1 Wildlife Drive, Sanibel, FL 33957.

Directions: Cross the causeway to Sanibel Island ($3 toll) and, at the T intersection, turn right on Periwinkle Road. Follow it to the end and turn left on Tarpon Bay Road. Drive 0.5 mile; the preserve entrance is on the right just after the pedestrian crosswalk sign.

The Hike: Cross the boardwalk over to the dike and walk up to the map on the kiosk to choose your route from several loops around the freshwater impoundments. The area is an interesting mix of habitats, with the freshwater pools in the middle and mangroves and buttonwoods and tropical hardwoods around the edge.

Highlights: You'll find shell mounds topped with gumbo limbo and cabbage palms, and excellent views of the impoundments to watch for alligators and birds.

Logistics: All trails are shared with bicycles. The trails are marked by a series of colored arrows.

Other Activities: The birdwatching from all of the trails is great! Visit the rest of the refuge (hikes SG-30 through SG-32) off Sanibel-Captiva Road.

Indigo Trail

J. N. "Ding" Darling National Wildlife Refuge

SG-30 $ 📖 🚻 ♿

Location: Sanibel Island [N26°26.750' W082°06.774'].

Length: 4 miles round-trip.

Map: Rough map in refuge brochure; ask in visitor center for a map of hiking trails in the refuge.

Contact Information: J. N. "Ding" Darling National Wildlife Refuge (941-472-1100), 1 Wildlife Drive, Sanibel, FL 33957.

Directions: Cross the causeway to Sanibel Island ($3 toll) and, at the T intersection, turn right on Periwinkle Road. Follow the "Captiva" signs through Sanibel to Sanibel-Captiva Road. Drive 5.1 miles to the park entrance on the right, and park near the visitor center.

The Hike: From the parking lot, the Indigo Trail passes under the building alcove with the soda machines. Interpretive markers aid in your understanding of the flora along the trail. After you cross a boardwalk and Wildlife Drive, the trail becomes a dike walk between mosquito control impoundments, shaded in the early morning by buttonwoods.

Highlights: Enjoy a nice view of the mangrove marshes from the end of the trail, and take the short Cross Dike Trail to an observation deck over the marshes, where a permanent set of binoculars lets you scan the horizon for birds.

Logistics: The visitor center is open 9:00–5:00 daily from November through April, and 9:00–4:00 from May through October. The refuge is open sunrise to sunset but closed on Fridays. Bicycles are permitted on this trail but must be walked along the boardwalk sections. The boardwalk may be slippery. There is a $1 walk-in fee to hike the trail, collected at a drop box along the trail route. Expect mosquitoes at dawn and dusk and during the summer rainy season.

Other Activities: Don't miss the interpretive displays in the visitor center. Drive the 5-mile Wildlife Drive to explore the interior of the refuge and to obtain access to the Wulfert Keys Trail (SG-31) and the Shell Mound Trail (SG-32).

Wulfert Keys Trail

J. N. "Ding" Darling National Wildlife Refuge

SG-31 $

Location: Sanibel Island [N26°28.486' W082°08.938'].

Length: 0.5 mile round-trip.

Map: Rough map in refuge brochure; map of hiking trails in the refuge available at visitor center.

Contact Information: J. N. "Ding" Darling National Wildlife Refuge (941-472-1100), 1 Wildlife Drive, Sanibel, FL 33957.

Directions: Cross the causeway to Sanibel Island ($3 toll) and, at the T intersection, turn right on Periwinkle Road. Follow the "Captiva" signs through Sanibel to Sanibel-Captiva Road. Drive 5.1 miles to the park entrance on the right, and follow Wildlife Drive to the Wulfert Keys parking area beneath the power lines.

The Hike: This hike provides a short walk along a canal to the edge of Hardworking Bay, named for the difficult work of the fisherman there who set their traps by hand for crabbing. Cross the bridge and walk along the mangrove-lined canal, where the mangroves create a tangled jungle through which the snowy egrets and ibises pick their way.

Highlights: The trail ends on the bay with a sweeping view of the Wulfert Keys, which serve as rookeries for herons, egrets, and roseate spoonbills in the spring.

Logistics: The visitor center is open 9:00–5:00 daily from November through April, and 9:00–4:00 from May through October. The refuge is open sunrise to sunset but closed on Fridays. There is a $5 fee to drive Wildlife Drive. Expect mosquitoes at dawn and dusk and during the summer rainy season.

Other Activities: Don't miss the interpretive displays in the visitor center, where the Indigo Trail (SG-30) begins. Drive the 5-mile Wildlife Drive to explore the interior of the refuge and the Shell Mound Trail (SG-32).

Shell Mound Trail

J. N. "Ding" Darling National Wildlife Refuge

SG-32 $ &

Location: Sanibel Island [N26°28.437' W082°09.144'].

Length: 0.4-mile loop.

Map: Rough map in refuge brochure; map of hiking trails in the refuge available at visitor center.

Contact Information: J. N. "Ding" Darling National Wildlife Refuge (941-472-1100), 1 Wildlife Drive, Sanibel, FL 33957.

Directions: Cross the causeway to Sanibel Island ($3 toll) and, at the T intersection, turn right on Periwinkle Road. Follow the "Captiva" signs through Sanibel to Sanibel-Captiva Road. Drive 5.1 miles to the park entrance on the right, and follow Wildlife Drive to the parking area for the Shell Mound Trail, beyond the Wulfert Keys Trail.

The Hike: Follow the boardwalk into a tropical hardwood hammock and keep to the left at the fork to circle a massive shell mound carpeted in dense tropical vegetation. Dropping down off the shell mound, the trail loops into a mangrove forest where white mangroves create a canopy more than thirty feet above the trail. Exit to the left as you complete the loop.

Highlights: The mangrove forest is an awesome tangle of roots and limbs.

Logistics: The visitor center is open 9:00–5:00 daily from November through April, and 9:00–4:00 from May through October. The refuge is open sunrise to sunset but closed on Fridays. There is a $5 fee to drive Wildlife Drive. Expect mosquitoes at dawn and dusk and during the summer rainy season. The boardwalk may be slippery in places.

Other Activities: Don't miss the interpretive displays in the visitor center, where the Indigo Trail (SG-30) begins. Drive the 5-mile Wildlife Drive to explore the interior of the refuge and the Wulfert Keys Trail (SG-31).

Note: This trail was damaged by Hurricane Charley. Check with the land manager for status.

Sanibel-Captiva Conservation Foundation

SG-33 $ 📖 🚻 👥

Location: Sanibel Island [N26°26.322' W082°05.838'].

Length: 3-mile trail network with 2.1-mile perimeter loop and lots of shorter options.

Map: Available at desk on entering preserve.

Contact Information: Sanibel-Captiva Conservation Foundation (941-472-2329), 3333 Sanibel-Captiva Road, Sanibel, FL 33957.

Directions: Cross the causeway to Sanibel Island ($3 toll) and, at the T intersection, turn right on Periwinkle Road. Follow the "Captiva" signs through Sanibel to Sanibel-Captiva Road. Keep alert for the small "Sanibel-Captiva Conservation Foundation" sign on the left after 4.1 miles, and turn left into the entrance.

The Hike: The trail network introduces you to an interesting mosaic of habitats in the middle of this barrier island, from the freshwater marshes and tropical hammocks to the mangrove-lined brackish Sanibel River and ridges comprised of ancient Calusa shell mounds.

Highlights: Walk out to the observation tower along the Sanibel River for an eagle's-eye view of the preserve and the river. Visit Alligator Hole to walk the boardwalk around this freshwater pond, where an observation deck lets you sit and watch the birds.

Logistics: The trails are open 8:00–3:00 weekdays year-round, and on weekends as well from November through April. There is a $3 entry fee, children under 17 and members free.

Other Activities: Explore the nature center's exhibits, which provide an understanding of Sanibel Island's habitats and history. There is also a native plant nursery and a small store on the site.

Note: These trails were damaged by Hurricane Charley. Check with the land manager for status.

Matanzas Pass Preserve

SG-34 ♿ 🚸

Location: Fort Myers Beach [N26°26.957' W081°56.278'].

Length: 2 miles of interconnecting pathways.

Map: Displayed at trailhead parking area.

Contact Information: Lee County Parks and Recreation (941-461-7400), 3410 Palm Beach Boulevard, Fort Myers, FL 33916.

Directions: From US 41 in Fort Myers, take Summerlin Road west to Estero Boulevard (SR 865); follow Estero Boulevard south through Fort Myers Beach to Bay Road. Turn east. The trailhead is at the end of the road.

The Hike: Part boardwalk, part footpath, this network of trails takes you through a tropical hardwood hammock and a mangrove forest along Matanzas Pass, and then continues into an area that was once cleared and is now reforested with a mixture of plants.

Highlights: Watch mangrove crabs scuttle along the boardwalk and mangrove roots in the mangrove forest; watch for dolphins and manatees from the observation platform on Matanzas Pass. It's a haven for wildlife on this developed barrier island—watch too for raccoons and opossum.

Logistics: The preserve is open sunrise to sunset. Once you leave the boardwalk, the trails are subject to tidal flooding. The boardwalk section is wheelchair accessible.

Other Activities: There's a canoe launch (bring your own watercraft) for exploration of Matanzas Pass.

Black Island Trail

Lovers Key State Park

SG-35 **$** 📖 👫

Location: Lovers Key [N26°23.673' W081°52.581'].

Length: 5-mile double loop.

Map: Available at ranger station at park entrance; map and interpretive brochure available at trailhead kiosk.

Contact Information: Lovers Key State Park (941-463-4588), 8700 Estero Boulevard, Fort Myers Beach, FL 33931.

Directions: From I-75 exit 116, drive west on CR 865 (Bonita Beach Road), crossing US 41 after 3.7 miles. Watch for the park entrance sign after 10.9 miles. Turn left and follow the entrance road 0.8 mile to parking lot 2, and park at the trailhead on the left.

The Hike: The trail system at Black Island consists of two separate loops linked by an unpaved service road. Both loops follow fingers of land that were created by dredging many years ago (the better to create developable waterfront property along Estero Bay), the land colonized by plants of the coastal scrub and tropical hammock habitats. As a result, the trails create long and slender loops down each peninsula, with cross trails to shorten the hikes.

Highlights: There are great views along the canals as you hike. Take the side trail over to the laurel fig tree to marvel at its size—it's reminiscent of a large banyan tree.

Logistics: The trail is shared by bicycles. After a rain, part of the trail will be under water—expect to wade through large puddles. There is a picnic area partway along the first loop.

Other Activities: Visit the slender strand of shell beach along the Gulf of Mexico, with its picnic benches and swimming area; rent a canoe or kayak and explore the miles of waterways, or take a guided ecotour.

Estero Scrub Preserve

SG-36

Location: Estero [N26°26.540' W081°50.057'].

Length: 5.5-plus miles in a network of trail.

Map: Displayed and available in brochure at trailhead kiosk.

Contact Information: Estero Bay Preserve State Park (941-463-3240), 700-1 Fisherman's Wharf, Fort Myers Beach, FL 33931.

Directions: From US 41 south of Fort Myers, drive 4.2 miles south of Allico Road to Broadway. Turn right and follow the road west for 1.4 miles to the "No Outlet" sign. Turn right in front of the Florida Power & Light substation and park at the trail entrance.

The Hike: Start your hike on the outer Pine Flatwoods Loop, blazed with red markers, which leads through wet flatwoods with islands of scrub and cypress domes; melaleuca crowds out the cypresses in places. The Fiddler Crab Loop provides the shortest loop, 2.5 miles, if you follow it out to the mud flats; the outer loop is 4.5 miles long. The linear Blue Trail, often flooded, leads to the Estero River and is 1 mile long.

Highlights: Walk along the tidal marsh on the edge of the estuary, where fiddler crabs scurry in large crowds and rocks jut out of the thick, sticky mud.

Logistics: The preserve is open sunrise to sunset. As the area is an estuarine preserve, it is prone to tidal flooding. This is a trail for the adventuresome only: since much of the preserve encompasses wetlands, expect to wade through sections of the trail. Carry a map and keep careful track of the trail markers. Most of the hike is in full sun, so bring plenty of water; a hiking stick will help you keep your balance on slippery mud and as you wade.

Other Activities: Birdwatching is best along the tidal marsh, where you're likely to see roseate spoonbills, Louisiana herons, and white ibis grazing the flats at low tide.

Nature Trail

Koreshan Historic State Park

SG-37 **$** 📖 🚻 🎯 🧒 🐴

Location: Estero [N26°26.254' W081°49.103'].

Length: 0.5 mile one-way.

Map: Rough map in park brochure available at ranger station.

Contact Information: Koreshan Historic State Park (239-992-0311), PO Box 7, Estero, FL 33928.

Directions: From I-75 exit 123, follow Corkscrew Road west to US 41. Cross US 41; the park entrance is immediately on the right.

The Hike: Mangroves and slash pine meet along the banks of the Estero River, and this short interpretive trail clambers up and down the river bluffs, offering great scenic views as it connects the picnic area with the historic Koreshan settlement.

Highlights: There is an interesting mix of native and non-native plants introduced by the Koreshans in the 1890s, including gigantic bamboo, snake plants, and masses of cacti dangling from the tops of cabbage palms.

Logistics: Inside the park, follow the entrance road around to the picnic area and canoe launch. The trail starts along the Estero River beyond the picnic area; walk along the river's edge until you find the sign. The footpath is rugged in several places. Keep to the left at each fork to end up at the settlement; forks to the right lead to the campground.

Other Activities: Tour the historic settlement. Picnic, fish—or paddle upriver or out to Mound Key, a significant archaeological site from the Calusa culture; there's an outfitter just east of the park at the bridge on US 41.

CREW Marsh Trail System

CREW Management Area

SG-38 ♦♦♦ 🛖

Location: Lake Trafford [N26°29.383' W081°32.117'].

Length: Over 5 miles in five loop trails.

Map: Displayed at trailhead kiosk and available in brochure.

Contact Information: CREW Land and Water Trust (941-332-7771), 2301 McGregor Boulevard, 3rd Floor, Fort Myers, FL 33901.

Directions: From I-75 exit 123, Corkscrew Road, drive east for 19 miles to the preserve entrance on the right.

The Hike: Follow the orange blazes to explore the northwestern boundary of the 5,000-acre Corkscrew Marsh on this series of trails that ranges through pine flatwoods, oak hammocks, and palm hammocks. The Marsh Trail Loop leads to an observation tower over the vast sawgrass marsh, with a short boardwalk that ends at an observation deck over a seasonal pond. The linear Hammock Trail meanders through a lush palm hammock with an understory of tropical plants like wild coffee and marlberry, and leads to the primitive campsite at the southwestern end of the trail system. The Pine Flatwoods Trail Loop is a mowed grassy trail through the uplands. The shorter Jabberwocky Trail and Raccoon Way are new additions to the preserve.

Highlights: There are great views into the marsh from the observation tower on the Marsh Loop, and abundant wildflowers and numerous types of carnivorous plants in the bogs.

Logistics: The kiosk will have information on trail conditions. The trail system is always flooded during the wet season. This is a very remote area; take appropriate safety precautions. A permit (free) is necessary for using the primitive campsite; call the land manager. There's a portable toilet at the parking area, and several picnic tables along the Hammock Trail.

Other Activities: This is an excellent birdwatching spot, especially from the observation tower and decks along the trails. Hunting is permitted seasonally; check www.floridaconservation.org for details and wear blaze orange during hunts.

Corkscrew Swamp Sanctuary

SG-39 $ 🔲 👪 ♿ 👫 ❄️

Location: Immokalee [N26°22.547' W081°36.227'].

Length: 2.3-mile boardwalk, with shortcut for a shorter loop.

Map: Available at information desk.

Contact Information: Corkscrew Swamp Sanctuary (239-348-9151), 375 Sanctuary Road West, Naples, FL 34120.

Directions: From I-75 exit 111, drive east on CR 846; after 15.6 miles, turn left at the "Corkscrew Marsh Sanctuary" sign onto CR 849. Follow this road for 1.5 miles to the parking sign for the sanctuary.

The Hike: Florida's longest and oldest boardwalk trail winds through swamp forests of incredible beauty, with a high canopy of cypress, open marshes, quiet ponds circled by alligator flag and pond apple, and sluggish tannic streams. Follow the side trails to scenic points, and take your time to savor this very special preserve.

Highlights: In addition to protecting the largest nesting colony of wood storks in the United States, this 2,800-acre preserve contains the largest stand of virgin bald cypress in the world, with trees up to 600 years old; the slash pines behind the nature center are more than 200 years old.

Logistics: The preserve opens daily at 7:00 a.m.; closing time is 7:30 p.m. from April 11 to September 30 and 5:30 p.m. from October 1 to April 10. There is an admission fee of $8 for adults, $3.50 for children, $5 for Audubon members. Strollers and wheelchairs can traverse the entire boardwalk. Numerous benches and covered shelters provide protection against sudden rains. Part of the boardwalk is closed during wood stork nesting season.

Other Activities: After you enter the Blair Audubon Center, take the time to browse the exhibits and watch the film before heading out on the hike. Birdwatchers will want to bring their binoculars and field guides to identify the many species along the trail.

Sabal Palm Trail

Picayune Strand State Forest

SG-40 ⛺

Location: Naples [N26°05.719' W081°38.045'].

Length: Nested loops of 2.2 and 3.5 miles.

Map: Displayed and in brochure at trailhead kiosk.

Contact Information: Picayune Strand State Forest (941-348-7557), 2121 52nd Avenue SE, Naples, FL 34114.

Directions: From I-75 exit 101, take CR 951 (Collier Boulevard) south 4.8 miles to Sabal Palm Road. Turn left and follow the road, which becomes dirt. After 3.4 miles, keep alert for a driveway on the right leading back to the trailhead parking and kiosk.

The Hike: Take a walk on the wet side. Built by Boy Scouts, this stroll through swampland celebrates the preservation of a segment of the Big Cypress Swamp that was once a part of the biggest real estate scam in Florida. As befits a swamp, the trail is partially under water in all but the dry spring months, so you'll be wading through the cypress sloughs en route to the campsite, which is near the intersection of the two loops.

Highlights: Colorful pine lilies poke out of the grass under the pines, and a variety of orchids bloom in the canopy of cypress trees throughout the strand.

Logistics: This hike is in a very remote area and is best visited with a companion. During the wet season, you will wade knee-deep in places. The return route is not clearly signposted; be alert for landmarks, or use a map and compass. Wear insect repellent!

Other Activities: Hunting is permitted in the forest during certain seasons; wear blaze orange if you hike the trail during hunting season.

Royal Palm Hammock Trail

Collier-Seminole State Park

SG-41 $ 📖 🚻 🅰

Location: Royal Palm Hammock [N25°59.304' W081°35.640'].

Length: 0.9-mile loop.

Map: Rough sketch in park brochure.

Contact Information: Collier-Seminole State Park (941-394-3397), 20200 East Tamiami Trail, Naples, FL 34114.

Directions: From I-75 take exit 101, Naples / Marco Island. Drive south on CR 951 for 7.1 miles to US 41. Turn left and go east 8.5 miles to the park entrance. Follow the park entrance road to the marina to find the trailhead.

The Hike: This trail is a wild but gentle introduction to the habitats protected by this park: although the boardwalks are old and slippery, you can explore the coastal prairie and mangrove marsh without getting your feet wet. The trail starts out in a tropical hammock and then reaches a fork; turn left to walk clockwise around the loop.

Highlights: Walk beneath the regal royal palms, and savor the view from the lookout over the Everglades.

Logistics: This park is legendary for its mosquitoes, so apply the insect repellent liberally and use protective clothing. The boardwalk may be slippery in places.

Other Activities: Take an ecotour trip from the marina, or launch a canoe or kayak for a paddling trip. Enjoy the shaded campground, and visit the National Historical Mechanical Engineering Landmark, the walking dredge used to build the Tamiami Trail. For adventuresome hikers, there is a longer trail (SG-42) across the street.

Collier-Seminole Hiking Trail

Collier-Seminole State Park

SG-42 **Ⓕ** **$** ⬚ ⬚ ⬚

Location: Royal Palm Hammock [N25°59.402' W081°34.698'].

Length: 6.5-mile loop.

Map: Rough map available from park, detailed backpacking map from Florida Trail Association.

Contact Information: Collier-Seminole State Park (941-394-3397), 20200 East Tamiami Trail, Naples, FL 34114.

Directions: From I-75 take exit 101, Naples/Marco Island. Drive south on CR 951 for 7.1 miles to US 41. Turn left and go 8.5 miles east to the park entrance. Ask the ranger for the gate combination and a trail map.

The Hike: This loop is a real workout! Start at the parking area and use the blue connector to reach the orange-blazed main trail. Turn right to walk counterclockwise around the loop. You'll wade through thick cypress strands and across sloughs, splash through wet flatwoods, cross wildflower-dotted prairies, and appreciate the high ground in the tropical hammocks.

Highlights: It's a true immersion into the Big Cypress environment, with fascinating royal palm hammocks and shady cypress swamps.

Logistics: Bring dry clothes: you *will* get wet on this hike! Full mosquito protection is recommended: long pants, long shirt, and a head net. If you're backpacking, check with the rangers first before camping out for the night. There is a small fee for overnight camping.

Other Activities: There's canoeing, a nature trail (hike SG-41), picnicking, historic displays, and guided pontoon boat ecotours into the Everglades on the south side of the park, as well as an excellent campsite.

Big Cypress Bend Boardwalk

Fakahatchee Strand Preserve State Park

SG-43   📖 ♿ 🚻 🎏

Location: Copeland [N25°56.514' W081°28.168'].

Length: 1.2 miles round-trip.

Map: Displayed on trailhead kiosk.

Contact Information: Fakahatchee Strand Preserve State Park (941-695-4593), PO Box 548, Copeland, FL 33926.

Directions: The trailhead is along US 41 (Tamiami Trail), 8.6 miles east of Collier-Seminole State Park (hikes SG-41 and SG-42) and 6.9 miles west of SR 27.

The Hike: Start your hike along the limestone path, which leads to the boardwalk through a stand of bald cypress that escaped the logging that decimated most of the massive cypress in the Big Cypress Swamp. The understory is dense with ferns, and plants of the tropical hammock cover the high spots. The boardwalk ends at an overlook over a deep flag pond, where you'll likely spot an alligator.

Highlights: It's an incredible walk beneath ancient cypresses, which are swaddled in bromeliads.

Logistics: The park is open sunrise to sunset. There is limited parking; do not block the entrance. Expect mosquitoes—wear insect repellent.

Other Activities: There is a picnic bench at the trailhead. Bring your binoculars to watch for activity in the eagles' nest along the boardwalk.

South Central

Desoto, Hardee, Highlands, Glades, Okeechobee, Hendry

Backpackers on the Seminole section of the Florida Trail.

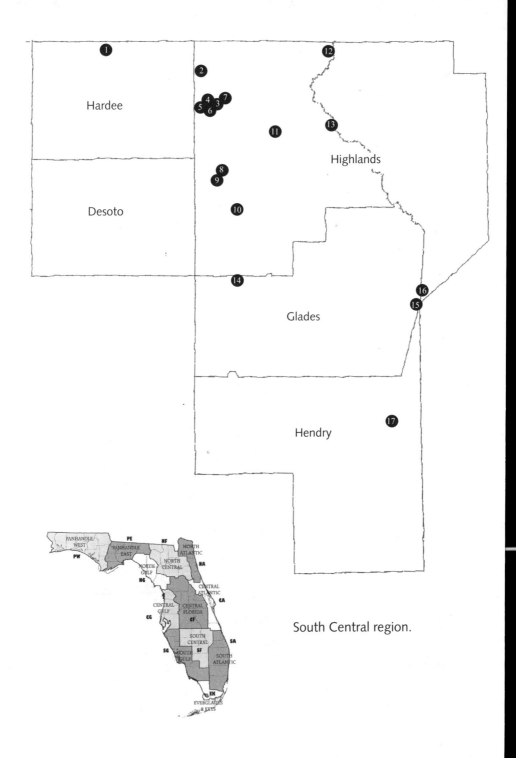

South Central region.

Paynes Creek Historic State Park

SF-1 $ 📖 🚻 👫 🐾

Location: Bowling Green [N27°37.403' W081°48.557'].

Length: 2.9 miles in two trails.

Map: Rough map in park brochure.

Contact Information: Paynes Creek Historic State Park (941-375-4717), 888 Lake Branch Road, Bowling Green, FL 33834.

Directions: From US 17 in Bowling Green, follow Main Street 0.3 mile east to Lake Branch Road. Turn right. After 1.1 miles you reach the park entrance on the right. Make the first right on the entrance road to park in front of the visitor center.

The Hike: Start at the Fort Chokonikla Trail, which circles a high spot where this Seminole War–era fort once stood, and follow the trail down into the shady hammocks along Paynes Creek. A spur trail crosses the creek on a swinging bridge, terminating at a memorial for Captain George S. Payne and Dempsey Whiddon, who died during a Seminole attack. The creekside trail continues past a picnic area as the Peace River Trail, a loop that reaches the confluence of Paynes Creek and the Peace River.

Highlights: It's certainly worth walking down to the confluence! There are great views of the river and creek along both trails.

Logistics: Before hiking, stop at the visitor center for a better understanding of the historical context of these trails.

Other Activities: There's a picnic area and a playground.

The Preserve at Sun n' Lakes

SF-2 🐎

Location: Sebring [N27°31.952' W081°33.124'].

Length: 4-plus miles.

Map: In brochure at trailhead kiosk.

Contact Information: Highlands County Parks and Recreation (863-402-6812) 636 South Fernleaf, Sebring, FL 33870.

Directions: From US 27, follow Sun n' Lakes Boulevard 3 miles west to where it ends at a T with Balboa Road. Turn right, then immediately make a left into the parking area.

The Hike: Tucked away inside a large residential community, this 1,347-acre patch of natural lands includes wet flatwoods and bayheads, flatwoods ponds, mesic pine flatwoods, and open palmetto scrub. The trail system starts at the trailhead kiosk and runs in loops around the ponds in addition to following the county line with Hardee County, creating loop options of as little as half a mile to explore.

Highlights: Meander out around the flatwoods ponds to watch the birds. Bring a lunch and settle in at one of several picnic tables along the route.

Logistics: The preserve is day use only. There are several walk-in entrances along Balboa Road, but only one trailhead. Some portions of the trails are shared with bicycles. Yellow markers indicate the trail route. The trails will be flooded during the wet summer season.

Other Activities: Fishing is permitted in the ponds.

Hickory Trail

Highlands Hammock State Park

SF-3 $ 📖 🚻 Ⓒ 🧒 🐴

Location: Sebring [N27°28.352' W081°32.565'].

Length: 2.9 miles in five trails.

Map: Rough map in park brochure.

Contact Information: Highlands Hammock State Park (863-386-6094), 5931 Hammock Road, Sebring, FL 33872.

Directions: From US 27 north of downtown Sebring, follow Hammock Road (CR 634) for 2.8 miles west to the park entrance. Continue down the park road to Hammock Drive, and turn right. Park your car at the first pulloff on the right.

The Hike: The Hickory Trail enters a dense hammock of ancient hickories and oaks, leading you across a boardwalk to the Big Oak Trail loop. Follow a spur trail to the right past the Big Oak to cross the park entrance road to access the Wild Orange Grove Trail, a linear trail through a hydric hammock. Leaving the parking area in the opposite direction, follow the fern-lined Fern Garden Trail to the Richard Lieber Memorial Trail, a boardwalk over a sluggish swamp.

Highlights: The oaks in this hammock are enormous, with the knobby Big Oak having a base more than 36' around. It's thought to be more than a thousand years old.

Logistics: Sections of this trail are low-lying and may flood. Be careful of slippery boardwalks.

Other Activities: The trail system ends at a clearing with a concession stand (where they sell great wild orange ice cream and pie) and the Civilian Conservation Corps museum. There are numerous other short trails in the park—see hikes SF-4 through SF-7.

Young Hammock Trail

Highlands Hammock State Park

SF-4 $ 📖 🅐 🚻 🏕

Location: Sebring [N27°28.398' W081°32.773'].

Length: 0.6-mile loop.

Map: Rough map in park brochure, interpretive brochure available at kiosk.

Contact Information: Highlands Hammock State Park (863-386-6094), 5931 Hammock Road, Sebring, FL 33872.

Directions: From US 27 north of downtown Sebring, follow Hammock Road (CR 634) for 2.8 miles west to the park entrance. Continue down the park road to Hammock Drive, and turn right. Park your car at the third pulloff.

The Hike: Circling through a relatively young (for this park, not for Florida) hammock of oaks, hickory, and sweet gum, this trail skirts a bayhead before completing the loop through a climax forest of oaks succeeding the surrounding pine flatwoods.

Highlights: Look for catfaces on the slash pines, a reminder of the pre-1930s turpentine industry that touched this region.

Logistics: There may be puddles in the trail through the bayhead.

Other Activities: In addition to the Civilian Conservation Corps museum, there are numerous other short trails in the park—see hikes SF-3 through SF-7.

Cypress Swamp Trail

Highlands Hammock State Park

SF-5 $ 📖 🄰 ♿ ❋

Location: Sebring [N27°28.301' W081°33.143'].

Length: 0.4-mile loop.

Map: Rough map in park brochure.

Contact Information: Highlands Hammock State Park (863-386-6094), 5931 Hammock Road, Sebring, FL 33872.

Directions: From US 27 north of downtown Sebring, follow Hammock Road (CR 634) for 2.8 miles west to the park entrance. Continue down the park road to Hammock Drive, and turn right. Drive 1 mile, passing both the amphitheatre parking and a pulloff for bike trails before arriving at the large parking area on the right.

The Hike: Starting out as a broad wheelchair-accessible boardwalk, the boardwalk tapers down to a narrow, winding two-board walkway through a cypress swamp along Little Charlie Bowlegs Creek.

Highlights: There are numerous observation points along the trail; take the time to pause and watch the wildlife.

Logistics: Once you get off the broad boardwalk, the original walkways are narrow and require a good sense of balance. It's easy to get startled by waterfowl and alligators moving underneath them.

Other Activities: In addition to the Civilian Conservation Corps museum, there are numerous other short trails in the park—see hikes SF-3 through SF-7.

Ancient Hammock Trail

Highlands Hammock State Park

SF-6 $ 📖 🅰 👫 🐕 ⛺

Location: Sebring [N27°28.211' W081°32.916'].

Length: 0.6-mile loop.

Map: Rough map in park brochure.

Contact Information: Highlands Hammock State Park (863-386-6094), 5931 Hammock Road, Sebring, FL 33872.

Directions: From US 27 north of downtown Sebring, follow Hammock Road (CR 634) for 2.8 miles west to the park entrance. Continue down the park road to Hammock Drive, and turn right. Drive 2.2 miles around the loop to the parking area on the right.

The Hike: Cross the bridge to access the start of the loop in front of the "Prayer of the Woods" sign. This is a place for contemplation, a forest in an ancient floodplain, where the trees make you feel very small. Ferns carpet the forest floor.

Highlights: This is a true immersion into the forest primeval, and the oaks along this trail are amazing in size.

Logistics: Since this is a low-lying area, portions of the trail may be mushy or flooded at times.

Other Activities: In addition to the Civilian Conservation Corps museum, there are numerous other short trails in the park—see hikes SF-3 through SF-7.

Allen Altvater Trail

Highlands Hammock State Park

SF-7 $ 　□　◉　⛫　🐎

Location: Sebring [N27°28.395' W081°31.823'].

Length: 0.6-mile loop.

Map: Rough map in park brochure.

Contact Information: Highlands Hammock State Park (863-386-6094), 5931 Hammock Road, Sebring, FL 33872.

Directions: From US 27 north of downtown Sebring, follow Hammock Road (CR 634) for 2.8 miles west to the park entrance. After you pass the entrance station, turn right into the campground. Stay to the right to find the trailhead near site 115.

The Hike: Follow the trail across a bridge to access the loop. Walking counterclockwise, you enter upland pine flatwoods and climb to sandhills before dropping back down to the creek.

Highlights: Wildflowers amid the pines attract colorful butterflies.

Logistics: Do not block campsite spaces; pull off the road to access the trail. Portions of the trail may be damp at times.

Other Activities: In addition to the Civilian Conservation Corps museum, there are numerous other short trails in the park—see hikes SF-3 through SF-6.

Bobcat, Eagle, and Deer Trails

Lake June-in-Winter Scrub State Park

SF-8 **$** 🐾

Location: Lake Placid [N27°17.790' W081°25.467'].

Length: 3.3 mile network of three trails.

Map: Rough map in park brochure.

Contact Information: Highlands Hammock State Park (863-386-6094), 5931 Hammock Road, Sebring, FL 33872.

Directions: From US 27 north of Lake Placid, follow CR 17/621 west for 4 miles. Keep left at the fork. After another 0.3 mile, turn left on Daffodil Street and follow it for 2 miles to the park entrance on the left. Park your car *outside* the gate to access the trail system, which starts along the fence line.

The Hike: Following the fence line, the Bobcat Trail leads south, crossing Tomoka Run on a jeep trail, to the intersection with the Eagle Trail. Turn left and continue up along the bright ribbon of sand through the diminutive scrub forest. Make a right at the next junction to continue along the loop. At the next junction you reach the Deer Trail, which goes down a spur trail to a youth camp along the lakeshore to the left, or completes the loop back to the Bobcat Trail to the right.

Highlights: This hike is a botanist's delight, with scrub plum, scrub hickory, spike moss, scrub beargrass, and other gems of the Lake Wales Ridge. Stop at the "Eagle Nest Overlook" sign and look to your right for the eagle's nest.

Logistics: Since you're out in the midst of "Florida's desert," dress and act accordingly: this is a hot, dry environment with no shade and no water resources. Tomoka Run flows across the trail along the fence line and has no bridge—you may have to wade it.

Other Activities: There is a short nature trail, hike SF-9, inside the park, with a canopied picnic table at the trailhead.

Out in the scrub of the Lake Wales Ridge.

Tomoka Run Trail

Lake June-in-Winter Scrub State Park

SF-9 $ 📖 🚻 👥 🐕

Location: Lake Placid [N27°17.808' W081°25.203'].

Length: 0.3-mile loop.

Map: Rough map in park brochure.

Contact Information: Highlands Hammock State Park (863-386-6094), 5931 Hammock Road, Sebring, FL 33872.

Directions: From US 27 north of Lake Placid, follow CR 17/621 west for 4 miles. Keep left at the fork. After another 0.3 mile, turn left on Daffodil Street and follow it for 2 miles to the park entrance on the left.

The Hike: This brief but enjoyable nature trail takes you on a quick loop through the scrub habitat of the Lake Wales Ridge, where tannic Tomoka Run slices through the bright sand, creating a microclimate around which a hardwood hammock has formed.

Highlights: It's a delight to walk along a burbling stream through the shady forest.

Logistics: Numerous benches make this an easy walk for all ages.

Other Activities: There is a picnic table at the trailhead, and a much longer hike through the scrub that starts at the park entrance—see hike SF-8.

Florida Scrub Nature Trail

Archbold Biological Station

SF-10 📖 🕴️ 👫

Location: Lake Placid [N27°10.781' W081°21.115'].

Length: 0.5-mile loop.

Map: On kiosk and back of visitor guidebook.

Contact Information: Archbold Biological Station (863-465-2571, www.archbold-station.org), PO Box 2057, Lake Placid, FL 33862.

Directions: From the junction of US 27 and SR 70, go west 1 mile to Old SR 8, just before the railroad tracks. Turn south and follow the road for 1.7 miles to the gate on the right; turn right and drive in on the entrance road. Stop at the kiosk and sign a release form, and then continue to the far end of the parking lot, to your left. Park on the pavement; on foot, follow the dirt path through the residential area to the trailhead. Signs point you in the right direction.

The Hike: Follow the loop through the hilly scrub habitat, where numbered posts correspond to a very detailed interpretive guide (available at the kiosk and main building) explaining the interrelationships of the scrub ecosystem. At marker 11 the trail joins an old jeep track and there is less tree cover. Follow the signs. After marker 21 the trail joins another jeep track, making a left past the weather station into the research complex. Arrows point the way. Walk around the garage to complete the loop at the parking lot.

Highlights: This is a close-up look at the Lake Wales Ridge scrub habitat. Keep alert, and you may see or hear Florida scrub-jays!

Logistics: Be sure to sign a release form before hiking the trail. Be alert for alligators—you wouldn't expect them in the scrub, but they do inhabit the canals and ponds.

Other Activities: Interpretive activities include a video on the Lake Wales Ridge. There is a gift shop in the main building (Mon–Fri 8:00–5:00) and a butterfly and native plant garden near the trailhead.

Bee Island Boardwalk

Istokpoga Park

SF-11 ♀♂

Location: Lorida [N27°26.596' W081°17.144'].

Length: 0.4 mile round-trip.

Map: None available.

Contact Information: Highlands County Parks and Recreation (863-402-6812) 636 South Fernleaf, Sebring, FL 33870.

Directions: From US 27 south of Sebring, follow US 98 for 8 miles to Lorida.

The Hike: The boardwalk leads from the parking lot to the boat ramp area, where you have your choice of following it in either direction: around to the other side of the channel, or straight out to your left to the lake. There is a kiosk with information about the restoration of Lake Istokpoga.

Highlights: The boardwalk from the parking area goes through a dark cypress swamp. You'll find great views of the lake from the end of the boardwalk on the east side of the canal.

Logistics: The park is open sunrise to sunset. There are no railings along the boardwalk, so it is not recommended for children or wheelchairs. Keep alert for alligators.

Other Activities: There are picnic tables with grills, a boat launch, and fishing from the boardwalks.

Florida Trail

Upper Kissimmee River

SF-12 **F** 🏕 🎣

Location: Along the Kissimmee River between Bluff Hammock and River Ranch [N27°47.240' W081°12.669'].

Length: 29.2 miles linear.

Map: Rough map from South Florida Water Management District; detailed backpacking map available from Florida Trail Association.

Contact Information: South Florida Water Management District (800-250-4200), 205 North Parrott Avenue, Suite 201, Okeechobee, FL 34973.

Directions: For the northern trailhead, follow SR 60 west from Yeehaw Junction to River Ranch; drive south on River Ranch Road to the crossover or the Kicco WMA trailhead. For the southern trailhead, follow US 98 west from Okeechobee past Fort Basinger to Bluff Hammock Road east of Lorida; follow Bluff Hammock Road to its end.

The Hike: This linear hike follows the floodplain of the Kissimmee River along a historic trail once trod by cattle drovers when Florida's settlers moved down along the river in the 1800s, seeking homesteads near Lake Okeechobee.

Highlights: The ghost town of Kicco along the Kissimmee River has remnants of old sidewalks and buildings; the Old Kissimmee Cemetery is near the location of the Seminole War–era Fort Kissimmee.

Logistics: This is a lengthy, remote section of trail. Bring adequate food and water filtration equipment for the two-to-three-day journey. There are six campsites along the route. Check on water level reports with SFWMD before hiking the trail, as this section may flood. When crossing the Avon Park Air Force Range, be alert to military operations and do not touch anything resembling munitions.

Other Activities: There's good birdwatching along the river.

Florida Trail

Hickory Hammock

SF-13 🅵 ⛺ 🏕 ⛰

Location: Following the Kissimmee River from the US 98 trailhead [N30°08.564' W083° 50.308'] to Bluff Hammock.

Length: 9.1 miles linear.

Map: Rough map from South Florida Water Management District displayed and available at kiosk; detailed backpacking map available from Florida Trail Association.

Contact Information: South Florida Water Management District (800-250-4200), 205 North Parrott Avenue, Suite 201, Okeechobee, FL 34973.

Directions: Follow US 98 west from Okeechobee, crossing the Kissimmee River and the Istokpoga Canal before arriving at the large trailhead parking area on the north side of the highway. For the northern trailhead for this section, follow US 98 west to Bluff Hammock Road; drive north to where the road ends near the river; there is a trail kiosk at the parking area.

The Hike: This is one of the most beautiful linear hikes in south central Florida, as it follows the newly meandering course of Istokpoga Creek and the Kissimmee River, winding through dark hydric hammocks and shady uplands with a dense canopy of live oaks; beneath the oaks, you can see the river in the distance. The trail becomes more difficult as it follows the edge of a ranch fence along the river, crossing a tall bridge before continuing along a boardwalk to Bluff Hammock.

Highlights: Your proximity to the river means many scenic views along this section.

Logistics: From US 98, follow the blue blaze to meet the main trail, and turn left to hike north. Obtain a free permit for the Hickory Hammock campsite in advance by contacting the SFWMD. Check on water level reports with SFWMD before hiking this section, as the trail is prone to flooding.

Other Activities: Separate equestrian trails leave the same trailhead; there's great birding along the marshes.

Platt Branch Mitigation Park

SF-14 📖 🐎

Location: Venus [N27°02.831' W081°22.680'].

Length: Up to 5 miles, with 2.7-mile inner loop.

Map: Displayed on kiosk at trailhead.

Contact Information: Florida Fish and Wildlife Conservation Commission (863-648-3203), Southwest Region, 3900 Drane Field Road, Lakeland, FL 33811-1299.

Directions: From US 27 in Venus (north of Palmdale, south of Lake Placid), follow CR 731 west for 1.2 miles to Detjens Dairy Road. Drive south 1.3 miles. After you pass Placid Farms Drive, make the next right on the jeep road and follow it 0.8 mile to the kiosk at the beginning of the trail.

The Hike: The trail system follows old jeep roads throughout this former ranchland, circling a vast flatwoods pond as you traverse scrubby flatwoods, oak scrub, and open prairies at the southernmost tip of the Lake Wales Ridge. Watch for blazes and signs to direct you around the loops.

Highlights: There is an observation deck on the flatwoods pond. Lined with cypresses, Fisheating Creek is the last wild and scenic waterway winding its way into Lake Okeechobee.

Logistics: The trail system is under development, so signage is sporadic; carry a compass or GPS, as it's easy to get turned around in the vast open prairies. There are plans for a backpackers' campsite along Fisheating Creek.

Other Activities: Enjoy birdwatching along the flatwoods pond.

Florida Trail

Lake Okeechobee

SF-15

Location: Circling Lake Okeechobee, passing through the towns of Lakeport, Moore Haven, Clewiston, Lake Harbor, South Bay, Belle Glade, Pahokee [N26°49.505' W080°39.990'], Canal Point, and Port Mayaca.

Length: 109-mile loop.

Map: Basic maps available from Office of Greenways and Trails and from Army Corps of Engineers, detailed backpacking maps in a set from Florida Trail Association.

Contact Information: U.S. Army Corps of Engineers South Florida Operations Office (941-983-8101), 525 Ridgelawn Road, Clewiston, FL 33440-5399.

Directions: Major trailheads are at Fisheating Creek on SR 78; Alvin Ward Park, Moore Haven; Clewiston Recreation Area; John Stretch Park, Clewiston; South Bay Recreation Area; Rardin Park, Belle Glade; Pahokee Marina; Canal Point Recreation Area; Port Mayaca Recreation Area; and Parrott Avenue Wayside, Okeechobee. Numerous smaller trailheads can be found off US 441, US 27, and SR 78 around the lake.

The Hike: It's an eight-to-ten-day walk on varying surfaces—grass, limestone, gravel, and more—around the second largest freshwater lake entirely within the United States.

Highlights: You're 35 feet above the lake—the views are incredible! Top scenic spots include Port Mayaca to Taylor Creek, Indian Prairie, and Fisheating Creek to Moore Haven.

Logistics: The dike is open and shadeless; consider walking only during the morning hours. There are designated campsites along the lake. Every Thanksgiving week, the Loxahatchee Chapter of the Florida Trail Association organizes a nine-day supported walk around the lake, the Big O Hike.

Other Activities: The trail is now paralleled in places by a paved bicycle path. This is a prime spot in Florida for birding, where sightings of wood storks, sandhill cranes, and even white pelicans are commonplace.

Florida Trail

Lower Kissimmee River

SF-16 **F** 🐿 🏕

Location: Along the Kissimmee River between Fort Basinger and the Okeetanie Recreation Area [N27°09.163' W080°52.042'] on Lake Okeechobee.

Length: 30.6 miles linear.

Map: Rough map available from South Florida Water Management District, detailed backpacking maps from Florida Trail Association.

Contact Information: South Florida Water Management District (800-250-4200), 205 North Parrott Avenue, Suite 201, Okeechobee, FL 34973.

Directions: Follow US 98 west from Okeechobee, crossing the Kissimmee River and the Istokpoga Canal before arriving at the large trailhead parking area on the north side of the highway. The southern terminus is on SR 78 west of Okeechobee, across from Okee-tanie Recreation Area.

The Hike: This section of the Florida Trail follows open dikes along the Kissimmee River, with occasional detours down back roads.

Highlights: There are great opportunities for birdwatching along the dikes. The Yates Marsh and Basinger sections provide respite from walking along the roads.

Logistics: Follow the orange blazes! This trail is best hiked south to north because of logistical issues involved in crossing the S-65D lock. There is very little shade and limited camping.

Other Activities: Birdwatch and fish.

Florida Trail

Seminole Section

SF-17 Ⓔ ⛰

Location: Northern terminus, John Stretch Park [N26°41.799' W080°48.465']; southern terminus, Big Cypress Seminole Reservation [N26°19.864' W080°52.925'].

Length: 36.1 miles linear.

Map: Detailed backpacking map available from Florida Trail Association.

Contact Information: South Florida Water Management District (800-250-4200), 205 North Parrott Avenue, Suite 201, Okeechobee, FL 34973.

Directions: The northern terminus is along US 27 at John Stretch Park between Clewiston and South Bay. The southern terminus is at the north end of the Big Cypress Seminole Reservation at the L-3 canal.

The Hike: This section of the Florida Trail follows open dikes along the L-3, L-2, L1-E, and Miami Canals through sugarcane fields and cattle ranches. It is a remote, unusual section where wildlife is common—you may see bobcats and deer crossing the sugarcane fields.

Highlights: The short walk through the Rotenberger Wildlife Management Area is an immersion into the Everglades of a century ago, before the region was drained and diked.

Logistics: There is very little shade, and camping opportunities are limited; orange blazes are few, given the lack of trees and posts. It is not safe to leave a car at either end of the section, so you'll need to arrange a shuttle.

Other Activities: The birdwatching in Rotenberger WMA is fabulous. Fishing is popular at the Roberts Road bridge.

South Atlantic

St. Lucie, Martin, Palm Beach, Broward, Miami-Dade

View of the savannas from the Hawks Bluff Trail.

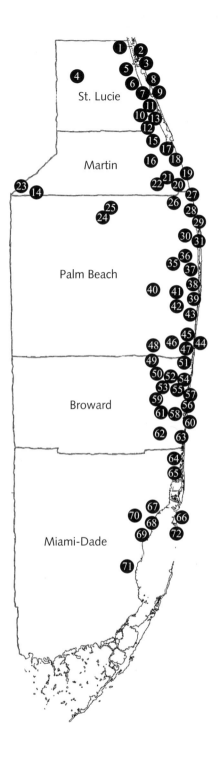

St. Lucie

Martin

Palm Beach

Broward

Miami-Dade

South Atlantic region.

St. Lucie
- SA-1   Indrio Savannahs Natural Area
- SA-2   Jack Island Preserve
- SA-3   Coastal Hammock Trail, Fort Pierce Inlet State Park
- SA-4   Pinelands Natural Area
- SA-5   Sweetwater Hammock Natural Area
- SA-6   Oxbow Eco-Center
- SA-7   Halpatiokee Nature Trail, St. Lucie River Preserve State Park
- SA-8   Ocean Bay Nature Trail
- SA-9   Turtle Beach Nature Trail
- SA-10 Oak Hammock Park
- SA-11 Spruce Bluff Preserve

Martin
- SA-12 Savannas Preserve State Park
- SA-13 Hawks Bluff Nature Trail, Savannas Preserve State Park
- SA-14 Florida Trail, Dupuis Management Area
- SA-15 Halpatiokee Regional Park
- SA-16 Phipps Park
- SA-17 South Fork Hiking Trail, South Fork St. Lucie River Management Area
- SA-18 Seabranch Preserve State Park
- SA-19 Sand Pine Scrub Oak Trail, Hobe Sound National Wildlife Refuge
- SA-20 Florida Trail, Jonathan Dickinson State Park
- SA-21 Hobe Mountain Trail, Jonathan Dickinson State Park
- SA-22 Kitching Creek Nature Trail, Jonathan Dickinson State Park
- SA-23 Rafael Sanchez Trail, Okeechobee Ridge Park

Palm Beach
- SA-24 Florida Trail, J. W. Corbett Wildlife Management Area
- SA-25 Hungryland Boardwalk and Trail, J. W. Corbett Wildlife Management Area
- SA-26 Riverbend County Park
- SA-27 Blowing Rocks Preserve
- SA-28 Jupiter Ridge Natural Area
- SA-29 Juno Dunes Natural Area
- SA-30 Frenchman's Forest Natural Area
- SA-31 Satinleaf Trail, John D. MacArthur Beach State Park
- SA-32 North Trail System, Grassy Waters Preserve
- SA-33 Raincatcher Boardwalk, Grassy Waters Preserve
- SA-34 Royal Palm Beach Pines Natural Area
- SA-35 Okeeheelee Nature Trail, Okeeheelee Park
- SA-36 Wetland Hammock Trail, Pine Jog Environmental Education Center

SA-37   Custard Apple Trail, John Prince Park
SA-38   Rosemary Scrub Natural Area
SA-39   Seacrest Scrub Natural Area
SA-40   Loxahatchee National Wildlife Refuge
SA-41   Wakodahatchee Wetlands
SA-42   Nature Trail, Morikami Park
SA-43   Delray Oaks Natural Area
SA-44   Gumbo Limbo Nature Center
SA-45   Spanish River Boardwalk, James A. Rutherford Park
SA-46   Serenoa Glade Preserve
SA-47   Sugar Sand Park
SA-48   Cathy Burdett Nature Trail, South County Regional Park
Broward
SA-49   Doris Davis Foreman Wilderness Area
SA-50   Tall Cypress Natural Area
SA-51   Deerfield Island Park
SA-52   Pond Apple Trail, Tradewinds Park South
SA-53   Fern Forest Nature Center
SA-54   Colohatchee Natural Park
SA-55   Habitat Restoration Nature Trail, Easterlin Park
SA-56   Beach Hammock Trail, Hugh Taylor Birch State Park
SA-57   Exotic Trail, Hugh Taylor Birch State Park
SA-58   Secret Woods Nature Center
SA-59   Woodmont Natural Area
SA-60   Barrier Island Nature Trail, John U. Lloyd Beach State Park
SA-61   Ann Kolb Memorial Trail, Plantation Heritage Park
SA-62   Tree Tops Park
SA-63   Ann Kolb Nature Center, West Lake Park
Miami-Dade
SA-64   Greynolds Park
SA-65   Arch Creek Park
SA-66   Bear Cut Nature Preserve
SA-67   Nature Trail, A. D. Barnes Park
SA-68   Hammock Trail, Matheson Hammock Park
SA-69   Old Cutler Hammock Nature Trail, Bill Sadowski Park and
         Nature Center
SA-70   Nature Trail, Kendall Indian Hammocks Park
SA-71   Castellow Hammock Park
SA-72   Bill Baggs Cape Florida State Park

Indrio Savannas Natural Area

SA-1

Location: Indrio [N27°31.757' W080°21.709'].

Length: More than 5 miles in three loops.

Map: Posted and available at trailhead kiosk.

Contact Information: St. Lucie County Environmental Resources (772-462-2526; www.co.st-lucie.fl.us.gov/erd), 6120 Glades Cutoff Road, Fort Pierce, FL 34981.

Directions: From I-95 exit 138, follow Indrio Road 6 miles east to US 1. Turn north and drive 0.6 mile to Tozour Road, on the left; follow signs down to trailhead parking next to the lake.

The Hike: A trail system blazed in three different colors creates stacked loops through 423 acres of protected scrub, scrubby flatwoods, marshes, and hydric hammocks. Follow the orange trail from the parking lot along the south shore of the lake to the first trail junction, and then select your route based on your planned length of hike.

Highlights: Enjoy fabulous birding along the impoundment areas. An observation tower on the blue loop and a lengthy boardwalk on the orange loop provide sweeping vistas.

Logistics: Many parts of the trails have limited shade; wear sunscreen and a hat. Leashed pets are permitted, but along the orange trail, be alert to heavily used alligator crossings between the canal and the impoundment.

Other Activities: There is picnicking, birdwatching, and fishing along the shoreline of the lake. Nonmotorized craft are permitted in the lakes and impoundments.

Jack Island Preserve

SA-2

Location: Fort Pierce [N27°30.099' W080°18.499'].

Length: 5-plus miles, with a 4.2-mile perimeter loop.

Map: None available.

Contact Information: Fort Pierce Inlet State Park (772-468-3985), 905 Shorewinds Drive, Fort Pierce, FL 34949.

Directions: From Florida's Turnpike or I-95, follow SR 70 into Fort Pierce to US 1. Turn north on US 1 and drive 3.2 miles to North A1A (North Beach Causeway); turn right. Cross the bridge and continue 2.4 miles to the traffic light just past Fort Pierce Inlet State Park. Turn left and drive north 1.2 miles; the entrance is on the left.

The Hike: Cross over the bridge from the parking area to start your walk around the trail system, which offers several options—a hike along the perimeter of the island, or on one of several interior walkways. You are immersed in mangrove habitat, and the island has been ditched for mosquito control; the walkways are on the dikes.

Highlights: An observation tower on the west side provides a great view of surrounding islands. The southern end of the island offers sweeping vistas of the Indian River Lagoon and its hundreds of tiny islands. You'll almost always hear and see osprey over the open water. Look for several species of crab sharing space under the mangroves.

Logistics: Parking is limited. There is no shade on the trail system, so bring adequate sun protection and plenty of water.

Other Activities: The bridge connecting the parking area to the island is a popular fishing spot. Bring your binoculars to look out from the observation deck over rookeries on islands in the Indian River Lagoon.

Coastal Hammock Trail

Fort Pierce Inlet State Park

SA-3 $ 📖 🚻 👫

Location: Fort Pierce [N27°28.559' W080°17.623'].

Length: 0.4-mile loop.

Map: Rough map in park brochure; interpretive brochure available at trailhead or ranger station.

Contact Information: Fort Pierce Inlet State Park (772-468-3985), 905 Shorewinds Drive, Fort Pierce, FL 34949.

Directions: From Florida's Turnpike or I-95, follow SR 70 into Fort Pierce to US 1. Turn north on US 1 and drive 3.2 miles to North A1A (North Beach Causeway); turn right. Cross the bridge and continue 2.2 miles to the park entrance on the right.

The Hike: Enter the deep shade of red bay and live oak and turn right at the beginning of the loop. Interpretive markers correspond to the guide as you walk through the dense tropical hammock, where wild coffee, ferns, and saw palmetto fill the understory beneath sugar hackberry, Spanish stopper, and bay.

Highlights: It's a pretty trail, and the strong salt and bay leaf aroma makes you feel like you've stepped into an Italian kitchen when you enter the hammock.

Logistics: To find the trailhead after paying your entrance fee, continue 1.4 miles on the park entrance road to the farthest parking area; the trailhead is on the return loop and is marked by a large brown sign.

Other Activities: This park offers picnicking and beaches, and is one of the top surfing destinations on the Atlantic Coast.

Pinelands Natural Area

SA-4 🦅

Location: Fort Pierce.

Length: Nearly 6 miles on outer loop; options as short as 1 mile.

Map: Displayed at trailhead kiosk and available as brochure.

Contact Information: St. Lucie County Environmental Resources (772-462-2526; www.co.st-lucie.fl.us.gov/erd), 6120 Glades Cutoff Road, Fort Pierce, FL 34981.

Directions: From SR 70 (Okeechobee Road) in Fort Pierce, drive 14.5 miles west of Florida's Turnpike; turn left on VPI Grove Road and follow signs to the park entrance.

The Hike: Three stacked loops (blue, orange, and white) wind their way through a variety of habitats that have one thing in common—pines. Palmetto prairies, wet flatwoods, and uplands have a vast open understory great for spotting wildlife.

Highlights: The isolated nature of this tract makes it a haven for wildlife. Look for bald eagles, wood storks, and sandhill cranes as well as wild turkey and white-tailed deer. There is an observation tower halfway along the outer loop, great for wildlife viewing.

Logistics: The park is open dawn to dusk, day use only. This is an extremely remote part of the county; make sure you bring plenty of water and adequate sun protection, as many portions of the trails are out in open scrub.

Other Activities: It's a great spot for early morning birdwatching.

Sweetwater Hammock Natural Area

SA-5 ▢ ▨ ▨

Location: Fort Pierce [N27°23.463' W080°20.989'].

Length: 0.4-mile loop.

Map: Displayed and in brochure at trailhead kiosk.

Contact Information: St. Lucie County Environmental Resources (772-462-2526; www.co.st-lucie.fl.us.gov/erd), 6120 Glades Cutoff Road, Fort Pierce, FL 34981.

Directions: From I-95 exit 126, CR 712 (Midway Road), drive east to 25th Street and turn north. The park entrance is on the right side of the road.

The Hike: This short interpretive loop trail leads you through shady oak hammocks thick with bromeliads and ferns en route to a river view, dropping through a hydric hammock and floodplain forest on its way.

Highlights: It's a beautiful trail—the oak hammocks are lush, and the trail briefly overlooks the scenic North Fork of the St. Lucie River.

Logistics: The park is open dawn to dusk. The trail can be accessed via a canoe dock on the river, as well.

Other Activities: A picnic table is provided near the river.

Oxbow Eco-Center

SA-6 ⬜ 🚻 ♿ 👫 🐕 🎆

Location: Port St. Lucie [N27°21.219' W080°21.285'].

Length: 4-mile trail system, offering loops up to 3.8 miles.

Map: Displayed at trailhead and available in Trail Map brochure.

Contact Information: Oxbow Eco-Center (772-785-5833; www.stlucieco.gov/erd/oxbow), 5400 NE St. James Drive, Port St. Lucie, FL 34983.

Directions: From I-95 exit 126, CR 712 (Midway Road), drive east to 25th Street (St. James Drive). Turn right on St. James Drive and follow it south to the park entrance on the left.

The Hike: An interconnecting series of trails enables you to explore the natural wonders of this 220-acre preserve along the North Fork of the St. Lucie River, meandering through dense oak hammocks, pine flatwoods, hydric hammocks, and open prairie, and along high bluffs on the river's edge. Boardwalks provide a limited amount of access for wheelchairs. Plan to spend several hours on the trails, where you'll spot wildlife and an interesting variety of plants.

Highlights: There are fabulous views of the river from the high bluffs along the Otter Trail, and pitcher plants growing in bogs along the Blue Heron Trail. The interpretive signs provide a great amount of detail on plants and habitats.

Logistics: The trails are open dawn to dusk, the nature center 1:00–5:00. No bicycles are allowed. A canoe dock on the river affords paddlers access to the trail system.

Other Activities: Visit the nature center for an overview of the preserve's habitats.

Halpatiokee Nature Trail

St. Lucie River Preserve State Park

SA-7 📖

Location: Port St. Lucie [N27°18.328' W080°18.562'].

Length: 0.8 mile round-trip.

Map: Displayed on trailhead kiosk.

Contact Information: Savannas Preserve State Park (772-340-7530), 9551 Gumbo Limbo Lane, Jensen Beach, FL 34957.

Directions: On US 1, 0.7 mile north of Walton Road, in Port St. Lucie, the park entrance is on the west side of the highway.

The Hike: Tunneling through dense floodplain forest vegetation, the nature trail provides an intimate look at a variety of ecosystems between the uplands near US 1 and the mangrove-lined channel at Evan's Creek. Return along the Fire Trail for a different look at the habitats.

Highlights: Learn to do a balancing act on strategically placed bog bridges along both trails! Dense ferns abound in the junglelike wetlands.

Logistics: Follow the white blazes. A hiking stick is recommended for keeping your balance on the bridges. Several benches provide resting spots along the way.

Other Activities: Birdwatch along Evan's Creek. Or launch your kayak, if it's lightweight enough to carry that far, at the canoe platform at the end of the trail; use the straight-line Fire Trail to get there.

Ocean Bay Nature Trail

SA-8 📖 🚸 🐕 🏕️

Location: Hutchinson Island [N27°19.541' W080°13.773'].

Length: 0.3-mile loop.

Map: Displayed and in brochure at trailhead kiosk.

Contact Information: St. Lucie County Environmental Resources (772-462-2526; www.co.st-lucie.fl.us.gov/erd), 6120 Glades Cutoff Road, Fort Pierce, FL 34981.

Directions: Take SR 732 (Jensen Beach Boulevard) east from US 1 to A1A. Drive north on A1A about 4.5 miles to the park entrance on the ocean side.

The Hike: This short shady walk through a coastal dune habitat tunnels through a tropical canopy of sea grapes, gumbo limbo, strangler fig, and sugarberry that creak and groan in the perpetual sea breeze; you can hear the roar of the waves nearby. Past marker 15, the trail drops down to the left and leaves the sea, working its way through a breezeway of palms and willows to return to the parking area.

Highlights: As you wander through the tunnels of sea grapes, notice the textures of fallen leaves on the forest floor. It's a natural funhouse of tight passageways between the trees, cool and shady.

Logistics: From the trailhead, take the first left to follow the nature trail, following the black arrows and red blazes past interpretive posts.

Other Activities: Visit the beach! The jeep track leads to an ocean crossover.

Turtle Beach Nature Trail

SA-9 📖 🚸

Location: Hutchinson Island [N27°21.372' W080°14.497'].

Length: 1 mile round-trip.

Map: Interpretive brochure available from Florida Power & Light at the Energy Encounter Center on Hutchinson Island.

Contact Information: Florida Power & Light (877-FPL-4FUN), PO Box 025576, Miami, FL 33102.

Directions: The trailhead is off A1A north of the Florida Power & Light Hutchinson Island Nuclear Power Plant. Stop at gate 2 for an interpretive guide from the Energy Encounter Center and to sign in as a recreational user. Drive north of the power plant and turn right after crossing the creek. Follow the narrow dirt road out to the trailhead at the beach.

The Hike: Walk along the footpath of wood chips and sand behind the dunes to access the boardwalk trail. The boardwalk loops through a dense mangrove forest with tidal creeks, and has numbered stops corresponding to the interpretive brochure.

Highlights: Watch for mangrove crabs scuttling along the mangrove prop roots, and ibises and herons roosting and feeding in the forest.

Logistics: The gates are locked at 8:00 p.m. The 0.1-mile access trail along the dunes can be deep in soft sand. The Energy Encounter Center at FPL gate 2 is open Sun–Fri 10:00–4:00; you may still use the trail without signing in, but they prefer that you check in if the office is open. The center offers "eco-detective backpacks" for the kids, to make exploring the trail and its habitats more fun.

Other Activities: Fish, swim, and sun along the Atlantic Ocean.

Oak Hammock Park

SA-10

Location: Port St. Lucie [N27°16.750' W080°24.466'].

Length: 1.5 miles of trails in two loops and a connector.

Map: None provided.

Contact Information: City of Port St. Lucie (772-878-2277), 2195 SE Airoso Boulevard, Port St. Lucie, FL 34984.

Directions: From FL 716 (Port St. Lucie Boulevard), drive west from the Florida's Turnpike entrance for 0.7 mile to Del Rio Boulevard. Turn right; drive north 0.9 mile on Del Rio Boulevard to California Boulevard. Turn left and drive west 1.2 miles to the sign for the park on the left at Pamona; follow signs through the neighborhood to the park entrance at 1982 Villanova Road.

The Hike: Oak Hammock Park provides two gentle loops, the Oak Trail and the Pine Trail, plus a connector trail that leads out to the local neighborhood. The trails radiate in opposite directions from the trailhead. After following the canal briefly and passing a large midden, the Oak Trail enters the deep shade of an oak hammock dense with fern-draped ancient live oaks. The Pine Trail loops through a hammock of tall slash pines and cabbage palms.

Highlights: The sheer size and age of oaks along the Oak Trail are a wonder to behold, and the midden (with plenty of "Keep Off" signs around it) is rather large.

Logistics: There are plenty of benches to make this an easy walk for all ages. Watch your children carefully en route to the Oak Trail, since there is a canal and a slough paralleling the trail.

Other Activities: You'll find a playground, picnic pavilions, a fishing deck on the canal, and a butterfly garden.

Spruce Bluff Preserve

SA-11 📖 🏇

Location: Port St. Lucie [N27°15.334' W080°19.992'].

Length: 2 miles in two linear trails.

Map: Posted on trailhead kiosk; brochures with map available at kiosk.

Contact Information: St. Lucie County Environmental Resources (772-462-2526; www.co.st-lucie.fl.us.gov/erd), 6120 Glades Cutoff Road, Fort Pierce, FL 34981.

Directions: From Florida's Turnpike, drive 1.5 miles east on Port St. Lucie Boulevard to Floresta Drive. Turn right on Floresta and drive south 0.7 mile to Southbend. Turn left on Southbend, then make a left on Peru Street. After 0.5 mile turn left on Dar Lane, and left into the entrance for the preserve. Park your car in front of the kiosk on the left.

The Hike: On the south side, the trail leads through sand pine scrub and scrubby flatwoods to unexpected vistas along a series of boardwalks across vast freshwater marshes busy with wading birds. The trail loops around a tree-topped midden before returning to the marshes. On the north side, the trail follows an abandoned entryway to a thwarted development through scrubby flatwoods and scrub, terminating in a loop around a historic pioneer-era cemetery.

Highlights: You'll find fabulous views of the wetlands, and a bit of history to explore. The South Trail provides a very pleasant hike.

Logistics: The preserve is open dawn to dusk. Parking is limited; do not block the road or gates.

Other Activities: Bring your binoculars! You will see a lot of wading birds on the marshes.

Savannas Preserve State Park

SA-12 📖 🚻 🐕

Location: Jensen Beach [N27°14.779' W080°14.994'].

Length: 1.5 miles.

Map: None.

Contact Information: Savannas Preserve State Park (772-340-7530), 9551 Gumbo Limbo Lane, Jensen Beach, FL 34957.

Directions: From US 1, follow CR 707A (Jensen Beach Boulevard) east to the state park entrance on the left.

The Hike: Starting behind the restrooms, this interpretive trail meanders off into wide open scrubby flatwoods on a blazed forest road, headed for the Savannas—a broad open freshwater marshland only a mile from the saltwater Indian River Lagoon.

Highlights: The trail passes ephemeral ponds as it wends its way across the scrub. The open understory makes for excellent birding.

Logistics: Follow the blue blazes to stay on the trail. Unlike at the main tract of this state park (on Walton Road, to the north), no horses are permitted on this trail. Bicycles and pets are allowed. The trail is open and sunny, so carry plenty of water and wear skin protection.

Other Activities: Picnic at the trailhead picnic area.

Hawks Bluff Nature Trail

Savannas Preserve State Park

SA-13 ☆☆

Location: Jensen Beach [N27°15.617' W080°14.410'].

Length: 1.1 miles.

Map: Rough sketch on state park map.

Contact Information: Savannas Preserve State Park (772-340-7530), 9551 Gumbo Limbo Lane, Jensen Beach, FL 34957.

Directions: From US 1, follow CR 707A (Jensen Beach Boulevard) east 2.2 miles to CR 723 (Savannah Road). Turn left and drive 1.1 miles to the crest of the hill; park on the grassy shoulder on the left side of the road.

The Hike: Follow the blazes clockwise for the most interesting hike, starting off with a steep uphill to rise to the top of relict coastal dunes topped with sand pines and cocoplum. As the trail descends, it passes through sand pine scrub where fallen bromeliads grow in a thick carpet on the forest floor. Looping around through oak scrub, you emerge on the edge of the freshwater marshes and enter an oak hammock, then have the opportunity to walk out a slender spit of land for a close communion with the marshes. The trail ascends through a cabbage palm flatwoods to complete the loop.

Highlights: Visit five different habitats in less than a mile, and enjoy sweeping views of the freshwater savannas.

Logistics: Parking is limited. Pull off the residential street onto the shoulder and do not block the gate.

Other Activities: Fish and birdwatch along the savannas.

Florida Trail

DuPuis Management Area

SA-14 🅕 $ ⏶ 🏕

Location: Indiantown.

Length: Stacked loops of 5, 7.2, 11.7, and 15.6 miles, plus 6.8-mile Corbett Connector.

Map: Available from land manager and may be found at trailhead kiosk; detailed backpacking map available from Florida Trail Association.

Contact Information: DuPuis Management Area (800-432-2045), 23500 SW Kanner Highway, Canal Point, FL 33438

Directions: Follow SR 76 for 6 miles west from its junction with SR 710 in Indiantown to the park entrance on the left.

The Hike: This vast preserve near Lake Okeechobee encompasses nearly 22,000 acres of pine flatwoods, open prairies, and numerous other habitats, including unexpected delights like cypress strands. The four loop trails offer a variety of day hike and backpacking options, with several designated primitive campsites along the way. Expect to see wildlife! The western side of Loop 4 and the Corbett Connector—a link to the Florida Trail in Corbett WMA (SA-24)—are part of the 72-mile Ocean to Lake Trail.

Highlights: Enjoy colorful wildflowers in the cypress strands and comfortable campsites in the pines.

Logistics: The preserve is open dawn to dusk. Day use fee is $3 per vehicle, permit for primitive camping $5. Obtain permit at the trailhead at gate 2, near the Governor's House. Orange blazes mark the perimeter loop; blue blazes mark the cross trails and side trails to campsites.

Other Activities: There are equestrian trails, and seasonal hunting. Check www.floridaconservation.org for hunting dates; wear blaze orange during hunting season.

Halpatiokee Regional Park

SA-15   📖   🚻   🐎

Location: Stuart [N27°06.252' W080°15.104'].

Length: 1.3 miles in two trails.

Map: None available.

Contact Information: Martin County Parks (772-221-1418), 2401 SE Monterey Road, Stuart, FL 34996.

Directions: From I-95 exit 101, SR 76 (Kanner Highway), drive east to the first right turn, Lost River Road; follow Lost River Road for 0.5 mile to the park entrance on the left. Take the park entrance road all the way to the back of the park, behind the ball fields, to access the nature trails.

The Hike: From the end of the parking circle, follow the paved bicycle path for a short distance to reach the trailhead at the hiker sign, and walk down to the right to a T intersection with the Gopher Tortoise Trail. To the left, the trail rounds several small marshes and stays along the edge of an oak hammock before returning you to the paved path. The trail to the right is far more interesting—it ducks through the hammocks past a picnic spot and follows the river down to where the new Riverside Trail takes you along the rugged bluffs through the saw palmetto above the river.

Highlights: Enjoy great river views and challenging hiking along the Riverside Trail, and a burbling mini-waterfall in the canal, as well as hundreds of bromeliads and orchids in the trees along the river.

Logistics: The park is open sunrise to sunset.

Other Activities: This is a county park with picnic tables, ball fields, and other recreational activities; a canoe livery is just up the road.

Phipps Park

SA-16

Location: Stuart [N27°06.964' W080°16.719'].

Length: 1 mile.

Map: None available.

Contact Information: Martin County Parks (772-221-1418), 2401 SE Monterey Road, Stuart, FL 34996.

Directions: From I-95 exit 101, follow SR 76 west for 0.6 mile to Locks Road. Turn right and drive 1.2 miles to the park entrance on the right. Continue along the park entrance road to the far side of the campground, where a trailhead sign marks the beginning of the trail.

The Hike: This trail, created as an Eagle Scout project, winds 0.3 mile through the open sun of a meadow that is starting to fill in with small trees, then descends into a dense hammock along a stream draining down toward the St. Lucie River. Tall ferns and giant wild coffee crowd the footpath (which is mushy in places) through the palm hammock.

Highlights: Look for gopher tortoise activity in the open area.

Logistics: The trails inside the hammock are not well maintained—consider this a hike for adventurers only! Green trail markers lead the way.

Other Activities: There's a campground (some waterfront spaces, none with shade), birding in open fields and along the canal, bank fishing, and a playground.

South Fork Hiking Trail

South Fork St. Lucie River Management Area

SA-17 🅵 ⛺

Location: Stuart.

Length: 1.1 miles linear, plus 0.8-mile connector and 0.2-mile loop.

Map: Map with trail data available from South Florida Water Management District; detailed map available from Florida Trail Association.

Contact Information: South Florida Water Management District (800-432-2045), 3301 Gun Club Road, West Palm Beach, FL 33416.

Directions: From I-95 exit 61, FL 76, drive east to Cove Road. Turn right and continue east. Turn right on Gaines Avenue, and drive south to where it ends at the county park. From here, the rest of the trip is by water!

The Hike: This is not your normal hike—you have to paddle down to the trailhead before starting your walk. From the canoe landing, the trail climbs out of the hydric hammock and skirts the edge of pine flatwoods, intersecting with a 0.2-mile loop trail on the island before climbing up on the river bluffs. When the trail ends at the main grade, you can use it as a connector to return to the trailhead, or retrace the scenic trip along the river bluffs.

Highlights: There are scenic views from the river bluffs, and pleasant bridges and boardwalks through the hydric hammocks.

Logistics: Primitive camping is permitted at the canoe landing, but you must obtain a permit (free) in advance from the South Florida Water Management District.

Other Activities: Paddle the South Fork of the St. Lucie River.

Seabranch Preserve State Park

SA-18 **F** 🚻 🐕

Location: Hobe Sound [N27°07.831' W080°10.171'].

Length: 5.1 miles in two loops and a connector.

Map: Posted and available in brochure at trailhead kiosk; detailed map available from Florida Trail Association.

Contact Information: St. Lucie Inlet Preserve State Park (561-744-7603), 16450 SE Federal Highway, Hobe Sound, FL 33455.

Directions: From I-95 exit 61, FL 76, follow Cove Road east for 4.5 miles, crossing US 1, to reach CR A1A just after the railroad tracks. Turn right and continue 1.5 miles south. Make a left into the small parking area across from the VFW.

The Hike: A jeep trail leads from the trailhead to the actual start of the loop, a trail junction with signs "North Loop 3.2 miles" and "South Loop 1.9 miles." While the South Loop is an easier walk, and passes under some very old sand pines, the North Loop is where you're more likely to see wildlife. It winds through patches of older sand pine scrub, young Lilliputian forests of scrub oaks, and a scrubby flatwoods.

Highlights: Florida scrub-jays and gopher tortoises inhabit this miniature landscape, and it's likely you'll see both! The bayhead at the east end of the park is rare for the region, as it drains into the brackish Indian River Lagoon.

Logistics: There is a composting privy at the trailhead. Much of the trail is in open sand pine scrub, so bring plenty of water, wear sun protection, and expect to walk through some stretches of soft sand. If you walk the outer perimeter of both trails, it's a 4.8-mile loop.

Other Activities: There are picnic tables at the trailhead.

Sand Pine Scrub Oak Trail

Hobe Sound National Wildlife Refuge

SA-19 📖 🚻 👫

Location: Hobe Sound [N27°02.216' W080°06.714'].

Length: 0.4-mile loop; add 0.2 mile to visit Intracoastal Waterway beaches.

Map: None available; trail shown on locator map for refuge.

Contact Information: Hobe Sound National Wildlife Refuge (772-546-6141), PO Box 645, Hobe Sound, FL 33475.

Directions: Along US 1, just south of Old CR A1A in Hobe Sound, turn in on the east side of the highway at the Hobe Sound National Wildlife Refuge Visitor Center.

The Hike: Start at the kiosk near the chickee used as an outdoor classroom, from the south side of the visitor center parking lot. The trail traverses a sliver of coastal scrub between US 1 and the Intracoastal Waterway, enjoying some noticeable elevation gain on the relict dunes. Past the second bench, the trail loops back toward the entrance. It passes under a massive slash pine, which rains needles on the footpath from its spreading crown. Emerging into an open sandy area, the trail completes the loop at the chickee.

Highlights: Enjoy the rugged terrain, patches of scrub mint, and miniature moss forests under the rosemary bushes.

Logistics: The refuge is open dawn to dusk. The restrooms are open only when the visitor center is open.

Other Activities: The visitor center, with small gift shop and bookstore, is open limited hours on weekdays. By the restrooms, walk down 47 steps through the forest to the Intracoastal Waterway, where you can sit on a bench and watch the birds, or fish from the banks.

Florida Trail

Jonathan Dickinson State Park

SA-20 **F** **$** ⬚ 🚻 🅲 △ 🐎 ⌘

Location: Hobe Sound [N27°00.246' W080°06.087'].

Length: 17 miles in two loops and a connector.

Map: Rough map available at ranger station, detailed backpacking map from Florida Trail Association.

Contact Information: Jonathan Dickinson State Park (561-546-2771), 16450 SE Federal Highway, Hobe Sound, FL 33455.

Directions: Use Florida's Turnpike exit 116 or I-95 exit 87A, SR 706 (Indiantown Road), Jupiter. Drive east 5 miles to US 1. Turn left and continue north 5.1 miles to the park entrance on the left. Park your car at the parking area adjacent to the ranger station at the entrance.

The Hike: One of Florida's most awesome weekend backpacking trips, the trail system in Jonathan Dickinson consists of the East Loop—a rugged 9.7-mile trail traversing rolling relict dunes topped in sand pine scrub, open prairies, cypress swamps, pine flatwoods, and more—and the Kitching Creek Loop, a 3.9-mile wander through tropical hardwood hammocks and prairies.

Highlights: You'll find challenging dunes to climb, sweeping views across the prairies, and a bountiful array of unusual wildflowers, including carnivorous plants and terrestrial orchids.

Logistics: You must check in at the ranger station to ensure you can camp along the trail. Campsites are at 4.9 miles (Scrub-jay Camp) and 8.6 miles (Kitching Creek Camp), with the latter being the more pleasant location. Pitcher pumps are available for nonpotable water at both locations. Much of the trail is dry and open, so use sun protection and carry water. At certain times of year, parts of the trail will flood.

Other Activities: This park is jam-packed with activities—an ecotour up the Loxahatchee River to a historic site, paddling (rentals available), rugged mountain bike trails, equestrian trails, picnic pavilions, and two major campgrounds. There are also two other hiking trails (SA-21 and SA-22) within the park.

Hobe Mountain Trail

Jonathan Dickinson State Park

SA-21 $ 📖 Ⓐ 🚻

Location: Hobe Sound [N27°01.010' W080°06.610'].

Length: 0.4 mile round-trip.

Map: Rough sketch on park map.

Contact Information: Jonathan Dickinson State Park (561-546-2771), 16450 SE Federal Highway, Hobe Sound, FL 33455.

Directions: Following the directions for hike SA-20, continue past the ranger station to the T intersection. Turn right and follow the entrance road to Hobe Mountain Tower Road. Turn right and drive up the hill to a small parking area.

The Hike: This boardwalk-and-staircase trail clambers up over tall relict dunes topped in sand pine scrub to an observation tower atop Hobe Mountain, which at 86 feet is the highest natural hill south of Lake Okeechobee.

Highlights: Admire the 360° view from the top of the tower. You can see the Atlantic Ocean to the east; the ribbon of dark green to the west is the cypresses along the Loxahatchee River.

Logistics: It's a steep but short climb to the top of the tower. Hold on to your hat—the wind off the ocean can blow it away!

Other Activities: This park is jam-packed with activities—an ecotour up the Loxahatchee River to a historic site, paddling (rentals available), rugged mountain bike trails, equestrian trails, picnic pavilions, and two major campgrounds. There are also two other hiking trails (SA-20 and SA-22) within the park.

Kitching Creek Nature Trail

Jonathan Dickinson State Park

SA-22 $ 🔲 🚻 🅐 🚸 🐎

Location: Hobe Sound [N26°59.570' W080°08.837'].

Length: 1.3-mile loop.

Map: Available from park ranger at entrance station and in map holder at trailhead.

Contact Information: Jonathan Dickinson State Park (561-546- 2771), 16450 SE Federal Highway, Hobe Sound, FL 33455.

Directions: Following the directions for hike SA-21, continue past the ranger station to the T intersection. Turn right and follow the entrance road all the way to the back of the park, where it reaches another T intersection. Turn right and park in the parking area near the picnic pavilion. The trailhead is at the north edge of the parking lot.

The Hike: This pleasant short loop provides an introduction to several of the ecosystems found in the park, including pine flatwoods, scrubby flatwoods, and the cypress-lined Kitching Creek. You cross a bridge over Wilson Creek at 0.3 mile, and reach a spur trail to an observation deck on Kitching Creek at 0.7 mile. The trail parallels the creek for some time before meeting up with the Wilson Creek Trail again and crossing the creek, following it upstream briefly to complete the loop.

Highlights: Take some time to sit and savor the view at the observation deck overlooking Kitching Creek. Watch for ripening blueberries and blackberries along the trail in May!

Logistics: For an even shorter hike, follow the well-marked 0.5-mile Wilson Creek Trail along the trickling waterway.

Other Activities: This park is jam-packed with activities—an ecotour up the Loxahatchee River to a historic site, paddling (rentals available), rugged mountain bike trails, equestrian trails, picnic pavilions, and two major campgrounds. There are also two other hiking trails (SA-20 and SA-21) within the park.

Rafael Sanchez Trail

Okeechobee Ridge Park

SA-23 **F**

Location: Port Mayaca [N26°59.215' W080°37.016'].

Length: 5 miles linear.

Map: Available from Florida Trail Association.

Contact Information: Martin County Parks (772-221-1418), 2401 SE Monterey Road, Stuart, FL 34996.

Directions: From the city of Okeechobee, drive south on US 441 to the Port Mayaca bridge, take the turnoff to the right just before the bridge and make a left under the bridge to find the trailhead. Alternatively, use SR 76 from Indiantown to reach US 441 and drive north across the bridge to access the recreation area.

The Hike: It's a meandering walk along a ribbon of dense hardwood hammock sandwiched between US 441 to the west and sugarcane fields to the east, with surface outcrops of limestone and large cypress trees.

Highlights: This is the only protected remnant of the original shoreline of Lake Okeechobee, prior to the creation of the Herbert Hoover Dike in the 1930s.

Logistics: The park is open for day use only. It's possible to leave a car at both ends and make this a one-way linear walk; the intent is to have the northern end of the trail tie in eventually to the Florida Trail at Lake Okeechobee to provide an 11-mile round-trip hike.

Other Activities: The trail connects, via the entrance road under the Port Mayaca bridge, to the Florida Trail on Lake Okeechobee (SC-15) and the paved bicycle trail leading north to Okee-tanie Recreation Area.

Florida Trail

J. W. Corbett Wildlife Management Area

SA-24 **F** $ ⌂

Location: Royal Palm Beach [N26°51.345' W080°18.163'].

Length: 17 miles linear.

Map: Heavy waterproof map is sold by Friends of Corbett WMA, and detailed backpacking map by Florida Trail Association.

Contact Information: Florida Fish and Wildlife Conservation Commission (561-625-5122), 8535 Northlake Boulevard, West Palm Beach, FL 33412.

Directions: From I-95 exit 77, take Northlake Boulevard (CR 850) west for 12 miles, where it ends at Seminole-Pratt-Whitney Road. Turn right; follow the road, which turns to dirt, 3 miles to the entrance. Turn left and continue to the youth camp; keep to the right and then make a left at the "Hungryland Boardwalk" sign. Follow the jeep track to the trailhead.

The Hike: At the "FT" sign, sign the trailhead register before taking off into the wilds of this northernmost relict portion of the Everglades. After the first mile, a blue-blazed low-water loop gives you an alternative to wading through a deep wet prairie. For more than half the length of the hike, you'll skirt dozens of these prairies and slip through pine flatwoods before reaching the rugged mosaic of dwarf cypress prairies, cypress strands, and wet flatwoods that make up the western side of the preserve.

Highlights: Views across the wet prairies are spectacular, and backpackers will enjoy a wade through the Hole in the Wall, a half-mile-wide cypress strand blooming with brilliant bromeliads.

Logistics: Follow the orange blazes. This is a rugged backpacking trip, recommended for experienced hikers only. You will encounter a lot of wading, even in the dry season, as you traverse the cypress sloughs. The trail connects to Dupuis Management Area (SA-14) via a 6.8-mile connector trail. An out-and-back trip to Little Gopher Campsite, 12 miles each way, is doable as a weekend trip, but extremely strenuous.

Other Activities: This trailhead is adjacent to the Hungryland Boardwalk (SA-25).

Hungryland Boardwalk and Trail

J. W. Corbett Wildlife Management Area

SA-25 $ 📖 🚻

Location: Royal Palm Beach [N26°51.350' W080°18.167'].

Length: 1.1-mile loop.

Map: None available.

Contact Information: Florida Fish and Wildlife Conservation Commission (561-625-5122), 8535 Northlake Boulevard, West Palm Beach, FL 33412.

Directions: See hike SA-24; the two trails share a trailhead.

The Hike: After crossing a boardwalk over a wet prairie, the trail meanders through pine flatwoods to start the main boardwalk loop into Hungryland Slough, a dense strand of cypresses thick with colorful bromeliads and tall ferns.

Highlights: This walk offers great views across the prairies, and a pleasant immersion into the peace and quiet of the cypress slough.

Logistics: Stop at the self-service pay station and drop off your entrance fee of $3 per person. Numerous benches make this an easy walk for all ages. Portions of the trail may flood during the wet season.

Other Activities: This trailhead is adjacent to the Florida Trail trailhead for the Corbett section of the Ocean to Lake Trail (SA-24).

Riverbend County Park

SA-26 | ♦♦ | ♿ | ♦♦

Location: Jupiter Farms [N26°57.357' W080°10.209'].

Length: 2.5-mile loop, with evolving options.

Map: Available in park brochure.

Contact Information: Palm Beach County Parks and Recreation Department (561-966-6660), 2700 6th Avenue South, Lake Worth, FL 33461.

Directions: West of Florida's Turnpike and I-95 on Indiantown Road (SR 706), the park entrance is just west of the Loxahatchee River, on the south side of the highway.

The Hike: A winding network of hard-packed pathways leads through this 800-acre park with its variety of habitats that focus on water: wet flatwoods, depression marshes, cypress strands, and cabbage palm hammocks along the Loxahatchee River.

Highlights: Linger in pleasant palm hammocks and enjoy birding along the impoundments on the Loxahatchee River floodplain.

Logistics: If the park is not yet fully open, inquire at the park office about hiking the trails that are currently in place. The hard-packed surface is ideal for wheelchairs with assistance. A portion of the trail system is a part of the new 72-mile Ocean to Lake Trail, connecting with Jonathan Dickinson State Park and Loxahatchee Slough Natural Area.

Other Activities: Paddlers can rent canoes and kayaks at the east entrance for put-in. A picnic area is under development.

Blowing Rocks Preserve

SA-27 **$** 📖 🚻

Location: Jupiter Island [N26°58.738' W080°05.041'].

Length: 2 miles in three trails.

Map: None available.

Contact Information: Blowing Rocks Preserve (772-744-6668), 574 South Beach Road, Hobe Sound, FL 33455.

Directions: Use Florida's Turnpike exit 116 or I-95 exit 87A, SR 706 (Indiantown Road), Jupiter. Drive east 5 miles to US 1. Turn left and continue north 1.3 miles to CR 707 (Beach Road). Turn right and follow the road north along Jupiter Island for 2.4 miles to the park entrance on the right—keep alert for the small parking area sign.

The Hike: From the nature center on the west side of the road, stairs lead down to the Restoration Trail along the Indian River Lagoon, which creates a loop through an open area that has been cleared of Australian pine and other invasive exotics and replaced with native plants, many of which have showy and fragrant blooms. The Sea Grape Path starts at the entrance kiosk at the parking lot and leads through a tunnel of sea grapes down toward the beach. At the dune crossover, turn left to follow the Dune Trail north, where it continues to be shaded by grapes but pops in and out of spots with sweeping scenic views of the Atlantic Ocean, eventually ending at a staircase that takes you down to the beach. Walk along the beach to create a loop.

Highlights: On the beach below the Sea Grape Path are the namesakes of this preserve, a tall outcropping of Anastasia limestone right at the shoreline, where wave action has created sea caves that you can visit at low tide. During a rough high tide, waves break up through chimneys in the caves, spurting upward to create the "blowing" rocks.

Logistics: The preserve is open 9:00–5:00 daily, but the parking area closes at 4:30 p.m. There is no charge to hike the Restoration Trail, but to use the Sea Grape Trail to visit Blowing Rocks Beach, there is an admission fee of $3, children 12 and under free.

Other Activities: Visit the nature center for an excellent overview of habitats in the area and an understanding of the Anastasia limestone formation. No swimming at this rocky beach!

Jupiter Ridge Natural Area

SA-28 ☐ 🚻 ♿ ⁂

Location: Jupiter [N26°54.966' W080°04.384'].

Length: 2.3 miles in two loops.

Map: On trailhead kiosk and in park brochure.

Contact Information: Palm Beach County Department of Environmental Resources Management (561-233-2400) 3323 Belvedere Road, Building 502, West Palm Beach, FL 33406-1548.

Directions: Use Florida's Turnpike exit 116 or I-95 exit 87A, SR 706 (Indiantown Road), Jupiter. Drive east 5 miles to US 1. Take US 1 south; the park entrance is on the right after 1 mile.

The Hike: The trail system consists of the Little Blue Heron Nature Trail, a wheelchair-accessible sidewalk which is the gateway into the preserve, crossing a boardwalk over a scrub pond before reaching the access to two unpaved loops: the Scrub Lizard Hiking Trail, a rugged 1.7-mile long loop over relict dunes, and the Pawpaw Hiking Trail, which leads 0.6 mile along a mangrove swamp and through open scrub.

Highlights: This is an incredibly beautiful patch of coastal scrub that was saved from development. Although the Scrub Lizard Hiking Trail is rough and deep in sand in places, as you clamber over the dunes, the bright white sand evokes images of ski slopes. Look for fingerlings of spike moss along the trail near the Indian River Lagoon.

Logistics: The park is open sunrise to sunset. There is a portable toilet at the trailhead. Bring plenty of water and sun protection for walking the shadeless paths through the open coastal scrub.

Other Activities: Launch or land your canoe along the trail on the Intracoastal Waterway. The Scrub Lizard Hiking Trail is a great birdwatching site for Florida scrub-jays.

Juno Dunes Natural Area

SA-29 📖 ♿ 👫

Location: Juno Beach [N26°53.139' W080°03.342'].

Length: 0.7-mile loop.

Map: Displayed and available with interpretive guide at main entrance kiosk.

Contact Information: Palm Beach County Department of Environmental Resources Management (561-233-2400), 3323 Belvedere Road, Building 502, West Palm Beach, FL 33406-1548.

Directions: The preserve is on US 1, south of Indiantown Road (SR 706), on the beach side of the road inside Loggerhead Park. Follow signs for "Beach Parking" rather than "Nature Trail." The trailhead is on the left, opposite the playground area.

The Hike: This short but pleasant hike through the diminutive coastal scrub preserved by this 576-acre tract affords a view of the scenery enjoyed by passengers on the Celestial Railroad circa 1889. Sliced in two by US 1, the preserve encompasses several habitats. The paved wheelchair-accessible trail leads over relict dunes to a high point with an observation shelter. From the shelter, you can look out across the Atlantic Ocean and to the preserve on the other side of US 1. The nearby scrub vegetation looks like a beautiful quilt of love vine and saw palmetto textured in orange and green. Follow the unpaved yellow-dot- blazed Royal Tern trail downhill and turn right at the trail junction to create a loop hike.

Highlights: This hike is great for kids because of its short length and the fun activities surrounding it. Large painted leaf (wild poinsettia) and coral beans show off bright red blooms in winter. Use the interpretive guide to track down some of the more unusual denizens of this forest, like the poisonwood—but don't touch!

Logistics: Park near the playground and start your hike at the kiosk. The preserve is open sunrise to sunset.

Other Activities: A short nature trail leading into coastal scrub from Loggerhead Park playground leads to an observation tower overlooking the Atlantic Ocean. Visit the Marinelife Center of Juno Beach to see sea turtles in rehab, or head down to the beach for swimming and sunning. A playground and picnic area provides a place for the kids to unwind.

Frenchman's Forest Natural Area

SA-30 📖 ♿

Location: Palm Beach Gardens [N26°51.420' W080°04.347'].

Length: 2.7 miles in three loops.

Map: Displayed and in brochure at trailhead kiosk.

Contact Information: Palm Beach County Department of Environmental Resources Management (561-233-2400) 3323 Belvedere Road, Building 502, West Palm Beach, FL 33406-1548.

Directions: From the intersection of PGA Boulevard and Prosperity Farms Road, east of the Gardens Mall, turn north and follow Prosperity Farms Road for 2 miles to the parking area on the left, just after you cross the creek.

The Hike: A pleasant set of three trails leads through a variety of ecosystems, including pine flatwoods, scrub, mangrove swamp, palm hammocks, cypress dome, and oak hammocks. The access trail through the uplands is wheelchair accessible; the yellow-blazed Saw Palmetto Hiking Trail is the main loop, with the red-blazed Cypress Trail a spur that crosses a cypress dome and loops through scrub habitat.

Highlights: Look for terrestrial orchids in the shady palm hammock at the end of the boardwalk across the cypress dome; enjoy the many large and old South Florida slash pines still standing in this forest. Gopher tortoises live in the sandy hills along the paved access trail.

Logistics: The park is open sunrise to sunset. No pets are allowed. The short paved portion of the trail is open to bikes.

Other Activities: There is good birdwatching from the covered observation platform on Lake Worth Creek.

Satinleaf Trail

John D. MacArthur Beach State Park

SA-31 $ ⬜ 🛉🛉 🛉🛉 🏠

Location: Singer Island [N26°49.710' W080°02.620'].

Length: 0.3-mile loop.

Map: Rough map in park brochure.

Contact Information: John D. MacArthur Beach State Park (561-624-6950), 10900 SR 703, North Palm Beach, FL 33408.

Directions: From I-95 exit 79A, drive east on PGA Boulevard, which becomes A1A after you cross US 1; watch for the park entrance road on the left after 4.7 miles. Once you pay your entrance fee, follow the "Nature Center" signs and park in the first parking area on the left. The trailhead is near the playground.

The Hike: Introducing a sliver of tropical hammock along the Lake Worth Lagoon, this quarter-mile loop immerses you in a jungle of unusual plants like tall mastic, gumbo limbo, and paradise trees, slender (and stinky) white stopper, pigeon plum, and blolly, and a dense tangle of marsh ferns, wild coffee, and silvery green saw palmettos in the understory. Interpretive markers introduce these denizens of South Florida's coastline.

Highlights: Walk down a corridor of paradise trees, their fern-like fronds shading the path, and pause for a break in the shade of a pigeon plum.

Logistics: Pick up an interpretive brochure at the kiosk for a better understanding of the tropical forest. Some of these plants are poisonous (such as the poisonwood), so be careful what you touch!

Other Activities: Enjoy the excellent nature center, the butterfly garden, a broad bridge across the lagoon great for birding, kayak rentals, and, of course, one of the most beautiful beaches in the region.

North Trail System

Grassy Waters Preserve

SA-32

Location: West Palm Beach [N26°48.931' W080°10.412'].

Length: 0.6-mile round trip and 1-mile loop.

Map: None available.

Contact Information: Grassy Waters Preserve (561-627-8831), 8264 Northlake Boulevard, West Palm Beach, FL 33412.

Directions: From Florida's Turnpike, follow PGA Boulevard 4.2 miles west to the Beeline (SR 710). Drive south 3.4 miles to Northlake Boulevard (CR 709A). Continue 1 mile west to the park entrance on the right, just beyond the south entrance.

The Hike: The 0.3-mile Eagle Trail starts at a pier and picnic tables on the north side of the lake, entering a narrow passage through a tropical hardwood hammock with myrsine, wild coffee, and cocoplum. The trail ascends a boardwalk through sawgrass on the edge of the marsh and comes to a dead end; return the same way. The 1-mile Hammock Trail traces the edge of the slough and then enters a dark palm hammock to make a loop.

Highlights: The observation deck at 0.2 mile has great views of the marshes and cypress sloughs. Watch for wading birds and alligators.

Logistics: The footpath is very rocky in places. Numerous signs keep you on the right trail. Do not attempt to circle the lake past the "Trail Ends Here" sign, as alligators are prevalent along the abandoned loop section of the trail.

Other Activities: Classes and interpretive programs are offered at the nature center on the south side of Northlake Boulevard (SA-33). There's picnicking and fishing, and birdwatching along the lake.

Raincatcher Boardwalk

Grassy Waters Preserve

SA-33 📖 🚻 ♿ 👫 ❄️

Location: West Palm Beach [N26°48.542' W080°10.209'].

Length: 0.8-mile boardwalk loop.

Map: Map with interpretive information available at nature center.

Contact Information: Grassy Waters Preserve (561-627-8831), 8264 Northlake Boulevard, West Palm Beach, FL 33412.

Directions: From Florida's Turnpike, follow PGA Boulevard 4.2 miles west to the Beeline (SR 710). Drive south 3.4 miles to Northlake Boulevard (CR 709A). Continue 0.9 mile west to the park entrance on the left.

The Hike: This interpretive boardwalk provides an excellent introduction to the Loxahatchee Slough, a slow-flowing "river of grass" through Palm Beach County. You walk beneath cypresses decked out in bromeliads and under tall slash pines. After the first 0.2 mile the Never Ending Boardwalk (always under construction) branches out to the right as a spur trail, passing by a chickee en route to the depths of the swamp, with an overlook over a broad wet prairie. Return along the same route, and continue to follow the loop back around to the nature center.

Highlights: The chickee is a place for quiet contemplation amid the bay trees. Enjoy the vast panoramas of wet prairie from the overlooks.

Logistics: The preserve is open 9:00–5:00 daily. A donation of $1 per person or $5 per carload is suggested.

Other Activities: Classes and interpretive programs are offered at the nature center. There's biking on the dike trails, canoe rentals at the nature center, and great birdwatching at the open overlook next to the parking area.

Royal Palm Beach Pines Natural Area

SA-34 📖 🚻 ♿ 👫

Location: Royal Palm Beach [N26°43.873' W080°14.958'].

Length: 3.6 miles in two loops.

Map: Displayed and in brochure at trailhead kiosk.

Contact Information: Palm Beach County Department of Environmental Resources Management (561-233-2400) 3323 Belvedere Road, Building 502, West Palm Beach, FL 33406-1548.

Directions: From Florida's Turnpike, take Okeechobee Boulevard (SR 704) west 5.8 miles to Royal Palm Beach Boulevard. Drive north 1.6 miles to Crestwood Boulevard; turn left. Drive 0.6 mile to the entrance of the Saratoga Pines subdivision, where you'll see a tiny brown "RPB Park" directional sign. Turn right, then right onto Saratoga Boulevard West, which makes a sharp curve to the right. After 0.7 mile, turn left on Natures Way, which ends in the parking lot of the preserve.

The Hike: A rare slice of the ancient Everglades habitat, this preserve encompasses nearly 770 acres of pine flatwoods and delicate prairies, part of the Loxahatchee Slough. From the trailhead, a short wheelchair-accessible trail leads to a nice view over a prairie pond. Two hiking trails, the Slash Pine Hiking Trail (blazed red) and the Pine Lily Hiking Trail (blazed yellow), create connected loops through the preserve, rounding the prairies.

Highlights: This is a great respite from surrounding suburbia, a place to get away into the woods. Enjoy beautiful prairie wildflowers all year long.

Logistics: The preserve has gated access, 9:00–sunset. There is a portable toilet at the parking area. The short wheelchair-accessible trail is suitable for small children, but the longer loops are not.

Other Activities: Birdwatch along the open prairies. There is a separate equestrian trail system (accessed from a separate trailhead).

Okeeheelee Nature Trail

Okeeheelee Park

SA-35 ▢ 👫 ♿ 👫 🐴

Location: West Palm Beach [N26°40.021' W080°10.085'].

Length: 2-plus miles, with 1.5-mile perimeter trail and shorter options.

Map: Detailed map with information on common plants and trees available at nature center and at trailhead.

Contact Information: Palm Beach County Parks and Recreation Department (561-966-6660), 2700 6th Avenue South, Lake Worth, FL 33461.

Directions: From I-95, drive west on Forest Hill Boulevard into Greenacres; one mile west of Jog Road, watch for the park entrance on the right at 7715 Forest Hill Boulevard. Follow the park entrance road back 1 mile to the nature center. The trail system starts behind the nature center.

The Hike: A network of wheelchair-accessible paved paths and hardpacked limestone natural walkways leads through pine flatwoods, oak hammocks, and along the edges of open meadows. Several overlooks provide scenic views over the ponds and over a fenced enclosure with deer.

Highlights: Enjoy the cypress pond overlook, walking through dense palm hammocks, and the natural-surface trails leading to blinds along the East Marsh.

Logistics: The trails are open daily from sunrise to sunset, the nature center and restrooms Tue–Fri 1:00–4:45, Sat 8:15–4:45, Sun 1:00–4:45. Guided tours are given; ask at the desk for details.

Other Activities: Okeeheelee is one of the county's largest recreational parks for day use, with fishing, boating, water skiing, ball fields, paved bike trails, golf, tennis, playgrounds, and numerous picnic pavilions.

Wetland Hammock Trail

Pine Jog Environmental Education Center

SA-36 📖 👫 👬

Location: West Palm Beach [N26°39.845' W080°08.466'].

Length: 0.5-mile loop.

Map: In interpretive brochure available at office or at kiosk in front of office.

Contact Information: Pine Jog Environmental Education Center (561-686-6600), 6301 Summit Boulevard, West Palm Beach, FL 33415.

Directions: From Florida's Turnpike, take Southern Boulevard east to Jog Road. Turn right and drive south 1 mile to Summit Boulevard. Turn left; the nature center entrance is on the left within 0.2 mile.

The Hike: Directly across from the parking area, the trail starts by meandering past a birdhouse to a loop around a large flatwoods pond. Keep to the right to walk around the far edge of the pond, where the next side trail leads you into a side loop through pine flatwoods and oak hammocks at various stages of growth. The trail completes its loop by coming back along the edge of the pond.

Highlights: This is a wonderful immersion in the habitats that have long been obliterated throughout West Palm Beach. Walking around the pond gives you great views across the water, and the opportunity to watch wading birds and frogs.

Logistics: The center is open 9:00–5:00 weekdays, 2:00–5:00 Sundays. In 2005, plans are to expand the trail system and to open the trail to the public on Saturdays. Benches along the way make this an easy walk for all ages. Some parts of the trail may flood after heavy rains.

Other Activities: The exhibit center offers information about habitats in the region.

Custard Apple Trail

John Prince Park

SA-37 ⬡ 🐕 👫

Location: Lake Worth [N26°36.121' W080°04.973'].

Length: 1 mile of trails, with walks from 0.3 to 0.5 mile.

Map: None available.

Contact Information: Palm Beach County Parks and Recreation Department (561-966-6660), 2700 6th Avenue South, Lake Worth, FL 33461.

Directions: The northern entrance of the park is on Lake Worth Road, 0.5 mile east of Congress; the southern entrances are off Congress north of Lantana Road at Prince Drive and 6th Avenue. From all entrances, head south on the main park road; follow signs toward the campground. Trailhead parking is on the left and the trail on the right 0.7 mile south of the Prince Drive entrance soon after a sharp left turn; watch for the trailhead sign.

The Hike: Meandering through tropical hammocks and open marshy areas, the trail system connects to the campground and includes five short named trails (Coot, Custard Apple, Cypress, Dahoon, Heron) as well as numerous unnamed beaten paths through the hammocks. Use Dahoon, Cypress, Custard Apple, and Heron to create a loop, or simply explore.

Highlights: Don't miss the trail's namesakes, several tall old custard apple trees (also known as pond apple) along the Custard Apple Trail. An unbroken forest of these trees once stretched from Lake Okeechobee to this region. Although an essential food for wildlife, their large green apples are not palatable. Watch for wading birds off the unmarked trails leading from the Cypress Trail to the marsh, and butterflies on the wildflowers in the open areas.

Logistics: The park is open sunrise to sunset. Restrooms are located at the secondary trailhead at the campground entrance.

Other Activities: John Prince Park offers numerous recreational opportunities, including lakeside camping (265 sites), picnicking, fishing, canoeing, golfing, and birding. There is both a bark-chip fitness trail and a lengthy paved biking/skating trail on-site.

Rosemary Scrub Natural Area

SA-38 ▢ ♿ 🚼

Location: Boynton Beach [N26°33.464' W080°04.048'].

Length: 0.4 mile in two loops.

Map: Displayed and in interpretive guide at trailhead kiosk.

Contact Information: Palm Beach County Department of Environmental Resources Management (561-233-2400) 3323 Belvedere Road, Building 502, West Palm Beach, FL 33406-1548.

Directions: From I-95 take Hypoluxo Road east to the first traffic light; turn south on Seacrest Boulevard and follow it 1 mile. The trailhead and parking are on the west side of the road.

The Hike: After starting out on the paved Red Bay Nature Trail, follow the yellow-dot blazes along a loop through open scrub on the Gopher Apple Hiking Trail, where this disturbed habitat is bouncing back to good health. Continue the trek on the paved trail under tall sand pines and silk bay to complete both loops.

Highlights: Although it encompasses only fourteen acres, this natural area protects an increasingly vanishing habitat for this region—a coastal scrub. Look for spike moss, fragrant tarflowers, and scrub mint returning to the open scrub, as well as the burrows of gopher tortoises and armadillos.

Logistics: The preserve is open sunrise to sunset. Parking is limited.

Other Activities: None.

Seacrest Scrub Natural Area

SA-39 📖 ♿ 🚻

Location: Boynton Beach [N26°29.754' W080°04.272'].

Length: 1 mile in two loops.

Map: Displayed and in interpretive guide at trailhead kiosk.

Contact Information: Palm Beach County Department of Environmental Resources Management (561-233-2400) 3323 Belvedere Road, Building 502, West Palm Beach, FL 33406-1548.

Directions: From I-95 take Boynton Beach Boulevard east to Seacrest Boulevard; turn right and drive south on Seacrest Boulevard to the park entrance on the left.

The Hike: The paved wheelchair-accessible Gopher Tortoise Trail leads through a scrub restoration area, where slash pines tower over the sand pines. Take a right and head down the natural footpath of the Sand Pine Trail to enjoy a 0.7-mile loop through the sand pine scrub habitat.

Highlights: Look for brilliant fall wildflowers along the Sand Pine Trail, and the opportunity to see gopher tortoises grazing through the scrub.

Logistics: The preserve is open sunrise to sunset. Be sure to close the gate behind you so the gopher tortoises don't escape!

Other Activities: Birdwatching.

Arthur R. Marshall Loxahatchee National Wildlife Refuge

SA-40 $ 🕮 🚻 👫 ♟

Location: Boynton Beach: Cypress Swamp Boardwalk [N26°29.961' W080°12.721'], Marsh Trail [N26°29.805' W080°12.800'].

Length: 1.2 miles in two marked trails, plus endless dikes to walk.

Map: Available at visitor center.

Contact Information: A.R.M. Loxahatchee National Wildlife Refuge (561-734-8303), 10216 Lee Road, Boynton Beach, FL 33437-4796.

Directions: From Florida's Turnpike, follow Boynton Beach Boulevard west for 1.9 miles until it ends at US 441. Turn left and drive 2 miles south to the park entrance on the right.

The Hike: Starting at the visitor center, the 0.4-mile Cypress Swamp Boardwalk surrounds you with the beauty of a cypress slough dense with bromeliads, orchids, and ferns. Follow the sidewalk and footpath across the entrance road to the picnic area near the chickee to find the start of the 0.8-mile Marsh Trail that loops around impoundment C-7, providing excellent views of the marshes and their inhabitants.

Highlights: The Cypress Swamp Boardwalk shouldn't be missed; it's a window into a precious Florida habitat that has long vanished from this region. Climb the observation tower along the Marsh Trail for a bird's-eye view of bird activity in the impoundments.

Logistics: The refuge is open sunrise to sunset. Dike trails are shared with bikes and are open and shadeless—use adequate sun protection and carry plenty of water.

Other Activities: Stop by the visitor center for an overview of the habitat before heading out on the trails. There is a canoe launch at the end of the park entrance road. Birding is great along the entire dike trail system—you'll see rare Everglades snail kites here.

Wakodahatchee Wetlands

SA-41 📖 ♿ 🚻

Location: Delray Beach [N26°28.669' W080°08.694'].

Length: 0.8-mile boardwalk.

Map: Map displayed and interpretive brochure available at trailhead kiosk.

Contact Information: Palm Beach County Water Utilities (561-641-3429), 13026 Jog Road, Delray Beach, FL 33446.

Directions: From Florida's Turnpike, follow Atlantic Boulevard east to Jog Road. Drive 1.6 miles north on Jog Road; the entrance is on the right.

The Hike: It's an easy stroll along an elevated boardwalk through a wetlands reclamation area used by Palm Beach County to filter treated wastewater. You walk above successive stages of marsh, from bulrush in the shallows to deeper water with alligator flag. A quarter-mile linear trail leads to a half-mile loop through the marsh.

Highlights: Marvel at the proximity of wading birds—they're everywhere. The sound of birds is incessant. Purple gallinules will hop right up on the railings as you walk by. Bring your camera! Creative purple martin birdhouses line one of the islands.

Logistics: The boardwalk is open sunrise to sunset. Covered gazebos and benches provide spots to sit and watch the birds.

Other Activities: Most folks who visit are here for the birds!

Nature Trail

Morikami Park

SA-42

Location: Delray Beach [N26°25.582' W080°09.332'].

Length: 0.6-mile loop.

Map: None.

Contact Information: Palm Beach County Parks and Recreation Department (561-966-6660), 2700 6th Avenue South, Lake Worth, FL 33461.

Directions: Drive 0.7 mile south on Jog Road from Linton Boulevard, and turn right on Morikami Park Road. Continue 0.5 mile west to the park entrance—go beyond the Morikami Museum entrance and turn left into the parking area.

The Hike: Somewhat abandoned since the development of Morikami Museum as an attraction, this interesting little loop introduces you to the pine flatwoods habitat and skirts areas once farmed in pineapples and other tropical produce. The shell path crosses a paved road twice, looping down past agricultural areas and through relict cypress domes thick with bromeliads.

Highlights: It's worth doing this walk just to read the beautiful interpretive signs and learn a little about George Morikami's contributions to farming and the local community.

Logistics: The trailhead is unmarked, so head down to the bus turnaround to find the trail starting on your left, where it soon passes a kiosk. Restrooms are available in the community center.

Other Activities: Both the Morikami Museum & Japanese Gardens and the American Orchid Society Botanical Gardens are adjacent to the park.

Delray Oaks Natural Area

SA-43 📖 ♿ 🚸

Location: Delray Beach [N26°25.628' W080°05.558'].

Length: 1-mile loop.

Map: Map displayed and interpretive brochure available at trailhead kiosk.

Contact Information: Palm Beach County Department of Environmental Resources Management (561-233-2400) 3323 Belvedere Road, Building 502, West Palm Beach, FL 33406-1548.

Directions: Trailhead parking is on the west side of Congress Avenue at 29th Street, just north of the Boca Raton city limits.

The Hike: Two trails provide access to this beautiful 25-acre oak hammock. The paved trail leads through deep shade to an observation platform over what was once the edge of the Yamato Marsh. Branching off to the south, the natural footpath blazed with yellow dots on posts creates a loop through the hammock and out into a relict patch of scrub.

Highlights: Enjoy the shady walk under the oaks; watch for large gopher tortoise burrows along the natural footpath.

Logistics: The trails are open sunrise to sunset.

Other Activities: More than sixty species of wildlife live on this patch of preserve—keep your eyes open!

Gumbo Limbo Nature Center

SA-44 📖 🚻 ♿ 👫

Location: Boca Raton [N26°21.983' W080°04.201'].

Length: 1 mile in two trails.

Map: None provided.

Contact Information: Gumbo Limbo Nature Center (561-338-1473), 1801 North Ocean Boulevard, Boca Raton, FL 33432.

Directions: From I-95 exit 44, Palmetto Park Road, drive east for 3.3 miles to A1A (Ocean Boulevard). Turn left and continue 1.1 miles north to the park entrance on the left, just beyond Red Reef Park.

The Hike: The wheelchair-accessible Coastal Hammock Boardwalk starts on the south side of the building, snaking through a dense tropical hammock out to the mangrove-lined shores of the Spanish River. Interpretive markers aid you in plant identification. Follow the many pathways and loops through the tangled jungle of forest, where an observation tower gets you up over the tree canopy. On the north side of the building, the North Loop meanders through a butterfly garden and through a grove of Australian pine to another walk along the river before looping back through the hammock.

Highlights: Several vantage points, including the top of the observation tower, provide great views of the Spanish River. Watch for giant land crabs lurking beneath the boardwalks.

Logistics: The center is open Mon–Sat 9:00–4:00, Sun 12:00–4:00. Admission is free, but a $2 donation is appreciated. If the parking area is full, park your car just south at Red Reef Park, where a connecting boardwalk links you to the trail system. Frequent benches make this an easy walk for all ages.

Other Activities: Don't miss the exhibits in the nature center!

Spanish River Boardwalk

James A. Rutherford Park

SA-45 ♿ 👫 ⛲

Location: Boca Raton [N26°22.087' W080°04.514'].

Length: 0.7 mile round-trip.

Map: None available.

Contact Information: City of Boca Raton (561-393-7700), 201 West Palmetto Park Road, Boca Raton, FL 33432.

Directions: Off US 1 (Federal Avenue) in Boca Raton, turn east onto NE 24th Street to enter the park.

The Hike: Follow the boardwalk along the edge of the Spanish River (Intracoastal Waterway) and into the depths of an old and grand forest of red and white mangroves. Ibises pick through the shady shallows. Trail's end is at an observation platform along a beach across from Gumbo Limbo Nature Center (SA-44).

Highlights: Numerous observation platforms provide sweeping views of the waterway. Watch the mangrove limbs and trunks for scuttling mangrove crabs, and look down into the clear water of the Spanish River for stingrays, pufferfish, and small sharks.

Logistics: The boardwalk has several entrances from the parking lot. For an optimal stroll, park in the first parking area just beyond the "Canoe Livery" sign and start your walk at the north end of the boardwalk.

Other Activities: Rent a canoe and explore the mangrove waterways, or take the kids up to the playground area set under shady banyan and fig trees. There's picnicking (with tableside grills in the fig grove), a soccer field, and a fitness trail. Enjoy birding from the boardwalk.

Serenoa Glade Preserve

SA-46 📖 🚻 ♿ 👫

Location: Boca Raton [N26°21.844' W080°06.523'].

Length: 0.5-mile loop.

Map: At beginning of loop on interpretive kiosk, with interpretive guides available.

Contact Information: City of Boca Raton (561-393-7700), 201 West Palmetto Park Road, Boca Raton, FL 33432.

Directions: From I-95, take Glades Road 0.5 mile east. Turn south on NW 10th Avenue, then west on NW 15th Street to the entrance to George Snow Park on the right. Park and head back toward the tennis courts to find the entrance to Serenoa Glade Preserve hidden in the trees.

The Hike: Half of the loop is paved (accessible to wheelchairs), half earthen, as you meander through scrub and pine flatwoods along one of Boca Raton's high points, the Atlantic Coastal Ridge, with lots of shade under gnarled oaks. Green numbered markers along the trail correspond to the interpretive guide. After you round the corner past marker 4, the broad earthen footpath takes off to the left into the scrub through saw palmetto and wiregrass, returning to the main loop after 0.2 mile.

Highlights: This is a rare piece of the Atlantic Coastal Ridge with a transition zone, from scrub on the ocean side to pine flatwoods on the Everglades side, which was fortunately preserved from becoming yet another office complex.

Logistics: The preserve is open 8:00 a.m. to sunset.

Other Activities: Adjacent George Snow Park has picnic tables, a playground, and basketball and tennis courts.

Sugar Sand Park

SA-47 ▢ ▨ ⌂

Location: Boca Raton: Sand Pine [N26°20.754' W080°07.508'], Slash Pine [N26°20.694' W080°07.612'].

Length: Two separate 0.3-mile loops.

Map: Interpretive brochure for each trail available at front desk of Community Center.

Contact Information: Sugar Sand Park (561-347-3913), 300 South Military Trail, Boca Raton, FL 33486.

Directions: The entrance to Sugar Sand Park is on the east side of Military Trail between Palmetto Park Road and Camino Real in Boca Raton. Follow the park road 0.2 mile to the Explorium parking, and park near the playground. Marked with a "Nature Trail" sign, the Sand Pine Nature Trail starts from the eastern (forested) edge of the parking lot. The Slash Pine Nature Trail starts on the opposite side of the Explorium.

The Hike: Lined with bark chips, the Sand Pine Nature Trail meanders through a shady sand pine scrub with scattered Chapman oaks in the understory; the Slash Pine Nature Trail takes you through an upland slash pine and palmetto forest. Green markers correspond to the interpretive brochures. On each trail, you can either return by the same path or use the paved bike trail to loop back to the parking area.

Highlights: Enjoy the fragrant tarflowers in bloom, and watch for gopher tortoise burrows along the trail. Look for strangler figs wrapped around their cabbage palm hosts.

Logistics: The park is open 8 a.m. to sunset.

Other Activities: This 132-acre park provides numerous facilities, including ball fields, a paved trail, a large children's playground, and the Children's Science Explorium, a free science center with interactive activities and programs.

Cathy Burdett Nature Trail

South County Regional Park

SA-48 📖 🚻 ♿ 👫

Location: Boca Raton [N26°22.762' W080°13.542'].

Length: 0.6-mile boardwalk.

Map: Displayed at trailhead.

Contact Information: Daggerwing Nature Center (561-488-9953), 11200 Park Access Road, Boca Raton, FL 33498.

Directions: From US 441 in Boca Raton, take Glades Road west to Cain Boulevard. Drive 0.3 mile north to Park Access Boulevard; follow this road 1 mile to the nature center, just past the water park.

The Hike: The boardwalk starts from the nature center and crosses a wetlands area into a dark tropical hammock dense with large pond apple trees, strangler fig, and myrsine. A spur trail leads to an observation tower that looks out over the canopy. The woods are a riot of green, with ferns carpeting the forest floor. The boardwalk ends at interpretive marker 10; plans are for future expansion of the walkway. Return to the nature center by retracing your path.

Highlights: The boardwalk stands high above the forest floor, so you have a great up-close view of the canopy. This is an old forest, with massive strangler fig and pond apple trees, Jamaican satinleaf, and giant leather ferns. The roots dangling from strangler figs make it look like a jungle!

Logistics: The nature center and restrooms are open Tues–Fri 1:00–4:30, Sat 9:00–4:30, closed Sun–Mon.

Other Activities: This is a large county park with many facilities, including a water park just across the road from the nature center.

Doris Davis Foreman Wilderness Area

SA-49 📖 ♿ 👫

Location: Parkside [N26°19.258' W080°13.357'].

Length: 0.5-mile loop.

Map: Displayed at trailhead kiosk.

Contact Information: Broward County Parks and Recreation (954- 357-8100), 950 NW 38th Street, Oakland Park, FL 33309-5982.

Directions: From US 441/SR 7, 1.7 miles north of the Sawgrass Expressway, turn west on Loxahatchee Road. Drive 1.2 miles to Parkside Drive; turn south. Parking at the trailhead entrance is on the east side of the road, just past the elementary school.

The Hike: Although this patch of wilderness is only twenty acres, the loop trail stays deep in the woods, giving this urban walk a truly wild feel. Follow the paved trail clockwise to an outdoor amphitheatre; turn right to start along the lengthy boardwalk across a cypress stand. The trail loops back through pine flatwoods to its beginning point.

Highlights: It's a botanical delight—blooming bromeliads in the trees, pond apples and cocoplums along the trail, and numerous varieties of ferns amid the cypresses.

Logistics: The park is open 8:00–6:00.

Other Activities: Geocaching.

Tall Cypress Natural Area

SA-50 📖 🚻 ♿ 👫

Location: Coral Springs [N26°16.575' W080°12.813'].

Length: 0.5-mile loop.

Map: Displayed at trailhead kiosk.

Contact Information: Broward County Parks and Recreation (954-357-8100), 950 NW 38th Street, Oakland Park, FL 33309-5982.

Directions: From the intersection of US 441 and Sample Road, drive west 3 miles to Turtle Run Boulevard. Turn right and follow the road 0.1 mile to the preserve entrance on the left.

The Hike: This boardwalk trail winds its way through a cypress slough that is a wonderland of ferns. A profusion of giant sword ferns, marsh ferns, giant leather ferns, and many others fill the understory. Tropical trees grow on the matted soil: pigeon plum, paradise tree, satinleaf, and strangler figs. The trail leads upward into a pine flatwoods, emerging into full sun under tall slash pines. Pond cypresses rise above you as you come to a T intersection; to the left is a gazebo overlook on the pine flatwoods. Continue to the right to complete the loop.

Highlights: Come for the deep green "bowl" of ferns beneath the cypresses, and the many types of tropical trees scattered throughout the wetlands.

Logistics: The trail is open 8:00–6:00. There are soda machines at the trailhead, and benches provided at comfortable intervals.

Other Activities: This is an excellent spot for birding—watch for woodpeckers in the pines.

A riot of ferns at the Tall Cypress Natural Area.

Deerfield Island Park

SA-51 📖 🚹🚺

Location: Deerfield Beach [N26°18.883' W080°04.897'].

Length: 1.3 miles in two loop trails.

Map: In park brochure; self-guided interpretive brochure available at park office.

Contact Information: Deerfield Island Park (954-360-1320), 1720 Deerfield Island Park, Deerfield Beach, FL 33441.

Directions: From US 1 (Federal Highway) drive east on Hillsboro Boulevard to the Chamber of Commerce building on the left; turn north on Riverview Road and follow it to the end. You must use the park's free shuttle boat or your own private craft to get to the park.

The Hike: A paved trail leads from the information kiosk to the two nature trails. The Coquina Trail runs 0.5 mile through the hardwood hammock, with an observation platform overlooking the Intracoastal Waterway. The Mangrove Trail starts off in the other direction and has a boardwalk through a mangrove forest.

Highlights: This is a designated urban wilderness area, with great views of the Intracoastal Waterway.

Logistics: Shuttle boats depart from the dock on a regular schedule; call for times and days. A marina is available for private boats on a first-come-first-served basis.

Other Activities: There's picnicking, and horseshoes and volleyball.

Pond Apple Trail

Tradewinds Park South

SA-52 📖 ▦

Location: Coconut Creek [N26°15.801' W080°10.620'].

Length: 0.5-mile boardwalk loop.

Map: None available.

Contact Information: Tradewinds Park (954-968-3880), 3600 Sample Road, Coconut Creek, FL 33073.

Directions: The entrance to Tradewinds Park South is just west of Florida's Turnpike on Sample Road. Follow the park road 1.2 miles south to its end at Frittilary Shelter and disc golf course. From the parking lot, walk along any of the paved trails toward the canal; look for the boardwalk entrance with its "Slippery When Wet" sign.

The Hike: Hidden in a back corner of this popular urban park, the well-worn boardwalk circles a primeval pond apple and cypress swamp, immersing you in a slice of the long-departed Everglades habitat that once thrived on this side of the Atlantic Coastal Ridge. Follow the loop clockwise. Numbered pond apples painted on the railing correspond to an interpretive brochure.

Highlights: Enjoy this peaceful relict of what Coconut Creek used to look like before land reclamation efforts in the early 1900s. Scan the black water for alligators, and marvel at the massive pond apple and cocoplum trees.

Logistics: The boardwalk is very slippery when wet. And this is a swamp—expect mosquitoes and wear repellent. There's a park entrance fee of $1 on weekends only.

Other Activities: Numerous activities include picnicking, disc golf, and the Butterfly World attraction.

Fern Forest Nature Center

SA-53 📖 🚹 ♿ 🚼 ❄️

Location: Coconut Creek [N26°13.780' W080°11.209'].

Length: 2.2 miles in four trails.

Map: In park brochure, available at nature center.

Contact Information: Fern Forest Nature Center (954-970-0150), 201 Lyons Road South, Coconut Creek, FL 33063.

Directions: On Atlantic Boulevard (FL 814), drive west from Florida's Turnpike or I-95 to Lyons Road. Turn right just beyond the traffic light, at the "Fern Forest Nature Center Ramp" sign. The loop turns you southbound on Lyons Road; after 0.3 mile the park entrance is on the right.

The Hike: The trail system encompasses four trails: the wheelchair-accessible Cypress Creek Trail, a boardwalk that circles the floodplain of what was once Cypress Creek; the Prairie Overlook Trail, which loops through cabbage palms and slash pines en route to an overlook on an open prairie; the Wetlands Wander, a ribbon of trail following a dark slough; and the Red Maple Walk, a slippery foray into a red maple swamp.

Highlights: At least thirty-four species of ferns grow in this park—you'll marvel at how lush and dense they are along the Cypress Creek Trail, where the rocky edges of now-dry Cypress Creek are a sobering reminder of how the draining of the eastern Everglades changed this region forever.

Logistics: The park is open daily 8:00–6:00. No pets. If you attempt the Red Maple Walk, you will get wet, muddy shoes; bring spares!

Other Activities: Visit the interactive nature center before setting off on your walk, and bring a picnic lunch to enjoy in the picnic area.

Colohatchee Natural Park

SA-54 📖 🚻 ♿ 👥

Location: Wilton Manors [N26°09.231' W080°07.761'].

Length: 0.3-mile boardwalk loop.

Map: None available.

Contact Information: Colohatchee Natural Park (954-390-2130), 1975 NE 15th Avenue, Wilton Manors, FL 33305.

Directions: From I-95, take the Sunrise Boulevard exit for Fort Lauderdale. Follow Sunrise east to NE 15th Avenue, and turn left. Continue north into Wilton Manors on NE 15th Avenue for 1.1 miles. After the traffic circle, you cross the South Fork of the Middle River. The park is on the left side of the road; a boat ramp is on the right.

The Hike: Starting at the parking lot, the interpretive boardwalk winds its way through a dark forest of young red and black mangroves along the South Fork of the Middle River to access the park's open recreational area. In the 1890s, settler William C. Collier planted an orange grove near here and traded with the Seminoles, who named the river "Colohatchee" in his honor. Salt water intrusion up the river now brings mangroves to this inland area, where it is likely a hammock of cypresses and pond apples once thrived.

Highlights: Watch for mangrove crabs scuttling along the boardwalk and on the mangrove trunks. There's great birding in the open understory, and a nice little observation deck along the river.

Logistics: The park is open 9:00–5:00 daily except Tuesday. There is a $1 entrance fee on weekends and holidays. The fenced parking area has a limited number of spaces; use the boat ramp parking if the main parking lot is too crowded. Expect mosquitoes.

Other Activities: Launch boats, canoes, and kayaks at the boat ramp, picnic in the mangrove forest, or play basketball, volleyball, or horseshoes in the park.

Habitat Restoration Nature Trail

Easterlin Park

SA-55 ▢ 🚻 ⛺ 🐕

Location: Oakland Park [N26°10.387' W080°09.731'].

Length: 0.9-mile loop.

Map: Outline in park brochure.

Contact Information: Easterlin Park (954-938-0610), 1000 NW 38th Street, Oakland Park, FL 33309.

Directions: From I-95 exit 31A, drive one block east to Powerline Road. Take this north for 0.4 mile to NW 38th Street, and turn left. The park entrance is on the left after 0.2 mile.

The Hike: A loop around the perimeter of this designated Urban Wilderness Area, the broad trail meanders through an ancient forest of cypresses and royal palms past marshlands with standing water, where ferns and pond apple thrive. Although the constant roar of vehicles makes it sound like you're walking down the interstate, you can't see them, you just hear them—a strange juxtaposition with the dense forest. After 0.7 mile the trail ends at the far edge of the campground, and you must walk around the lake to return to the trailhead.

Highlights: Although surrounded by a cocoon of traffic noise, the footpath winds through a gorgeous hammock with cypresses more than two centuries old, their knees pushing up from dark rich soil.

Logistics: Visitors pay a $1 entrance fee on weekends and holidays. Check in at the park office for an interpretive brochure. The trail may be wet and squishy in places. This is one of the few hikes I've encountered where wearing headphones and listening to music while walking the trail would enhance the experience.

Other Activities: There's camping, picnicking, fishing, and two playgrounds.

Beach Hammock Trail

Hugh Taylor Birch State Park

SA-56 **$** 📖 🚻 🚫

Location: Ft. Lauderdale Beach [N26°08.364' W080°06.257'].

Length: 0.3-mile loop.

Map: Rough sketch on park map.

Contact Information: Hugh Taylor Birch State Park (954-564-4521), 3109 East Sunrise Boulevard, Fort Lauderdale, FL 33304.

Directions: From I-95, follow Sunrise Boulevard east across the Intracoastal Waterway to Fort Lauderdale Beach; the park entrance is on the left 1 mile east of US 1.

The Hike: Starting off by heading down between impounds where coots play, the trail enters a shady coastal tropical hammock. Turn right at the trail junction and walk beneath the ancient sea grapes and strangler fig, gumbo limbo and myrsine. Coming back around the loop, you can gaze out over the pond from the high relict dunes before returning to the trailhead.

Highlights: Although you can hear traffic from the nearby roads, the beauty of the hammock is a counterpoint to the noisy reality of Fort Lauderdale Beach.

Logistics: After you enter the park, turn right into the first parking area to find the trailhead. Be wary of raccoons that ramble through the area looking for handouts.

Other Activities: You can picnic, swim, fish on the Intracoastal Waterway, and bicycle around the park road loop. The visitor center is on the beach side along A1A north of Sunrise Boulevard, and there is a second nature trail (SA-57) that starts at the main picnic area.

Exotic Trail

Hugh Taylor Birch State Park

SA-57 **$** 📖 🚻 👫 🐕

Location: Fort Lauderdale Beach [N26°08.714' W080°06.746'].

Length: 0.5 mile round-trip.

Map: Rough sketch on park map.

Contact Information: Hugh Taylor Birch State Park (954-564-4521), 3109 East Sunrise Boulevard, Fort Lauderdale, FL 33304.

Directions: From I-95, follow Sunrise Boulevard east across the Intracoastal Waterway to Fort Lauderdale Beach; the park entrance is on the left 1 mile east of US 1.

The Hike: Begin your walk near the picnic area and playground, following the brown posts with yellow numbers as you enter a hammock filled with noninvasive non-native plants, mostly planted in the 1890s as part of Terramar, the estate of Hugh Taylor Birch, a Chicago attorney. Although the park is surrounded by city, you'll encounter a lot of wildlife, from rabbits and squirrels to lizards and giant land crabs. Built by Boy Scouts, this trail showcases some of the more unusual plants on the former estate, like traveler's palm and sapodilla, all growing in a natural forest setting.

Highlights: Make sure you get a copy of the interpretive brochure to fully appreciate the unusual species of plants along this trail!

Logistics: Ask for the interpretive brochure at the ranger station. The trail may be damp in places. Instead of retracing your steps after a quarter mile, you can also use the paved bike path to continue on a 2-mile walk around the park.

Other Activities: You can picnic, swim, fish on the Intracoastal Waterway, and bicycle around the park road loop. The visitor center is on the beach side along A1A north of Sunrise Boulevard, and there is a second nature trail (SA-56) at the first parking area.

Secret Woods Nature Center

SA-58 📖 🚻 ♿ 👫

Location: Dania [N26°05.341' W080°10.639'].

Length: 1 mile in two trails.

Map: In park brochure.

Contact Information: Secret Woods Nature Center (954-791-1030), 2701 West SR 84, Fort Lauderdale, FL 33312.

Directions: From I-95, use exit 25. Follow SR 84 west over the bridge to the park entrance on the right.

The Hike: From the trailhead, two trails head off in opposite directions. The Laurel Oak Trail is a bark chip footpath that meanders through upland forest and around a cypress swamp, and the New River Trail is a wheelchair-accessible boardwalk that winds through floodplain forest and mangroves en route to the edge of the New River.

Highlights: Get up close and personal to giant land crabs along the Laurel Oak Trail, and watch ibises and herons roost along the New River Trail, where it's fun to walk through the tangled jungle of mangroves.

Logistics: The park is open 8:00–6:00. No bicycles or pets are permitted. Numerous benches along both trails make this an easy walk for all ages.

Other Activities: The nature center is Broward County's first, and includes interpretive displays and a living beehive.

Woodmont Natural Area

SA-59 📖 ♿ 🚻 🎣

Location: Tamarac [N26°12.756' W080°15.492'].

Length: 0.4-mile loop.

Map: None provided.

Contact Information: Broward County Parks and Recreation (954-357-8100), 950 NW 38th Street, Oakland Park, FL 33309-5982.

Directions: From Florida's Turnpike exit 62, SR 870 (Commercial Boulevard), drive west 2.8 miles to University Avenue. Follow University Avenue north 1 mile. Turn on McNab Road, and continue 0.3 mile to NW 80th Avenue. Drive 0.2 mile north; the park is on the right.

The Hike: This is a combination paved trail and boardwalk through the last patch of undeveloped land in Tamarac, 22 acres of pine flatwoods surrounded by suburbia. The understory of the forest has colorful lantana, beautyberry, and wild coffee, as well as mounds of wild balsam apple and grapevines. Strangler fig roots dangle from the upper canopy. The trail parallels a canal across from an apartment complex on the return trip.

Highlights: The boardwalk crosses a pond cypress swamp. Birdsong is constant; listen for the hooting of barred owls and the rat-a-tat-tat of the pileated woodpecker.

Logistics: The park is open 8:00–6:00. There are no facilities except a parking area.

Other Activities: Birders will enjoy this patch of urban habitat—listen for chirps and calls throughout the woods.

Barrier Island Nature Trail

John U. Lloyd Beach State Park

SA-60 **$** 📖 🚻 👫

Location: Dania Beach [N26°04.117' W080°06.746'].

Length: 0.5-mile loop.

Map: Rough map in park brochure.

Contact Information: John U. Lloyd Beach State Park (954-923-2833), 6503 North Ocean Drive, Dania Beach, FL 33304-3044.

Directions: From I-95 exit 21, drive east on Sheridan Street to North A1A; turn left and continue 1.5 miles to the park entrance.

The Hike: This is a natural footpath through a coastal hammock altered by invasive species such as Australian pines, Brazilian pepper, and melaleuca. In the spots where the original hammock of strangler fig, wild coffee, myrsine, and sea grapes still shades the trail, the vegetation crowds in close. At 0.1 mile there is a shortcut across the loop to provide a shorter walk. Stay on the outer loop for the full walk, or do a figure-8: turn right and duck under the sea grapes to reach a mangrove-lined canal; turn left to walk north along the marsh. The trail turns back to the south through the invasive species to complete the loop.

Highlights: Along the marsh you can hear the sound of the surf breaking behind the mangroves. This beach was once part of the route of the Barefoot Mailman, who walked between Lake Worth and Miami in the 1880s to deliver the mail.

Logistics: Tall folks will find themselves frequently ducking under branches on this trail! There are several unmarked forks on the trail, but the slender spit of land prevents the possibility of getting too far off course.

Other Activities: This is a popular beach for swimming and sunning. During turtle nesting and hatching season, volunteers offer nighttime walks on the beach; call the park for details.

Ann Kolb Memorial Trail

Plantation Heritage Park

SA-61 🚻 🚺 🐕

Location: Plantation [N26°06.440' W080°13.321'].

Length: 0.2-mile loop.

Map: Route shown in park brochure in red (yellow is fitness trail).

Contact Information: Plantation Heritage Park (954-791-1025), 1100 South Fig Tree Lane, Plantation, FL 33317.

Directions: Take I-595 west to University Drive, and drive north 1.3 miles to Broward Avenue. Turn right and continue 1.5 miles east to Fig Tree Lane. Alternatively, head west from US 441 for 1.5 miles on Broward Avenue. Drive south on Fig Tree Lane to the park entrance on the left. Follow the park road past the office. When the road forks after 0.5 mile, keep right and park your car next to the playground.

The Hike: This park is the site of a former University of Florida agricultural experimentation farm, and the trail loops through part of the farm with representative native plant communities, including tropical hardwood hammock, coastal strand, and pine flatwoods. The trail starts next to the pedestrian side entrance to the park—look for the bark chip path. The path makes a sharp right after you see the bus station on the corner, entering deep shade under gumbo limbo, mimosa, and flamebush before emerging within sight of the playground.

Highlights: It's a tiny oasis of trees in the urban mass, and you skirt rare fruit orchards.

Logistics: The park is open 8:00–7:30. Stop at the office for a map. Visitors pay $1 entrance fee on weekends and holidays. The path can be indecipherable in places, so look for bark chips to lead the way.

Other Activities: There are picnic shelters, a playground, a fitness trail, and fishing.

Tree Tops Park

SA-62 🚻 ♿ 🧒 🐴

Location: Davie [N029°04.469' W080°16.531'].

Length: 3.1 miles in two trails.

Map: Rough map displayed at park office.

Contact Information: Tree Tops Park (954-370-3750), 3900 SW 100th Avenue, Davie, FL 33328.

Directions: From I-595 take exit 4, Nob Hill Road; drive south for 2.6 miles to the park entrance on the left. Follow the park entrance road back to the park office.

The Hike: The trail to Pine Island Ridge begins behind the park office, and is a paved path leading through the hammock out to a slender ridge that was once a tree island surrounded by the sawgrass of the Everglades, the site of a significant Seminole village. Two footpaths branch off the paved path to further explore the island. In front of the park office, follow the sidewalk to the west to the "Hiking Trail" sign to enter a network of footpaths meandering through oak hammocks and out to the edge of a large flatwoods pond.

Highlights: Climb up the observation tower for an up-close look at the live oak canopy, or sit along the pond and watch the wading birds as they fish for their dinners.

Logistics: The park is open 8:00–sunset. Visitors pay a $1 entrance fee on weekends and holidays.

Other Activities: You'll find a canoe rental near the park entrance, fishing in the ponds and wetlands, a butterfly garden, picnic groves, and a playground and Safety Town for kids.

Ann Kolb Nature Center

West Lake Park

SA-63   📖   🚻   ♿   👫

Location: Hollywood: Lake Observation Trail [N26°02.322' W080°07.201'], Mudflat Trail [N26°02.273' W080°07.166'].

Length: 1 mile in two round-trip trails.

Map: Available at nature center.

Contact Information: West Lake Park (954-926-2410), 1200 Sheridan Street, Hollywood, FL 33019.

Directions: From I-95 exit 21, drive east on Sheridan Street to the park entrance on the left, just before the bridge over the Intracoastal Waterway.

The Hike: The Lake Observation Trail is a boardwalk that drops down from the base of the observation tower into the mangrove forest and out onto West Lake, a large brackish lagoon, to an observation platform. The Mudflat Trail is not an interpretive trail, but it crosses a boardwalk to an island of Australian pines past the holes of giant land crabs, and briefly becomes a paved trail through the mangrove forest to another boardwalk, which ends at a shaded observation platform with seats on a cove of West Lake.

Highlights: Mangroves, mangroves, and more mangroves—plus a tall observation tower (with elevator!) to look out over the tidal flats.

Logistics: Interpretive markers along the Lake Observation Trail correspond to numbers in a $2 booklet available at the visitor center. The trails are shadeless, so use sun protection. No dogs are permitted.

Other Activities: Ecotours depart from the dock near the nature center. Before walking the trails, explore the nature center for a better understanding of the habitats around West Lake. This is a popular site for paddlers; kayak and canoe rentals are available. A bike trail, shown on the hiking map, leads to the south end of the park.

Greynolds Park

SA-64 👫

Location: North Miami Beach: Lakeshore Trail [N025°56.384' W080°09.182'], Oleta River Trail [N025°56.537' W080°09.171'].

Length: 1.7 miles in two trails.

Map: In brochure available at park office.

Contact Information: Greynolds Park (305-945-3425), 17530 West Dixie Highway, North Miami Beach, FL 33160.

Directions: From I-95 exit 19, drive east on Miami Gardens Drive for 2.1 miles to NE 22nd Avenue. Turn right. The park entrance is immediately on the left. Once inside, turn right and drive along the park road to Paradise Park Circle. Park at the far end near the stone bridge.

The Hike: The Lakeside Nature Trail meanders around impoundments created by rock quarries created in the 1890s; tropical trees surround the rock-lined waterways. Starting by the boathouse, the Oleta River Nature Trail is a boardwalk through a dense mangrove forest along the Oleta River, leading to a paved trail that takes you down along the river to an observation platform.

Highlights: You have the chance of seeing a crocodile in the Oleta River, and feral iguanas resting on tree limbs around the waterways.

Logistics: A $1 entrance fee is charged on weekends and holidays.

Other Activities: This is a popular picnicking park, with several playgrounds. Fishing is permitted from boardwalks and platforms on the ponds; boats are available for rental at the boathouse.

Arch Creek Park

SA-65 📖 👫 👫 🦮

Location: North Miami [N25°54.049' W080°09.742'].

Length: 0.3-mile trail system.

Map: Self-guiding trail map with interpretive information available at park museum.

Contact Information: Arch Creek Park (305-944-6111), 1855 NE 135th Street, North Miami, FL 33181.

Directions: From US 1 (Biscayne Boulevard), turn west on NE 135th Street, several blocks north of NE 125th Street and the Bal Harbor Causeway. The park entrance is on the right within the first block.

The Hike: This tropical hammock was the site of a Tequesta Indian village between 500 BC and AD 1300. Gentle natural footpaths wind through the dark forest, where plant identifications add to your knowledge of South Florida's tropical plants.

Highlights: Even though the natural arch of Arch Creek collapsed several decades ago, the limestone canyon is still worth a look. The arch was the original "Gateway to Miami" and a bridge on the military trail of the 1800s.

Logistics: The park is open 9:00–5:00 daily. Parking is limited near the museum; consider parking farther down the road and accessing the trail system from its far end. Numerous benches and chickees provide rest stops.

Other Activities: Stop in at the museum to learn about the long history of this intriguing archaeological and geological site.

Bear Cut Nature Preserve

SA-66 $ 📖 🚻 ♿ 🚻

Location: Key Biscayne: Osprey Beach Trail [N25°42.621' W080°09.026'], Tequesta Hammock Trail [N25°42.966' W080°09.057'], Bear Cut Nature Trail [N25°42.961' W080°09.047'].

Length: 2.2 miles in three loops.

Map: On kiosk near parking lot, and in brochure available at nature center.

Contact Information: Bear Cut Nature Preserve (305-361-6767), 6767 Crandon Boulevard, Key Biscayne, FL 33149.

Directions: Take I-95 exit 1A to the Rickenbacker Causeway ($1 bridge toll) to Key Biscayne. Continue on Crandon Boulevard to Crandon Park ($4 parking fee). The preserve is at the north end of the North Entrance beach parking area on the left.

The Hike: Start out behind the nature center with a walk down the 1.3-mile Osprey Beach Trail, a broad mowed path along the coastal dunes with several beach crossovers. Where it meets the paved path (the 1.3-mile Fossil Reef Bike Trail), continue straight ahead to a boardwalk that leads out to a scenic view. Retrace your path or use the paved path (left fork) to return to the nature center, where the 0.3-mile Bear Cut Nature Trail and 0.3-mile Tequesta Hammock Trail create short rugged loops through the tropical hardwood hammock.

Highlights: Enjoy the constant sound of the waves strumming the sand from the Osprey Beach Trail, where ultraviolet morning glories drape over the vegetation. At the end of the boardwalk you'll see a 6,000-year-old fossilized mangrove forest reef—well worth the trip!

Logistics: Crandon Park is open 9:00–5:00 daily. There is no shade on the Osprey Beach Trail. The Bear Cut Nature Trail is short but very rugged. Before you hike, pick up an interpretive guide at the nature center. Wheelchairs can use the bike trail to access the boardwalk to the fossil reef overlook on Biscayne Bay.

Other Activities: Enjoy swimming and sunning at the beach, and picnicking under the shade of the sea grapes. Don't miss the exhibits, artwork, and gift shop at the Marjorie Stoneman Douglas Nature Center.

Nature Trail

A. D. Barnes Park

SA-67 📖 🚻 ♿ 🚼 🐕‍🦺

Location: Miami [N025°44.306' W080°18.535'].

Length: 0.6-mile paved trail system.

Map: None available.

Contact Information: A. D. Barnes Park (305-666-5883), 3401 SW 72nd Avenue, Miami, FL 33155.

Directions: From FL 976, follow Bird Road (SW 40th Street) east 0.5 mile to SW 72nd Avenue. Turn left. The park entrance is immediately on the right. Inside the park, turn left and follow the park road around to the Leisure Center. Enter the trail system on a walkway through the beautiful tiled mural.

The Hike: The paved path leads through pine flatwoods back to the Sense of Wonder Nature Center, where it forks into several options, continuing through a shady oak hammock to an observation deck set under the forest canopy, where strangler figs and sword ferns thrive.

Highlights: Savor the burbling water down oolite boulders overgrown in ladder brake ferns, the butterfly garden, and the tiny slice of pine rockland habitat tucked in the back corner.

Logistics: The Leisure Center entrance to the trail system must be used when the nature center is closed.

Other Activities: The Sense of Wonder Nature Center is open Mon–Fri 9:00–6:00, Sat–Sun 10:00–6:00.

Hammock Trail

Matheson Hammock Park

SA-68 📖 ❄️

Location: Coral Gables [N25°40.927' W080°16.296'].

Length: 1.4 miles round-trip.

Map: On trailhead kiosk.

Contact Information: Matheson Hammock Park (305-666-6979), 9610 Old Cutler Road, Coral Gables, FL 33156.

Directions: From US 1, take Red Road east to Old Cutler Road. Turn north and drive past Fairchild Gardens before reaching Matheson Hammock Park on the right. Park your car in the nearest parking area to the park entrance. The trailhead kiosk is along the paved path to the picnic area.

The Hike: From the kiosk, follow the paved path back past the picnic area and restrooms to the start of the trail; turn right and walk through a short stretch of tropical hammock. You emerge at Old Cutler Road. Carefully cross the road and continue to the trailhead for the West Hammock Trail. This trail forms a loop through a shady tropical hammock, with dense foliage and outcroppings of limestone.

Highlights: Watch for caves and sinkholes along the trail, where ferns grow lushly around their edges. Just imagine—this is what much of Coral Gables used to look like!

Logistics: The numbered signposts correspond to an interpretive guide available at the trailhead. The trail is rather rocky and rugged. The mosquitoes can be fierce—use insect repellent.

Other Activities: If you continue farther down the park road, there is an entrance fee to enter the main part of the park, which has swimming, a marina, concession facilities, sea kayaking, and a paved bike trail.

Old Cutler Hammock Nature Trail

Bill Sadowski Park & Nature Center

SA-69   📖   🚻   👫

Location: Cutler Ridge [N25°36.497' W080°19.139'].

Length: 0.4 mile round-trip.

Map: None available.

Contact Information: Bill Sadowski Park & Nature Center (305-255-4767), 17555 SW 79th Avenue, Coral Gables, FL 33156.

Directions: Follow Old Cutler Ridge Road south from Coral Gables to the traffic light at SW 176th Street; drive 1 mile west and look for the park entrance on the right.

The Hike: Starting behind the nature center, the trail is a bark chip path winding through a rejuvenating tropical hammock which was nearly leveled by Hurricane Andrew in 1993. Short fences demarcate deep solution holes in the oolitic Miami limestone. A bridge spans what was once the drainage of a natural creek; a boardwalk takes you up and over a remnant of the rocky limestone Cutler Ridge. The trail ends at a canal, where you can turn left and walk down along the grassy open strip to the canoe launch area, or return back through the leafy forest to the trailhead.

Highlights: This is the only place you'll see what Cutler Ridge looked like before development—South Florida's rocky ridges are long buried under grassy lawns. Several massive fig trees survived the hurricane and provide dark bowers in the forest. Look for small caves in the solution holes.

Logistics: During summer and fall, hundreds of spiders spin webs across the trail—duck under, or use a stick to clear the way.

Other Activities: You'll find a canoe launch, a picnic area, a native tree arboretum, a butterfly garden, and a playground. Fishing is permitted in the canal. The public observatory is open Saturday nights 8:00–10:00. There is a nature center with a live animal exhibit.

Nature Trail

Kendall Indian Hammocks Park

SA-70 📖 👬 🐾

Location: Kendall [N25°41.723' W080°22.429'].

Length: 0.7-mile loop with intersecting pathways.

Map: In interpretive guide, available at trailhead or park office.

Contact Information: Kendall Indian Hammocks Park (305-596-9324), 11345 SW 79th Street, Miami, FL 33173.

Directions: From Florida's Turnpike, take the North Kendall Drive exit (SW 88th Street) and drive east to SW 107th Avenue. Turn left (north) and continue 0.4 mile to the park entrance on the left. The trail begins at the "Nature Trail" sign near the west end of the first parking lot on the left.

The Hike: Meander through one of urban Miami's last stands of natural forest—a hardwood hammock known as the Snapper Creek glade. Were it not for the sounds of civilization intruding, you'd swear you were in the midst of a large tropical hammock, with wild coffee rising over your head, and willow bustic and mastic creating a dense canopy. A network of trails runs through the hammock; follow the numbered posts for the main loop.

Highlights: This is a true oasis in the urban mass: enjoy the wild junglelike atmosphere, with scattered chunks of oolitic limestone rising from the forest floor; feel like a kid again when you clamber over and under fallen trees.

Logistics: Numerous side trails lead through dense tropical vegetation; it's easy to get lost—but not for long, given the small size of the hammock. Use personal safety precautions: this is an urban park.

Other Activities: There are ball fields, a playground, and a picnic shelter.

Castellow Hammock Park

SA-71 ⊔ 🛉 🛉🛉 🐕

Location: Redland [N25°33.530' W080°27.097'].

Length: 0.5 mile round-trip.

Map: In interpretive guide available at nature center.

Contact Information: Castellow Hammock Park (305-242-7688), 22301 SW 162nd Avenue, Miami, FL 33170.

Directions: From US 1 in Goulds, take Hainlin Mill Drive west. Once you pass Monkey Jungle, continue 1.5 miles to 162nd Avenue (Farmlife Road). Turn left and drive 0.5 mile to the park entrance on the left.

The Hike: It's an immersion into a remnant of the tropical forest that once covered this region, a dense tropical hammock with limestone outcrops. Mastic, gumbo limbo, paradise trees, and Jamaican dogwood trees knit a dense canopy overhead, with wild coffee and giant sword ferns carpeting the forest floor. The winding trail passes numerous deep and narrow solution holes before creating a short loop through the forest.

Highlights: Peer into deep oolite solution holes, and marvel at massive trees, including a multi-trunked gigantic gumbo limbo at marker 16.

Logistics: The gate is closed at 5:00 p.m., although the park is open sunrise to sunset; park outside the gate and walk in. Markers along the trail correspond to the interpretive guide. The trail starts behind the nature center.

Other Activities: There is a nature center for the kids to explore, a "hummingbird and butterfly" garden, and picnic tables.

Bill Baggs Cape Florida State Park

SA-72 $ 👫 🐾

Location: Key Biscayne [N25°40.055' W080°09.444'].

Length: 1.5 miles linear, or 1- or 2-mile loop.

Map: In park brochure.

Contact Information: Bill Baggs Cape Florida State Park (305-361-5811), 1200 South Crandon Boulevard, Key Biscayne, FL 33149.

Directions: Take I-95 exit 1A to the Rickenbacker Causeway ($1 bridge toll) to Key Biscayne. Continue on Crandon Boulevard for 7 miles to the end of the road; the park entrance is on the right. Follow the park entrance road to its end at the parking area nearest the bayside. The nature trail starts in the cut between the two parking areas. Look for the "Nature Trail" sign.

The Hike: Walk along an old jeep trail on the ecotone between a tropical hardwood hammock and open freshwater cattail marshes, passing a cluster of large ficus trees and scrambling up and over relict dunes before crossing the marina road to follow the mangrove forest along Biscayne Bay.

Highlights: There are numerous fragrant wildflowers in bloom, from woodlands phlox to yellow nickerbean. From the bike trail, you can see Stiltsville, a village of houses in Biscayne Bay.

Logistics: The trail is open and mostly shadeless; use adequate sun protection and carry lots of water. At the first road crossing, turn left, passing a restroom, to reach the bike trail (turn left again) for a pleasant 1-mile return loop along the water's edge through the shady tropical hammock. The second road crossing, at the marina, provides access to the bike trail (to the left) for a 2-mile loop.

Other Activities: Tour the lighthouse at Cape Florida, swim and sun on the beaches, rent bicycles to explore the bike path, or rent sea kayaks at the marina.

Everglades and Keys

Big Cypress National Preserve, Everglades National Park, and the Florida Keys

Pine rocklands on the Jack C. Watson Wildlife Trail.

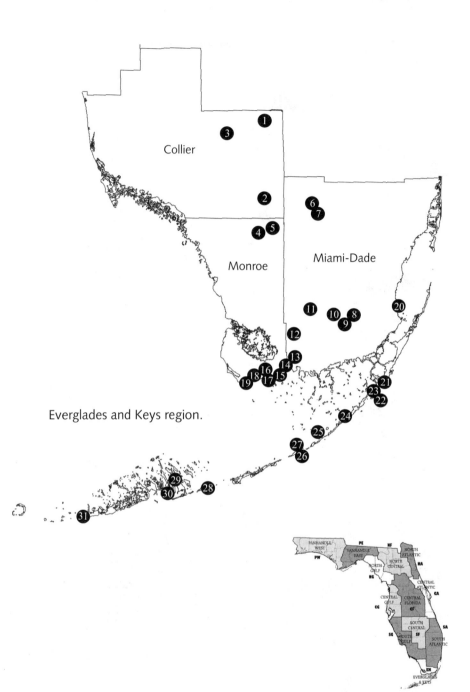

Collier

Monroe

Miami-Dade

Everglades and Keys region.

Big Cypress National Preserve (Collier, Monroe)
- EK-1   Florida Trail, Alligator Alley to Big Cypress Seminole Reservation
- EK-2   Florida Trail, Oasis to Alligator Alley
- EK-3   Fire Prairie Trail
- EK-4   Florida Trail, Loop Road to Oasis
- EK-5   Tree Snail Hammock Trail

Everglades National Park (Miami-Dade, Monroe)
- EK-6   Bobcat Boardwalk, Shark Valley
- EK-7   Otter Cave Hammock Trail, Shark Valley
- EK-8   Anhinga and Gumbo Limbo Trails
- EK-9   Old Ingraham Highway
- EK-10   Pinelands
- EK-11   Pa-hay-okee Overlook
- EK-12   Mahogany Hammock Trail
- EK-13   Mangrove Trail, West Lake
- EK-14   Snake Bight Trail
- EK-15   Rowdy Bend Trail
- EK-16   Bear Lake Trail
- EK-17   Christian Point Trail
- EK-18   Eco Pond Loop
- EK-19   Coastal Prairie Trail

The Keys (Monroe)
- EK-20   Biscayne National Park
- EK-21   Dagny Johnson Key Largo Hammock Botanical State Park
- EK-22   Mangrove Trail, John Pennekamp Coral Reef State Park
- EK-23   Wild Tamarind Trail, John Pennekamp Coral Reef State Park
- EK-24   Windley Key Fossil Reef Geological State Park
- EK-25   Lignumvitae Key Botanical State Park
- EK-26   Golden Orb Trail, Long Key State Park
- EK-27   Layton Trail, Long Key State Park
- EK-28   Silver Palm Trail, Bahia Honda State Park
- EK-29   Wilderness Trails, National Key Deer Refuge
- EK-30   Torchwood Hammock Preserve
- EK-31   Fort Zachary Taylor Historic State Park

Florida Trail, Alligator Alley to Big Cypress Seminole Reservation

Big Cypress National Preserve

EK-1 **F** 🏕 ⛺

Location: Ochopee [N26°10.150' W081°04.347'].

Length: 8.5 miles linear, or 14.9-mile loop.

Map: In Big Cypress National Preserve brochure; detailed backpacking map available from Florida Trail Association.

Contact Information: Big Cypress National Preserve (239-695-2000), HCR 61 Box 110, Ochopee, FL 34141.

Directions: The southern trailhead is at the I-75 rest area 0.3 mile west of mile marker 63; the section ends at the Big Cypress Seminole Reservation boundary.

The Hike: Following Nobles Road north, the Florida Trail parallels a canal dug out of the limestone, where the cypress strands are festooned with bromeliads and wading birds pick through the shallows. A loop trail veers off to the east, providing both a day hike and a backpacking loop through the wilds of palm and pine, cypress and sawgrass. The main trail crosses a stream and ascends into a cabbage palm flatwoods en route to the reservation.

Highlights: Strands of cypress line Nobles Road. A tropical hammock surrounding a stream at 5.5 miles offers the first shade along the main route.

Logistics: If you plan on camping, inform the security officer at the rest area that you will be leaving a car overnight. There are two designated campsites along the loop trail—Carpenter Camp and Panther Camp. Carry water into the campsites. Start on the north side of I-75; walk along the fence line up the ramp until you find the gate. Open it (it looks like it is locked) and close it behind you. If you plan to enter the Seminole Reservation, contact the Florida Trail Association (877-HIKE-FLA) at least two weeks in advance to obtain permission.

Other Activities: This area is open to seasonal hunting. Be aware of hunt dates and wear blaze orange.

Florida Trail, Oasis Ranger Station to Alligator Alley

Big Cypress National Preserve

EK-2 **F** ⛺

Location: Ochopee [N25°51.432' W081°02.019'].

Length: 28.8 miles linear.

Map: In Big Cypress National Preserve brochure; detailed backpacking map available from Florida Trail Association.

Contact Information: Big Cypress National Preserve (239-695-2000), HCR 61 Box 110, Ochopee, FL 34141.

Directions: The southern trailhead is at the Oasis Visitor Center on US 41; the northern trailhead is at the I-75 rest area 0.3 mile west of mile marker 63.

The Hike: This is by far the most remote section of the Florida Trail, a rough and rugged hike through cypress sloughs and sawgrass prairies, a hike that requires three to four days of strenuous backpacking, with hip-deep wading in places. More than sixty inches of rain fall here each year, mostly in summer, nourishing the swamp and the sawgrass prairies and mangrove islands to the south.

Highlights: You'll see spectacular hanging forests of bromeliads and orchids in the cypress strands—and you'll welcome the dry islands of pine and palmetto.

Logistics: Register at the Oasis Ranger Station before starting off, or fill out a self-service card at the kiosk. Most backpackers who hike this section leave a car at the I-75 rest area or arrange to be picked up. Some carry a hammock because of the scarcity of dry spots for camping. In the spring, water may be difficult to find.

Other Activities: Visit the Oasis Ranger Station for a short film and interpretive information about the unique Big Cypress ecosystem, and walk the boardwalk to see alligators in the ditch.

Fire Prairie Trail

Big Cypress National Preserve

EK-3 🐎

Location: Ochopee [N26°05.807' W081°15.900'].

Length: 5.2 miles round-trip.

Map: Trail shown on overall Big Cypress National Preserve map.

Contact Information: Big Cypress National Preserve (239-695-2000), HCR 61 Box 110, Ochopee, FL 34141.

Directions: Leaving the Oasis Ranger Station on US 41, drive 14.7 miles west to Turner River Road (CR 839), just after H. P. Williams Roadside Park. Turn right and drive 14.6 miles north, passing the Concho Billy Trailhead and Wagon Wheel Road, to the trailhead on the left.

The Hike: Starting out as a green tunnel between cypress strands, the trail—which is a high and dry roadway built years ago to facilitate oil exploration—opens up after a half mile into broad open prairies, a panorama that stretches to the far horizons. As you walk through the prairie, notice the textures of grasses and the colorful wildflowers in this vast wet wilderness. The trail ends at a former oil rig site; return along the same route.

Highlights: The vistas across the prairie are truly breathtaking, with distant clouds providing a backdrop for the sights and sounds of this habitat.

Logistics: Sign the hiker register at the trailhead. Since more than half the hike is in full sun, use sun protection and bring plenty of water.

Other Activities: Go fishing and kayaking on the adjacent Turner River.

Florida Trail, Loop Road to Oasis Ranger Station

Big Cypress National Preserve

EK-4 **F** 👫 ⛺

Location: Pinecrest [N25°45.614' W081°02.060'].

Length: 7.8 miles linear.

Map: In Big Cypress National Preserve brochure; detailed backpacking map available from Florida Trail Association.

Contact Information: Big Cypress National Preserve (239-695-2000), HCR 61 Box 110, Ochopee, FL 34141.

Directions: To get to the southern trailhead from US 41 (Tamiami Trail) at Forty Mile Bend, follow Loop Road south through the Miccosukee Indian Reservation; the pavement turns to dirt. Keep alert: within 2 miles you will see the Florida Trail kiosk on the right side of the road. The northern trailhead is at the Oasis Visitor Center on US 41.

The Hike: This is one of the most beautiful and remote sections of the Florida Trail, but a rough and wet walk. This is where the trail begins, where sawgrass and cypress meet, and you walk through haunting forests of dwarf cypress trees and rare patches of pine rocklands with jagged limestone karst. The trail works its way around Robert's Strand, a chain of deep cypress-lined ponds with fern forests and pond-apple swamps; it is always shady here. Marvel at the bromeliads and orchids growing in profusion in the cypress strands.

Highlights: You won't easily forget slipping across vast marl sawgrass prairies, or entering the fern forest where giant sword ferns wave over your head, or walking the slender piece of land through Robert's Strand beneath colorful orchids and bromeliads.

Logistics: Register at the Oasis Ranger Station before starting off, or fill out a self-service card at the kiosk. Most hikers who hike this section have someone shuttle them to Loop Road to hike to US 41. Depending on the time of year, it can be very, very wet—bring a hiking stick to steady yourself as you wade through cypress sloughs. Expect to walk at no more than a mile-an-hour pace, even in relatively dry conditions (March and April).

Other Activities: Visit the Oasis Ranger Station for a short film and interpretive information about the unique Big Cypress ecosystem, and walk the boardwalk to see alligators in the ditch.

Tree Snail Hammock Trail

Big Cypress National Preserve

EK-5 📖 👫

Location: Pinecrest [N25°44.788' W080°56.871'].

Length: 0.3-mile loop.

Map: Trail shown on overall Big Cypress National Preserve map.

Contact Information: Big Cypress National Preserve (239-695-2000), HCR 61 Box 110, Ochopee, FL 34141.

Directions: From US 41 at the west end of the Miccosukee Reservation, turn south on Loop Road and follow it through Pinecrest until you see the Everglades Environmental Center on the left. Park there; the trail starts across from the center on the north side of the road.

The Hike: It's a loop through a dense, dark tropical hammock, where the small trees create a tunnel through which the trail passes. Surface limestone outcrops along the trail, and sword ferns grow along the edge of a sluggish slough. A whisk fern perches in a strangler fig. In this hammock, you enter a world inhabited by rare and tiny creatures—the colorful and endangered *Liguus* tree snails of South Florida's hammocks.

Highlights: Look for *Liguus* snails grazing on algae on smooth-barked trees such as Spanish stopper and Jamaican dogwood. An outdoor classroom surrounds the remnants of a whiskey still from circa 1881.

Logistics: Yellow ropes delineate the footpath. Numerous benches make this an easy walk. Expect to encounter mosquitoes.

Other Activities: Across the road, the Everglades Environmental Center is open to youth groups and educators for specialized environmental programs; contact them for details.

Bobcat Boardwalk

Everglades National Park

EK-6 **$** 📖 👪 ♿ 🚻

Location: Shark Valley [N25°45.348' W080°45.984'].

Length: 0.3-mile loop.

Map: Trail shown on map in Everglades National Park brochure.

Contact Information: Everglades National Park (305-242-7700), 40001 SR 9336, Homestead, FL 33034.

Directions: From the junction of SR 997 (Krome Avenue) and US 41 west of Miami, drive 18 miles to the Miccosukee Reservation; the park entrance is on the south side of the highway.

The Hike: Accessed just up the canal from the visitor center, this gentle boardwalk takes you through a tropical hammock and under a shady tunnel of cocoplums, emerging into the open to showcase the sawgrass prairie. At the end, turn left and use the paved tram loop road through the prairie to complete the loop back to the parking area.

Highlights: Get a good up-close look at the rough limestone beneath the surface of the clear water in the sawgrass prairie, and at the trees of the tropical hardwood hammock. Look for colorful *Liguus* tree snails on the smooth-barked trees.

Logistics: The parking area is open 8:30–6:00. Wear insect repellent. Follow the paved loop south to the start of the trail. Return the same way you came, or use the paved loop to return to the parking area.

Other Activities: The visitor center and gift shop are open 9:00–4:30. There is a tram tour (additional fee) on a 14-mile loop road through the River of Grass, with a stop at an observation tower. You may bicycle or walk the loop, but there is no shade.

Otter Cave Hammock Trail

Everglades National Park

EK-7 $ 🚻

Location: Shark Valley [N25°44.834' W080°45.991'].

Length: 1-mile loop.

Map: Trail shown on map in Everglades National Park brochure.

Contact Information: Everglades National Park (305-242-7700), 40001 SR 9336, Homestead, FL 33034.

Directions: From the junction of SR 997 (Krome Avenue) and US 41 west of Miami, drive 18 miles to the Miccosukee Reservation; the park entrance is on the south side of the highway.

The Hike: Walk south along the paved tram road paralleling the canal to reach the trailhead for Otter Cave, which is on the left side of the road 0.2 mile past the entrance to the Bobcat Boardwalk (EK-6). The trail starts and ends here, making a loop through the tropical hardwood hammock as it skirts many solution holes. Bridges help you cross some of the wettest spots.

Highlights: It's an immersion into a tropical hardwood hammock with an up-close look at solution holes in the limestone bedrock.

Logistics: The parking area is open 8:30–6:00. Use the paved tram road to access the trail. At times of high water, the trail will be flooded and warnings will be posted at the trailhead. You may still get your feet wet on this hike even when the trail is open.

Other Activities: The visitor center and gift shop are open 9:00–4:30. There is a tram tour (additional fee) on a 14-mile loop road through the River of Grass, with a stop at an observation tower. You may bicycle or walk the loop, but there is no shade.

Anhinga and Gumbo Limbo Trails

Everglades National Park

EK-8 **$** 📖 🚻 ♿ 👫 ❋

Location: Royal Palm Hammock [N25°22.951' W080°36.570'].

Length: 1.2 miles in two loops.

Map: Trail shown on map in Everglades National Park brochure.

Contact Information: Everglades National Park (305-242-7700), 40001 SR 9336, Homestead, FL 33034.

Directions: From the park entrance on CR 9336, drive south 1.6 miles to the turnoff on the left for Royal Palm Hammock. Continue another 1.9 miles to the parking area. Walk behind the exhibit hall to access the trails.

The Hike: Royal Palm Hammock is the gateway to the park's two most popular nature trails: the Anhinga Trail and the Gumbo Limbo Trail. Virtually every visitor to the park walks the Anhinga Trail, where the alligators draw close to the wall next to the trail and climb atop mounds to sun along Taylor Slough. Birds are everywhere—cormorants and anhingas, herons and ibises. Follow the boardwalk across the islands of pond apple to walk the loop. The Gumbo Limbo Trail immerses you in a lush tropical hammock, where gumbo limbo, mastic, and Jamaican dogwood jostle for space, shading rocky solution holes.

Highlights: You're guaranteed wildlife sightings along the Anhinga Trail. On the Gumbo Limbo Trail, look carefully at trees with smooth bark, and you may spot a *Liguus*—a Florida tree snail.

Logistics: Numerous benches make this an easy hike for all ages. Arrive early in the day for optimum wildlife viewing; the parking area and trails become more crowded with visitors as the day wears on. The Anhinga Trail is wheelchair accessible.

Other Activities: Visit the exhibit hall before heading out on the trail, and the many other trails (EK-9 through EK-19) throughout this massive park.

Old Ingraham Highway

Everglades National Park

EK-9 $ ⛺

Location: Royal Palm Hammock [N25°22.502' W080°37.339'].

Length: Up to 22 miles round-trip.

Map: Trail shown on map in Everglades National Park brochure; detailed map available from either visitor center.

Contact Information: Everglades National Park (305-242-7700), 40001 SR 9336, Homestead, FL 33034.

Directions: From the park entrance on CR 9336, drive south 1.6 miles to the turnoff on the left for Royal Palm Hammock. After 0.8 mile, turn right at the "Daniel Beard Research Center" sign. Drive another 0.5 mile to the "Hidden Lake Environmental Education Center" sign, and continue straight; the road becomes rough. Continue 1.5 miles to gate 15 and park alongside the road; do not block either gate.

The Hike: Starting behind gate 15, this trail follows the crumbling pavement of the Old Ingraham Highway, opened in 1922 as the first road connecting Homestead and Flamingo. After the first mile's worth of dense vegetation (heavy with poisonwood), the trail parallels the canal created to provide fill for the road, and has vast panoramic views of the sawgrass prairies and tree islands that comprise the northern Everglades. There are two primitive campsites along the trail, the Ernest Coe at 3.5 miles, and the Old Ingraham at 11 miles.

Highlights: This is one of the few places in the park where you can walk for miles and miles along the vastness of the River of Grass.

Logistics: The trail is shared with bicyclists. There are no trail markings—follow the road. If you plan to backpack this trail, check in at one of the visitor centers beforehand so they know where you are. Be alert for alligator activity along the canals. There is virtually no shade, so use sun protection and carry enough water for your journey.

Other Activities: This trail is part of the Long Pine Key and Royal Palm Hammock complex, which includes the campground, more trails (EK-8), and Pinelands (EK-10). There are numerous unmarked trails accessible from Long Pine Key campground.

Pinelands

Everglades National Park

EK-10 $ 📖 🅐 ♿ 🚻

Location: Long Pine Key [N25°25.362' W080°40.787'].

Length: 0.4-mile loop.

Map: Trail shown on map in Everglades National Park brochure.

Contact Information: Everglades National Park (305-242-7700), 40001 SR 9336, Homestead, FL 33034.

Directions: From the park entrance on CR 9336, drive south 6 miles to the turnoff on the right for Pinelands.

The Hike: This 0.4-mile paved nature trail provides a sample of the complex pine rocklands habitat, of which Long Pine Key is one of the largest remaining examples in the state. The path winds through the forest beneath Dade County slash pines, circling numerous deep solution holes.

Highlights: Peer into the jagged solution holes for a closer look at the karst landscape sculpted by rain out of the limestone bedrock beneath the pines.

Logistics: Wooden boards call attention to places where the solution holes come right up to the edge of the pavement. Take care not to step off the path.

Other Activities: Set up base camp at the nearby Long Pine Key campground, and visit the many other trails (EK-8 through EK-19) throughout the park.

Pa-hay-okee Overlook

Everglades National Park

EK-11 $ 📖 ♿ 👫

Location: Long Pine Key [N25°26.435' W080°47.003'].

Length: 0.2-mile loop.

Map: Trail shown on map in Everglades National Park brochure.

Contact Information: Everglades National Park (305-242-7700), 40001 SR 9336, Homestead, FL 33034.

Directions: From the park entrance on CR 9336, drive south 12.1 miles to the turnoff on the right for Pa-hay-okee, passing the turnoffs for Royal Palm Hammock (EK-8) and Pinelands (EK-10) en route. Drive 1.3 miles down the side road to the parking area.

The Hike: This is a short walk that provides an excellent perspective of the cornerstone of the Everglades, the River of Grass. The broad boardwalk leads upward into the treetops to an observation tower with an incredible view. Walk down the stairs to a boardwalk just inches above the watery prairie for a different take on the habitat.

Highlights: The panoramic view of the sawgrass prairie is a humbling sight; you'll feel small by comparison to the immense landscape before you.

Logistics: Steps connect the two boardwalks at the observation tower, so wheelchairs cannot traverse the entire loop but can approach it from both ends.

Other Activities: Set up base camp at the Long Pine Key campground, and visit the many other trails (EK-8 through EK-19) throughout the park.

Mahogany Hammock Trail

Everglades National Park

EK-12 $ 🕮 ♿ 🚻

Location: Long Pine Key [N25°19.414' W080°49.925'].

Length: 0.4-mile loop.

Map: Trail shown on map in Everglades National Park brochure.

Contact Information: Everglades National Park (305-242-7700), 40001 SR 9336, Homestead, FL 33034.

Directions: From the park entrance on CR 9336, drive south 19.1 miles to the turnoff on the right for Mahogany Hammock, passing the turnoffs for Royal Palm Hammock (EK-8), Pinelands (EK-10), and Pa-hay-okee (EK-11) en route. Follow the side road to the parking area.

The Hike: This boardwalk trail leads you through one of the many tree islands found throughout the sawgrass prairies of the Everglades; this particular island is home to a dense tropical hardwood hammock dominated by mahogany—including the largest mahogany tree in the United States.

Highlights: Look carefully on the trunks of smooth-barked trees such as Jamaican dogwood for the colorful *Liguus* tree snails of the Everglades.

Logistics: Don't forget the insect repellent! The farther south you travel in the park, the more troublesome the mosquitoes become.

Other Activities: Set up base camp at either the Long Pine Key campground or the Flamingo campground or Flamingo Lodge, and visit the many other trails (EK-8 through EK-19) throughout the park.

Mangrove Trail

West Lake, Everglades National Park

EK-13 $ ⬚ ⬚ ♿ ⬚

Location: Flamingo [N25°12.869' W080°51.046'].

Length: 0.4-mile loop.

Map: Trail shown on map in Everglades National Park brochure.

Contact Information: Everglades National Park (305-242-7700), 40001 SR 9336, Homestead, FL 33034.

Directions: From the park entrance on CR 9336, drive south 30.1 miles to the turnoff on the left for West Lake, passing the turnoffs for Royal Palm Hammock (EK-8), Pinelands (EK-10), Pa-hay-okee (EK-11), and Mahogany Hammock (EK-12) en route. Park your car and walk over to the boardwalk under the mangroves.

The Hike: The Mangrove Trail is a boardwalk through a dense tangle of mangrove forest where, like an ibis, you walk amid the roots of massive trees. Bromeliads decorate the mangrove limbs. At the fork, keep left to walk out over the open water of West Lake; the trail bends back around into the mangrove tunnel to complete the loop.

Highlights: The contrast between the shady mangrove tunnels and the expansive view of West Lake is striking.

Logistics: Mosquitoes will be fierce here. Restrooms are inside the building at the canoe launch.

Other Activities: Launch canoes from the observation deck and dock on West Lake. Set up base camp at Flamingo campground or Flamingo Lodge, and visit the many other trails (EK-8 through EK-20) throughout the park.

Snake Bight Trail

Everglades National Park

EK-14 $

Location: Flamingo [N25°12.667' W080°52.479'].

Length: 3.6 miles round-trip.

Map: Trail shown on map in Everglades National Park brochure.

Contact Information: Everglades National Park (305-242-7700), 40001 SR 9336, Homestead, FL 33034.

Directions: From the visitor center in Flamingo, drive 5.4 miles north to the pulloff for Snake Bight; park on the right.

The Hike: The trail follows an old road that once led to the E. C. Knight Fish Company processing plant on Snake Bight, an inlet off Florida Bay. The tropical hardwood hammock is so dense that you feel like you're walking down a long green tunnel, with a canal adjoining on the left. The trail emerges into open coastal prairie after 1.7 miles and arrives at a boardwalk, ending at an observation deck on Snake Bight.

Highlights: Enjoy the view from the end of the trail, across the salt flats of Snake Bight—it's one of the only places in the United States where you might see flamingos in the wild.

Logistics: Bicycles share the trail. It's possible to connect with the Rowdy Bend Trail (EK-16) to make a 7.6-mile loop using the Main Park Road to return to your car. The entrance to the Rowdy Bend Trail is not marked, but it's the only wide gap on the south side of the trail near the coastal prairie. Mosquitoes are fierce along this trail, even in winter. Wear long-sleeved shirt and pants when hiking. Have a mosquito head net handy; one can be purchased in the marina store. Expect to walk through slippery marl mud in the coastal prairie; use a hiking stick to steady yourself.

Other Activities: Set up base camp at Flamingo campground or Flamingo Lodge, and take an ecotour out of the Flamingo marina, or rent a kayak to ply the waters of Florida Bay. From Flamingo, you have easy access to hikes EK-14 through EK-19.

Rowdy Bend Trail

Everglades National Park

EK-15 $

Location: Flamingo [N25°10.504' W080°54.303'].

Length: 5.2 miles round-trip.

Map: Trail shown on map in Everglades National Park brochure.

Contact Information: Everglades National Park (305-242-7700), 40001 SR 9336, Homestead, FL 33034.

Directions: From the visitor center in Flamingo, drive 2.7 miles north of Flamingo; park on the grass just after the "Rowdy Bend Road" sign on the right.

The Hike: Follow Rowdy Bend Road to find the trailhead. This trail showcases the coastal prairie habitat, with occasional diversions into the shade of a tropical hardwood hammock; the natural footpath becomes a deep rut through prairie grasses and crosses stretches of open marl before meeting the Snake Bight Trail after 2.6 miles. For a scenic view of Florida Bay, turn right and walk down to the observation platform.

Highlights: Gaze at panoramas across the open prairies, including the eerie sight of ghostly wind-and-salt-bleached dead buttonwood trees lying like giant pieces of driftwood.

Logistics: Bicycles share the trail. It's possible to connect this trail with Snake Bight Trail (EK-15) to make a 7.6-mile loop using the Main Park Road to return to your car; this trail ends at Snake Bight Trail. Mosquitoes are fierce here, even in winter. Wear long-sleeved shirt and pants when hiking. Have a mosquito head net handy. Expect to walk through slippery marl mud in places; use a hiking stick to steady yourself. Much of the trail is in open coastal prairie, so use sun protection and carry a lot of water.

Other Activities: Set up base camp at Flamingo campground or Flamingo Lodge, and take an ecotour out of the Flamingo marina, or rent a kayak to ply the waters of Florida Bay. From Flamingo, you have easy access to hikes EK-14 through EK-19.

Bear Lake Trail

Everglades National Park

EK-16 $

Location: Flamingo [N25°08.938' W080°55.389'].

Length: 3.5 miles round-trip.

Map: Trail shown on map in Everglades National Park brochure.

Contact Information: Everglades National Park (305-242-7700), 40001 SR 9336, Homestead, FL 33034.

Directions: From Flamingo in Everglades National Park, follow the Main Park Road north for 0.5 mile to Bear Lake Road on the left. If the gate is open and the road is passable, you may proceed along this dirt road for 1.7 miles to the trailhead. If not, park outside the gate and walk up the road.

The Hike: The trail officially starts at the parking area with the canoe symbol, behind the "No Parking Beyond This Sign" sign, immediately plunging into a shady tropical hammock to parallel the Bear Lake Canal, which provides paddlers access to Bear Lake. As the canal broadens, the habitat transitions to a mangrove forest where roots dangle over your head. You emerge on a marl spit of land along Bear Lake, where the trail ends at the water.

Highlights: There is a nice view of mangrove-lined Bear Lake from the end of the trail. Watch for eruptions of motion in the water signaling the breathing behavior of schools of *Clarias batrachus*, better known as the walking catfish.

Logistics: Bear Lake Road is frequently closed to traffic after it rains, so you may find it necessary to hike up the road for 1.7 miles to access the trailhead for the Bear Lake Trail, doubling the length of the hike. The trail is shared with bicycles. Mosquitoes are fierce along this trail, even in winter. Wear long-sleeved shirt and pants when hiking. Have a mosquito head net handy; one can be purchased in the marina store.

Other Activities: Set up base camp at Flamingo campground or Flamingo Lodge, and take an ecotour out of the Flamingo marina, or rent a kayak to ply the waters of Florida Bay. From Flamingo, you have easy access to hikes EK-14 through EK-19.

Christian Point Trail

Everglades National Park

EK-17 $

Location: Flamingo [N25°09.109' W080°55.102'].

Length: 3.6 miles round-trip.

Map: Trail shown on map in Everglades National Park brochure.

Contact Information: Everglades National Park (305-242-7700), 40001 SR 9336, Homestead, FL 33034.

Directions: From Flamingo in Everglades National Park, follow the Main Park Road north for 1 mile to the "Christian Point" sign on the right.

The Hike: Starting off in a mangrove forest, the trail works its way through a hammock of buttonwood and a tropical hardwood hammock before heading across an open coastal prairie, slick underfoot with marl mud. The trail ends at a tangle of mangroves edging Florida Bay near Christian Point.

Highlights: There are hundreds of bromeliads clinging to the buttonwood trees. Enjoy the views across the coastal prairie and from the end of the trail.

Logistics: Mosquitoes are fierce along this trail, even in winter. Wear long-sleeved shirt and pants when hiking. Have a mosquito head net handy. Expect to walk through slippery marl mud in places; use a hiking stick to steady yourself. Much of the trail is in open coastal prairie, so use sun protection and carry a lot of water.

Other Activities: Set up base camp at Flamingo campground or Flamingo Lodge, and take an ecotour out of the Flamingo marina, or rent a kayak to ply the waters of Florida Bay. From Flamingo, you have easy access to hikes EK-14 through EK-19.

Eco Pond Loop

Everglades National Park

EK-18 $ 📖 🚻 🅰 ♿ 🚻

Location: Flamingo [N25°08.322' W080°56.242'].

Length: 0.5-mile loop.

Map: Trail shown on map in Everglades National Park brochure.

Contact Information: Everglades National Park (305-242-7700), 40001 SR 9336, Homestead, FL 33034.

Directions: From the visitor center in Flamingo, drive 0.8 mile south on the Main Park Road and park in the parking area on the right. A boardwalk leads to an observation platform that marks the start of the trail.

The Hike: The trail circles a man-made wetland created to naturally filter and cleanse treated wastewater from the visitor center and lodge complex in Flamingo. Start at the observation deck and walk counterclockwise around the loop. The trail leads to another observation platform about a quarter of the way around the pond. As the trail curves around the far side of the pond, you get a nice panorama of the coastal prairie before facing the pond again for great views over the open water as you complete the loop.

Highlights: This is one of the easiest spots in the park to go birding. Visit at dawn or dusk for the stunning sight of thousands of wading birds, mostly ibises, roosting in the island of buttonwoods in the middle of the lake. Roseate spoonbill sightings are common.

Logistics: Although the observation deck is wheelchair accessible, the footpath is a natural surface along a solid berm and may not be accessible without assistance. Wear insect repellent! Restrooms are at the nearby visitor center.

Other Activities: Set up base camp at Flamingo campground or Flamingo Lodge, and visit the many other trails (EK-8 through EK-19) throughout the park. In particular, the Coastal Prairie Trail (EK-19) with its shorter Bayshore Loop and the Bear Lake Trail (EK-16) start nearby. Take an ecotour out of the Flamingo marina, or rent a kayak to ply the waters of Florida Bay.

Coastal Prairie Trail

Everglades National Park

EK-19 $ 📖 🄯 ⛺

Location: Flamingo [N25°08.213' W080°56.919'].

Length: 1.3-mile loop or 14 miles round-trip.

Map: Trail shown on map in Everglades National Park brochure.

Contact Information: Everglades National Park (305-242-7700), 40001 SR 9336, Homestead, FL 33034.

Directions: Drive all the way to the end of the Main Park Road and enter the campground at Flamingo. Tell the campground attendant you're here to hike the trail. When the campground road forks, keep right at the "B-C" loop junction, following the outer road until you see the "Coastal Prairie Trail" sign on the right side of the road; park on the grass.

The Hike: The 7-mile (one way) main trail follows an old cotton pickers' road from the 1930s out to Clubhouse Beach through one of the Everglades' most interesting habitats, the desertlike coastal prairie. An easier walk is the Bayshore Loop, a 1.3-mile trail under the mangroves and buttonwoods along Florida Bay through what was once the village of Flamingo. The loop lets you sample both the mangrove forest and coastal prairie habitats.

Highlights: Enjoy great views of Florida Bay and the unusual coastal prairie environment.

Logistics: The marl prairie is very slippery when wet. Use a hiking stick to steady yourself and don't expect to walk fast. While the Bayshore Loop is partially shaded, the Coastal Prairie Trail is in full sun—use sun protection and carry a lot of water. If you plan to camp overnight on Clubhouse Beach, register at the visitor center so they know you're out there. Mosquitoes are especially fierce along this trail—full body protection is recommended, even in winter, as a rain can stir them up. A mosquito head net is a must, and can be purchased in the marina store.

Other Activities: Set up base camp at Flamingo campground or Flamingo Lodge, and take an ecotour out of the Flamingo marina, or rent a kayak to ply the waters of Florida Bay. From Flamingo, you have easy access to hikes EK-14 through EK-19.

Biscayne National Park

EK-20 📖 🛉🛉 ⛺

Location: Homestead.

Length: 9 miles, in three short nature trails plus 7-mile road walk.

Map: In park brochure.

Contact Information: Biscayne National Park (305-230-PARK), 9700 West 328th Street, Homestead, FL 33033-5634.

Directions: From US 1 in Homestead, follow SW 328th Street (North Canal Drive) east to Homestead Bayfront Park to the park headquarters and Dante Fascell Visitor Center, where you can obtain information on how to reach the keys by boat.

The Hike: There are nature trails on three of the keys that comprise Biscayne National Park. Elliott Key has a self-guided interpretive trail through a tropical hardwood hammock, and the opportunity to walk the shadeless Spite Highway, a seven-mile stretch of old roadwalk erected by a developer before the land was bought by the government. Boca Chica Key and Adams Key each have short nature trails through the hammocks.

Highlights: Enjoy views of beautiful Biscayne Bay and immersion into tropical hammocks.

Logistics: The park is open daily 8:00–5:30. All three islands can be accessed only by boat. Private boaters can use the boat docks. Restrooms are on Elliott Key and Adams Key. Overnight camping is permitted on Boca Chica Key (primitive tent camping) and Elliott Key (developed campground). There is a docking fee of $15 per night on Boca Chica and Elliott Keys.

Other Activities: Try sea kayaking, snorkeling, and diving the offshore reefs. There are also picnic areas.

Dagny Johnson Key Largo Hammock Botanical State Park

EK-21 📖 🛉🛉 ♿ 👯

Location: Key Largo [N25°10.559' W080°22.172'].

Length: 1.1-mile loop.

Map: Displayed at trailhead and available in park brochure.

Contact Information: John Pennekamp Coral Reef State Park (305-451-1202), PO Box 487, Key Largo, FL 33037.

Directions: Driving north on US 1 from John Pennekamp Coral Reef State Park, keep right at the fork for SR 905 (Card Sound Road). The trailhead parking area is on the right after 0.5 mile, in front of a large archway.

The Hike: Using a paved road (built to be the entrance to a condo development) and several side trails, you work your way through the largest tropical hammock in the United States. Look into the forest at the range of unusual bark textures and colors, and keep alert for *Liguus* tree snails on smooth-barked trees. The side loop takes off into the forest at the "Nature Trail" sign and leads you to the rim of an old quarry.

Highlights: There are fourteen National Champion trees in this hammock, the highest concentration on one piece of land in the United States. However, being tropical trees at the northern extent of their range, none are more than thirty feet tall.

Logistics: Parking is limited. Guided hikes are offered at 10:00 a.m. on Thursday and Sunday. Stay on the pathways—there are poisonwood and machineel trees throughout the hammock, both of which can cause severe reactions for anyone allergic to poison ivy. Looking for adventure? Check in at John Pennekamp Coral Reef State Park for a day-use-only backcountry permit to wander the network of jeep trails throughout the 3,000-acre park.

Other Activities: Birdwatchers will appreciate sighting the rare white-crowned pigeon, which feeds on the fruit of the poisonwood tree. Visit nearby John Pennekamp Coral Reef State Park (EK-22 and EK-23) for more hiking and other outdoor activities.

Mangrove Trail

John Pennekamp Coral Reef State Park

EK-22 $ 📖 🚻 Ⓐ ♿ 🚸

Location: Key Largo [N25°07.435' W080°24.169'].

Length: 0.8-mile boardwalk.

Map: Rough map in park brochure.

Contact Information: John Pennekamp Coral Reef State Park (305-451-1202), PO Box 487, Key Largo, FL 33037.

Directions: The park entrance is at MM (mile marker) 102.5 on US 1, Key Largo. Follow the park entrance road to the farthest parking area inside the park. The trailhead is on the left.

The Hike: It's an interpretive boardwalk that immerses you in the mangrove forest along a tidal creek. Halfway through the loop, the trail emerges into the open along shorter mangroves, paralleling the creek. A staircase leads up to an observation deck.

Highlights: Enjoy a refreshing walk through an aesthetically pleasing tangled jungle of white mangroves, thanks to the cool salt breezes off the Atlantic. The observation tower provides great overview of the mangrove forest. Keep alert for iguanas!

Logistics: The trail is best visited in winter; mosquito repellent is crucial the rest of the year.

Other Activities: John Pennekamp Coral Reef State Park is best known as the first underwater state park in the United States, protecting part of the living coral reef that surrounds the Keys. Take a reef tour, rent a sea kayak and ply the channels, or grab your snorkel and follow the underwater trail. Enjoy swimming, sunning, and picnicking, and be sure to stop by the visitor center for a look at aquariums filled with fish native to the offshore coral reef habitat.

Wild Tamarind Trail

John Pennekamp Coral Reef State Park

EK-23 $ ⬚ ⛨ ⬛ ⛨ ⛺

Location: Key Largo [N25°07.530' W080°24.427'].

Length: 0.3-mile loop.

Map: Rough map in park brochure.

Contact Information: John Pennekamp Coral Reef State Park (305-451-1202), PO Box 487, Key Largo, FL 33037.

Directions: The park entrance is at MM 102.5 on US 1, Key Largo. Drive in on the park entrance road and turn right at the fork. Park your car on the right adjacent to the trailhead.

The Hike: It's a short but beautiful introduction to a dark and shady tropical hardwood hammock, dense with gumbo limbo, torchwood, crabwood, mastic, and other denizens of the West Indian forest. The trail meanders around solution holes and past large trees, creating a loop. A side trail leads to the right to end at the campground; walk down the trail to check out the tidal pond.

Highlights: Look carefully at the tree limbs and trunks as you walk the loop; you may spy a *Liguus* tree snail feeding. Pause by the tidal pond and watch herons fishing.

Logistics: The footpath is outlined with limestone. Small tags identify the various plants along the route.

Other Activities: John Pennekamp Coral Reef State Park is best known as the first underwater state park in the United States, protecting part of the living coral reef that surrounds the Keys. Take a reef tour, rent a sea kayak and ply the channels, or grab your snorkel and follow the underwater trail. Enjoy swimming, sunning, and picnicking, and be sure to stop by the visitor center for a look at aquariums filled with fish native to the offshore coral reef habitat.

Windley Key Fossil Reef Geological State Park

EK-24 **$** 📖 🚻 👪 🎋

Location: Windley Key [N24°57.004' W080°35.733'].

Length: 1.4 miles in a loop and a spur trail.

Map: In park brochure; detailed interpretive guide sold at visitor center.

Contact Information: Windley Key Fossil Reef Geological State Park (305-664-2540), PO Box 1052, Islamorada, FL 33036.

Directions: Drive 0.5 mile south of MM 85 on US 1; the park entrance is on the right.

The Hike: This interpretive walk introduces you to the underpinnings of the Florida Keys—the fossilized reefs upon which the islands were formed. You follow interpretive stations around two quarries from which ornamental stone was carved until the 1960s, and walk a loop through the tropical hardwood hammock on the Hammock Trail. The Sunset Trail is a spur trail on the ridge above the Windley Quarry, looking down on the mangrove forest along Florida Bay.

Highlights: See fossilized corals such as brain coral and star coral embedded in the limestone walls of the quarries. Pay attention to the interpretive signs—there are many rare plants in the hammock, including the white ironwood tree and prickly cordgrass.

Logistics: Hours are limited to Thu–Mon 8:00–5:00. Collecting of fossil rock or plant materials is strictly prohibited.

Other Activities: Stop at the visitor center before starting off on your hike for a better understanding of the geology of the Florida Keys and the history of these quarries. There is a picnic area in the Flagler Quarry.

Lignumvitae Key Botanical State Park

EK-25 **$** 📖 🚻

Location: Lignumvitae Key [N24°54.180' W080°41.736'].

Length: Guided hike of 1 to 1.5 miles on 3.5-mile trail system.

Map: None available.

Contact Information: Lignumvitae Key Botanical State Park (305-664-2540), PO Box 1052, Islamorada, FL 33036.

Directions: Lignumvitae Key can be visited only by boat. Launch a sea kayak from nearby Lower Matecumbe Key, dock your own boat, or be at Robbie's Marina (south of MM 78) 45 minutes before tour time. Advance reservations are recommended (305-664-9814). The ferryboat ride costs $15 round-trip.

The Hike: Depending on the mosquitoes and the weather, your hike route will vary, but the primary focus is on the dense tropical hardwood hammock and its riotous variety of unusual and rare plants as well as its deep solution holes. Most of the walk is shaded. A spur trail leads out to the island's shore at the south end and a loop trail at the north end passes through a coastal berm and mangrove forest.

Highlights: This state park protects many rare plants, including its namesake tree, the lignum vitae. The tree's wood is so dense that it sinks in water, and it's the only tree on earth whose branches crisscross each other at sharp angles. Along the hike, you'll see the National Champion lignum vitae, a gnarled tree more than a thousand years old, spreading its limbs above a large solution hole.

Logistics: Hikers may visit the park only on guided walks, held at 10:00 a.m. and 2:00 p.m. daily. No pesticides are used on the island, so wear full mosquito protection: a head net, long- sleeved shirt, and long pants are recommended. Most visitors come from November through March; mosquitoes are fierce the remainder of the year.

Other Activities: You'll visit the historic Matheson House, circa 1919, where the island's caretakers once lived. Ask at Robbie's Marina about snorkeling trips to the reefs surrounding Lignumvitae Key.

Golden Orb Trail

Long Key State Park

EK-26 $ 📖 🚻 🅰 ❄

Location: Long Key [N24°48.851' W080°49.285'].

Length: 1.2-mile loop.

Map: Rough map in park brochure.

Contact Information: Long Key State Park (305-664-4815), PO Box 776, Long Key, FL 33001.

Directions: The park entrance is 0.5 mile south of MM 68 on the left. Follow the park entrance road and keep to the left at the fork; the trail starts along the boardwalk behind the restrooms.

The Hike: Leaving the access boardwalk through the mangrove forest, the trail follows the water's edge, dipping in and out of shady tropical hammocks, until you cross a bridge over a mangrove-lined canal and rise into the open, desertlike coastal berm with its salt-rich soil and stunted plant life. After skirting tidal flats and mangrove forest, you enter a tropical hammock and walk along the edge of a mangrove forest on the inner lagoon before returning to the far end of the parking area.

Highlights: This walk provides fabulous scenic views along the calm Atlantic Ocean (the waves break out of sight on the coral reefs) as well as a great introduction to the unusual coastal berm habitat of the Keys, where the "soil" underfoot is sun-bleached pieces of coral.

Logistics: A boardwalk connects the trailhead with the campground, with a scenic walk along the Atlantic Ocean. Expect mosquitoes; use insect repellent. Do not touch oozing tree bark in the tropical hammock—there are poisonwood trees scattered throughout the hammock.

Other Activities: Long Key State Park offers a popular seaside campground, as well as oceanfront picnic tables and kayak and canoe rentals. The Layton Trail (EK-27) is a short interpretive trail on the undeveloped Florida Bay side of the park.

Layton Trail

Long Key State Park

EK-27 📖 ⚓

Location: Long Key [N24°49.381' W080°49.059'].

Length: 0.2-mile loop.

Map: Rough map in park brochure.

Contact Information: Long Key State Park (305-664-4815), PO Box 776, Long Key, FL 33001.

Directions: From the main entrance to Long Key State Park, drive north on US 1 for 0.6 mile (just past MM 68) for the trailhead on the left at the "Layton Trail" sign; park on the shoulder.

The Hike: The trail makes a loop through a shady tropical hardwood hammock, past thatch palms, gumbo limbo, pigeon plum, and poisonwood. Keep to the left at the loop junction to head out to the limestone edge of Florida Bay. Turn right and walk along the shoreline, which is thick in dried grasses and debris. At an interpretive marker, the trail turns to the right to reenter the tropical hammock and complete the loop.

Highlights: Enjoy a sweeping view of Florida Bay where the trail emerges from the tropical hammock to the shoreline.

Logistics: The trail is not well marked along the shoreline. Stay behind the buttonwoods and look for the interpretive marker to tell where the trail turns.

Other Activities: The campground and the Golden Orb Trail (EK-26) are across US 1 in the main portion of the park.

Silver Palm Trail

Bahia Honda State Park

EK-28 **$** 📖 🚻 ♿ 👫

Location: Bahia Honda Key [N24°39.889' W081°15.455'].

Length: 0.6-mile loop or round trip.

Map: Rough map in park brochure; interpretive guide available at ranger station.

Contact Information: Bahia Honda State Park (305-872-2353), 36850 Overseas Highway, Big Pine Key, FL 33043.

Directions: Enter the park from MM 37 on US 1 on Bahia Honda Key, on the Atlantic Ocean side. At the T intersection, turn left and drive north on the park road past the Sandspur Camping Area and a beach parking area. After 1.3 miles you reach the end of the road at another beach parking area. The trailhead is at the northern end of the parking area.

The Hike: Follow the trail into the tropical hardwood hammock just behind the dunes, where it leads you down behind a screen of mangroves along an inner lagoon busy with wading birds. As the trail rises into the dunes, you walk through a grove of slender silver palms before reaching the coastal strand, where the trail ends on the beach after 0.3 mile.

Highlights: This is the largest grove of silver palms (*Coccothrinax argentata*) in the United States. Botanists have discovered hundreds of rare and unusual species of plants on this island, ranging from the Geiger tree to the small-flowered lilythorn. Birders will want to spend some time along the lagoon, as roseate spoonbills are often sighted here.

Logistics: Create a loop by walking along the beach back to the parking area, or walk back along the same route. Wear sun protection.

Other Activities: The beach is one of the highest rated in Florida for its beauty, and the two campgrounds are very popular during the winter months. Drive down to the south end of the park to explore the Butterfly Garden and the Old Bahia Honda Bridge; rent a sea kayak or snorkeling gear to head out on the calm waters; swim in the sheltered bay.

Wilderness Trails

National Key Deer Refuge

EK-29 □ &. 👫 ⁂

Location: Big Pine Key [N24°42.571' W080°22.948'].

Length: 1.1 miles in a round trip and a loop.

Map: Trail shown in park brochure; interpretive brochure available at trailhead kiosk; detailed information about hikes in the refuge at visitor center in shopping center on Key Deer Boulevard.

Contact Information: National Key Deer Refuge (305-872-0774), PO Box 430510, Big Pine Key, FL 33043.

Directions: From US 1 on Big Pine Key, follow Key Deer Boulevard for 3.2 miles to the "Wildlife Trails" sign; turn left to enter the trailhead parking lot.

The Hike: Two separate but adjacent trails start at this trailhead: the Fred Manillo Trail, with a surface of hard-packed emulsified gravel and numerous benches, and the Jack C. Watson Wildlife Trail, a wilder foray into the pine rocklands. The 0.3-mile round-trip Manillo Trail meanders through the pine rocklands to end at a boardwalk overlooking a freshwater wetland. Along the 0.8-mile Jack C. Watson Wildlife Trail, you loop through the pine rocklands, passing alligator holes, solution holes, and wetlands.

Highlights: Both trails provide an excellent immersion into the pine rocklands habitat. Keep alert for rustling in the bushes, since Key deer are frequently spotted along the trails.

Logistics: Only the Fred Manillo Trail is wheelchair accessible; it is also a good introduction to the habitat for small children. Along the Watson Trail, droopy-leaved poisonwood crowds close to the footpath; if you are allergic to poison ivy, do not let poisonwood touch your skin.

Other Activities: Stop at the visitor center for an overview of the refuge and its most important inhabitant, the Key deer. Visit Blue Hole (just south on Key Deer Boulevard) for an unmarked walk along the edge of the island's biggest fresh water source, where deer come to drink, and explore the many unmarked trails outlined in the "National Key Deer Refuge Hiking and Bicycling Trails" flyer available at the visitor center.

Torchwood Hammock Preserve

EK-30 📖

Location: Little Torch Key.

Length: 0.4-mile loop.

Map: Interpretive guide and map available from The Nature Conservancy.

Contact Information: The Nature Conservancy, Key West Office (305-745-8402), 201 Front Street, Suite 222, Key West, FL 33040.

Directions: Obtain permission for access and directions to the preserve from The Nature Conservancy.

The Hike: Showcasing five of the Keys habitats, this short loop trail leads you through a rocky tropical hammock dense with West Indian trees like mastic, blolly, and torchwood. Emerging along a coastal rock barren, the trail crosses a narrow gutterlike ditch cut through the rock as a mosquito control canal, and reaches the bleached coastal berm, where you can see a good distance across the mangrove-lined tidal flats. The trail meanders back through the tropical hammock to complete the loop.

Highlights: Look for *Liguus* snails on smooth-barked trees in the hammock, and rare white-crowned pigeons feeding on the fruit of the poisonwood tree. Key deer may be seen.

Logistics: The preserve is gated; access must be obtained from The Nature Conservancy. Parking is extremely limited. Follow the markers to stay on the footpath. Stay on the path, not just to minimize impact on the habitat—there are poisonwood trees throughout the hammock. Plant identification markers aid you in learning the plants of these habitats. Wear insect repellent!

Other Activities: Birdwatch throughout the preserve, but especially along the tidal flats—look for mangrove cuckoos and reddish egrets in spring.

Fort Zachary Taylor Historic State Park

EK-31 $ 📖 🚻 👫

Location: Key West [N24°32.779' W081°48.650'].

Length: 1.2 miles round-trip.

Map: Rough sketch in park brochure.

Contact Information: Fort Zachary Taylor Historic State Park (305-292-6713), PO Box 6560, Key West, FL 33041.

Directions: Follow US 1 south to Mile 0. Continue to the sign for Fort Taylor; turn left, follow the road through the condo complex into the air station, and turn right into the entrance for Fort Taylor. Pay your fee at the gate and follow the entrance road to the very end, near the harbor.

The Hike: Follow the Point Trail through a forest of Australian pines down to the westernmost point of Key West on the farthest-south hike you can do in the continental United States. Granted, the landscape isn't pretty—all of the land surrounding the fort is fill, so there isn't a lot of vegetation. But the views across the water are spectacular. When you come up to a sign that says "Foot Traffic Only," cross the jeep trail and clamber up the slope to the seawall to follow that north. Across the open field, follow the footpath around to the fort along the moat, where you meet the Fort Trail leading into Fort Taylor. Return along the same pathway to the parking area.

Highlights: Built prior to the Civil War, Fort Taylor is an imposing sight and well worth a tour.

Logistics: Bicycles share the footpath in places. Cruise ships slip past on their way to drop anchor off Mallory Square, so you may be startled by the sound of air horns.

Other Activities: With picnicking, sunning, surfing, and fishing, this is inarguably Key West's best beach, so enjoy!

Sandra Friend is an active volunteer with the Florida Trail Association and a member of the Outdoor Writers of America and the Florida Outdoor Writers Association. She has written 18 books, including *50 Hikes in Central Florida*, *50 Hikes in North Florida*, *50 Hikes in South Florida*, and (with photographer Bart Smith) *Along the Florida Trail*.